*er*

**Print envelopes of various sizes. See "Envelopes and Labels,"** *page 256.*

**Use templates to create documents with standard formats. See "Using the Style Gallery,"** *page 399.*

**Let Word enter today's date for you automatically. See "DATE and TIME Fields,"** *page 660.*

**Insert pictures, charts, and other objects. See "Frames: Positioning Text and Graphics on the Page,"** *page 481.*

**Create a chart with Word's Graph utility. See "Creating Charts with Microsoft Graph,"** *page 541.*

**Store text or graphic objects to insert as AutoText entries. See "Using AutoText,"** *page 128.*

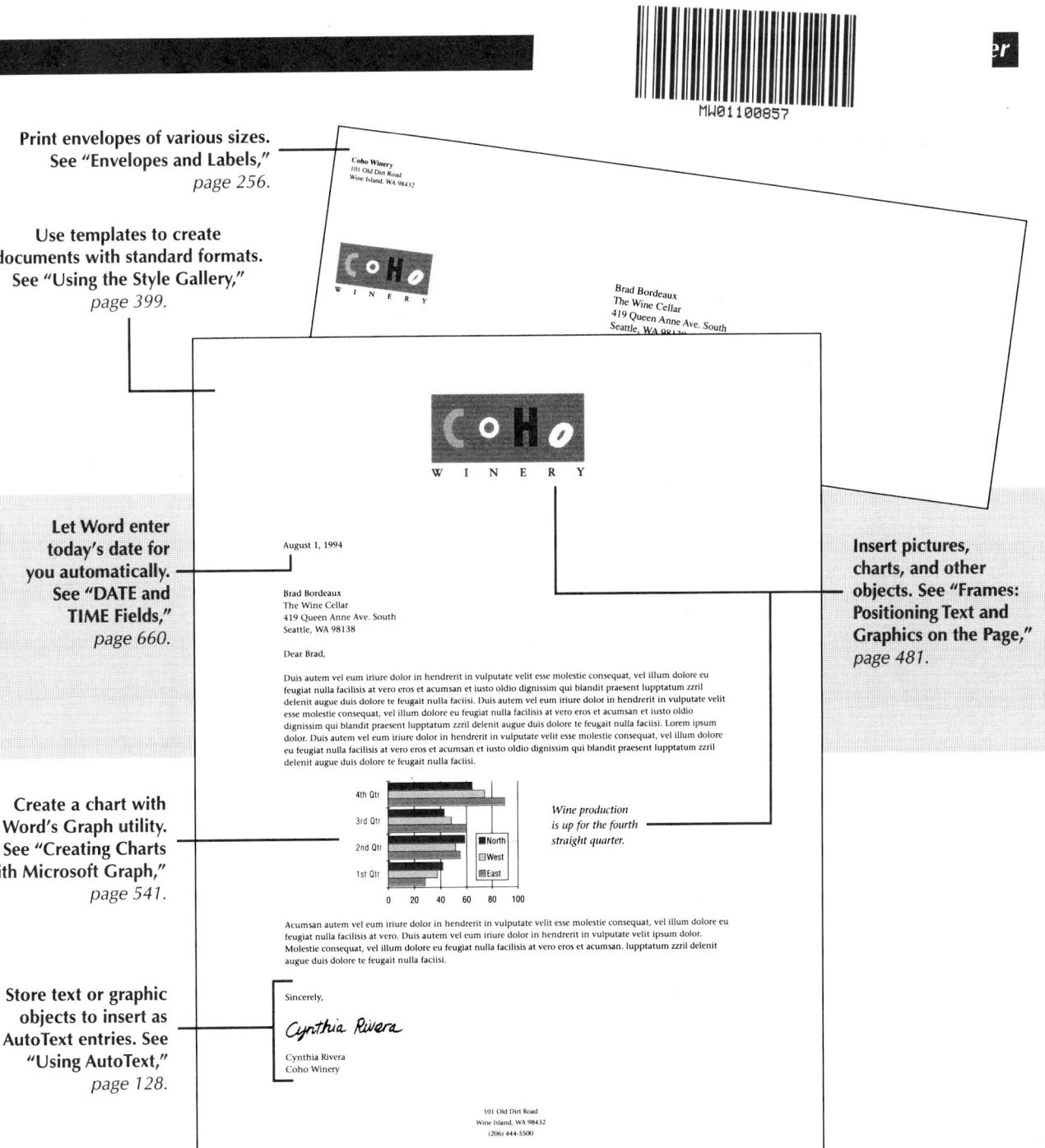

*More ideas inside back cover…*

# Word 6
## *for the Macintosh*
# Companion

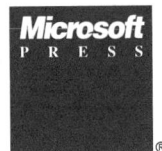

The Cobb Group
M. David Stone & Alfred Poor
and Mark Crane

PUBLISHED BY
Microsoft Press
A Division of Microsoft Corporation
One Microsoft Way
Redmond, Washington 98052-6399

Library of Congress Cataloging-in-Publication Data
Microsoft Word 6 for the Macintosh companion / the Cobb Group, M.
    David Stone & Alfred Poor, and Mark Crane.
        p.    cm.
    Includes index.
    ISBN 1-55615-644-8
    1. Microsoft Word.    2. Word processing.    I. Stone, M. David.
II. Poor, Alfred E.    III. Crane, Mark W.    IV. Cobb Group.    V. Title:
Microsoft Word six for the Macintosh companion.
Z52.5.M52M48    1994
652.5'536--dc20                                              94-30460
                                                                CIP

Printed and bound in the United States of America.

1 2 3 4 5 6 7 8 9 QFQF 9 8 7 6 5 4

Distributed to the book trade in Canada by Macmillan of Canada, a division of Canada Publishing Corporation.

A CIP catalogue record for this book is available from the British Library.

Microsoft Press books are available through booksellers and distributors worldwide. For further information about international editions, contact your local Microsoft Corporation office. Or contact Microsoft Press International directly at fax (206) 936-7329.

**Acquisitions Editor:** Lucinda Rowley
**Project Editors:** Marianne Moon, Ron Lamb
**Manuscript Editors:** Marianne Moon, Rebecca Gleason
**Technical Editor:** Stuart J. Stuple

*For Bebe, Anna, and Alex:*
*we made it through another one!*
*Thanks for the loving and patient support.*
—AEP

*For Marie, again, and always.*
—MDS

*...and to all our rowdy Mac fans—family and friends alike!*

# Contents

## PART ONE: Getting Started

# PART TWO: Basics

# PART THREE: Advanced Word

# PART FOUR: Power Tools

## PART FIVE: Customizing Word

# Acknowledgments

It takes a lot of work from many people to create a book of this size, and we appreciate the support and assistance we have received in this project.

We are especially grateful to Nathaniel Poor, who not only helped by taking most of the screen shots in this book but also took personal responsibility for seeing that we stayed as true as possible to the conventions and concepts of the Macintosh interface and applications. This book is much better as a result of his efforts.

We also want to thank all the folks at Microsoft Press who worked so hard to help get this book to you in such a short time.

# Introduction:
# Before You Begin

Welcome to the *Word 6 for the Macintosh Companion*. Word 5.1 has been so popular with Macintosh users that it is difficult to imagine that many improvements could be added to it. The fact is, however, that Word 6.0 represents a major overhaul providing dozens upon dozens of new, powerful features. For example, you can create more powerful links between programs, making it easier to share the same information between Word and spreadsheet, graphics, and database programs.

# What's New in Word 6.0 (and Where to Find It in This Book)

**NEW!**

If you are already familiar with a prior version of Word, you will find a lot of familiar features in Word 6.0. You'll also find hundreds of significant changes. Some are improvements to old features, some are replacements for features found in older versions, and some are completely new from the ground up. You'll find these new features discussed throughout the 28 chapters of this book, but to help you spot them, we've flagged the most significant changes with a "New!" icon in the margin, just like the one next to this paragraph. We don't have room to list them all, but here's a quick look at some of the new and exciting features you will find.

## More toolbars

You no longer get one toolbar with Word, you get more than a dozen, including specialized toolbars for specific functions, such as drawing, outlines, and borders. The ToolTips feature lets you see what a toolbar button does without clicking on it. You also have more options than ever to create custom toolbars, giving you instant access to the commands and macros you use the most. You can even create your own toolbar buttons, if you want. Another new feature lets you place toolbars anywhere you want. (See Chapters 1 and 9.)

## Wizards

As with many other recent versions of Microsoft programs, Word 6.0 now has wizards. These are like "supertemplates" that guide you through the creation of complex document formats, from fax cover sheets to book layouts, from letterhead designs to calendars. All you have to do is fill in the blanks in a series of dialog boxes to create personalized document designs. And it's easy to use a wizard to create a template, so you can use your new layouts over and over again. (See Chapter 9.)

## AutoCorrect and AutoText

Word 6.0 can automatically correct your common typing errors with the new AutoCorrect feature. And the Word 5.1 "glossary" feature has been replaced with AutoText, which you can use to enter everything from a company name to a signature at the touch of a key. (See Chapter 5.)

## More help features

Word 6.0 has a new context-sensitive help feature, which can provide specific help screens for menu commands or other items, as well as display the paragraph and character formatting in use for a section of text. Word also has a HyperCard stack of automated demos to step you through basic procedures. You can even get help on Help—after starting Help, select Using Microsoft Help from the Help menu. (See Chapter 1.)

## Context-sensitive menus

Holding down the Control key when you press the mouse button provides handy information with Word 6.0; under many conditions, you get context-sensitive menus listing the commands you are most likely to need at that point. (See Chapter 1.)

## Full Screen view

Some people like to have all of Word's commands, toolbars, and other features visible while they work, while others prefer to work with nothing on the screen but their text. Word's new Full Screen view option lets you show as much or as little as you want on your screen while you're editing. (See Chapter 9.)

## Template features

Templates let you predefine any and all format and layout features, which you can then use over and over again to create new documents with those features. Templates also provide nearly endless opportunities to automate and customize Word. You can attach more than one template to a given document. You can create templates that serve as tool kits, with macros, style definitions, and other customized features, and then attach them to your documents as global templates to make their features available. You can also move style definitions, macros, and other customizations between templates using the new Organizer feature. (See Chapter 27.)

## Multiple-level Undo

In Word 5.1, you could undo only the last edit change you made. With Word 6.0, you can undo multiple steps—either one step at a time or all at once. (See Chapter 3.)

## Forms

Create on-screen forms that make it easy to collect information such as names and addresses. You can even create custom prompts, default entries, and other features that most people associate only with sophisticated database programs. (See Chapter 21.)

## AutoFormat

Let Word apply formatting automatically to your documents with the new AutoFormat feature. (See Chapter 12.)

## Character styles

In Word 5.1, you could define formatting styles for entire paragraphs, but if you wanted to apply formatting to just a portion of a paragraph, you had to apply it explicitly. Word 6.0 adds character styles, making it as easy to apply consistent formatting to certain words or phrases as it is to apply formatting to an entire paragraph. (See Chapter 12.)

## Envelope and label features

Word 6.0 makes it easier to print envelopes by picking the address right out of your document. You can also add U.S. Postal Service Postnet bar codes to your addresses automatically. A new label feature makes it easy to create labels in a variety of formats. (See Chapter 8.)

## Improved mail merge

You can create complex documents by merging lists of information from other programs with text to create form letters, catalogs, and other types of printed documents. New features make it easy to create mailing labels as well. (See Chapter 21.)

## More page layout options

You can create complex page layouts with Word 6.0, including sophisticated multiple-column designs with columns of different widths. (See Chapter 14.)

## Access to other applications through OLE

Word 6.0 makes it easy to create links with other applications with the addition of support for OLE. OLE lets you open a linked file—such as a drawing or an Excel spreadsheet—and edit it using the original program without leaving Word. Word 6.0 also includes a number of useful mini-applications that have OLE support, such as WordArt 2, which lets you use any TrueType font to create impressively formatted headlines for your documents. (See Chapters 15 and 23.)

## Improved Find File features

The Find File command has been expanded and improved. You can use it to search using complex criteria across multiple directories, and then you can store your search specification to use again in the future. You can also perform a wide variety of useful file management tasks using Find File. (See Chapter 17.)

## Fields

Word 6.0 uses fields, which provide access to Microsoft's powerful WordBasic programming language. You don't have to remember all the arcane details, however, to take advantage of fields. The Insert Field command will help you find the field you want and enter the correct codes to make it do what you want. Word can insert many of the fields automatically when you create a table of contents or an index, making the task even easier. (See Chapters 20 and 22.)

## Improved keyboard shortcuts

Word 6.0 lets you create two-keystroke assignments, making it easy to group similar commands, as well as giving you more combinations from which to choose. (See Chapter 28.)

## A special note for Word 5.1 users

It is easy to make the transition from Word 5.1 to Word 6.0, thanks to a Word 5.1 toolbar option.

# Setting Up Word

In the rest of this introduction, we'll show you how to get ready to run Word 6.0. First we'll describe the hardware you need to run the program, and we'll talk about some of the optional hardware accessories you might want for your system. Then we'll cover how to install the program on your hard disk.

Although the information in this introduction is sufficient to get you started with Word, we suggest that you also consult the *Quick Results* manual that comes in the Word for the Macintosh package. You can call Microsoft for help if you have trouble installing and loading the program. The telephone number for Microsoft's Product Support Line is listed in the materials included in your Word for the Macintosh package.

## Hardware requirements

Word 6.0 requires a Macintosh or Power Macintosh running System 7 with at least 1700 kilobytes (K) of memory available after loading the system software. (Word 6.0 will not run on a 68000 Macintosh.) As shipped, the preferred and suggested sizes for Word 6.0 are set at 2500 K, but allocating additional memory will result in better performance. We suggest setting both preferred and suggested memory sizes to 4000 K. To do this, click on the Microsoft Word icon, choose the File menu, and then choose Get Info. This opens the Microsoft Word Info dialog box. Move to the Memory Requirements section in the lower right corner and enter the new values. When you are done, close the dialog box to save your changes.

Your computer must also have disk storage, and plenty of it. You'll need a floppy-disk drive for loading the program. (The Word package comes with 1.44-megabyte (MB), 3.5-inch floppy disks; you can request 800 KB disks instead if your system does not have a high-density drive.) Your hard disk must have at least 24 MB of free space to install the program and all its supporting files. (If you can do without all the extra features, including the Word Help files, you can install the program in less than 5 MB of hard-disk space.)

## Installing Word

Assuming you have the appropriate hardware and the Word program itself, you're ready to install Word on your hard disk. Although Word's program files occupy several floppy disks, the installation process is straightforward.

You must have System 7 already installed on your system before you start installing Word. Insert the first disk in the floppy drive, open the disk's window, and double-click on the Microsoft Word Setup icon you find there.

The Setup program checks to see that you have sufficient disk space, and then asks whether you want to perform a Typical, Complete/Custom, or Minimum installation. We recommend that you choose the Complete/Custom installation option if you have enough disk space available. Keep in mind that if you do not choose the Complete/Custom installation option, the Setup program may not install all the files we refer to throughout this book.

The installation program will copy the various files to the appropriate places on your hard disk. A dialog box will keep you posted on the installation progress by reporting the percentage completed and showing at all times the name of the file that is currently being installed. The Setup program also displays some "infomercials" about various Word features and reminders to send in your registration card (which we recommend you do, by the way, to ensure that you get notices of upgrades).

The Setup program will copy files into a number of folders, including one named Microsoft Word, which will contain icons for Word, Word Help, and Word Readme Help, as well as several folders. Setup will also install a separate Microsoft folder containing items that can be shared by Microsoft products. At this point, you are ready to run Word. After starting the program as described in Chapter 1, you might want to take a tour of the new features by selecting Quick Preview from the Help menu.

### Mininum Installation

As we already mentioned, the Setup program also offers a Minimum installation option which installs essential files, including Word, its Help files, and the spelling checker. This "minimum" installation will take up between 4 MB and 5 MB of disk space.

Fortunately, there is another approach for those with little disk space available. The Complete/Custom installation option in the Setup program lets you pick and choose which sets of files you want to install. The program provides a running total of the estimated disk space needed to accommodate your selections, so you can tailor the installation to match the space available. If you pick just the Word program files (and not the Help files, spelling checker, sample files, or anything else), the installation will take about 5 MB.

## Conventions Used in This Book

With Word installed, you are ready to put it to work. This book is designed to help you make the most of the program's power and flexibility right from the start. Before we begin, however, let's take a moment to go over some of our assumptions and the conventions we'll use in the following chapters.

First and foremost, we assume that you have a basic understanding of how to work with the Macintosh and its applications in general. We explain many of the fundamentals as we go along, but if you are not familiar with the Macintosh, you may want to have a general reference handy.

We have placed the emphasis on telling you what you need to know in order to get a specific task accomplished, and we have done our best to write our explanations in as readable and enjoyable a form as we can. As a result, there are topics where we have chosen not to use the official Macintosh or Word terminology, because we feel those terms are misleading. When we do choose to substitute our own words, however, we are careful to explain when and why we are doing so. For example, Word has dialog boxes with multiple layers that look like index cards with tabs on their top edges to hold labels.

Word calls these different layers *tabs*, but we feel that this could be confusing since most people will think of the tab as the small label area at the top. Instead, we have chosen to call these layers *cards* because that's what they look like. In another departure from strict nomenclature, we use the term *option buttons* for the objects that are often referred to as *radio buttons*.

We already mentioned the "New!" symbols that appear in the margins next to features that are new or significantly changed in Word 6.0. You will also find two other marginal symbols. The "Note" symbol indicates information that may be a little tangential to the main discussion but that provides important background information, highlights how the discussion relates to other material, or supplies details that may be essential in certain situations. And pay special attention to the "Tip" markers, because they flag information that you're not likely to find anywhere else. These tips can save you time by showing you some handy tricks, or save you aggravation by helping you avoid some potential pitfalls.

We have also provided many cross-references between different sections of the book. This will make it easier and faster to find the information you need when you need it.

When discussing keyboard commands, we name the keys you are to press, such as Option or Delete or Right arrow. Keep in mind that most Macintosh keyboards have both a Delete key (located above the Return key) and a Del key (located with the other movement keys to the left of the numeric keypad).

If you are meant to press two keys at a time, we'll combine them with the hyphen (-) symbol, as in z -D or Control-Shift-2. If you are meant to press a series of keys in sequence, we'll separate them with commas, as in F10, O, O, K. Note that we have written this book assuming you are using an extended keyboard. As a result, we may describe keystrokes that are not available on a standard or PowerBook keyboard. And there may be some actions that you cannot carry out unless you have an extended keyboard. For example, the only way to switch between displaying field codes and the field results is with Shift-F9, which is not available on keyboards that do not have function keys. We've also taken care to identify boxes that have drop-down lists, which can be easily opened from the keyboard.

When you use the menu commands in Word, you have several different ways to make selections:

- You can click on the menu name with the mouse and then hold the mouse button down while dragging to a command within that menu.

- You can use the F10 key to activate the menu bar and then use the arrow keys to navigate through the options, press Return to open the drop-down menu, use the arrow keys to highlight a menu command, and then press Return to choose the command.

- Or, after pressing the F10 key to activate the menu bar, you can press the letter that's underlined in the menu name to open the menu and then press the letter that's underlined in the menu command to choose the command.

- In addition, in many cases there are shortcut keys for choosing the same commands or buttons you can choose with the mouse.

Finally, we assume that you are starting with the default settings for Word 6.0 as they are initially set by the Setup program. As we've already suggested and as you will see in later chapters, there are dozens of useful ways to customize the program: changing the menus and their options, adding new commands through macros, assigning new shortcut keys for commands, and more. To start with, however, we assume that you have not made any changes of this sort.

Now that we've gone over the ground rules, let's take a quick look at the program itself.

# PART ONE

# Getting Started

# TOPIC FINDER

# A Brief Tour

his chapter provides an overview of Word for the Macintosh. If you're new to Word, you'll want to read the chapter carefully because it lays the groundwork for everything that follows. If you've used earlier versions of Word, you might skim the chapter to be sure you know the basics of the program, especially new features or changes that you might otherwise overlook. New features are marked, so you can find them easily.

We'll start by showing how to run Word and by taking a tour of the screen and the help system. We'll end by discussing a few customization options that are critical to making you feel comfortable while working with the program.

## Starting Word for the Macintosh

As you'll soon discover, Word usually gives you more than one way to do things. In fact, that's one of the program's major strengths. You even have a number of choices for starting the program.

### How to start Word from the Finder

Most often you'll already be in the Finder when you want to start Word. Because the Word installation program creates a separate folder for Word on your hard disk, you should see something similar to the screen in Figure 1-1 on the next page.

FIGURE 1-1

Your hard disk will
include a folder for
Microsoft Word
after you install the
program.

If you see the Microsoft Word folder, you can use the mouse to double-click on it or highlight it and press ⌘-O to open it. If you don't see the folder, maximize the hard disk window using the Zoom box, or use the window's scroll bars or the keyboard arrow keys to move around within the window until you locate the folder. Note that if someone has installed Word and set up your system so that the Word program or folder is installed in a different folder, you'll have to check the other folders in the Finder or ask that person where the Word for the Macintosh folder is.

## How to start Word using the Word for the Macintosh icon

After you open the Word folder, you can start the program. To start Word with the mouse, double-click on the icon. If you prefer using the keyboard, you have to select the icon using Tab or the arrow keys and then press ⌘-O.

Here's a quick way to select an icon within a window: Type the first letter of the title of the icon. For example, to select the Word icon, which has the default title *Microsoft Word*, press M. If there is more than one icon with the same initial letter in its title, the first icon with that letter will be highlighted. If you hold down the Option key when you choose the Special menu, the first command will become Clean Up By Name, which will sort the icons in alphabetical order in the window, making it easy to find the icon you want. You can also press Tab to highlight the icons in alphabetical order, no matter how they are arranged in the window.

You can tell which icon is selected in two ways: there is a colored block around the icon's title, and the icon becomes darkened. If the Word icon isn't highlighted when you open its folder, you can select it with either the keyboard or the mouse.

# How to start Word and open a document simultaneously

Word normally opens a blank document named Document1 when you begin a new Word session. However, you can also start the program and open an existing document in one step.

## How to start Word and open a document using an icon

Having Word automatically load a particular document can be handy, especially if it's a document that you edit or reprint on a regular basis. As shown in Figure 1-2, all you have to do is either double-click on the icon for the document, or highlight it and press ⌘-O. Word will run and automatically load the file.

 You can also click on an alias icon for a document to run Word and open the document. You can create an alias icon in a folder using the Finder's File Make Alias command.

**FIGURE 1-2**

To start Word and load a specific document, simply double-click on the document icon in its window, or highlight it and press ⌘-O.

Documents
12 items    34.3 MB in disk    119.9 MB av

Letters    Memos    Reports

New NRBQ    Revision    Monthly

Cars    Callouts    Names

Sales 1    Sales 2    Numbers

 You can open multiple files at the same time using icons. Simply select all the files you want to open (either by clicking and dragging around the ones you want or by holding down the Shift key as you click on them) and then press ⌘-O or double-click on one of the selected icons. Word will start and open all the documents.

# The Word Screen

No matter which method you use to start Word, the first thing you'll see when Word is loaded will be the copyright notice. When it disappears, you'll see a screen similar to the one in Figure 1-3. (This discussion assumes that you are using the default settings. It's easy to change the appearance of this screen, however, as we'll discuss elsewhere in this chapter.)

The window in the center of the screen in Figure 1-3 displays a "Tip Of The Day" that points out useful tricks and shortcuts for using Word. You can press Return (or click on OK) to close the box and then proceed to the Word editing screen.

**FIGURE 1-3**

This screen will appear each time you begin a new Word session.

The Tip Of The Day tips are a painless way to learn a wide variety of tricks and shortcuts in Word. However, if you decide you don't want to see a Tip Of The Day every time you start the program, click on the X next to "Show Tips At Startup" or press ⌘-S, and the window will no longer appear each time the program starts.

As you can see from the name in the title bar in Figure 1-4, Word creates a new, blank document named *Document1*, ready for typing. (You can save the document under any name you like. We'll show you how in the next chapter.) If you've worked with other Macintosh programs, many of the screen elements will be familiar.

FIGURE 1-4

Word creates an empty
document named
*Document1* when you
first start the program.

The large, empty area that occupies the bulk of the screen is the document window—your workspace. This is where you will create, edit, format, and view your documents.

At this point, the document window will be empty except for a blinking vertical bar called the *insertion point,* or *cursor,* and a horizontal line below it called the *end-of-document marker.* Note that the cursor is different from the *mouse pointer*, which some people refer to as the *mouse cursor;* we'll discuss the *mouse pointer* later in this chapter. The cursor indicates your current position in the Word document. Each time you type a text character, the cursor moves one space to the right. You also use the cursor to specify the location you want to edit in existing text. If you have used other word processors, you'll find Word's cursor familiar.

## The title bar

At the very top of the document window is the title bar, shown in Figure 1-5.

FIGURE 1-5

The title bar.

If your Word document window is less than full screen, as shown in Figure 1-6 on the next page, you'll see something slightly different from the figures in this book. To get a closer match, you can click on the Zoom box in the right corner of the title bar or double-click on the title bar to change the window to a full-screen window.

FIGURE 1-6

A document window in Word.

The title bar provides two important pieces of information. First, it displays the name of the document in the document window. This is the name Word will use when you choose the File Save command. Second, the title bar changes color depending on whether or not the window is selected so that you can easily see which window is active if you have several windows showing.

## The menu bar

The top line of the screen is the menu bar, shown in Figure 1-7. (If Use Short Menu Names is selected on the Tools Options General card, the Insert, Format, and Window menus are abbreviated as Ins, Fmt, and Wnd.) You can use the menus on the menu bar to initiate many of the Word commands. You can redesign the menus if you want to add commands that aren't there; for now, however, we'll stay with Word's default menus. For details on customizing menus, see "Customizing the Menus" on page 904 and "Renaming, Adding, and Deleting Menus" on page 914.

FIGURE 1-7

The menu bar.

There are eight menus in addition to the Apple, Help, and Application menus: File, Edit, View, Insert, Format, Tools, Table, and Window. Each menu has its own set of commands, as shown in Figure 1-8.

Each of Word's first-level menus offers its own set of commands.

Briefly, you use the Apple menu at the left edge of the menu bar to access utility programs, such as the Apple Calculator. The Apple menu also has an About Microsoft Word command, which opens a box containing information about Word, as shown in Figure 1-9. The About dialog box displays the version of the program, copyright information, the name and company name of the person the copy is licensed to, and the serial number. Choose the System Info button at the bottom of this dialog box to run the Microsoft System Information application, which displays lots of useful information about your system and how it is configured. For example, you can see a list of graphics filters or text file converters that are installed. System Info can give you information you need to diagnose and solve problems, and there is an option that allows you to save the information in a file for later reference.

**FIGURE 1-9**

The About Microsoft Word dialog box has a button to display system statistics that can be helpful in troubleshooting a problem.

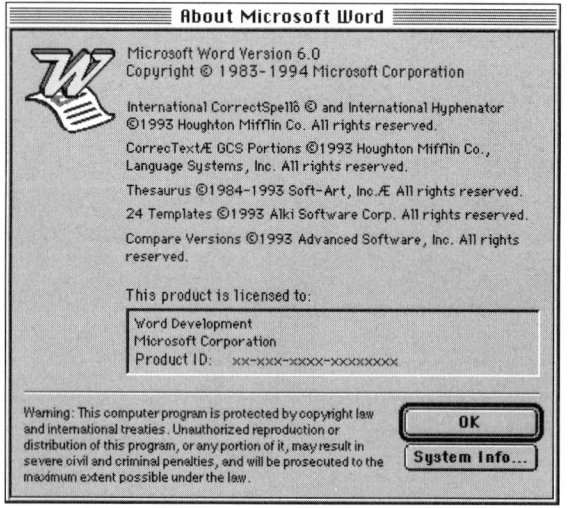

The File menu concentrates on file-handling and printing commands. The Edit menu lets you copy and move text, search for text, replace text, and otherwise edit your document. The View menu lets you control some of the options for what appears on the screen; you can switch between Normal and Outline view, for example, and choose whether to see headers, footers, footnotes, and annotations. The Insert menu lets you insert page breaks, footnotes, page numbers, index entries, files, pictures, and more. The Format menu lets you control the way your text, pictures, and other elements of your document look. The Tools menu offers a wide range of ancillary tools, such as a spelling checker, a thesaurus, and a utility for handling envelopes, as well as tools for customizing the program. The Table menu is itself a powerful tool for creating and formatting tables within your document. The Window menu lets you rearrange and switch among document windows and create new windows to view different parts of a single document. The Help menu offers assistance when you need information on how to perform a task, and the Application Menu lets you switch between open applications.

## How to issue commands

Another feature for which Word offers you freedom of choice is the way in which you give commands. You can use either the mouse or the keyboard for most commands, and in each case you have a variety of choices.

To choose a command from a menu, you can use the mouse to point to the menu name on the menu bar and then hold down the mouse button to pull down the menu options. Drag the mouse pointer to highlight the command you want, and release the mouse button.

To choose a menu command with the keyboard, press F10 or ⌘-Tab to activate the menu bar; then open a menu either by typing the letter that's underscored in the name of the menu you want to use or by using the Left arrow and Right arrow keys to move to that menu and then pressing Return or the Down arrow key. With the menu open, you can choose the command either by typing the letter that's underscored in the command name or by using the Up arrow and Down arrow keys to move to the command and then pressing Return.

If you use F10 or ⌘-Tab to turn on the underscores that indicate the menu shortcuts, Word will also display underscores for the shortcut keys in dialog boxes. If you open a dialog box using a mouse, Word will not display the underscores. You can get them to be displayed, however, by pressing the ⌘ key once.

## Keyboard shortcuts

As you glance through the Word menus, you'll notice that several key names, such as ⌘-Option-L and ⌘-N, appear to the right of some commands. These notations indicate shortcut keys you can press to choose commands without going through the menus. The ⌥ represents the Option key. The Shift key is represented with ⇧. For example, the key combination ⌘-S is next to the File Save command; you can press ⌘-S to save a document. Similarly, you can press ⌘-Option-L instead of choosing Tools and then Spelling. Although it doesn't show on the menu, you could also use F7 in place of choosing Tools and then Spelling. Note that Word also has other such keyboard shortcuts that aren't listed on the menus. For example, pressing Shift-⌘-P twice opens the dialog box you would see by choosing Format Font with the Font Size list box selected. (The first Shift-⌘-P selects the Font Size list on the Formatting toolbar.)

## Context-sensitive menus

In addition to pull-down menus on the menu bar, Word 6.0 offers context-sensitive menus at the click of the mouse button; just hold down the Control key as you click the button. As shown in Figures 1-10A and 1-10B, these menus vary depending on what you're pointing at when you hold down the Control key as you click on the button. If you're pointing at a toolbar (and you have an arrow pointer), the menu appears with a set of commands related to toolbars. If you're pointing to text in the document, the menu appears with a set of editing and formatting commands. The menu works just like the pull-down menus, so you can choose commands with the mouse, dragging the pointer until the command you want is highlighted and then releasing the button.

**FIGURE 1-10A**

Context-sensitive menus pop up when you hold down the Control key before clicking. As shown here, and in Figure 1-10B, the menus vary depending on what the mouse is pointing at when you click.

There are no commands on the context-sensitive menus that aren't also available through the pull-down menus. The advantage of the context-sensitive menus is that if you are working with your text, mouse in hand, you can Control-click to get to the commands you're most likely to need. For example, if you want to format a block of text and you prefer selecting text with the mouse rather than with the keyboard, you can select a block and immediately Control-click while pointing to the selected text to display the menu commands for Cut, Copy, Paste, Font, Paragraph, and Bullets And Numbering.

**FIGURE 1-10B**

## The Standard toolbar

The horizontal strip below the menu bar is the Standard toolbar, shown in
Figure 1-11. This row of 22 buttons provides immediate access to such varied
commands as Cut, Paste, Undo, and Spelling (spelling checking). To use the
Standard toolbar, simply point with the mouse to the button that represents
the command you want, and click.

**FIGURE 1-11**

The Standard toolbar.

In addition to the Standard toolbar, Word 6.0 comes with many other
toolbars and lets you create more. You can customize each of the individual
toolbars, and you can show or hide each one independently. For details on
customizing toolbars, see "Customizing Toolbars" on page 288.

For now, we'll focus on the default settings for the Standard toolbar.
Figure 1-12, starting on the next page, lists the 22 buttons and the actions that
they represent.

You don't need to refer to this list to find out what a given button does,
however. Simply place the mouse pointer on a button, and within a second or
so, you'll see a small box immediately below the pointer showing a short description of the button's function. (This is the ToolTips feature, which can be
turned on and off using the View Toolbars command.) When the ToolTip is
displayed, you'll also find a more complete explanation on the bottom line of
the window. (This bottom line is called the *status bar*. If you turn off the status
bar, the detailed message will not appear.)

| Button | Button Name | Action |
|---|---|---|
| | New | Creates a new document with default settings |
| | Open | Opens an existing document |
| | Save | Saves the current document |
| | Print | Prints the current document |
| | Print Preview | Displays pages as they will be printed |
| | Spelling | Checks the spelling in the active document |
| | Cut | Cuts the current selection and puts it on the Clipboard |
| | Copy | Copies the current selection and puts it on the Clipboard |
| | Paste | Inserts a copy of the Clipboard's contents |
| **NEW!** | Format Painter | Copies the formatting of the current selection to a specified location |
| **NEW!** | Undo | Reverses, or undoes, the previous actions, one at a time |
| **NEW!** | Redo | Restores, or redoes, the previous actions that were undone, one at a time |
| **NEW!** | AutoFormat | Automatically formats a document |
| | Edit AutoText | Creates an AutoText entry if you've first selected some text, or inserts an entry |
| | Insert Table | Inserts a table, or lets you modify one that already exists |
| | Insert Microsoft Excel Worksheet | Inserts a worksheet from Microsoft Excel |

*(continued)*

**FIGURE 1-12**

Word's Standard toolbar buttons.

**FIGURE 1-12** *continued*

| Button | Button Name | Action |
|---|---|---|
| | Columns | Changes the column format of the selected sections |
| | Drawing | Toggles between showing and hiding the Drawing toolbar | NEW! |
| | Insert Chart | Inserts a Microsoft Graph object |
| | Show/Hide ¶ | Toggles between showing all nonprinting characters (such as tabs) and hiding any nonprinting characters that are not specifically set to be visible |
| 115% | Zoom Control | Scales the editing view | NEW! |
| | Help | Provides Help information on a command, a screen region, or text properties | NEW! |

## The Formatting toolbar

If you installed Word with the default installation and haven't changed any settings, you'll see Word's Formatting toolbar immediately below the Standard toolbar, as shown in Figure 1-13. You can use the Formatting toolbar to choose the most commonly used formatting commands. As with all toolbars, you can point to a button with the mouse pointer to see an explanation of the button's function.

**FIGURE 1-13**

The Formatting toolbar.

The first text box in the Formatting toolbar shows the current paragraph style for the selected text. (The default style is Normal.) The second text box shows the current font. The third shows the font size in points. (A point is a typographical measurement that equals approximately $1/72$ inch.) For more information on how font size is determined, see "Font Formatting" on page 223.

After the three text boxes come four groups of buttons. The three buttons in the first group are labeled with letters that stand for bold, italic, and underlined character formatting. The four buttons in the second group affect paragraph formatting: left aligned, centered, right aligned, and justified. The four buttons in the third group control other paragraph formatting features. The first adds automatic numbering to the paragraphs in the current selection of text or removes automatic numbering for text that's already numbered. The second button works much the same way except that it adds or removes bullets from bulleted lists. The next two buttons decrease and increase the amount of left indention for the current paragraph or paragraphs by one tab stop.

The last button on this toolbar looks like a window with four panes. This button displays (or hides) the Borders toolbar, which you can use to add borders around and between paragraphs or table cells, and to add shading.

## The ruler

The horizontal strip below the Formatting toolbar is the ruler, shown in Figure 1-14. The ruler serves two functions: You can use it to see the width of your text lines and also to format your text. The ruler shows the left and right margins, tab settings, and any indentions or extensions into the margin for a paragraph. You can move markers on the ruler to change these settings. For more information about how to use the ruler to change the appearance of your text, see "Paragraph Formatting" on page 204.

**FIGURE 1-14**

The ruler.

## The scroll bars

The Word screen also has scroll bars—one horizontal and one vertical, as shown in Figure 1-15. These scroll bars indicate where you are in the document and give you a means of moving through it. As you move from the beginning of the document to the end, the box in the vertical scroll bar moves from the top of the bar to the bottom; its position is an indication of your relative location within the document.

The horizontal scroll bar works in a similar way. When the left edge of your document is showing, the box in the horizontal scroll bar is at the far left. It moves to the right as the display shifts to the right.

You can use either scroll bar in three ways. You can click on the arrows at either end to move in small increments. You can point to the empty space on either side of the box and click to move in larger increments. Or you can drag the box to move it to the position you want. For more information about using the scroll bars for moving through your document, see "How to navigate with the mouse" on page 63.

**FIGURE 1-15**

The scroll bars.

## How to change the View mode

The horizontal scroll bar has three buttons at its left end. You click on them to select Normal, Page Layout, and Outline views—the same options as the first three commands on the View menu. For most writing and editing, you'll probably want to use the default choice, Normal view, which is the leftmost button. For more information on these different views and when you might want to use them, see "Viewing Your Document" on page 267.

## How to split a window

There is a small black box, called the *split box,* just above the top arrow in the vertical scroll bar. You can use this to divide your document window into two parts, or panes. If you place the mouse pointer over this box, the pointer will change to the horizontal split pointer. See "The mouse pointer" on page 20 for more information on the different pointers. When you see the split pointer, click the mouse button and hold it down. Drag the pointer downward until you've divided the window in the proportions you want, and then release the mouse button. You can also double-click on the split box to divide the window in half.

Alternatively, you can split your document window by choosing the Split command on the Window menu, which will also divide the window in half.

NEW!

The current document will show in both panes of the window, but each pane will have its own vertical scroll bar. This means that you can look at two different sections of the document at the same time and scroll them independently. You can return to a single pane by double-clicking on the split box or by moving the pointer over the split box so that the split pointer shows and then holding the button down while you drag the split pointer to the top or bottom outside the document window. If you prefer to use the keyboard, choose the Split command by using F10, W, P to return to a single pane.

## The status bar

The horizontal strip at the bottom of the Word window is the status bar, shown in Figure 1-16. Word uses the status bar to show information about your document and to show prompts and messages when you use certain commands.

FIGURE 1-16

The status bar.

While you're writing or editing, Word uses the status bar to show both your position in the document and the settings for some features, such as Overtype mode. Figure 1-17 shows a Word document and its status bar. Figure 1-18 shows some of the codes you will see in the status bar as you work.

**FIGURE 1-17**

When you're writing or editing, Word shows information about your document in the status bar.

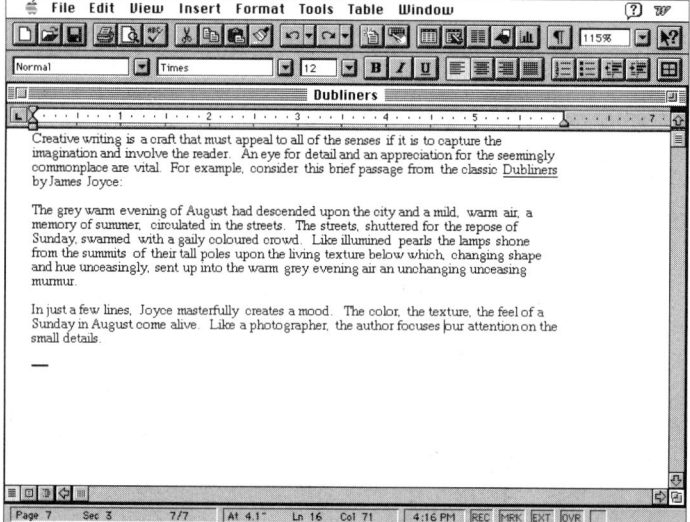

In some cases, more than one message may appear at a given spot. For example, the EXT and COL messages both appear in the box to the right of the Mark Revisions space.

Some of the status items in Word 6.0 do double duty by also letting you toggle a setting or open a dialog box. For example, you can turn on Extend Selection by double-clicking on the EXT indicator and turn on Overtype mode by double-clicking on OVR. In both cases, you can double-click again to turn the feature off. Similarly, you can open dialog boxes by double-clicking on MRK for marking revisions, and REC for macro recording. Note that the text for each of these status items is grayed when the setting is off. When you turn the feature on, the item appears as solid text.

| Indicator | Meaning |
|-----------|---------|
| Page 7 | Page 7 is currently displayed. |
| Sec 3 | Section 3 is currently displayed. |
| 7/7 | Page 7 of a 7-page document is currently displayed. |
| At 4.1" | The cursor is 4.1 inches from the top edge of the page. |
| Ln 16 | The cursor is in the sixteenth line of the current page. |
| Col 71 | The cursor is 71 characters from the left margin. |
| REC | The macro recorder is on. |
| MRK | Word is in Mark Revisions mode. |
| EXT | Extend Selection (F8) is on. |
| COL | Column Selection (⌘-Shift-F8) is on. |
| OVR | Word is in Overtype mode. |

**FIGURE 1-18**

Status bar messages and their meanings.

When you activate a menu, as shown in Figure 1-19, Word displays a short message in the status bar that explains the purpose of the highlighted menu item.

**FIGURE 1-19**

When you highlight a menu command, Word replaces the usual status bar information with a short message explaining the purpose of the command.

# The mouse pointer

There is one more important element on the Word screen: the mouse pointer. Unlike the other elements, the pointer has no fixed location or shape. Rather, you can use the mouse to point to any location on the screen, and the pointer will take on different shapes in different locations.

If you position the pointer on one of the bars at the top of the screen or on a scroll bar, you'll see an arrow pointing up and to the left. We'll refer to this as the *left-arrow pointer.* You use this pointer to choose menu commands, click on toolbar buttons, use scroll bars, and place or move tab and margin markers on the ruler, among other tasks. If you move the pointer to the document window, it will change to look like a capital I; this is called the *I-beam pointer.* It indicates that the mouse is set to work with text.

These are just two examples from the many pointers shown in Figure 1-20. Each pointer indicates that the mouse is set to perform a different function.

The I-beam pointer appears when your cursor is over text and helps you select the proper insertion point. The italic I-beam appears whenever the cursor is over italic text and slants with the italic characters.

The arrow that points diagonally to the right appears only when you move the pointer into the invisible selection area at the left edge of the document window. When you see the right-pointing arrow, you can use the mouse to select lines, paragraphs, or the whole document. For details on this feature, see "How to select text by using the selection bar" on page 76.

The watch indicates that Word is busy. When you see it, you have to wait for Word to finish its current task before you can continue.

The cross-hair pointer appears when you insert a frame in your document; you can use it to define the size and position of the frame. For a discussion of frames, see "Frames: Positioning Text and Graphics on the Page" on page 481.

The horizontal split pointer appears when you choose the Split command from the Window menu or when you position the pointer on the split box on the vertical scroll bar. For details on using this pointer, see "How to split a window" on page 17.

You'll see the vertical split pointer when the pointer is between the style area and the rest of the document window. For details about the style area and styles, see "Displaying the Style Area" on page 427.

The pointer takes on the downward-pointing arrow shape when you move it over the top of a table column. You can use this pointer to select an entire column of a table. For more information about this technique, see "Special table selection techniques for the mouse" on page 346.

| Pointer | Name |
|---|---|
| | I-beam pointer |
| | Italic I-beam pointer |
| | Left-arrow pointer |
| | Right-arrow pointer |
| | Watch |
| | Cross-hair pointer |
| | Horizontal split pointer |
| | Vertical split pointer |
| | Downward-pointing arrow |
| | Horizontal outline pointer |
| | Vertical outline pointer |
| | Four-headed outline pointer |
| | Graphics repositioning pointer |
| | Left diagonal pointer for frames |
| | Right diagonal pointer for frames |
| | Cropping pointer |
| | Magnifying pointer |
| | Drag-and-drop pointer for moving |
| | Drag-and-drop pointer for copying |
| | Format Painter pointer |
| | Macro-recording pointer (the arrow is transparent) |
| | Finger-pointing hand |
| | Arrow-and-question-mark pointer |

**FIGURE 1-20**

Pointers and their names.

The four-headed outline pointer appears when you point to a heading or body-text icon while in Outline view. It changes to the vertical outline pointer when you drag the heading vertically. It changes to the horizontal outline pointer when you drag the heading left or right to promote or demote the heading. We'll cover Word's outlining features in Chapter 19.

The horizontal and vertical outline pointers also appear when you're moving or resizing graphics or frames, as do the two diagonal pointers and the graphics repositioning pointer. The cropping pointer is used to change how much of a graphic is visible. For a discussion of frames, see "Frames: Positioning Text and Graphics on the Page" on page 481.

The magnifying pointer appears in Print Preview mode and can be used to increase magnification of the document. We cover all of the Print Preview features in Chapter 8. One of the two drag-and-drop pointers appears when you drag a section of selected text or a framed object from one location to another. You can turn this feature off for text if you prefer. For details on turning the feature off and on, see "How to use the mouse to drag and drop text" in the Tip on page 92.

The pointer for the Format Painter appears when you choose the Format Painter button on the Standard toolbar. The Format Painter enables you to copy character formatting, paragraph formatting, or both. We cover the use of this new feature in Chapter 7. The macro-recording pointer appears in the document window while you are recording a macro to remind you that Word doesn't record mouse movements as part of a macro. The pointer disappears when you start typing, but it reappears when you then move the mouse. We'll cover macros in detail in Chapter 24.

If you're concerned about how your text looks, you may find yourself going regularly to the Format menu, just to confirm that your text is formatted correctly. Word 6.0 can give you that information quickly. Display the arrow-and-question-mark pointer by pressing ⌘-Shift-? or by clicking on the Help button on the Standard toolbar. Then point to the text you want information about and click. Word will display the information in an information box similar to the one in Figure 1-21.

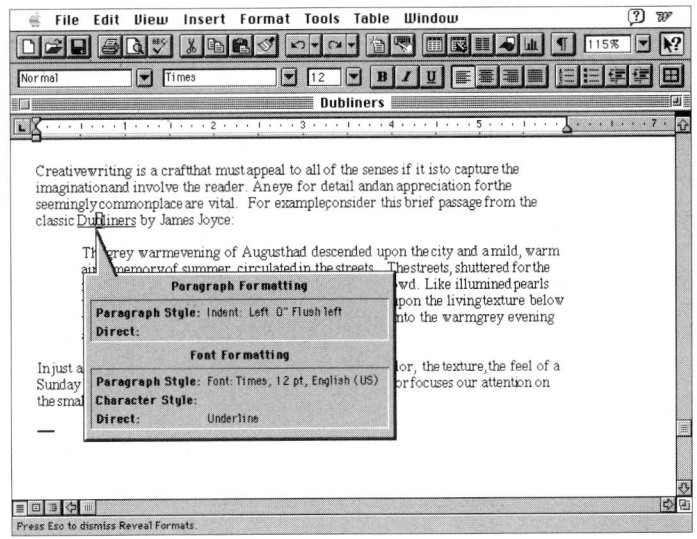

**FIGURE 1-21**

Word can let you see how your text is formatted without going to the Format menu.

You'll see the finger-pointing hand when you position the pointer on an underlined term in a Help window. Clicking the mouse button when this hand shape is showing brings up information about that term.

Finally, you'll see the arrow-and-question-mark pointer when you press ⌘-Shift-? or Shift-Help to get context-sensitive help or when you click on the Help button on the Standard toolbar.

# Getting Help

If you forget how to use a command or other feature (or haven't yet learned it), you can use Word's online Help to get information about how the feature works. There are two ways to get help. You can search through Word's extensive help information by using the Help menu. Alternatively, you can call up context-sensitive Help by using the Help key.

## How to use the Help menu

If you display the Help menu, you'll see the seven commands shown in Figure 1-22 on the next page. About Balloon Help describes the Balloon Help feature, which displays small messages in a cartoon-like balloon, describing the object under the mouse pointer. Show Balloons turns this feature on, at which point the command in the menu will change to Hide Balloons so you can turn it off again.

The Microsoft Word Help command opens a window, shown in Figure 1-23, that lists the major topics available in the Help system. Search For Help On lets you look up topics by using keywords. The Help Index command opens a window, shown in Figure 1-24, that displays an alphabetic list that covers most commands and procedures.

**FIGURE 1-22**

You can get help by simply selecting the commands on Word's Help menu.

**FIGURE 1-23**

If you choose the Microsoft Word Help command, you'll see this window.

You can also use the row of buttons that show across the top of the window to jump to the contents page in Help; search for specific topics; step back through the last screens you viewed; see a list, or history, of the Help screens you've viewed (so that you can return to any of them directly); or go to the Help index.

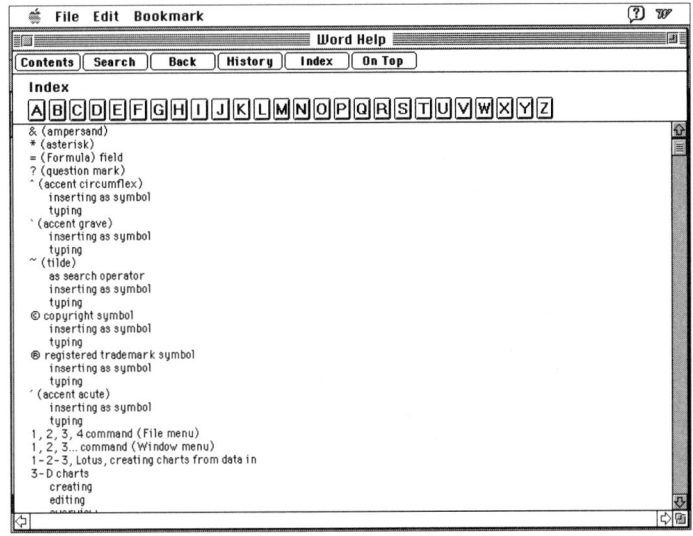

**FIGURE 1-24**

If you choose the Index command, you'll see this window.

On most Help screens, you'll see words and phrases that appear with a solid underline. Word calls these *jump terms.* You can think of jump terms as cross-references. When you point to one, the pointer will take on the shape of a pointing finger. If you click the mouse button while pointing to a jump term, a Help window on that topic will open. You can also use the Tab key to move to and highlight a term on the screen and then press Return to open the term's Help window. After you read the jump term's Help window, you can return to the original Help window by clicking on the Back button.

In addition to the jump terms, you'll also see words and phrases with dotted underlines, called *glossary terms.* As with jump terms, the pointer changes to a pointing-finger shape when it is on a glossary term. Click on the word to open a window containing the definition of that term. Click again, and the definition will disappear. To bring up a glossary term's definition from the keyboard, use the Tab key to highlight the appropriate term, and then press the Return key. Press Return again to remove it.

You can close the Help window by clicking on the Close box in the upper left corner of the Help window or by pressing ⌘-W.

## Other commands on the Help menu

The Quick Preview and Examples And Demos commands were described in the Introduction.

The next command is Tip Of The Day, which brings up the same Tip dialog box you see when the program is first loaded. This box shows you a useful tip or trick to make Word easier and faster to use. (Word chooses the day's tip at random.) If you want to see all the tips rather than wait for them to come up at random, choose More Tips for a list of tip topics.

The Technical Support command on the Help menu provides information about Microsoft technical support, along with some hints and advice on solutions to try before you call the support lines.

## How to get context-sensitive Help

In addition to the Help menu screens, Word offers context-sensitive Help, which you can use with either the keyboard or the mouse.

### Using the keyboard

To bring up context-sensitive Help with the keyboard, first use the keyboard to either highlight the command on the appropriate Word menu, open the dialog box, or generate the message you want information on. Then press the Help key. Word will display the related Help screen. If you do not activate a command, dialog box, or message before you press the Help key, Word will display the Help window shown in Figure 1-24.

### Using the mouse

To bring up context-sensitive Help with the mouse, first press Shift-Help or click on the Help button at the right end of the Standard toolbar. The pointer will take the shape of a question mark over an arrow. Then click the command or screen area you want information on, and Word will display the related Help screen. If you change to the arrow-and-question-mark pointer and then decide you don't want help after all, press the Esc key to return the pointer to its usual shape.

## More about Help

The Help system has still more features you may want to explore. The Edit Copy command on the menu bar, for example, will copy help information to the Clipboard so that you can paste it into your documents. Even more useful, the Edit Annotate command lets you add your own annotations to the Help system. Simply choose Edit Annotate, type in a note, and choose Save.

If you add an annotation to a Help screen, Word will add a paper-clip icon to the screen to indicate that there's some information there. To see the note later, simply choose Edit Annotate or click on the paper-clip icon.

You can also print information from the Help system with the File Print Topic command, and you can insert bookmarks with the Bookmark Define command. Bookmarks will let you quickly find a particular section later. The best way to learn more about the Help system is to explore the menus.

# Essential Customization Options

There is one additional issue you should consider before you start working with Word.

Word's customization features give you the ability to match the program to the way you work. You can, in fact, change most of the features discussed in this chapter. You can rename the menu commands; redesign or hide the Standard and Formatting toolbars; hide the ruler, status bar, and scroll bars to display more text; reassign shortcut-key combinations; and even build your own commands.

Elsewhere in this book, you can learn how to use all of these features and more. For now, however, you shouldn't make too many changes to Word. The examples in this book use the default settings, and until you're familiar with the program, you should stay with the defaults so that your screen will look much like the illustrations in the book. Even so, there are several customization options you should know about now because they will affect how comfortable you are when using the program—particularly if you're used to another word processor and expect Word to behave in certain ways. Here, then, is a quick tour of the customization options you may want to consider right away.

## The View menu

Start by opening the View menu, shown in Figure 1-25.

Notice that there is a check mark next to the Ruler command. This indicates that the command is active and that its associated screen element is displayed. You can display or hide the ruler by choosing the command.

**FIGURE 1-25**

The View menu has commands that control the appearance of the Word screen, including whether the ruler is visible.

```
View
• Normal
  Outline
  Page Layout
  Master Document

  Full Screen

  Toolbars...
✓ Ruler

  Header and Footer
  Footnotes
  Annotations

  Zoom...
```

Notice also the command named Toolbars. This command opens a dialog box that lets you choose whether to display any (or all) of the ten Word toolbars, including the Standard and Formatting toolbars that are displayed by default.

 You can also display a shortcut menu controlling the toolbar features by holding down the Control key when clicking in the toolbar with the mouse button.

You might want to hide the ruler or toolbars for either of two reasons: You don't use them or you want to see more text on your screen.

You can display or hide any of these items at any time, but note that some of our examples in later chapters use the ruler or toolbars and assume that they are showing.

## The Options dialog box

Most of the menu-based customization choices are available through the Options dialog box. Choose Tools Options, and Word will display the dialog box shown in Figure 1-26. The Options dialog box looks much like a set of file cards with tabs showing. If you move from card to card, you'll find that the options in the box vary. The figure shows the View options.

**FIGURE 1-26**

When you choose the Tools Options command, Word will open the Options dialog box.

You can choose a card by clicking on its tab with the mouse. You can also use the keyboard; ⌘-Page Down will move to the next card, and ⌘-Page Up will move to the previous one.

## View options

If a card other than View is showing on your screen, click on the View tab or press ⌘-Page Up to move from card to card. (Use ⌘-Page Down to move to the previous card.)

There are only a few items on the View card that you need to know about now. First, in the section labeled Window, are check boxes for the Horizontal Scroll Bar and the Vertical Scroll Bar. An X in a check box tells Word to display the item on your document screen. An empty, or *cleared*, check box tells Word not to display it. A check box toggles between checked and cleared each time you choose it. You can hide either or both of the scroll bars to give you more room on your screen for text.

Another important option, Draft Font, is listed in the Show box. When this check box is checked, Word will use a draft font that has little relationship to what your text will look like when printed. If you want the text on screen to be as close to the text on the printed page as possible, be sure that this check box is cleared (that is, there is no X in it). Word's default setting is for Draft Font off. For a thorough discussion on matching the screen and the printed page, see "Understanding Screen Fonts and Printer Fonts" on page 553.

If speed is a problem with your system and you don't need to see how text will look on the printed page while you're writing or editing, check the Draft Font check box on the View card. Word usually runs faster with this option turned on.

The Nonprinting Characters box includes check boxes for various items that don't appear on a printed page but that you might want to see on the screen while editing: tabs and spaces, paragraph marks, nonprinting characters, optional hyphens, and hidden text. If you check the Tab Characters and Spaces check boxes, Word will show tab characters on the screen as small arrows pointing to the right and spaces as small dots between words. This can help you distinguish tabbed spacing from sequences of character spaces. You can select either of these options independently.

If you check the Paragraph Marks check box, Word will display paragraph marks, showing you at a glance whether Word will treat a given line as a line within a paragraph or as a paragraph by itself. Checking the All check box is equivalent to checking all of the check boxes in the Nonprinting Characters box—Word will display all nonprinting items on the list. You can also toggle the All option by clicking on the Show/Hide ¶ button at the right end of the Standard toolbar.

## Edit options

The second card to the right of View is labeled Edit, as shown in Figure 1-27.

The Edit card in the Options dialog box lets you change some Word editing settings.

The first check box, Typing Replaces Selection, needs some explanation. If this box is checked (as it is by default) and you have highlighted some text in a document, Word will replace the highlighted text with the newly entered text when you start typing. If the check box is cleared, Word will not replace a highlighted block; instead, it will insert the new text before the highlighted block.

The second choice is a bit safer, but the first approach also has advantages. If you want to replace one block of text with another, the Typing Replaces Selection option lets you do it in one step instead of two. Which option you choose is a matter of your preference.

**NEW!**      If you have Word set so that typing will replace a selection and you accidentally delete a block of text, you can recover the text immediately after typing by choosing the Edit Undo command. Word 6.0 has a multiple-level Undo feature that can undo many previous steps. This feature will let you recover easily from accidentally replacing a section of text (or from other mistakes), even after you take other actions.

The Drag-And-Drop Text Editing option is another one that most people have strong preferences about, either for or against. If checked, this check box lets you drag a text selection to change its position. This feature is checked by default, and if you don't like it, you can clear it here.

The Automatic Word Selection check box affects how the highlight moves **NEW!** when you click and drag over text. Without it, the highlight moves one character at a time. With it, the highlight selects only complete words, and it will jump to include the entire next word as soon as the mouse pointer moves to the start of that word. For more details on this feature, see "How to extend a selection word by word" on page 74.

The next check box worth noting is Use The INS Key For Paste. If this is checked, you can use the Shift-Ins key combination to paste data from the Clipboard into your document. (The Ins key is the Help key if you don't also press Shift.) Whether you select the Use The INS Key For Paste option or not, ⌘-V will paste data from the Clipboard into your document.

The Overtype Mode check box sets Overtype as the default mode. Most users prefer to work in Insert mode, in which new text is inserted at the cursor, pushing the old text ahead of it. However, some prefer Overtype mode, in which new text replaces old text character by character, much like typing over a character on a typewriter.

> Whether or not you have selected the Use The INS Key For Paste option, you can still use Control-Ins to toggle between Insert and Overtype modes when you are working in a document.

## Save options

The next card of immediate interest, labeled Save, is shown in Figure 1-28 on the next page. There are four Save options you should be aware of from the start: Always Create Backup Copy, Allow Fast Saves, Prompt For Summary Info, and Automatic Save.

Checking the Always Create Backup Copy check box tells Word to save the old version of an existing file—a backup—before it saves a new version of that file. If a backup version already exists, it's replaced by the new backup version. This means you always have a one-generation-old version of a file available. This can be helpful if you decide you don't like a change that you made in the current version. It also gives you a recent version to go back to in case the current version is corrupted on disk.

The Allow Fast Saves option speeds document saving while you are creating or editing a document. Rather than save the entire file each time, Word attaches the changes to the end of the file. It will save the entire file every tenth save or when you close the document. Checking this box makes the intermediate save operations faster, but the file will grow longer and longer until you finally close the document. This option is selected by default.

**FIGURE 1-28**

The Save options let you specify Word's actions when it saves document files.

The Prompt For Summary Info check box, which is cleared by default, tells Word to ask for details about your document—title, subject, author, keywords, and comments—the first time you save a new document (or save an existing document with a new name). This information is useful for managing your documents. If you check this box, Word will always remind you to add the information to each file.

The Automatic Save option tells Word to save the current file at whatever interval you specify in the Minutes text box, although sometimes it might interrupt you while you're in the middle of writing a sentence, so you might find it distracting. We recommend using this feature and setting it to no more than 10 to 15 minutes.

The *Automatic Save* name for this feature is a little misleading because your work is not saved in the same way as it is when you choose the File Save command. Instead, Automatic Save protects you from losing information only in the event of a system crash or power failure. All Automatic Save files are cleared when you exit Word normally. As a result, you should not rely solely on Automatic Save to protect your work; we recommend that you also save your work manually at regular intervals, such as every paragraph or every page.

## User Info options

The User Info card is the last Tools Options card of immediate interest. As shown in Figure 1-29, this card displays basic information about the user.

**FIGURE 1-29**

The User Info options card displays information about the user that other features in Word can take advantage of.

Word uses the entry in the Name text box to fill in the Author information in the Summary Info dialog box. It uses the entry in the Initials text box to mark annotations you insert in a document. And it uses the Mailing Address entry as the return address for the envelope-printing utility. If you entered this information properly when you installed Word, it will be correct here as well. If not, simply type the changes in the appropriate text box. You'll also need to enter the rest of your address information, after your name and company name.

There are many other settings accessible through the Options dialog box. Browse through them and set any that you think are worthwhile. However, note that most of these options won't mean much to you until you're more familiar with Word. We'll come back to them later. Now it's time to begin working with documents.

# Topic Finder

# 2

# File Handling

earning how to use any word processor involves more than learning how to enter, edit, and format text. It also involves learning an entirely new filing system. When you enter text on your screen in Word—or in any other word processor, for that matter—your work isn't saved until you store it in a file on your computer's disk. And you'll find that you can quickly build up a large collection of files—so large that it can become unwieldy to keep track of them.

So before you invest time and energy in building a document, you'll want to be sure you understand how to open, close, and save files. You'll also want to become familiar with filling out the Summary Info dialog box. The information you supply in this dialog box can help you find specific files when you need them.

In this chapter, we'll look at the basic file-handling commands for creating new files, opening existing files, deleting files, and saving the files you're working on. For a discussion of Word's more sophisticated file-handling features, see Chapter 17.

# Creating and Opening Documents

As we discussed in Chapter 1, there are several ways to start Word. If you simply double-click the Microsoft Word icon in the Finder, for example, Word will create a new, blank document and name it *Document1*. Alternatively, you can open one or more existing documents along with Word. For example, you can highlight one or more document icons in the Finder and double-click on one of them to run Word and open the documents at the same time. Odds are good, however, that you'll be running Word already when you want to create or open a file. For more information on starting Word, see "Starting Word for the Macintosh" on page 3.

## How to create a new document

If you want to create a new document while running Word, simply choose File New. Word will open the dialog box shown in Figure 2-1.

**FIGURE 2-1**

Use the New dialog box to open a new document in Word.

The New dialog box lets you make two choices—one in the Template list box on the left and one in the New option box on the right—to designate the file as either a document or a template. Templates are useful for creating standard formats for your documents; we'll discuss them briefly at the end of this chapter and in more detail in Chapters 9 and 27.

As you can see in Figure 2-1, Word also has a large number of wizards listed in the Template list box. Wizards automate the creation of complex documents and even of customized templates. We'll ignore wizards in this discussion, but we'll cover specific wizards as appropriate throughout this book. For a discussion of wizards in general, see "Wizards: Automated Documents" on page 294.

For the moment, all you really need to know to start a new file is that you want to create a document rather than a template and that you want to use the template called Normal. Because Word defaults to both of these options in any case, you can open a new document by simply choosing OK.

You can also create a new document that uses the Normal template by clicking on the leftmost button on the Standard toolbar.

As you create documents during any given session, Word will number them sequentially: Document1, Document2, Document3, and so on. Word will create a new document window for each new document.

## How to open an existing document

If you want to retrieve an existing document from disk while you're in Word, choose File Open or ⌘-O or click on the Open button—second from left on the Standard toolbar. Word will display a dialog box like that shown in Figure 2-2.

**FIGURE 2-2**

You use this dialog box to retrieve files.

> **Select a Document:**
>
> 🗁 Documents ▼       ⊂ Macintosh HD
>
> 🗀 Callouts        79360K available
> 🗀 Cars
> 🗀 Letters         [ Open ]   [ Eject ]
> 🗀 Memos
> 🗀 Monthly         [ Cancel ]  [ Desktop ]
> 🗀 Names
> 🗀 New NRBQ        [ Find File... ] [ Help ]
>
> **List Files of Type:**      ☐ Read Only
>
> Readable Files  ▼    ☐ Confirm Conversions

At the top left of the dialog box, there is a prompt to select a document. The first box shows the current folder; you can open this box to choose a different folder. You can also choose the Desktop button at the right of the dialog box to go to the Desktop level so that you can choose a different disk or open a folder or file that is on the Desktop.

The list below the folder box shows the files (and folders) in the current folder in alphabetic order. You can open a file in the current folder by double-clicking on its name or highlighting the name and pressing Return. (To highlight a name with the keyboard, either use the arrow keys or type the first letter of the filename, and Word will move the highlight to the first name in the list that starts with that letter.)

You can limit the files that are displayed in the file list by using the List Files Of Type box at the bottom left of the dialog box. This defaults to Readable Files, but you can choose other types of files as shown in Figure 2-3 on the next page.

**FIGURE 2-3**

The List Files Of Type list provides a choice of file types to be displayed in the file list.

You can use this feature to show only Word documents, or text files, or documents from Microsoft Excel for the Macintosh version 3.x, 4, or 5. Figure 2-3 shows many of the options available.

We'll discuss the details of importing and exporting files in Chapter 18; see "Opening Documents Stored in Other Formats" on page 589.

Word will do its best to identify a file format created by a different program and convert it to Word format. If you check the Confirm Conversions check box in the dialog box for opening files, Word will first display its guess and then give you the opportunity to change its selection if you know that the file is in a different format.

## How to find a document

At times when you can't remember which directory a file is in, its exact name, or even the disk it's stored on, the Find File button on the right side of the dialog box for opening files can be helpful. For now, just be aware that this button is equivalent to the Find File command on the File menu. In either location, this feature provides a number of useful capabilities, including the ability to search for files in more than one directory as well as to print, delete, and copy multiple files. We'll discuss this feature in detail in "Retrieving Documents" on page 571.

## How to access a network

If your computer is connected to a network, you can open a file stored on a network drive. When you connect to a network drive, you can access that drive as if it were a hard drive on your computer; you can switch to the network drive by selecting the drive from the Desktop.

## How to use the Read Only check box

In the lower right corner of the dialog box for opening files is a check box labeled *Read Only*. If you check this box before you open a file, Word will let you browse through the document and even make changes to it, but it will not let you save the document under its original name. If you want to save any changes, you'll need to save the file under a new name, using the File Save As command. (We'll discuss the File Save and File Save As commands in a moment.) This Read Only feature gives you the ability to protect an important original from accidental changes but still use that original to create a revised version with a new name.

## How to open recently used documents

If you create long documents, you'll often find yourself returning to Word to work with documents you worked on in a previous writing session. There's an easy way to reopen the documents you've used most recently. As you can see at the bottom of Figure 2-4, the File menu lists the last few document files you've opened. To reopen any of these, simply select the filename from the menu or type the number that appears to the left of the name.

**FIGURE 2-4**

The filenames at the bottom of the File menu provide an easy way to reopen the documents you've used most recently.

| File | |
|---|---|
| New... | ⌘N |
| Open... | ⌘O |
| Close | ⌘W |
| Save | ⌘S |
| Save As... | |
| Save All | |
| Find File... | |
| Summary Info... | |
| Templates... | |
| Document Layout... | |
| Page Setup... | |
| Print Preview | |
| Print... | ⌘P |
| 1 Callouts | |
| 2 Revision | |
| 3 New NABQ | |
| 4 Monthly | |
| Quit | ⌘Q |

You can change the number of recently opened files listed at the bottom of the File menu. By default, the File menu lists up to four names, but if you choose Tools Options and then choose the General card, you'll find an option labeled Recently Used File List. You can change this to any number from 1 through 9, or you can turn the feature off entirely.

# Saving Your Work

As you work in Word, the documents you create reside in your computer's random access memory (RAM) and in temporary files on your disk. However, when you leave Word, the information held in RAM and the links to the temporary files are both lost. To store a document so that you can retrieve it and work with it later, you must save it as a file on your disk. After it is saved on disk, the file will remain there until you delete it.

 Remember that even saved files are still at risk because you can have a problem with your hard disk. As with all computer programs, you should protect the time and effort you invest in your work by making frequent backups—that is, additional copies—of any Word document files you can't afford to lose. There are many strategies for creating backups—including adding a tape backup system or additional hard disks to your computer. If you're new to computers, however, the simplest approach is to save a second copy of important files on a floppy disk, using Word's save feature. The extra work involved will pay off when (not if!) you lose a file from your hard disk.

The tools you'll normally use to save a document are the File Save and File Save As commands. The first time you use either command when working on a new document (or try to save changes to a Read Only file), Word will display the Save As dialog box, shown in Figure 2-5. After you've named and saved a document, you can bypass this dialog box by choosing File Save. Note that clicking on the Save button—the third button from the left on the Standard toolbar—is equivalent to choosing the File Save command.

**FIGURE 2-5**

Word displays the Save As dialog box when you choose File Save As. It also shows this dialog box when you choose File Save to save a file for the first time.

The first time you save a file, you must specify a filename. By default, Word suggests the current folder and displays the folder name above the file list box. If you want to create a new folder within the current folder, choose the New button, type a name for the folder, and choose the Create button.

If you want to store the document on a different drive, you can go to the Desktop by choosing the Desktop button and then selecting a drive from the top left box.

After you've specified the appropriate drive and folder, type the name for the file in the Save Current Document As text box and choose OK. (We'll ignore the Options button for the moment.) Depending on how you've set Word's save options, you may then see Word's Summary Info dialog box, shown in Figure 2-6. To complete the save operation, choose OK in this dialog box. (Note, in passing, that the Summary Info dialog box has several important features to help you manage your document files. We'll discuss them later in this chapter, under "Summary information.")

The Summary Info dialog box is displayed automatically only if you have checked the Prompt For Summary Info check box on the Save card in the Options dialog box. To check the setting, you can choose the Options button in the Save dialog box, or choose Tools Options and then choose Save.

**FIGURE 2-6**

The Summary Info dialog box appears when you choose OK in the Save As dialog box.

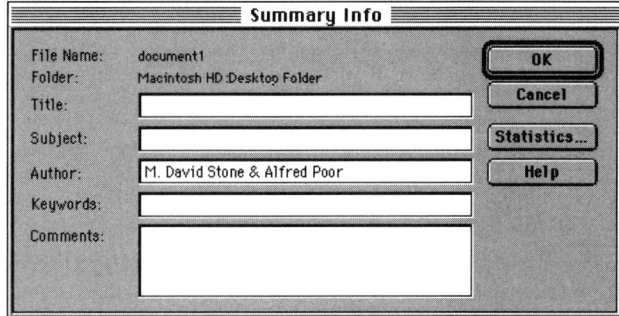

## Filename rules

When naming Word documents, follow the standard Macintosh naming conventions. You can use uppercase and lowercase letters, spaces, numbers, and any punctuation mark except a colon. You are limited to a total of 31 characters in a filename.

## File Save As options

In addition to the filename, folder, and drive, you can specify other options with the File Save As command. These options are available through the Options button in the Save As dialog box.

The Options button in the Save As dialog box takes you to the Options dialog box shown in Figure 2-7. This is the same dialog box, with the same Save card, that you can get to by using the Tools Options command, except that you can't change to any of the other cards as you can when you open the dialog box by choosing Tools Options. You'll find some of these options discussed in Chapter 1, but one option is important enough to repeat the discussion here: Automatic Save. We strongly recommend that you take advantage of Word's Automatic Save feature. It will minimize your chances of losing your work in case of a power outage or system failure.

**FIGURE 2-7**

Choosing the Options button in the Save As dialog box lets you choose any of several saving options. It opens the same dialog box that is available through the Tools Options Save command.

For those who need to safeguard important files, Word's File Sharing Options group at the bottom of the Save card offers ways to protect a file from changes and from prying eyes. The File Sharing Options group includes two text boxes for passwords: the Protection Password text box and the Write Reservation Password text box. You can use each type of password independently of the other, but note that you can also use both together, with the protection password controlling who can see a file and the write reservation password controlling who can modify it.

Either password can be up to 15 characters long, using uppercase letters, lowercase letters, spaces, and punctuation marks. As you type, Word will substitute a dot for each character. To ensure that you typed the password correctly, Word will ask you to type it again after you choose OK. If the two entries match, the program will accept the password and return to the Save As dialog box. If you then choose OK to close the dialog box and finish saving, the password will take effect.

If you assign a protection password, you won't be able to open the file without entering the correct password. If you assign a write reservation password, you'll be able to read the file without knowing the write reservation password, but you won't be able to save changes to the file.

When opening a file that includes a write reservation password, you have a choice of entering the password, which will let you make changes to the file, or selecting the Read Only button in the Password dialog box. If you open the file as read-only, you can make changes and save the file under a new name. The new file will automatically inherit the same password or passwords as the original version unless you go to the Options dialog box and specifically remove the passwords.

Be careful when using protection passwords. If you don't know the password, there is no way to get to your text. This obviously makes for a secure system, but you need to be careful not to forget the password. Note also that the passwords are case sensitive, so that *hi there*, for example, will not match *Hi There* or *HI THERE*. When you enter a password, be sure to remember the case you used, as well as the characters themselves. We suggest maintaining a list of filenames and their corresponding passwords, but be sure to keep the list in a safe place. Too many security systems are defeated because users leave the passwords in an obvious location, such as in a desk drawer or even taped to the system monitor.

When used by itself, Word's protection password provides reasonably good security, as long as you don't give the password to anyone who might resave the file—or save a copy of the file—with the password removed. However, if you take advantage of the write reservation password to let some people read a file without being able to modify it, the security is limited at best. Using both types of passwords on the same file makes it more difficult for anyone to get to or change the file, but once you have a file open for reading, it's a simple matter to choose File Save As and then Options and remove the passwords to save an unprotected version of the file under another name. Write reservation passwords work well as a way to keep specific files intact, but don't rely on them if you want to keep information secret.

The third option in the File Sharing Options group is a Read-Only Recommended check box. If you select this option for a file, Word will display a dialog box similar to the one shown in Figure 2-8 each time the file is opened, recommending that the file be opened as read-only. If you choose Yes, Word will open the file as read-only. If you choose No, you'll be able to change the file and save the changes. Note, however, that if you have assigned a write reservation password to a file, the Read-Only Recommended check box will not bring up the dialog box shown in Figure 2-8.

**FIGURE 2-8**

If you choose the Read-Only Recom-mended check box before saving a file, Word will display a dialog box similar to this whenever a user tries to open the file.

## How to change a filename or folder

The File Save As command offers one other capability. Word has no direct way to change a filename or move a file to another folder from within the pro-gram. However, you can create a copy of the file under a different filename, in a different folder, or both, by using the File Save As command and specifying the appropriate folder and filename. You can then delete the original file, us-ing any file-deletion technique you're comfortable with. This is a less than ideal workaround, but it yields the same effect as if you had simply renamed or moved the file.

## Summary information

If the Prompt For Summary Info box is checked on the Save card in the Tools Options dialog box, the first time you save a document Word will display a Summary Info dialog box similar to the ones shown in Figures 2-6 and 2-9. You can use this feature to make it easier to organize your documents and find files on your system.

It's a good habit to make sure you have appropriate entries in the Sum-mary Info dialog box when you save a document for the first time. Alterna-tively, you can fill in the dialog box when you start a new document before you actually create the document, by choosing the Summary button in the File New dialog box. You can also open the current document's Summary Info dialog box at any time by choosing File Summary Info.

## How to enter summary information

Word automatically includes the filename and directory information at the top of the dialog box, and as already noted, you can't change these directly from within Word. However, all other entries in this dialog box are under your control.

You can enter a descriptive title in the Title text box. Titles in the Title text box can be up to 255 characters long and can include any character or symbol that you can type on your keyboard, including spaces and colons. For example, if you're writing a newspaper article about Mick Jagger of the Rolling Stones, you might save the document under the filename *Jagger* but enter the title *Mick Jagger and the Rolling Stones Still Rocking* in the Title text box, as we've done in Figure 2-9.

**FIGURE 2-9**

We've entered some sample information in this Summary Info dialog box.

| | | |
|---|---|---|
| File Name: | Jagger | OK |
| Folder: | Macintosh HD:Microsoft Word 6.0:Documents | Cancel |
| Title: | Mick Jagger and the Rolling Stones Still Rockin | Statistics... |
| Subject: | Mick Jagger still has the right stuff, after 25 y | Help |
| Author: | M. David Stone & Alfred Poor | |
| Keywords: | Jagger Stones rock music article | |
| Comments: | Feature story for Sixties Rock magazine May 1993 | |

In addition to specifying a title, you can describe the subject of the document in the Subject text box. As with the Title text box, the Subject text box will accept up to 255 characters. For our sample, we've entered the text *Mick Jagger still has the right stuff, after 25 years*.

By default, Word fills in the Author text box using the name currently entered in the Name text box on the User Info card in the Tools Options dialog box. You can modify this entry, as we have here, to include additional authors, or you can change the name altogether. To change the default name, choose Tools Options, select User Info, and enter a new name.

You can create an index for your document by entering a list of keywords in the Keywords text box. The keywords should indicate the document's contents. For example, for our sample document, you might enter the words *Jagger, Stones, rock,* and *music*. Notice that in Figure 2-9 we've used a space between each keyword and the next keyword. You can enter up to 255 characters of keywords, including spaces. The main benefit of using keywords is that you can later find and open the document by searching for those words with the File Find File command. For information on the Find File command, see "Retrieving Documents" on page 571.

The last option in the Summary Info dialog box is the Comments text box. You can type any remarks you want in this text box. Here again, you can use up to 255 characters, including symbols. In our sample Comments text box, we've entered *Feature story for Sixties Rock magazine May 1993*.

## How to get statistical information about a document

The Summary Info dialog box includes a button labeled Statistics. If you choose it, you'll see some useful information about your document, as shown in Figure 2-10.

**FIGURE 2-10**

The Document Statistics dialog box shows you information about your document.

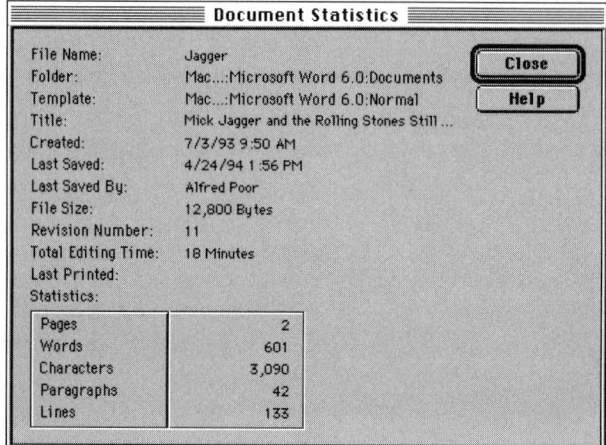

The Document Statistics dialog box shows you the filename, folder, associated template, document title, date and time of creation and last revision, most recent author (or editor, or typist) to save the file, file size in bytes, revision number, total editing time, and date of last printing. It also shows the number of pages, words, characters, paragraphs, and lines in the document. You can't edit any of this information directly. To return to the Summary Info dialog box, choose Close.

## Possible problems in saving

If you don't have enough room on the current disk to save your document, you'll see a message box like the one shown in Figure 2-11 when you try to save. If so, choose OK; Word will close the message and return you to the document window. Then you can choose the File Save As command to save the document on a different disk, or you can delete some of the files on the disk. (We'll show you how to do this shortly, in the section "Deleting a File.")

**FIGURE 2-11**

You'll see this message box if there isn't enough room to save your document on the active disk.

If the name you enter in the Save Current Document As text box duplicates a name that already exists in the current directory, you'll see a message box asking whether you want to replace the existing file. To replace the existing file with the document you're trying to save, choose Replace. Otherwise, choose Cancel to return to the Save As dialog box.

## How to save a document again

After you save a document, you don't need to use the File Save As command again unless you want to save that file under a new name or change one of the file options. To save the changes to a file that you've previously saved, simply choose File Save or click the Save button on the Standard toolbar. Word will save the current version and let you continue editing.

Word provides shortcut keys for various tasks. You can use ⌘-S to save the current file.

If you choose File Save As to save a file that you've previously saved, you'll see the Save As dialog box containing the current name in the Save Current Document As text box. If you mean to save the file under its original name, choose OK, and Word will save the file as if you had chosen File Save. If you want to save the document under a new name, however, type that name in the Save Current Document As text box and choose OK. Word will then save the new version of the document under the new filename and leave the original file unchanged.

## How to save a read-only document

If you try to save a file you opened with the Read Only option turned on, Word will display a message reminding you of the file's read-only status.

Choose OK, and Word will display the Save As dialog box. If you again try to assign the same name to the altered file, Word will again display the message box. To save your changes to the file, you must give the file a new name. As should be clear, the Read Only option is a convenient way to protect your files from unintended changes.

## How to save everything at once

In addition to saving individual files one at a time, you can save everything that's open (including documents, templates, macros, and glossaries) by choosing File Save All. The File Save All command is particularly handy when you've split a single document into several files—as you might with long sections of a single report, for example—or when you're creating or editing AutoText entries or macros. We'll discuss AutoText in "Using AutoText" on page 128. We'll discuss macros in Chapters 24 through 26.

When you choose File Save All, Word will try to save all open documents and all changes in macros and AutoText entries. It will automatically save each open document (assuming the document isn't read-only) and each additional item.

## How to close files without leaving Word

The File Close command is meant to let you close files without leaving Word. For example, if you've opened three files to transfer data among them and you finish your work with one of the three, you can choose the File Close command so that you have only two windows left to work with. If you haven't made changes to the document since you last opened or saved it, Word will immediately close the file.

If you have made changes, however, or if you've entered anything in a new document, Word will display a message box asking whether you want to save the changes to the document. If you choose Yes and the current document has previously been saved, Word will save the document under its current name and then close it. If the document has never been saved, Word will display the Save As dialog box. If you choose No, Word will close the document without saving the changes. If you choose Cancel, Word will return you to the document without saving it or closing it.

The File Close command is equivalent to clicking on the Close box in the upper left corner of the document window. The shortcut key for closing a document window is ⌘-W.

## How to close files and exit Word

The File Quit command tells Word to close everything that's currently open and return to the Finder. If you haven't made any changes since the last time you saved the open files, Word will simply close up shop. If you have made changes or entered anything in a new document, however, you'll see a message box asking whether you want to save your changes. Word will try to save all documents and all changes in macros and glossaries, stopping to ask whether to save each item, including each document. You can save or discard your changes by choosing Yes or No for each item. You can also cancel the Quit command any time that the message box is displayed simply by choosing Cancel.

You can also close Word by pressing ⌘-Q.

# Deleting a File

You can always use the Finder to delete files. You can use the Application menu to switch to the Finder, or if your document windows are not at full size, you can click on the Desktop behind the Word document windows to activate the Finder. There you can highlight one or more document icons and drag them to the Trash to delete the files. However, you may find it easier to delete files without leaving Word.

To delete a file from within Word, first choose File Find File. Word will display a Find File dialog box similar to the one shown in Figure 2-12 on the next page. (The first time you use this feature, Word may display a Search dialog box first; simply choose OK to search for all Word document files on the current drive.)

The Find File dialog box offers a wide range of sophisticated file search and file management functions, which we'll cover in detail in Chapter 17. For the moment, however, we're concerned only with the ability to delete files by using this dialog box. By default, the Find File dialog box will list all Word files on the current drive. (If you don't see the file you want, even after scrolling through the choices, you can change the search specification with the Search button, as we'll discuss in Chapter 17.)

FIGURE 2-12

**FIGURE 2-12**

You can use the Find File dialog box for many tasks, including deleting a file.

To select a file to delete, simply click on the filename, or use the Up and Down arrow keys to move the highlight to the filename, or type the first letter in the filename. (If more than one filename starts with the same letter, you can type the same letter repeatedly to cycle through the choices.) When you've highlighted the file you want to delete, choose Commands and then choose Delete (or press the Del key). Word will display a message box asking whether you want to delete the file. Choose Yes to confirm the deletion or No to have Word return you to the Find File dialog box without deleting the file.

## How to delete multiple files

If you want, you can delete more than one file at a time. To select a group of adjacent files, highlight the first name and hold down the Shift key as you move over the list. To select multiple filenames with the mouse, hold down the mouse button as you extend the selection over adjacent files, or click on the first filename in the batch that you want to delete and then hold down the Shift key as you click on the last name in the list. Word will highlight all file-names between the two you selected. To select nonadjacent filenames with the mouse, hold down the ⌘ key while you click on each name. To remove a file from the list, hold down the ⌘ key and select the entry.

After you highlight the names of the files to delete, choose Commands and then choose Delete (or press the Del key). Word will prompt you to con-firm the deletion. Watch out when you're deleting multiple files—you can easily highlight an extra name and delete the file accidentally. Pay careful at-tention to your selections because Word asks you only once to confirm all of the deletions.

# Templates

There is one last topic related to file handling that you ought to be familiar with, if only on a superficial level: templates. We've mentioned templates in passing several times in this chapter. Word templates are a somewhat complex feature that we won't discuss in detail until much later. However, the concept of a template is so central to Word that you need to be aware of it, even at this early stage.

With most word processing programs, a template is a document that you create as a model for other documents. A letter template, for example, might include your return address, an automatic date entry, and some appropriate formatting commands. Depending on the program, you can use the template either by copying it to another file first and then loading that file or by opening a new file and loading the template.

Templates in Word are similar in concept. You can even create them and edit them in the same way you create and edit standard document files. The difference is that Word recognizes template files as being different from document files.

To avoid being buried in a wealth of choices, we also strongly suggest that you use only the Normal template until you are thoroughly familiar with Word. However, note that Word templates also provide far more potential for customization than you would probably expect. As we'll discuss in Chapter 28, you can even create a different customized set of menus for each template. Note too, as mentioned elsewhere, that Word 6.0 comes with a large number of wizards that automate the process of creating complex templates and related documents. For a general discussion of wizards, see "Wizards: Automated Documents" on page 294.

## How to use templates

Templates in Word work differently from how you might expect. When you attach a template other than the Normal template to an existing document, Word does not detach the Normal template—even though the program gives little indication that it is still attached. Similarly, if you open a new document and specify some other template, Word will still attach the Normal template.

In fact, the second template serves as an additional, or supplementary, template. In general, any customization that you saved in the Normal template is still available in a document that has a supplemental template attached, unless you've overridden the Normal template modifications by additional customization in the supplemental template.

Although templates serve a function that is similar—at least in part—to the Macintosh Stationery Pad feature, they are fundamentally different. When you "open" a Stationery Pad, it creates a new document based on the Stationery Pad. If you open and edit a Word template, however, you make changes to the original document, not a copy. Instead, Word uses a template as the source when creating a new document or when changing the attributes of an existing document by attaching a different template to it.

Unless told otherwise, Word uses its default settings as the Normal template. You can specify the Normal template with every file you create, or you can create a separate Letter template, Memo template, Report template, and so on for each kind of document you regularly use. In fact, Word comes with several sample templates that you can use as well.

If you don't fully follow this introduction to templates, don't let it throw you. Just be aware, for now, that templates exist. We'll come back to templates later in discussing features ranging from basic editing tools to some of Word's most sophisticated customization capabilities. Now we can move on to the basic skills for working with an actual document.

# Topic Finder

# 3

# Essential Skills

fter you open a new document, you'll want to enter text, edit it, and format it to suit your needs. In this chapter, we'll show you how to enter text, and we'll introduce some navigation and selection techniques you'll need so you can view, edit, and format that text. We'll also cover some basic editing skills to set the stage for our discussion of Word's editing, proofing, and formatting features in Chapters 4 through 7.

You'll find many keyboard shortcuts in this chapter. We urge you to practice these; they will help you work more efficiently in Word because they let you keep your fingers on the keys rather than reach for the mouse all the time.

## Entering Text

Entering text in Word is actually easier than typing on a typewriter. As with most word processing programs, the *wordwrap* feature lets you type continuously, without manually entering a carriage return at the end of each line. If you are new to word processing, you may be tempted to press the Return key as you near the end of each line of text. Don't give in to the habit. If there's not enough room on the current line for the word you are typing, Word will move the entire word to the start of the next line automatically. The only time you need to press the Return key while entering text is when you want to start a new paragraph.

More important than the fact that you don't have to enter the carriage return at the end of each line is the fact that you shouldn't. A carriage return at the end of each line makes it more difficult to edit and reformat text. You should press Return only at the end of a paragraph (or a line that you want Word to treat as a paragraph).

## A sample document

To illustrate some basic entry, selection, and editing techniques, we'll use the text in Figure 3-1. To work along with us, you can enter this text in a Word document yourself, or you can type in any other text. If you've just started Word, you can enter your text in the file titled Document1. If you need to open a new file, however, choose File New. When the New dialog box appears, choose OK to bring up the new, blank document.

**FIGURE 3-1**

We'll use this text as a sample document to illustrate text entry, selection, and editing techniques.

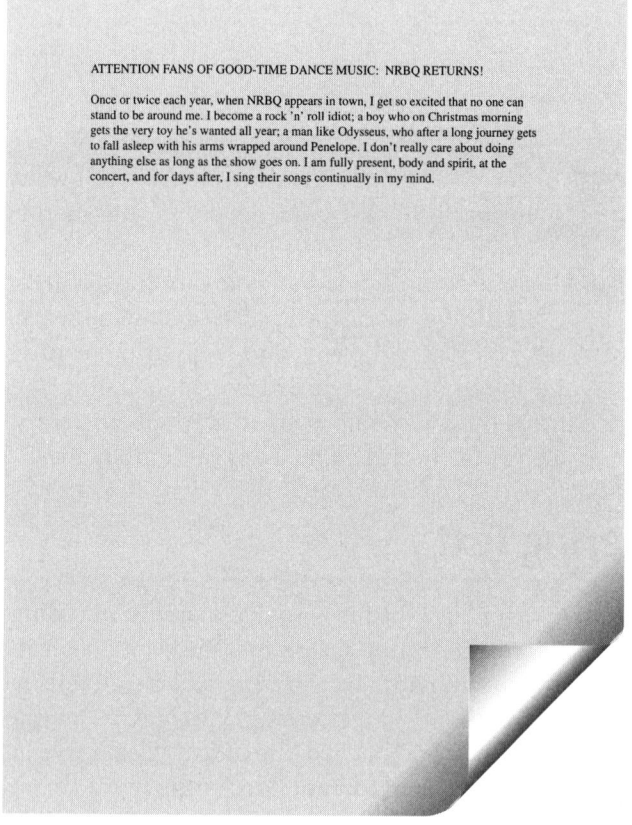

ATTENTION FANS OF GOOD-TIME DANCE MUSIC: NRBQ RETURNS!

Once or twice each year, when NRBQ appears in town, I get so excited that no one can stand to be around me. I become a rock 'n' roll idiot; a boy who on Christmas morning gets the very toy he's wanted all year; a man like Odysseus, who after a long journey gets to fall asleep with his arms wrapped around Penelope. I don't really care about doing anything else as long as the show goes on. I am fully present, body and spirit, at the concert, and for days after, I sing their songs continually in my mind.

## What you'll see

Word displays your documents in one of four basic views: Normal, Page Layout, Outline, or Master Document (a variation of Outline view for long documents). Throughout this chapter, we will use Normal view. You'll find it easier to follow our examples if your screen is set the same way as ours. To verify that it is, open the View menu and make sure there is a bullet (a small dot) next to the Normal command. (The bullet indicates which of the four mutually exclusive choices is currently chosen.) If there isn't a dot, choose the Normal command to change to Normal view.

Next, choose Tools Options and select the View tab. Verify that the check box labeled Draft Font is cleared. If this check box is checked, the fonts and type sizes in your document will not be accurately displayed, nor will the line breaks appear as they will on the printed page. Although this can speed up performance a bit, you lose the ability to see how your document will look when it's printed, which is one of any Macintosh word processor's main strengths. To make sure that your screen matches our illustrations, do not use the Draft Font option.

You will also want to make sure that Word's zoom feature is set appropriately. If the zoom percentage is too high, the characters on your screen will be far larger, proportionately, than they'll appear in the illustrations. If the percentage is too low, the screen characters will be far smaller. Mouse users can click in the Zoom Control pull-down list box on the Standard toolbar, as shown in Figure 3-2. Keyboard users can choose View Zoom to open the Zoom dialog box shown in Figure 3-3 on the next page, choose from the Zoom To settings, and then choose OK.

NEW!

**FIGURE 3-2**

You can tell Word to zoom in or out on a document by using the Zoom Control drop-down list box.

**FIGURE 3-3**

You can also tell Word
to zoom in or out on a
document by using the
Zoom dialog box.

To improve the legibility of the screen images in this book, we have
used a zoom setting of 115%. If you want a zoom level different
from those Word provides on its built-in list, you can simply type
the level, either in the Zoom text box on the Standard toolbar or in
the Percent text box in the Zoom dialog box.

The default font for a new document will depend on the printer you've
installed, but it will typically be a 12-point version of Times, or something
similar. (The issues of printer and screen fonts can get quite complex; we'll
discuss them in more detail in Chapter 16.)

You can choose a different point size by opening the Font Size drop-down
list on the Formatting toolbar, either with the mouse or with the shortcut keys
(⌘-Shift-P, Down arrow). By the way, this and all other references to shortcut
keys assume you are using the default settings for Word's keys. We strongly
recommend that you not reassign any keys until you are thoroughly familiar
with the program. (If you want to change keyboard assignments, however,
we'll explain how to do so in Chapter 28.)

When you open the Font Size drop-down list, you should see a list similar
to the one in Figure 3-4, although the actual choices will depend on your printer
and other factors.

## How to enter text

With 12-point type and Normal view selected, begin entering text. As you
type, notice the blinking vertical cursor. The cursor moves one space to the
right with each character you type, indicating your position in the document.

If you make an error, press the Delete key to move the cursor back one
space at a time and erase your mistakes. Then resume typing as usual. If you
don't notice an error until you are well past it, don't worry about it at this
point. We'll show you how to correct those mistakes later in this chapter.

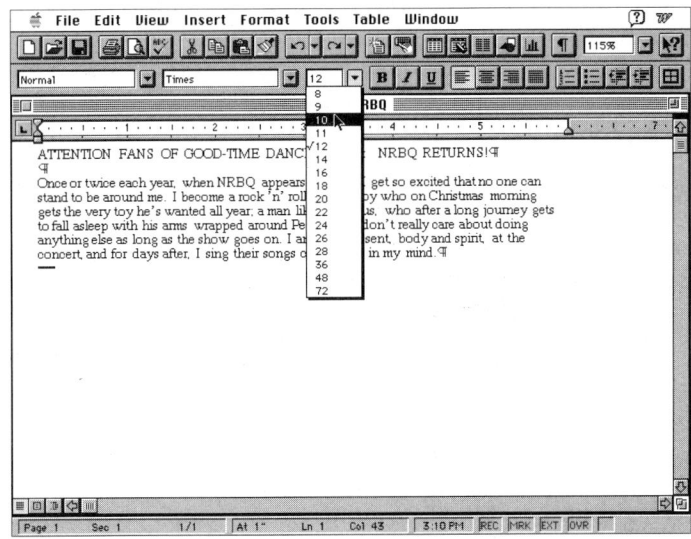

**FIGURE 3-4**

You can change the point size of your text using the Formatting toolbar.

You will notice that at the end of the first line in Figure 3-2 there is a symbol you won't find on your keyboard. It is shaped like a backwards P and is called the *paragraph symbol*. There's another on a line by itself below the first line. These paragraph symbols mark the points at which you should press the Return key if you are entering our sample document. When you press Return, the cursor will move to the start of the next line. Depending on how Word is configured, you may or may not see the paragraph symbols on your screen; as mentioned in Chapter 1, you can display and hide these by choosing Tools Options, then choosing View, and selecting the Paragraph Marks option. You can also click on the Show/Hide ¶ button on the Standard toolbar to show all nonprinting characters. For more information, see the next section, "Displaying Special Marks."

When you type text, press Return only when you need to begin a new paragraph. If you like, you can emphasize paragraphs by pressing Return twice between paragraphs or by pressing the Tab key at the beginning of each paragraph. However, be aware that there are easier ways to get the same effect, as we'll discuss in Chapter 7. Don't worry if some of the text scrolls off the top of the screen. As you'll see in a moment, you can use Word's scrolling features to bring text back into view.

# Displaying Special Marks

One of Word's most striking features is its graphical interface, which can show a close approximation on the screen of what your text will look like on paper. This on-screen display is often referred to as WYSIWYG, an acronym for "What You See Is What You Get."

You might be surprised to learn that you actually enter special coding information every time you create a new paragraph or make a formatting change. Behind the scenes, Word keeps track of formatting changes with a series of nonprinting characters that indicate paragraphs, blank spaces, optional hyphens, and so forth.

As we discussed in Chapter 1, you can set Word to display some or all of these special marks. The Tools Options View card offers a set of check boxes for nonprinting characters, including one labeled All. Putting an X in the All check box displays all hidden formatting characters on the screen. The Show/Hide ¶ button, just to the left of the Zoom Control button on the Standard toolbar, has the same effect as the All check box.

There are times when it can be handy to see some or all of these nonprinting characters—to see whether you've used spaces or tabs, for example, for positioning. In general, though, whether you display some or all of the nonprinting characters is strictly a matter of taste. Figure 3-5 shows our sample with all nonprinting characters displayed.

**FIGURE 3-5**

We've turned on the display for all non-printing characters in our sample document.

The paragraph mark (¶) not only represents the end of a paragraph in your Word document, it also holds the formatting for the paragraph, as we'll discuss in Chapter 7.

The dots (·) between words and sentences in Figure 3-5 represent blank spaces. It is easy to distinguish space marks from periods, since they are much higher on the line, nearly level with the middle of lowercase letters.

# Basic Elements of a Document

Before we explain how to select, edit, and format, it's important that you understand how Word deals with text. Word has its own definitions for characters, words, sentences, paragraphs, and blocks, and you need to know what those are. The concepts aren't difficult to grasp, but they may differ from what you expect. And it's easy to become frustrated if you use one set of definitions while Word uses another.

## Characters

The most basic element of text in Word is the character. A character can be any element you enter: a space, a tab, a letter, a number, a punctuation mark, or any of the nonprinting characters mentioned earlier. Words, sentences, paragraphs, and blocks are combinations of characters.

Word will treat some groups of characters as more than one word for purposes of moving the cursor or selecting text, but it will treat them as a single word in determining where to break a line. Consider, for example, a non-breaking space. A non-breaking space is a special character that you enter by pressing Control-Shift-Spacebar. If you are displaying nonprinting characters, Word shows this as a space dot with a tilde (~) over it. You might use a non-breaking space between *Room* and *2A*, for example, to tell Word to treat *Room 2A* as a single word at the end of a line. Without the non-breaking space, Word might put *Room* as the last word in one line and *2A* as the first word in the next. With the non-breaking space, Word will keep the two together. If you select the text one word at a time, however, you can select only *Room*; you have to select *2A* separately.

## Words

To Microsoft Word, a word can be any combination of alphabetic and numeric characters—*Document1*, for example, and *Room2A* are acceptable words. The program recognizes words as groups of characters that are set apart from other text by one or more blank spaces, by any punctuation mark other than an apostrophe, or by one of Word's nonprinting characters.

For selecting text or moving through text, spaces don't count as words, but punctuation marks and symbols do. So Word considers *abc def* as two words, for example, but *abc=def* as three. The first line of our sample document (the title), in Figure 3-5, has 12 words, according to Word—including the hyphen between GOOD and TIME, the colon after MUSIC, and the exclamation point at the end.

 Word does not use the same rules for counting words as for selecting them. Although *abc=def* is treated as three separate words for selection or navigation purposes, Word will count it as a single word if you ask for a word count by choosing Tools Word Count, or by choosing File Summary Info and then Statistics. For details, see "How to get statistical information about a document" on page 46.

## Sentences

A sentence is a group of characters and words set apart by a period, exclamation point, or question mark. You can also use a paragraph mark or a forced line break to mark the end of a sentence. (A forced line break, entered with Shift-Return, is represented on screen by the ↵ symbol.) The character that marks the end of a sentence also marks the end of the last word in that sentence. For example, consider the first sentence in the first full paragraph in our sample. The sentence ends with "...to be around me." The period after the word *me* marks the end of the sentence, as well as the end of the word *me*.

## Paragraphs

A paragraph can be any combination of characters, words, and symbols that are set apart by a paragraph mark. Keep in mind that the paragraph mark at the end of a paragraph is part of that paragraph. In fact, Word treats the paragraph mark as an individual word.

## Blocks

In Word, a block of text is any group of characters—or even a single character—that you've highlighted. The highlight, or selection, tells Word to treat a
group of characters as a single unit. Often a block of text will consist of a sentence, a paragraph, or several paragraphs. However, a block can be any arbitrary length and can start or end in the middle of a paragraph, sentence, or word.

## Where the elements matter

These definitions for character, word, sentence, paragraph, and block may
seem a bit esoteric at this point. However, they will become important when
you begin moving around in your document and selecting blocks of text. If
you select or move text and get unexpected results, referring to these definitions may help you understand what happened.

# Navigation

Most documents are longer than the 20 or so lines that fit in a typical document window, so it's likely that most of your document won't be visible as
you enter and edit text. If you are not familiar with this effect, it may help you
to think of your words as written on a continuous scroll of paper that's
wound on rollers hidden at the top and bottom of your screen. Text that
comes before the section you're currently looking at has, in essence, scrolled
off the top of the screen. If you move up in your document, the document will
scroll down, revealing previous parts of the document, and subsequent parts
of the document will scroll off the bottom of the screen. You can move down
in your document to scroll these parts of the document back into view.

To move around in a large document, you'll need to use Word's navigation techniques. Some of these use the mouse; others use the keyboard. Which
one you will prefer to use is largely a matter of taste, so we'll show both ways,
starting with the mouse-based choices.

## How to navigate with the mouse

When you navigate through a document with the mouse, there's one key
point you'll need to keep firmly in mind: Your cursor will remain where it
was before you moved unless you tell Word to move the cursor also. In fact, if

you use the mouse to view another part of your document and then start typing, you'll find that Word returns you to your starting point and that anything
you've typed is entered at the original cursor position.

You can use this feature as a convenient way to look at something elsewhere in your document and then return to the section you're currently working on. However, if you actually want to work on the other part of your
document rather than just view it, place the I-beam pointer at the spot you
want to move the cursor to, and then click the mouse button. You can also use
this point-and-click technique to move the cursor anywhere within a single
screenful of text.

## The scroll bars

Among the most basic mouse-based navigation tools are the horizontal and
vertical scroll bars. As we mentioned in Chapter 1, the boxes within the scroll
bars are called scroll boxes, and the arrows at either end of each scroll bar are
called scroll arrows.

You can turn the vertical and horizontal scroll bars on and off. If either or both scroll bars don't show on your screen, choose Tools
Options, select the View tab, and make sure the Vertical Scroll Bars
check box and the Horizontal Scroll Bars check box are checked.
The scroll bars will also disappear—along with most toolbars—if
you choose View Full Screen to see more text. (To turn off the Full
Screen option, press Esc.)

**How to use the vertical scroll bar.**   To move through your document a line at a
time with the vertical scroll bar, simply click on the scroll arrow at the top or
bottom of the vertical scroll bar. Click the bottom arrow to scroll down—or
forward—through a document and the top arrow to scroll up—or backward.
To move through a document a full screen at a time, click anywhere within the
scroll bar—above the scroll box to scroll up, or below the box to scroll down.
Word will scroll the next screen into view and carry over two lines from the
earlier screen to help you get your bearings. As shown in Figure 3-6, the distance that Word scrolls depends on the current size of the document window.
If you've reduced the size, as in this figure, Word will still scroll one screen at
a time, although there will be fewer lines per screen.

To move long distances through a document, you can drag the scroll box
to the appropriate position in the scroll bar. The distance you travel by dragging the scroll box depends on the length of your document.

**FIGURE 3-6**

We've reduced the document window to four lines to show how window size affects scrolling. Note that the number of lines Word scrolls when you click below the scroll box is based on the size of the window. Note also the two lines carried over from the previous screen to help you keep track of where you are.

The scroll box position on the vertical scroll bar represents your relative position in the document. In a short document, the box will move a long distance if you scroll to the next screenful. In a long document, it will hardly move at all. Scrolling works the other way too: The distance you travel by dragging the scroll box depends on the length of your document. If you have a sense of where you want to move to, you can drag the scroll box to the appropriate position. For example, to move to page 25 in a 50-page document, drag the scroll box to the middle of the scroll bar. The screen will not change until you release the mouse button.

**How to use the horizontal scroll bar.** If you're working with a document that is too wide to fit on one screen—for example, if you're using a wide page width or a window that doesn't fill the entire screen—you can use the scroll arrows at either end of the horizontal scroll bar to move right and left. Horizontal scrolling is much like vertical scrolling: Use the scroll arrows to move short distances, click on either side of the scroll box to move by a full screen, or drag the scroll box to reposition the window manually.

Unlike the vertical scroll bar's relative positioning, which changes depending on how long the document is, the horizontal scroll bar's positioning is constant. Word allows a maximum document width of 22 inches and will let you scroll the full 22 inches with any document. If you drag the scroll box to the extreme right end of the horizontal scroll bar, you'll travel the full 22 inches; if you drag it to the middle of the scroll bar, you'll travel to the 11-inch mark—no matter where the right margin is in the current document.

## How to navigate with the keyboard

For navigating, many people find the mouse easier to learn at first because of its straightforward point-and-click strategy; however, the keyboard commands are in many ways easier to use, once you've learned them. A little time invested in learning the keyboard commands can yield big dividends in efficiency because you can keep your fingers on the keyboard rather than reach for the mouse. Figure 3-7 summarizes the keystrokes we'll cover in this section.

 **NOTE** One important difference between using the keyboard and using the mouse is that when you use the keyboard, the cursor will travel with you as you move through your document.

| These Keys... | Move the Cursor... |
|---|---|
| Left arrow | Left one character |
| Right arrow | Right one character |
| Up arrow | Up one line |
| Down arrow | Down one line |
| Home | To the beginning of the current line |
| End | To the end of the current line |
| Page Up | Up one screen |
| Page Down | Down one screen |
| ⌘-Left arrow | Left one word |
| ⌘-Right arrow | Right one word |
| ⌘-Up arrow | Up one paragraph |
| ⌘-Down arrow | Down one paragraph |
| ⌘-Home | To the top of the document |
| ⌘-End | To the bottom of the document |
| ⌘-Page Up | To the top of the screen |
| ⌘-Page Down | To the bottom of the screen |
| ⌘-Option-Page Up | To previous page |
| ⌘-Option-Page Down | To next page |
| Shift-F5 or ⌘-Option-Z | To a previous location |
| F5 or ⌘-G | To a specified location |

**FIGURE 3-7**

Keyboard navigation.

You can also use the numeric keypad for navigation. If you are familiar with a PC-compatible keyboard, the assignments are the same: 4 is Left arrow, 8 is Up arrow, 6 is Right arrow, 2 is Down arrow, 7 is Home, 1 is End, 9 is Page Up, and 3 is Page Down.

## How to move short distances

The Left, Right, Up, and Down arrow keys are tremendously convenient for moving short distances. When you use the Up and Down arrow keys, your cursor will move more or less in a straight line. (Because line lengths vary and characters occupy different amounts of space, your cursor may jump around a bit as you move from line to line.) If you press the Up arrow key at the top of the document window or the Down arrow key at the bottom, Word will scroll the next lines of text into view.

When you press the Right or Left arrow key, the cursor will move one character to the left or right. (Be aware that a tab, which will show on screen as a right arrow ($\rightarrow$), is treated as a single character, no matter how much of a jump it represents.) Press the Left arrow key at the beginning of a line, and the cursor will move to the end of the previous line. If you press the Right arrow key at the end of a line, the cursor will move to the beginning of the next line.

If you press the Left arrow key when the cursor is at the beginning of the first line on the screen, or the Right arrow key when the cursor is in the bottom line on the screen, Word will scroll the document as well as move the cursor to the next line.

## How to move by words or paragraphs

Word offers ⌘-key shortcuts that you can use to move the cursor by words or paragraphs. To move from one word to the next, press ⌘-Right arrow or ⌘-Left arrow. The cursor will land immediately to the left of the next (or previous) word.

To move through your document a paragraph at a time, use ⌘-Up arrow and ⌘-Down arrow. If your cursor is currently in the middle of a paragraph, ⌘-Up arrow jumps you to the beginning of that paragraph. If your cursor is already at the beginning of a paragraph, ⌘-Up arrow will take you to the beginning of the previous paragraph. Similarly, pressing ⌘-Down arrow will take you to the beginning of the next paragraph.

## How to move by screenfuls

To move through your document a full screen at a time, you can use the Page Up and Page Down keys. To move up, press Page Up; to move down, press Page Down. The amount of text scrolled will depend on the size of the current document window; Word will carry over two lines from the previous screen to help you find your place. As you scroll new portions of the document into view, the cursor remains in the same relative screen position—unless the beginning or end of the document is already on screen. If the beginning of the document is on screen, the Page Up key will move the cursor to the beginning of the document. If the end is on screen, Page Down will move the cursor to the end.

## How to move by pages

If your document is longer than one page, you can move forward one page at a time with ⌘-Option-Page Down. To move back a page, press ⌘-Option-Page Up.

## How to move to the beginning or end of your document

You can also use the ⌘ key with the Home and End keys to move the cursor to the beginning or end of your document. ⌘-Home will move it to the beginning of the document; ⌘-End will move it to the end.

## How to move the cursor to its previous location

When you edit text, you will likely find yourself skipping from one spot to another to move text, make minor changes, or remind yourself what you wrote elsewhere. Word offers a choice of navigation features to help streamline this process: the Shift-F5 and ⌘-Option-Z keyboard shortcuts.

When you press Shift-F5 or ⌘-Option-Z, the cursor will move to the last place where you made a change. (This is not necessarily the last place the cursor was located; you have to have made some editing change for this keyboard shortcut to work.) Word will keep track of the last three locations where you made changes and will let you cycle through those locations and your current position with Shift-F5 or ⌘-Option-Z, moving from the most recent change to the oldest one and then back to the place you started from.

The Shift-F5 or ⌘-Option-Z technique is useful for toggling between two areas of your document when you need to compare two portions of text. For example, suppose you have a table on page 3 and a discussion of the table on page 4 and you want to keep moving between the text where you're discussing the table and the table itself. To tell Word to remember a point in the table, make a trivial change there, such as adding a space and then deleting it by pressing the Delete key. Then you can move back and forth with Shift-F5 or ⌘-Option-Z.

## How to use the Go To command

Moving by character, line, screen, and so forth is useful, but there will be times when you want to jump to a specific place. If you know the page or other specific location—or even if you don't—you can use the Go To command to get there. Start by either choosing Edit Go To or pressing F5 or ⌘-G. Word will respond with the Go To dialog box, shown in Figure 3-8.

**FIGURE 3-8**

You can use the Go To dialog box to browse through your document by page, section, line, or other item.

You can also bring up the Go To dialog box by double-clicking anywhere on the position information on the status bar—that is, anywhere in the box that includes page and section information or in the box that includes inch, line, and column information.

**NEW!**

The Go To What list box shows the different kinds of items you can move to. By default, Word suggests Page unless you've used a different choice since you last loaded Word. If you want to go to the immediately following page— for example, page 4 when you're currently on page 3—you can simply choose Next. Word will move the cursor to the beginning of the first line on the next page. Notice, however, that Word will not close the dialog box unless you choose Close or press Esc or click on the close box.

**NEW!**

Because Word keeps the Go To dialog box open until you explicitly close it, you can continue to move through the document one step at a time, choosing Next to move forward or Previous to move back. This technique will work with any of the items in the Go To What list box, taking you to the next or previous section, line, and so on. In effect, you can browse through your document until you find the item you're looking for.

**NEW!**

If you know the page number you want to move to, you can simply type it in the Enter Page Number text box, as shown in Figure 3-9 on the next page. Word will change the Next button to read Go To and will dim the Previous button. Choose Go To, and Word will move the cursor to the beginning of the first line on the specified page and display the page in the document window. It will also show the page number in the status bar to indicate the actual position of the cursor. (Note, in passing, that the status bar indicates the page numbers for the document as it will appear when it is printed.)

**FIGURE 3-9**

You can use the Go To dialog box to move quickly to a specified page or other location in your document.

You can also specify relative position in the Enter Page Number text box. For example, enter +2 to advance two pages or – 3 to move back three pages. You can enter + or – alone to move one page forward or back, but it's easier to use the Next and Previous buttons, as just described.

Moving through your document using any of the other choices in the Go To What box is similar to moving by pages. One of the few differences is that the heading over the text box labeled Enter Page Number in Figures 3-8 and 3-9 will change, depending on the item you've selected in the Go To What list box. If you select Bookmark, for example, the label will change to Enter Bookmark Name. (A bookmark is a kind of placeholder you can insert into your document by choosing Edit Bookmark, entering a name, and choosing Add.) With some choices, including bookmarks, the text box will become a drop-down list box containing all relevant items—bookmark names, for example. (For more information about bookmarks, see "Bookmarks" on page 303.)

## Other methods of moving through your document

In addition to commands meant specifically for moving through your document, Word offers two navigation techniques that aren't usually thought of that way: the Edit Find command and Outline view.

## How to use the Edit Find command to navigate

You can use the Find dialog box, shown in Figure 3-10, to move to a location in your text defined by specific text; to a specific character, paragraph, or style formatting; or to any combination of these. You can begin a search from any point in your document and search forward from the cursor (by selecting Down in the Search box); backward from the cursor (by selecting Up); or through the entire document, starting at the cursor, going to the end of the document, and then starting again at the beginning (by selecting All).

**FIGURE 3-10**

The Find dialog box lets you look for any combination of text and formatting.

After you define what to search for and choose Find Next, Word will highlight the first instance of the item that it finds. You can then choose Cancel to close the dialog box and remain at that location, or Find Next to look for another instance of the search item. If you begin the search in the middle of your document, Word will ask whether to continue searching from the beginning of the document when it reaches the end (if searching down) or continue searching from the end when it reaches the beginning (if searching up). For details about the Edit Find command and its companion, Edit Replace, see "Using the Edit Find and Edit Replace Commands" on page 95.

## How to use Outline view to navigate

Word's Outline view is meant primarily for organizing your writing by using an outline. Outline view includes the ability to collapse an outline to show headings only, as shown in Figure 3-11 on the next page. Collapsing the outline makes it easy to view the overall structure of your document and to move entire sections. It also gives you a way to move through your text quickly.

You can take advantage of this feature even if you use the outliner for nothing else. You have only to format your section titles with any arbitrary heading level. We'll show you how when we cover outlining later in this book, and we'll show you how to collapse and expand the outline with the mouse as well as with the keyboard. For the moment, simply be aware that it can be done. And you'll probably want to learn at least this much about the outline feature, even if outlining doesn't match the way you work. For details, see Chapter 19.

**FIGURE 3-11**

Word's collapsible outliner lets you see only your section headings and move through a document quickly by moving to a different heading.

If you need to move through a long report or other document, you have only to choose View Outline to switch to Outline view. Then choose the lowest level of heading you want to see (by using Control-Shift-1 for level 1 headings, Control-Shift-2 for level 2 headings, and so forth, or by using the numbered buttons), move the cursor to the heading for the section you want to move to, expand the section by pressing the plus key on the numeric keypad or clicking on the Expand button on the Outlining toolbar, move the cursor to the part of the section you want to work with, and go back to Normal view by choosing View Normal. (This sounds more complicated than it really is. All the collapsing and expanding involves just six keystrokes.) Note that Word will not always expand the document to show you the current cursor position. However, you will move there immediately if you type any printing character, such as a letter of the alphabet or a number.

## Selecting Text

Second in importance only to knowing how to move through your document is knowing how to select blocks of text. Before you can edit or format a given portion of text, you have to tell Word which text you want to work with. In most cases, you do that by selecting the text.

When you select text, Word will display the selected block of characters in inverse video—white text and graphics on a black background rather than the normal black on white (if you are using the default colors). Throughout this book, we'll refer to this inverse video as *highlighted text* or *selected text.* As with navigation techniques, Word offers many ways to select text, both with the mouse and with the keyboard. Each approach offers its own advantages. We strongly encourage you to explore all the methods discussed here so that you can find the ones that work best for you. Once again, we'll start with mouse-based techniques.

# How to select with the mouse

As with navigation techniques, many people find it easier at first to use the mouse for selecting text. But you may be surprised at how many choices you have with the mouse alone.

## How to drag across text

The most basic mouse selection technique is dragging across the text you want to select. For example, suppose you want to select the words *twice each year* in line 3 of the sample document. Begin by positioning the I-beam pointer just to the left of the letter *t* in the word *twice*. Next, press and hold down the mouse button and, without releasing the button, drag to the right until you've highlighted the entire phrase, as shown in Figure 3-12. When you release the mouse button, the characters will remain highlighted. You can use dragging to select any size block of text, from a single character to an entire document.

**FIGURE 3-12**

You can select a block of text by dragging across the block.

To select more text than appears on the screen, start your selection and drag past the top or bottom of the document window. Word will scroll the document and extend your selection until you release the mouse button or until you move the cursor back into the document window. However, selecting text by dragging is best suited for relatively small blocks that fit on one screen. There are more efficient ways to select larger blocks.

## How to select a word by double-clicking

To select an entire word with the mouse, simply double-click (press the mouse button twice in quick succession) anywhere on that word. Word will highlight the entire word and any space characters to its immediate right.

If you double-click on a word that is followed by a period, a comma, or some other delimiting character, you will not highlight the delimiting character. For example, if you double-click on the word *year* in the third line of our sample text, Word will highlight only the characters *year*—not the comma following that word or the space after the comma. Instead, punctuation characters are treated as separate words. In fact, if you double-click on the comma, Word will highlight the comma and the space.

## How to extend a selection word by word

If you're familiar with selecting text by dragging in almost any Macintosh program, you probably know that when you extend a selection by dragging across text it's sometimes difficult to start and end the selection at the right place. The mouse is not a precision pointing device; sometimes you'll start a selection on the second or third character in a word when you wanted to start at the beginning, or you'll overshoot or undershoot the end of a word when you wanted to extend precisely to its end.

As we mentioned in Chapter 1, Word 6.0 includes a new option, Automatic Word Selection, that can make this selection task much easier. You can see the current setting for the option—and turn it on or off—by choosing Tools Options Edit. If you want the feature on, make sure the check box labeled *Automatic Word Selection* is checked. If you want it off, make sure it's not checked.

If Automatic Word Selection is on, you can start selecting text anywhere in a word. As soon as you extend past the end of that word, Word will select the entire word. In addition, each time you extend the selection into the next word, the program will select the full word.

If you don't always want to select complete words, you may well prefer to turn Automatic Word Selection off. Even with the feature off, however, you can get the same effect. Simply start by double-clicking on the first word you want in the selection, to highlight the whole word, and hold the button down on the second click. Then, as you drag the mouse to extend the selection, Word will extend it a full word at a time.

## How to select a paragraph by triple-clicking

To select an entire paragraph with the mouse, simply triple-click (press the mouse button three times in quick succession) anywhere in the paragraph. Word will highlight the entire paragraph, including the paragraph mark.

You can continue to hold down the mouse button on the third click and drag to expand your selection a paragraph at a time.

## How to select a sentence with ⌘-click

Word also offers a simple technique for selecting an entire sentence. Just hold down ⌘ as you click anywhere in the sentence. Word will highlight the sentence, as well as the period and any blank characters after the sentence. If the sentence is the last one in a paragraph, Word will not highlight the paragraph mark, which it treats separately from the sentence.

You can continue to hold down the mouse button after a ⌘-click and drag to expand your selection a sentence at a time.

## How to select a block without dragging

Dragging the mouse to highlight line after line of text takes time. But Word offers a faster choice: the Shift-click method. First click at the beginning of the block you want to select. Then move the pointer to the end of the block, hold down the Shift key, and click. Word will highlight the entire block.

When you select a block with the Shift-click technique, the end of the selection can be anywhere in the document and you can get there using any of the mouse navigation techniques we've discussed, as long as you don't click in the document window at any other position. You can also click at the end of the block first and then go to the beginning, and you can adjust the extent of the selection by holding down Shift and clicking again.

If the Automatic Word Selection check box on the Tools Options Edit card is cleared, Word will let you start and end the selection in midword. But if the check box is checked and you click in the middle of a word and drag past the beginning or end of the word, your selection will automatically include the entire word.

## How to select text by using the selection bar

Word has an invisible selection bar on the left side of the document window. Although you can't see it, you can use the selection bar to select a line, a paragraph, or the entire document. You will know you are in the selection bar when the mouse pointer changes to a right-pointing arrow.

To select an entire line of text, just move the pointer to the left side of the document window until it changes to the right-pointing arrow; then, with the arrow immediately to the left of the text, point to the line of text you want to select, and click. To select an entire paragraph, move your pointer to the selection bar and double-click.

To select the entire document, move the pointer to the selection bar and either triple-click or press the ⌘ key as you click once. This technique is particularly helpful when you need to make a global change to your document, such as changing the type style for all your text.

You can set Word to show the formatting style for each paragraph at the left of the screen, in an area called the *style area*. To display the style area, choose Tools Options View and enter a setting in the Style Area Width text box. As Figure 3-13 shows, the selection bar lies between the left edge of the text and the right edge of the style area, indicated by the vertical line. If you move into the style area and click, you will select the entire paragraph. If you double-click, the Style dialog box will open. For details on styles and the style area, see Chapter 12.

**FIGURE 3-13**

You can use the style area to select a paragraph of text with the mouse.

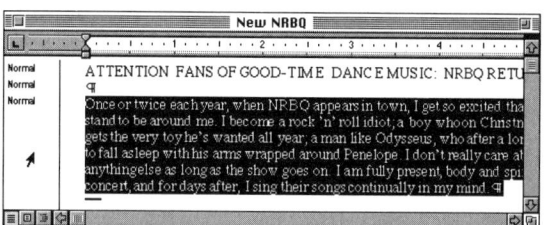

## How to make column selections

Up to this point, all our selections have been for sequential blocks of characters—all the characters in a sentence, line, or paragraph. But there are times when you'll want to select only a vertical column of text, as with the table of text shown in Figure 3-14.

You can select a
column of text with
the mouse by using the
Option key with the
mouse button.

To select a column of text, position the pointer at one corner of the text you want to select. Next hold down the Option key as you press the mouse button, and drag to the opposite corner of the block. Word will highlight the text without regard for words, sentences, or paragraphs. If your document is in a proportional font, some of the characters in the selection may be only partially highlighted. When you make column selections, Word considers any character that is more than half highlighted to be part of the selection.

## How to select with the keyboard

As with navigation, Word provides a full set of techniques for selecting text with the keyboard. And again, many people find it faster and easier to use the keyboard than to reach for the mouse.

### How to use Extend Selection mode

One of the most useful selection tools is the Extend Selection key: F8. When you press F8, the letters *EXT* in the status bar turn solid and dark, indicating that Extend Selection mode is active. While you are in this mode, you can highlight text by using all the same keystrokes that you use for navigation, as listed in Figure 3-7 (except for Shift-F5 or ⌘-Option-Z, which cancel Extend mode). With Extend Selection active, however, these keystrokes will now select text as you move through your document. The initial position of the cursor serves as the anchor for one end of the selection. The cursor's current position marks the other end.

NEW!

You can also turn Extend Selection mode on and off by double-clicking on the *EXT* indicator in the status bar at the bottom of the screen.

For example, if you press F8 and then press ⌘-Right arrow, the cursor will move to the space following the current word and will highlight the text and the space simultaneously. Similarly, if you press F8 and then End, the cursor will move to the end of the current line, highlighting the text from the starting point to the end of the line. (You can also use the F8 key in combination with the mouse to extend a selection. Click at the beginning of the selection, press F8, and then click at the end of the selection.)

> The F8 key has additional selection features. After you've pressed F8 once to turn on Extend Selection mode, you can press it a second time to highlight the word the cursor is currently in. Press it a third time to highlight the sentence the word is in, a fourth time to highlight the paragraph, and a fifth time to select the entire document. To cancel Extend Selection mode, press the Esc key and then any cursor-movement key to remove the highlight.

> F8 has one more trick in its bag: searching for and extending the selection to a designated character. Press F8 once to activate Extend Selection mode; then press a key corresponding to any character: a letter, a number, or a punctuation mark. Word will search for the first occurrence of that character and highlight all text from the cursor through the character, including the character as part of the selection. At this point, you can press the key for the same character (or a different one) to extend the selection again.
>
> For example, you can press F8 and then the period key to extend to the end of the current sentence; then repeatedly press the period key to extend the selection a sentence at a time. Similarly, you can press F8 and then the Return key to extend to the end of the current paragraph; then repeatedly press Return to extend the selection one paragraph at a time.

## How to select with Shift-navigation keys

As an alternative to the Extend Selection method, you can hold down the Shift key to turn the navigation keys into selection keys. Place the cursor where you want to begin your selection, and then press and hold down Shift while using almost any of the keys listed in Figure 3-7. You will simultaneously move the cursor and highlight the text.

### How to select the entire document

To select your entire document with the keyboard, press ⌘-A or press the F8 key five times.

# Basic Editing Techniques

The most common needs when you're editing text are inserting new characters, deleting existing characters, and overwriting the characters you want to change. These are also Word's most basic and most important editing techniques. Although we'll talk more about editing in Chapter 4, we'll introduce these techniques here because they relate closely to the selection and navigation techniques we've just explored.

As we mentioned earlier, Word wraps your text within a paragraph whenever you make editing or formatting changes. As you work with the insertion, deletion, and overwriting techniques, notice how Word reflows your text to adjust for the changes.

## How to insert new text

Inserting text is as easy as typing, but first you have to be in Insert mode, not Overtype mode. In Insert mode, Word moves any text to the right of the cursor as you type. In Overtype mode, Word overwrites text to the right of the cursor. Press the Control-Ins key several times; the *OVR* (for Overtype) flag should toggle on (dark text) and off (grayed) in the status bar with the repeated key presses. As with the Extended Selection feature, you can also turn this on and off by double-clicking on the *OVR* flag in the status bar. Once you know how to turn the *OVR* flag on and off, make sure it is off.

Next, using the keyboard or the mouse, move the cursor to the spot where you want to insert the text. If you use the mouse, remember to reposition the cursor by moving the I-beam pointer to the desired spot and clicking. Then begin typing. As you type new characters, Word will push the existing characters to the right. Words at the end of the line will move to the beginning of the next line.

## How to delete text

The easiest way to delete a character is to place the cursor to the right of it and press the Delete key. Word will delete one character to the left of the cursor, pulling characters at the right of the cursor one space to the left. If you prefer, you can place the cursor to the left of the character you want to delete and press the Del key. In this case, Word will delete the character to the immediate right and move all following characters to the left.

To delete several characters at once, you can select them and then press either Delete or Del. Word will delete the block and fill in the gap by pulling the remaining text in your document up and to the left.

If you press the Delete key while your cursor is at the beginning of a line within a paragraph, Word will move the cursor to the end of the previous line and delete the last character in that line (usually a space). If this action joins two words, the newly joined word may be too long to fit on the previous line and may wrap to the line you started from. If you press Delete while the cursor is at the beginning of a paragraph, Word will delete the paragraph mark at the end of the preceding paragraph and reflow your text to combine the two paragraphs.

Word 5.1 prevented you from deleting the paragraph marker between two paragraphs with different formatting. Word 6.0 no longer prevents this, however.

### Deletion shortcuts

Word offers some keyboard shortcuts for deleting text. For example, instead of pressing the Delete key to delete characters one at a time, you can press ⌘-Delete to delete everything from the cursor to the beginning of the word immediately left of the cursor. To delete the space to the right of the word as well, position the cursor to the right of that space before you press ⌘-Delete.

If you position the cursor in a word and press ⌘-Delete, Word will delete all the characters to the left of the cursor up to but not including the blank space that separates the current word from the previous word.

You can delete from the cursor to the end of the word at its right by pressing ⌘-Del or ⌘-Option-G. If you position the cursor to the left of the first character of a word, ⌘-Del will delete all of that word and the following space. If you position the cursor in the middle of a word, ⌘-Del will delete all characters to the right of the cursor up to but not including the space that separates that word from the next.

## How to overwrite text

Most users prefer to do all their editing in Insert mode and follow it up by deleting any text they mean to replace. In general, this is the safest procedure because you can easily retrieve the text you started with if you decide you want it back. However, you may prefer to write over the text you're replacing.

If so, you need to use Overtype mode, pressing the Control-Ins key to toggle between it and Insert mode, as we discussed earlier in this chapter, in the section "How to insert new text."

After you toggle to Overtype mode (the OVR flag will appear as solid text in the status bar), all you need to do to overwrite text is move the cursor to the appropriate spot and start typing. The process is similar in concept to typing over characters on a typewriter except that Word fully replaces the existing characters you're typing over, leaving no telltale evidence that you've changed anything. Note that Word lets you overwrite text only within a paragraph. When you reach the end of the paragraph, anything more that you type stays in the same paragraph if you don't press Return, or goes into a newly created paragraph if you do press Return. Subsequent paragraphs move down, just as with Insert mode.

## How to overwrite text by selecting it

Whether you are in Overtype mode or Insert mode, Word is set by default to delete any selected text when you start typing and replace it with the text you're typing. You can turn this option on or off by choosing Tools Options Edit and checking or clearing the Typing Replaces Selection check box.

> Be careful with the Typing Replaces Selection option. Unlike Overtype mode, which replaces one character at a time, the Typing Replaces Selection option immediately deletes all selected text as soon as you type a single character. If you are in Overtype mode as well, additional keystrokes will overtype additional text. But if you do accidentally delete a large block of text this way, don't panic. Word's multilevel undo feature will let you recover all the missing text. (We cover the undo feature later in this chapter, under "How to undo an action or multiple actions.")

Finally, be aware that you cannot overwrite a paragraph mark by selecting it and typing over it unless you select a block of text that ends after the paragraph mark. If you select a block that includes a paragraph mark and replace it by typing, Word will combine the current paragraph with the paragraph below it and will assign the paragraph formats from the second paragraph to the combined paragraph. For more details, see "Paragraph Formatting" on page 204.

## How to cut text

In addition to the techniques we've discussed so far, Word provides the Edit Cut command, as well as the shortcut key ⌘-X, for deleting text. You can also click on the Cut button—the one with the scissors icon—on the Standard toolbar to cut selected text. Unlike the deletion techniques, however, the Edit Cut command and equivalent shortcuts store the deleted text in a special place called the *Clipboard.* Although the Clipboard is actually a large chunk of memory, you can think of it as a temporary storage place. For now, just note that after you place something on the Clipboard with the Edit Cut or Edit Copy command, you can paste the Clipboard's contents anywhere in your Word document (or, indeed, in documents in other programs) by using the Edit Paste command. We'll talk more about these commands and the Clipboard in the next chapter.

# Canceling and Repeating Actions

When you insert, delete, or overwrite text, Word remembers your last set of keystrokes, as well as any text you deleted in the process. This short-term memory makes it possible to undo most editing changes or automatically repeat a command or another series of keystrokes.

## How to undo an action or multiple actions

The Edit Undo command is one of the most important in Word because it gives you a second chance when you make a mistake or change your mind. To undo your most recent editing changes, simply choose Edit Undo, click the Undo button on the Standard toolbar, or press ⌘-Z (or Option-Delete). Edit Undo can be a real lifesaver when you find that you have accidentally altered a critical passage of text.

Edit Undo is context sensitive; it changes to reflect your last action. If you insert new text or overtype selected text and then open the Edit menu, you'll see the Undo Typing command at the top of the menu. If you use the Del key to delete a selection, you'll see the Undo Clear command.

You can even undo an Edit Undo command. If you choose Edit Undo to undo some typing and then open the Edit menu again, the second menu command will be Redo Typing. Choose this command to restore the text.

*NEW!*     One of the most powerful new features in Word 6.0 is its multiple-level Undo command. You can choose Edit Undo (or the Undo button on the Standard toolbar) repeatedly until you have completely reversed your edits.

There is also a pull-down list attached to the Undo button on the Standard toolbar. The list shows all the edits that can be undone. Simply highlight through the point you want to return to, release, and your work will be restored to its status at that point.

Be aware that the undo feature will undo all of your work back to the point you return to. If you realize you've made a mistake several steps earlier, however, you can still correct the mistake without losing the changes you've made since then.

Here's how to do it: Suppose, for example, that you've accidentally deleted a block of text and have since inserted additional text and added formatting. To retrieve the text, first give the Edit Undo command repeatedly until the deleted block of text reappears (or use the pull-down list to find the action you want to return to and go directly to that point). Then open a new document window with the File New command and copy the text to the new document, using any of Word's standard copy commands (such as Edit Copy and Edit Paste). Next return to the original document and use the Redo command to restore all of the changes you have just undone but wanted to keep. Finally copy the text back from the second document to the original.

The multiple-level undo feature can undo nearly any editing change, but keep in mind that there are other types of actions that can't be undone. For example, if you use the File Find File command to erase a file or you accidentally overwrite a file with the File Save As command, you won't be able to reverse those actions. The moral: Be careful when handling files.

## How to repeat an action

As we've already mentioned, in addition to being able to undo your last action, you can also repeat it by using the Edit Repeat command.

Like the Edit Undo command, Edit Repeat is context sensitive, so it will change to reflect your last action. For example, if you use the Format Font command to change the format of some text, you'll see the command Repeat Font Formatting below the Undo Font Formatting command. You can then select blocks of widely separated text and reformat them one at a time by choosing Edit Repeat Font Formatting. The keyboard shortcut is ⌘-Y.

If your last action was an undo operation, Edit Repeat becomes Edit Redo, and you can redo ("undo the undo" on) the operation that you've just undone. Like Undo, Redo (which is also available on the Standard toolbar, immediately to the right of the Undo button and pull-down list) can reverse multiple actions in sequence—which is handy in case you execute a number of Undo commands and overshoot the point where you wanted to stop. Unlike Undo, however, the Redo queue of commands is emptied as soon as you give a command other than Undo or Redo.

## Where We Go from Here

The concepts and commands in this chapter form the basis for most of what you'll do when working with Word. If you learn nothing more than what's in this chapter, you'll be able to enter and edit text. In the next part of this book, we'll show you everything you need to know about entering and editing text, as well as about proofreading, formatting, and printing your text.

# PART TWO

# Basics

# TOPIC FINDER

# 4

# Editing Text

n Chapter 3, we covered the most basic editing tasks: how to enter, select, delete, and overwrite text. However, there are at least two other editing tools that almost any Word user is likely to need on a daily basis.

These core tools are the cut-and-paste feature and the search-and-replace feature. We'll cover both in this chapter. Keep in mind that, as we discussed in Chapter 3, your first task in editing often is to select the text you want to change. As you practice with the features we'll discuss here, you may find it helpful to refer back to the selection and navigation techniques covered in Chapter 3; learning how to select text quickly will speed your editing significantly.

## Copying and Moving Text

Word's Edit Cut, Edit Copy, and Edit Paste commands are the scissors and glue that make editing a snap. With just a few keystrokes or mouse clicks, you can reorganize your document or duplicate a block of text—perhaps to edit it experimentally or to add a copy of it elsewhere in a document. You can also copy or move items from one Word document to another, or even between

Word and another program. In this chapter, we'll cover copying and moving text within Word. In Chapter 18, "Sharing Data with Other Programs," starting on page 587, we'll show you how to share information with other programs.

In general, you copy or move text in Word by selecting the text, copying or cutting the selection, and then choosing the location where you want to insert—or paste—it. You can also copy formats without text; we'll come back to formatting issues after we look at the Edit Cut, Edit Copy, and Edit Paste commands.

# How to copy text

Rather than retyping a given block of text when you need a copy, you can use the Edit Copy command to copy the text to the Clipboard, which is a temporary holding area for data, and then use the Edit Paste command to paste the text in one or more locations in your document. For obvious reasons, the Edit Copy command can save a great deal of time when you need to duplicate more than a word or two.

To copy a block of text, first select it, and then choose the Edit Copy command or click on the Copy button on the Standard toolbar. Next position the cursor where you want the copied block to appear, and choose Edit Paste or click on the Paste button on the Standard toolbar. Word will insert a copy of the text to the left of the cursor, leaving the cursor at the end of the pasted block. The original block of text will remain unchanged.

It's often a good idea to work on a copy of your text rather than on the original. Suppose, for example, that you're working with the document shown in Figure 4-1 on the next page, and you're not happy with the first paragraph of body text. Instead of working with the existing paragraph, and perhaps needing to restore it to its original form if you decide you don't like your changes, you can select the entire paragraph, choose Edit Copy, position the cursor to the left of the first word in the paragraph, and choose Edit Paste. You can then work with the duplicate paragraph, as shown in Figure 4-2 on the next page.

## Keyboard shortcuts for copying text

Keyboard shortcuts make the copying process even easier. After you've selected a block of text, press ⌘-C or F3 to copy the text to the Clipboard. Then move to where you want the text to appear, and press ⌘-V or F4 to paste. If you check the Use The INS Key For Paste check box on the Tools Options Edit card, you can also press Shift-Ins for pasting.

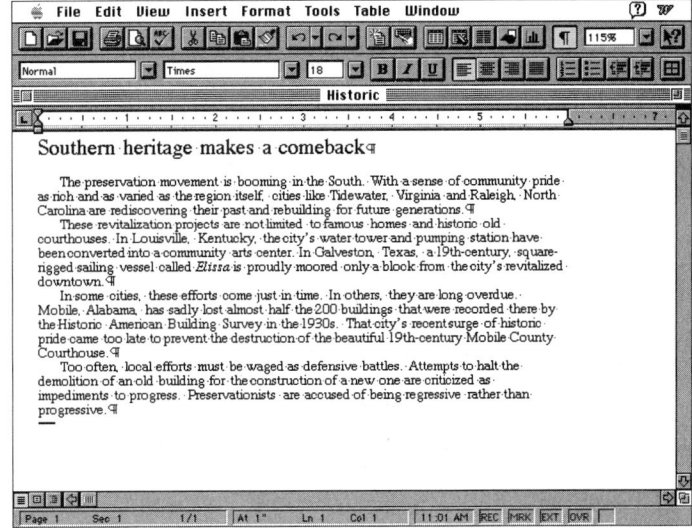

**FIGURE 4-1**

You need a copy of the first paragraph to edit experimentally while leaving the original untouched.

**FIGURE 4-2**

When you choose the Edit Paste command, Word will insert the copied paragraph just before the cursor. The copied paragraph in this case is the first paragraph of body text.

## The Clipboard

We've mentioned the Clipboard several times in describing the Edit Copy and Edit Paste commands. You can view the Clipboard's contents at any time by opening the Clipboard window. Simply choose Show Clipboard from the Window menu. Figure 4-3 on the next page shows the contents of the Clipboard after you copied the paragraph from the document shown in Figure 4-2.

**FIGURE 4-3**

The Clipboard window contains the last selection you cut or copied.

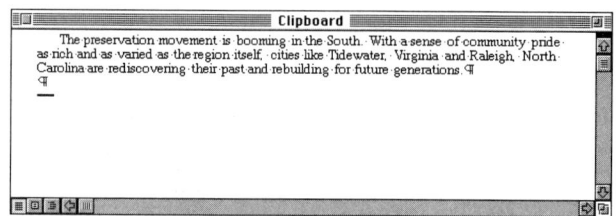

Although the Clipboard can accommodate a text block of any size—from one character to an entire document (memory permitting)—it's important to understand that the Clipboard can hold only one selection at a time. If you select text and choose the Edit Copy or Edit Cut command (which we'll discuss shortly) and then make another selection and choose either command again, Word will erase the first selection from the Clipboard and replace it with the second. Of course, if you copied the first block of text, you have lost nothing but time. But if you cut the first block of text and then cut or copied another block of text before pasting the first one, you'll lose the first block. If you want to collect a series of items, see "Using the Spike" on page 139.

If you lose a block of text this way, you can recover it with the Edit Undo command. This command will not undo the changes to the Clipboard, but it will recover the lost text, placing the text back in your document in its original position, without affecting the contents of the Clipboard.

Once text is on the Clipboard, and until you overwrite it with another Edit Cut or Edit Copy command, you can paste it as many times as you like. The Macintosh will remember the Clipboard contents even if you choose other commands or edit your document before you paste. You can also open and edit new documents (or even move to a different program) without losing the current contents of the Clipboard. However, the Clipboard contents are lost when you shut down your computer.

## How to copy text without using the Clipboard

In some situations, you'll want to copy text without using the Clipboard. For example, the Clipboard may already contain text that you want to paste later, but you need to perform another copy operation first.

This is where Word's Copy To feature comes in handy. You can use the mouse to drag-and-drop a block of text. Start by selecting the text you want to copy. Then hold down the Option key as you click and drag the mouse pointer to the destination; the mouse pointer will change to a drag symbol with a small plus sign. When you release the mouse button, a copy of the selected text will appear at the mouse pointer's position.

If you prefer using the keyboard, highlight the text and press Shift-F2. Word displays a prompt in the status bar (assuming the status bar is showing) that asks *Copy to where?* Move the cursor to the new position (where it is displayed as a dotted line rather than the usual solid line), and press Return to insert the copy.

# How to move text

Moving a block of text is similar to copying one, except that Word removes the block from its original location. To use the Clipboard to move text, select a block of text, choose Edit Cut, move to the new location, and then paste the text by choosing Edit Paste.

## Keyboard shortcuts for moving text

The keyboard shortcuts for cutting text are ⌘-X and F2; like ⌘-C and F3, both shortcuts give the same result. Pasting text that was cut to the Clipboard is the same as pasting text that was copied to the Clipboard. Move to where you want the text to appear, and press ⌘-V or F4 to paste.

## How to move text without using the Clipboard

As it does for copy operations, Word also has a way to move text that bypasses the Clipboard. This relies on the mouse and also uses a drag-and-drop technique. Start by selecting the text you want to move. Then drag the selection to its new location. Unlike the copy procedure, however, there is no keyboard command to move text without placing it on the Clipboard first.

If you forget the shortcuts for the Clipboard operations, you can open the Edit menu and look at the keyboard shortcuts that appear to the right of the appropriate commands. Figure 4-4 summarizes the keyboard shortcuts for Edit Cut, Edit Copy, and Edit Paste and the shortcuts for copying and moving without the Clipboard.

| Command | Keyboard Shortcut |
|---|---|
| **With the Clipboard** | |
| Cut | ⌘-X or F2 |
| Copy | ⌘-C or F3 |
| Paste | ⌘-V or F4 or Shift-Ins (when Use The INS Key For Paste option is turned on) |
| **Without the Clipboard** | |
| Copy | Shift-F2 |

**FIGURE 4-4**

Keyboard shortcuts for cutting, copying, and pasting.

You can turn off the drag-and-drop feature for copying and moving blocks of text. Some users will find the drag-and-drop feature intuitive and useful. Others won't like it because it affects selection procedures: If you highlight text with the mouse when the drag-and-drop feature is active and then decide you want to select a smaller portion of that text, you must remove the highlight completely before changing the selection. Fortunately for both groups of users, you can turn this feature on and off by checking or clearing the Drag-And-Drop Text Editing check box on the Tools Options Edit card. For more details about the drag-and-drop feature, see "Essential Customization Options" starting on page 27.

## How to replace text as you paste

Whether you are copying or moving text, you can have Word paste over, or replace, an existing block of text when you paste the copied or moved text. First be sure that the Typing Replaces Selection check box on the Tools Options Edit card is checked. Then cut or copy the text you want to paste. Select the text you want to replace, and choose the Edit Paste command.

Returning to the sample document shown in Figure 4-1 on page 89, suppose you want to replace the last sentence in the first paragraph of body text with the last two sentences from the second paragraph. Highlight the last two sentences of the second paragraph and choose Edit Copy. Next highlight the last sentence of the first paragraph and choose Edit Paste. As shown in Figure 4-5, Word will overwrite the highlighted text with the copied text.

**FIGURE 4-5**

If you select a block of text before you paste, and the Typing Replaces Selection option is on, Word will overwrite the selected text when you paste.

If the Typing Replaces Selection feature doesn't suit the way you work, remember that you can turn off the feature by clearing the Typing Replaces Selection check box on the Tools Options Edit card. For more information about using this feature, see "Essential Customization Options" starting on page 27.

## How to copy or move text between two documents

Occasionally you may want to use the same block of text in two or more Word documents or move text from one document to another—between two chapters of a book, for example. Rather than retyping the text, you can copy or move the original block. For example, consider the two document windows shown in Figure 4-6. Suppose you want to copy the paragraph that appears in the top document window (Sales 1) and place it after the first paragraph in the second document (Sales 2). (To display two documents at the same time, open both files and then choose Window Arrange All. This command displays both document windows with one in the top half of the screen, and the other in the bottom half. You can then move back and forth between the two documents either with the Windows menu or by pressing ⌘-F6.)

**FIGURE 4-6**

You want to copy the paragraph from the top document window into the bottom document window.

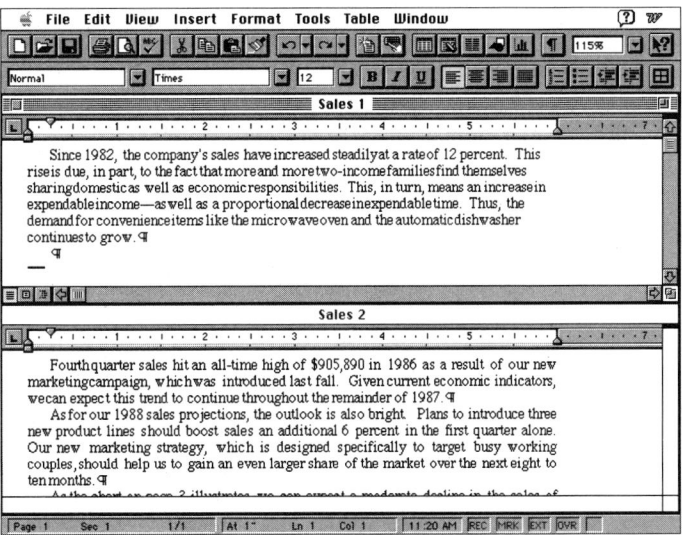

To copy the paragraph, first activate the Sales 1 document window, highlight the paragraph, and choose Edit Copy or click on the Copy button. Next activate the Sales 2 document window, move the cursor to the left of the word *As* in the second paragraph, and choose Edit Paste or click on the Paste button. As shown in Figure 4-7, Word will insert a copy of the paragraph in the Sales 2 document window. When you want to move text rather than copy it, simply use Edit Cut instead of Edit Copy. Just as it does when you are working within a single document, Windows will remember your copied block of text until you choose Edit Cut or Edit Copy again or until you quit Windows.

A copy of the paragraph now appears in the bottom document window as well.

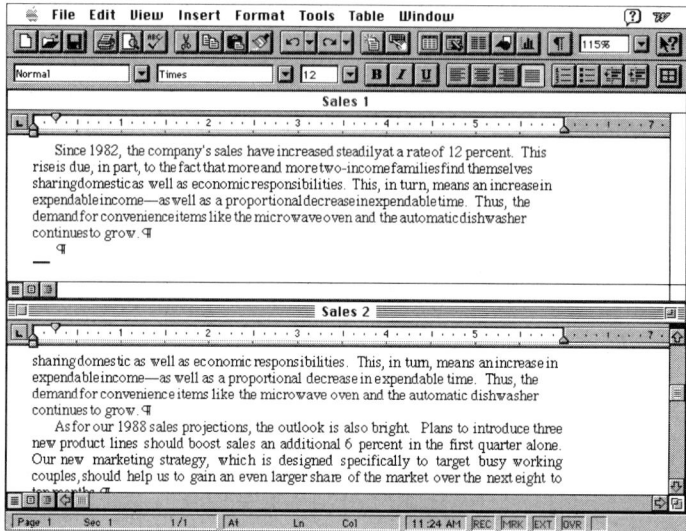

Note that you can use Word's File menu commands to open new documents and retrieve existing files in order to paste text into them or to cut or copy text from them. Similarly, you can use the Window menu commands to move to any open document window before pasting.

If you prefer to use the drag-and-drop method for copying or moving text, you'll find that Word will also let you drag and drop between windows. Simply select the text you want to move or copy, and drag it from one document window to another. The mouse pointer will become a circle with a slash when it is between the document windows and will turn back into the drag-and-drop pointer when you move it into a document again.

## Formatting issues

When you copy or move a block of text, Word will generally retain the original character formatting of the text when it pastes the characters in the new location. Similarly, when you copy or move an entire paragraph, Word will retain the paragraph formatting of the copied or moved text, provided that you include the paragraph mark (¶) in the selection.

In either case, you may need to revise the character and paragraph formatting of the pasted text to match the formatting of the surrounding text. You'll find these formatting issues covered in Chapter 7, starting on page 191, along with shortcuts for adjusting the formatting of pasted text.

## How to use Smart Cut And Paste

Word has an option that makes it easier to paste text into an existing sentence or paragraph. On the Tools Options Edit card, you'll find a check box labeled Use Smart Cut And Paste. If this option is checked, Word will do its best to preserve correct spacing between words and punctuation when you paste text.

For example, assume you've copied a block of text that has a space at the end, such as "block of text ". If Smart Cut And Paste is not turned on and you paste this block immediately after the first word of the phrase "paste here", you will get "pasteblock of text  here"—with no space between *paste* and *block*, but with two spaces between *text* and *here*. When the Smart Cut And Paste option is turned on, however, Word will automatically insert a space between the first two words and remove the extra space between the last two. This feature is a worthwhile time-saver, and we recommend that you use it.

# Using the Edit Find and Edit Replace Commands

Like most word processors, Word lets you search through a document for a particular word or a sequence of characters. It also lets you search for a character sequence and replace it with a different one. Typically, the character sequence—often called a *string* of characters, or a *text string*—will be one or two words. It can, however, be several sentences long.

Searching and replacing are two of the most useful features in any word processing program. Word takes these features a step further than most by letting you look for and change formats and styles as well as characters. In this section, we'll show you how to use the Edit Find and Edit Replace commands. As you'll see, there are some less-than-obvious ways to use these features and some potential problems you need to be aware of.

## How to search for text with the Edit Find command

To search for a character sequence, choose Edit Find (the shortcut key is ⌘-F) to open the dialog box shown in Figure 4-8 on the next page. When it first appears, you'll see a blinking cursor in the Find What text box. Type the characters you want to locate (we'll refer to this as your *search text*), and then choose Find Next to begin the search.

**FIGURE 4-8**

To search for a specific character sequence, enter your search text in the Find What text box.

The Find What text box can show only about 30 to 40 characters, depending on your display and the characters in the search text, although the search text itself can be as long as 255 characters. Text on the left side of the box will scroll out of view as you type beyond the right end of the text box, but you can bring the hidden portion into view by using the Left or Right arrow key to move left or right or by using the mouse to drag to the left or right. You can also jump to the beginning or end of the search text by using the Home and End keys.

You can click on the down arrow at the right of the Find What box (or press the Down arrow key) to open a list box that shows the last four text strings you searched for during the current Word session.

Below the Find What text box is the Search text box, which defaults to All if no text is selected. The pull-down list for this box offers two other options: Down and Up. The All setting tells Word to begin the search at the current cursor location, scan forward to the end of the document, and then continue the search from the start of the document to the search's starting position. The Down setting tells Word to scan forward from the cursor location to the end of the document. The Up setting tells Word to search backward from the cursor location to the beginning of the document.

Choose Find Next to begin a search. If you're searching with the Down option selected and with the cursor located anywhere other than before the first character of the file, Word will display the message box shown in Figure 4-9 when it reaches the end of the document. If you're using the Up option, you'll see a similar message when you reach the beginning. In either case, if you want Word to jump to the other end of the document and continue the search, choose Yes. If you want to halt the search, choose No.

**FIGURE 4-9**

To continue a search
from the beginning
of your document,
choose Yes in response
to this message box.

Regardless of the setting in the Search box, if Word reaches the starting point for the search without finding a match, it will halt and display the message box shown in Figure 4-10.

**FIGURE 4-10**

Word will display
this message box if it
cannot find the search
text.

If Word does find your search text, it will scroll the found text into view, highlight the match on screen, and halt the search. You can then choose Cancel to close the Find dialog box, leaving the cursor at that location, or you can continue searching by choosing Find Next again. If you choose Cancel, you have two choices for continuing the search later: You can use the Edit Find command again and choose Find Next, or press Shift-F4 to repeat the search.

If you close the dialog box and then press Shift-F4 to continue searching, Word will not redisplay the Find dialog box. Rather, it will immediately scan for the search text you last typed in the Find What box. In fact, the search text will not change until you replace it, remove it, or quit Word. You can even open another document file to search for the same text in another document. However, the next time you choose the Edit Find command, Word will highlight the contents of the Find What text box so that you can overwrite the search text easily.

You can close the Find dialog box to edit the found text, but you don't have to. If you press Control-Tab or point to the document with the mouse and click, Word will leave the Find dialog box on the screen but will activate the document so that you can edit it. If you need to edit a substantial amount of text, you can also move the dialog box out of the way. When you finish editing, you can press Control-Tab or click on the dialog box again to return to it.

If Word did not find the text you were searching for, but you're neverthe-less convinced that the text is in the document, check the entry in the Find dia-log box carefully. Keep in mind that unless you've told Word otherwise (in ways that we'll get to shortly), Word looks for exact matches. If you've en-tered extra blank spaces or typed a character incorrectly in the Find What text box, Word won't be able to locate the search text. (Capitalization doesn't mat-ter unless you have checked the Match Case check box, which we'll also cover in a moment.)

Note that you can paste text into the Find What text box. If you spot one instance of your search text in your document, you can highlight it, copy it by pressing ⌘-C, and paste it into the Find What box by pressing ⌘-V. This should guarantee that the string is entered correctly. Of course, you may still have trouble finding a match if you have mistyped the text in your document.

You can also use the Edit Find command to jump quickly to any part of your document—to make revisions, for example. Suppose you want to edit a section of your text that comes immediately after the heading *Part II.* You can search for *Part II*, and Word will take you to that section heading, where you can revise your text as necessary.

## How to use the options in the Find dialog box

The Find dialog box offers four check boxes: Match Case, Find Whole Words Only, Use Pattern Matching, and Sounds Like.

**Match Case.** With the Match Case option, you can limit your search to in-stances of the search text that exactly match the capitalization of what you enter in the Find What text box. If you don't check the Match Case check box, Word will ignore case (uppercase and lowercase) when it looks for the search text. For example, if you enter *Microsoft* as the search text and do not check Match Case, Word will also find *microsoft*, *MicroSoft*, and *MICROSOFT*. If you use Match Case, however, Word will find only *Microsoft*.

The Match Case option can be helpful when you're searching for a proper noun that has the same spelling as a common noun. Suppose, for example, you want to search for a reference to the Word program. To avoid stopping for the word *word*, simply enter *Word* as your search text and then be sure to check the Match Case check box. This option can also be useful if you're look-ing for a word or phrase that you know is at the beginning of a sentence.

 Using the Match Case option has one possible disadvantage. If you've accidentally used the improper case in some instances in your text—typing the name of the software as *word* or *WOrd* instead of *Word*—the search will not find these occurrences. For the greatest assurance that you've found all the instances of a word— to check the correct case throughout the document, for example— it's safer to cast a wider net.

**Find Whole Words Only.** The Find Whole Words Only option is useful when you're searching for a short word, such as *action*, that is also likely to be contained within a larger word. Unless you check this check box, Word will also find text that occurs within another word. For example, if you search for *action*, Word will stop for such matches as *reactionary* and *actionable*. By checking the Find Whole Words Only check box, you're telling Word to ignore these matches.

On the other hand, performing a search without the Find Whole Words Only option can often be useful. For example, if you can't remember whether you wrote *We will look at...* or *We'll be looking at...*, you can search for *look* and find either phrase. Of course, if Word is finding many unwanted matches during a search, you can always turn on the Find Whole Words Only option at any time.

**Use Pattern Matching.** The Use Pattern Matching option determines whether Word looks for an exact match for the characters you enter in the Find What text box or interprets them as pattern symbols. For example, the question mark is the wildcard character for matching any symbol. If you enter *th?* in the Find What text box and check the Use Pattern Matching check box, Word will treat *the* as a match as well as matching *th?* in a sentence such as *Did you finish fourth?* On the other hand, if you type *th?* and don't check the Use Pattern Matching check box, Word will look for a literal match, matching *th?* but not *the*.

There is much more to be said about pattern matching. We'll cover the feature in detail shortly.

**Sounds Like.** The fourth check box, Sounds Like, is one of Word's most sophisticated search options. It lets you match words even when their spelling differs from the spelling used in the search text. For example, if you type *nyff* or *nighf* in the Find What text box and check the Sounds Like check box, Word will treat *knife* as a match. The feature has its limitations, however; while *numona* will match *pneumonia*, for example, *numonya* will not (even though the spelling checker will correctly suggest *pneumonia* as the correct spelling for *numonya* but not *numona*). Note that Use Pattern Matching and Sounds Like are exclusive; you can have only one active at a time.

## NEW! How to use pattern matching

Word's pattern-matching feature lets you cast a wider net when looking for matches. As we just discussed, Word will take advantage of pattern matching only if you have checked the Use Pattern Matching check box in the Find dialog box (or in the Replace dialog box, which we'll discuss later in this chapter).

Assuming you've checked the Use Pattern Matching check box, Word will recognize the question mark symbol (?) as a wildcard character. Each question mark in your search text will match any one character in a potential match. For example, if you enter *ba?e* as your search text, Word will find *bale*, *base*, *bane*, and *bake*.

Word also can use the asterisk (*) to match any number of characters. For example, the search text *ba\*e* not only will find *bale*, *base*, *bane*, and *bake* but also will match *balance*, *backstage*, and *baccalaureate*. Unlike the question mark, the asterisk will also match zero characters; in other words, the search text *ba\*e* would also match *bae*.

One minor problem with using the asterisk wildcard is that you can't then limit the search to whole words only. Look for *ba\*e*, for example, and Word will also match the *base* in *baseball*. Nor can you limit the search to whole words by adding a space at the end of the search text. If you try, Word will look for the next word that ends with *e*. For example, if you end one paragraph with the words *baseball park* and start the next with *Whatever happened to the...*, Word will match everything from the *base* in *baseball* through *the*, including the period and the paragraph mark. The moral: You'll want to verify each match carefully when using the asterisk as a wildcard.

## NEW! 

Square brackets ([ ]) serve a number of purposes. If you put two or more letters between the brackets, Word will match any one of the letters in that position. For example, *ba[lr]e* will match *bale* and *bare*. Put two letters separated by a hyphen within the brackets to define a range; *ba[k-n]e* will match *bake*, *bale*, and *bane*. Put an exclamation mark before the first character within the brackets to match any word that does not have the specified characters in that position. For example, *ba[!rs]e* will not match *bare* or *base* but will match *bake* and *bale*. Similarly, you can put an exclamation mark before a range of characters within the brackets (indicated by a hyphen), and Word will match any word that does not contain any of the characters in the range in that position. For example, *ba[!m-z]e* will not match *bare* or *base* but will match *bake* and *bale*.

Curly brackets ({ }) indicate numeric patterns. A number within the brackets will match any word with exactly that number of adjacent occurrences of the prior character; *be{2}*, for example, will match *beers* and *bee* but not *bed*. Including a number and a comma requires at least that many occurrences of the prior character; *be{1,}*, for example, will match *beers*, *bee*, and *bed*. Two numbers separated by a comma indicate a range of occurrences of the prior character; *10{1,3}* will match *10*, *100*, or *1000* but not *1*. (It will also match *10000*, which is *1000* plus an extra *0*.)

The @ symbol signals one or more occurrences of the prior character. For example, *be@r* will match *berry* or *beer*.

The less than (<) and greater than (>) symbols will let you match characters at the beginning or end of a word. Type *<ho* in the Find What box to match *how*, *house*, and *hose* but not *roughhouse*. Type *ge>* in the Find What box to match *huge*, *rouge*, and *page* but not *get*.

Finally, you can use parentheses to group characters and to control the sequence of matching, in much the same way you use parentheses to control the order of processing in arithmetic or algebraic expressions.

## How to search for a pattern-matching character

If you have checked the Use Pattern Matching check box and you need to use one or more of the pattern-matching characters (or operators) as a literal match, simply precede the character with a backslash (\). For example, to search for a question mark when the pattern-matching feature is turned on, type \? to have Word match literal question marks rather than matching any character.

If you want to search for a question that begins with *Why*, you can turn on pattern matching and type *Why*\?* in the Find What box. To search for a literal backslash character when the Use Pattern Matching check box is checked, you need to type a second backslash (like this: \\).

Word 6.0 uses the caret as an indicator of special characters, such as ^t to indicate a tab. To search for a caret when pattern matching is turned on, you must type ^^.

## How to find special characters

Another useful feature of the Edit Find command is that it can find special characters such as paragraph marks, non-breaking spaces, and optional hyphens. Word even provides a feature that will automatically insert most of the relevant codes for special characters into the Find What text box for you.

Figure 4-11 shows the list that opens when you choose the Special button at the bottom of the Find dialog box without checking the Use Pattern Matching check box. The location of this box can vary, depending on the position of the Find dialog box on your screen when you choose Special. To insert a special search code in the Find What text box, simply select the element you want to find from the selection box, and Word will insert the appropriate code.

**FIGURE 4-11**

When you choose the Special button in the Find dialog box without pattern matching, Word will display this list of special characters whose codes can be added to the Find What text box.

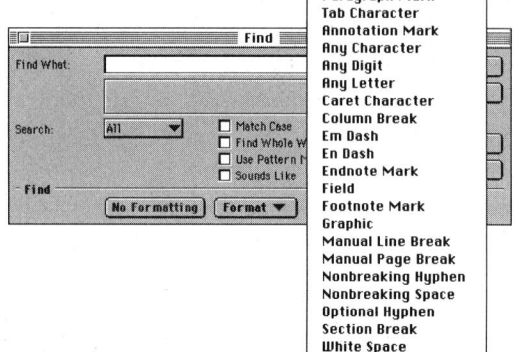

When the Use Pattern Matching feature is turned on, Word will not recognize certain codes for special characters—those for paragraph marks or for blank space, for example. It will recognize others, however, such as ^t for tab. Note that choosing the Special button when pattern matching is turned on will produce a different set of entries in the selection box, as shown in Figure 4-12.

**FIGURE 4-12**

When Use Pattern Matching is checked, Word displays the special characters that it can use for patterns.

If you know the code for the special character you want to find, you can type the code directly into the Find What text box. The table in Figure 4-13 lists the characters you can search for and gives the corresponding keyboard code for each. At the risk of getting ahead of ourselves, but to make this a more useful reference, we've also listed several codes that you can use only when replacing text. We'll come back to these codes later in this chapter, in "How to replace text with the Edit Replace command" on page 108, which covers Word's search-and-replace feature.

| This Code... | Represents This Character... |
|---|---|
| **Codes that work in the Find What or Replace With box** | |
| ^t | Tab mark (→) |
| ^0*nnn* | ASCII character in *nnn* (decimal) form (case-sensitive when pattern matching is on) |
| ^^ | Caret character (single caret also finds a single caret when pattern matching is not on; to find two carets, you must enter four carets) |
| ^n | Column break (dotted line across a column) |
| ^l | Manual line-break character (↵) |
| ^m | Manual page break (also matches section breaks when pattern matching is on) |
| ^+ | Em dash |
| ^= | En dash |
| ^s | Non-breaking space (~) |
| ^~ | Non-breaking hyphen |
| ^- | Optional hyphen |
| ^p | Paragraph mark (¶) (only works in the Find What text box when pattern matching is not on) |
| **Codes that work in the Find What box only** | |
| ^a | Annotation reference |
| ^g | Any graphic |
| **Codes that work in the Find What box only and work only when pattern matching is on** | |
| ? | Question mark (treated as a character otherwise) |
| * | Asterisk (treated as a character otherwise) |

*(continued)*

**FIGURE 4-13**

Search-and-replace codes for special characters.

**FIGURE 4-13** *continued*

| This Code... | Represents This Character... |
|---|---|
| **Codes that work in the Find What box only and work only when pattern matching is off** | |
| ^e | Endnote |
| ^d | Field |
| ^f | Footnote |
| ^b | Section break (when pattern matching is on, ^*m* matches both page and section breaks) |
| ^w | White space (any combination of normal spaces, non-breaking spaces, and tab marks) |
| ^? | Any character (equivalent to *?* used by itself when pattern matching is on) |
| ^# | Any digit |
| ^$ | Any letter |
| **Codes that work in the Replace With box only** | |
| ^c | Clipboard contents |
| ^& | Find What text box contents |

The codes used to search for special characters are case-sensitive; you must use lowercase letters.

Several codes listed in Figure 4-13, such as *^w*, need further explanation. When you specify *^w* as your search text, Word will find the blank space that appears between any two printing characters in your document, including the single spaces between words, as well as tabs. This *^w* code will not treat paragraph marks as white space.

The codes for ASCII characters in decimal form also require some explanation. You can search for any ASCII character by entering a caret followed by a zero and the character's three-digit ASCII code. For example, if you enter *^0097* as your search text, Word will find every occurrence of the letter *a*. Even though *097* is the ASCII code for a lowercase *a* and *065* is the code for an uppercase *A*, Word will find every *a*, regardless of case, unless you check either the Match Case check box or the Use Pattern Matching check box.

Be aware that your search text can include any combination of special characters and other text. For example, to find every instance of a paragraph that begins with *For*, you can choose the Edit Find command and enter *^pFor* in the Find What text box. When you choose OK, Word will highlight the paragraph mark at the end of the preceding paragraph as well as the word *For* at the beginning of the following paragraph.

> Word can find many special characters even when they're not visible on the screen. For example, if you haven't checked the Paragraph Marks check box on the Tools Options View card, the paragraph mark at the end of each paragraph will not be displayed on your screen. However, if you search for the code *^p*, Word will highlight the space following each paragraph. Similarly, Word can find tab marks, optional hyphens, and end-of-line markers even when they aren't displayed.

## How to find hidden text

Word cannot find matches in text that has been formatted as hidden unless you first set the program to display the hidden text. If hidden text is currently hidden from view, you can display it either by clicking on the Show/Hide ¶ button on the Standard toolbar or by checking the Hidden Text check box on the Tools Options View card. You can then begin the search.

## How to find formatting attributes and styles

As mentioned earlier in this chapter, Word lets you search not only for a character sequence but for font, paragraph, and style formats as well. You even have the choice of searching for a format by itself or in combination with a particular character sequence. For example, suppose you use the Heading 3 style at the start of each section in a document. By searching for the style, you can rapidly move from section to section using Shift-F4 to repeat the last Edit Find command. Similarly, you can go to a particular heading by searching for both the style and a keyword in that heading. For information about styles, see Chapter 12, "Styles & AutoFormat," starting on page 389.

At the bottom of the Find dialog box, shown in Figure 4-8 on page 96, are the No Formatting and Format buttons. Until you specify some formatting as part of your search text, the No Formatting button will remain grayed. If you specify a format as part of the search text, however, the button will become available, and you can choose it to remove the format from the search criteria.

Choose the Format button, and Word will offer a menu with seven choices: Font, Paragraph, Tabs, Border, Language, Frame, and Style. Most of these open Find dialog boxes that are similar to the formatting dialog boxes you'll see when you choose the corresponding command on the Format menu. The one exception is the Language choice, which opens the Find Language dialog box that is similar to the dialog box available when you choose Tools Language. In all of the dialog boxes available through the Format button, you can specify which format and language attributes to search for, using essentially the same procedure you would use to assign those attributes to your text.

Because these dialog boxes are essentially identical to the dialog boxes used for applying formats, we won't work through each one here. Note, however, that when designating formats to search for or replace, you have three choices, as opposed to the two you have when assigning formats. For example, when you assign formats, you must define text as either bold or not bold. But when searching or replacing, you can specify that the text must be bold, that it must not be bold, or that it can be either. Unless you specify otherwise, Word will assume that any given type of format—bold, italic, typeface, font size, and so on—is irrelevant. But if you open the various dialog boxes available through the Format button, you can specify those formats you want to look for.

Note too that in these dialog boxes, the check boxes can toggle through three states: gray (the default) to indicate that the state for that format option doesn't matter; blank to indicate that you want to match only text that lacks that format; or checked to indicate that you want to match only text that has that format. In much the same way, you can leave text boxes blank to tell Word to ignore the setting for that format; any entry in a text box will restrict matches to matching formats. For details on some of these formatting features and on how to use their dialog boxes, take a look at "Paragraph formatting" on page 204 and "Font formatting" on page 223. You'll also want to refer to all of Chapter 12, "Styles & AutoFormat," starting on page 389, which includes a discussion of the Language dialog box.

You can also use the Formatting toolbar buttons to apply formatting criteria to the Find and Replace boxes.

**Toolbar shortcuts for format attributes and styles in Find.**  For those who prefer toolbar shortcuts, Word offers toolbar buttons for specifying most common formatting attributes in the Find dialog box. Figure 4-14 shows all these buttons.

| Press This... | To Specify This Format... |
|---|---|
| **Lists for selecting a setting** | |
| Normal ▾ | Style |
| Times ▾ | Font |
| 12 ▾ | Font size |
| **Buttons on the formatting toolbar that toggle between three states: attribute included in the search, attribute excluded, and attribute ignored** | |
| **B** | Bold |
| *I* | Italic |
| U | Underline |
| **Buttons on the formatting toolbar that toggle the setting on and off** | |
| ▤ | Left alignment |
| ▤ | Centered alignment |
| ▤ | Right alignment |
| ▤ | Justified Alignment |

**FIGURE 4-14**

Toolbar shortcuts for specifying formats when searching or replacing.

# How to replace text with the Edit Replace command

The Edit Replace command (shortcut key ⌘-H) is closely related to the Edit Find command. In fact, if you choose the Replace button in the Find dialog box, Word will expand the dialog box and rename it Replace. This Replace dialog box, shown in Figure 4-15, is identical to the Replace dialog box you can open by choosing Edit Replace. As the name implies, it differs from the Find dialog box primarily in that it lets you automatically replace found text with new text rather than simply searching for text. You can also use it to search for and replace styles and other formats.

**FIGURE 4-15**

The Replace dialog box lets you find and replace text, formats, and styles in a single step.

The options and operation of the Replace dialog box are nearly identical to those of the Find dialog box, except for the addition of a Replace With text box. At its simplest, you use the replace feature by typing the search text in the Find What text box and the replacement text in the Replace With text box. If you leave the Replace With box blank, Word will replace the search text with nothing—that is, it will simply delete the search text.

Like the Find What box, the Replace With text box can display only about 30 to 40 characters but can hold up to 255 characters. You can scroll the text left or right with the Left or Right arrow key or by using the mouse to drag to the left or right. You can also jump to the beginning or end of the search text by using the Home and End keys.

As is the case with Edit Find, after you choose the Edit Replace command and specify settings, Word will remember the entries in the text boxes, and those entries will be the new defaults until you delete them, replace them, or quit the program.

After you enter the search text and the replacement text, choose Find Next if you want to see each match before replacing it, or choose Replace All to change every match without reviewing any of them. If you choose Find Next, Word will stop at each match and scroll the match into view with the text highlighted, as shown in Figure 4-16. Choose Replace to overwrite the found text with the replacement text. When Word pastes the replacement text into your document, the new text will take the same format as the search text it replaces unless you've specified a new format in one of the dialog boxes available through the Format button. Word will also attempt to match the capitalization of the text you replace, as explained more fully later in this chapter.

**FIGURE 4-16**

When Word finds the search text using Find Next, it highlights the match in your document.

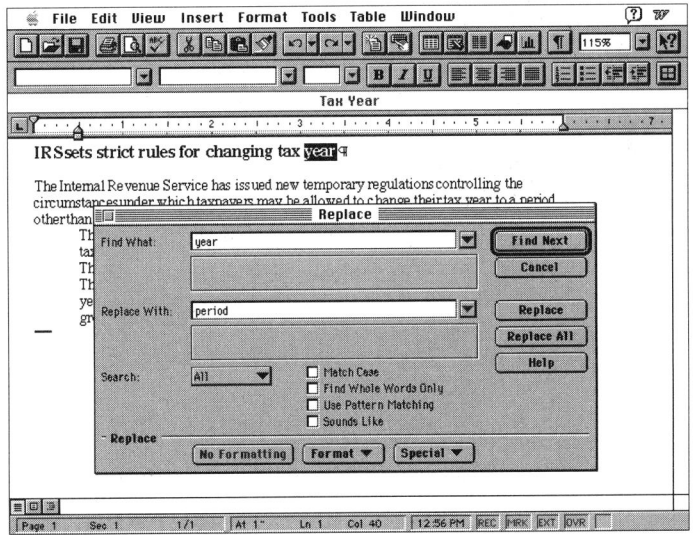

## How to use the Replace All option

Suppose you're working in the document shown in Figure 4-16 and you decide to change every occurrence of the word *year* to the word *period*. Assume that the cursor is at the beginning of the third paragraph (the second paragraph of body text) when you open the Replace dialog box. Type *year* in the Find What text box and *period* in the Replace With text box. Then choose Replace All. Word will start the replace procedure. If you've set the Search box to All, rather than Up or Down, Word will make all the replacements and then display the message box shown in Figure 4-17 on the next page.

**FIGURE 4-17**

Word has replaced all seven occurrences of the word *year* with the word *period*.

**FIGURE 4-18**

If you have not selected All as the Search setting for a replace operation, Word will display a message like this when it reaches the end (or the beginning) of the document.

If you select either Up or Down for the Search setting, Word will start replacing at the cursor position and then pause at the beginning or the end of the document to ask whether you want to continue the replacement for the remainder of the document. Figure 4-18 shows the message you'll see for searching Down.

If you choose Yes in the message box to continue the replacement procedure, Word will continue making changes until it reaches the point where it started. When Word completes all the changes, it will display a message box indicating the number of changes it made.

## How to selectively replace text

In many cases, you won't want to replace every occurrence of your search text. Sometimes you'll want to examine each match before you tell Word it's OK to change the text. At other times you'll want to confine the replacement to a selected portion of your document. Word lets you use either of these strategies.

**Single replacements.** If you want to see each match before deciding whether to change it, use the Replace button instead of Replace All. After you choose the Find Next button the first time, Word will highlight the first match and then wait. If you choose Replace, Word will make the replacement and move on to highlight the next occurrence of the search text. If you don't want to make the replacement, choose Find Next, and Word will continue the search without replacing.

Using the Replace button rather than the Replace All button is particularly helpful when you believe that your document might contain several variations of the search text. For example, suppose you are changing the word *walk* to *run*. As you go through the document, Word may match the past-tense form *walked*. If you have chosen Replace All, *walked* would become *runed*. When you check each match, however, you can click in your document with the mouse or press Control-Tab to switch to the document, replace the word *walked* with *ran*, and then click on the Replace dialog box or press Control-Tab to return to the dialog box and continue the search.

**Replacements within a selected block of text.** To change all matches within a specific block of text, simply select the text before you choose the Edit Replace command. If you want to change the word *year* to *period* within only the first paragraph of body text, for example, select that paragraph before choosing Edit Replace. You can then type *year* in the Find What text box and *period* in the Replace With text box. When you choose the Replace All button, Word will change every occurrence of the search text within the selected paragraph and will indicate the number of changes in the subsequent message box.

## How to use the Match Case option

When you check the Match Case check box in the Find dialog box, Word will find only that text whose capitalization exactly matches that of the search text. This same rule applies when you use the Edit Replace command. In this case, however, the Match Case option also affects your replacement text.

If you do not turn on the Match Case option and you type your replacement text in lowercase letters, Word will replace all instances of the search text, regardless of case, and will follow the existing capitalization of each occurrence to determine the capitalization of the replacement. If you use uppercase in your replacement text, however, Word will follow this capitalization. If you use the Match Case option, Word will match case for both the search text and the replacement text.

For example, suppose you want to replace the word *May* with the word *April* throughout the sample document shown in Figure 4-19 on the next page. If you type your search text and your replacement text in all lowercase letters and do not turn on Match Case, Word will find all occurrences of *may*, ignoring case, and replace them with the word *april* when you choose Replace All, as shown in Figure 4-20 on the next page.

FIGURE 4-19

You want to change
the word *May* to *April*
throughout this
document.

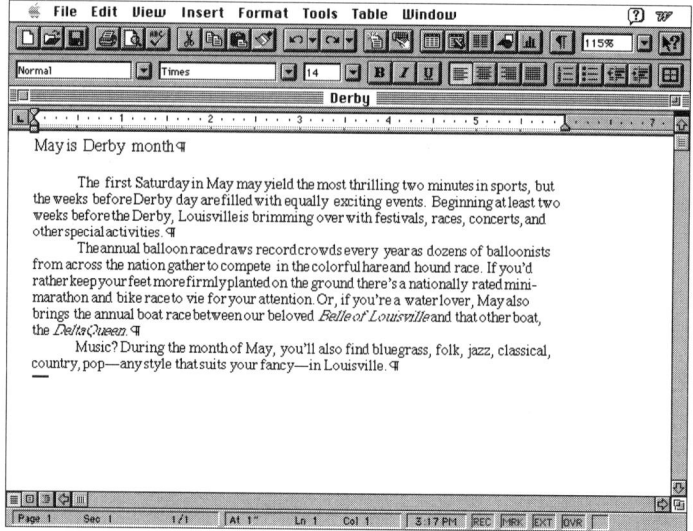

FIGURE 4-20

If you type your search
text and your replace-
ment text in all lower-
case letters and do not
use the Match Case
option, Word will
retain the document's
existing capitalization.

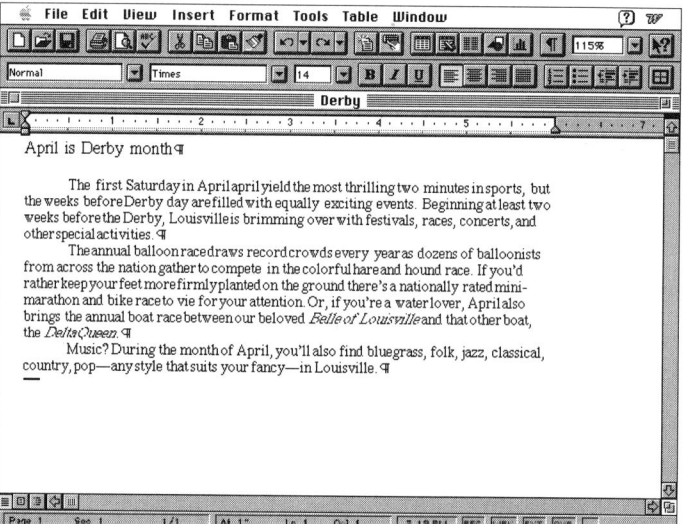

Notice that in every instance where the word *may* was capitalized, Word
also capitalized the replacement text *april*. But if you want to ensure that *April*
will be capitalized in every instance, you should type it that way in the Replace With text box. This feature is handy when you've inadvertently capitalized a word incorrectly throughout your text—typing *MicroSoft*, for example,
rather than *Microsoft*—and you want to use the search-and-replace feature to
automatically fix the capitalization.

In the first paragraph of body text in Figure 4-20, notice that Word changed the phrase *May may yield* to *April april yield*, although you obviously want to change only the month names. You can avoid this by using the Match Case option. Figure 4-21 shows the effect of the Edit Replace command—replacing *May* with *April*—on our original sample document with the Match Case option turned on. Notice that the phrase *May may yield* is now changed, correctly, to *April may yield*.

**FIGURE 4-21**

When you use the Match Case option, Word will change only those words that exactly match the capitalization of the search text.

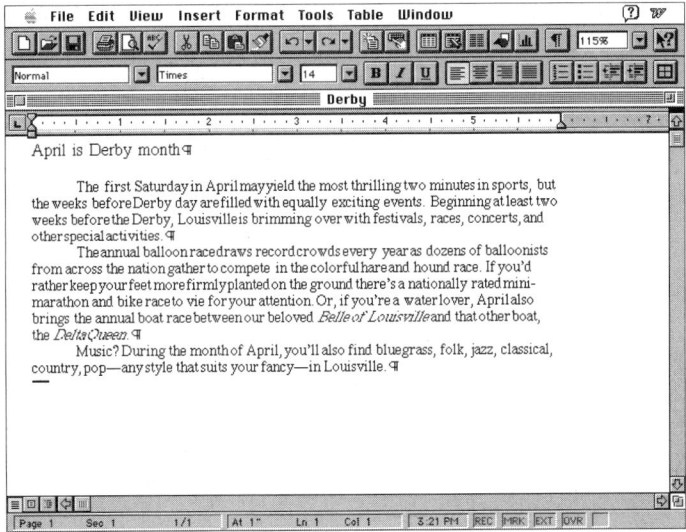

At the risk of repeating ourselves, the rule is this: With the Match Case box checked, Word will find only those instances of the search text whose capitalization exactly matches the capitalization of the text you type in the Find What text box. In addition, with the Match Case box checked, Word will always paste your replacement text into your document exactly as you typed it in the Replace With text box.

## How to use wildcards with Edit Replace

As we detailed earlier in Figure 4-13, you cannot use wildcards in the Replace With box. If you use pattern-matching characters in the Find What box, however, Word will replace all matches with the text in the Replace With text box.

For example, suppose that you want to replace every occurrence of the words *software* and *hardware* with the phrase *computer supplies*. Choose Edit Replace, type *????ware* as your search text, and check the Use Pattern Matching check box (or type *^?^?^?^?ware* without using pattern matching). Then type *computer supplies* as your replacement text, and choose the Replace All button. Word will look for all words that begin with four letters followed by *ware* and will replace those words with *computer supplies*.

### How to replace hidden text

The Edit Replace command will affect hidden text only if the text is displayed on screen. By default, Word won't display any text that is formatted as hidden, and it will ignore that text during a search-and-replace operation. If you want to change hidden text, check the Hidden Text check box on the Tools Options View card or click on the Show/Hide ¶ button on the Standard toolbar before you begin the search-and-replace operation.

### How to replace formatting attributes and styles

The Edit Replace command can search for and replace formats using exactly the same search capabilities that we discussed for the Edit Find command.

You can specify formatting for the replacement text using the same procedures and toolbar shortcuts that you use for the search text. The position of the cursor—in either the Find What or the Replace With text box—determines whether the attribute is applied to the search text or the replacement text. When you specify a format, it's easy to confirm that you specified it correctly by looking at the settings below each text box.

As we noted when discussing the Find feature, it's often useful to look for specific text based on its formatting. It's sometimes even more useful to specify the formatting and style of the replacement text. For example, suppose you've been using the term *widget* as the name of a new product. The marketing department has now decided that the official name is *WidJet* and that it should always be printed in bold italics. Word's ability to specify formatting for the replacement string makes replacing *widget* a simple task. Similarly, you might have a document in which you need to replace all bold text with italics. Here again, the ability to search for and replace formats makes it a simple matter of specifying bold for the search text and specifying italic and not bold for the replacement text.

### How to use special characters with Edit Replace

Earlier in this chapter, we discussed the special codes you can use in the Find What text box to search for special characters in a document. For example, if you want to include a paragraph mark as part of your search text, you can type ^p. You can use many of these same codes, and some others, in the Replace With text box as part of your replacement text. If you want an extra carriage return after each paragraph, for example, you can search for ^p and replace it with ^p^p.

Figure 4-13 lists the codes available for both the Find What box and the Replace With box. You cannot use some of these codes in the Replace With text box; the codes for white space and for any field, for example, would make no sense as part of replacement text. Other codes, such as ^b for section break, would make sense as replacement text, but they work only for finding text. As you can with Find What, you can click on the Special button to display a list of available characters.

Figure 4-13 also includes two codes that work only in the Replace With box: ^c, which inserts the Clipboard contents; and ^&, which uses the search text as part of the replacement text. Both of these are worth a closer look.

**How to replace from the Clipboard.** Word provides an unusual option for search-and-replace operations by letting you store the replacement text on the Clipboard. Storing replacement text on the Clipboard offers two advantages: First, the Clipboard is not bound by the 255-character maximum that applies in the dialog box, so you can use the Clipboard when the replacement text is unusually long. Second, replacement text pasted from the Clipboard is pasted into your document with formatting intact. This makes the Clipboard the preferred choice when you have a mix of formats in the replacement text. (This is true only for text that is formatted directly. If you are formatting with styles, the replacement text will not retain its formatting. For a discussion of style formats, see Chapter 12, "Styles & AutoFormat," starting on page 389.) And you can also use the Clipboard to replace text with a graphic.

To use the Clipboard's contents as the replacement text, be sure that the cursor is in the Replace With text box, choose the Special button, and then select Clipboard Contents from the list. You can also simply type the characters ^c in the Replace With text box.

**How to use search text as part of the replacement text.** The second code that works only in the Replace With box is ^&, which inserts the search text as part of the replacement text. This code can save you time and effort for certain kinds of search-and-replace operations. For example, if you've been referring to someone by his or her last name throughout your text and you want to add a title, you need to type the last name only once, in the Find What box. To change *Schlagenhauffer* to *Dr. Schlagenhauffer* throughout your text, enter *Schlagenhauffer* in the Find What text box and *Dr.* ^& in the Replace With text box.

A more interesting use for the ^& code involves combining this code in the Replace With box with the wildcard codes in the Find What box. Suppose, for example, you've written a report that includes the phrases *hardware sources*, *software sources*, and *information sources*. To avoid confusion, you want to change the first two references to *hardware vendors* and *software vendors*. By taking advantage of the wildcard character with pattern matching selected, you can search for *????ware sources* to find instances of both *hardware sources* and *software sources*. If you type *^& vendors* as replacement text, Word will replace *hardware sources* with *hardware sources vendors* and replace *software sources* with *software sources vendors*. You can then replace all occurrences of *sources vendors* with *vendors* alone to complete the change.

## More on editing

As we've demonstrated in this chapter, you can use Word's Edit Find and Edit Replace commands to make rapid changes in your text. Part of the flexibility comes from the generalized nature of these features. However, Word offers other, more specialized, editing tools as well for altering text in your documents. We'll cover some of these in the next chapter.

# TOPIC FINDER

# 5

# Additional Editing Tools

ord has a number of specialized tools that make certain kinds of text entry and editing tasks easier. Some of these—such as the tool for footnotes—are so specialized that you may find them indispensable or you may use them rarely, if at all, depending on your personal taste and the kind of writing you do. However, there are several tools that most people will need at least occasionally. These include the AutoCorrect and AutoText features, the Thesaurus, special characters and symbols, and tools to create and edit headers and footers.

In many ways, these tools are more sophisticated than the basic editing features we discussed in Chapter 4. Where Word's search-and-replace feature, for example, is best described as a sophisticated version of a basic word processing function, the program's AutoCorrect and AutoText features are sophisticated in concept as well as in implementation. They are, in fact, supremely elegant tools for entering text and other data. Much the same can be said of the other tools we'll discuss in this chapter.

## NEW! Similarities and Differences Between AutoCorrect and AutoText

AutoText and one of the AutoCorrect options perform similar functions: They both store frequently used text and graphics so you can insert them in your document with minimal effort. In both cases, the stored text can be as short as a single character or as long as several pages. The entries may be signature blocks, long passages of boilerplate text, specially formatted phrases such as a company trademark, graphics (such as a company logo), preformatted tables, or just about any other kind of data that you may need to enter repeatedly.

Both AutoText and AutoCorrect can speed text entry by reducing the number of keystrokes it takes to type a block of boilerplate text or other item you use often. In addition, both features offer the significant benefit of improving accuracy; you can use them to make certain that you never again misspell the name of an important client or an important person in your organization. And in both cases, once the new text (or other data) is inserted into your document, you can edit and format it.

Although the two features share similar functions, they are also quite different. Both have *auto* in their names, but AutoCorrect is more automatic. Specifically, AutoCorrect will replace an abbreviation with its full text, or definition, as soon as you enter a space, tab, or carriage return to signal the end of the abbreviation. (This also happens when you have one or more punctuation characters—such as a comma or a period—after the abbreviation; AutoCorrect makes the replacement and retains the punctuation.) In contrast, AutoText works only when you tell Word to replace the abbreviation, and only when the cursor is within or immediately follows the abbreviation.

Also, as the name implies, AutoCorrect is meant to help you catch and correct common typing mistakes. For example, it can automatically convert *teh* to *the* without your having to notice the mistake or even think about it. And AutoCorrect offers several options that turn some elementary correction features on and off without your having to define any special abbreviations or definitions. We'll cover these in the section immediately after this.

## NEW! Using AutoCorrect

AutoCorrect is designed to correct mistakes automatically. If you've set any of the AutoCorrect options to work (some are on by default when you first install Word), they'll watch over your typing from the time you start the program; Word will correct the specified mistakes as you make them. If none of the AutoCorrect options are set to work, it's simple enough to activate them.

Whether you choose AutoCorrect or AutoText to store a given definition will depend partly on how often you intend to use the definition, partly on the abbreviation you intend to use, and partly on the reason you need it. For abbreviations that you use frequently—and that you're not likely to type for some other purpose—AutoCorrect is the preferred choice because it doesn't wait for you to give a specific command before it expands the abbreviation into the full definition. Similarly, if there are any typing errors you habitually make, AutoCorrect is the better choice, since you're likely to make the errors without being aware of them.

For abbreviations that you use infrequently, you'll generally be better off using AutoText so that having to give a command isn't bothersome. AutoText is also better for abbreviations that you might use for another purpose—for example, *pc* used as an abbreviation for *personal computer*.

**NEW!**

## How to use AutoCorrect

To see the current settings for the AutoCorrect options, choose Tools AutoCorrect. Word will display the AutoCorrect dialog box, shown in Figure 5-1. The figure shows the dialog box as it appears with the default settings. The first four check boxes govern some straightforward correction features.

Use the AutoCorrect dialog box to select options that make Word identify and correct mistakes as you type.

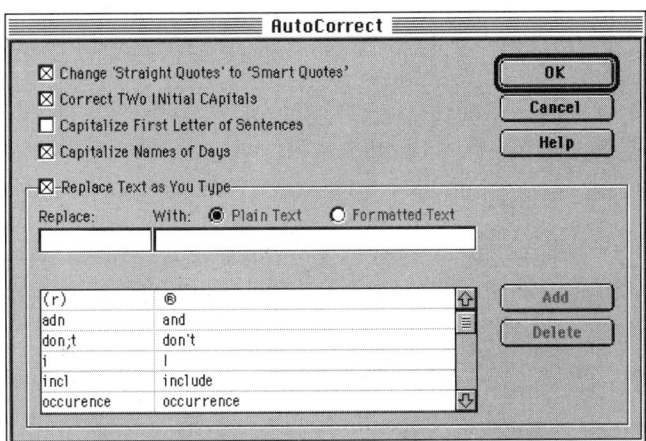

The Change 'Straight Quotes' To 'Smart Quotes' option will automatically change quotation-mark characters as you type. If you're not familiar with typographic conventions, you might not be aware that there are different

kinds of quotation marks. Many people simply use the straight quotes: ' and ".
From a typographical viewpoint, however, these should be used only to sig-
nify certain units of measure, such as ' for feet and " for inches. For dialog or
for quoted excerpts and terms, the preferred choices are pairs of opening and
closing quotation marks, such as

    'this'

and

    "this"

Word's approach to Smart Quotes doesn't always make the right
choice between opening and closing quotation marks. In particular, if you have a quotation within a quotation, as in
    "I said, 'What kind of quotes do you want?'"
Word will sometimes choose the wrong quotation marks. In this
example, if you don't add a space between the final single quotation mark and the final double quotation mark, Word will end with
a closing double quotation mark—as it should. But if you add a
space, Word's Smart Quotes feature will guess wrong and insert an
opening double quotation mark instead of a closing one. In general, whether or not you add a space depends on whether you feel
the particular font crowds the three quotation marks together. So
although there is no hard-and-fast typographical rule about
whether to add a space or not, you may well prefer to add one.

There are several ways around this problem, including some
that take advantage of macros—an advanced feature that we'll
cover in the last section of this book (but without dealing with this
particular problem). If you use the Smart Quotes feature, however,
you should at least be aware of the problem. And note that the simplest fix is to type all combinations of single and double quotation
marks without spaces and then use Word's search-and-replace
feature to search for '" and replace them with ' ". If you need to replace curly quotes, note that to insert them into the Find or Replace
dialog box, you need to use special shortcut keys. The opening
quotes are Option-[ for " and Option-] for '. The closing quotes are
Shift-Option-[ for " and Shift-Option-] for '. Finally, when using the
Find or Replace feature, curly quotes match exactly (an opening
quote matches only an opening quote), but the straight quotes inserted from the keyboard match any quote (" matches ", ", or ").

These are widely known as *curly quotes*. The reference to Smart Quotes means that the feature can automatically determine whether a given curly quote should be the opening or closing quotation mark. If there's a check in this check box, Word will convert all quotation marks in your documents to curly quotes.

The second check box is Correct TWo INitial CApitals. This is one of our favorite additions to Word 6.0, since we both occasionally fail to release the Shift key quickly enough to prevent the second letter of a word from being capitalized by accident. If you check this check box, Word will correct such typos—for example, it will change *WOrd* to *Word*—even if you don't notice the mistake. At the same time, it will leave recognizable abbreviations, such as NY and CA, alone.

The next check box, Capitalize First Letter Of Sentences, will automatically capitalize the first word of a sentence. By default, this box is not checked, on the assumption that most people shift case on their own at the start of a sentence and there are times when they may not want to. But if you sometimes forget to capitalize the first letter in a sentence, or you find it a chore, you can check this check box and Word will take care of the capitalization for you.

The Capitalize Names Of Days check box controls the last of the four basic AutoCorrect options. This feature can recognize the days of the week. Add a check here, and if you forget to capitalize *friday*, Word will automatically turn it into *Friday* for you.

## Replace text as you type

NEW!

The last check box in the AutoCorrect dialog box—the Replace Text As You Type check box—determines whether Word pays any attention to the rest of the AutoCorrect dialog box. If the check box is checked, Word will watch for words or abbreviations listed in the Replace column, and when you type one, it will swap that text for the text (or other data) in the With column.

The Replace Text As You Type option is the AutoCorrect feature that's similar to AutoText—that is, you can use it to store frequently used text and other data. The list in the Replace column shows the abbreviations, or names, for the complete entries. For our purposes, we'll use *AutoCorrect name* to refer to an item that AutoCorrect puts in the Replace list. The *AutoCorrect definition* is the full text that's represented by the AutoCorrect name. In contrast, an *AutoCorrect entry* refers to the complete item—both the AutoCorrect name and the text it represents.

### How to name AutoCorrect entries

For obvious reasons, it helps to use AutoCorrect names that are easy to remember. Word provides plenty of flexibility for names; you can create names up to 31 characters long. This should be plenty—you'll want to keep the abbreviations as short as possible so that you can type them quickly. On the other hand, you won't want to make them so short that you can't remember which is which.

There are a few rules to keep in mind for AutoCorrect names. They must be single words, which means they cannot contain any spaces. They can use virtually any character you can type at the keyboard, including numbers and punctuation characters. AutoCorrect names are not case-sensitive, at least in the sense that Word will treat *teh* and *TEH* as the same abbreviation; however, the capitalization of the abbreviation will affect how Word inserts the AutoCorrect text, as we'll explain in the next section.

The AutoCorrect definition can be text or graphics or both. If it's text, you can type up to 255 characters into the With text box directly. You can insert much larger selections—several pages long— or graphics by entering your text or graphics in a document, selecting what you've entered, and choosing Tools AutoCorrect. Word will assume you want to create a new definition and will insert the text or graphic into the With text box. You need only add an abbreviation in the Replace box and choose Add.

### Capitalization complications

The way the AutoCorrect feature treats case is a bit complex, but you can use the feature to your advantage. If you create an AutoCorrect name in lowercase, Word will recognize text exactly as you type it in your document if you type it in lowercase, with an initial capital, or in all capitals. So if you enter *teh* as an AutoCorrect name, Word will match the case of each letter when you type *TEH*, *Teh*, or *teh*, but Word will not recognize the AutoCorrect name if you type it as TeH, tEh, or tEH.

If you put one or more capital letters in the name when you create it, Word will match words you type in your document only if they have exactly the same capitalization.

Word also follows some complex rules about case when it replaces the AutoCorrect name with the full text of the definition. If the name, as shown in the Replace column of the AutoCorrect dialog box, has any capital letters in it, Word will replace it without making any changes to the capitalization of the full definition as you stored it in the AutoCorrect dialog box. On the other hand, if the name is stored in lowercase, Word will, under some conditions, change the capitalization of the text it inserts. For example, Word will capital- ize the first word if you type the name in your document with the first letter capitalized; or Word will capitalize every letter in the definition if you type the name in your document in all caps. There is an important exception to this rule, however: If the first word of the stored definition is capitalized, Word will not alter the case of any of the text under any circumstances when it in- serts *the definition* in your document. If a letter in any word other than the first word of the definition is capitalized, that capital will be preserved no matter how the name is entered.

Given the complexity of capitalization with the AutoCorrect fea- ture, it helps to follow a simple rule of thumb: If you want Word to follow the capitalization of the name as you type it in your docu- ment, be sure to type your AutoCorrect names and definitions in lowercase in the AutoCorrect dialog box. If you want Word to al- ways insert text with a specific capitalization, you should include a capital letter in the name as you store it in the AutoCorrect dialog box and be sure to type it in your document with the same capitali- zation.

## How to add AutoCorrect entries

Word comes with a number of predefined AutoCorrect entries, some of which are illustrated in Figure 5-1. You will likely want to add your own, however.

For example, you might have a colleague whose name you have to write frequently, such as *M. David Stone*. You could type the complete name each time you use it. Or you could let Word type it for you, by assigning an AutoCorrect name—using, for example, the initials *mds*—to a definition con- sisting of the entire name.

Word provides several ways to define this combination. One of the easiest is to choose Tools AutoCorrect and then type *mds* in the Replace text box and *M. David Stone* in the With text box. As soon as you type an acceptable entry in each text box, the Add button in the dialog box will change from grayed to active. You can then choose the Add button to add the entry to the list at the bottom of the dialog box.

Word arranges the AutoCorrect entries in alphabetic order, as determined by the Replace abbreviation. If there are more entries than will fit in the list box at one time, Word will display a scroll bar at the right of the list so that you can scroll through the list.

As mentioned already, you can also enter text or other data directly in your document, then select a block, and then choose Tools AutoCorrect. Word will insert the selected block in the With text box. All you have to do then is type a word in the Replace text box and choose the Add button to create the AutoCorrect entry. This approach is particularly handy when you want to define a large block—from a paragraph to several pages—as an AutoCorrect item. It also works for pictures and similar objects other than text. We'll discuss additional aspects of pictures and other objects in Chapter 15, "Drawing, Graphics, & Other Objects," starting on page 521.

When you use this block method with text, the Plain Text and Formatted Text radio buttons in the dialog box will not be grayed the way they are if you type the definition text in the With text box directly. You use these buttons to retain the formatting of the With text.

If you want your AutoCorrect text to include specific formatting when Word inserts it into your document—as you would with a letterhead or company logo, for example—choose the Formatted Text option when defining the AutoCorrect entry. Otherwise, choose the Plain Text option, and the inserted text will take on the same formatting as the name it replaces. Be aware, however, that you cannot store plain text definitions longer than 255 characters. For longer entries, you *must* use formatted text.

Finally, you can use the Clipboard to paste text into the With text box. This makes it possible for you to paste text copied from programs other than Word. When you're using text that originated in Word, however, the Clipboard is not as useful as selecting text on the screen because it won't give you the option of storing the definition as formatted text.

## How to change AutoCorrect names and definitions

After you've created an AutoCorrect entry, you may want to change its name or definition.

**To change an AutoCorrect name.** First choose Tools AutoCorrect to open the dialog box. Then select the entry you want to change in the list box. Word will insert that entry in the text boxes above the list box. Make the changes in the Replace text box, choose Add, and Word will add the new item to the list box. Then select the original item and choose Delete. Word will remove the item from the list box without asking for confirmation.

**To change an AutoCorrect definition that's short enough to fit in the With text box.** Follow the steps described for changing an AutoCorrect name to place the name and definition in the text boxes. Make any changes desired to the definition and choose Replace. (The Add button changes to Replace whenever you edit a definition.) Word will display the message shown in Figure 5-2 asking you to confirm that you want to replace the definition. Choose Yes to proceed with changing the definition.

**To change the formatting for the definition.** If the definition is too long to fit in the text box, or you want to change the formatting of the definition, start by inserting the definition in your document. Then make whatever changes you want. When you finish modifying (or creating) the new text, select the text in your document and choose Tools AutoCorrect to open the dialog box; Word will insert the selection in the With text box. Next you type the name for the entry you want to change and then choose the Replace button. Word will display the message shown in Figure 5-2 asking you to confirm that you want to redefine the entry. Choose Yes to proceed with the change.

**FIGURE 5-2**

Word will warn you with this message before you change the definition of an AutoCorrect item.

## How to delete AutoCorrect combinations

To get rid of an AutoCorrect item, highlight the item in the list box at the bottom of the AutoCorrect dialog box, and then choose the Delete button.

Be careful when using the Delete button. Word will delete the highlighted item from the list box without asking for confirmation first. You cannot recover the deleted entry with the Undo feature.

# How to override AutoCorrect changes

There may be times when you don't want Word to replace an abbreviation with AutoCorrect text. For example, assume you're writing a technical paper that refers to a device with the acronym *TEH*. To prevent Word from replacing the acronym with *THE* each time you type it, you could turn off the AutoCorrect Replace Text As You Type feature. But that would mean having to do without the feature entirely.

There's a better way. Word treats the AutoCorrect process as an editing step, in the same way as it treats typing, deleting, or moving text. As a result, you can undo an automatic correction. If Word applies any of the AutoCorrect features to an exception that you don't want changed, simply choose the Undo command with ⌘-Z (or any other method you prefer) and continue typing. If you plan to use a given exception often, however, you may want to remove the abbreviation from your AutoCorrect list and re-create it as AutoText.

# Using AutoText

As we discussed at the beginning of this chapter, AutoText works much like the Replace Text As You Type option in the AutoCorrect feature. The key difference is that with AutoText, Word does not replace the AutoText name with the full definition until you tell it to. As with AutoCorrect, however, you can create an AutoText definition as text, pictures, or a combination of the two.

We'll discuss how to create AutoText entries shortly, but first we'll look at how to insert an AutoText entry. This will help clarify the difference between the semiautomatic AutoText and the fully automatic AutoCorrect.

 Users familiar with older versions of Word may recognize AutoText as a new name for the Glossary feature from those earlier versions of the program. Although the feature is essentially unchanged, the new name is a more immediately understandable description of what the feature does.

## How to use AutoText

There are two ways to use an AutoText entry. Which approach you choose is largely a matter of taste. Of course, for either method to work, you must first create an entry.

One approach is to pick the entry from a list. If you choose Edit AutoText (with nothing selected in your document), Word will open the AutoText dialog box, shown in Figure 5-3. You can then select the name you want from the list box in the top half of the dialog box. For our purposes, and in parallel with our definitions for the AutoCorrect feature, the *AutoText name* refers to an item in this list box. The *AutoText definition* is the full text that is represented by the name. An *Autotext entry* refers to the complete AutoText item—both the name and the text it represents. Notice that the list box shows only the AutoText names—the abbreviations for the actual entries.

If there are more AutoText names than can fit in the list box at once, the vertical scroll bar at the right of the list box will become active, and you can scroll though the list. As you select each one, you can see as much of the text for that entry as will fit—in the box labeled Preview in Figure 5-3. When you find the item you want, choose the Insert button to insert the text in your document.

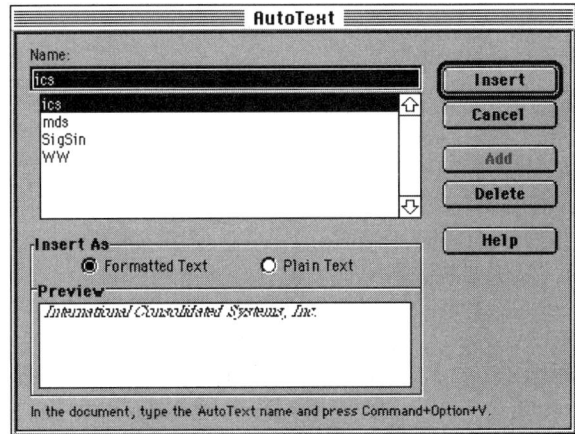

**FIGURE 5-3**

You can use the AutoText dialog box to select an AutoText entry from a list of names.

If you know the AutoText name for an entry, you can use either a keyboard or a mouse shortcut instead of choosing from a list. Suppose, for example, that you regularly type your company name, *International Consolidated Systems, Inc.*, but you sometimes need to use the abbreviation *ICS* as well. This is a good candidate for an AutoText, rather than AutoCorrect, entry because it's a long name that you need to use repeatedly, and its obvious abbreviation—*ICS*—is also something that you'll occasionally need to use. We'll discuss how to create the entry shortly. For the moment, assume that it already exists, with *ICS* as the AutoText name.

To use the entry, you first type the abbreviation *ICS* in your document. If you want the abbreviation only, you can continue typing; Word will leave the *ICS* as is. If you want to replace the abbreviation with the full definition, however, you can simply give a shortcut command to replace it. For keyboard users, the command is ⌘-Option-V. If you prefer using the mouse, you can point to the AutoText button on the Standard toolbar—the icon resembles a hand pointing to a keyboard—and click.

The primary difference between AutoCorrect and AutoText is that AutoCorrect replaces an entry's name without needing a command, whereas AutoText waits until you tell it to replace the name with a definition. That frees you to use abbreviations that are meaningful and that you might use as words by themselves—as in the example in this section.

## How to add a new AutoText entry

Before you can use an AutoText entry, of course, you have to create one. The first step for creating a new entry is to create the AutoText definition anywhere in your document and then select the definition. (As with AutoCorrect entries, you can highlight any part of your document to create an entry, including pictures and other objects.) Next choose Edit AutoText to open the AutoText dialog box, shown in Figure 5-4. You can use the menu or click on the AutoText button on the Standard toolbar.

**FIGURE 5-4**

The AutoText dialog box contains options for creating, modifying, and deleting AutoText entries.

Word will show as much of the selected text, picture, or other object as will fit in the Selection box at the bottom of the dialog box, and it will display the first few words in the Name box at the top. (If the selected item does not contain any text or other characters you can type at the keyboard, or if it includes certain special characters such as paragraph marks, Word may leave the Name box blank.) At this point, you can edit the text in the Name box to change the name to anything you prefer. Finish by choosing the Add button to add the item to the list of AutoText entries.

When you type an AutoText name, there are a few rules to keep in mind. First, if you enter a name that already exists, Word will display a message box, as shown in Figure 5-5, that asks whether you want to redefine the AutoText entry. Choose Yes to replace the old entry with the new text that you've selected or No to return to the AutoText dialog box without changing the entry.

**FIGURE 5-5**

If you try to assign an existing name to a new AutoText entry, Word will ask whether you want to redefine the entry.

You can also use the Clipboard to create the AutoText name. Copy the text you want for the name to the Clipboard, and then highlight the block of text you want for the definition. Next choose Edit AutoText. Word will insert the selected text as the AutoText definition. You can then simply press ⌘-V to paste the text from the Clipboard into the Name text box, and you can choose Add to finish adding the item.

## Naming the entries

AutoText, unlike AutoCorrect, lets you include spaces in an entry's name. In fact, you can use any characters you want, including punctuation marks, that you can generate with the keyboard. Being able to contain spaces means the AutoText name can consist of two or more words—for example, *Sig Sin* instead of *SigSin* for a signature block using *Sincerely Yours*. However, the name cannot exceed 32 characters (including spaces). This shouldn't be an issue, since, as with AutoCorrect entries, you'll want to keep the AutoText names as short as possible so that you can type them quickly. As with AutoText names, also, you'll want to avoid making the names so short that you can't remember what each one is for.

Try to use meaningful AutoText names. Also, try to group similar entries to make them easier to remember. If you use *HeadLtr* to store the heading boilerplate for letters, *HeadMem* is a good choice for memos, and *HeadRep*, for reports. And because Word lists AutoText entries in alphabetic order based on their names, you can group related entries such as these together simply by adding the same prefix to each of their names.

Unlike AutoCorrect, AutoText pays no attention to the capitalization of either the AutoText name itself or the way you type it in your document; Word will match the two regardless of case. Also unlike AutoCorrect, the

AutoText feature will not change the capitalization of the AutoText definition under any circumstances when it inserts the text into your document. This means that Word will interpret any attempt to define the AutoText name *ICS* as redefining *ics*. It also means that you can use capitalization to help increase the readability of AutoText names without making it harder to type the names when you want to use them. For example, you can create the AutoText name *SigSin* and insert its definition into your text by typing *sigsin* and pressing ⌘-Option-V.

Although you can change the entry in the Name box while adding an AutoText item, you cannot change the contents in the Selection box. To change the AutoText definition, you have to choose Cancel to close the AutoText dialog box, make the changes in the text within the document, highlight the modified block of text, and reopen the AutoText dialog box.

## Formatted AutoText entries

When you select text for a new AutoText entry, Word stores the current format for that text along with the entry. Using an earlier example, if you italicize the words *International Consolidated Systems, Inc.*, before defining them as an AutoText entry, Word will insert them with italic formatting, by default, whenever you use the AutoText name *ics* (combining it with any formatting of the AutoText name). If you want to insert the text without the original formatting, you have to insert it from the AutoText dialog box, rather than using a shortcut; before choosing the Insert button, choose Insert As Plain Text. (In a case like this, however, you may find it just as easy to reformat the text after it is inserted by AutoText.)

In addition to storing formats such as bold or italic, Word will store fonts, point size, superscript, subscript, and any other character formats you assigned to the text before defining it as AutoText. If your AutoText definition includes one or more paragraph marks, Word will store the paragraph formatting as well—including line spacing, indention, and so forth.

NEW!

When you open the AutoText dialog box and select a name in the Name box, Word will show you as much of the definition for that name as will fit in the Preview box. The Preview box always shows the text formatted the way Word will insert it. By default, Word sets the option for Formatted Text, so the text in the Preview box will match the text as formatted when you defined the entry plus any format you've applied to the name. If you choose the Plain Text option instead, the text will match the format currently applied to the point where you are about to insert the entry. In other words, if you choose the Plain Text option, the entry will take on the format applied to the AutoText name.

## How to revise an existing AutoText entry

If you use the AutoText feature often, you will occasionally need to change the definition for a given entry. Changing the definition is similar to creating a new entry. Rather than editing the definition within the AutoText dialog box, you have to replace it with new text. For a short entry, you can simply type the new text anywhere in a document. For a longer entry, you will probably want to insert the text as AutoText and then edit it.

After you edit the definition, you can highlight it, open the AutoText dialog box, and select the AutoText name whose definition you want to replace. At this point, the Preview box will show the currently stored definition for the entry. After confirming that you've selected the correct entry, choose the Add button. When Word asks whether you want to redefine the entry, choose Yes to redefine it and return to the document.

## How to delete an AutoText entry

You might also occasionally need to delete an AutoText entry. To delete an entry, open the AutoText dialog box, select the AutoText name you want to get rid of, and choose the Delete button. Word will remove the selected entry and leave the dialog box open so that you can insert or delete other entries.

Word will let you delete only one AutoText entry at a time. This is an important safety feature, since the program doesn't stop to ask for permission before deleting. If you need to delete several entries, you have to delete each one individually.

## How to rename an AutoText entry

If you want to change the name of an AutoText entry, you must use the Organizer. We will discuss the Organizer in detail in "Organizer: Moving Styles, AutoText, Toolbars, and Macros Among Templates," starting on page 896.

For now, just follow these steps to open the Organizer and change an AutoText entry's name. Choose File Templates to open the Templates And Add-Ins dialog box, and then choose the Organizer button. Word will open the Organizer dialog box. Choose the AutoText card, as shown in Figure 5-6 on the next page. In this example, the current document is attached only to the Normal template, which is why the figure shows the entries for Normal on both sides of the Organizer dialog box. (We'll touch on saving AutoText entries in other templates elsewhere in this chapter.)

**FIGURE 5-6**

You can use the Organizer's AutoText card to change the name of an AutoText entry.

You can highlight the appropriate AutoText entry in either Normal list box, and Word will display its text in the Description box at the bottom of the card. Then choose the Rename button. Word will display a Rename dialog box, in which you can enter a new name for that entry. Type the new name, and choose the OK button; Word will return you to the AutoText card in the Organizer dialog box. Choose the Close button to return to your document.

## How to insert an AutoText definition with the AUTOTEXT field

We've already mentioned three ways to insert AutoText definitions into your document: by typing the AutoText name and pressing ⌘-Option-V, by typing the name and then clicking on the AutoText button on the Standard toolbar, and by choosing the entry in the AutoText dialog box.

Still another way to insert an AutoText definition is with the AUTOTEXT field. Although fields are an advanced subject that we won't examine in detail until Chapter 20, it makes sense to look at the AUTOTEXT field with other AutoText issues.

Briefly, the AUTOTEXT field is a marker that takes the place of the actual AutoText definition. When you insert the field, the marker maintains a permanent link to the AutoText entry it refers to. If you then change the AutoText definition for that entry, Word can automatically update all instances of the entry in your document.

To create an AUTOTEXT field, press ⌘-F9 to insert a pair of curly brackets in your document, like this:

{}

The cursor will appear within the brackets. Do not enter these brackets by typing them. The resulting brackets may look the same on the screen, but Word will not recognize them as indicating a field.

The AUTOTEXT field takes the form {AUTOTEXT AutoTextName}, where *AutoTextName* is the name of the entry you want to insert. With the cursor inside the curly brackets, type the word *AUTOTEXT*, a space, and the appropriate AutoText name. Then press F9 to update the field with AutoText's current text. If necessary, press Shift-F9, and Word will show the field results rather than the field code.

After you have inserted an AUTOTEXT field in your document, you can update it whenever you modify the text for that entry. Simply select the entire document, pressing ⌘-A, and then press F9. Word will update all fields in the selection to match the new text.

Note that you can also store other kinds of fields as part of your AutoText definition, so you can enter and easily update such items as date, time, or page number. We'll cover fields in more depth in Chapter 20.

## How to store pictures as AutoText

Although you'll probably use AutoText mainly for text, you can also use it for pictures. As we've already mentioned in passing, the mechanics of storing pictures as AutoText are essentially identical to the mechanics of storing text. But before you can use pictures for AutoText entries, you have to know how to work with them in your documents directly. For details on working with pictures and other objects, see Chapters 14 and 15.

## How to choose a template

One last important difference between the AutoCorrect and AutoText features is that all AutoCorrect entries are available to all documents in Word. AutoText entries, in contrast, may not be.

Word stores its AutoText entries in special files, called *templates*. Unless you tell Word otherwise, it stores all AutoText entries in the standard template, Normal. In general, the Normal settings amount to your default settings for the program; they are available while you work in any Word document—not just documents based on the template Normal—unless you override the settings with supplementary templates.

If you're working with a document that's based on a template other than Normal, you can tell Word to save an AutoText entry in that document's supplementary template instead of Normal. When you save the entry in any template besides Normal, however, you can use that entry only with documents that are based on that supplementary template.

As a concrete example, suppose you are working with a document that is based on the supplementary template Memo. If you save an AutoText entry in Normal and then open any other document, you will be able to use that AutoText entry. But if you save the entry in Memo and then open a document that isn't based on Memo, you will not be able to use the AutoText entry while working with the second document.

There is one further complication. In addition to the Normal template and supplementary templates, Word 6.0 will also let you designate so-called global templates. To avoid getting bogged down in detail here, simply note that if you designate a template as a global template, its AutoText entries will be available to all open files. However, you won't be able to save new entries to the template directly. For a detailed discussion of this and other template issues, see Chapter 27.

When you add an AutoText entry with the AutoText dialog box, you can indicate your choice of template for storing the entry in the Make AutoText Entry Available To text box. This text box appears only when you are creating a new entry. If you open the pull-down list in this box, you will see a list of templates (other than global templates) that are attached to the document, as shown in Figure 5-7. You can then select the template in which to store the AutoText entry before you choose the Add button.

**FIGURE 5-7**

The pull-down list box attached to the Make AutoText Entry Available To box shows the templates attached to the current document.

Until you become thoroughly familiar with templates, we recommend that you store all changes in the default Normal template. When you are familiar with templates, you can move AutoText entries to any template you like. For details, see "Organizer: Moving Styles, AutoText, Toolbars, and Macros Among Templates," starting on page 896.

## How to save the AutoText entries on disk

Word doesn't actually save your AutoText entries on disk when you define or change them. Left to its own devices, it simply keeps the AutoText entries in memory, eventually saving the changes in one of two ways. If you make changes to the entries in Normal, the Prompt To Save Normal setting on the Tools Options Save card controls whether Word asks before saving the changes. If this option is not checked, Word will save the changes whenever it does an automatic save and when you quit the program. If Prompt To Save Normal is checked, Word will not automatically save the changes when it does an automatic save and when you choose File Quit. Instead, Word will ask whether you want to save the changes, by way of the message box shown in Figure 5-8. You can then choose Yes to save the changes, No to throw them away, or Cancel to go back to Word.

**NEW!**

**FIGURE 5-8**

Word will ask whether to save your AutoText entry changes to Normal when you exit from Word.

Word treats changes to a supplementary template somewhat differently from changes to Normal. If you've made any AutoText changes in a supplementary template, Word will ask whether to save them when you close the document that's based on that template. When you choose File Close, Word displays the message box shown in Figure 5-9. As with changes to Normal, you can then choose Yes to save the changes, No to throw them away, or Cancel to go back to the document rather than close it.

**FIGURE 5-9**

Choose Yes in this message box if you want to update the changes you've made to the template's AutoText entries.

## How to save AutoText entries with the File Save All command

As anyone who has ever lost work to a power blackout or a system crash can tell you, leaving a large amount of data in memory without saving it on disk is a good way to lose your work. Fortunately, Word provides a simple way to save the AutoText changes on command. Choose File Save All, and Word will try to save all open files with any changes since the last save, as well as any changes to the AutoText entries in both Normal and any supplemental templates currently open. For each template, Word will display a message box asking whether you want to save your changes. You can choose Yes or No for each one, or you can return to your document without saving by choosing Cancel.

## How to print the AutoText entries

If you use a lot of AutoText entries, you'll find that it can quickly become difficult to remember them all. Fortunately, Word provides a straightforward way to print your AutoText entries so that you can keep a handy reference near your computer. First open a document that's attached to the template containing the AutoText list you want to print. (Any document will do for those in Normal.) Next choose File Print, select AutoText Entries from the Print What drop-down list, and choose OK. Word will print a list containing each AutoText name and its definition. Figure 5-10 shows a sample AutoText list.

**FIGURE 5-10**

You can print a list of your AutoText entries to keep as a handy reference.

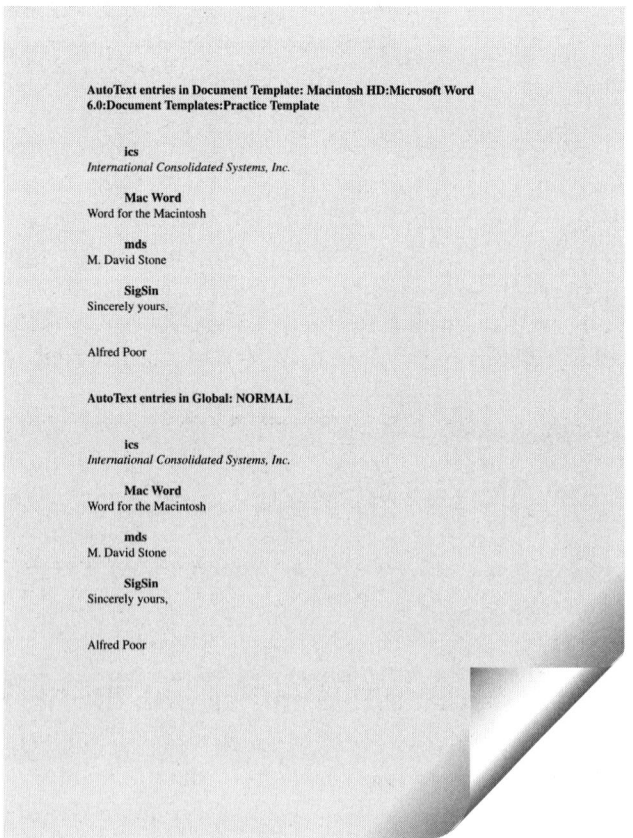

# Using the Spike

Word offers a special AutoText entry called the Spike. The Spike gets its name by analogy to the physical spike that some businesses use to hold bills, receipts, and other loose pieces of paper.

## What is the Spike?

To understand how the Spike works, imagine you own and operate a small hardware store. Next to your cash register, you keep a spike to hold copies of your sales receipts. Each time a customer buys something in the store, you hand one copy of the receipt to the customer and place the store's copy on the spike. At the end of the day, you take all the receipts off the spike and log each sale in a journal. When business begins the next day, the spike is empty, ready for a new day's receipts.

Like a physical spike, Word's Spike is useful for collecting and storing multiple pieces of related information and then depositing that information at a single location. Of course, the information on Word's Spike isn't a group of receipts or bills—it's text or pictures that you want to insert in your document. After you've stored something on the Spike, you can insert the contents at a single location in your text.

The Spike is actually a special AutoText entry named Spike. The main difference between the Spike AutoText name and other AutoText names is that when you store text or a picture on the Spike, Word doesn't replace the current contents with the new text or picture; instead, it adds the new text or picture to what's already there. In all other respects, the built-in Spike entry behaves as any other AutoText entry does.

## How to place text or pictures on the Spike

To move an item to the Spike, first select the text or picture you want to move, and then press ⌘-F3. Word will remove the selected item from the document and add it to the Spike. Word inserts a paragraph mark following each item that you add to the Spike's contents. To add another item, simply repeat the process. Each time you press ⌘-F3, Word will add the current selection.

## How to insert the Spike's contents

You have two choices for inserting the contents of the Spike: You can empty the contents into your document, or you can copy the contents without emptying the Spike. (You cannot insert a portion of the Spike's contents into a document.)

## How to empty the Spike

To empty the Spike into a document, place the cursor in the appropriate spot and press ⌘-Shift-F3. Word will transfer the contents from the Spike to the document, emptying the Spike in the process.

## How to copy from the Spike

To copy the Spike's contents into a document without emptying the Spike, you can use any of the three standard commands for inserting AutoText entries. Type the word *spike* and then press ⌘-Option-V; or type *spike* and then choose the AutoText button; or choose the Edit AutoText command, select Spike in the list box, and then choose Insert. In each case, Word will insert a copy of the Spike's contents but leave the Spike unchanged so that you can either continue adding to it or insert additional copies elsewhere.

## Techniques for using the Spike

Occasionally, you may want to add text to the Spike but not delete the text from your document. Unfortunately, Word does not have a built-in command to copy text directly to the Spike. But there is a simple technique that will serve the same purpose. Select the text you want to add to the Spike, and then, before you press ⌘-F3, copy the selection to the Clipboard. (⌘-C is a handy way of copying to the Clipboard.) Next add the selection to the Spike by pressing ⌘-F3. This procedure will delete the selection, but you can now replace it by using the Edit Paste command if you do so before copying anything else to the Clipboard. (You may find the ⌘-V keyboard shortcut the most convenient way of pasting.)

Another technique that isn't immediately obvious is to clear the Spike if you decide you don't want to insert the accumulated text anywhere after all. Of course, you can always use ⌘-Shift-F3 to empty the Spike, and then delete the text from your document. But a more elegant choice is to choose Edit AutoText, select Spike in the Name list box, and choose Delete. Word will clear the Spike and remove Spike from the list of AutoText names.

You can define an AutoText entry named Spike with the standard AutoText procedures. The AutoText entry you define this way will act as if it were the initial entry for the Spike, and it will clear any text or other data already stored on the Spike. Word will ask for confirmation before clearing the current text or other data on the Spike, but it's still best to use this technique with care.

# Using the Thesaurus

The Word Thesaurus provides a storehouse of synonyms—as well as some antonyms—that you can use much like you use a book-bound thesaurus. In particular, you may find the feature helpful for avoiding unnecessary repetition in your writing. And if you're a careful writer who cares about word choice, the Thesaurus can be invaluable when you are looking for just the right word to say precisely what you mean.

To use the Thesaurus, type the word for which you want a synonym or an antonym. Then highlight the word, or put the cursor anywhere on the word, or leave it on the space immediately after the word. Next press ⌘-Option-R, or choose Tools Thesaurus. Word will open the Thesaurus dialog box.

As shown in Figure 5-11, Word will display the currently selected word in the Looked Up text box. (In some cases, such as when the cursor is between two paragraph marks, Word will not consider any text selected and will display the Thesaurus dialog box without any text entered.) If you highlight more than one word before choosing Tools Thesaurus, Word will try to match the entire phrase, as shown in Figure 5-12. In either case, if the Thesaurus does not find a match, it will show the label of the text box as Not Found and provide an alphabetic list of possible words to choose from, as in Figure 5-13 on the next page.

**FIGURE 5-11**

The Thesaurus dialog box displays the current selection in the Looked Up text box.

**FIGURE 5-12**

If you highlight more than one word, the Thesaurus will try to match the entire phrase.

FIGURE 5-13

If the Thesaurus does not find a match, it will show you a list of similarly spelled words to choose from.

## How to find the right synonym

Note that the Replace With Synonym list box shows the synonyms for the definition currently selected in the Meanings list box. In Figure 5-11, for example, it shows the synonyms of *world* (the word we looked up) for the definition *earth*. If you highlight a different definition in the Meanings list box, Word will change the list in the Replace With Synonym box to match it. In this case, if you select *realm* in the Meanings list box, you will get the list shown in Figure 5-14. Notice that both definitions in the Meanings list box show the part of speech in the context of the definition.

FIGURE 5-14

The list of synonyms in the Replace With Synonym list box depends on which definition you select in the Meanings list box.

Often you will want to see synonyms for a word that shows up in the Replace With Synonym box. For example, after you open the dialog box shown in Figure 5-11, you may want to see synonyms for the word *orb*. Simply highlight the word and choose the Look Up button (or double-click on the word). Word will respond by putting the selected word in the Looked Up text box, and it will show you the appropriate entries in the Meanings and Replace With Synonym list boxes.

Some words will also show an item labeled *Antonyms* in the Meanings box. Select this word to see a list of antonyms in the list box where Word normally displays synonyms.

## How to recall other words

You can review the full list of words you've looked up during any Thesaurus search by opening the Looked Up list. For example, after browsing through synonyms for *earth* and *orb*, you can return to the original list of synonyms by selecting *world* from the Looked Up list. You can also step back through the words you have looked up by choosing the Previous button. This button will be grayed when there are no more previously looked-up words to recall.

Word will retain the list of looked-up words only as long as the Thesaurus dialog box is open. When you close it, the list is emptied.

## How to replace the old word with a new one

After you identify a suitable synonym, simply select that word in the Meanings or Replace With Synonym list box. Word will place the selected word in the text box at the top of the Replace With Synonym list. Choose the Replace button, and Word will close the Thesaurus dialog box and replace the original word in your document with the synonym you specified.

When you're trying to find an appropriate word and you can think of several that aren't quite right, it's sometimes useful to type your near misses in the Thesaurus dialog box and have the Thesaurus look up each word. The Thesaurus can manage this task easily enough, but not the way you might expect. Rather than entering your near miss in the Looked Up text box, you need to enter it in the Replace With Synonym text box and choose the Look Up button. Word will move the word to the Looked Up text box and look up the word. If it finds a match, it will show the appropriate synonyms and definitions.

# Using Symbols and Special Characters

There are times during the creation of a document when your problem isn't a matter of finding the right word—it's a matter of finding the right character. The Macintosh has its own built-in way to insert special characters using the Option key in combination with other keys; you can use the Key Caps desk accessory on the Apple menu to see which symbols are available this way. Word offers its own way to insert special characters, and includes many special formatting characters that are not available through Key Caps. These characters include non-breaking spaces, optional hyphens, non-breaking hyphens, and characters such as an en space. In addition, Word offers a wide range of symbols, such as copyright marks and foreign language characters. You will probably find it to be a matter of personal preference whether you use the Key Caps, Word's Insert Symbol command, or the keyboard shortcuts to add special characters to your documents.

## How to insert special characters

There are two built-in ways to add symbols and special characters to your documents with Word: through the Symbol dialog box and through keyboard shortcuts. The keyboard is quicker, but the dialog box is easier until you learn the shortcut keys. And because the dialog box will show you the shortcut keys as you choose each symbol, you can use it as a tool to learn the keyboard shortcuts as well.

### The Insert Symbol command

To use the Symbol dialog box, start by placing the cursor at the point in your document where you want to insert a symbol or a special character. Then choose Insert Symbol. Word will open the Symbol dialog box, which has two cards labeled Symbols and Special Characters. Figure 5-15 shows the dialog box, with the Symbols card showing.

**FIGURE 5-15**

The Symbols card makes it simple to put special symbols in your documents.

**Symbols.** At the top of the Symbols card is the Font text box, which in Figure 5-15 shows that the currently selected font is Symbol. The major portion of the card is filled with a grid of 224 squares, showing the printable characters available in the Symbol font's character set. You can choose from other available fonts by opening the Font list box; the list of fonts will vary depending on how your copy of Word is set up. In general, your choices will include MT

Extra, Symbol, and MS LineDraw, which are all TrueType fonts, plus the choice (normal text) that shows the characters available in most other TrueType fonts.

When you first open the dialog box, one square on the grid will be highlighted to indicate that it's the currently selected character. To see an enlarged view of a character, you can point to it with the mouse and click, or you can use the Tab key to move to the grid and use the arrow keys to move around the table. After the first keypress, Word will show an enlarged view of each symbol as you highlight it. As you can see in Figure 5-15, there are several buttons along the bottom of the Symbols card. Choose the Insert button, or double-click on any character in the grid, and Word will insert the selected symbol at your cursor location.

After you insert a character with the Insert button or by double-clicking, Word will not close the Symbol dialog box. This lets you easily insert several symbols without the chore of having to reopen the dialog box repeatedly. You can click on your document and then move the cursor position—or even edit the document—before inserting each symbol. Word will make the document active while leaving the Symbol dialog box on top of the document on the screen. After you move the cursor to the new position, click on the dialog box to make it active.

After you insert the first symbol, Word will rename the Cancel button to Close.

## How to assign a shortcut key to a symbol

You can use the Shortcut Key button to assign a keystroke combination so that, in subsequent usage, you can insert a symbol without opening the Symbol dialog box. First select the symbol and then choose the Shortcut Key button, and Word will open the Customize dialog box with the Keyboard card showing, as in Figure 5-16 on the next page.

We've arranged the figure so that you can see the Symbol dialog box behind the Customize dialog box. In this example, we have chosen the MS LineDraw font and selected the lower right box. This symbol is a box that's particularly useful for creating checklists and survey forms. That makes it a prime candidate for a character that you might use repeatedly.

**FIGURE 5-16**

The Customize
Keyboard feature lets
you assign shortcut
keys to symbols.

When you open the Customize dialog box this way, Word limits the possibilities for customization. Specifically, you can use only the Keyboard card, and only to assign a keystroke to the character you selected before opening the Customize dialog box. Notice that the Categories list box is grayed, with only one choice—All Commands—available in any case, and that the Commands list box is limited to one choice as well—Symbol—with the actual symbol showing in the lower right corner of the card, just above the Save Changes In box. As you might suspect, you can use this dialog box for far more sophisticated customizing as well. We'll cover the keyboard customizations in depth in Chapter 28.

In Figure 5-16, we have pressed Control-B (as a mnemonic for *box*), and Word displays the key combination in the Press New Shortcut Key text box. The Current Keys list box is empty, indicating that there are no shortcut keys currently assigned to this symbol, and the Currently Assigned To area, just under Control-B, indicates that this shortcut key is not assigned to any other character or command. If it were already assigned, Word would show you the assignment. You could then backspace to remove Control-B from the text box and then press another key combination for the new shortcut key. Alternatively, you could go ahead and assign Control-B to the box, overriding the previous assignment. The Description box indicates that this is character number 255 in the font that's named MS LineDraw.

As with AutoText entries, shortcut keys are stored in templates, and all of the same considerations about templates apply. Briefly, the Save Changes In box lists the templates to which the current document is attached. Normal is the default selection, and storing a shortcut key in Normal will make the shortcut available to all documents you create. Until you're familiar with templates, and unless you have a specific reason for storing your shortcut keys elsewhere even then, we recommend that you store your shortcut key customizations in Normal. For more on templates, see "How to choose a template" on page 135.

When you're satisfied with the settings, choose the Assign button to assign the shortcut key. Word will remove the keystroke combination from the Press New Shortcut Key text box and add it to the Current Keys box. Should you change your mind and decide that you want to remove the key assignment, simply select the key combination in the Current Keys box, and then choose the Remove button.

To close the Customize dialog box, choose the Close button, and Word will return you to the Symbols dialog box. The shortcut key is now assigned to the symbol, and when you're working in your document you'll be able to insert the box from the MS LineDraw font simply by pressing Control-B. Note also that Word will show you the shortcut key for any character as you select it from the grid on the Symbols card. The keystroke is displayed after the words Shortcut Key, to the right of the Font box at the top of the card.

You can define more than one shortcut key for the same symbol. You might want multiple shortcut keys for any of several reasons. For example, if more than one person uses the same computer and each user prefers different keystrokes, each user can use the keystrokes he or she prefers. To define additional shortcut keys, simply repeat the procedure just described. As you assign each one, Word will add the new key to the Current Keys box.

If you want to insert a symbol several times in a given document but don't expect to use it again in future documents, you don't need to assign a shortcut key. After you insert the symbol once, close the Symbol dialog box, and use the Edit Repeat command (this is fastest with the ⌘-Y shortcut) to repeat the Insert Symbol operation wherever you need that symbol in your document. The drawback to this technique is that you'll need to insert all the symbols before performing any other editing task: Your next editing operation will change the Edit Repeat function.

## Special Characters

The second card in the Symbol dialog box is labeled Special Characters. Select it, and the dialog box will look like the one in Figure 5-17 on the next page.

The card shows a list of characters, their names, and their shortcut keys (if any are assigned). The buttons along the bottom of the card are the same as for the Symbols card, and they work the same way. To insert one of the special

**FIGURE 5-17**

The Special Characters
card in the Symbol
dialog box makes it
easy to select a special
character to insert in
your document.

characters, for example, you select it in the list and choose the Insert button
(or double-click on the entry to be inserted). Word will insert the selected
character and keep the dialog box open until you choose the Close button.
Similarly, the Shortcut Key button will open the Customize dialog box, in
which you can assign or remove a shortcut key as just described.

If you browse through the list box on the Special Characters card, you can
see that there is some overlap with the characters on the Symbols card—with
choices, for example, that include the Copyright, Registered, and Trademark
symbols. However, you'll also find characters that aren't available on the
Symbols card. For the most part, these are meant for typesetting or desktop
publishing needs, so you may not be familiar with them.

Depending on your needs, you may want to take advantage of these typesetting characters, or you may want to stay with the typewriter-style equivalents. However, there are also some characters that you may find helpful even
if all you're interested in is typewriter-style output. Here's a quick rundown
of the characters and their uses, in their order within the Character list. You'll
also find a list of the keyboard shortcuts for easy reference, following the discussion of the various characters.

## Em dashes and en dashes

Many people use a hyphen, or two hyphens together, when they want to
insert a dash in their text. From a typographical viewpoint, however, the
hyphen should be used only for hyphenated words or to mark the break in a
word at the end of a line. At other times, you should use an em dash or an en
dash. The em dash is defined as a line that is as long as an uppercase M is
wide, whereas an en dash is defined as a line that is as long as an uppercase N
is wide. You can use either one to replace a hyphen or a double hyphen in
your text. The en dash is meant for use with large fonts, where the em dash
would take up too much space. The shortcut keys for both use either the hyphen on the top row or the minus key located on the numeric keypad. The
shortcut for the em dash is Option-Shift-hyphen or Option-Shift-minus, and
for the en dash, Option-hyphen or ⌘-minus.

If you're used to typing two hyphens in a row but prefer the way an em dash looks, use Word's AutoCorrect feature, covered in the first part of this chapter, to replace two hyphens with an em dash whenever you type them.

## Hyphens

Word offers three kinds of hyphens: regular, optional, and non-breaking. For the most part, Word treats a regular hyphen, which you enter by pressing the hyphen key, like any other character in your document. If the hyphenated word falls at the end of a line, however, Word will split the word between two lines, keeping the hyphen and all characters to the left of the hyphen on the first line.

## Non-breaking hyphens

Use a non-breaking hyphen when you don't want a word to break at the hyphen under any conditions. For example, suppose you're writing about the software program Lotus 1-2-3. To prevent Word from breaking *1-2-3* at the end of a line, use non-breaking hyphens. The shortcut key for a non-breaking hyphen is ⌘-Shift-hyphen (not the minus key on the numeric keypad). Non-breaking hyphens are always displayed on your screen, but their format changes depending on whether or not optional hyphens are being displayed. To display optional hyphens (discussed in the next paragraph)—as well as to change the display of non-breaking hyphens—choose Tools Options and then the View card, and add a check to either the Optional Hyphens or the All check box in the Nonprinting Characters section. Alternatively, you can click on the Show/Hide ¶ button on the Standard toolbar. When Word is set to display optional hyphens, non-breaking hyphens appear with a tilde (~) above a regular hyphen; otherwise, they appear identical. On your printouts, however, non-breaking hyphens always look exactly like regular hyphens.

## Optional hyphens

An optional hyphen is printed only when the hyphenated word is broken at the end of a line. When you use the Tools Hyphenation command to insert hyphens automatically, Word will insert only optional hyphens. (We'll discuss the Tools Hyphenation command in the next chapter.) To create an optional hyphen manually, press ⌘-hyphen (not the minus key on the numeric keypad). If Word is set to display all optional hyphens (as discussed previously), optional hyphens are displayed on the screen as dotted hyphens. If you choose not to display optional hyphens, Word will show only the ones that happen to fall at line breaks. These will look exactly like regular hyphens.

We recommend that you use an optional hyphen whenever you hyphenate a word at the end of a line. If you later revise your document, Word will not print the hyphen if the word has moved to the middle of a line.

## Em spaces and en spaces

The em space and en space are similar to the em dash and en dash in that their widths match the widths of the uppercase letters M and N. Use these when you need extra space between a pair of letters or words but do not want to change the spacing for all letters or words. There is no default shortcut key for either of these.

## Non-breaking spaces

A non-breaking space is a space that Word treats like a printing character in some ways. If you place one or more non-breaking spaces between two words, Word will not put the words on different lines when they fall at a line break. Rather, Word will treat the two words and the non-breaking space as a single unit when wrapping text.

To create a non-breaking space, press Control-Shift-Spacebar. If Word is set to display spaces, each non-breaking space will look like a tilde above a normal space dot on your screen. These special characters will not appear in your printed document; Word will print a blank space.

Non-breaking spaces can be useful when you want to keep two or more words together on the same line. For example, when you enter a date, such as July 23, 1992, you may want to enter non-breaking spaces between *July*, *23*, and *1992*. You might also use non-breaking spaces between the different portions of a multipart number, such as a social security number.

One important characteristic of a non-breaking space is that it maintains a specific width. You may have noticed that in a justified paragraph the width of a regular space will vary as Word adjusts the space between words. A non-breaking space, on the other hand, is always about as wide as a lowercase *n*. However, Word adjusts the width of non-breaking spaces according to the point size and character formatting of your text (just as the size of the lowercase *n* would change). For example, a non-breaking space in the middle of boldface text will be slightly larger than one that falls in the middle of plain text.

## Copyright, registered, and trademark symbols

These three characters are available on both the Symbols card and the Special Characters card. The versions available on the Special Characters card are drawn from the character set of the current font in your document—meaning the font Word will use if you close the dialog box and simply type text at the cursor position. This is also the same version of the symbols that you'll find on the Symbols card if you select (Normal Text) in the Font box. However, they are different from the similar symbols available in other specific fonts, such as the Symbol font. The shortcut keys for these three symbols are Option-G for Copyright, Option-R for Registered, and Option-2 for Trademark.

## Ellipses

An ellipsis, which looks like three periods in a row, is generally used to represent text that has been omitted. In fact, you can get a nearly identical effect by entering three periods. The advantage of using the special character is that Word treats it as a single character and will not break it into two parts if it falls at the end of a line. The shortcut key is Option-semicolon.

## Single and double opening and closing quotation marks

As we discussed in the AutoCorrect section earlier in this chapter, opening and closing curly quotes (' ' and " ") are much preferred over straight quotes (' and ") by those who care about such things, except for a few special purposes that require straight quotes, such as ' for feet and " for inches. In general, it's easier to use the AutoCorrect feature for curly quotes, but you can use these choices on the Special Characters card to get the same effect.

You can also use keyboard shortcuts to insert these characters into a document. See Figure 5-18 on the next page.

## Keyboard shortcuts

Although you can create your own shortcut key assignments for any symbol or special character, as we described earlier in this chapter, Word comes with a large number of shortcut keys already defined for special characters, most of which are the same as in the Key Caps desk accessory. These include the shortcuts we've mentioned while describing the characters available on the Special Characters card. For reference, Figure 5-18 lists these characters and their default shortcut key assignments.

## Foreign-language characters

Word also offers a wide range of foreign-language characters that you can insert by pressing predefined shortcut keys, which again are largely the same as in the Key Caps desk accessory. These include letters with various diacritical marks, such as $\grave{a}$, as well as diphthongs, as shown in Figure 5-19 on the next page.

| Special Character | Shortcut Key |
| --- | --- |
| Em dash | Option-Shift-hyphen or Option-Shift-minus |
| En dash | Option-hyphen or ⌘-minus |
| Non-breaking hyphen | ⌘-Shift-hyphen |
| Optional hyphen | ⌘-hyphen |
| Non-breaking space | Control-Shift-Spacebar |
| Copyright symbol | Option-G |
| Registered symbol | Option-R |
| Trademark symbol | Option-2 |
| Ellipsis | Option-semicolon |
| Single opening quote | Option-] |
| Single closing quote | Option-Shift-] |
| Double opening quote | Option-[ |
| Double closing quote | Option-Shift-[ |

**FIGURE 5-18**

Word provides predefined shortcut keys for certain special characters.

| Character(s) | Shortcut Key |
| --- | --- |
| à, è, ì, ò, ù | Option-grave accent, *letter* |
| À, È, Ì, Ò, Ù | Option-grave accent, Shift-*letter* |
| á , é, í, ó, ú | Option-e, *letter* |
| Á, É, Í, Ó, Ú | Option-e, Shift-*letter* |
| â, ê, î, ô, û | Option-i, *letter* |
| Â, Ê, Î, Ô, Û | Option-i, Shift-*letter* |
| ã, ñ, õ | Option-n, *letter* |
| Ã, Ñ, Õ | Option-n, Shift-*letter* |
| ä, ë, ï, ö, ü, ÿ | Option-u, *letter* |
| Ä, Ë, Ï, Ö, Ü, Ÿ | Option-u, Shift-*letter* |
| å, Å | Option-a *or* Option-A |
| æ, Æ | Option-' *or* Option-" |
| œ, Œ | Option-q *or* Option-Q |
| ç, Ç | Option-c *or* Option-C |

**FIGURE 5-19**

*(continued)*

These shortcut keys make it easy to insert foreign-language characters in your documents.

**FIGURE 5-19** *continued*

| Character(s) | Shortcut Key |
|---|---|
| ø, Ø | Option-o *or* Option-O |
| ¿ | Option-Shift-? |
| ¡ | Option-1 |
| ß | Option-s |

# Creating Headers and Footers

There is one other kind of text that you're likely to need at least occasionally: headers and footers. As the names imply, headers normally go at the top of each page in your document and footers go at the bottom. In general, both headers and footers serve as guideposts for the reader. In magazines, for example, they offer information such as the name, volume, issue, and date of the publication. In books, they often include a chapter or section name. But even in something as short as a two-page letter, a header or footer can be useful for showing the page number if nothing else.

Word's system for creating, formatting, and editing headers and footers is one of the most flexible of any word processor's. You can create headers and footers that range from a single character to multiple paragraphs. You can format them using many of the same features you use for body text. And you can also add graphics, such as a logo, to headers and footers. You can define different sets of headers and footers for odd and even pages, and a different set for the first page of a section or document. You can even control the position of headers and footers to place them anywhere on the printed page. We will cover some of the advanced techniques in later chapters. For now, we'll stick to the basics.

Except when you check spelling, Word doesn't display headers or footers in Normal or Outline view. If you're in either of these views when you choose a command to work with a header or footer, Word will switch to Page Layout view, in which it will show the headers and footers—and let you edit them—in their proper positions as they will be printed. You can also see the layout of headers and footers with the Print Preview command.

**NEW!**

Because headers and footers are essentially identical in behavior, differing only in where they are located on the page, we'll concentrate on headers in this discussion. Except where explicitly stated otherwise, however, the following comments apply to footers as well as headers.

# How to add page numbers to your printed document

Probably the most common need with headers and footers is that they contain the page number for each page. The need is so common, in fact, that Word offers an Insert Page Numbers command that you can think of as a kind of minimal header-and-footer feature. More important, if all you want in your header or footer is a page number and (optionally) a chapter number, Insert Page Numbers is the easiest way to put it there.

You can choose Insert Page Numbers from Normal or Page Layout view. Word will respond with the dialog box shown in Figure 5-20.

**FIGURE 5-20**

The Page Numbers dialog box helps you add page numbers to your document quickly and easily.

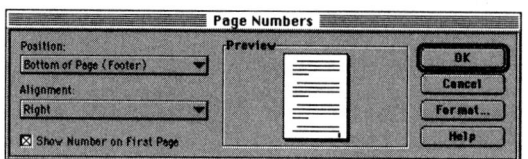

As Figure 5-20 shows, the Page Numbers dialog box has two list boxes, for Position and Alignment, plus a check box labeled Show Number On First Page. You can use these to tell Word where to print the page numbers. The Preview box will show the effects of your choices on a thumbnail sketch of a page.

The Position list box has two choices: Top Of Page (Header) and Bottom Of Page (Footer). These mean just what they say; you use them to assign the vertical position of the number.

The Alignment list box is a bit more complex, with five choices. The first three choices—Left, Center, and Right—will position the page number at the left side, the center, or the right side of the page, whichever you select. The remaining two—Inside and Outside—are not quite self-explanatory. These two are meant for documents that are to be printed on both sides of the paper and bound along one edge, as in a book. Choose either of these, and the preview box will change to show two pages so that you can see the layout of the page numbers on a pair of facing pages, as shown in Figure 5-21.

**FIGURE 5-21**

In the Page Numbers dialog box, you can format page numbers for facing pages.

The Show Number On First Page setting is not reflected in the Preview **NEW!**
box, but if you check this box, the first page number will appear on the first
page of the document. This is frequently the preferred choice for a report, but
most people do not number the first page of a letter or memo. If you don't
want the first page numbered, verify that the box is cleared.

In addition to setting position, alignment, and first-page numbering in the
Page Numbers Dialog box, you can choose the Format button to display the Page
Number Format dialog box, shown in Figure 5-22.

**FIGURE 5-22**

Use the Page Number
Format dialog box to
tell Word how to
number your pages.

The Page Number Format dialog box has three sections. The top section
contains a single item: Number Format. If you open this list box, you'll see
examples of different numbering formats: Arabic numbers, uppercase or lowercase alphabetic characters, and uppercase or lowercase Roman numerals.
Most often you'll probably want the default selection of Arabic numbers.
Simply choose the format to use in any case.

In the bottom section of the dialog box, you tell Word to start numbering
at a number of your choice, using the Start At text box, or to continue numbering from the preceding document section. This feature is useful if you have a
long document, such as a book, broken into several files because it lets you set
the starting page number for each file in order to maintain a continuous numbering scheme. (Note, however, that any changes in page length in one file
will throw off the numbering in other files.) For a better way to handle page
numbering over multiple files, see "Working with Long Documents" on page
559. You can also use Start At to return the page count to 1 at the beginning of
each section of your text. You create new sections with the Insert Break command, which we'll cover in Chapter 13.

Between the top and bottom sections of the dialog box is a section that **NEW!**
starts with a check box labeled Include Chapter Number. If the box is cleared,
the rest of this section will be grayed. If the box is checked, however, the remaining options are available. As the name suggests, you can use this option
to add a chapter number to your numbering system; for example, you can

number pages in Chapter 1 as 1-1, 1-2, 1-3..., pages in chapter 2 as 2-1, 2-2, 2-3..., and so on.

> Simply adding a check in the Include Chapter Number check box will not add chapter numbers to your headers—even with appropriate settings for the rest of the entries in this section of the dialog box. To have Word add chapter numbers along with page numbers in the headers or footers, you also have to add heading numbers with the Format Heading Numbering command. In addition, if you want to start the page numbering at 1 for each new chapter, you'll have to put each chapter in its own section. For details on adding numbers to headers, see "Numbering Headings" on page 453. For details on dividing documents into sections and making use of those sections, see "Multisection Documents" on page 455.

You use the Chapter Starts With Style list box to specify which style you've used to format the chapter headings. We'll discuss styles in Chapter 12. For now, simply be aware that if you want to include a chapter number in your header, you must be consistent about using a specific style—from Heading 1 to Heading 9—to format your chapter headings, and you cannot use the style for anything else. If you've used the Format Heading Numbering command to number the headings, then each time Word encounters a paragraph formatted with the specified style, it will advance the chapter count by one.

You use the remaining option in this section, Use Separator, to specify the character that will separate the chapter from the page number; the choices are hyphen, period, colon, em dash, and en dash. For a more detailed discussion of adding chapter numbers to headings, take a look, once again, at "Multisection Documents" on page 455.

When you finish with the Page Number Format dialog box, choose OK to close it and return to the Page Numbers dialog box. To create the header, select Top Of Page (Header) in the Position box. Choose OK to close the dialog box and return to your document.

When Word returns you to your text, it will also insert the {PAGE} field into your header. We'll discuss fields in detail in Chapter 20. For the moment, it's enough to know that the field is a marker that tells Word to put the current page number at that spot. If the program is set to view field codes, when you look at your document in Page Layout view you will see the field {PAGE}. If the program is set to show field results, you will see a page number. In either case, when you print your text, Word will insert the page number.

If you have already defined a header, using the techniques that we'll explain in the next section, and you give the Insert Page Number command, Word will not warn you about the potential conflict with the header that's already there. In fact, the conflict is more apparent than real. Word inserts page numbers in the header (or footer) area within a frame, without deleting or otherwise affecting any text already in the header. You may have to adjust the position of the page number frame or adjust the position of the text to make the layout of the two elements visually attractive, but you won't accidentally replace the old header with a page number and then have to re-create it.

## The View Header And Footer command

Although you can use the Insert Page Numbers command for some header and footer functions, you'll need to use Word's View Header And Footer command to add information such as the document name or the current date. If you like, you can also use the View Header And Footer command simply to insert a page number.

### The Header And Footer toolbar

When you choose View Header And Footer, Word opens the Header And Footer toolbar, shown in Figure 5-23 on the next page. In addition, if you are in Normal or Outline view, the program switches to Page Layout view. When you choose the Close button on the Header And Footer toolbar, Word will remove the toolbar from your screen and switch back to the view you were using when you started.

When you choose View Header And Footer, Word moves your cursor to the header. To move to the footer, you can either scroll to the bottom of the current page or click the leftmost button on the Header And Footer toolbar (the Switch Between Header And Footer button).

You can use the next two buttons on the toolbar—Show Next and Show Previous—for switching to the next or previous header defined within the document. This may mean moving between even and odd headers, moving to the first page header, or even moving between headers in different sections. The fourth button is used for controlling whether the current header is linked to the previous section. When headers are linked, changes in one section are duplicated in all linked sections. When the button is pressed, the Same As Previous message appears on the upper right border of the header. When the button is raised, the header is not linked and can be changed independently of headers in other sections. Of course, when you are viewing the footer, the Show Next and Show Previous buttons move between footers and the Same As Previous button links between footers. See "Multisection Documents" on page 455.

**FIGURE 5-23**

You create and edit headers and footers in Page Layout view, as shown here.

## How to add page, date, and time to a header

In addition to header text such as a report title, which will stay the same on each page, you'll usually put some information in a header or footer that will change. The page number is the most likely candidate in this category. You may also want to include the current date and time when printing.

As we mentioned when discussing Word's Insert Page Numbers command, Word provides a special kind of entry for this kind of variable information. The entries are called fields. You can press Shift-F9 to toggle between seeing the fields themselves—such as {PAGE}, {DATE}, and {TIME}, for example—and seeing the results of those fields, such as the actual page number, date, and time. Alternatively, you can switch between field codes and field code results by checking and clearing the Field Codes check box on the Tools Options View card. (See Chapter 20 for more information on how to change the format of the information displayed by these fields.)

The next three buttons on the Header And Footer toolbar—starting with the fifth button from the left—will insert the field codes for page numbers, date, and time. If you want to add these to a header, you can simply position the cursor where you want the information to appear, and choose the appropriate button.

If you prefer, you can insert any of these fields from the keyboard. Start by pressing ⌘-F9 to insert Word's field marker, a pair of curly brackets, which will appear on the screen with the cursor between them. You can then simply type *page* or *date* or *time* and then press F9 to update the code. Press Shift-F9 to display field results rather than the field codes. When you finish, the result will be exactly the same as using the buttons in the Header And Footer toolbar.

The fields that Word inserts when you choose the date and time buttons from the Header And Footer Toolbar (or type those same fields in directly, as just described) give the current date and time as registered in your system. These can serve as a date and time stamp for the document each time you print it; however, you may prefer to show a specific date and time that will remain constant. To convert a date or time field to text that won't change as the system date and time change, select the date and time field (or field results), and then press ⌘-Shift-F9.

## How to get different headers and footers on odd and even pages

To the right of the Time button on the Header And Footer toolbar is the Document Layout button. Click this to open the Document Layout dialog box with the Layout card showing, as in Figure 5-24.

For the moment, the only section of interest on this card is the center section on the left side, labeled Headers And Footers. Your choices will affect the thumbnail sketch of a document in the Preview section of the card. We will discuss the rest of the Document Layout dialog box options in Chapter 17.

**FIGURE 5-24**

You can use the Layout card to create different headers and footers for facing pages, as well as special first-page headers and footers.

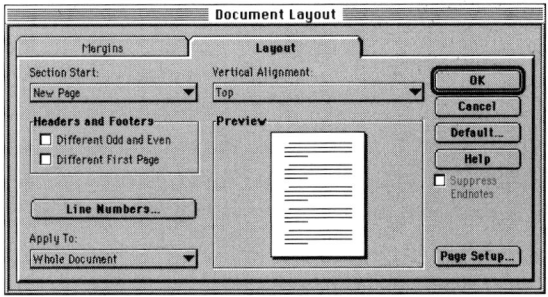

You use the Different Odd And Even check box to create different sets of headers and footers on facing pages. For example, you might want to have the page numbers and a report title on the odd (right-hand) pages, and the date on the even (left-hand) pages.

### How to print a different header and footer on the first page

You use the Different First Page option to specify a different header and footer for the first page only. Check this box if you want the header on the first page to be different from those in the rest of the document. You also check this box if you want no header on the first page but are using a header in the rest of the document.

### How to hide the body text while editing a header or footer

The next button on the Header And Footer toolbar is the Show/Hide Document Text button. There are times when you might want to focus on the contents of a header or footer and not be distracted by the body text of your document. Click on this button to switch between displaying the full page and displaying only the header or footer.

### How to leave the header or footer area

The last button, labeled Close, will close the Header And Footer toolbar, leaving the header and footer areas so that you cannot edit them. If you were in Page Layout view when you chose View Header And Footer, choosing the Close button will return the cursor to your body text and gray the header or footer text. If you were in Normal or Outline view, choosing the Close button will return you to whichever view you started in. You can choose the Close button either by clicking on it or by pressing Control-Shift-C.

You can also close the toolbar and hide the header or footer by double-clicking on the body text area in the document. This will have exactly the same effect as choosing the Close button.

## How to create a header or footer

When you first choose the View Header And Footer command for a document that doesn't already have a header, Word positions your cursor at the first character space in the header area, much as it does when you open a new document window. In fact, the header area functions much like the standard document area in most ways. You can, for example, use the Formatting toolbar and the Ruler to control formatting.

Just above the header area, Word displays the label Header. For a footer area, it displays Footer. Other possible labels include First Page Header, First Page Footer, Even Page Header, Even Page Footer, Odd Page Header, and Odd Page Footer, depending on the settings you have chosen on the Document Layout Layout card and which page you are editing. (You can use the Show Next and Show Previous buttons to move between areas.) In a multi-section document, the label will also indicate which section of the document the header is in, adding the word *Section* and the section number. (Once again, we will cover multisection documents, along with even and odd page layouts, in detail in Chapter 13.)

Whenever the cursor is in the header area, you can create the header simply by typing and formatting the text you want. For example, suppose you're writing an article about the Kentucky Derby and you want *Off to the Races* printed at the top of each page. You have only to type the phrase in the empty header area, as shown in Figure 5-25.

Press the Tab key to separate elements in a header or footer. By default, Word defines tab stops for the center and flush-right positions.

As the ruler in Figure 5-25 shows, the header is initially set flush left, with a centered tab at 3 inches and a right-aligned tab at 6 inches. If you are using Word's default settings, the header area's right-indent marker will fall at the 6-inch mark. Of course, the ruler settings will vary according to the formatting options you specify, just as they do in the body of your document.

**FIGURE 5-25**

To create a header, just type the text you want in the header area.

## How to format and position the header text

Word's default positioning for a header is 0.5 inch from the top of the page, with the body text 0.5 inch below the header (1 inch from the top of the page). It's also 1.25 inches from the left side of the page, aligned with the body text.

You can use almost all of Word's formatting features—which we will discuss in detail in Chapter 7, "Formatting"—on your header text. For example, you can right-align the text, right-align a multiline header, or use borders to visually separate headers from body text.

Word also has options, such as the From Edge settings on the Document Layout Margins card, that change the spacing and location of your headers and footers. We will discuss these in Chapter 16.

## How to delete headers and footers

To delete a header or footer, simply move the cursor to the header or footer area, select all of the text, and then press the Del key or choose Edit Cut.

## How to use editing and proofing tools in headers and footers

If you start the spelling check with the cursor in the body text of your document, Word will check the body text first and then the headers and footers. If you start the spelling check from the header area, however, Word will check only the header. If you start from the footer area, Word will check only the footer.

Interestingly, if you are in Normal or Outline view when you start a spelling or grammar check, Word will remain in that view and open a separate pane at the bottom of the document window. This split into two panes looks similar to the result of using the Window Split command except that the lower pane contains either a header or a footer.

When you finish the spelling check, Word will close the second pane for you. If you choose the Cancel button during the spelling check, however, Word will leave the extra pane open. You can then edit the header or footer in the pane, and when you finish, you can either choose the Close button or press Control-Shift-C to close the pane.

Now that we've covered the basics of typing and editing text, we're ready to explore the three proofing tools—for checking spelling, grammar, and hyphenation—in the next chapter.

# Topic Finder

# 6

# Proofing

nce you have entered and edited your text, Word stands ready to help provide a final polish to your words with three proofing tools. The spelling checker will help you locate and change misspelled words. The grammar checker will help you check common usage and grammar errors. Automatic hyphenation will help you hyphenate words correctly at the ends of lines. Each of these tools can help you make a better impression with your writing.

## Checking Spelling

Spelling errors are among the more distracting mistakes you can make. Misspell a common word, and it makes your work look sloppy. Misspell an unusual word, and you appear unfamiliar with it. Misspell someone's name, company, or product, and you stand a good chance of offending the reader. Word's spelling checker can help you avoid all of these mistakes.

Word identifies misspelled words by comparing them to one or more lists of correctly spelled words. The program comes with a dictionary of 106,000 words. In addition to this main dictionary, you can also develop custom dictionaries. Typically, these custom dictionaries will contain proper nouns, technical terms, and other specialized words that match your needs. You may also find that Word's standard dictionary is missing quite a few nontechnical words that you use frequently. Fortunately, you can build these dictionaries painlessly over time as you use the spelling checker.

To check spelling, open the document you want to check, and choose Tools Spelling, or click on the Spelling button on the Standard toolbar, or press the ⌘-Option-L shortcut keys. Word will begin the spelling check. When it encounters the first questionable spelling, Word will highlight the word in the text and open the Spelling dialog box, shown in Figure 6-1.

**FIGURE 6-1**

The Spelling dialog box.

## A quick tour of the Spelling dialog box

A tour of the Spelling dialog box will tell you most of what you need to know about the spelling checker. The title bar shows the dictionary currently in use—in this case, English (US), the dictionary with American spellings (*color*, for example, rather than *colour*). At the top of the Spelling dialog box is the Not In Dictionary text box, where Word will show you any word that it can't find in its dictionary. Below that text box is another text box with an attached list box. The second text box is labeled Change To, and the list box is labeled Suggestions. By default, when Word can't identify a word in your text, it suggests alternative spellings. This is an option you can turn off if you like, as we will discuss shortly.

### Ignore and Ignore All

There are six buttons along the right side of the dialog box, plus another five along the bottom. The top two on the right side are labeled Ignore and Ignore All. If you don't want to change a word that the spelling checker considers suspect (as it might with someone's name or the name of a product, for example), you can tell the spelling checker to ignore that word. The Ignore button tells Word to skip just the one instance. The Ignore All button tells Word to skip all occurrences for the rest of the current editing session.

That last point is worth special emphasis: Once you choose the Ignore All command for a given word, the spelling checker will continue to ignore that word even during later spelling checks during the same session. You can tell Word to stop ignoring words, however, with the Reset Ignore All button available on the Tools Options Spelling card, which we'll discuss later in this chapter. Word will also stop ignoring the words if you quit Word and restart it.

## Change and Change All

Below the Ignore and Ignore All buttons are the Change and Change All buttons. You can select a replacement for a suspect word from the Suggestions list box, or you can type the correct spelling directly in the Change To text box. If you choose Change, the spelling checker will replace the suspect word for the single instance that is currently highlighted in the document. If you choose Change All, the spelling checker will make the same change for any identically misspelled words it finds.

## Add and Suggest

If you choose the Add button, the spelling checker will add the suspect word to the custom dictionary currently in the Add Words To box. If no custom dictionary is selected in the Add Words To box, the Add button will be grayed out. (We'll show you how to create and use a custom dictionary shortly.)

In general, you should add words that are correctly spelled but not recognized if you expect to use them in other documents and if you're sure you'll never type the word accidentally when you mean something else. If you write about computer software, for example, you may use a term like *.txt fairly often. But if you add *txt* to your dictionary, you risk missing a misspelling of *text*.

The Suggest button next to the Add button will be grayed out by default; Word makes suggestions automatically unless you change a setting on the Tools Options Spelling card, as we'll discuss in a moment.

## AutoCorrect

The first of the five buttons across the bottom is labeled AutoCorrect. When Word finds a word with questionable spelling or capitalization, this button will be active. (When Word finds a repeated word in your text, the AutoCorrect button will be grayed.) If you choose AutoCorrect, Word will store the words currently in the Not In Dictionary box and the Change To box as an AutoCorrect entry, so the program will automatically correct the error in the future when you type it. This feature makes it easy to build up AutoCorrect entries for your most common spelling and typing mistakes.

Think twice when adding AutoCorrect entries from the spelling checker. If the questioned word is actually spelled correctly but isn't the word you meant to use, adding it as an AutoCorrect entry will tell Word to change it for you even when you do intend to use it. For example, you might type *ti* instead of *it*, but if you designate these as an AutoCorrect entry, Word will change a passage about musical notes from *sol la ti do* to read *sol la it do*—which significantly alters the meaning (not to mention the fact that it makes the passage more difficult to sing).

## Options

Choosing the Options button takes you to the Tools Options Spelling card. We'll skip that for now, but we'll discuss the Spelling card as soon as we finish looking at the remaining buttons.

## Undo Last

The Undo Last button lets you back up if you realize you've accidentally chosen the wrong button. When you choose it, the spelling checker returns to the previous suspect word and undoes whatever instructions you gave about that word.

Even if the Undo Last button is grayed, you can still undo other spelling changes in the document if they were made during the current editing session—meaning since the document was opened for editing. Because Word treats spelling changes as editing actions, you can use the Edit Undo feature to reverse them. For details on the Edit Undo command, see "How to undo an action or multiple actions" on page 82.

As with Word's Edit Undo feature, you can back up multiple steps to reverse spelling changes. In general, you can undo changes back to and including the first change since you started the current spelling check. If you undo all changes you've made during the current spelling check, Word will gray out the Undo Last button.

### Cancel and Help

The Cancel button aborts the spelling check, closes the Spelling dialog box, and leaves the last suspect word highlighted. This changes to the Close button after the first time you use the Change or the Change All button.

The Help button takes you directly to help for the Spelling command.

## The Tools Options Spelling card

Choosing the Options button takes you to the same screen as choosing Tools Options Spelling, as shown in Figure 6-2.

### The Suggest options

At the top of the card, you'll see an area labeled Suggest, with two check boxes, both of which are checked by default. The first is Always Suggest. If this box is checked, Word will always look for and show suggested corrections for words it can't find in its dictionaries. The second box is From Main Dictionary Only. As the name suggests, this option lets you limit Word's search for suggestions to the main dictionary only.

N$\text{EW}$!

As we've already mentioned, Word checks the Always Suggest check box by default; however, you may want to clear it to speed performance. Searching for suggestions can take time, and you have to wait while Word displays its list of alternative spellings. If most of your misspellings tend to be typing errors, you may find you can spell most words correctly when Word brings the error to your attention. (Don't worry about mistakes. Word will check your corrections as well.) And you can always resort to the Suggest button to find the spelling for any individual word you really need help with. If spelling is not one of your strong points, however, you probably won't gain anything by clearing the Always Suggest check box.

## The Ignore options

The next section, labeled Ignore, offers two check boxes and a button.

The two check box options are Words In UPPERCASE and Words With Numbers. By default, these are not checked. If you check the first of these options, the spelling checker will ignore words that appear entirely in capital letters, on the grounds that these are likely to be trademarks, acronyms, or other special-purpose words with unusual spellings. If you check the second choice, the spelling checker will skip words that contain numerals, for the same reason.

We strongly suggest that you use these options sparingly; it is better to add your acronyms and other special-purpose words to the custom dictionary than to risk missing misspelled words.

The Reset Ignore All button will be grayed out unless you've used the Ignore All button in the Spelling dialog box during the current editing session. When the Reset Ignore All button is active, you can use it to tell Word to stop ignoring the words you've designated with Ignore All. This feature comes in handy when you discover you've inadvertently told Word to ignore a word that is actually misspelled.

The combination of the Ignore All and Reset Ignore All features can help speed spelling checks on a rough draft of a document. If you are working with a draft that's filled with abbreviations, notes, the initials of the person who wrote each note, and other items that the spelling checker will question, you can tell it to ignore them during preliminary spelling checks with the Ignore All button. When you're ready for the final version and you want to be sure you've cleaned out all the notes from the rough draft, use the Reset Ignore All button to tell Word to stop ignoring those items.

### The Custom Dictionaries options

The Custom Dictionaries section at the bottom of the card lets you manage custom dictionaries.

This section includes a list box that shows the available custom dictionaries and shows which ones are active. You can activate up to 10 dictionaries simply by adding a check in each dictionary's check box. (Toggle the check on or off by pointing with the mouse and clicking, or by highlighting the choice and pressing the Spacebar.)

The four buttons along the right side of this section let you create and manage custom dictionaries. The New button lets you create a new dictionary file. Choose it, and Word will open a dialog box that will let you specify a folder and a name for the file.

The Edit button lets you open and edit the currently highlighted dictionary file as a Word document—a process we'll discuss in a moment. If you opened the card from the Spelling dialog box, the button will be grayed out. If you want to edit a custom dictionary with this command, you need to open the dialog box with the Tools Options Spelling command.

The Add button will open a dialog box that will let you specify a dictionary file to add to the Custom Dictionaries list. Note that you can't add files that don't already exist. If you want to create and add a new dictionary, you'll have to do it in two steps, creating it first with the New button.

The Remove button will remove a file from the list. Simply highlight the file you want to remove, and then choose the button. Word will not stop to ask for confirmation. If you accidentally remove the wrong file, it's easy enough to add it back to the list by choosing the Add button.

The Language box lets you choose a language setting for the currently highlighted custom dictionary. As with the Edit button, this option will be grayed out unless you opened the dialog box with the Tools Options Spelling command.

**NEW!**

### How to close the Tools Options Spelling card

After you make the changes you want on the Spelling card, choose OK to save your changes, or choose Cancel to discard any changes to the check boxes. (Note, however, that choosing Cancel won't cancel the Reset Ignore All command or cancel any changes you made to the list of custom dictionaries.) If you opened the dialog box by using the Options button in the Spelling dialog box, Word will return you to that dialog box.

## How to find and correct misspelled words

You now know most of what you need to about spelling checker basics except how to designate the text to check. You have two choices, depending on whether you want to check your entire document or just a portion of it.

Most often you'll want to check all of your text (including annotations and footnotes, even if they are not showing). With the cursor anywhere in your document and no text selected, simply choose Tools Spelling, press ⌘-Option-L, or click on the Spelling button on the Standard toolbar. Word will check the entire document starting from the cursor's current position to the end of the document, then from the start of the document to the cursor's current position. When the spelling checker reaches the point where you started, Word will show you a message stating that the spelling check is complete.

### How to check the spelling in a selection

Word will also let you check only a portion of your text, even as small a portion as a single word. Simply select the text you want to check. Then either choose Tools Spelling, press ⌘-Option-L, or click on the Spelling button on the Standard toolbar. If Word finds a suspect word in the selection, it will show you the word in the Spelling dialog box. When it finishes checking the selection, Word will show you a message asking whether to continue checking the rest of the document. Choose Yes or No as appropriate.

## Custom dictionaries

To use the spelling checker efficiently, you will almost certainly want to create one or more custom dictionaries to supplement the main dictionary. No matter what business you're in or what type of writing you do, chances are that you frequently use a specialized vocabulary that isn't in the main dictionary. At the very least, you probably use a specialized set of proper nouns, product names, and acronyms. It can quickly become annoying to have Word flag these words as unknown every time you use them. If you add them to a custom dictionary, however, Word will recognize them as legitimate words.

The easiest way to add words to a custom dictionary is with the Add button in the Spelling dialog box, which we described earlier in this chapter. However, there are some issues you should know about when you add words to a custom dictionary. First, Word does not provide a built-in option to remove a word should you make an incorrect entry. There is a way around this problem, as we'll show you in a moment, but the easiest solution is to avoid it in the first place. As much as possible, be sure to type a new word correctly the first time.

### Capitalization

Capitalization is another issue you need to be aware of. If you add a word to a dictionary in all lowercase letters, the spelling checker will accept that word in your text as long as it is all lowercase, all uppercase, or lowercase with an initial capital letter.

If you capitalize the first letter in the word when you add it, however, Word will recognize only occurrences that are capitalized the same way or are in all capital letters. For example, suppose you add the name *Cesarini* to a custom dictionary. When it checks spelling, Word will flag any occurrence of this name where the C is not capitalized or where not all of the letters are capitalized; *cesarini, CEsarini,* and *cEsarini* would all be flagged, but *Cesarini* and *CESARINI* would be accepted. If the dictionary entry has two or more letters capitalized, as in *McDonald,* the capitalization must match exactly for Word to accept it.

As much as possible, then, you'll want to add common terms in all lowercase letters. Use uppercase letters when you want the spelling checker to use capitalization as part of the basis for recognizing a word, as in the case of proper names. If the word is at the beginning of a sentence the first time the spelling checker finds it, you can add it with the initial capital letter if you like, but you'll have to add it again later in all lowercase if it shows up in the middle of a sentence.

Capitalization also affects the way Word shows alternatives in the Suggestions list box. If the suspect word is capitalized, Word will show the alternatives as capitalized also, and it will capitalize any replacement word you accept.

## How to edit a custom dictionary

As mentioned earlier, Word does not offer an option to delete mistakes from a custom dictionary. However, you can handle this chore fairly easily.

Custom dictionaries are essentially text files, with each word on a separate line in alphabetic order. Word identifies these as Custom Speller Dictionary type. You can open these files for editing in Word by choosing File Open and setting the List Files Of Type option to All Files. But the easier way is to use the Edit button on the Tools Options Spelling card. When you choose this button, Word shows you a message box stating that this operation will let you edit the custom dictionary as a Word document, and asking if you want to continue. You can then choose No to cancel the edit, or Yes to open the currently highlighted custom dictionary.

After you open a custom dictionary file, you can add, edit, or delete words at will. Note that you do not need to keep the file in alphabetic order; Word will reorder it for you the next time you add a new word from within the Spelling dialog box.

You can also use this technique to add words from other lists or from dictionaries created in other programs. If you can edit the other file so it contains one word per line, you can use the Insert File command to add those words to an existing custom dictionary. After merging the files, use the Table Sort Text command with the Case Sensitive option turned off; that way, you can scan through the file and look for duplicate entries. Then save the file. (Word will automatically save it as Speller Custom Dictionary type.) Your custom dictionary will contain all the added words. We'll discuss the Table Sort command in "Sorting" on page 749.

## NEW!   How to exclude words

There are times when you may want the spelling checker to question words it would ordinarily accept. For example, if you have a habit of transposing letters, you might type *teh* or *fro* when you intend to type *the* or *for*. While *teh* is not a word, *fro* is, as in *moving to and fro*.

You can tell Word not to accept *fro* by creating a new file called an *exclude dictionary*. Before you can create it, however, you need to know the name of the main spelling dictionary Word is using. You can find the name by looking through the Microsoft folder, which you should find at the hard disk level. The folder stores files, such as dictionaries, that two or more Microsoft programs can share. It should have been created either by the Word installation program or by another Microsoft installation program, if you have other Microsoft programs such as Excel on your Macintosh.

To find the filename, use the Finder to open the Microsoft folder, and choose View By Kind to sort the folder's contents by kind of item. Then scroll down the list, looking for files identified in the Kind column as MS Spelling 2 Documents. The folder should have at least two of these files—the Custom Dictionary and the main dictionary—which will be the English Dictionary if you're using the US version of the English language dictionary. You should also see the names of any other custom dictionaries that you created in the Microsoft folder. In any case, simply ignore the custom dictionaries. The one dictionary that's left over should be the main dictionary.

When you find the name for the main dictionary, write it down; you'll need it for naming the exclude dictionary. Next start Word, if it isn't already running, and then open a new document and type the words you don't want Word to recognize, using one line per word. Save this file as a Speller Exclude Dictionary using the Save File As Type pull-down list and giving it the same name as the main dictionary but adding the word *Exclude* before the word *Dictionary*. Be sure to store it in the same folder as the main dictionary. For example, if your main dictionary file is named English Dictionary and is in the Microsoft folder, save the file in the Microsoft folder as English Exclude Dictionary.

Word will then refer to this file whenever you run a spelling check, and if it finds one of the words that's in the exclude file, it will treat that word as if it were not in the dictionary file.

## The (no proofing) language option

After Word finishes a spelling check, you may see the message shown in Figure 6-3, indicating that Word found text formatted with the (no proofing) language option.

**FIGURE 6-3**

Word will notify you if it found text formatted with the (no proofing) language option.

The point of the message is to tell you that Word skipped over some or all of your text during the spelling check—a valuable piece of information if you applied the (no proofing) format by accident. The most likely way you might make this mistake is by accidentally defining the Normal style with (no proofing). We will discuss styles in more detail in Chapter 12, but for now, you can check the setting by choosing Format Style and highlighting Normal in the Styles list. If the Description box includes the words *(no proofing)*, you should change it. Choose the Modify button, open the Format pull-down list, choose Language, and then pick a language from the Mark Selected Text As list box. This option defines which dictionary to use; most American English speakers will want the English (US) option. Choose OK to close the language dialog box, OK again to close the Modify Style dialog box, and Close to close the Style dialog box.

You can use the (no proofing) format option to advantage. For example, you might have a table of organization names with their acronyms. To keep the spelling checker from stopping at each one, you could select the table, choose the Tools Language command, and select the (no proofing) option.

# Checking Grammar and Style

It's one thing to know whether you've spelled your words correctly. It's another thing entirely to know whether you've put them together in a readable combination. Word helps solve this problem with a second tool: the grammar checker. The Word grammar checker tool will identify possible errors in grammar and style, suggest improvements, and provide a readability rating for your text. What's more, you have a great deal of control over the kinds of issues the grammar checker will flag for you.

## A quick tour of the Grammar dialog box

To start the grammar checker, choose the Tools Grammar command. Word will then scan your entire document sentence by sentence, starting with the sentence the cursor is in.

> As with the spelling checker, the grammar checker will ignore any text that is formatted with the (no proofing) option.

In its default setting, Word will also check spelling at the same time that it checks grammar. Spelling comes first, so if Word does not recognize a word in a sentence, you'll see the Spelling dialog box before you see the Grammar dialog box for that sentence. (If you like, you can turn off the spelling check, as we will explain later in this chapter.) After the program checks the spelling in a sentence, it checks for grammar and syntax. If it finds any suspect grammar, it will open the Grammar dialog box, shown in Figure 6-4.

**FIGURE 6-4**

The Grammar dialog box will notify you of possible grammar and style errors.

When the grammar checker flags a possible problem, it will show you the current sentence in the Sentence text box. If you want to make any changes, you can edit the text in this box.

### Suggestions and explanations

Below the Sentence text box is the Suggestions box, where Word will offer suggestions for changes that might improve the sentence. Be careful about taking the program's advice. Remember that the English language is complex, and no one has yet written a grammar checker that has a real understanding of grammar or syntax.

Basically, the grammar checker follows rules that tell it when to flag something as being suspicious. And although the grammar checker is extremely sophisticated compared to a spelling checker, it will often make suggestions that are blatantly wrong. Even more often, the suggestions will be arguable. For example, Word will flag a sentence that starts with *And* or *But* and will tell you that it is preferable to avoid a sentence beginning with either. But there are times when breaking the rule makes for stronger writing. In short, you need to evaluate the sentence yourself and decide whether the suggestions make sense.

If you don't understand why Word is making a given suggestion, choose the Explain button at the bottom left of the Grammar dialog box. As shown in Figure 6-5, Word will offer an explanation of the rule and sometimes even suggest when it's OK to break the rule. These explanations can help you decide whether the suggestion applies to your sentence.

**FIGURE 6-5**

When you choose the Explain button in the Grammar dialog box, Word will provide an explanation of the rule it's basing the suggestion on.

**Explain**

**Rule: Passive Verb Usage**
Excessive use of the passive voice can make a document unclear. Try rewriting the sentence using a more direct verb. 'Documentation will be included with the delivery' might become 'Each delivery will include documentation.'

## How to find and fix the problem

When the grammar checker finds a possible problem, as in Figure 6-4, it highlights the relevant word or phrase in the Sentence text box (by showing it in bold and red). It also highlights any corresponding words in the Suggestions box. The highlights make it easier to locate the problem in the original sentence. If the suggestion includes a possible text change, Word may offer to make the change for you, in which case it will make the Change button active so you can choose it. If there's more than one suggestion, you can highlight one before choosing the change button to accept it. Alternatively, you can accept a suggestion by double-clicking on it. Also choose the Change button to accept any changes you've made to the text in the Sentence text box.

If you make a change and then decide you shouldn't have, you can choose the Undo Last button at the bottom of the Grammar dialog box. This will reverse the last change you made. You can also use the Edit Undo feature to reverse the changes after closing the Grammar dialog box.

You can also make edits directly in the document window if you prefer. To get to your text, you can use the mouse to click on the window, or you can switch to the window with Control-Tab. In either case, the Grammar dialog box will stay on the screen. When you've completed your changes, you can return to the Grammar dialog box by clicking on the box or pressing Control-Tab, and you can continue the grammar check by choosing the Start button.

### How to tell Word to move on without making a change

If you decide not to take Word's suggestion (as will probably happen more often than not), you can skip the suggestion by choosing the Ignore button. If you think the sentence is right as it stands and you don't want Word to check it for any other possible errors, choose the Next Sentence button. If you completely disagree with the rule Word is following to make the suggestion, you can choose the Ignore Rule button. You can also exclude rules on a permanent basis with the Grammar configuration options available through the Options button; we'll discuss these in a moment.

Finally, if you want to halt the grammar check entirely and return to your document, choose Cancel or Close (the Cancel button changes to a Close button as soon as you make a change in your text through the dialog box). Word will close the dialog box, and return you to the document window.

## Readability measures and how to use them

If you let Word complete a grammar check, assuming you're using the default settings, the grammar checker will display a Readability Statistics dialog box for your document, as in Figure 6-6.

It's important to realize that these statistics are based only on the section of the document covered by the grammar checker in its most recent session. If you close the Grammar dialog box to edit your text and then restart the grammar checker, the grammar checker will restart its tracking of the statistics as well. Also note that the statistics do not include any text formatted with the (no proofing) option.

The first section of the Readability Statistics dialog box lists some basic information: the number of words, characters, paragraphs, and sentences. The middle section uses these numbers to calculate average sentences per paragraph, words per sentence, and characters per word.

The bottom third of the box reports some readability ratings. The first is the percentage of sentences containing constructions in the passive voice. Note that some sentences may be mistakenly flagged as passive.

**FIGURE 6-6**

After it completes a grammar check, Word will show you some statistics about the readability of your document.

| Readability Statistics | |
|---|---|
| Counts: | |
| Words | 156 |
| Characters | 774 |
| Paragraphs | 5 |
| Sentences | 6 |
| Averages: | |
| Sentences per Paragraph | 1.20 |
| Words per Sentence | 26 |
| Characters per Word | 4.78 |
| Readability: | |
| Passive Sentences | 16.6 % |
| Flesch Reading Ease | 52.5 |
| Flesch-Kincaid Grade Level | 11.96 |
| Coleman-Liau Grade Level | 13.75 |
| Bormuth Grade Level | 11.20 |
| OK | Help... |

In general, you should avoid passive voice where possible because it can make your writing seem stuffy and will definitely make it harder to read. For example, *He wrote the book* is livelier and easier to read than the passive construction *The book was written by him.* Some people insist it sounds more objective to write *It has been determined that...*, rather than *I discovered that....* In truth, the second form is not only stronger and easier to read, it's more honest because it tells the reader who determined whatever you are about to say.

The other four readability ratings are based on formulas that analyze sentence length and the number of multisyllable words. Text with longer sentences and bigger words is typically more difficult to read and therefore rates higher on these scales. The Flesch Reading Ease score is based on a 100-point scale with lower numbers indicating easier-to-read text. Standard writing typically falls within the 70-to-80-point range.

The other three scores, Flesch-Kincaid, Coleman-Liau, and Bormuth Grade Levels, are reported in U.S. school grade levels. Text that scores between 7th and 8th grade level is considered easily readable by most adults. Note, however, that these measures will usually report different grade levels. Lower scores are theoretically even easier to read; higher scores, more difficult.

Note too that these measures aren't absolute. The following selection scores between 11th and 15th grades (college-level) according to the Readability Statistics criteria:

The National Football League Championship is called the Superbowl, and the Philadelphia Eagles are one of the favorites this year.

In contrast, the next selection rates between 3rd and 8th grade levels:

The bit count starts with the hex offset address. The first 2 bytes point to the last register in the FIFO segment.

All three readability scores rate the first sentence as more difficult to read, but most people will find the second much more difficult to understand. One reason is that the second sentence relies heavily on specialized terms—jargon. These small words make the selection more readable according to the grammar checker formulas, but not in real life. The moral: Take the Readability Statistics results with a large grain of salt.

## How to use the grammar-checking options

As we mentioned earlier in this chapter, you can change the way the grammar checker works by specifying which rules it uses. You can change these settings on the Tools Options Grammar card, shown in Figure 6-7. To reach the card, choose the Options button in the Grammar dialog box; alternatively, choose Tools Options and then Grammar. Notice that by default, Word checks both the Check Spelling and Show Readability Statistics check boxes. You can turn either of these features off if you like by clearing the appropriate check box.

**FIGURE 6-7**

The Tools Options Grammar card lets you configure the grammar checker.

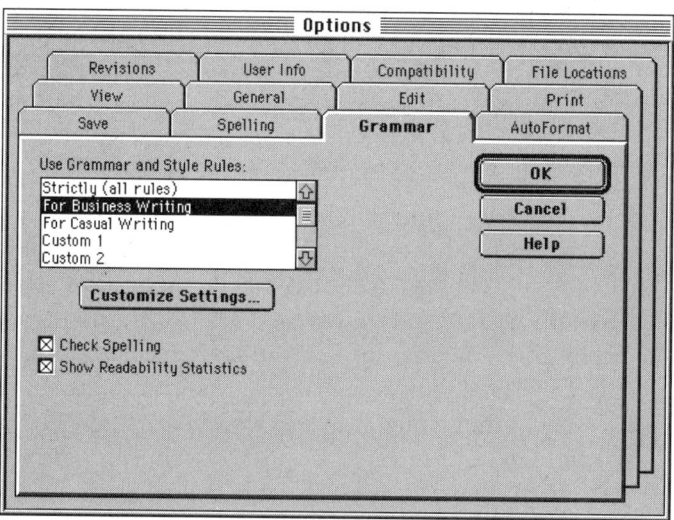

The Use Grammar And Style Rules list box lets you choose a set of grammar rules for the Grammar checker to follow. Word can store six sets of rules, and will let you define any of them however you like. As shipped, the Strictly (All Rules) option is set to use all the grammar rules available to the program. The For Business Writing option, which is the default choice, uses fewer rules, and the For Casual Writing option uses the fewest. The other three sets are simply named Custom 1, Custom 2, and Custom 3. To customize any of these sets of rules, on a rule-by-rule basis, choose the Customize Settings button to open the Customize Grammar Options dialog box shown in Figure 6-8.

The top item in the dialog box—the Use Grammar And Style Rules box—includes a pull-down list box to let you pick which set of rules to modify. The example in the figure is set for business writing.

Second from the top are the Grammar and Style option buttons. These determine which type of rules Word will show in the list box immediately below the option buttons.

Most of Word's grammar rules, such as agreement between subject and verb, are clear-cut issues of right and wrong. Most style rules, such as the acceptability of starting a sentence with *And* or *But*, are open to debate (and regularly broken by writers of the highest caliber). However, this distinction is not strictly true. For example, Word lists homonyms (words that sound alike but mean something different, such as *affect* and *effect*) as a style rule. But using the right word is not a matter of taste. Similarly, Word lists informal usage as a grammar rule. But usage is normally considered an issue of style.

As you can see in Figure 6-8, some rules have checks next to them, indicating that they're currently active. The scroll bar on the side of the list box indicates that there are more rules than the list box can show at once. You can scroll through the list for each kind of rule.

**FIGURE 6-8**

The Customize Grammar Options dialog box lets you fine-tune the grammar checker rules to your needs.

| Customize Grammar Options |
|---|
| Use Grammar and Style Rules: |
| For Business Writing ▼        Reset All |
| ● Grammar        ○ Style |
| √ Agreement with Here or There        OK |
| √ Clause Errors |
| √ Commonly Confused Words        Cancel |
| √ Double Negatives |
| √ Format Errors        Explain... |
| √ Informal Usage |
| √ Jargon Words        Help |
| **Catch** |
| Split Infinitives:        By More Than One Word ▼ |
| Consecutive Nouns:        More Than Three in a Row ▼ |
| Prepositional Phrases:        More Than Three in a Row ▼ |
| Sentences Containing More Words Than:        35 |

If you are not sure what one of the rules refers to, you can highlight the rule in the list box and then choose the Explain button. Word will open an Explain message box similar to the one shown in Figure 6-9.

**FIGURE 6-9**

Word can provide explanations for the rules listed in the Customize Grammar Options dialog box.

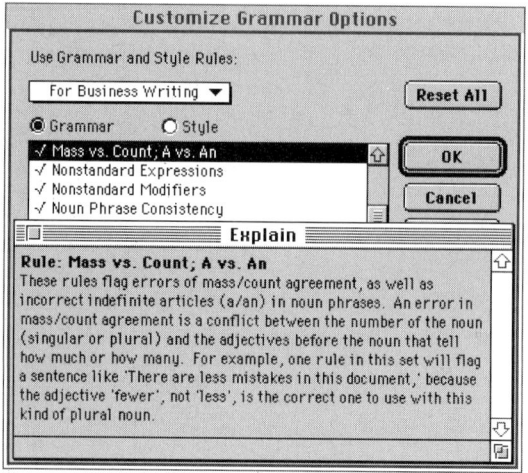

The default setting For Business Writing (the choice showing in the Use Grammar And Style Rules box in Figures 6-8 and 6-9) activates most, but not all, of the rules listed in the box under the Grammar and Style option buttons. More important, you can turn rules on or off to customize the grammar checker. For example, if you know you tend to use weak modifiers such as *nice*, you might add the Weak Modifiers rule to the business writing configuration. Simply choose the Style option button, and add a check to the Weak Modifiers rule in the Style list box—either by clicking to the left of the rule (where the check will appear) or by highlighting the rule and pressing the Spacebar.

As already mentioned, you can redefine all six sets of rules: Strictly (All Rules), For Business Writing, For Casual Writing, and the three Custom choices. If you go to the Use Grammar And Style Rules pull-down list, you'll see that the choices of rules change when you pick a different set from the list. More important, you can define your personalized profile for each set of rules independently of the others. Note that the Strictly (All Rules) choice becomes something of a misnomer if you choose to leave out some rules, but you can still use the choice to include the maximum number of rules you want to follow.

If you have made changes to any set of rules, you can choose the Reset All button at any time to tell Word to return the set to its default rules. Simply open the Customize Grammar Options box and choose Reset All. Note that this will change only the set of rules currently shown in the Use Grammar And Style Rules box.

**NEW!**

Finally, note the Catch section at the bottom of the dialog box. You can use the three pull-down lists to tell the grammar checker to point out split infinitives, strings of nouns, and consecutive prepositional phrases. More important, you can customize these to suit your taste. The choices in the Split Infinitives pull-down list are Always, Never, By More Than One Word, By More Than Two Words, and By More Than Three Words. The default For Business Writing choice is By More Than One Word. The choices for Consecutive Nouns and for Prepositional Phrases are Never, More Than Two In A Row, More Than Three In A Row, and More Than Four In A Row. The default For Business Writing choice for both is More Than Three In A Row.

The final item in the Catch section is a text box labeled Sentences Containing More Words Than. Word will flag any sentence with more words than the number in this box; the default setting in all cases is 35 words.

**NEW!**

## A strategy for using the grammar checker

Word's grammar checker is certainly not one of the program's strongest features, but that's the nature of all grammar checkers today. While it can catch mistakes that you might miss when proofreading, and while you can configure it to suit your needs and tastes, it is slow and not completely reliable. Used on well-written text, it suggests more mistakes than actually exist, a tendency that can quickly become tiresome. On the other hand, one mistake in a document can be too many, and if the program catches just one error, the improvement can be worth the time and effort.

In truth, the grammar checker's most valuable feature is simply that it will help make you aware of your writing. But for actually checking grammar, the grammar checker works best if you already know how to write well and you've taken the time to customize it. You'll want to turn off rules for mistakes you don't make, to avoid bothersome false alarms. And be sure to turn on the rules for mistakes that you do make. It's a good idea, also, to make the grammar check the last step (with the possible exception of hyphenation) in preparing your text.

# Hyphenation

Word's hyphenation feature is another tool you can use to improve the final appearance of your text. Hyphenation is particularly helpful when you are using justified paragraphs or narrow columns. By hyphenating words, you can avoid the unsightly extra spaces that Word will occasionally insert to maintain a justified right margin. If you are using left-aligned paragraphs instead of justified paragraphs, hyphenation helps make lines more nearly equal in length.

*NEW!*

Word can hyphenate words as you enter text. If you find that distracting, you can use the Tools Hyphenation command on text you've already created. Either choice is far more efficient than manually inserting optional hyphens with ⌘-hyphen, and either one frees you to concentrate on your writing while you enter or edit text. Note too that you can hyphenate an entire document or just a selected portion of text.

As with the Spelling and Grammar checkers, hyphenation will skip over any text formatted with the (no proofing) Tools Language option. Although you can use this feature to good advantage, be careful not to format text for no proofing unless that's really what you want. If you simply want Word's hyphenation feature to ignore a section of text but you still want the spelling checker and grammar checker to check that section, you should format the text with Word's Don't Hyphenate option.

To format text as Don't Hyphenate, first place the cursor or selection in the paragraph or paragraphs you want to format. Then choose Format Paragraph, go to the Text Flow card, check the Don't Hyphenate check box, and choose OK. We'll cover paragraph formatting in detail, starting on page 204.

## How to use the Tools Hyphenation command

Before looking at the mechanics of Word's hyphenation feature, it's important to understand that Word actually has two very different hyphenation features, though both are available through the Tools Hyphenation command. The fully automatic hyphenation feature will insert all hyphens in a document without asking for your approval. The so-called manual hyphenation feature is semiautomatic. Choose manual hyphenation, and Word will stop at each word it thinks needs a hyphen, and let you accept, reject, or change the position for the hyphen.

If you want to hyphenate your text with the semiautomatic feature, first select the portion you want to hyphenate, or, if you want to hyphenate the entire document, make sure there is no text selected. The selection, or lack of selection, will have no effect on the fully automatic feature.

To start the hyphenation, choose Tools Hyphenation. Word will show you the Hyphenation dialog box, shown in Figure 6-10.

**FIGURE 6-10**

The Tools Hyphenation command opens the Hyphenation dialog box, where you can make configuration changes or start the hyphenation process.

If you check the Automatically Hyphenate Document check box at the top of the Hyphenation dialog box, Word will do all of the work for you. (Word will make its decisions based on the settings in the dialog box for the Hyphenation Zone and Limit Consecutive Hyphens To boxes, which we'll explain in a moment.) If you prefer to make your own choices, use the Manual button—which we'll also explain shortly. If the Automatically Hyphenate Document check box is not checked and you choose the OK button, Word will return to your document without making any changes—just as if you chose Cancel.

Automatic hyphenation has a distinct advantage over other choices for hyphenation in that it will readjust the hyphenation if you change the font or size of your text or if you change other formatting settings. It will also let you undo all hyphenation in a single stroke. Word stores the automatic hyphenation setting with each file. And you can remove hyphenation by simply clearing the Automatically Hyphenate Document check box.

The two disadvantages of automatic hyphenation are that you lose control over where the hyphens go and your computer's performance can slow down because of the extra work Word does to determine where the hyphens should go. If your system is fast enough, the second disadvantage is not an issue. In general, if you use hyphenation, we recommend using the automatic choice unless you absolutely insist on controlling the position for each hyphen.

### The Hyphenate Words In CAPS option

The Hyphenate Words In CAPS check box in the Hyphenation dialog box lets you tell Word to either hyphenate or ignore words that are in all uppercase letters. If you don't want to hyphenate words that are in all caps, make sure this check box is not checked.

In general, you will not want this box checked if you are letting Word hyphenate automatically. The danger is that you could end up hyphenating an acronym that's in all caps.

### The Hyphenation Zone text box

The Hyphenation Zone text box lets you set the allowable distance between the right indent and the end of the line, an area that Word calls the hyphenation zone. By adjusting the width of the zone, you can adjust the unevenness of lines along the right margin in a ragged-right format. This setting also affects the number of words that will be hyphenated overall. The larger the zone, the fewer the words that will be hyphenated.

If the distance between the indention and the end of the line is greater than the value in the Hyphenation Zone text box, Word will try to hyphenate the first word on the next line so that part of the word will appear on the preceding line. The default measurement is 0.25 inches. If you want to decrease the raggedness of the words along the right margin, or you want to reduce the amount of space that appears between words in justified text, enter a smaller Hyphenation Zone setting. On the other hand, if you want to hyphenate as few words as possible, or you dislike seeing short single syllables at the beginnings of lines, enter a larger Hyphenation Zone setting.

### Limit Consecutive Hyphens To

The Limit Consecutive Hyphens To text box controls how many consecutive lines can end in hyphens when Word hyphenates automatically. A value of 0 or No Limit allows a hyphen on every line. Most people, however, prefer to limit the number of successive hyphenated lines to one or two. To limit the number, simply enter 1 or 2 in the text box. (The limit for the box is 32,767 lines, but anything over 3 or 4 in this text box will be effectively the same as entering a 0.)

## Manual hyphenation

If, instead of using automatic hyphenation, you choose the Manual button in the Hyphenation dialog box, Word will search for the first candidate for hyphenation. It will then display the Manual Hyphenation dialog box, shown in Figure 6-11.

When you use manual hyphenation, Word will automatically switch to Page Layout view.

As you can see in Figure 6-11, at this point Word will show you the word broken into syllables in the Hyphenate At text box. You cannot see it in the figure, but Word will position a blinking cursor at the proposed location for a hyphen. Word will also highlight the suggested word break in your document, where it will show the recommended hyphenation in context.

**FIGURE 6-11**

When Word finds a candidate for hyphenation, it will suggest a word break.

If you want to accept the hyphenation Word suggests, simply choose Yes. If you want to change the hyphenation, use the mouse to move the blinking cursor to a new hyphenation point in the Hyphenate At text box, and then choose Yes. When you choose Yes, Word will insert an optional hyphen character at that point. (We covered optional hyphens and other special characters in "Special Characters" on page 147.)

If you don't want to hyphenate the word, choose No to skip it, or choose Cancel to end hyphenation and return to the document. Note that if you specify a hyphenation point that comes after the line break (marked by a gray vertical line in the Hyphenate At text box), Word will add an optional hyphen at that point, but the word will wrap to the next line. If you edit or reformat your text later, however, so that the word's position shifts in the line, Word may be able to take advantage of the optional hyphen.

Word will let you hyphenate a word between any two letters—you do not have to break the word between syllables. If you place the cursor somewhere other than at a syllable break in the text box, Word will display a vertical cursor at that point rather than highlighting the break. You will find this flexibility in controlling word breaks helpful in those rare situations when none of Word's proposed syllable breaks are acceptable.

If you start hyphenation for an entire document from the middle of a document, Word will begin at the start of the current paragraph and proceed to the end of the document. It will then start hyphenating at the beginning of the document again and continue to the original cursor position. If you selected a block of text before starting hyphenation, Word will first hyphenate the selected block and then open a message box asking whether you also want to hyphenate the rest of the document. After you hyphenate the full document, Word will open a message box telling you that the hyphenation is complete.

## Save hyphenation for last

If you use Word's manual (actually semiautomatic) hyphenation feature, you will generally be better off if you complete your writing, editing, and formatting before you hyphenate. In particular, if you make substantial changes to a document after you've hyphenated it, you will almost certainly change the location of any number of hyphenated words, moving them to the middle of the lines they're in. In addition, you'll probably need to hyphenate a number of words that have moved to the ends of lines. Because hyphenation affects only the appearance of the final printed document, it is a waste of time to run the hyphenation feature repeatedly.

Having to rehyphenate is not an issue with automatic hyphenation, of course, because Word will adjust the hyphens for you as you change your text. Even with automatic hyphenation, however, you may be better off waiting until you've finished writing, editing, and formatting before turning the feature on. Having automatic hyphenation break a word as you're typing it, and having it adjust line breaks as you write or edit, can be distracting. Depending on your system, you might also find that it slows your computer's performance noticeably.

Most important, if you wait until you're finished and then check the Automatically Hyphenate Document check box, you'll get the same result as if you had had the feature on from the moment you started writing the document. If you take this route, however, we recommend that you look through your document before printing it, since hyphenation will affect line breaks and can therefore affect page breaks.

## How to delete unwanted optional hyphens

Note that if you use manual hyphenation, you don't have to remove unnecessary optional hyphens from your text, because Word doesn't print them unless they appear at line breaks. Even if you don't delete them, they won't affect the appearance of your printed text in any way. If you work with nonprinting characters showing, however, we recommend that you delete unnecessary optional hyphens before you rehyphenate. Otherwise, your screen will be cluttered with optional hyphens.

The easiest way to remove optional hyphens is with the search-and-replace feature described in Chapter 4. Use ^- (caret, hyphen) as the Find What text, and leave the Replace With text box blank to replace the hyphens with nothing. (The ^- is a special search-character combination that will find only optional hyphens. It will not find standard hyphens or non-breaking hyphens. You can enter it in the text box by opening the Special pull-down menu and choosing Optional Hyphen from the pull-down list.) If you've hyphenated your text recently, you also have the option of using the Edit Undo command.

The spelling and hyphenation tools covered in this chapter can play an important part in making your documents look better from a mechanical point of view, and the grammar tool can help make them read better. If you want to dress up your words visually, however, you'll need to format them to take advantage of your system's—and particularly your printer's—capabilities. In the next chapter, we'll cover fundamental formatting.

# TOPIC FINDER

# 7

# Formatting

s a full-featured word processor, Word for the Macintosh offers you far more features than an ordinary text editor, but it stops short of equaling a desktop publishing program. Word gives you control over many formatting aspects of a document—page size, margins, text size, font, and line spacing, to name just a few. And the Macintosh interface lets you see what a formatted page will look like before you print it. Word doesn't offer quite the sophisticated formatting and typographic control of a high-end desktop publishing program, but it is capable of just about any desktop publishing task most users will ever need.

We'll discuss Word's advanced formatting features in later chapters. For now, we'll stick to basics. Be forewarned that even the basic features can get a bit intimidating, but one concept can make them easier to understand.

Formatting in Word takes place at four levels: the overall document, the section, the paragraph, and the character. (Note that Word 6.0, unlike earlier versions, refers to character formatting as *font* formatting.)

There is a distinction between formatting directly and formatting by style. We'll stay strictly with direct formatting in this chapter and save styles for Chapter 12.

# Top-Down Document Design

Most formatting changes made at one level can affect the formatting at lower levels. For example, if you change the margins for your whole document (a document-level formatting change), you'll affect the width of every paragraph in the document. Because the different levels are interrelated, it makes sense to design your documents from the top down.

To design your document from the top down, you should decide first on the most general aspects of your document layout—paper size and margins, for example—and then fine-tune such factors as paragraph and font formats. You'll find that this approach simplifies document design and eliminates a lot of backtracking. Figure 7-1 lists some of the features you can set at each formatting level.

**FIGURE 7-1**

You can simplify document design by moving from the general to the specific.

**Document Formatting**
Paper size
Orientation
Left and right margins
Top and bottom margins
Mirror margins or gutter
Footnote positions

**Section Formatting**
Section breaks
Number of columns
Space between columns
Header and footer positions
Page numbers

**Paragraph Formatting**
Alignment
Line spacing
First-line indention
Left and right indention
Paragraph spacing
Tab settings
Borders

**Font Formatting**
Font
Size
Style
Position
Spacing

This chapter looks at document, paragraph, and font formatting. We'll save section-level formatting for later, because it comes into play only in complex documents in which you need to change certain characteristics—such as the number of columns or the header or footer—from one part of a document to another. We'll also save columns for later. You'll find a discussion of section-level formatting in "Multisection Documents" on page 455. For information about columns, see "Multicolumn Formatting" on page 469. Note that we've already covered the basics of page numbering and headers and footers in "Creating Headers and Footers" on page 153.

# Document Formatting

The first step is to establish your page layout. In most documents, the only factors that affect the layout are paper size, margins, and print orientation. Since the size of your available text area will affect the appearance of every paragraph, you should establish these three settings before any other formatting. If you change the size of your text area after you've changed paragraph or font formats, you may have to go back and reapply your paragraph or font formats.

## How to determine the size of the text area

Figure 7-2 shows Word's default page layout. Word assumes that you're using 8½-by-11-inch pages in portrait orientation—that is, positioned so that the

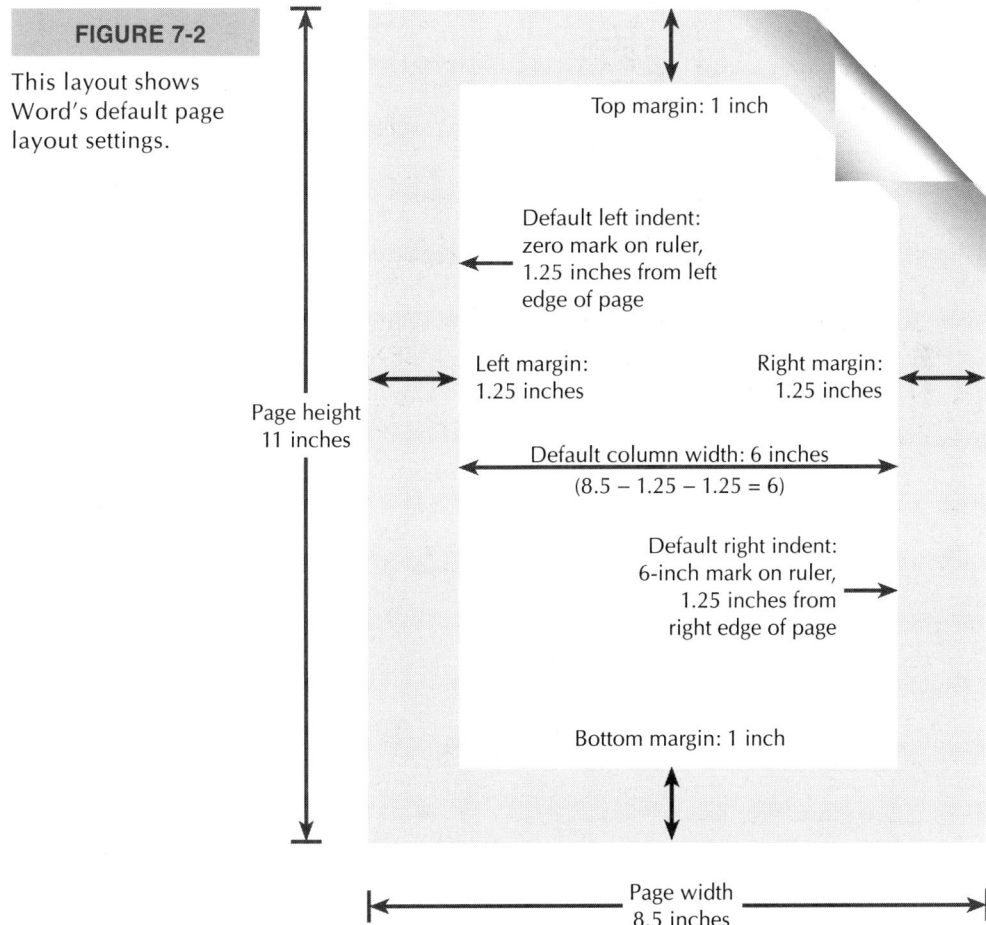

**FIGURE 7-2**

This layout shows Word's default page layout settings.

Top margin: 1 inch

Default left indent: zero mark on ruler, 1.25 inches from left edge of page

Left margin: 1.25 inches

Right margin: 1.25 inches

Page height 11 inches

Default column width: 6 inches
(8.5 − 1.25 − 1.25 = 6)

Default right indent: 6-inch mark on ruler, 1.25 inches from right edge of page

Bottom margin: 1 inch

Page width 8.5 inches

lines of text print running parallel to the short sides of the paper. The default left and right margins are 1.25 inches each. The top and bottom margins are 1 inch each. These margins define the amount of blank space between the edge of the paper and the edge of your text.

The combination of paper size, margins, and page orientation delimits your available text area. The width of the text area, for example, is the width of the paper minus the left and right margins. With Word's default settings, the text area on each page is 6 inches wide (8.5 minus 1.25 minus 1.25) and 9 inches high (11 minus 1 minus 1).

You can change paper size by choosing File Page Setup, which will open the Page Setup dialog box, as shown in Figure 7-3.

**FIGURE 7-3**

The Page Setup dialog box's contents will vary depending on the printer you have installed using the Chooser.

In general, you can pick the paper size and orientation (portrait or landscape) in the Page Setup dialog box. Figure 7-4 on the next page shows the default layout settings for a landscape page. Some printers will offer additional options, such as the Printer Effects check boxes shown in Figure 7-3. Most printers will also offer a Custom page size, which you can use to set specific page dimensions.

Top margin: 1 inch

Left margin:
1.25 inches

Right margin:
1.25 inches

Paper width

Column width: 8.5 inches
(11 − 1.25 − 1.25 = 8.5)

Bottom margin: 1 inch

Paper height

**FIGURE 7-4**

When you use landscape orientation, the page is wider than it is tall.

Note that at the bottom left of the dialog box, there is a box labeled Apply Size And Orientation To, and it defaults to the Whole Document choice. There is another choice, This Point Forward, which will insert a section break and apply the Page Setup settings only to that section. (For more information about sections, see Chapter 13, "Bullets, Numbering, & Sections.") If your document already has one or more section breaks, there will be a third choice—which will be the default choice—named This Section.

For some printers, there will be an Options button available at the top right of the Page Setup dialog box, which you can choose to change settings that are specific to that printer. The Print button takes you to the Print dialog box, and the Default button lets you set the current Page Setup choices as the default for the current template. For more details about templates, see Chapter 27.

The Margins button takes you to the Document Layout dialog box shown in Figure 7-5. This is the same dialog box you reach using the File Document Layout command. This dialog box has two tabbed cards: Margins and Layout.

The Document Layout dialog box also has some buttons along the right edge. The Default button works in the same way as the Default button in the Page Setup dialog box; it saves the current settings as in the document's template. The Page Setup button will open the same Page Setup dialog box as we just described, with one notable difference; there will not be an Apply Size And Orientation To box available.

## Margins

As you can see in Figure 7-5, the Margins card contains options for adjusting the top, bottom, left, and right margins. You need only enter a new setting in the appropriate text boxes along the top of the card. Note that you can also set top and bottom margins to either At Least or Exactly. The At Least choice allows the margin to be increased if necessary to accommodate a larger header or footer.

The Preview box in the center shows a thumbnail sketch of a formatted page. As you change the margin settings, the sketch will change to show the effect of the new settings.

The Mirror Margins check box in the lower right lets you set different inside and outside—rather than left and right—margins. This is a common requirement if you plan to print your document on both sides of the paper and you want the text area on both sides to match up, even if the left and right margins are different. If you check this box, the Left and Right margin labels will change to Inside and Outside, and the Preview box will change to represent a pair of facing pages.

**Binding margins.** You use the Gutter setting if you want to create a binding margin, which is important for pages that you plan to bind in a booklet, for example. (Do not confuse this Gutter setting with the concept of a gutter between columns, which Word refers to as the space between columns.)

If you enter a Gutter setting without checking the Mirror Margins check box, the binding margin will go on the left side of each page. If you check Mirror Margins, the binding margin will go along the inside edge of the facing pages, as shown in Figure 7-6.

**FIGURE 7-6**

Check the Mirror Margins check box, and Word will change the Left and Right margin labels to Inside and Outside. It will also show two facing pages and the effect of the Gutter settings along the inside of both pages.

 In a sense, the Gutter setting is redundant; you can get the same result on your printed page with or without it. For example, say that you want a 1-inch binding margin plus an additional inside margin of 1.25 inches and an outside margin of 1.25 inches. To get it, you can check the Mirror Margins check box and set the Inside margin to 2.25 inches, the Outside margin to 1.25 inches, and the Gutter to 0 inches. Or you can set the Inside margin to 1.25 inches, the Outside margin to 1.25 inches, and the Gutter to 1.0 inch. The two combinations of settings are equivalent.

You use the Apply To pull-down list in the lower right corner of the Margins card to specify whether the settings will affect the whole document (the default) or everything from the current cursor position to the end of the document. Word may offer other options depending on your document's contents and whether a block of text is highlighted when you open the dialog box.

Finally, note the Header and Footer text boxes in the From Edge box. These help determine the placement of headers and footers, but we'll ignore them for now. For details, see "Defining the Position of a Header or Footer" on page 558.

The text boxes in Figures 7-5 and 7-6 use Word's default units of measure: inches. You can change the unit of measure to centimeters, points, or picas, if you prefer, in the Measurement Units list box on the Tools Options General card. Even if you don't change that setting, you can still use any of the units that Word recognizes. To set a margin of 2.54 centimeters, for example, simply type *2.54 cm* in the appropriate text box and then choose OK. Word will convert the entry to inches, and the next time you open the Page Setup dialog box, the setting will read 1". Note that when you increase the top or bottom margin, you decrease your text area and, therefore, the number of lines that fit on each page. When you decrease a margin, you increase the text area.

## Layout

The Layout card, shown in Figure 7-7, contains some options that we've covered earlier and others that belong in a discussion of advanced features. We'll ignore this card for now. For a discussion of the Headers And Footers options, take a look at "Creating Headers and Footers" on page 153. For a discussion of the advanced features on this card, see "Multisection Documents" starting on page 455.

**FIGURE 7-7**

The Layout card in the Document Layout dialog box contains more options that affect your document's format.

## The horizontal ruler

Word's horizontal ruler contains several symbols that indicate your current page and paragraph formats. The symbols double as tools that you can use to adjust these formats. For the moment, we'll concentrate on the symbols related to page format. Note that Word also contains a vertical ruler, which we'll discuss shortly.

If you're using Word's default settings and you're working in Normal view, the ruler will look like Figure 7-8. The zero point is at the left edge of the white section of the ruler, and it always indicates the left edge of your text column, regardless of your left margin setting, paper size, or page orientation. For example, Word's default left margin setting is 1.25 inches from the left edge of the paper. If you change the margin setting to 3, the zero point on the ruler will represent a position 3 inches from the left edge of the paper.

**FIGURE 7-8**

This is the horizontal ruler with Word's default settings in Normal view.

The right margin, as defined by the Format Page Setup command, is indicated by the right edge of the white section of the ruler. This edge may not be visible, depending on several factors including the settings for your side margins, your Zoom setting, and your monitor type. In Figure 7-8, the zero point is at the left, and the right margin is at the 6-inch mark on the ruler.

Unless told otherwise, Word will align the right indent marker for your paragraph with the right margin. Similarly, Word will align the first-line and left indent markers with the zero point unless instructed otherwise. Do not confuse the indent markers with the left and right margins. The key point: You can change the indent markers to affect one or more paragraphs without affecting the overall margins for your document. To put it another way, changing the indents merely changes the position of text relative to the margins. (We'll say more about this when we discuss paragraph formatting later in this chapter.)

## How to change left and right margins

Word provides two approaches for changing margins: through the ruler and through the Page Setup dialog box. If you like, you can use the mouse for this task; change to Page Layout view by choosing View Page Layout, or change to Print Preview by choosing File Print Preview. Then move the mouse pointer to the edge of the margin, on the horizontal ruler. The pointer will change to a left-and-right-pointing arrow, as shown in Figure 7-9 on the next page. To move the margin, hold down the mouse button and drag in either direction. Note that when you hold down the mouse button, Word will display a vertical dashed line down the entire page, as in Figure 7-10 on the next page, to show where the new margin will fall. To accept the new margin setting, simply release the button.

**FIGURE 7-9**

When you move the mouse pointer over the margin edge on the horizontal ruler in Page Layout view or Print Preview, the pointer will change to a left-and-right-pointing arrow, indicating that you can drag the margin indicator.

**FIGURE 7-10**

When you're dragging the margin marker with the mouse, Word displays a vertical dashed line to indicate where the margin boundary will fall in relation to the text.

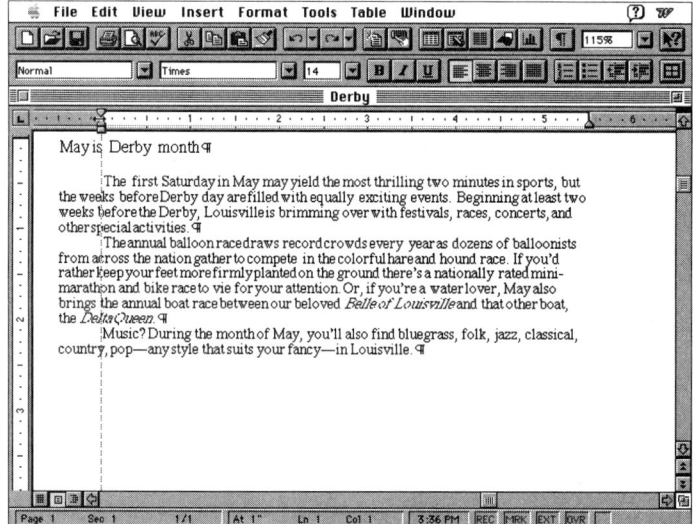

If you prefer using the keyboard to change the margins, choose File Document Layout, and choose the Margins card. Then change the left and right margin settings (or the inside and outside settings if the Mirror Margins option is active) in the appropriate text boxes.

You can adjust margins with the mouse and ruler only when in Page Layout view or Print Preview. If you work mostly in Normal view, you can usually change the margin settings more quickly through the Document Layout dialog box. Note, too, that changing the settings through the dialog box is generally more accurate in any case because you type precise measurements rather than judge margin size by eye.

## The vertical ruler

When you switch to Page Layout view or Print Preview, Word adds a vertical ruler to the left side of the screen. As Figure 7-10 shows, the vertical ruler is similar to the horizontal ruler; its white section delineates the body text area for a page, and the gray represents the margin. (More precisely, the white section will represent the currently active text area on the page, which will be the header or footer if that's what you're working with.)

## How to change top and bottom margins

You can use the vertical ruler to adjust the top and bottom margins by dragging with the mouse, much as you can use the horizontal ruler to adjust the side margins. Figure 7-11 shows the top margin in the process of being adjusted, with the horizontal dashed line indicating the current position of the margin.

**FIGURE 7-11**

In Page Layout view or Print Preview, you can use the vertical ruler to change top and bottom margins by dragging.

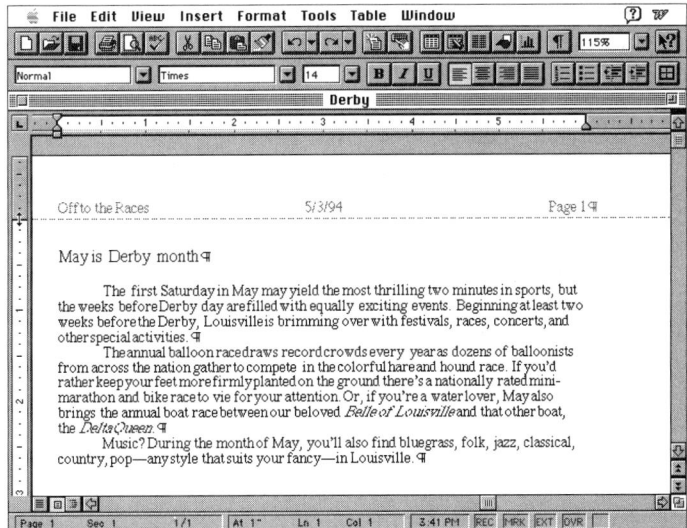

Again, if you prefer using the keyboard to change the margins, choose File Document Layout and then select the Margins card. Change the top and bottom margin settings in the appropriate text boxes. As with side margins, changing the settings through the dialog box is generally more accurate than dragging.

You can also use the vertical ruler to adjust the header and footer positions. For details on adjusting header and footer placement, see "Defining the Position of a Header or Footer" on page 558.

# Controlling Line and Page Breaks

The size of the text area usually determines how long individual lines of text can be and how many lines can fit on a page. Sometimes you might want to override these settings, however, and make a line or a page end earlier.

## How to force line breaks

Word automatically breaks lines at the right margin; however, you can also force line breaks. You can, of course, press the Return key to start a new paragraph. However, you will sometimes want to start a new line without starting a new paragraph. To start a new line without starting a new paragraph, press Shift-Return. Word will mark the line break on your screen with a ↵ symbol. The new line will still be a part of the same paragraph as the line preceding it and will be treated that way for all formatting purposes.

## Page breaks and repagination

Word also automatically calculates where page breaks will fall. If you like, you can have Word calculate page breaks only when you tell it to, by clearing the Background Repagination check box on the Tools Options General card. Doing so may increase your computer's speed slightly when you work in Normal or Outline view. Word will automatically repaginate when you print or when you're working in Page Layout view or Print Preview.

On the status bar, Word displays the page number of the cursor's current location. This page number will be accurate if you've selected the Background Repagination option. If Background Repagination is off, however, you shouldn't trust the page number on the status bar except when you're in Page Layout view or Print Preview.

### Manual page breaks

Sometimes you'll want to force a page break at a particular position in your document. You might, for example, want to ensure that some material stays together on the same page. To insert a page break, move the cursor to the spot where you want the new page to begin, and press Shift-Return. Alternatively, choose Insert Break, select Page Break, and choose OK. Either technique will insert a manual page-break marker at the cursor position.

NEW!     Notice that the dots in the horizontal line marking a manual page break are closer together than those in a line marking an automatic page break. (The former may even appear as a solid line, depending on your screen.) And, in case that's too subtle a distinction for you, the manual break is marked in the middle with the label Page Break. Figure 7-12 compares the automatic and manual page-break markers.

The dots in a manual page-break marker are more closely spaced than those in an automatic page-break marker. The manual break is also clearly labeled Page Break.

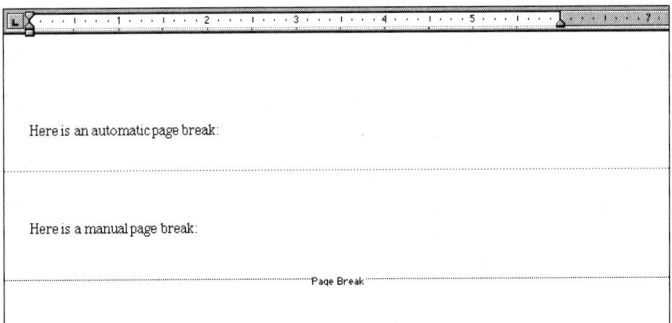

Here is an automatic page break:

Here is a manual page break:

Page Break

Keep in mind that automatic page-break markers will change position each time you repaginate your document. Manual page breaks, however, will stay at the location where you inserted them. Because of this, we suggest you use manual page breaks sparingly. Otherwise, if you reformat or change your document in any way, the manual page breaks could cause unwanted gaps and awkward breaks on your printed page. Note that a manual page break is a single character to Word, and you can delete it just like any other character.

If you want to force a new page so that a certain paragraph is always at the top of a page, you may want to assign the Page Break Before formatting option to that paragraph rather than insert a manual page break. We'll discuss that possibility later in this chapter, when we discuss the Paragraph dialog box.

## Other factors that affect page breaks

Other factors affect where a page will end. Widows and orphans—that is, single lines that get stranded at the top or bottom of a page—are one such factor; Word has a way to prevent these automatically, as we will discuss shortly. Headers and footers can also affect page breaks. In addition to the simple headers and footers discussed in Chapter 5, you can create multiline headers or footers that can have an even greater effect. Multisection documents and footnotes are also factors in where pages break. We'll discuss these topics in later chapters.

# Paragraph Formatting

After you establish a document's page layout, you're in a better position to format individual paragraphs. Word's paragraph formatting options cover a lot of territory, including indentions, alignment, line spacing, and before-and-after spacing. In many documents, your paragraphs may all conform to one or two formats, so you won't need to format many individual paragraphs. In other documents, however, you may need a variety of paragraph formats.

Word's paragraph formatting commands always apply to whole paragraphs. To indicate which paragraph you want to format, place the cursor anywhere in that paragraph or select any or all of its text. If you want to format two or more paragraphs at once, first you must extend the selection to include some text in each of those paragraphs.

In this section, we'll cover direct paragraph formatting only. As we mentioned earlier, Word also provides formatting by styles, which we'll cover in Chapter 12. Styles are a powerful formatting tool, particularly for complex documents. We firmly recommend that you learn to format by styles, and the present discussion is important as a foundation for moving on to styles.

Word also has a feature called AutoFormat, which you'll find on the Format menu. AutoFormat analyzes your document and automatically applies paragraph and font formatting. This is a useful tool, but since it relies on predefined styles for the actual paragraph and font settings that it applies, we'll postpone our discussion of AutoFormat to Chapter 12.

## The defaults

Word's default settings for a paragraph are flush left and single spaced (based on the tallest character), with no first-line, left, or right indent. Flush left refers to how the text is aligned—with an even left margin and a ragged right margin. Single spacing refers to the amount of *leading* (pronounced "ledding") between lines of text. Word automatically adds 2 points of space (approximately $1/36$ inch) between lines to create buffers between the ascenders and descenders of characters on adjacent lines. You can increase or decrease this line spacing as needed.

The default indent settings of no left, right, or first-line indent mean that all text is aligned within the text area established by your page margins. However, you can increase or decrease the width of one or more paragraphs as needed. For example, if you want to set a quotation off from the rest of your text, you first put it in its own paragraph and then adjust the left and right indent markers to narrow that paragraph. You can also format a paragraph to indent its first line automatically, and then you won't need to press the Tab key at the beginning of each paragraph.

 A note of warning: You may be tempted to change your margin settings by moving the indent markers on the horizontal ruler. We strongly urge you to resist this temptation. As we've pointed out earlier, if you later make any changes to your page size, margins, or print orientation, Word will move the indent markers on the ruler to reflect the new settings, thereby scrambling the "margins" you set with the indent markers.

## How to apply paragraph formats with the mouse

There are a wealth of options for formatting paragraphs. You can use the mouse or the keyboard. The Formatting toolbar and the horizontal ruler are especially handy if you use the mouse. Figure 7-13 shows the Standard and Formatting toolbars and the horizontal ruler.

**FIGURE 7-13**

You can use the Standard and Formatting toolbars and the horizontal ruler to format your paragraphs.

The Formatting toolbar contains pull-down lists for styles, fonts, and font sizes. We'll cover styles in Chapter 12 and the two font list boxes later in this chapter. The first three buttons to the right of the pull-down lists are for font formatting, which we'll cover toward the end of this chapter. The next set of four buttons relates to paragraph alignment.

Keep in mind that all of the techniques described in the following discussion change only the current paragraph or paragraphs—that is, the paragraph containing the cursor, or all paragraphs in which some text is selected. To change all paragraphs in a document, you need to select the entire document first.

## Alignment

The Formatting toolbar's four paragraph alignment buttons are labeled with thumbnail sketches of what they do, as shown in this table:

| Button | Alignment | Button | Alignment |
|--------|-----------|--------|-----------|
|        | Left      |        | Right     |
|        | Centered  |        | Justified |

To use these buttons, place the cursor or selection anywhere in the target paragraph and click on the button for the format you want to apply. Notice that you can tell the alignment of any paragraph from these toolbar buttons; when the cursor is in the paragraph, the appropriate alignment button will appear depressed. In Figure 7-14, and Figure 7-15 on the next page, for example, you can see that the left alignment button is depressed.

**FIGURE 7-14**

The second paragraph in this sample document is a quotation.

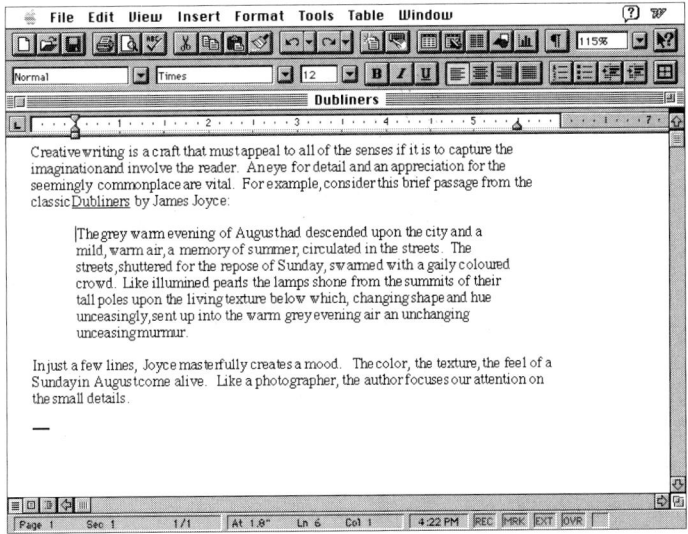

**FIGURE 7-15**

To indent the left and right edges of a paragraph, move the indent markers on the ruler.

## Indents

As we discussed earlier, document margins are controlled by the margin settings in the Document Layout dialog box or by the margin markers on the ruler in Page Layout view or Print Preview. By default, Word will align the first-line and left indent markers with the left margin and the right indent marker with the right margin. (See Figure 7-13.) You can move these markers to change the width of the text in one or more paragraphs.

## How to change indents with the mouse and the ruler

To change the width of a paragraph with the mouse, first make sure that the cursor or current selection is somewhere in the paragraph or paragraphs you want to change. Then drag the left or right indent marker as appropriate.

For example, the second paragraph in Figure 7-14 is a quotation from James Joyce's *Dubliners*. To set it off by indenting, first move the cursor to the paragraph or select any portion of it. Then move the mouse pointer to the rectangle below the left indent marker (the bottom of the two indent markers on the left side of the horizontal ruler), hold down the mouse button, and drag the marker to the 0.5-inch position. (Dragging the rectangle will move both the top and bottom markers at the same time.) To indent the right edge of the paragraph, drag the right indent marker to the 5.5-inch position. Figure 7-15 shows the result.

The left indent marker is split into two triangles. The top triangle controls the indent for just the first line of a paragraph, and the bottom triangle indents all subsequent lines in the paragraph. You can use this feature to indent the first line of a paragraph or to create a hanging indent, in which the first line extends to the left of the rest of the paragraph. Note that when you drag the rectangle below the bottom triangle, as in our example, the top triangle moves with it. But if you drag either the top or bottom triangle by itself, the other will not move.

## How to change indents with the Formatting toolbar

You can also move the left indent to the next tab setting by clicking on the Increase Indent and Decrease Indent buttons on the Formatting toolbar:

| Button | Action |
|---|---|
| | Increase Indent |
| | Decrease Indent |

By default, these are the second and third buttons from the right on the Formatting toolbar. Each click on the Increase Indent button will move the left indent one tab stop to the right. (Tab stops are 0.5 inches apart in Word's default settings.) Each click on the Decrease Indent button will move the left indent one tab stop to the left. Note that you cannot use the Decrease Indent button to move the left indent beyond the left margin.

## How to set tabs with the mouse

Although Word has a sophisticated table feature (which we will cover in Chapter 11), you can also create columns of tabular information simply by using tab stops. As with a typewriter, you set the places where the cursor will stop when you press the Tab key. Unlike a typewriter, Word offers four different kinds of tab settings, allowing you to easily align numbers, names, or other data in columns.

These tab stops are controlled by the button at the left end of the horizontal ruler. The shape of the icon indicates which kind of tab will be inserted when you click on the ruler.

| Button | Tab Alignment | Button | Tab Alignment |
|--------|---------------|--------|---------------|
| ⌞L⌟ | Left | ⌐⌐ | Right |
| ⊥ | Centered | ⊥ | Decimal |

A left-aligned tab aligns the left edge of text with the tab stop. A right-aligned tab aligns the right edge of text with the tab stop. Centered tabs center text on the tab stop. Decimal tabs—usually the best choice for a column of numbers—align numbers on the decimal point (or after the last digit if there is no decimal).

To set a tab stop with the mouse, start by clicking on the Tab button at the left side of the ruler until it displays the type of tab you want. If you need to enter a column of numbers, for example, click until you see the decimal tab icon. Then click on the ruler at the position where you want the tab stop. To change the position, you can drag the tab stop to a new position. To delete a tab, simply drag it down and off the ruler.

## How to apply paragraph formats with the keyboard

There are keyboard shortcuts for some, but not all, of the mouse techniques we have just described. There are also some keyboard shortcuts for paragraph formatting features that aren't readily accessible with the mouse.

### Paragraph formatting shortcut keys

Word offers a number of shortcut keys for paragraph formatting. Several are mnemonic (⌘-L for left-aligned and ⌘-R for right-aligned, for example), making them easy to remember. Figure 7-16 lists these shortcuts.

| This Key Combination... | Moves... |
|-------------------------|----------|
| ⌘-M | Left indent and first-line indent one tab stop to the right |
| ⌘-Shift-M | Left indent and first-line indent one tab stop to the left |
| ⌘-T | Left indent but not first-line indent one tab stop to the right (hanging paragraph) |
| ⌘-Shift-T | Left indent but not first-line indent one tab stop to the left |

*(continued)*

**FIGURE 7-16**

Shortcut keys for paragraph formatting.

**FIGURE 7-16** *continued*

| This Key Combination... | Sets Paragraph To... |
| --- | --- |
| ⌘-L | Left alignment |
| ⌘-E | Centered alignment |
| ⌘-R | Right alignment |
| ⌘-J | Justified alignment |
| ⌘-1 | Single spacing |
| ⌘-5 | 1½ spacing |
| ⌘-2 | Double spacing |
| ⌘-0 (digit 0) | Adds or deletes a line of space before the paragraph |

## Left indent shortcut keys

The left indent shortcuts work similarly to the Formatting toolbar's Increase Indent and Decrease Indent buttons. ⌘-M moves the left indent and the first-line indent one tab stop to the right; ⌘-Shift-M moves them both one tab stop to the left. (By default, Word sets tab stops every ½ inch along the ruler.) As with the equivalent toolbar button, you cannot use ⌘-Shift-M to move the indent marker beyond the left margin. Note that you can also move the left indent without moving the first-line indent. ⌘-T moves the left indent to the right; ⌘-Shift-T moves it to the left.

## Paragraph alignment shortcut keys

Using the shortcut keys for paragraph alignment is equivalent to clicking on the Formatting toolbar paragraph alignment buttons. ⌘-L formats to left alignment, ⌘-R to right alignment, ⌘-J to justified alignment, and ⌘-E to centered alignment.

Three of these four shortcut keys are easily remembered mnemonics. It may help you to think of ⌘-E as Entered Centered. Alternatively, if you're willing to give up ⌘-C for copying text to the Clipboard, you could redefine ⌘-C for centering, using the techniques we'll describe in Chapter 28.

## Line-spacing shortcut keys

By default, Word automatically adds 2 points of leading (spacing) between lines of text. This results in single spacing based on the tallest character in the line. More precisely, for point sizes typically used in body text (10-12 points), Word allows 2 points of space between the tallest ascender on one line and the lowest descender on the line immediately above. For example, if you're using 10-point Times type, Word will allow 12 points from the bottom of one line to the bottom of the next line, creating 2 points of separator space between lines.

In addition to single-spaced lines, you can easily create double-spaced and 1½-spaced lines. The first format is standard for manuscript pages because it gives you extra room on the printed page for writing notes and corrections. The second is often useful for making a long report easier to read. With double spacing, Word will insert a full line of blank space above each line of text. For 10-point Times type, this means 12 points of leading. With 1½-spaced lines, Word will insert one half-line of blank space above each line of text, or about 6 points of leading. Figure 7-17 shows examples of single spacing, 1½ spacing, and double spacing.

**FIGURE 7-17**

You can set single spacing, 1½ spacing, or double spacing with keyboard shortcuts.

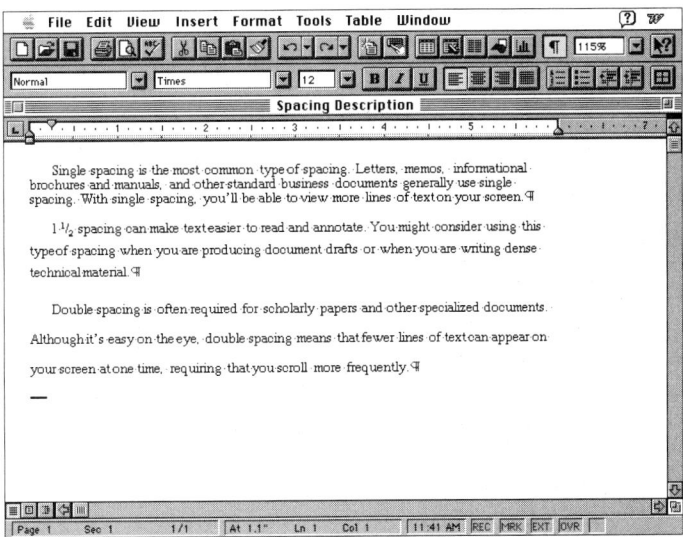

Word's shortcut keys for spacing are ⌘-1 for single spacing, ⌘-2 for double spacing, and ⌘-5 for 1½ spacing.

You can use the Paragraph dialog box to control the line spacing more precisely, and with many more options. You can create line spacing that's larger than double spacing or smaller than single spacing. We'll discuss this later in this chapter.

## Paragraph-spacing shortcut keys

Paragraph spacing is similar to line spacing except that the spacing applies only to the space above the top line of the paragraph, as shown in Figure 7-18 on the next page. There are two settings available with keyboard shortcuts:

⌘-0 (the digit 0) toggles between one extra line of space before the paragraph and no extra space.

Use paragraph spacing to create extra space between paragraphs. The top two paragraphs do not have extra spacing; the bottom one does.

If you set paragraph spacing with the Paragraph dialog box (which we'll discuss shortly), you can insert space before or after the paragraph and specify precisely how much space to insert.

## About paragraph spacing

If you generally use single spacing and you separate paragraphs by a blank line, you're probably used to creating the blank line manually by pressing the Return key twice at the end of each paragraph. This technique is inferior in at least one important way to using the Before or After setting in the Spacing group.

These settings make it easier to reformat if you decide to change the amount of space between paragraphs. With Before or After, you need only select the paragraphs and then change the Before or After setting. This one change will reformat all of the selected paragraphs at once. (You can also use style sheets to make this type of wholesale formatting change even easier, as we'll discuss in Chapter 12.)

# The Paragraph dialog box: Indents And Spacing

To exercise full control over your paragraph formats, you need to use the Format Paragraph command. Format Paragraph opens a dialog box with two cards: Indents And Spacing and Text Flow. Figure 7-19 shows the Indents And Spacing card.

**FIGURE 7-19**

The Paragraph dialog box controls the formatting of the current paragraph.

Both cards share a Preview area with a thumbnail sample of your text. The paragraph marked in bold in the sample will reflect any changes you make to the settings in this dialog box. Both cards also share a Tabs button that opens the Tabs dialog box, which we will explore later.

 You can open the Paragraph dialog box by choosing the Format Paragraph command or by popping up a context-sensitive menu. To use the context-sensitive menu, place the cursor or selection in the paragraph or paragraphs you want to format and then press Shift-F10, or move the mouse pointer anywhere within the paragraph or selection and hold the Control key as you click the mouse button. Choose Paragraph to open the same Paragraph dialog box as with the Format Paragraph command.

## Indentation

The first two Indentation text boxes define the paragraphs's indention from the left and right margins. The default measurement is inches, but you can use any other unit of measure that Word recognizes. These are the same indentions you can set with the Increase Indent and Decrease Indent toolbar buttons and the equivalent keyboard shortcuts. With the Paragraph dialog box, however, you can specify indents more precisely.

**NEW!**

You can specify a measurement by typing it in the appropriate text box or by clicking on the arrows at the right side of each box. Note that you can create a negative indent—to start the lines in the margins—by specifying a negative (minus) number in either box.

You use the Special pull-down list to define a first-line indent or a hanging indent. These settings affect the starting position of the paragraph's first line relative to the remaining lines. If you choose First Line, the first line of the paragraph will be indented by the amount displayed in the By text box. If you choose Hanging, the first line will start at the point indicated by the Left indentation setting, and the remaining lines will be indented farther to the right by the amount shown in the By text box.

## Spacing

You use the Spacing options to specify the amount of space between paragraphs and between the lines within paragraphs.

The Before and After text boxes control the amount of spacing between paragraphs. The default is no extra space, but you can specify any amount from 0 through 1584 points. The default unit of measure is points, but you can use any other unit Word recognizes, provided that you add the correct abbreviation for the units: *cm* for centimeters, *in* or ″ for inches, *li* for lines, *pi* for picas, and *pt* for points.

**NEW!**

The Line Spacing pull-down list has a number of predefined settings. Single, Double, and 1.5 Lines match the settings for the keyboard shortcuts we discussed earlier. The Multiple setting, last on the list, lets you define any line spacing by entering a number in the At text box (default is 3 lines). If you choose At Least, Word adjusts the spacing as required for different fonts but lets you specify a minimum spacing in the At text box. (Note that single, 1.5, double, and multiple line spacing are treated as At Least settings.) If you prefer, you can specify a precise spacing by selecting Exactly and entering a value in the At text box—but keep in mind that this will prevent Word from making any automatic adjustments should you change text size.

As with the Before and After text boxes, you can specify any unit of measurement that Word recognizes, as long as you use the correct abbreviation for the units. You cannot specify a negative value.

## Alignment

The Alignment pull-down list in the lower right corner offers the same four options as the toolbar buttons and the equivalent shortcut keys: left aligned, center aligned, right aligned, and justified.

# The Paragraph dialog box: Text Flow

The Text Flow card in the Paragraph dialog box, shown in Figure 7-20, controls where Word will break text to start a new line or a new page.

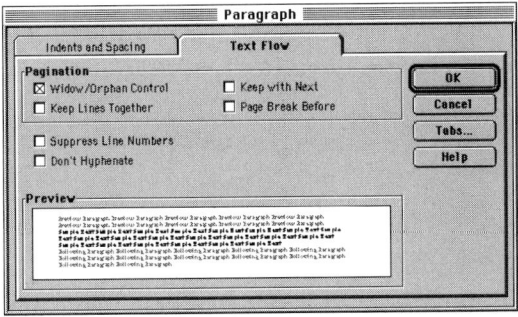

## Pagination

The Pagination box has four check boxes that help Word determine where to place automatic page breaks.

**Widow/Orphan Control.** Although it is none-too-progressive jargon, the term *widow* refers to those straggling single lines of text that sometimes appear at the top of a page, separated from the rest of their paragraph. The first line of a paragraph left alone at the bottom of a page is called an *orphan*.

In general, you should keep at least two lines of a paragraph on a given page. If there isn't room for two lines, you should push the entire paragraph to the beginning of the next page. And if there is room at the bottom of a page for all but one line of a paragraph, you should push an extra line to the top of the second page.

When checked, the Widow/Orphan Control check box on the Text Flow card ensures that no single line of text from a paragraph will stand alone on a page, unless it is a single-line paragraph. If you use this option, Word will adjust your page breaks so that at least two lines of a paragraph always appear on a page. In some cases, this means that Word will print fewer than the maximum number of lines on a page, making your bottom margin slightly larger.

**Keep Lines Together.** This option tells Word not to allow a page break within a paragraph. Use it when you want to keep an entire paragraph together. For example, if you've formatted tabular columns with forced line breaks so that the entire table is one paragraph, checking the Keep Lines Together check box will ensure that the table will be printed on a single page.

**Keep With Next.** This option tells Word not to break a page between the current paragraph and the next one so that at least a portion of each will appear on the same page. This is useful for section headings, to make sure that the heading will not be printed at the bottom of a page separately from the next paragraph.

**Page Break Before.** This option tells Word to place the current paragraph at the top of a new page, no matter how much empty space that would leave on the preceding page. You might want to use this option for a paragraph (such as a chapter title or other heading) that marks the beginning of a new topic or section.

### Suppress Line Numbers

We will discuss line numbering in Chapter 13. For now, simply be aware that if you have Word set to add line numbers to a document, you can turn this feature off for any paragraph or paragraphs by checking the Suppress Line Numbers check box.

### Don't Hyphenate

Checking the Don't Hyphenate check box tells Word not to apply hyphenation to the current paragraph when Word is set to hyphenate the document automatically. We discussed hyphenation in "Hyphenation" on page 184.

## Tabs

To open the Tabs dialog box, shown in Figure 7-21, choose the Tabs button on either card in the Paragraph dialog box. When the Paragraph dialog box is not open, you can open the Tabs dialog box by choosing Format Tabs.

**FIGURE 7-21**

You can use the Tabs dialog box to add, delete, and modify tab settings for a paragraph.

Figure 7-21 shows the default Word settings for the Tabs dialog box. In the Default Tab Stops text box, at the top center, you can specify a set of evenly spaced tabs for the paragraph. By default, this is set to 0.5".

As you define custom tab settings for a paragraph, they appear in the Tab Stop Position list box at the left of the dialog box, as shown in Figure 7-22 on the next page. You can also see the tabs on the ruler in the background. Note that when you create custom tab stops, you clear all of the default tab stops to the left of those you create.

**FIGURE 7-22**

Word lists custom tab stops in the Tab Stop Position list box by their location on the horizontal ruler, measured in inches.

The Alignment and Leader areas show the definition for the tab stop position currently displayed in the Tab Stop Position text box. The ruler shows the specifications for all tab stops set for the current paragraph. In Figure 7-22, for example, the marker on the ruler indicates that the tab stop at 4 inches is decimal aligned.

The first four options in the Alignment area are the same as those controlled by the four tab-stop markers on the ruler. The fifth option, Bar, is not a tab in the usual sense. A bar tab by itself doesn't function as a tab stop; you can't tab to it, and inserting it doesn't clear any of the default tab stops to its left. Instead, the bar tab creates a solid vertical line that runs through the text of a paragraph at that position.

The bar tab can be quite helpful if you are building a table by using tabs, rather than Word's table feature, and you want to separate the columns with vertical lines. Build the table by using left, right, centered, and decimal tabs, as appropriate. Then insert the bar tabs between columns. The result will look similar to Figure 7-23.

**FIGURE 7-23**

The bar tab adds vertical lines to tables you build with tabs.

Sales by Region for the Past Four Months

| Region | Aug | Sept | Oct | Nov |
|--------|-----|------|-----|-----|
| East | 123 | 273 | 251 | 342 |
| Central | 432 | 325 | 234 | 435 |
| West | 341 | 287 | 246 | 141 |

A leader on a tab is a pattern of characters—usually alternating periods and spaces—that fills the space between the points where the tab begins and ends. The default is to have no leader, but a leader can help make lists of names or numbers easier to read. Figure 7-24 on the next page shows a table of contents that uses a leader between chapter titles and the starting page numbers.

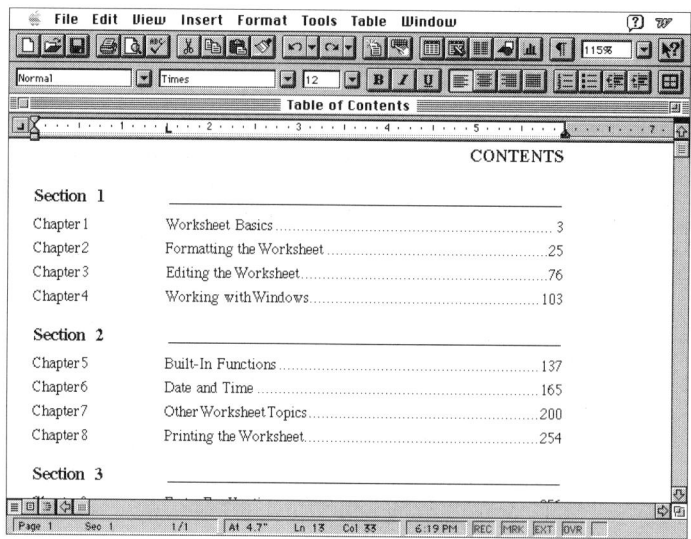

**FIGURE 7-24**

A tab leader can make it easier to read formatted lists, such as this table of contents.

You can add a new tab stop by typing a value in the Tab Stop Position text box, setting the Alignment and Leader options, and choosing the Set button or OK. You can also modify the alignment and leader settings for any tab stop by selecting the tab in the Tab Stop Position list box, changing the options in the Alignment and Leader boxes, and then choosing Set or OK. In both cases, if you choose Set, Word will leave the dialog box open. If you choose OK, Word will close the dialog box.

To delete a tab stop, select it in the Tab Stop Position box, and then choose the Clear button. If necessary, you can delete all tab stops at once by choosing the Clear All button. In either case, Word will delete the tab stops from the list box but will not throw them away completely. Instead, it will either maintain a list of each tab stop to clear, titled Tab Stops To Be Cleared, or display the notation All at the bottom of the Tabs dialog box. If you decide you don't want to clear those tabs after all, choose Cancel, and Word will close the dialog box without deleting the tab stops. To close the dialog box and accept the changes you've made, choose OK.

## Paragraph borders and shading

You can make individual paragraphs or groups of paragraphs stand out from the rest of your text by adding a border like the one shown in Figure 7-25 on the next page. You can add borders with the Border toolbar or with the Paragraph Borders And Shading dialog box, which you open by choosing Format Borders And Shading.

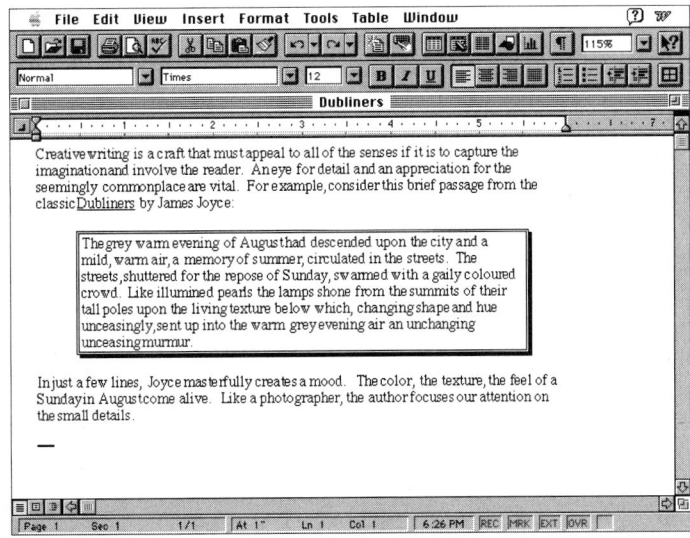

**FIGURE 7-25**

You can use borders, like the shaded border here, to make individual paragraphs stand out from surrounding text.

Before you can format a border, you must first decide whether you want the border to go around a single paragraph or several. If you extend a selection to include more than one paragraph before opening the dialog box or using the Borders toolbar, any border you define will include all of the paragraphs with text selected. If all paragraphs in the selection have the same indent settings, Word will enclose them in a single border. If the indents vary, however, Word will start a separate border outline each time an indent changes.

If a page break occurs between two paragraphs enclosed by a single border, Word will automatically add a bottom line to the border on the first page and a top line to the border on the second. If the page break falls in the middle of a paragraph, Word will break the border, so it will be missing a bottom line on the first page and a top line on the second. If you edit the text so that the page break changes, Word will continue to adjust the borders, following this same rule.

You can control whether Word will create full borders on both pages when a page break falls within a bordered area. If you want the border to break, delete any paragraph returns within the text surrounded by the border. To create text that looks like multiple paragraphs but is actually one long paragraph, use Shift-Return when you want to force a new line. If you want a complete border on each page, you can either make each line its own paragraph— which will work well for lists or tables created with tabs—or you can format the paragraphs with the Keep Lines Together option on the Text Flow card in the Paragraph dialog box.

## How to add a border using a dialog box

To add a border, place the cursor in the paragraph you want to add it to, or make a selection that extends from the first to the last paragraph you want to surround. Then choose the Format Borders And Shading command to open the Paragraph Borders And Shading dialog box. The dialog box has two cards, Borders and Shading. The Borders card is shown in Figure 7-26.

**FIGURE 7-26**

You can use the Borders card to add borders to one or more paragraphs.

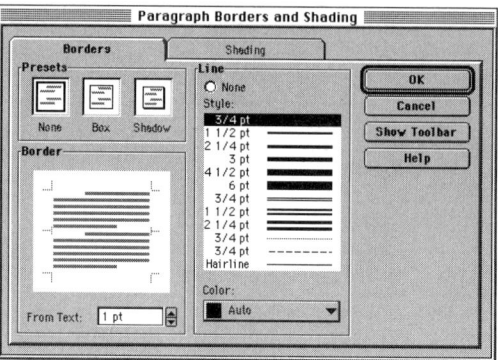

The Presets box displays the three options for borders: None, Box, and Shadow. (The Shadow option provides a slight 3-D effect.) These make it easy to quickly create a standard border. But you can also create your own settings if you prefer.

The thumbnail sketch in the Border box shows what your border will look like. The From Text box controls how far (in points) the border will be from the text in the paragraph or paragraphs.

Word requires a single From Text entry for all four sides of a border. If you need uneven spacing between the border and the text, you can adjust spacing manually. First set the From Text entry to match the setting you want for the right side of the text. Next, to adjust the top or bottom spacing, press Return to add a blank line in its own paragraph above or below the text, and adjust the height of the line by putting the cursor in that paragraph and choosing Format Paragraph. Set the line spacing option to Exactly, and enter the appropriate height in the At text box. To adjust the spacing at the left side of the text, choose Format Paragraph and format the text with the Hanging option in the Special box, using the By text box to adjust the space. Then add a tab in front of the first line to indent the first line by the same amount as the rest of the paragraph. We covered each of these settings in "The Paragraph dialog box: Indents And Spacing" on page 213.

Note that when you increase the setting in the From Text box, the size of the text area will shrink within the Border box. This can give you the wrong impression of how your page will look. In fact, the text for the paragraph or paragraphs stays constant, while the border around the text gets larger. The thumbnail sketch shows you the increase in space between text and border, not the increase in the border size.

The Line box displays the different line types you can select—thin lines, **NEW!** thick lines, single or double. You can also specify a dotted or dashed line. The Line box contains a Color pull-down list that you can use to apply a color to the border. (The shadow in a shadowed border is always black regardless of the color of the lines.)

If you don't want to use any of the predefined choices in the Presets box, you can create custom borders in the Border box. Guidelines at the corners of the thumbnail sketch indicate the allowable positions for border lines, and triangle-shaped handles indicate which border lines are active at any given moment. You can use the mouse to click on the guidelines and toggle the handles on or off, or you can press ⌘-R and then any of the arrow keys to cycle through different sets of lines. A line is active when the black triangles appear at the two ends of its handles; you can redefine all active lines at once by choosing a different style, color, or both in the Style and Color list boxes. By setting different lines as active, you can define any border you like. You can, for example, create a border with a single line at the top and bottom and a double line down the left and right side, using blue for the top and left and green for the bottom and right. Simply turn the individual lines on and off, and define the format for each separately.

Note, too, that there is an allowable line in the middle of the Border box that is not active in the default setting. You can activate this with the mouse or the keyboard. If you define a line for this position, it will surround each paragraph in a selection with its own border, rather than including all of the selected paragraphs within a single border.

## How to format a paragraph with shading

You can add any of various patterns and colors of shading to selected paragraphs with the Shading card, shown in Figure 7-27 on the next page. The Preview box shows the effect of the settings as you select them. By default, Word selects the None button, meaning no shading. To add shading, choose the Custom button, and then define the shading you want before choosing OK to apply it.

FIGURE 7-27

Use the Shading card
to add a shaded pattern
to a paragraph.

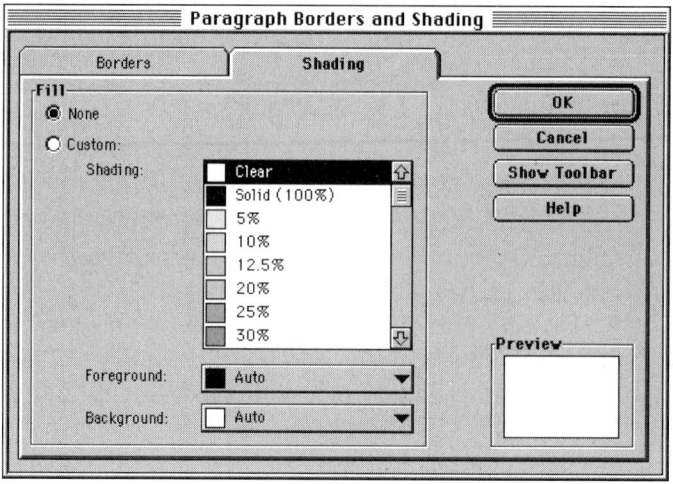

Start by choosing a pattern from the Shading list. The top of the list,
shown in Figure 7-27, is organized by percent of foreground color. The bottom
of the list, shown in Figure 7-28, contains dark and light patterns of lines.
Then choose a color for the pattern and its background from the Foreground
and Background pull-down lists.

FIGURE 7-28

The Shading list offers
various shading and
crosshatched patterns
to choose from.

Make test printouts of the different shading patterns and colors so
that you know what your printer's output will look like. Even with
a monochrome printer, your color choices can produce different
effects depending on your printer.

### How to add a border and shading with the Borders toolbar

Both cards in the Paragraph Borders And Shading dialog box have a Show Toolbar button. If you choose this, or the Borders button on the Formatting toolbar, Word will display the Borders toolbar, shown in Figure 7-29.

**FIGURE 7-29**

The Borders toolbar gives you quick access to most of the borders and shading options.

The Borders toolbar provides easy access to a subset of the features available on the Borders and Shading cards. The left pull-down box contains line style options for the border. The buttons in the middle of the toolbar let you designate which edges you want the line to apply to: top, bottom, left, right, inside, outside, and none. The right pull-down box contains shading pattern options. You cannot change line or shading colors from this toolbar; for that, you must choose the Format Borders And Shading command.

# Font Formatting

The fourth level of direct formatting is font formatting. Font formatting defines how text characters will look: the font you want to use; the size of the font; any special emphasis such as boldface, italics, and underlining; the position of the characters relative to each other; and the amount of space between characters. In the following section, we'll show you how to control these factors.

You can apply font formats as you type your text or afterward. If you've already entered the text, you will need to select the text before you apply formats to it. The text selection can be as small as a single character or as large as your entire document. Word will format only the text that you've highlighted.

If you prefer, you can format text as you create it. When you type new text in a Word document, it takes on the formatting characteristics of the text immediately preceding it. For example, if you move the cursor to the middle of a line formatted in 18-point boldface type, any new characters you type will also appear in 18-point bold. If you want to change formats in midstream, you can choose new formatting options without selecting any text; Word will apply those new formats to any text you type from that point forward. As you continue to type, the formatting characteristics will stay the same unless you apply new formats or move the cursor to another part of your document.

As with paragraph formats, you can change font formats with the mouse or the keyboard, and there are shortcuts for each. We'll start, as before, with the mouse shortcuts.

## How to apply font formats with the mouse

You can use the mouse to apply the font formats available on the Formatting toolbar. The choices you are likely to use most often are these three buttons:

| Button | Format |
| --- | --- |
| **B** | Boldface |
| *I* | Italic |
| U | Underline |

To change existing text, select the text and click on the button you want. To apply formatting to new text, position the cursor and then click on the button; any new characters you type will use the chosen format. You can apply more than one format to the same text; for example, you can apply both boldface and underline formats simply by clicking on both buttons.

When text containing one or more of these formats is highlighted, the corresponding button will appear as if it were pressed. You can then remove the format by clicking on the button. Similarly, as you type text, you can toggle formatting on and off at the cursor position.

To the left of these three buttons are three drop-down lists. The leftmost is the Style list, which we will cover in Chapter 12. The next two lists are the Font and Font Size lists.

### An aside: What's a font?

At one time, the term *font* referred to all characters of a given typeface in a given size—a definition from the days of movable type and printing presses, when each font was stored in a separate drawer. With the advent of personal computers, laser printers, and software that offers sophisticated formatting, the definition of this term has become fuzzy. In Word's context, a font is a family of type styles, including different sizes as well as medium, boldface, and italic versions of a given typeface.

In *monospaced* fonts, each letter is assigned the same amount of space on a line. Courier, for example, which has long been one of the most widely used fonts for typewriters, is a monospaced font. *Proportionally spaced* fonts, or simply *proportional* fonts, assign different amounts of space to different characters. These fonts give more space to a capital *M* than to a lowercase *i*, for example. You'll find them in most books, magazines, and newspapers.

Many fonts, such as the popular Times font, have little tails on the strokes of their letters. These tails are called *serifs*, and fonts that have them are called *serif fonts*. American readers tend to prefer serif fonts for the main text of documents. Fonts without the tails, such as Helvetica, are called *sans serif fonts*; these are better suited for headlines and tables. Figure 7-30 shows a sample of Times and a sample of Helvetica.

**FIGURE 7-30**

The serif font Times is popular for body text. The sans serif font Helvetica is well suited for headlines and tables.

## How to select a font and a font size with the mouse and the Formatting toolbar

You can use the mouse and the Formatting toolbar to change fonts and font size. To change the font, just select the text whose font you want to change, or position the cursor where you want to begin typing a new font. Then open the Formatting toolbar's Font list box, as shown in Figure 7-31, and choose the font you want to use. Note that the Macintosh and Word may not be able to display the characters on screen precisely as they will look when printed; see "Understanding Screen Fonts and Printer Fonts" page 553.

**FIGURE 7-31**

The Formatting toolbar's Font drop-down list lists the fonts available.

The Font Size drop-down list works similarly; select some text or reposition the cursor, and then open the list and choose the font size you want (in points).

If you want text the same size as Pica type from a typewriter (six lines per inch), you should select a 10-point font. (Note that font size defines the height—but not necessarily the width—of characters.)

If you format your paragraphs with a Line Spacing of anything but Exactly, Word will automatically adjust the line spacing to match larger or smaller font sizes.

## How to apply font formats with shortcut keys

Shortcut keys can duplicate all the formatting features of the Formatting toolbar and more. Many users will find shortcut keys the quickest method of formatting text. Figure 7-32 lists the shortcut keys for font formatting.

### Toggle shortcuts

The first set of commands in the table in Figure 7-32 are toggles. You press the keystroke combination once to apply the format and then press the keys a second time to remove it. For example, if you highlight some text and press ⌘-B once, the text will be boldface. Press ⌘-B again, and the boldface format will be removed.

| This Key Combination... | Toggles This Font Format... |
| --- | --- |
| ⌘-B | Boldface |
| ⌘-I | Italic |
| ⌘-Shift-D | Double underline |
| ⌘-U | Single underline (words and spaces) |
| ⌘-Shift-W | Single underline (words only) |
| ⌘-Shift-A | All capital letters |
| ⌘-Shift-K | Small capital letters |
| Shift-F3 or ⌘-Option-C | Cycle the case of letters |
| ⌘-= | Subscript (down 3 points) |
| ⌘-Shift-= | Superscript (up 3 points) |
| ⌘-Shift-H | Hidden text |
| ⌘-8 (not NumPad) | Display nonprinting characters |

**FIGURE 7-32**

*(continued)*

Shortcut keys for font formatting.

**FIGURE 7-32** *continued*

| This Key Combination... | Applies This Font Format Feature... |
|---|---|
| ⌘-Shift-F | Formatting toolbar Font list |
| ⌘-Shift-P | Formatting toolbar Font Size (Points) list |
| ⌘-Shift-> | Grow font (increase to next available size on the Formatting toolbar Font Size list) |
| ⌘-Shift-< | Shrink font (decrease to next available size on the Formatting toolbar Font Size list) |
| ⌘-] | Increase font size by 1 point |
| ⌘-[ | Shrink font size by 1 point |
| ⌘-Spacebar or ⌘-Shift-Z | Remove all direct font formatting |
| ⌘-Shift-Q | Use Symbol font |

Most of the toggle commands are self-explanatory; the underline options, however, deserve explanation. ⌘-Shift-D puts a double underline under all characters in the selected text. ⌘-U does the same, except that it uses a single underline. ⌘-Shift-W does something a little bit different; it uses a single underline, but only under the printable characters in the selection—not under the spaces.

Note, too, that Shift-F3 (Change Case) is not a toggle, because it cycles through three states instead of two. Shift-F3 will change the case of the selected text each time you press it: for example, from all lowercase, to initial capitals, to all capitals, and then back to all lowercase again.

Shift-F3 will work differently depending on the text you've highlighted. **NEW!** If the text includes periods or other punctuation to indicate that it contains full sentences, Word will try to find and capitalize the first letter of each sentence for the initial capitals part of the cycle. If there's no indication that the text consists of sentences, Word will capitalize the first letter of each word instead. If you don't have a keyboard with function keys, you can use the alternate ⌘-Option-C shortcut instead.

Two other shortcut keys need further explanation: ⌘-Shift-H (Hidden Text) and ⌘-8 (Nonprinting Characters). Word will not normally print text formatted as hidden, but you can set Word to print hidden text with the Tools Options Print card. Similarly, Word will not display hidden text unless you check the Hidden Text check box on the Tools Options View card or, alternatively, set Word to display all nonprinting characters; you can do the latter either by checking the All option on the View card, by clicking on the Show/Hide ¶ button on the Standard toolbar, or by pressing ⌘-8.

## How to change fonts and font sizes from the keyboard

The next six keyboard shortcuts in Figure 7-32, beginning with ⌘-Shift-F, cover fonts and font sizes. If you have the Formatting toolbar displayed, you can use ⌘-Shift-F to activate the Font list box and ⌘-Shift-P to activate the Font Size list box. Once the list boxes are activated, you can then choose a font or size, as appropriate, by using the Up and Down arrow keys and then pressing Return to complete the selection.

If the Formatting toolbar is not displayed, Word will open the Font dialog box when you press ⌘-Shift-F or ⌘-Shift-P. If the Formatting toolbar is displayed, Word will open the Font dialog box when you press ⌘-Shift-F or ⌘-Shift-P a second time—after the Font list box or Font Size list box is active. (We will look at the Font dialog box immediately after this discussion of the shortcut keys.)

Both ⌘-Shift-> (Grow Font) and ⌘-] (Increase Font By 1 Point) will increase the font size of the currently selected text, but they take different approaches to increasing font size. ⌘-Shift-> will increase the font to the next size, as specified in the Points list box, so if the list box shows point sizes of 10, 11, 12, 14, 16, 18, 20, 22, 24, 26, 28, 36, 48, 72, the Grow Font shortcut key will change font size using just those choices, changing in steps of 1, 2, 8, 12, or 24 points. On the other hand, ⌘-Shift-] (Increase Font By 1 Point) will change size by 1 point, in all cases, no matter what the current setting. The same considerations apply to the ⌘-Shift-< (Shrink Font) and ⌘-[ (Shrink Font By 1 Point) keys.

## How to remove direct font formatting

There may be times when you want all characters within a selection to revert to their default settings. Simply select the text and press ⌘-Spacebar or ⌘-Shift-Z.

## How to switch to Symbol font

The ⌘-Shift-Q shortcut key is simply a quick and easy way to switch to Symbol font so that you can type Greek letters, mathematical symbols, and other special symbols directly from the keyboard. Pressing ⌘-Shift-Q is equivalent to choosing Symbol from the Font list box, but only for the next character you type. After you type one character, Word will switch you back to the default format for the text.

# The Font dialog box

As with paragraph formatting, you can apply font formats by way of a dialog box. This approach can give you more precise control over some of the features. You can open the Font dialog box either by choosing Format Font or by pressing the shortcut key ⌘-D. The Font dialog box has two cards: Font and Character Spacing. The Font card is shown in Figure 7-33.

**FIGURE 7-33**

Use the Font card in the Font dialog box to specify formatting features for the selected text.

Notice the Preview box in the lower right corner of the card. If you have some text selected, a portion of it will appear here, complete with any formatting you've applied to the text. If no text is selected, Word will use the font name as a sample. As you change the formatting choices in the Font dialog box, the Preview sample shows the effects of your settings.

The Font, Font Style, and Size text boxes have list boxes underneath them. You can choose a typeface and font size using the Font and Size lists. The Font Style box lists the available font styles—Regular, Italic, Bold, and Bold Italic. When you choose any item from one of these list boxes, Word displays it in the appropriate text box.

The Underline pull-down list offers five choices: four types of underlining plus None. In addition to the three underlining types we discussed in the shortcut key section, you can also choose a dotted underline.

The Color pull-down list lets you add color to your text. The default (Auto) is black. If you don't have a color printer, Word will print all of your text in black or a gray interpretation of any colors.

Even if you don't have a color printer but you do have a color monitor, you can still see the colors on the screen. For example, if you write notes to yourself in your text, you might define them with a distinct color so that you won't miss them later. Similarly, if you create on-screen forms, as we'll discuss in Chapter 23, you can use color to differentiate some parts of a form from others.

The Effects box offers a set of check boxes for additional formatting choices. Strikethrough puts a line through the middle of each character. Superscript and Subscript move the text to a position higher or lower than other text on the same line. By default, Superscript and Subscript move text up or down by 3 points and automatically convert the characters to a smaller size (although the setting in the Size box will not change). Superscript and Subscript are mutually exclusive, so you can apply only one at a time. Small Caps and All Caps are self-explanatory and, as with Superscript and Subscript, are mutually exclusive. We described the Hidden attribute in "Toggle shortcuts" on page 226.

Figure 7-34 shows the Character Spacing card. This controls some finer details of letter spacing, such as kerning. These features let you control the appearance of the text, and how many characters fit on a line. Unless you have some specific need for these features—such as crafted formatting for desktop publishing—you will probably leave these at their default settings.

If you change your mind about applying a font format, you can choose the Cancel button to go back to your document without making any changes. Choosing the OK button will apply any settings that you've chosen.

**FIGURE 7-34**

The Character Spacing card controls advanced spacing features that many users will never need.

## How to change your default font format

The Default button that is present on both the Font and Character Spacing cards will make the current settings on both cards the default for the current template. If you choose this button, Word will display a dialog box asking whether you want to make the change to the template. If you are working in a document that is based on the Normal template, this will reset the default for font formatting, so be careful before you make the change.

## How to change more than one selection of text

If you need to change more than one selection of text to the same new settings, remember the Edit Repeat command (and its shortcut key, ⌘-Y). You can use it to apply the same formatting repeatedly to different selections. After you've formatted the first selection, simply select the next and press ⌘-Y. You can re-peat this as many times as necessary. Also remember that you can use the Edit Replace command to change font formatting for specific strings of text.

# Copying and Moving Font and Paragraph Formats

When you copy or move a block of text, Word will generally retain any font formats you assigned directly to that text when it pastes the characters into the new location. (This is not true for formats applied through styles. In Chapter 12, we'll talk about the effects of editing text that's formatted with styles.) If you copy or move an entire paragraph, including the paragraph mark, Word will also retain the paragraph formats of the copied selection when you paste. However, if you copy or move any part of the paragraph and don't include the paragraph mark in your selection, Word will use the para-graph formats assigned to the text in the paste area.

In any case, you may need to revise the formats of the pasted text to match those of the surrounding text. Word provides both keyboard and mouse short-cuts to copy character or paragraph formats without copying any text.

## How to copy a paragraph mark

One easy way to copy a paragraph format—using either the mouse or the keyboard—is to copy just the paragraph mark from the end of one paragraph and then either paste it over the mark at the end of another paragraph or in-sert it before the old paragraph mark and then delete the old one. Because all paragraph formatting information is stored with the paragraph mark, Word will reformat the paragraph. Note that to use this technique, you'll need to display paragraph marks in your document either by choosing the Show/Hide ¶ button on the Formatting toolbar, by pressing ⌘-8 or by activating the Paragraph Marks or All option on the Tools Options View card. (Note also, in passing, that if the source paragraph is formatted with a named style, Word will apply that style to the destination paragraph. We'll talk about styles in Chapter 12.)

If you've moved a paragraph formatted with one set of paragraph formats to a section of text that's formatted with a different set, the easiest way to change formatting will often be to go to the end of the paragraph you've moved, delete the paragraph mark, and then press Return. Because Word stores all formatting with the paragraph mark, deleting the marker at the end of the first paragraph not only joins the two paragraphs but formats all of its text to match the second paragraph. When you press Return to create a new paragraph mark, the first paragraph retains the format it had when the text was joined. Also note that if you place the cursor at the end of the first paragraph and use the Del key to delete the paragraph mark, Word will delete the paragraph mark whether or not it is currently showing on the screen.

## How to use the Format Painter

Perhaps the easiest way to use a block of text as the model for other text is to use the Format Painter. The feature is available both on the Standard toolbar, using the button with an icon that looks like a paintbrush, and through the shortcut key ⌘-Shift-C.

### How to use the Format Painter with the mouse

Start by highlighting a portion of text whose format you want to apply elsewhere in your document. Then click on the Format Painter button. Your mouse pointer will change to look like the normal I-beam with a plus sign to its left. Hold down the mouse button and drag across the section of text that you want to apply the formatting to. Word will highlight the selection as you paint. When you release the mouse button, the text will take on the formatting of the source selection, and the mouse pointer will revert to the normal I-beam.

If you want to apply the same formatting to several sections, double-click the Format Painter button. Having started with a double click, you'll find that when you finish highlighting a section and release the mouse button, the mouse pointer will remain in the Format Painter mode so that you can repeat the process as many times as you want. To turn off the feature, press any key. Esc is probably the safest and most convenient choice; if you had text highlighted and pressed a character key, the highlighted text would be replaced with that character.

## How to use the Format Painter with the keyboard

You can also use essentially the same method to copy formats with the keyboard. Once again, start by selecting a block of text that has the format you want to apply elsewhere. Then press ⌘-Shift-C. Next highlight the destination text and press ⌘-Shift-V to apply the formatting to the new text.

 Copying formats with these shortcut keys is similar to using the Edit Copy and Edit Paste commands except that you're copying formatting only. In fact, the Word commands attached to these keystrokes are CopyFormat and PasteFormat, and it may help you remember the shortcut keys if you think of this as copying and pasting formats. As with the Edit Paste command, you can use ⌘-Shift-V to apply formatting to successive selections of text.

## Some general comments about the Format Painter

Whether you use the mouse or the keyboard to copy formats with the Format Painter, there are several points you should be aware of. Most important is that you can copy font formatting, paragraph formatting, or both. To copy font formatting only, select source text without a paragraph mark.

To copy paragraph formatting only (including any font formats applied to the paragraph as a whole), select only the paragraph mark as the source. For example, if you've applied boldface to an entire paragraph but not to the paragraph mark and you select the paragraph mark as the source, you will apply only the paragraph formatting to the target text. If you've applied the boldface format to the paragraph mark itself at the source, however, you'll also apply boldface to the target text.

To copy paragraph and font formatting together, select both the text and the paragraph mark. If the font formatting of the text is different from that of the paragraph mark, Word will copy the paragraph-level formats—for indentions, for example—but will use the font formatting from the source text.

If your selected text has more than one type of font formatting applied to it, Word will recognize only the first formatting that it encounters. For example, if the first word in the selection is bold and the second is italic and you attempt to copy the formatting to a different two-word selection, both words will be bold.

At this point, if you've read everything from the beginning of this book, you've covered everything you need to know to create documents and format them attractively. All that is left is getting the product onto paper. We'll cover that subject in the next chapter.

# TOPIC FINDER

# 8

# Printing

ord's printing features are straightforward if you want to accept the default settings. However, there are many options you may want to use. Before you can print with Word, you have to be sure your printer is correctly installed and configured. Even then, the results may not always be precisely what you had in mind. You may have to fine-tune PrintMonitor, the font selection, or the formatting before your pages are printed the way you want.

We'll start with setting up your printer. This process actually breaks into two procedures: printer installation and printer selection.

## Selecting a Printer with the Chooser

Before you can print anything with Word—or any other program on the Macintosh—you need to tell the computer about the printer (or printers) you have installed on your system. The system software automatically installs support for a number of Apple printer models. You can also install additional printers or alter the information about those you've already installed. Assuming that your printer and computer are hooked up properly, we'll take a quick look at how to install and configure printers on the Macintosh. For further details, refer to your Macintosh and printer manuals or contact your printer manufacturer.

# How to install a printer

If you have a printer that is not directly supported by the system software, you need to install driver software. This is typically provided on a floppy disk with the printer; insert the floppy disk in your computer and run the installation program. This adds the driver to the Extensions folder in your computer's System folder.

You can then run the Chooser desk accessory (which you can select at any time from the Apple menu), which will show all the installed printers, as shown in Figure 8-1. Some printers require that you connect them directly to either your printer or modem port, as the figure shows. Other printers use an AppleTalk connection, and you can choose the printer you want from the list of printers, as shown in Figure 8-2.

**FIGURE 8-1**

Use the Chooser to select and configure printers.

**FIGURE 8-2**

The Chooser is able to identify printers that are attached via an AppleTalk connection.

Only one printer can be designated as the active printer. In order to use a different printer, you must return to the Chooser and make a different selection.

## PrintMonitor

You will also notice that one of the figures shows a Background Printing option, but the other doesn't. This option is only available for some printers. Background printing offers the advantage of allowing you to continue editing or writing, but the system performance will be reduced while background printing is in progress.

Background printing is handled by the PrintMonitor utility. This is a program in the Extensions folder that starts automatically whenever you begin a background print job. It lets programs print to temporary files on disk and then sends them to the printer. This feature offers advantages because printing to disk is faster than printing to a printer. The result is that you'll be able to return to using Word sooner. Your document will be printed while you go on to other tasks. Bypassing PrintMonitor will generally speed the actual printing, but you will wait longer to regain control of your system.

PrintMonitor operates in the background while you continue to work. You can choose Off for Background Printing in the Chooser, but we don't recommend it unless you find that printing in the background makes your system so unresponsive that it's essentially unusable.

When PrintMonitor is running, you can use the Application menu to switch to it and see the status of the print jobs that are waiting to be printed, as shown in Figure 8-3. There are also configuration options available for PrintMonitor; see your Macintosh manuals for details.

**FIGURE 8-3**

The PrintMonitor utility makes Background Printing possible by spooling print jobs to disk, so you can continue working while your printer is printing.

## The Setup options

As mentioned in the last chapter, you will see different options on the File
Page Setup screen, depending on which printer is active. As Figures 8-4, 8-5,
and 8-6 show, the available options will vary with different printer drivers.

**FIGURE 8-4**

These are the Page
Setup options available
with the StyleWriter
printer driver.

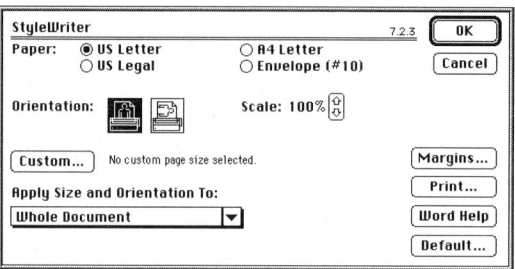

**FIGURE 8-5**

These are the
configuration options
available with the
Apple LaserWriter
printer driver.

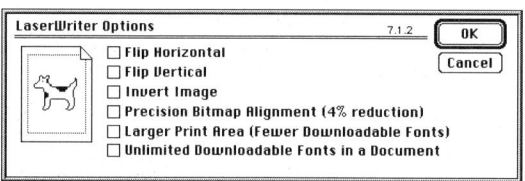

FIGURE 8-6

FIGURE 8-6

These are the
configuration options
available with the
Hewlett-Packard
LaserJet printer driver.

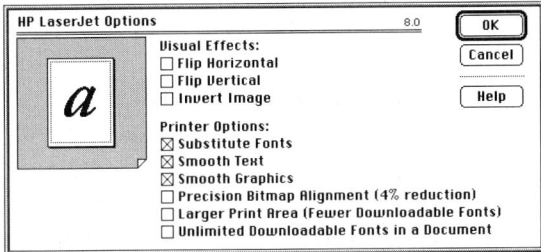

Choose from the available options for graphics resolution, page orientation, paper source, and so on.

Be aware that you won't have all options available for every printer. For example, of the three printers in the figures above, only the LaserWriter has Tabloid as an option for Paper. Few printers are large enough to offer this option.

Be aware that there are some complex issues involving printer memory, downloadable fonts, and the on-screen display of downloadable and cartridge fonts, most of which are beyond the scope of this book. As we'll discuss in Chapter 16, TrueType fonts can simplify these issues for most printers.

After you choose the settings you want, choose OK. If you choose Cancel or press Esc, the settings will not be stored.

## How to delete an installed printer

To "uninstall" a printer—after you change the printer on your system, for example—all you need to do is drag the driver's icon from the Extension folder and put it in the trash. Keep in mind that this removes the driver from your disk; if you should ever want to use that printer again, you will have to reinstall the driver first.

# Using the File Print Command

After you've installed and selected your printer, you can print in Word by choosing File Print, typing the keyboard shortcut ⌘-P, or clicking on the Print button on the Standard toolbar—fourth from the left, with an icon that resembles a printer.

When you choose the Print command, Word will always print the active document. It will not print any other documents that happen to be open unless you activate those windows individually and choose the print command for each. You can print more than one document at a time with the File Find File command; for details, see "How to print, delete, or copy one or more documents" on page 583.

If you click on the Print button, choose File Print, or press the shortcut key combination ⌘-P, Word will display a Print dialog box similar to the one shown in Figure 8-7. Notice that Word identifies the current printer at the top of the dialog box. If you want to change the printer, you must close the Print dialog box and use the Chooser, which you can access from the Apple menu.

**FIGURE 8-7**

Choose File Print to open the Print dialog box.

To print from the Print dialog box, choose OK to accept the default settings and send your entire document to the printer. (We'll cover the rest of the choices in this dialog box in a moment.) Word will display the Printing message box to indicate progress.

You can interrupt printing at any time while the Printing message box is displayed by pressing Esc or choosing the Cancel button in the Printing message box. If the print job has already been handed over to PrintMonitor, you'll need to go to PrintMonitor to halt the printing.

## How to work with PrintMonitor

If, for any reason, Word can't communicate with your printer while you are using PrintMonitor, Word will display a message box similar to the one in Figure 8-8. If you open the PrintMonitor window, you can then choose to cancel the print job or try again, as shown in Figure 8-9.

If you choose Cancel Printing, the print job will be deleted. If you choose Try Again, PrintMonitor will simply attempt to send the print job to the printer again.

**FIGURE 8-8**

Your Macintosh shows this message box if PrintMonitor cannot communicate with your printer.

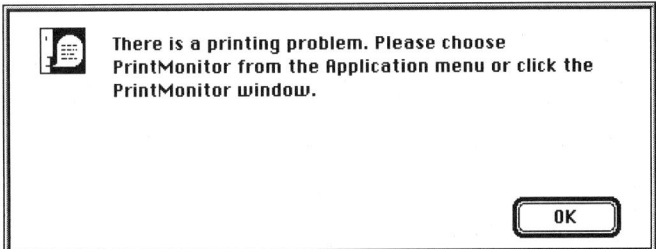

**FIGURE 8-9**

If you get the error message shown in Figure 8-8, open the PrintMonitor window using the Application menu. PrintMonitor will display this dialog box offering you the choice of canceling the print job or trying it again.

# File Print command options

Assuming you can successfully print a document, you can now explore the options in the Print dialog box, shown earlier in Figure 8-7. If all you ever want to print is your entire document, one copy at a time, you will never need any of these additional features. We expect, however, that you will use other options at least occasionally.

Note that you will see different options depending on the printer you have selected. We have shown the dialog box as it appears for a LaserWriter in Figure 8-7. We will skip the printer-specific items in this dialog box; consult your printer's manual for details about these choices. We'll only cover the options available for all printers, starting with the most commonly used options.

## Multiple copies and collating

You use the Copies text box in the Print dialog box to specify the number of copies to print. Notice the Collate Copies check box in the lower left corner of the dialog box. If this box is checked and you specify multiple copies, Word will send the print job to the printer repeatedly to make the requested number of copies.

## Pages and the Range button: How to print the entire document, specific pages, the current page, or a selection

By default, Word prints your entire document; however, you can choose to print only parts of it if you prefer. As shown in Figure 8-7, the Pages line has two option buttons: All and From/To. These features are provided by the Macintosh system and allow you to select either the entire document or a range of pages. Word offers a considerably more sophisticated range feature, however, which you access by choosing the Range button in the lower right corner of the dialog box; this calls up the dialog box shown in Figure 8-10.

**FIGURE 8-10**

The Range button in the Print dialog box opens this dialog box, which gives you greater control over the parts of your document that you want to print.

Any settings you make here will override the settings on the Pages line in the Print dialog box. The All option button simply prints the entire document.

Current Page refers to the page where the cursor is currently located; note that this isn't necessarily the same as the page that is currently displayed on the screen. If you have any question about the cursor's location, close the dialog box and check the page number in the status bar. Note that you can't check the location with the dialog box because Word uses the status bar for a message while the dialog box is open.

The Pages option includes a text box in which you can specify a set of **NEW!** pages to print. Simply enter the numbers of the pages in the text box. You can list individual pages, a range of pages (separate the starting and ending pages with a hyphen), or a combination of the two. Separate each page number or range from the following one with a comma. For example, to print pages 1, 3, 4, 5, and 7, you can enter *1,3-5,7*.

After you close the Range dialog box, its current settings will be displayed in the lower left corner of the Print dialog box, so you can see that the Pages settings will be overridden when you start the print job. To clear these settings, choose the Range button, choose Use Print Dialog Page Range, and then choose OK.

The Print Selection Only check box is at the lower left of the Print dialog box, and it will be grayed unless you selected some text before choosing the Print command. If you choose this option, Word will print only the selected text and will cancel any settings you may have chosen using the Pages or Range settings.

If you print a selection, the text will be correctly formatted, but any automatic page breaks will be ignored. This means that Word will print your selection starting at the top of the sheet of paper, no matter where it falls on the page displayed on the screen. Similarly, if your selection starts in the middle of a paragraph, Word will print the selection with the correct formatting for that paragraph, but it will format the first printed line as the start of a new paragraph, no matter where in the paragraph the text selection actually starts. Other page-formatting features, such as headers and footers, may also be printed differently from how they otherwise would be printed.

## How to simulate duplex printing: Odd Pages and Even Pages

Some printers are equipped with a duplex printing option. Each sheet of paper makes two passes through the printer, so that you can print one image on the front of the sheet and another on the back. Duplex printing can save lots of paper and make the finished document look more professional.

Even if your printer does not support duplex printing, it's easy to get equivalent results. The Print line near the bottom of the Print dialog box has two pull-down lists. By default, the first is set to Document, and the second is set to All Pages In Range. If you pull down the second list, you'll find that it contains three options: All Pages In Range, Odd Pages, and Even Pages. To print a document on both sides of the paper, print the odd pages first; then put the stack of pages back in the input tray and print the even pages.

Note that you will need to feed the pages in reverse order the second time. With a typical laser printer, for example, this means the pages need to be face down, with page 1 on top, followed by 3, 5, and so on.

If your printer doesn't have an optional paper path that will stack the output in this order, you can use the Reverse Print Order option on the Options Print card, which we will discuss later in this chapter.

Some laser printers have a difficult time when printing on the back of a page that was recently printed. For best results when printing odd and then even pages, be sure to use fresh paper that hasn't been moistened by exposure to high humidity. After printing the odd pages, give the paper a little time to dissipate some of the heat from the fuser rollers, and fan the stack to help eliminate static electricity. These steps should help reduce paper-feeding problems that can ruin a duplex print job.

## How to print supplementary information

As mentioned above, the default selection for the first pull-down list on the Print line is Document, but there are other choices—as you can see in Figure 8-11, which shows the opened list.

**FIGURE 8-11**

The first Print pull-down list in the Print dialog box enables you to print items other than your document.

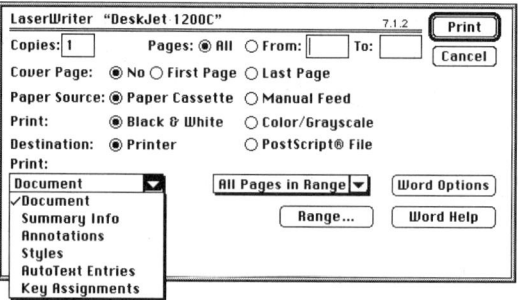

The Summary Info choice prints the information from the File Summary Info and Document Statistics dialog boxes, both of which we covered in

Chapter 2. Annotations prints a list of all annotations in the document, in order, along with the page number each annotation refers to. (We'll cover annotations in Chapter 10. Annotations are similar to footnotes except that they are comments about the document rather than a part of the document.) Styles prints the definitions of all style formats for the document. (We'll cover styles in Chapter 12.) AutoText Entries prints all AutoText entries, including any in the Normal template and the current supplementary template if there's one attached. Key Assignments is similar to the AutoText Entries choice: It prints any key assignments in the Normal and supplementary templates that are changed from the default settings.

You can print any one of these items by choosing it in the Print pull-down list. Note that you can also tell Word to print the Summary Info and Annotations with every document by using the Options settings.

## The Word Options buttons

There are two buttons in the Print dialog box worth mention. The Word Help button opens help screens about printing with Word. The Word Options button takes you to the Print card in the Options dialog box, shown in Figure 8-12. This is the same card that you see when you choose Tools Options and then choose Print.

**FIGURE 8-12**

The Word Options button in the Print dialog box opens the Options dialog box.

The card is divided into three group boxes: Printing Options, Include With Document, and Options For Current Document Only. Here's a look at each.

## Printing Options

Your choices in the Printing Options box define whether you print in reverse order or not and whether to update information while printing.

**Reverse Print Order.**  Checking the Reverse Print Order check box tells Word to print the document starting with the last page first. This is useful if you have a printer that stacks its output face up rather than face down; in this case, you'll have your pages in the correct order immediately upon printing.

This option can also be helpful if you need to print in reverse order to simulate duplex printing, which we discussed earlier in this chapter. If your printer doesn't offer an option for stacking pages in reverse order when you print the first side of the pages, checking the Reverse Print Order check box in Word will serve the same purpose.

**NEW!**    **Update Fields.**  Checking the Update Fields check box makes sure that all fields in the document are updated before they are printed. As we mentioned in Chapter 5, when discussing the PAGE, DATE, TIME, and AUTOTEXT fields, you can update fields at any time by selecting a block of text and pressing F9. If you make sure the Update Fields check box is checked, however, you don't have to remember to update fields manually before printing. Unless you have a specific reason for not wanting to update your fields each time you print, we suggest you check this box. We'll discuss fields in detail in Chapter 20, starting on page 639.

**NEW!**    **Update Links.**  Similar to the Update Fields option, Update Links will update any linked objects before printing. For more information on linked objects, see Chapter 15, "Drawing, Graphics, & Other Objects," starting on page 521, and Chapter 18, "Sharing Data with Other Programs," starting on page 587.

## Include With Document

In the Include With Document box, you can specify additional items to print with documents.

Earlier in this chapter, we described how you can tell Word to print the summary information or annotations, among other choices, from the Print dialog box. When you specify these choices in the Print dialog box, however, Word prints only the specified item. By adding a check to the appropriate check box here, you can tell Word to print these items automatically along with any document. Note that if you check the Annotations option, Word will check the Hidden Text option as well.

**Summary Info.** Check the Summary Info check box, and Word will print the information stored in the Summary Info and Document Statistics dialog boxes on a page by itself. The document will start on its own page (page 1 unless you've assigned a different number to the document's first page).

**Field Codes.** If this box is checked, Word will print the field codes instead of the field results for any fields in your document. In the majority of cases, you will probably not want to check this box. We will discuss fields in depth in Chapter 20.

**Annotations.** Annotations are notes, formatted as hidden text, that you can store in your document. Checking this box tells Word to print the notes. Word will print them after the document, starting on a separate page. If you check the Annotations check box, Word will also automatically check the Hidden Text check box. This makes sense; the markers for annotations are formatted as hidden text, and you need to print the markers as well—much as you need to see footnote references in your text to know what the footnotes refer to. For more information about annotations, including how to display them on your screen, see "Annotations" starting on page 306.

**Hidden Text.** Check the Hidden Text check box if you want Word to print text that you've formatted as hidden. Normally, of course, the point of formatting text as hidden is to hide it. For example, you might write yourself a note within a document to remind you to check a fact or identify the source of some information. Occasionally, however, you may want to print hidden text.

If you print a document complete with hidden text, keep in mind that this will result in a longer document. It will also change the pagination, throwing off page breaks. Note, too, that you can select Hidden Text without selecting Annotations, but not vice versa.

**Drawing Objects.** Word checks this check box by default. Clear the check box to tell Word not to print drawing objects along with the document. For more information about drawing objects, see Chapter 15, "Drawing, Graphics, & Other Objects," starting on page 521.

**NEW!**

## Options For Current Document Only

**NEW!**

There are three items in the Options For Current Document Only box. If the Print Data Only For Forms check box is checked and the document you're printing is a form, Word will print only the information in the form fields, and not the form itself. Unlike the other options on this card, which affect all documents you print with Word, the setting for this option is stored as part of each individual document file. For information on forms and how to create them, see Chapter 21, "Form Letters, Labels, & Forms," starting on page 679.

You can use the Fractional Widths check box to configure the printer to use more precise spacing between characters. This feature can improve the look of the final product, but it may make text on screen more difficult to read. If the uneven spacing on the screen is distracting, you can wait until you have finished editing your document and are ready to print before you turn this feature on.

The Print Postscript Over Text check box controls how PostScript instructions contained within your document are handled. PostScript instructions are text within a document formatted with the PostScript style and are frequently used to add special text or graphics to a document. Rather than being printed as part of the document, these instructions are interpreted by the printer. This setting controls whether the resulting output is formatted as though it were behind (the check box is cleared) or over the regular text and graphics in the document.

# Previewing a Printed Document

Given all of the formatting choices and printing options, it can be difficult to predict how all these elements will work together. To help avoid unpleasant surprises with the appearance of your printed document, Word offers two features that show you how your printed document will look before you print it: Page Layout view and Print Preview.

Both features let you see and work with anything from a bird's-eye view of multiple pages on up to a bigger-than-life-size view of part of a single page. With either feature, you see what amounts to a preview of your printed document, complete with headers, footers, and other special elements in place. And both features can help you avoid wasted time and effort on print runs that don't produce the results you have in mind. We'll look at the File Print Preview command first.

## Print Preview

When you choose File Print Preview (or click on the Print Preview button on the Standard toolbar), Word displays a screen like the one in Figure 8-13. Notice the word (Preview) following the filename on the title bar. Also notice the Print Preview toolbar, immediately below the menu bar. The text on the preview screen may or may not be readable, depending on the font size and the current Zoom setting.

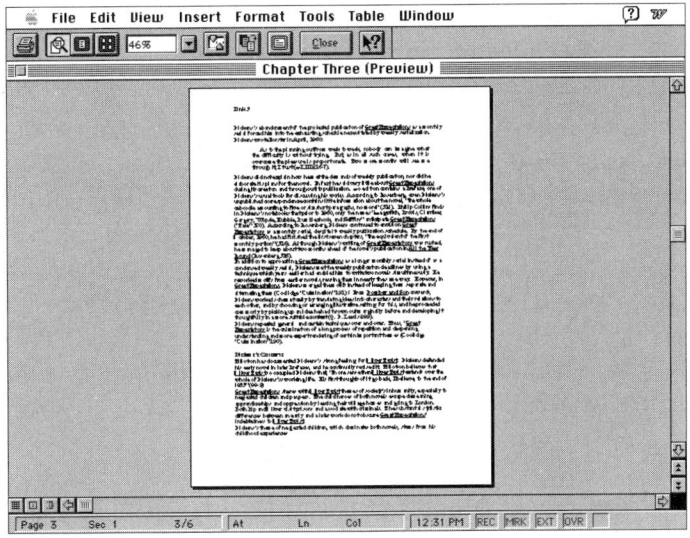

**FIGURE 8-13**

You can choose the
Print Preview com-
mand to preview and
alter your page layout.

## The Print Preview toolbar

The Print Preview toolbar makes it easy to adjust your screen display and use
the special features available in Print Preview. Here's a look at the toolbar
buttons and their functions.

| Button | Function |
|--------|----------|
| | Print |
| | Magnifier |
| | One Page |
| | Multiple Pages |
| | View Ruler |
| | Shrink To Fit |
| | Full Screen |

**Print button.** As with the Print button on the Standard toolbar, you can choose this button to bring up the Print dialog box. (Note that you can also print from Print Preview mode by choosing File Print from the menu bar.)

**Magnifier button.** The Magnifier button is actually a toggle that primarily controls the effect of a mouse click on the screen. Click on the button to toggle between the magnifier mode and normal text editing mode.

If this button is inactive, the mouse will behave just as it does in Normal or Page Layout view. However, if the button is active—in which case it will look as if it has been pressed—the mouse pointer will look like a magnifying glass whenever it is over a document, and it will have either a plus or a minus sign in the magnifying glass. This shape indicates that the mouse will provide a shortcut for zooming in (magnifying a page) or zooming out (making a page smaller) on the screen.

When the screen shows one or more full pages at a time, the magnifying glass will include a plus sign. If you click on a page to enlarge it, Word will zoom the page to the 100% zoom setting and position the image to show the portion of the page that you clicked on. When the image is displayed at a zoom size larger than 100% (or if you clicked to zoom to 100%), the mouse pointer will contain a minus sign, and if you click on the page, Word will zoom out to full page view.

You can edit your document in Print Preview just as if you were in Normal or Page Layout view. The key differences between Print Preview and Page Layout view are that in Page Layout view, the toolbars are the same as in Normal view—that is, you don't have the Print Preview toolbar. As a result, in Page Layout view, the magnifier button isn't available for zooming in and out. In both Page Layout view and Print Preview, however, you can see what amounts to a print preview with all formatting visible; and in both views you can make changes, deletions, and additions to your document and Word will reformat the document to reflect those changes. In both Page Layout view and Print Preview, your computer's performance will be slower than in Normal view.

NEW!     If you like, you can add a Magnifier button to your Standard toolbar that's similar in function to the Magnifier button on the Print Preview toolbar. Once you've done that, the difference between Page Layout view and Print Preview is almost nonexistent (except that Word doesn't display the Standard and Formatting toolbars in Print Preview). You'll find details on how to add this—or any other—button to a toolbar in "Customizing Toolbars" starting on page 288.

**One Page button.** Clicking the One Page button will set the zoom setting to display a single page. It will also set Word to use the same setting for the zoom-out shortcut with a mouse click if you use the Magnifier button as described earlier.

**Multiple Pages button.** This button displays more than one page at a time. If you simply hold down this button, you'll see the grid shown in Figure 8-14.

NEW!

**FIGURE 8-14**

Hold down the Multiple Pages button on the Print Preview toolbar, and you can then specify how many pages you will see on the screen at one time.

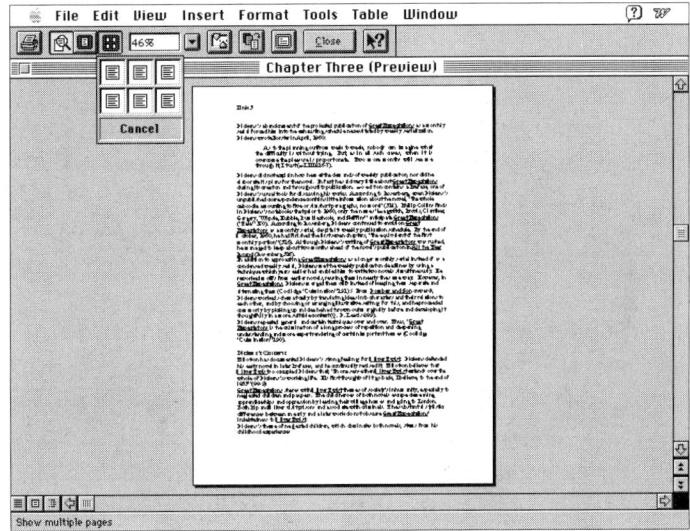

If you point to the Multiple Pages button and hold the mouse button down while you drag across the grid, you'll find that the grid will grow to as large as four rows of nine columns each.

If you have checked the Mirror Margins check box in the Page Setup dialog box (Margins card), the pages will be displayed as two-page spreads with a binding between the paired pages, as shown in Figure 8-15 on the next page. For more information on mirrored margins, see "Margins" on page 196.

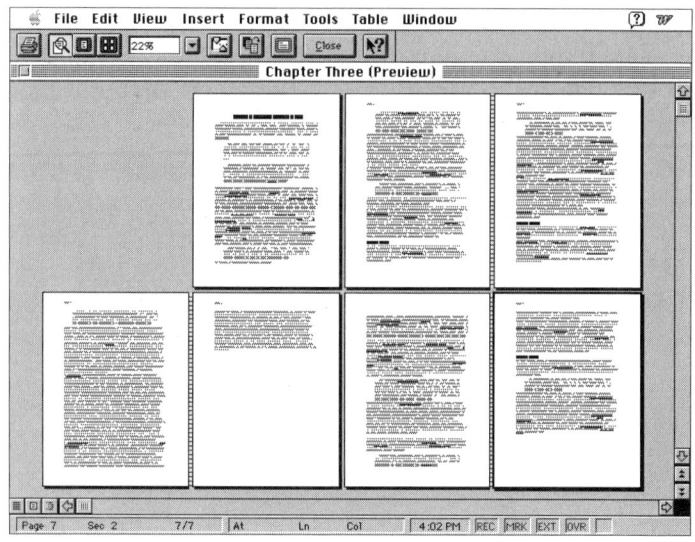

FIGURE 8-15

If you have specified mirrored margins as part of your page setup, the Print Preview screen will show pairs of facing pages when you use the Multiple Pages option.

**NEW!**    **Zoom Control text box.** The Zoom Control text box on the Print Preview toolbar shows the current scale—or zoom percentage setting—for the view; the smaller the percentage setting, the smaller the page on screen. Word sets this percentage when you use the Magnifier or click on the One Page or Multiple Pages button. But you can also set the zoom to other percentages.

The drop-down list that goes with this box, shown in Figure 8-16, offers a range of predefined settings, from 10% to 200% and from one-page width to two pages. You can also enter any zoom percentage you prefer, from 10 to 200.

FIGURE 8-16

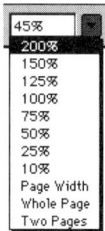

The Zoom Control box includes a drop-down list of options.

**NEW!**    **View Ruler button.** The View Ruler button toggles the rulers on and off. When the option is active, the View Ruler button will look as if it's pressed down. More important, you'll see the vertical and horizontal rulers for the current page, as shown in Figure 8-17. If Word is set to display more than one page at a time, you can move from page to page by clicking on a page with the mouse. The only way to move from page to page with the keyboard is to use the arrow keys to move through the text or use the Edit Go To command.

When you move to a different page, the ruler positions will change to match the page you're on.

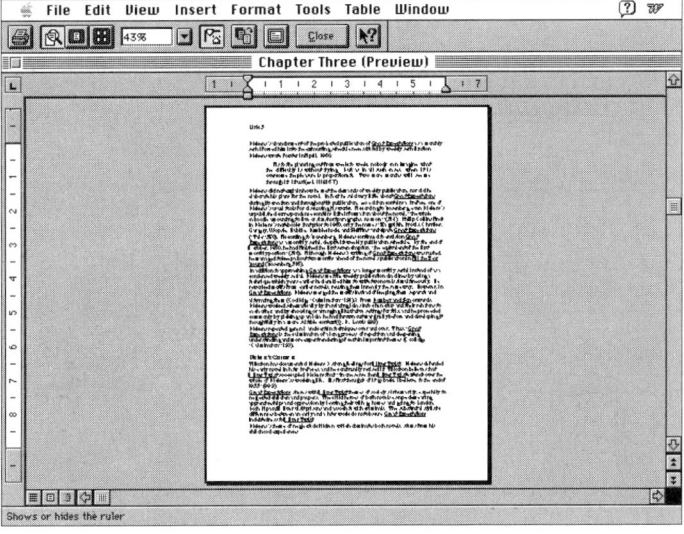

**FIGURE 8-17**

You can display rulers with your document in Page Preview.

Note that the top (horizontal) ruler indicates left and right margins, as well as the left, right, and first-line indent markers for the paragraph containing the cursor—just as in Normal view. And the tab icon in the left corner of the ruler also functions as in Normal view. We covered the horizontal ruler and tabs in Chapter 7.

**Shrink To Fit button.** Suppose you've written a letter or a memo, only to discover that a few lines—such as a signature block by itself—spill onto the last page. To fit those lines onto the next-to-last page, you could try moving the margins out a little or shrinking the fonts a bit; or you could click on the Shrink To Fit button, and Word will automatically reduce the font size in an effort to fit the document on one fewer page. Word will not remove manual (hard) page breaks, however. If there are any in your document, you may not be able to eliminate that extra page by clicking the Shrink To Fit button.

NEW!

Use this feature with caution. Word shrinks the document by reducing the font size. And it will try to comply with the command even if you choose it more than once. You could end up with text that is too small to read comfortably. Be sure to check the results before you decide to stick with them. And be prepared to use the Undo command.

**Full Screen button.** Choosing the Full Screen button is exactly equivalent to choosing the View Full Screen command. If you click on this button, Word will switch to Full Screen view, hiding the scroll bars and the status bar—and, indeed, everything but the menu bar, the title bar, and the Page Preview toolbar. (The View Ruler button acts independently in these two views; you can click it on in one view and off in the other if you choose.) The whole point of Full Screen view is to display as much of the page at one time as possible. You can toggle back to the default version of Print Preview, with the additional items displayed, by clicking on the Full Screen button again.

**Close and Help buttons.** The Close button will return you to the view your document was in when you chose the File Print Preview command. (Note, however, that if you are in Full Screen view when you choose the Close button, you will still be in Full Screen view when you return to the prior view.)

The last button on the Print Preview toolbar provides access to context-sensitive help, much like the Help button on the Standard toolbar. See "Getting Help" starting on page 23 for more information about online help.

## How to navigate in Print Preview

When you choose Print Preview, Word will always display the page that was currently visible on your editing screen—either as the only page (if Print Preview is set to show a single full page) or as one of multiple pages (when Print Preview is set to show more than one page). Before it displays the page, however, Word will automatically repaginate your document up to and including the pages it will preview on the screen.

If more than one page is displayed, the current page will be highlighted with a border around it. You can position the mouse pointer on a different page and click it to make that page active.

You can move through your document while in the Print Preview screen with the arrow keys, the Page Up and Page Down keys, or the vertical scroll bar. As in Page Layout view, the scroll bar buttons with two triangles move you a page at a time through your document if Word is set to show one full page at a time. If more than one page is displayed, these buttons will take you to the next screenful of pages. You can also press ⌘-Home and ⌘-End to jump to the first and last pages.

## How to change formats within Print Preview

As mentioned earlier, you can edit text in Print Preview. In fact, if you pull the Word menus down, you'll find that most choices are still available—including File Page Setup and Document Layout to adjust the margins and other page setup options. You can also use the rulers and the mouse to change other settings, such as indents and margins.

You can move the horizontal ruler's indent markers with a mouse while in Print Preview, exactly as you would in Page Layout or Normal view, by pointing to the appropriate marker, holding down the mouse button, and dragging the marker. You can also add, delete, or move tabs just as in Page Layout or Normal view. Keep in mind that changes to indents and tabs will affect only the current paragraph or paragraphs—meaning the paragraph or paragraphs containing the cursor or selection. **NEW!**

You can also adjust the margins with the rulers and the mouse exactly as you can in Page Layout view, by pointing to the margin marker on the appropriate ruler, holding down the mouse button, and dragging the marker. We discussed how to use Word's rulers to adjust indents and margins in "The horizontal ruler" starting on page 198, and tabs in the section "Tabs" starting on page 216. **NEW!**

Note that if you're working in a multisection document, your changes to the margins made with the mouse will apply to the current section only. If you want to change the format in more than one section, you can highlight some text that crosses the section breaks and then make your changes. We'll discuss multisection documents in detail in Chapter 13, "Bullets, Numbering, & Sections," starting on page 439.

The ruler scale is too small for precise adjustment of margins, tabs, and indents when you are viewing one or more full pages on the screen. You will find that such changes are easier if you zoom in for a close-up view of your page, which will also give you a more detailed ruler to work with. Don't forget that you can reverse changes with the Undo command if the result isn't what you wanted.

## Headers and footers

Although you can edit the text of your document in Print Preview, you cannot make changes to headers or footers. All you need to do, however, is either choose View Header And Footer or double-click on a header or footer. Word will switch to Page Layout view with the header or footer area active and the Header And Footer toolbar displayed. When you finish editing, choose Close on the Header And Footer toolbar. Word will leave you in either Page Layout or Normal view, whichever one you were in when you first switched to Print Preview.

You can also adjust the position and size of headers and footers. For details, see "Defining the Position of a Header or Footer" starting on page 558.

## How to use Page Layout view

Like Print Preview, Page Layout view displays a close approximation of your printed pages complete with margins, headers, page numbers, footnotes, and other assorted elements in place. The main difference is that in Page Layout view Word, by default, displays the Formatting and Standard toolbars rather than the Print Preview toolbar. In addition, you can edit headers and footers in Page Layout view.

In essence, Page Layout view offers a middle ground between Normal view and Print Preview, although it's closer to Print Preview. We'll cover the differences between Normal and Page Layout views in the next chapter, along with Word's other View menu commands. For the moment, it's enough to know that, as with Print Preview, Page Layout view displays all of the elements on your page while you edit and format your text.

There are several ways to switch to Page Layout view. We'll save most of these for the next chapter as well. For now, simply choose View Page Layout. And note that to change from Page Layout view to another view (such as Normal), you can, once again, choose the appropriate View menu command. If you're not sure which view you are currently in, take a look at the View menu. Word always indicates the active view by displaying a dot next to the appropriate command. (If you are currently in Print Preview, the active view, as indicated by the dot, is the one you will return to when you close Print Preview.)

### Limitations of Page Layout view

Page Layout view doesn't provide quite as accurate a representation of your printed document as Print Preview. In particular, if you've checked the Hidden Text check box on the Tools Options View card, any text formatted as hidden will appear in Page Layout view. This will be true even if you've set hidden text not to print, on the Tools Options Print card. In contrast, hidden text will show on the screen in Print Preview only if the Hidden Text check box on the Tools Options Print card is checked. And it will show even if Word is set not to show hidden text in Page Layout and Normal views.

# Envelopes and Labels

There is one last printing-related issue that virtually everyone has to deal with at least occasionally: envelopes and labels. Printing and formatting envelopes have traditionally caused problems for even the best word processors, and many offices equipped with the highest-quality laser printers and the latest software were obliged to keep typewriters within reach, just for addressing envelopes. Although such problems have not quite become a thing of the past, much progress has been made in envelope-printing with word processors—and Word 6.0 goes a long way toward making this chore quick and easy.

You can use the envelope-and-label feature without opening a document that includes the address you want, but if you do, you'll miss half the fun. When you choose Tools Envelopes And Labels, Word will first look at the current cursor position in the active document. If it doesn't see what looks like an address there, it will start at the top of the document and work its way downward, searching for anything that looks like an address. It will then open the Envelopes And Labels dialog box, as shown in Figure 8-18, with the Envelopes card displayed.

**FIGURE 8-18**

With the Envelopes And Labels dialog box, you can edit and print envelopes and labels from within your document.

How to create an envelope

If Word doesn't find anything it recognizes as an address, it will leave the Delivery Address text box empty. But if it finds text that looks like an address, it fills in the box.

Word shows quite a lot of intelligence in identifying the address. A series of short lines can confuse it, but it generally finds an address if one exists. If you want to make certain that Word finds the address, you can select the text or place the cursor in the address. But if you're curious, you might experiment a bit to see just how clever the program is at discovering an address on your page.

Word also inserts information in the Return Address text box. This is the Mailing Address entry currently stored on the Tools Options User Info card, but you can edit it in the Envelopes And Labels dialog box if you need to. If you make changes to the return address, Word will ask whether you want to use the revised address as your default return address when you print the envelope. Answer Yes, and Word will modify the information on the Tools Options User Info card. You can also check the Omit check box to have Word print only the Delivery Address. Use this option if you have preprinted envelopes that already include the return address.

The Preview and Feed areas show you how your envelope will look when printed and how the blank envelope should be oriented when fed into your printer. To change these settings, choose Options on the Envelopes card.

## How to change the format for an envelope

Figure 8-19 shows the Envelope Options dialog box, which Word will open when you choose the Options button on the Envelopes card. The box has two tabbed cards: Envelope Options and Printing Options; the Envelope Options card is illustrated in the figure.

**FIGURE 8-19**

The Envelope Options card contains a variety of options controlling how your envelope will appear when printed.

The first item on the Envelope Options card is the Envelope Size text box. The default setting is the standard Size 10 business envelope, but you can open the attached pull-down list to find 10 additional predefined sizes. You'll also find a Custom Size option; choosing this will open a dialog box in which you can enter the height and width of the envelope you want to use.

If you plan on using large envelopes (larger than 8.5 by 11 inches), make certain that your printer's paper path can handle the larger paper size. Most laser printers cannot take paper wider than 8.5 inches. If your envelope is too wide for your printer, you may find it convenient to print the address on a label instead. We'll cover Word's label-printing feature immediately after the envelope-printing feature.

**How to add Postnet and FIM bar codes.** The If Mailed In The USA box contains two check boxes. Check the Delivery Point Bar Code check box if you want Word to add a Postnet bar code to the envelope face. This bar code contains the ZIP code information from the delivery address in a machine-readable code that the U.S. Postal Service's automated mail-handling equipment can read. (Note, in passing, that if you tell Word to add the envelope to your file, it adds the Postnet bar code as a field, called the BARCODE field. You can also add a BARCODE field manually if you like. We will discuss fields in more detail in Chapter 20, starting on page 639.)

**NEW!**

The FIM-A Courtesy Reply Mail check box will be grayed unless the Delivery Point Bar Code check box is checked. If you check this second check box, Word will print a different bar code along the top of the envelope. This bar code helps the mail-handling equipment locate both the postage and the Postnet code. Check with your local post office for more information on FIM bar codes.

**How to format addresses.** Both the Delivery Address and Return Address boxes have a Font button and From Left and From Top text boxes. The Font buttons will open an Envelope Address dialog box for the delivery address and an Envelope Return Address dialog box for the return address. You can use these dialog boxes to modify the font formats for the address and return address, as appropriate. Use the From Left and From Top boxes to position the address blocks precisely. The default setting for all four is Auto, which will take care of placement for you.

**NEW!**

Note that there is no way to control the font format for individual words or lines in an address block. However, you can change these formats if you choose the Add To Document button on the Envelopes card and then format the individual words and lines within the document. We'll discuss the Add To Document button in a moment.

**How to set the envelope feed options.** Figure 8-20 on the next page shows the Printing Options card for envelopes. The items and choices on this screen will vary depending on your default printer. Word displays the printer name after the word Printer at the top of the card.

**NEW!**

**FIGURE 8-20**

The Printing Options card contains envelope feed options for your selected printer.

The Feed Method box in the middle of the card shows the available options for feeding envelopes into the current default printer. For most laser printers, the choices will include left-aligned, centered, and right-aligned positioning, with either the long or the short edge of the envelope being fed into the printer.

The Face Up, Face Down, and Clockwise Rotation buttons will appear on the Printing Options card for only some printers. You choose the Face Up or Face Down button to match the orientation of the envelope with your printer, as appropriate. Clockwise Rotation shifts the orientation for envelopes that are fed short edge first.

By default, Word will highlight the recommended Feed Method for the current printer. You can use the Reset button to return to Word's recommended settings.

## How to print the envelope

After you finish setting the envelope options, you can choose OK to return to the Envelopes And Labels dialog box. If you're satisfied with your settings, you can either print the envelope immediately by choosing the Print button or add the envelope to your document for later printing by choosing the Add To Document button.

If you print the envelope immediately, Word doesn't save it anywhere. If you add it to the document, Word will save it with the document and won't print it until you choose a print command. This option is particularly useful when you want to apply some special font formatting or when you want to edit the envelope further in some other way, such as by adding a picture or other object.

When you add the envelope to your document, Word adds a new section at the beginning of the file. We will discuss sections in Chapter 13; for now, it's enough to know that the envelope must be in a separate section because it's formatted with a page size and margins that differ from the rest of your document. (When Word changes these formats, the changes must apply to an entire section.)

## Labels

The Labels card, shown in Figure 8-21, is similar to the Envelopes card. You can use it to print one label or many labels.

**FIGURE 8-21**

With the Labels card, you can quickly print one or more labels.

To display the Labels card, choose Tools Envelopes And Labels and then choose the Labels card. Assuming that Word is able to identify an address in the current document, the Address box will contain the same address block as the Delivery Address on the Envelopes card. Instead of a return address, the Labels card contains a check box labeled Use Return Address, immediately above the Address box. If you check this box, Word will replace the destination address taken from your current document with the address from the Tools Options User Info card. In other words, the only address Word will print on the label is your return address.

The return address feature on the Labels card makes it easy to print one or more return address labels, but it isn't much help if you are trying to create a shipping label with both a return and a destination address on it. If you need to create a shipping label and the label comes in a one-across format, define the format as an envelope rather than a label. Choose the Custom Size option on the Envelope Options card for the envelope size, and specify the appropriate height and width. For details, see the discussion of printing envelopes, earlier in this chapter.

The Delivery Point Bar Code check box on the Labels card works the same way as on the Envelope Options card. The Label box displays a preview of the label and includes the label type, as defined on the Label options card, which we'll discuss in a moment.

The Print box, which contains two option buttons, is unique to the Labels card. The Full Page Of The Same Label option prints a full sheet of the same label. The Single Label option prints an individual label and also specifies the row and column position of the label on the sheet. The choices available for row and column number will vary depending on the type of label.

Note that the ability to specify a row and a column for printing a single label implies the ability to run the same label sheet through your laser printer any number of times, printing one label each time. Be aware that most printer label manufacturers do not recommend using a label sheet more than once. Each time you run the sheet through your printer, you increase the odds of having a label come off and stick to something inside the printer. That's particularly true if you've already used the label at the leading edge of the sheet in such a way that the label in the next row presents an edge to the printer. If a label comes off, it may cause serious damage— and, at the very least, will be a chore to find and remove. Some people use partially filled label sheets without any problems, but you may want to be more cautious and do this sparingly if at all. If you do try using partial sheets, print your labels so that you remove them from the bottom of the page first.

If you choose not to use partially filled sheets, you can minimize the number of wasted labels by dividing the sheets into smaller sheets. If you start with a sheet of 20 labels, for example, with two columns of 10, you can cut the sheet in half lengthwise and then cut each of the two halves in half. The final result is four sheets of five labels each. And each one will have a proper leading edge.

Instead of the Envelopes card's Add To Document button, the Labels card has a New Document button. Choosing this button creates a new document, formatted to produce the specified label (or page of labels). As with the equivalent option for envelopes, use this option if you want to edit the label further—to add font formatting to individual words or lines, for example, or to add graphics. You will also want to use this option if you plan to reprint the same page of labels at some later time, as with a sheet of return address labels.

## How to define the label to use: The Label Options dialog box

The Options button on the Labels card opens the Label Options dialog box, shown in Figure 8-22. You use this box to specify the type of labels being used.

**FIGURE 8-22**

The Label Options dialog box contains settings that control how your labels will appear when printed.

In the Printer Information box you choose a printer type (Dot Matrix or Laser).

You can select Dot Matrix even if your default printer is a laser printer. If you do, however, you may not get the results you want since the laser printer versions of labels in various sizes use a format different from that of the dot matrix versions. So be careful about changing the label type.

The Label Products box has a pull-down list of supported label brands, including Avery Standard, Avery Pan European, and Other. If you cannot find a choice that matches the labels you use, you can create your own custom format, as we will discuss in a moment.

The Product Number box lists the supported label formats for the Label Products group you specified. The majority of the available types are Avery products, and they cover everything from mailing labels to Rolodex cards. The Label Information box to the right of the Product Number box displays the type, width, height, and page size for the label that's currently highlighted in the Product Number list.

If you want to change the settings for a label or create your own custom settings, choose the Details button. This will open a dialog box, similar to the one in either Figure 8-23 or Figure 8-24, in which you can specify a custom format for a label sheet or tractor feed labels.

**FIGURE 8-23**

Choosing the Details button on the Label Options card will open a dialog box similar to this one and the one in Figure 8-24. This dialog box is typical for laser printers.

**FIGURE 8-24**

This dialog box is typical for dot matrix printers.

As you can see in the figures, the dialog box will vary depending on the setting for Printer Information in the Label Options dialog box. Figure 8-23 is an example of what you'll see for laser printers, Figure 8-24 for dot matrix printers.

For laser printers, you can define the top margin (distance from the top of a sheet to the top of the first label on the sheet), side margin (distance from the side of the sheet to the edge of the first label), vertical pitch (distance from the top of one label to the top of the next label), horizontal pitch (distance from the left edge of one label in a row to the left edge of the next), label height, label width, and number of labels in each row and column of a sheet. For dot matrix printers, you can define the same measurements. The settings for Number Across and Number Down determine which settings are available. In both cases, these choices are enough to let you easily create custom settings for virtually any label.

If you've been following along from the beginning of the book, by now you know enough about Word to go from a blank screen to final printed output. Unless you have specialized requirements such as footnotes and multiple columns, you know most of what you need to know. But we haven't covered everything that every Word user should know.

There are a number of ways in which you can reconfigure the Word program to suit your own needs and preferences, and so far we've barely touched on them. In fact, there are some straightforward settings that we haven't even looked at yet. In the next chapter, we'll show you some of the more straightforward ways of customizing Word to meet your needs.

# TOPIC FINDER

# Menu-Based Customization

f you've been following the discussion from the beginning of the book, you now know how to go from a blank Word screen to final printed output, unless you have some specialized requirements such as footnotes or multiple columns. Up to now, however, we have done most things Word's way, using most of the program defaults.

By now, you should have a sense of which defaults you'd prefer to change. In the final section of this book, we'll show you some sophisticated tricks for redesigning menus, reassigning keystrokes, and building macros. For now, we'll look at some relatively simple ways you can change Word to better match your tastes.

## Viewing Your Document

Among the most fundamental settings for Word is the way it displays your document on the screen. Depending on how you count them, there are at least five basic choices for viewing a document, and even more when you consider the scaling options. The basic views for editing are Normal, Outline, Page

Layout, and Master Document views, plus Print Preview. In addition, Normal, Outline, and Master Document views can appear with or without Draft mode turned on, and you can choose a Full Screen option for any view.

Some of these choices—Print Preview and Page Layout view, for example—are better suited to certain editing or formatting tasks than others. But you are likely to find each of the choices useful at some time or other. We've already mentioned some of these, and we covered Print Preview in depth in Chapter 8. Here's a look at the rest, starting with the one you have seen most often: Normal view, without Draft mode.

## Normal view

As the name implies, Normal is the view most people normally use for most of their work. And it's the view we've used for most of our examples up to this point. Normal view is generally considered to be WYSIWYG (What You See Is What You Get) because what you see on the screen is a close approximation of what you'll get on a printed page. By default, Normal view will show you all character and paragraph formatting, tab-stop alignment, line breaks, and page breaks (as a dotted line across the screen page).

Normal view has some limitations to its WYSIWYG features. It doesn't show headers, footers, footnotes, or side-by-side snaking columns as they'll appear on the printed page. Nor will Normal view show how text wraps around fixed-position paragraphs, tables, and pictures.

However, there are advantages to using Normal view as well. Because Word does not spend time calculating such details as headers and footers while in Normal view, working in Normal view is faster than working in the more fully WYSIWYG Page Layout view. In addition, because it doesn't show top and bottom margins on a page, Normal view will let you see the text at the bottom of one page and the top of another at the same time, as shown in Figure 9-1. This can be an important advantage when you're writing or editing and a page break falls in the middle of a sentence. For all of these reasons, you'll probably want to use Normal view most of the time.

**NEW!** To set your screen for Normal view, open the View menu, and make sure that a dot appears next to Normal. If you see a dot next to a different view choice, simply choose Normal. Alternatively, you can press the ⌘-Option-N shortcut keys to set Word for Normal view. Mouse users can click on the Normal View button, which is the leftmost of the three buttons that appear beside the horizontal scroll bar.

**FIGURE 9-1**

Normal view offers a useful balance between WYSIWYG features and system speed. It also lets you see the bottom of one page and the top of another at the same time.

## Normal view with the draft font

As your documents grow longer and more complex, it will take Word longer to display them and move through them. If you feel frustrated at the lack of speed, you may want to use Word's draft font when displaying your document. You can toggle the draft font on and off in Normal view with the Draft Font check box on the Tools Options View card.

Word operates much faster when displaying the draft font because it doesn't bother to show most character formatting on the screen. Word will display all of your text in the system font (the font used in the menu bar, typically Chicago). If you've added any character formatting such as boldface or italics, that text will display as underlined.

Figure 9-2 on the next page shows a sample document displayed using the draft font. Although this document is formatted with the Times font, as you can see by the Formatting toolbar, it's displayed with the Chicago font.

Word offers a separate option for graphics, the Picture Placeholders check box, on the Tools Options View card, as we'll describe later in this chapter. By dividing the Draft mode features into two separate settings, Word not only lets you use Picture Placeholders within Normal view but also enables you to view your pictures when using the draft font. In many cases, using Picture Placeholders rather than the Draft Font setting in Normal view will be the best compromise between speed and being able to see the formatting of your document.

**FIGURE 9-2**

Draft mode trades WYSIWYG capabilities for speed.

One instance where the draft font comes in handy is when you're editing text in a small font size. By working with the draft font, you will probably find it easier to read and select the small text. (You can also use Word's View Zoom command, however, which we will discuss later in this chapter.)

Keep in mind that the Draft Font setting controls only the way Word displays the document on your screen; it does not affect the way the document will look when you print it.

## Outline view

Word's Outline view is what's known as a collapsible outliner. If your document has headings of various levels defined (using styles, which we will discuss in Chapter 12), you can collapse the document to see only the headings. You can also choose to see headings up to a specified level. And you can move sections of your document around with ease, collapsing an entire section to a single line and then moving all of the text in that section by moving the one line. You can also use Outline view to collapse the document so that you can move through it quickly.

We'll cover the outlining features in Chapter 19. For now, it's enough to know that even if you don't generally use outlines, you may find Outline view helpful for such tasks as creating a table of contents.

**NEW!**
You can switch to Outline view by choosing View Outline, pressing ⌘-Option-O, or clicking on the Outline View button next to the horizontal scroll bar. (Note that the same button will switch you to Outline view or Master Document view, depending on which of the two views you were in most recently.)

Word will display a dot next to Outline on the View menu to indicate that it's set for Outline view. Figure 9-3 shows our sample document (uncollapsed) in Outline view. Notice the plus sign next to the title, indicating that the title is defined as a heading paragraph and that there is text under the heading. The indention of the other paragraphs indicates that they come under the heading. The small box next to each one indicates that they are defined as normal text, rather than headings.

**FIGURE 9-3**

Outline view shows the structure of your document. It is useful for creating a table of contents, moving through long documents, and rearranging large blocks of text.

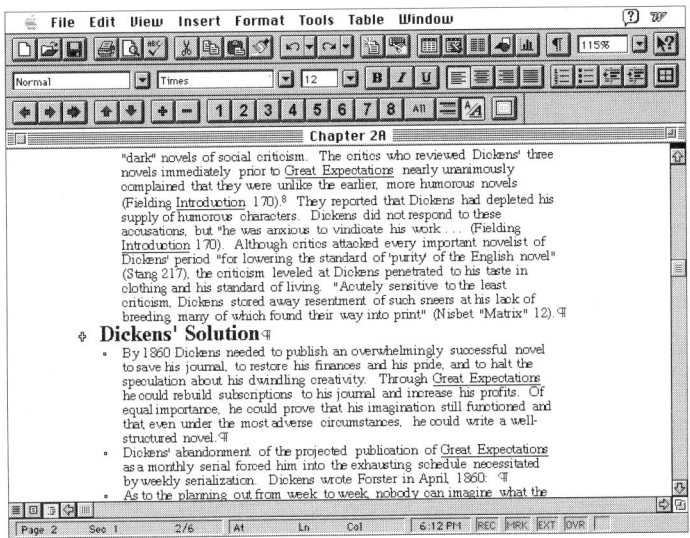

Outline view, like Normal view, works with or without Draft mode. You can use Draft mode in Outline view to gain the same speed advantage as in Normal view.

## Page Layout view

Page Layout view provides an on-screen representation of your printed document, yielding something very close to full WYSIWYG. In addition to the WYSIWYG features in Normal view, Page Layout view shows headers, footers, and footnotes as they will appear on the printed page. Page Layout view also displays snaking columns side by side and shows how text will wrap around fixed-position objects.

You switch to Page Layout view by choosing View Page Layout, pressing ⌘-Option-P, or clicking on the Page Layout View button (the middle button in the group of three beside the horizontal scroll bar). There are also a few commands, such as Insert Frame, that either automatically switch to Page Layout view or ask whether you want to. Whenever you're in Page Layout view, Word displays a dot next to the Page Layout command on the View menu.

NEW!

There is one important performance issue to consider with Page Layout view. Compared with Normal view, Page Layout view requires Word to work much harder—making complex calculations to determine the line and page formatting, and then creating the images to display on your screen. Given a complicated format, this can be a taxing load, even for a fast computer. As a result, you will probably find that you're best off typing and editing in Normal view, with or without Draft mode. We recommend that you reserve Page Layout view for when you absolutely need it.

When you're in Page Layout view, Word displays the top and bottom margins of each page, as well as the body text. For example, if your document has a 1-inch top margin with a header, the margin and header will appear at the top of each page. Similarly, the bottom margin will show at the bottom of each page, along with any footer you've created.

When you scroll vertically in Page Layout view, Word will also display the top and bottom edges of each page instead of marking page breaks with a dotted horizontal line as in Normal view. When you scroll horizontally, it will display the left and right edges of each page. For example, Figure 9-4 shows the bottom of one page and the top of another in Page Layout view after we've scrolled to bring the left edge of the pages into view. Notice the margins on both pages and the header at the top of the second page. The paragraph is broken in midsentence, making it clumsy to work with if you are writing or editing.

**FIGURE 9-4**

Page Layout view lets you see the elements of your document on the page, positioned as they will print.

When you are viewing the bottom of one page and the top of the next in Page Layout view, as shown in Figure 9-4, your page margins take up much of the available screen space. To see more of the pages without reducing the image size, you can use Full Screen mode, which we will cover later in this chapter.

## Text areas

In Page Layout view, Word treats different elements of your page layout as separate text areas. A simple document has only one text area—the single column of text that's bounded by the left, right, top, and bottom margins. In a multicolumn layout, each column is a separate text area. Each header and footer is also a text area.

The concept of text areas becomes significant as you move around and select text in Page Layout view. For example, each text area has its own ruler. Before we look at these issues, however, let's identify the separate text areas on a page.

## Boundary lines

To help you keep your bearings and distinguish text areas while in Page Layout view, Word can display boundaries, or dotted lines, around the different text areas of a document. To activate this feature, choose Tools Options, select the View card, and check the Text Boundaries check box in the Show group box. Figure 9-5 shows the same document you saw in Figure 9-4, but with text boundaries displayed.

**FIGURE 9-5**

You can tell Word to display boundary lines by selecting the Text Boundaries option on the Tools Options View card.

The View card shows a slightly different set of options in Page Layout view than it does in Normal view. In addition to the Text Boundaries check box, the card in Page Layout view contains a Drawings check box, an Object Anchors check box, and a Vertical Ruler check box. Choices available in Normal view (but not in Page Layout view) are the Draft Font and Wrap To Window check boxes and the Style Area Width option. In general, the choices that aren't available in one view aren't meaningful in that view. We'll cover each of these options later in this chapter.

Figure 9-5 shows two kinds of boundary lines. The vertical and horizontal lines that intersect below the header in the upper left corner of the page are the margin boundaries. If you scroll to any corner of the page, you will see similar intersecting lines. Above the header is the top of the header boundary. This top line is 0.5 inch from the top edge of the page—the position specified as the From Edge setting for the header, on the File Document Layout Margins card. If a page contains a footer, the bottom boundary of the footer will be marked by a similar line. There are also short horizontal and vertical lines that meet just outside the corner of the text area; these marks are similar to crop marks that layout artists use to mark the corners of a page.

## How to navigate in Page Layout view

In addition to the usual commands for navigating in Page Layout view, you can use the Page Back and Page Forward buttons at the bottom of the vertical scroll bar.

| Button | Name |
| --- | --- |
| ⬆ | Page Back |
| ⬇ | Page Forward |

When you click on the Page Back button, Word will move back one full page. If you start with the top of the current page showing, Word will move back to show the top of the previous page; if you start with the bottom of the current page showing, Word will move you back to the bottom of the previous page. Similarly, clicking on the Page Forward button will move you forward one full page.

As you navigate through your document in Page Layout view, you'll notice that Word always aligns the zero point of the horizontal ruler with the left boundary of the current text area. For example, consider the two-column document in Figures 9-6 and 9-7. With the cursor in the left column (as shown in Figure 9-6), Word aligns the zero point of the horizontal ruler with the left boundary of that text area. With the cursor in the right column (as shown in Figure 9-7 on the next page), the ruler's zero point is the left boundary of that text area.

Word also offers shortcut keys for moving around in Page Layout view. Option-Down arrow moves the cursor to the beginning of the next frame, object, or column on the current page; Option-Up arrow moves to the beginning of the previous frame, object, or column on the current page. Note that Word's idea of what comes next might not always match yours. For example, if you have a page with two frames surrounded by text, and you start at the bottom of the page, Option-Up arrow may move you in a continuous cycle to the columns on either side of the frame, then to the top of the page, then to the frame, and then to the columns surrounding the frame. If you're at the top or bottom of one page and want to move to the next, the Up and Down arrow keys by themselves will move you from the current page. Note also that if you use the arrow keys by themselves to move around in a multicolumn document in Page Layout view, you have to use the Left and Right arrow keys to move from the end of one column to the beginning of the next. Pressing the Down arrow key while you're in the last line of the first column, for example, will take you to the next page, not the next column.

**FIGURE 9-6**

Word aligns the horizontal ruler's zero point with the left boundary of the cur-rent text area. Here the cursor is in the left text column.

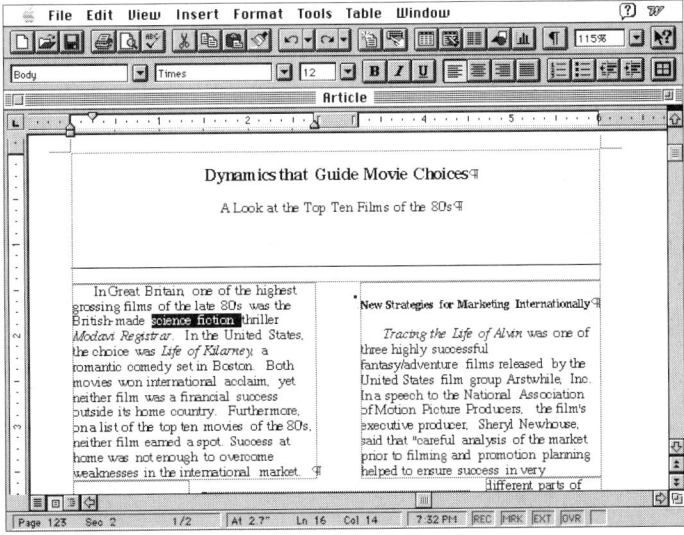

**FIGURE 9-7**

Now the cursor is in
the right text column;
the zero point on the
horizontal ruler has
also moved.

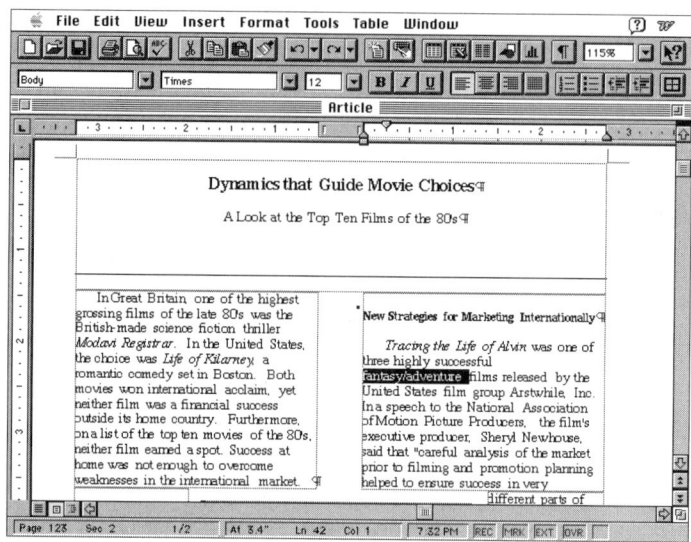

## How to select text in Page Layout view

Each text area in Page Layout view has its own selection bar. You can see evidence of this as you move the pointer around. When the pointer moves over the selection bar for a text area, it changes shape to a right-arrow pointer. For example, suppose you are working with a two-column layout. Your document window will have a selection bar on the far left, as it normally does. However, this selection bar is for the left column only. If you want to select text in the right column, you can use the right column's selection bar, located just to the left of the right column.

If you want to select all of the text in a document, move the pointer to any selection bar other than one for a header or footer and press the ⌘ key as you click the mouse button. You can also use all of Word's usual selection techniques. And you can select text on two or more pages by dragging to extend a selection beyond the top or bottom border of the text window. (You may find that this is much slower in Page Layout view than in Normal view.)

## How to edit and format in Page Layout view

Although you'll probably want to use Normal view for most of your editing and formatting, you'll often need to make minor changes while in Page Layout view as well. Of course, you can do everything in Page Layout view if you have a fast enough system and decide that you prefer to work this way. To make any changes, choose the same editing or formatting commands that you would choose in Normal view.

### Headers and footers in Page Layout view

Page Layout view shows you the position of each page's header and footer as they will appear when printed. To add new headers or footers, use the View Header And Footer command, as we discussed in Chapter 5. If you select the Different Odd And Even or Different First Page option for headers and footers on the File Document Layout Layout card, Word will label each header or footer—as Odd Page or Even Page, for example—but only while you are editing it. The labels will not show when you work with body text.

If you want to edit a header or footer that already exists, either choose View Header And Footer or double-click on the header or footer area. Word will activate the header or footer itself so that you can make changes, and it will display the Header And Footer toolbar. Word will apply any change you make to all appropriate headers or footers—meaning all headers on odd pages or even pages, for example, or all those in the current section. If your document has multiple sections, changing a header or footer on one page will affect any linked headers or footers in subsequent sections. We'll explain sectional headers and footers in "Section headers and footers" on page 463.

### Footnotes in Page Layout view

Footnotes function very much like headers and footers when you're in Page Layout view. When you choose Insert Footnote, Word will insert the footnote reference mark in the document's text and move the cursor to the footnote area at the bottom of the page. You can then type the footnote. If it already exists, you can move to it with the keyboard or mouse any time you're in Page Layout view and edit it as needed. We will discuss footnotes in more detail in "Footnotes and Endnotes" on page 560.

## Master Document view

NEW!

Master Document view is closely related to Outline view, except that it gives you a way to view, open, and manage many related files at once. This is particularly useful when you are working with a large document made up of many separate files—such as chapters of a book or sections of a long report. We will discuss Master Document view in more detail in "How to use Master Document view" on page 560.

## View Full Screen

NEW!

The View menu offers a command called Full Screen. This is available no matter which view you're in—even Print Preview.

Full Screen mode hides almost all of Word's on-screen window dressing. Switching to Full Screen mode will not remove the title bar and menu bar, but it can remove just about everything else. It may remove toolbars, rulers, scroll bars, and so on, depending on how you've set Word. In any case, the point is to display on one screen as much of your document as possible. Some users will prefer this over the regular Word display because it removes potentially distracting items and makes it easier to focus on writing. Figure 9-8 shows a document in Page Layout view in Full Screen mode.

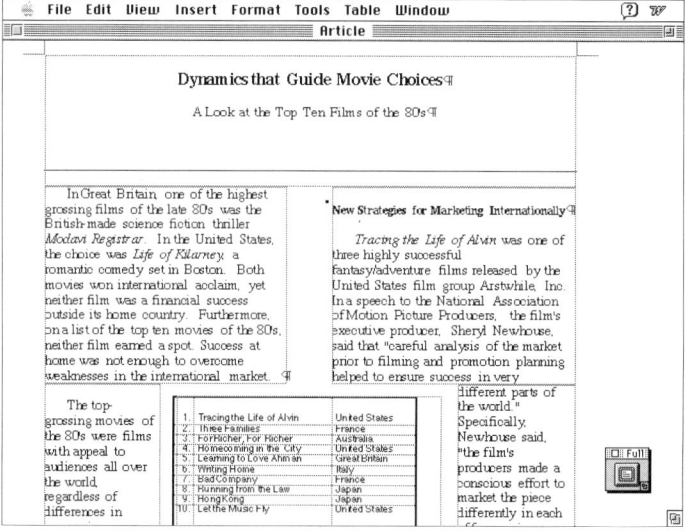

**FIGURE 9-8**

Word's Full Screen mode makes it easy to hide almost everything but your text.

Word remembers the settings you make in Full Screen mode for what to display and what to hide. You can change these settings the same way you change them when not in Full Screen mode—by choosing View Ruler to hide or display the rulers, choosing View Toolbars to open the Toolbars dialog box and hide or display individual toolbars, and checking or clearing the check boxes in the Window group box on the Tools Options View card.

More important, Word remembers separate sets of settings for Full Screen mode and non–Full Screen mode. So even if you don't want to use Full Screen mode for its obvious purpose—providing an uncluttered screen that shows more text—you might want to use it to toggle between two states, such as one that shows one set of toolbars and one that shows a different set. This can be quite useful if, for example, you've created some custom toolbars and want them available when you're formatting your document but not when you're writing or editing.

### How to turn Full Screen mode off

When you switch to Full Screen mode, Word will, by default, display a special Full Screen toolbar (although you can set Word not to show this either). The toolbar holds only one button, so it's only large enough to show the word "Full" on its title bar. This name is a bit misleading, however, because you click on the button to *leave* Full Screen mode. Alternatively, you can press the Esc key to leave Full Screen mode, or choose View Full Screen to toggle Full Screen off.

## Zoom settings

The Zoom command, at the bottom of the View menu, affects what you'll see in Normal, Outline, and Page Layout views, with the Draft Font option on or off, and whether or not you are in Full Screen mode. The Zoom command is one of Word's most useful viewing tools; it gives you control over how much of a page you can see at one time and how large the text characters and graphics will be on screen. The feature has much the same effect as a zoom lens on a camera, enabling you to zoom in for a close look or zoom out for a more sweeping view of your page.

You can treat the View Zoom command both as an aid to formatting and as a way to adjust text size for comfortable viewing. As a formatting aid, the feature will let you zoom out to see all or most of a page at once (or more than one page in Page Layout view) so that you can judge larger formatting issues, such as page and column breaks. It will also let you zoom in on your page so that you can see and control the precise placement of a picture or other graphic element.

Word will remember different zoom settings for Normal, Page Layout, and Outline views (with Outline and Master Document views sharing the same zoom setting). You can use this to good effect. For example, if you are creating a newsletter, you'll often need to make small changes in your text strictly for formatting purposes—as when you have to cut lines because a story doesn't quite fit the allotted space. By setting Page Layout view to show an overall view of the page and Normal view to display the text large enough to read easily, you can toggle back and forth between the two views— to Normal view so that you can quickly and easily make changes, and to Page Layout view so that you can see the effect of the changes on the overall layout.

Most of the time you'll probably want to see text in approximately the same size as it will be printed. With Word's View Zoom command, you can precisely control the text size by choosing a setting that's appropriate for your particular monitor and your individual taste.

## How to change zoom settings with the Zoom dialog box

To change the zoom setting in Word, you can choose View Zoom. Word will open the Zoom dialog box, shown in Figure 9-9.

**FIGURE 9-9**

The Zoom dialog box gives you control over the enlargement or reduction of your document on screen.

The Zoom To group box on the left side of the Zoom dialog box contains six option buttons, a text box, and a rather large toolbar-style button. The Preview box to the right of the Zoom To box will show the effect of your settings as you make them. If you're in Normal or Outline view, the small screen displayed within the monitor graphic will show the Normal style text as the text appears at that scale. If you are in Page Layout view, the box will show the outline of a page (or multiple pages) as the pages appear at that scale. In Page Layout view, Word adds a second preview area below the small monitor screen to show how the text will look.

Three of the option buttons in the Zoom To box are for preset zoom levels: 200% (useful for precise placement of graphics or text), 100% ("full size," appropriate for most writing and editing), and 75% (still large enough to be readable on many monitors, but showing more text than the 100% level).

The next three options are given in terms of a page rather than a percentage. Page Width will adjust the zoom scale to be large enough that the left and right margins both show on the screen. (Note, however, that if the style area is displayed at the left side of the screen, Word will not take it into account in adjusting the page width.)

**NEW!**　The Whole Page and Many Pages options are available only if you are in Page Layout view or Print Preview. Whole Page will fit a single page on the screen. The Many Pages option works with the large button just below it. This button works like the Multiple Pages button on the Print Preview toolbar, which we discussed in Chapter 8. As shown in Figure 9-10, you can click and drag on the grid to indicate how many rows and columns of pages you want to see on the screen at one time. These thumbnail views of pages are handy when you want to see the overall layout or form of a document.

You can set Word to display multiple pages in Page Layout view.

If none of the preset zoom choices serves your needs, you can specify any zoom level from 10% to 200% in the Percent text box. Word will use the setting until you either change it or choose one of the preset options.

## How to change zoom settings with the Standard toolbar's Zoom Control box

Word provides the Zoom Control box on the Standard toolbar for changing the zoom setting quickly with a mouse. When you click on the down arrow next to the box, you'll see a drop-down list of zoom setting choices, as shown in Figure 9-11.

The Zoom Control box on the Standard toolbar gives mouse users a quick way to change the zoom setting. The list on the left shows the choices available in Normal and Outline views; the one on the right shows the choices in Page Layout view.

As you can see in Figure 9-11, the choices available on the drop-down list depend on the view. In Normal or Outline view, the choices are 10%, 25%, 50%, 75%, 100%, 125%, 150%, 200%, and Page Width. In Page Layout view, Word adds Whole Page and Two Pages to the list.

# NEW!   Word Defaults

You can switch from one of Word's various views to another as often as you need to. However, Word also has a number of settings that you're likely to set once and then leave pretty much alone. These settings provide control over options that range from screen defaults to printing defaults to your default data directory. When you installed Word, all of these settings were predefined. But you can change any of them.

As we discussed at the end of Chapter 1, you can change many of the default settings from the various Tools Options cards. We've covered some of these settings in Chapter 1 and elsewhere; we'll discuss most of the rest now and refer back to those we've already looked at.

To open the Options dialog box, choose the Tools Options command. To display any card within the dialog box, choose the appropriate tab at the top of the dialog box. You can choose a tab by clicking on it with the mouse or by pressing ⌘-Page Down or ⌘-Page Up to move from one tab to the next.

## The View card

As shown in Figure 9-12, Word has a number of View settings that affect your screen display. We covered most of the Window options and the Nonprinting Characters options in Chapter 1, but we need to mention a few here.

**FIGURE 9-12**

The View card in the Options dialog box offers settings that affect how Word displays your document.

The options on the View card will change somewhat, depending on what view Word is currently set for. The options for Normal view and Outline view are the same, but those for Page Layout view are different. Note that in Figure

9-12, Word is set for Normal view, and the text at the top of the card reads *Normal View Options*. This text will change to reflect the view you're in.

When you're in Page Layout view, the View card contains several options that apply to features affecting only Page Layout view—for example, the Text Boundaries option (which adds dotted lines to indicate text areas on the page, such as body text and headers). The options contained only on the Normal and Outline versions of the card apply to features that affect only Normal and Outline views—for example, the Style Area Width option, which we'll discuss in a moment.

The Status Bar option in the Window group box on both cards determines **NEW!** whether the status bar will be displayed at the bottom of your screen. If you choose not to display it, you will still see most prompts and messages on the bottom line of your screen, but most of the time this line will be used as part of the document window. You will not see the brief help comments displayed when a command is highlighted.

The Style Area Width text box—available only in Normal, Outline, or Master Document view—lets you reserve a portion of the left side of the document window for displaying style names. Enter any measurement to have Word display the name of the current style for each paragraph while you are in Normal or Outline view. You can then adjust the size of the style area to see all or just part of each style name. We will discuss styles in Chapter 12, "Styles & AutoFormat," starting on page 389.

The Vertical Ruler check box—available only in Page Layout view—displays **NEW!** or hides the vertical ruler.

We covered most of the choices in the Nonprinting Characters group box in Chapter 1. Note that except for the All check box, which is equivalent to checking all of the other boxes, the choices in this group box let you selectively display or hide specific nonprinting characters, such as paragraph marks. Checking All is equivalent to clicking on the Standard toolbar's Show/Hide ¶ button.

If you choose to display tab characters, they will appear as small arrows pointing to the right. Spaces appear as dots that look much like periods but are raised off the text baseline to about the same level as the center of a lowercase o. We covered optional hyphens in Chapter 6. If you choose to display them, they will appear as dotted hyphens.

Hidden text, a font formatting option, is text that you don't usually want to see or print—notes to yourself, for example. If you display hidden text, it will appear with a dotted underline.

The check boxes in the Show group box control some finer points of how **NEW!** Word displays your document. Picture Placeholders speeds up display performance by using a box placeholder in a document instead of a picture's actual image. The Field Codes check box toggles Word between displaying fields themselves—for example, {DATE} or {TIME}—and displaying what Word calls the field results, such as *10/12/93* or *7:58 PM*. We'll discuss fields in detail in Chapter 20. For now, simply note that there are many more field codes that you might want to include in your document. At times, you'll want to see the field codes; at other times, the results.

**NEW!**   If you check the Bookmarks check box, Word will add square brackets around sections you've designated as bookmarks with the Edit Bookmark command. We'll discuss the Edit Bookmark command in Chapter 10. For now, just note that the Bookmarks check box will make it easy to visually identify the bookmarks in your documents.

**NEW!**   The Field Shading option provides a similar feature for fields, adding shading to fields to help you identify them. We'll explain how to use the Field Shading option when we cover fields in Chapter 20.

The Draft Font and Wrap To Window check boxes are available only on the Normal and Outline view versions of the View card. As we discussed earlier in this chapter, the Draft Font choice displays text in the system font, rather than the font the text is formatted in.

**NEW!**   Checking the Wrap To Window check box tells Word to adjust line breaks on screen to match the width of the document window rather than the actual margins of the document. This can come in handy if you're viewing one or more documents in partial screen windows, or if you're working with a document that's too wide to fit on screen. Figure 9-13 shows two windows, side by side, each with its own document. The one on the left is set with the Wrap To

**FIGURE 9-13**

The Wrap To Window check box, which is checked for the document window on the left in this figure and cleared for the window on the right, will wrap lines at the window edge rather than at the document margins.

Window check box checked; the one on the right is set with the check box cleared. The text in the left window is fully visible, wrapping at the edge of the window. The text in the right window is cut off at the edge of the window. We recommend that you check the Wrap To Window check box if you're working with partial screen windows or wide documents but that you leave it cleared otherwise.

The Drawings, Object Anchors, and Text Boundaries check boxes are available only on the Page Layout view version of the View card. As discussed earlier in this chapter, the Text Boundaries option will display lines around text areas when Word is in Page Layout view. Clearing the Drawings check box causes Word to display Word drawings as boxes, which can speed up display performance. The Object Anchors check box causes Word to display the location of each frame's anchor—the paragraph to which it is attached. For more details about frames, see Chapter 14, "Columns, Frames, & Pictures," starting on page 469. For more about Word drawings, see Chapter 15, "Drawing, Graphics, & Other Objects," starting on page 521.

## The General card

The General options affect the way certain commands and keys work. As with the View options, we covered some of these in Chapter 1; here's a look at the rest.

Checking the Background Repagination check box tells Word to continually recalculate the automatic page breaks in your document while you work on it. If you want to increase the program's speed, you can turn this option off; Word will still repaginate whenever you switch to Page Layout view or Print Preview, or when you print your document.

Two options affect the appearance of the screen: Blue Background, White Text and 3D Dialog And Display Effects. The first gives you an alternative to the typical Macintosh black text on a white background display. You still don't have much control over the color of your display, but at least you now have two choices. Check the check box to see the blue background alternative.

The 3D Dialog And Display Effects check box toggles the shaded effects of dialog boxes and other interface features on and off. These are on by default. You may prefer the simpler image you get without them; to see the effect, clear the check box.

The Beep On Error Actions check box controls whether Word makes a sound when indicating an error. To hear a beep (or other sound as specified in the system Sound Control Panel), make sure the box is checked. If you don't want to hear a beep, clear the check box.

NEW! The Update Automatic Links At Open check box controls whether Word automatically updates information that's linked to other files every time you open the document. We'll discuss this in the context of the features it affects in Chapter 18.

NEW! The Mail As Attachment check box enables you to attach documents to an electronic mail message. This is meaningful if your computer is on a local area network and has a supported electronic mail program installed. For more information on networks and mail, see your network administrator.

The last option in the General Options group box lets you choose how many of the most recently opened document files will be listed at the bottom of the File menu. The default is four, but you can set this option from zero to nine.

Finally, you can use the Measurement Units box to set the default measurements that Word will use. The choices in the attached list box are Inches, Centimeters, Points, and Picas.

## The Edit card

We discussed all but three of the options on the Edit card in Chapter 1, and the Use Smart Cut And Paste option in Chapter 4. The only two we haven't covered yet are the Allow Accented Uppercase and Picture Editor options.

NEW! The Allow Accented Uppercase option applies only to text formatted as another language, such as French. Add a check to this check box, and Word's proofing tool and change case features will suggest adding accents to uppercase letters where appropriate.

NEW! You use the Picture Editor option to designate the application you want to use for editing pictures. We'll discuss this in the context of working with pictures in Chapter 15.

## NEW!   The File Locations card

The File Locations card has a two-column list; one column is File Types and the other is Location. Location refers to where Word will look for the type of file indicated unless told otherwise; you can always instruct Word to use a file of a given type from some other folder.

You probably won't need to make many changes to these settings, but there is at least one that you should change. By default, Word saves new documents in the same folder in which the program was installed. But this is a little like organizing your file cabinets by throwing all your documents—office supply catalogs, incoming and outgoing letters, check stubs, reports, and so on—into one file folder without sorting them. You can use the options on the File Locations card to impose some order on your files.

We recommend that you create a separate folder specifically for your Word documents. Or, better yet, create a main data folder with a set of folders in it. Use any organizational scheme that makes sense to you. You might, for example, create a separate folder for each client and then, within each client folder, a separate folder for each project. Alternatively, you might create a separate folder for each kind of document—one for letters, one for reports, and so on. Use an organizational scheme that can be easily extended as needed and will readily guide you to a file you're looking for.

When you've decided on a main data folder, set the Documents file type to that folder. Highlight Documents in the File Types list, choose the Modify button, and then choose the folder you want from the list of folders. Notice that you can also create a new folder from the Modify Location dialog box: Choose the New button, and type a new folder name in the Name Of New Folder box. Now, whenever you choose File Save for a new file or choose File Open, Word will, by default, look in the main data folder you've specified, and you need only choose the appropriate folder. (Be aware, however, that once you tell Word to use some other folder, Word will continue to use that folder during the current editing session until you tell it otherwise.)

The same principles that apply to organizing your data files apply to other files as well. You should also consider taking advantage of the other file type choices on the File Locations card to sort your files into different folders. Here again, separating the files will make it easier to find a file when you're looking for it.

## The Save card

We discussed most of the choices on the Save card in Chapter 1, and we discussed the file-sharing options in Chapter 2. Of the four remaining choices, we'll save three for discussing in the context of the features they affect. The fourth, Prompt To Save Normal, determines whether Word asks you if you want to save changes such as AutoText entries to the Normal template when you close the program, or whether it automatically saves them. To have Word prompt you, make sure this box is checked. To have Word save the changes automatically, clear the check box.

**NEW!**

## The other Tools Options cards

We've covered only five of the twelve cards in the Options dialog box here; however, we've already covered some of the others. For details on the Print card, see "Printing Options" on page 246; on the User Info card, see "User Info options" starting on page 32; on the Spelling card, see "The Tools Options Spelling card" on page 169; and on the Grammar card, see "How to use the grammar-checking options" on page 180.

The remaining three cards affect features we haven't looked at yet. We will cover these cards in the context of the features they affect. For details on the AutoFormat card, see "The AutoFormat Feature" on page 390; on the Compatibility card, see "How to use the Tools Options Compatibility card" on page 600; and on the Revisions card, see "Revision Marks" on page 323.

# Customizing Toolbars

If you prefer the mouse over the keyboard, Word's toolbars are one of the program's most powerful and attractive features. They provide instant access to a wide range of commands—and also macros, if you care to add them to toolbars. In fact, you can think of the toolbars as "shortcut keys" for the mouse. As with many of Word's most attractive features, much of the appeal lies in the fact that you can easily customize the toolbars to suit the way you work.

## NEW!   Floating toolbars

As you may have noticed, not all toolbars are displayed neatly below the menu bar. Some of the specialized toolbars, such as the Full Screen and the Header And Footer toolbars, show up by default as floating toolbars that you can drag and place anywhere on the screen.

Less obvious is that you can also move the Standard and Formatting toolbars anywhere you like. You can even place a toolbar outside the Word document window altogether. Figure 9-14 shows a Word document window reduced to less than full screen, with the Standard toolbar moved into the document window and the Formatting toolbar outside the Word document window.

To move a toolbar from the top of the Word window, simply click on a space between buttons and drag the toolbar to a new location. Once a toolbar is floating, you can grab it and move it by pointing either to an empty space between buttons or to the toolbar's title bar and then dragging. To put any toolbar—including toolbars that float by default—at the top of the window, drag it to the position where you want it and drop it. Alternatively, you can simply double-click on the toolbar background or on the title bar.

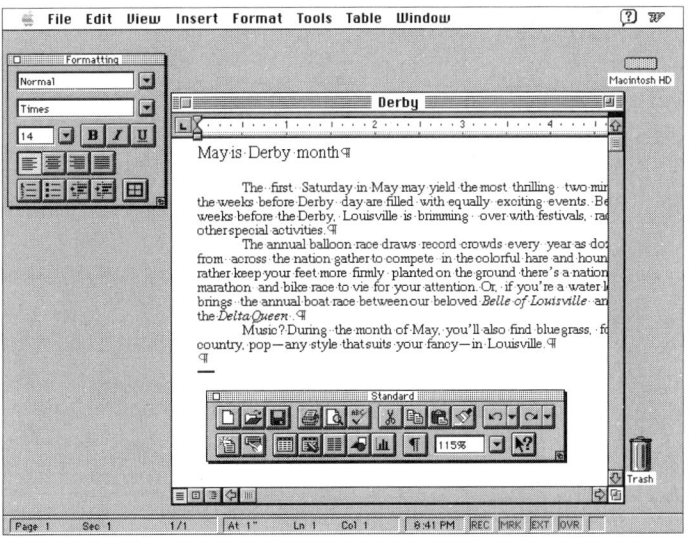

**FIGURE 9-14**

You can drag toolbars to new positions on the screen—even outside the Word document window itself, if you like.

You can even change the shape of a floating toolbar. Point to the Size box in the lower right corner of the toolbar border, and the mouse pointer will change to a two-headed arrow. Drag the lower right corner to make the window bigger or smaller; Word will automatically resize the other dimension and arrange the buttons to fit within the new space. (Notice that the toolbar snaps into place for its new positions, with the allowable dimensions determined by the number and size of buttons on the toolbar.) You can make a toolbar tall and thin or short and wide so that it will block the least amount of information on your screen while you're working.

In general, when you drop a floating toolbar at the top of the Word window, Word will try to insert it based on the position of the floating outline just before you dropped it. If the outline straddles two toolbar rows, for example, Word will generally insert the toolbar between the two.

## How to change or create a toolbar

NEW!

You can do much more than just move toolbars around the screen; you can also change the buttons on any toolbar, or even create new toolbars to suit your needs.

To create or change a toolbar, start by choosing the View Toolbars command, and then choose the Customize button; alternatively, choose Tools Customize, and then choose the Toolbars card. In either case, you'll see a dialog box similar to the one shown in Figure 9-15 on the next page.

**FIGURE 9-15**

The Tools Customize
Toolbars card enables
you to change Word's
toolbars by adding or
removing buttons for
commands or macros.

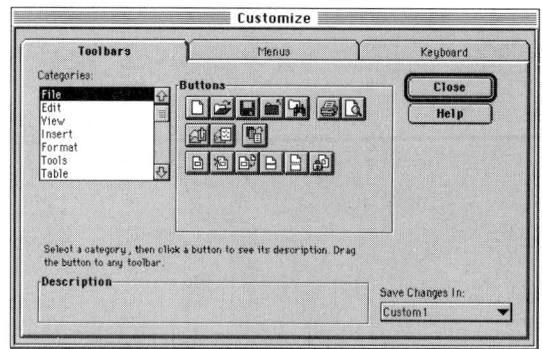

Note the Save Changes In list box in the lower right corner of the card.
We've chosen the Custom1 template, which is the supplemental template for
the current document. You could also store the changes as part of the Normal
template. We'll discuss templates later in this chapter; for the moment, it's
enough to know that Word always attaches the Normal template to each
document and that you can optionally attach a supplementary template as
well. If you're using only the Normal template, it will be the only choice available in the Save Changes In list box.

## How to delete a button

Whenever the Customize dialog box is open, toolbars and toolbar buttons are
not active: Clicking on a button will not execute a command.

You can remove any button from a toolbar to reduce the clutter or make
room for a different button. With the Customize dialog box open and the
Toolbars card displayed, click on the toolbar button that you want to remove,
drag it off the toolbar, and release it anywhere over the document window or
over the Customize dialog box. That's all there is to it.

## How to add a button

Adding a new button to an existing toolbar is nearly as easy as deleting one.
The Categories box on the Toolbars card lists various types of items that you
can add to the toolbar—all of the standard menu names (File, Edit, View, Insert, Format, Tools, Table, and Window and Help) plus choices for Drawing,
Borders, Mail Merge, All Commands, Macros, Fonts, AutoText, and Styles.
Figure 9-16 shows the Toolbars card with the Categories list scrolled down
partway.

Your choice in the Categories list box determines the options available in
the second box. If you choose any of the categories that match a name on the

menu bar (or choose Drawing, Borders, or Mail Merge), for example, Word will label the second box as Buttons and show a group of predefined buttons that you can choose from. To see a short description of any button's function, click on the button; Word will display the description in the Description box at the bottom of the card. To add a button to a toolbar, simply drag it to the toolbar and drop it in place. Word will automatically shift other buttons to the right, if necessary, to make room for the new one.

**FIGURE 9-16**

The Categories box lists categories of items to add as toolbar buttons.

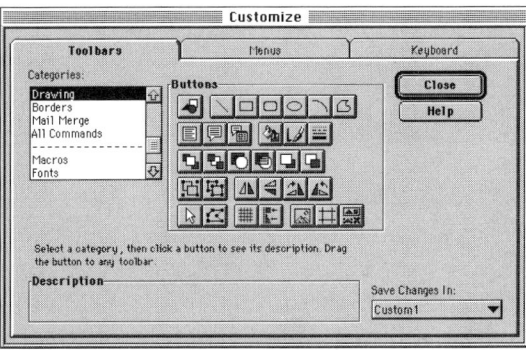

The last five items in the Categories list—All Commands, Macros, Fonts, AutoText, and Styles—do not display predefined buttons. Choose one of these, and Word will label the second box to match the category. Choose All Commands, for example, and Word will label the box as Commands. And instead of buttons, the second box will contain a scroll box filled with a list of commands (or other items). If you then drag an item that does not have a default button into the toolbar area, Word will open the Custom Button dialog box, shown in Figure 9-17, and you can choose a button for the particular item.

**FIGURE 9-17**

The Custom Button dialog box lets you choose an icon for a toolbar button.

The first choice in the Custom Button dialog box is Text Button. If you prefer buttons to be labeled in words instead of using icons that are often hard to remember, you can use this choice to create a button with a text label instead of an icon; you type the text in the Text Button Name box at the bottom of the dialog box. If you also define a shortcut key that uses the first letter of the button label, you'll be able to choose the item with either the mouse (by clicking on the button) or the keyboard (by using the keyboard shortcut). We'll show you how to define (or redefine) shortcut keys in "Keyboard Customization" on page 917. For now, simply be aware that it can be done.

Choose the Edit button in the Custom Button dialog box to alter an existing icon or create a new one. Figure 9-18 shows the Button Editor dialog box. To edit a button icon, click on the color you want to use—or click on the Erase pattern if you want to use that—and then draw the image, pixel by pixel, either by clicking the appropriate locations in the grid within the Picture box or by holding down the mouse button and dragging over the grid. The Clear button will replace the entire image with the Erase pattern. The Move buttons move the image up, down, left, or right by one row or one column of pixels.

**FIGURE 9-18**

Use the Button Editor to create your own button icons for toolbars.

You can edit any button's icon—not just the ones in the Custom Button dialog box. With the Customize Toolbars card showing, place the mouse pointer on any button on a toolbar, hold down Control, and click the mouse button. This will open a context-sensitive menu. Choose Edit Button Image to open the Button Editor with the button's icon already loaded. Note, too, that the context-sensitive menu also includes options for copying and pasting a button image, resetting a button to its original setting, and choosing a different button image. The first three choices are self-explanatory. The Choose Button Image choice opens the Custom Button dialog box, in which you can choose a different button icon to replace the icon of the button you clicked on.

## How to create a new toolbar

To create a new toolbar of your own design, simply drag a button or other item from the Toolbars card and drop it in the document window or on any part of the toolbars area that isn't already covered by a toolbar. Word will automatically create a new toolbar around the new button and will expand the toolbar as you add more buttons to it. If you start with an item other than a button, such as a style name, Word will also open the Custom Button dialog box when it creates the new toolbar so that you can define the icon or text for the button.

Word will treat your custom toolbars just like Word's default toolbars; they can either float or sit at one of the edges of the screen. And you can change their position and shape at will by dragging and dropping.

Word automatically names new toolbars in sequence, starting with *Toolbar 1*. While this name is functional, it hardly describes the toolbar's designed purpose. You can change the name with the Template Organizer. From the editing screen, choose File Templates and then the Organizer button; then choose the Toolbars card in the Organizer dialog box, as shown in Figure 9-19 on the next page. Highlight the toolbar whose name you want to change. Then choose the Rename button to open the Rename dialog box. You can then give the toolbar a more meaningful name, such as *Set Styles* for a toolbar with buttons that apply particular styles to paragraphs. When you've finished, choose OK to accept the new name, and then choose the Close button.

**FIGURE 9-19**

You can give toolbars more meaningful names with the Rename feature on the Toolbars card in the Organizer dialog box.

# The Tools Customize Menus and Keyboard Cards

The Customize dialog box has two more cards: Menus and Keyboard. You can use the Menus options to modify the Word menus, whether you want to rename a single command or completely restructure the entire Word menu system. You use the Keyboard options to assign new keyboard shortcuts to commands and macros. These are advanced features that we'll cover in detail in Chapter 28.

# NEW! Wizards: Automated Documents

Your documents themselves represent another category of important objects for customization. By using Word's wizards, you can automatically add complex, custom formats to some of the more common kinds of documents you create.

A wizard is a special type of file that can automatically create a document (or template) that uses sophisticated formatting. The essence of a wizard is that it will customize the result for you by prompting you for your formatting and text choices.

To create a new document with a wizard, choose File New, and then select one of the wizards in the Template list. For this example, we'll use the Fax Cover Wizard, which will create a fax cover sheet.

In general, a wizard presents one or more dialog boxes with options that offer you choices for customizing the format of the document. The first dialog box in the Fax Cover Wizard is shown in Figure 9-20, asking whether you want to format the page for portrait or for landscape orientation. The unlabeled preview box on the left displays the effect of your choice.

**FIGURE 9-20**

A wizard prompts you for information about how you want to customize a new document.

At the bottom of the screen are four buttons: Cancel, Back, Next, and Finish. The Cancel button cancels the creation of the new document; the Finish button tells Word to go ahead and create the new document using the information you've given to this point. The Back and Next buttons move you backward and forward through the wizard's dialog boxes, one step at a time. In the wizard's first dialog box, the Back button is grayed; when you reach the final dialog box, the Next button will be grayed.

Generally, you will want to go through all of a wizard's dialog boxes before choosing the Finish button. The only other time you should use this button is when you are certain that all questions in all of the dialog boxes have been answered as you want them.

The remaining dialog boxes for this particular wizard ask you to choose a style for your cover sheet (contemporary, modern, or jazzy); to enter or confirm your name, company, and address; and to enter or confirm your voice and fax phone numbers. When you've worked through all of these, Word will display a Finish dialog box, shown in Figure 9-21.

**FIGURE 9-21**

Word will present a Finish dialog box when you have answered all questions in a wizard's dialog boxes.

We won't cover other wizards here; the whole point of wizards is that they are fully self-explanatory. They give even the beginning Word user the benefit of elaborate formatting capabilities. Even the names of the wizards are self-explanatory: Fax Cover Wizard for creating a fax cover letter, Calendar Wizard for creating a monthly, weekly, or yearly calendar, and so on. However, we firmly recommend that you take the time to experiment with the wizards to see which ones suit your needs.

# An Introduction to Templates

To take fullest advantage of Word's flexibility and customizability—and even to take fullest advantage of wizards—it's important to understand the concept of templates. As we've mentioned earlier, templates hold information about your preferences for particular kinds of documents—allowing, for example, defaults for a letter that are different from those for a manuscript. The underlying concept of templates is simple. Learn to use templates, and you can unlock much of Word's power.

NEW!
## What is a template?

A template is a special type of Word document that serves as a pattern for other documents. Just as a shoemaker uses templates to make shoes of different sizes, so too can you use templates to create documents of different types.

Suppose, for example, that you print many of your Word documents on preprinted letterhead. Each time you begin a letter, you change the left margin from 1.25 inches to 1 inch and the top margin from 1 inch to 3 inches.

Instead of changing margins manually each time, you can create a template that automatically handles the task for you. After you've created the template, all you have to do is choose File New, choose the name of the template in the Template list box, and choose OK. Word will create a new document that has the correct margins. You can then begin typing the new letter.

A template can contain a lot more than margin settings. Among other possibilities, it can contain boilerplate text—blocks of text that you use in every document of the same type. These blocks can contain fields, such as a date field, which Word will automatically update for each new document. Templates can also have their own style settings (so that all documents created with the same template will have the same formatting and appearance) and their own AutoText entries (so that you can have different sets of AutoText entries in different kinds of documents), as well as specific macros, menus, and shortcut keys (so that each kind of document can have its own customized commands).

# Normal, document (supplementary), and global templates

Although Word now has three types of templates, only one is attached to all documents—the Normal template. Settings stored in the Normal template are available to all documents unless they are overridden by the settings in an attached template. In Word 6.0, it is possible to have several templates attached to the same document: the Normal template, the attached *document template* (or *supplementary template*), and multiple *global templates*. We will reserve the term *supplementary template* to refer only to a template that has been attached as the current document template. (You can also designate a third level of templates, called *global templates*. For now, it's enough to know that a global template makes its AutoText entries, macros, and customized features available to all open documents. We'll cover the subject in "Normal, Supplementary, and Global Templates," starting on page 890.)

If you attach a supplementary template, either by selecting it as the document template when creating the new file or by using the File Templates command, its name will be shown in the Document Template text box in the Templates And Add-Ins dialog box. If no supplementary template has been selected, you'll see the word *Normal* in the Document Template text box.

The supplementary template works in addition to, not instead of, the Normal template. Any settings stored in a supplementary template take precedence over those in the Normal template, but anything not specified in the supplementary template will follow the settings in the Normal template. That means that any AutoText entries, macros, keystroke assignments, or any other customized feature stored in a supplementary template will be available whenever you have that template attached to the file you're currently working in. Any such items that you've stored in the Normal template will be available as well—except for settings that conflict with the current supplementary template.

When you first install Word, there is no Normal file on your disk. Word simply uses the default settings that are part of the program to create a new Normal file the first time you open Word. This means that you can return to Word's document default settings by deleting Normal from your Word template folder or by renaming it with standard Macintosh commands.

So much for the general introduction to templates. To use templates, there are some specific techniques you need to understand: how to edit and create templates, how to create a new document based on any given supplementary template, and how to attach a template to and detach a template from an existing document.

## How to edit a template

There are two ways to change any template. You can create or modify features such as AutoText entries while working on a document; you can then save those changes in the Normal template or in the current supplementary template, if there is one. Alternatively, you can load the template and edit it directly. If you want to add boilerplate text to the template, editing the template is the only choice.

To open an existing template file for editing, choose File Open, select Document Templates in the List Files Of Type pull-down list, and choose the appropriate filename in the list box. You can then edit the file and change its settings just as you would with any document file. When you're done, simply save the file by choosing File Save.

## How to create a new template

Word comes with a starter set of templates and wizards that you can use to create new documents or templates. You'll be able to use some of these for your own work, but you'll probably want to create your own templates as well. To create a new template, choose the File New command, choose the Template option button in the New box, and then choose OK. Word will open a document window, but instead of using the name *Document1* in the title bar, it will use the name *Template1*. Make whatever changes you like to styles, margins, and other settings. Also add any text, headers, or footers that you want to define as part of this template. Word will automatically apply these settings to, and enter the text in, any documents you later create with this template attached.

You can save a template file using the same commands you would for saving a document. Word will prompt you for a filename. Enter a name, and then choose OK to finish saving. When you're done making changes, choose File Close. Once the template is created, you can use it as the basis for new documents or attach it to existing document files, as we'll discuss next.

## How to attach and detach templates

To attach any template to a new document, choose the template from the Template list box in the New dialog box. Keep in mind that the default is the Normal template; if you accept the default, you'll be using the Normal template only. If you choose a different template from the list, Word will attach that template. Word will treat this template as the document template, and it will also use the Normal template.

If you've already created a document with a supplementary template or with the Normal template alone, and you decide later that you want to use a different supplementary template, or add one, use the File Templates command. With the document open and active on your screen, choose File Templates. Word will display a dialog box like the one shown in Figure 9-22.

**FIGURE 9-22**

Choose the File Templates command to attach a different template to an existing document.

To see a list of available templates, choose the Attach button. The resulting Attach Template dialog box looks and functions just like the File Open dialog box. You can use it to find a particular template file and attach it.

If you choose the Normal template, Word will detach any template that's attached and will thereafter refer to the Normal template as the document template. If you choose any other template, Word will detach any supplementary template that's currently attached and replace it with the newly chosen template. Word will now refer to this newly chosen template as the document template. The Normal template will remain attached in any case.

As we mentioned earlier, you can tell Word whether to add customized features such as macros and AutoText entries to the Normal template or to the current supplementary template. In fact, you'll find a text box called something like Make AutoText Entry Available To in each item that you can assign to your choice of currently active templates. In general, unless you have a specific reason for doing otherwise, you should save customizations to the Normal template so that they will be available at all times.

## More about templates

This is the barest of introductions to templates. We can't cover most of the possibilities for customizing templates yet because we haven't covered the features themselves. As you learn new customization features, from styles (Chapter 12) to macros (Chapters 24–26), you can experiment with adding them to templates as it seems appropriate.

In the rest of this book, starting with the next chapter, we'll explore Word's advanced features. After we finish with them, we'll take a more detailed look at templates in Chapter 27.

# Advanced Word

# TOPIC FINDER

# 10

# Advanced Editing

hen you're fully comfortable with Word, you'll want to explore some of its advanced editing features. In this chapter, we'll discuss bookmarks, annotations, revision marks, and advanced Go To features, all of which will help you work with long and complex documents and help coordinate writing and editing tasks that involve more than one person. We will also cover a specialized type of editing, namely footnotes.

## Bookmarks

Word's bookmark feature gets its name by analogy to a real bookmark because it serves a similar purpose. After you define a bookmark, you can use the Go To command to move to that spot from anywhere in the document.

Word also uses bookmarks for other purposes. You can, for example, use them in references to number items automatically. We'll cover these other uses elsewhere, in the context of advanced techniques.

### How to define a bookmark

Defining a bookmark is similar to creating a new AutoText entry. Suppose you've created the document shown in Figure 10-1 on the next page, and you want a bookmark at the beginning of the introduction so that you can return to that section easily. First position the cursor or selection at the start of the introduction. Then choose Edit Bookmark to open the Bookmark dialog box, shown in Figure 10-2, and enter *Intro* in the Bookmark Name text box. Your screen should look like Figure 10-2. Choose Add to finish.

We'll use this document to demonstrate some bookmark basics.

To define a bookmark, position the cursor or selection in the text you want the bookmark to mark. Then open the Bookmark dialog box to assign a bookmark name.

## Bookmark names

Bookmark names follow a few simple rules. The name cannot exceed 40 characters, it must begin with a letter of the alphabet, and it can contain only letters, numbers, and the underline character. If you type an invalid character in the Bookmark Name text box, the Add button will be grayed. You'll have to change the name before the Add button will become active again.

## How to redefine a bookmark

Although you can't move or modify a bookmark, you can achieve the same effect by redefining the bookmark name to refer to a different location. Simply move the cursor or selection to the new location. Then choose Edit Bookmark and assign the bookmark name, either by typing it in the Bookmark Name box or by choosing it from the list. Finally, choose Add to close the dialog box and redefine the name. The bookmark feature is not case sensitive, so typing *INTRO*, *Intro*, or *intro* will all produce the same effect.

## How to delete a bookmark

To delete a bookmark, first choose Edit Bookmark. Then type the name to delete in the Bookmark Name text box (or choose it from the list), and choose the Delete button. Word will delete the bookmark and remove its name from the list box without asking for confirmation.

 If you delete text that includes a bookmark, you will also delete that bookmark.

## How to go to a bookmark

One of the advantages of bookmarks is that they make it easy to go to a specific place in a document. After you've defined a bookmark, you can move to it by using the Go To dialog box, shown in Figure 10-3. To open the dialog box, choose Edit Go To, press F5 or ⌘-G, or double-click on the status bar anywhere to the left of the time display.

**FIGURE 10-3**

Choose Edit Go To, press F5 or ⌘-G, or double-click on the status bar to open the Go To dialog box.

The Go To What list displays the kinds of items you can move to from this dialog box. If you highlight Bookmark, the label on the text box to the right will read Enter Bookmark Name, and the attached drop-down list will display all bookmarks in the current document. You can then enter the bookmark name in the text box (or choose it from the list) and choose the Go To button. If the bookmark you've specified marks a place in the document, Word will move the cursor to that position. If it defines a block of text, Word will move to that point and highlight the entire block. We'll cover the other choices later in this chapter.

# NEW!  Annotations

Annotations are hidden text that you can add as notes to a document without cluttering up your document. Word numbers each annotation automatically and marks it with its author's initials (based on information on the User Info card). If you have a document that a number of people are reviewing, annotations make it easy to keep track of who wrote what. You can also use annotations for notes to yourself—to remind you where you got certain information, for example, or to remind you to check your facts before printing or circulating the document.

As we'll discuss, you can lock a document for annotations, which means you can let others insert annotations while keeping them from making any changes to the document itself. And you can print a document's annotations.

## How to insert an annotation

To insert an annotation, move the cursor to the appropriate location or highlight the text you want to comment on; then choose Insert Annotation, and write your note. For example, suppose you want to insert the following annotation into the document shown in Figure 10-4:

Additionally, total expenditures for the month were well under budget.

Simply position the cursor where you want the annotation reference (or highlight the text you are annotating), and choose Insert Annotation. Word will insert a reference mark at the cursor location, open the annotation pane at the bottom of the window, as shown in Figure 10-4, and move the cursor to the annotation pane. You can then type the text, just as you would in a document window.

As you can see in Figure 10-4, the annotation reference mark consists of a pair of brackets ([ ]). These enclose the author's initials (in this case, AP) and a number that marks the annotation's order in the document. (In this case, it is the first annotation.) Note that Word uses the same reference mark both for the annotation itself, in the annotation pane, and for the annotation's position in your text.

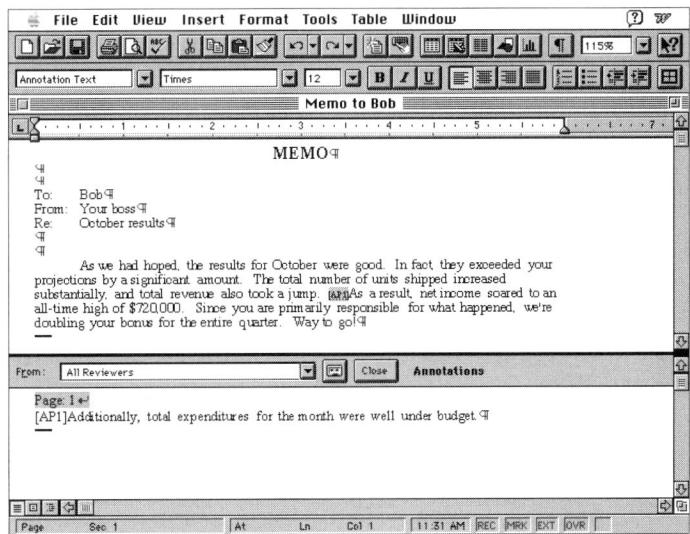

**FIGURE 10-4**

The Insert Annotation command opens the annotation pane so that you can type your annotation.

Word automatically formats the reference mark in your document as hidden text. However, the reference marks will be displayed whenever the annotation pane is open, whether you've set Word to show hidden text or not. When you are editing an annotation in the annotation pane, Word will highlight the corresponding mark in the document (and any associated text you selected when you created the annotation).

If you use annotations, we recommend that you either keep the annotation pane open while editing (by choosing the View Annotations command) or set Word to display hidden text (by checking the Hidden Text check box on the Tools Options View card). Being able to see the reference marks will keep you from accidentally deleting an annotation that you didn't know was there.

You can use the From list box at the top of the annotation pane to specify which annotations you want to view. If you are creating a new document, the only choices in the pull-down list will be All Reviewers and the current user as defined on the Tools Options User Info card. If the document has annotations from other users, however, the list will also include the name of each user. You can specify All Reviewers or select a specific reviewer to see notes only from that reviewer.

When you finish typing a note, you can close the annotation pane by choosing the Close button. (Click on it with the mouse, or press Control-Shift-C.) Alternatively, you can choose View Annotations to toggle the feature off. Any time you want to see your annotations, simply choose View Annotations again. If the annotation reference mark is showing, you can double-click on the reference mark to open the annotation pane.

## Voice annotations

The button between the From text box and the Close button has an icon of an audio cassette. If you have a microphone, you can click on this button—or choose Insert Object and pick Microsoft Voice Annotation from the Object Type list—to record voice annotations.

Keep in mind that sound files consume lots of disk space. Don't use this feature if you are short on disk space or if you need to keep file sizes small to minimize transfer time across phone lines or local area network connections.

## Annotation numbering

As you add annotations to a document, Word numbers the reference marks sequentially. If you insert an annotation above existing ones, Word will re-number annotations that come later. For example, if you insert an annotation at the top of the document, as shown in Figure 10-5, Word will number the new annotation 1 and will renumber the existing annotation 2.

**FIGURE 10-5**

Word marks each annotation reference with the initials stored on the Tools Options User Info card. It numbers the reference marks sequentially.

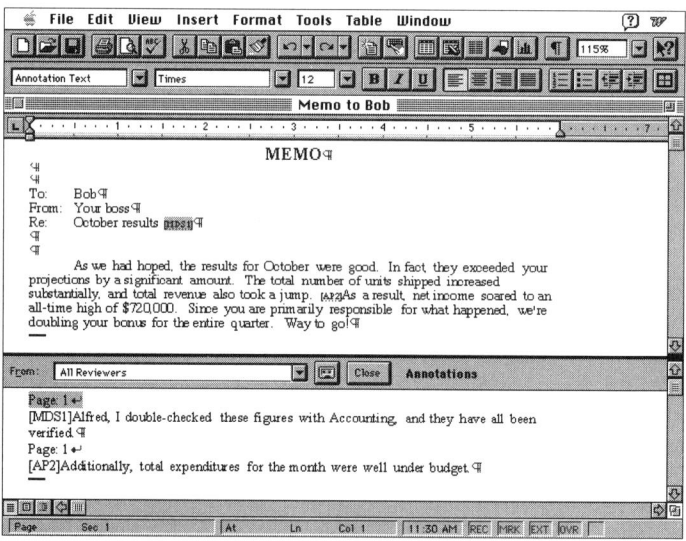

When you insert an annotation, Word creates the reference mark by using the initials currently stored on the Tools Options User Info card. If more than one person uses the same installed copy of Word to add annotations, all reference marks will have the same initials (unless each user remembers to change the information on the User Info card). However, if each individual adds the annotations on his or her own computer, each annotation will include that individual's initials. Figure 10-5 shows an annotation pane with notes written by two different people, MDS and AP. Notice that the reference marks are numbered sequentially, so [AP2] refers to the second annotation in the document, not the second one by AP.

### How to size the annotation pane

As you may have noticed, Word separates the document pane from the annotation pane with a split bar. You can adjust the size of the pane by adjusting the position of the split bar, using the techniques we covered in Chapter 1.

### How to move between the annotation and document panes

You can move between the annotation and document panes by either clicking on the pane you want to move to or pressing F6. Notice that if you scroll through either pane, Word will scroll the other so that you can see both an annotation and the text it refers to.

In addition to using annotations to write notes to yourself or to others, you can use them for any text you don't want in the document itself. For example, you might want to draft an alternative version of a given paragraph.

## How to work with annotations

Whatever you use annotations for, there will be times when you want to insert all or part of an annotation into your document and other times when you want to get rid of an annotation altogether. There may also be times when you want to move some text from your document to an annotation.

### How to move an annotation to or from the document pane

If you want to include text from an annotation in your document, cut or copy the text in the annotation and paste it into your document. (You can use any of the usual Word commands for cutting and pasting, such as Edit Cut and Edit Paste.) You can then delete the annotation reference mark by selecting the annotation mark in the document pane—so that it shows as the highlight color, not simply gray—and pressing Delete or Del.

You may also want to move text from the document to an annotation. For example, you may be considering deletion of a paragraph, but you have enough doubts that you aren't ready to throw the paragraph away yet. To move text to an annotation, first insert the annotation; then move back to the document, cut the text, move back to the annotation pane, and paste the text into the annotation.

## How to delete an annotation

You can delete all of the text in an annotation from within the annotation pane, but you can't delete the annotation itself in this pane. To delete an annotation, select the appropriate reference mark in the document so that it shows as highlighted rather than gray, and press Delete or Del. Word will remove the annotation mark and annotation entirely and automatically renumber subsequent annotations.

# How to lock a document for annotations

As we mentioned earlier, you can prevent others from making changes to your document but still let them insert annotations. To take advantage of Word's document protection feature, choose Tools Protect Document to open the Protect Document dialog box, shown in Figure 10-6.

**FIGURE 10-6**

The document protection feature lets you control the type of changes that can be made to a document.

The Protect Document For box contains three options: Revisions, Annotations, and Forms. We'll discuss the Revisions option later in this chapter and the Forms option in Chapter 21. For the moment, we're concerned only with the Annotations option.

If you choose Annotations and then choose OK, the only changes Word will let anyone make to the document will be the addition, deletion, and modification of annotations. If you add or change an annotation, Word will mark the changes as inserted text, using the current revision mark settings. (We'll cover these later in this chapter.) Note that Word will let you delete an annotation, but it won't necessarily erase it. More precisely, if you try to delete an annotation that you've added after applying document protection to the document, Word will erase the annotation. But if you try to delete one that you added before protecting the document, or one that some other user has added, Word will mark the annotation as deleted text using the current revision marks. (Here again, we'll discuss these later in this chapter.)

The Protect Document dialog box also includes a Password text box. If you type a password in it, Word will show only bullets and will prompt you to retype the password to confirm it. If you want to remove the protection from the document later, you'll be prompted to give the password.

### How to unlock a document

After you add protection to a document, the Tools menu command name changes to Unprotect Document. Choose this command to remove protection and allow normal editing of the document. If you defined a password when you protected the document, you'll be prompted to enter the password to remove protection.

## How to print annotations

To print a document's annotations by themselves, choose File Print to open the Print dialog box, choose Annotations from the Print pull-down list box, and choose OK. Word will print all of the annotations, showing each reference mark, associated text (if any), and the page each applies to.

If you want Word to print annotations along with a document, choose Tools Options and then the Print card (or choose File Print and then the Word Options button to display the Tools Options Print card). Make sure the Annotations check box is checked. Word will print your annotations at the end of the document, much like endnotes.

# Footnotes and Endnotes

The mere mention of footnotes can strike fear in the heart of anyone who has ever struggled through a term paper. Footnotes are cumbersome to deal with on typewriters and on many word processors. But Word's footnote feature, which is similar to its annotation feature, makes the job easy. You can add footnote text while you're working on the body of the document or later. Word will automatically number your footnotes and renumber them—even if you modify the document by adding and deleting footnotes or text or by inserting new footnotes between existing ones.

You can place footnotes at the bottom of each page, or you can make them endnotes located at the end of the document. You can also control how they are separated from the rest of your text. We'll start by showing you how to create a footnote.

## How to create a footnote

In the sample document shown in Figure 10-7 on the next page, we'll add a footnote reference mark at the end of the first paragraph of body text.

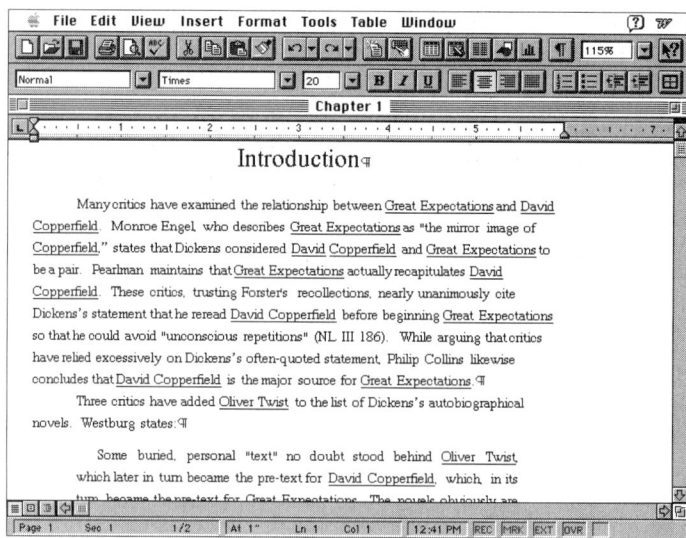

**FIGURE 10-7**

We'll insert a footnote reference mark into this document.

The first step is to position your cursor where you want the footnote reference mark. Then choose Insert Footnote to open the Footnote And Endnote dialog box, shown in Figure 10-8.

**FIGURE 10-8**

Use the Footnote And Endnote dialog box to insert footnotes into a document.

**NEW!**   In the Insert group box, you specify whether you are inserting a footnote or an endnote. Either choice will insert a reference mark in the document. Choose Footnote to print the note at the bottom of the same page. Choose Endnote to print it on a separate page (or pages) at the end of the document. Note that you can create both footnotes and endnotes in the same document. Word will maintain a separate numbering scheme for each.

The Numbering box contains two options: AutoNumber and Custom Mark. If you choose AutoNumber, Word will number all of the footnotes or endnotes in sequence, and it will automatically renumber them for you as needed. (We'll show how you can choose the numbering scheme you want in a moment.)

If you'd rather use a custom footnote reference mark, such as an asterisk, type the character you want in the Custom Mark text box. By default, the character (or characters) will be inserted in the same font as the adjacent text but in a smaller size and formatted as a superscript. You can type a character directly from the keyboard, or you can choose the Symbol button to open the Symbol dialog box and insert a symbol. The latter approach works similarly to the procedure we discussed in "The Insert Symbol command" starting on page 144.

You are not limited to single-character entries in the Custom Mark text box. Word will use up to 10 characters, including letters, spaces, and punctuation marks.

**Footnote options.** If you choose the Options button in the Footnote And Endnote dialog box, Word will open the Note Options dialog box, shown in Figure 10-9.

**FIGURE 10-9**

Use the Note Options dialog box to control how Word numbers and formats footnotes and endnotes.

The Place At pull-down list on the All Footnotes card offers two choices: Bottom Of Page and Beneath Text. Choose Bottom Of Page to put footnotes at the bottom margin of the page even if the body text ends above the bottom margin. Choose Beneath Text to put the footnotes just below the last line of body text on a page, regardless of where the body text ends.

NEW!

The Number Format list offers six predefined numbering schemes for the footnote reference marks: Arabic numbers, uppercase or lowercase letters, uppercase or lowercase Roman numerals, and a series of typographic symbols commonly used for footnotes.

In the Start At box, you can specify the number, letter, or symbol for the first footnote mark. The default choice is the first item in the sequence you chose in the Number Format box.

The three Numbering option buttons are Continuous, Restart Each Section, and Restart Each Page.

For most documents, you will probably want continuous numbering; this will number all footnotes sequentially for the entire document. If you've divided a document into sections, however, and those sections represent separate parts—such as chapters—you might want to use Restart Each Section. This will reset the numbering to the beginning of the sequence at the start of each section.

If you use the typographic symbol sequence, you might want to choose Restart Each Page because this is the conventional usage for these symbols. Choosing another numbering option for such symbols could yield an unexpected result; Word can number continuously using these symbols, but only by using multiples of the symbols—one of each the first time through, two of each the second time through, and so on. Since there are only four symbols, these multiple marks can easily become distracting if your document has many footnotes.

**Endnote options.** The options on the All Endnotes card, also shown in Figure 10-9, are similar to those on the All Footnotes card.

The Place At pull-down list contains two choices: End Of Section and End Of Document. If you choose End Of Section, Word will place the endnote text after the last line of a section and before the first line of the next section. If you choose End Of Document, the endnotes will appear after the last line of the document. The Number Format and Start At options are the same as those for footnotes.

There are two Numbering options: Continuous and Restart Each Section. The Continuous option works exactly as for footnotes, as does the Restart Each Section option when combined with the End Of Section placement option. However, if you've selected End Of Document in the Place At box, selecting Restart Each Section places all notes at the end of the document and numbers them sequentially by section. This is a useful feature for books in which endnotes are printed in a separate section subdivided by headings such as *Notes to Chapter 1*, *Notes to Chapter 2*, and so on.

**Footnote and endnote options.** Both cards include a Convert button that opens the same Convert Notes dialog box, which contains three options: You can convert all footnotes in the document to endnotes; you can convert all endnotes to footnotes; or you can swap the two, so that all footnotes become endnotes and all endnotes become footnotes. This feature can be handy if you change your mind about how you want your notes formatted.

**Finishing up.** When you close the Convert Notes dialog box, you will return to the Note Options dialog box. Close this, and you will return to the Footnote And Endnote dialog box.

If you choose OK at this point, Word will insert the footnote reference mark at the cursor position in your document (or the leftmost position of a selection). If you're in Normal or Outline view, Word will split your document window into two panes, as shown in Figure 10-10, with a corresponding footnote reference mark in the footnote pane at the bottom. The cursor will move to the footnote pane, just to the right of the footnote reference mark. If you're in Page Layout view or Print Preview, Word will insert the reference mark into the text and move the cursor to the area of the page where the footnote text will be printed.

**FIGURE 10-10**

When you choose OK in the Footnote And Endnote dialog box, Word will add a footnote reference mark and, if you're in Normal or Outline view, open a footnote pane.

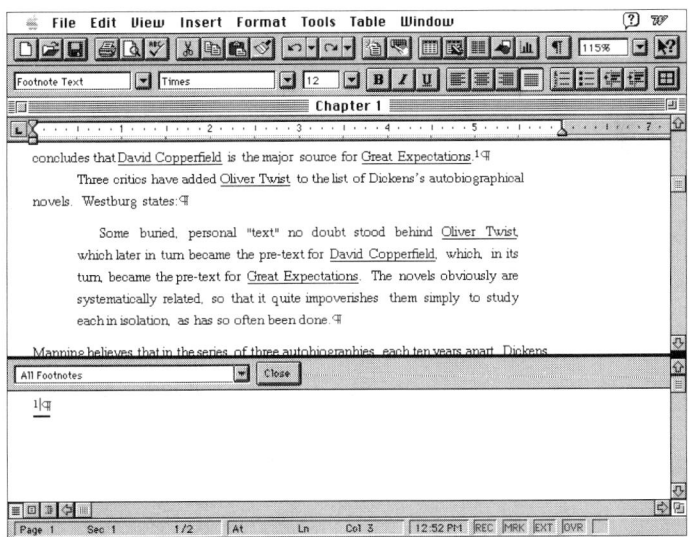

## How to work in the footnote pane

Now you can type your footnote in the footnote pane, just as if you were working in the document pane. If the footnote is too long to view in its entirety,

Word will scroll the pane as you type. You can also use the vertical scroll bar in that pane to bring additional text into view, or you can move the split bar to make the pane larger. See "How to split a window" starting on page 17 for details on how to move the split bar.

### How to move between the footnote and document panes

You can move between the footnote and document panes with the same techniques you use to move between the document and annotation panes: Press F6, or use the mouse to click anywhere in the pane you want to move to.

When you leave the footnote pane, Word will keep it open until you choose the Close button (with the mouse or with Control-Shift-C) or choose View Footnotes. You can reopen the footnote pane anytime by choosing View Footnotes again. Note, too, that you can quickly open the footnote pane with the mouse by double-clicking on a footnote reference mark. If you scroll through either pane, Word will scroll the other, and you will see both a footnote and the text it refers to.

## How to edit footnotes

After you've created a footnote, you can use Word's standard editing techniques to edit it. You can also find and replace footnotes, and you can use the Spelling, Thesaurus, and Hyphenate commands on them. We discussed finding and replacing in "How to find special characters" starting on page 101; the thesaurus tool in Chapter 5, "Additional Editing Tools," starting on page 119; and spelling and hyphenation tools in Chapter 6, "Proofing," starting on page 165.

### How to insert and delete footnotes

You insert and delete footnotes much as you do annotations. To delete a footnote, just highlight the footnote reference mark in your document pane and delete the mark. Word will delete the corresponding footnote text and renumber all subsequent footnotes automatically.

To insert a new footnote between existing footnotes, simply create the footnote as we've already described. Again, Word will renumber all subsequent footnotes automatically in both your document and footnote panes.

There are two keyboard shortcuts for inserting footnotes and endnotes. These bypass all of the dialog boxes we've discussed, so you may want to go through the menu process first to adjust the format settings. You can then use ⌘-Option-F to insert a footnote, or ⌘-Option-E to insert an endnote, at the current cursor position.

### How to copy footnotes

Here's a handy shortcut for repeating a footnote entry or copying it to another document. Select a footnote reference mark in the document, choose Edit Copy, and then paste the reference mark where you want the copy. Word will copy the reference mark for the footnote and insert the text in proper sequence in the footnote pane. If you copied an automatically numbered reference mark, Word will also renumber all footnotes appropriately.

### How to change a footnote's custom reference mark

If you've inserted a custom footnote reference mark (an asterisk, for example), and you decide to use a different reference mark, you'll need to change the mark in your document. If you try to edit the reference mark directly, Word will delete the entire footnote—both reference mark and text. To change the reference mark, select it in your document, choose Insert Footnote, and either type the new custom reference mark in the Custom Mark text box or choose the AutoNumber footnote option, as appropriate. Word will change the reference mark in both the document and the footnote pane.

## How to format footnotes

One of the most difficult aspects of manually inserting footnotes—whether with a typewriter or with a word processor that lacks a footnote feature—is formatting. Trying to determine how much space to leave at the bottom of the page, for example, can be a real problem, and dealing with a footnote that spills over to the bottom of the next page can be a headache. Word handles all these issues automatically.

### How to format footnote text and reference marks

When you insert a footnote in your document, Word adds two styles to the document's list of styles in use: Footnote Reference and Footnote Text. Similarly, when you insert an endnote, you'll find two other styles: Endnote Reference and Endnote Text. We will discuss styles in Chapter 12. For now, simply be aware that you can change the appearance of the footnote text, footnote reference marks, endnote text, or endnote reference marks by changing the style definitions. You can also use all of Word's direct formatting tools. Select the reference mark in the document text, or select the text you want to format in the footnote pane, and use the formatting commands just as you would for any other text in your document.

### How to change footnote and endnote separators

Unless told otherwise, Word will add a short horizontal line between the document text and footnote text to separate the two when you print a document that includes footnotes. Also, when a footnote is too long to fit entirely on the same page as the referenced text, or when all the footnotes for a page won't fit at the bottom of that page, Word will automatically place the remaining text on the next page. To indicate that the footnote text on the second page is a continuation, Word uses a horizontal line that extends from margin to margin. Similar separators are used for endnotes.

If you prefer, you can create custom separators. First make sure that you're in Normal view with the footnote pane open. (Choose View Footnotes if necessary.)

The list box in the upper left corner of the footnote pane should be displaying *All Footnotes* or *All Endnotes,* depending on which kind of notes you're working with. If you open the pull-down list, however, you'll see other choices.

If the box says *All Footnotes*—and assuming you have both footnotes and endnotes in the document—the pull-down list will contain five choices: All Footnotes, All Endnotes, Footnote Separator, Footnote Continuation Separator, and Footnote Continuation Notice. If the box shows *All Endnotes*, the last three choices will be for endnotes instead of footnotes.

Choose the item you want to change, and Word will display the current version of that item in the footnote pane. If the current item is still the default line that Word normally uses, as shown in Figure 10-11, you can't edit it; however, you can add to it, delete it, or replace it.

**FIGURE 10-11**

From within the footnote pane, you can customize the separator that divides footnotes from body text.

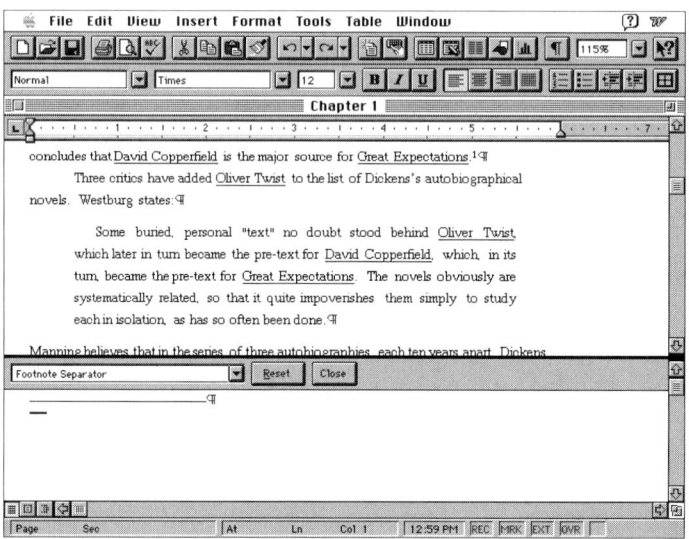

To add anything before or after the default line, position the cursor and type any characters you want to add. To delete the line, select the entire line and press Delete or Del. To replace the line, highlight the line and type the replacement. When you type the first character, Word will delete the line. You can then type any additional characters. If you like, you can open Microsoft Draw (which we will discuss in Chapter 15) and create a custom separator as a drawing object. And you can insert fields so that you can add a dynamic page number to your separator, for example.

The Footnote Continuation Notice and Endnote Continuation Notice are blank by default. You can create any message you like; however, keep in mind that the continuation notice will be visible only when the footnote or endnote continues onto the next page.

Figures 10-12, 10-13, and 10-14 show custom versions of the footnote separator, footnote continuation separator, and footnote continuation notice. Figure 10-15 shows how the custom separator and continuation notice appear in Page Layout view.

**FIGURE 10-12**

In this custom footnote separator, the word *Footnotes* replaces Word's default separator.

**FIGURE 10-13**

This custom footnote continuation separator is defined as *Footnotes (continued)*.

**FIGURE 10-14**

You can also add a footnote continuation notice.

**FIGURE 10-15**

Page Layout view shows the custom footnote separator and continuation notice.

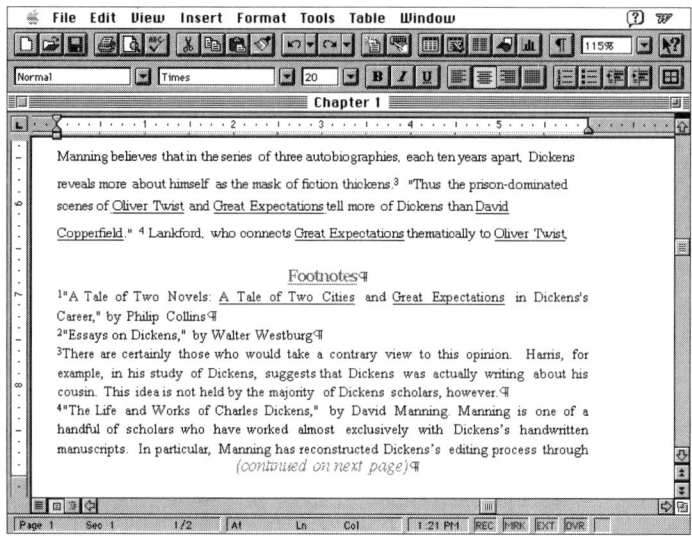

To go back to the default setting for any of these items—the footnote or endnote separators, continuation separators, or continuation notices—you can simply select the item in the pull-down list so that the current version of the item shows in the footnote pane, and choose the Reset button.

Any customizations you make for the footnote or endnote separators, continuation separators, or continuation notices are document specific. However, you can copy these to another document by copying between windows. You can also store customized separators as AutoText entries so that you can easily insert them in any document.

# Advanced Go To Techniques

NEW!

We've discussed using the Edit Go To command to jump to a bookmark. In addition, you can use the Go To command to jump to a page, section, line, annotation, footnote, endnote, field, table, graphic, equation, or object.

If you choose Edit Go To, press ⌘-G, press F5, or double-click on any of the positional information in the status bar, Word will display a Go To dialog box like the one shown in Figure 10-16. The Go To What list box contains the types of items you can jump to. The label for the text box to the right of the list box changes depending on which type you choose. With some types of items, the text box offers an attached drop-down list containing, for example, a list of bookmark names.

**FIGURE 10-16**

You can navigate through long documents by using the Go To dialog box.

After you choose the item in the Go To What list, you can use the Next and Previous buttons to move through your document. You can also type numbers in the text box to go directly to a particular item—or, for most kinds of items, enter a plus or minus sign along with a number to go forward or backward that number of items: Typing *+4* and then choosing the Go To button will take you forward four pages, four lines, four sections, and so forth. And don't forget that after using the Go To command, you can use Shift-F5 to return to a previous position.

## How to use the Go To command to move to specific kinds of items

Although the Go To command works similarly for all types of items, there are some differences you should be aware of. Here are some points to keep in mind for specific items.

**Going to a page.** To go to a particular page in the document, simply enter the page number in the Enter Page Number text box.

The page number specifies the number of pages from the beginning of the document—not necessarily the number assigned to the page. If you're working with a two-section document with two pages in section 1 and four separately numbered pages in section 2, entering 4 will jump you to the second page in section 2. Remember also to repaginate before jumping to a page. Word repaginates your document whenever you switch to Page Layout view or Print Preview; repagination will take place continuously if you've checked the Background Repagination check box on the Tools Options General card.

**Going to a bookmark.** If you choose Bookmark in the Go To What list, you must select a specific bookmark to go to. If you try entering a relative number, such as +5, to go forward that number of bookmarks, Word will interpret the entry as a bookmark name and display an error message stating that the bookmark does not exist.

**Going to an annotation.** When you pick Annotation in the Go To What list, the text box changes to Enter Reviewer's Name, and you can choose among all annotations or choose only those inserted by a specific user. You can also enter the annotation's number or use the plus/minus notation.

**Going to a footnote or an endnote.** To go to a specific footnote or endnote, choose Footnote or Endnote in the Go To What list and type a number in the text box. As it does for page numbers, Word counts the actual footnotes or endnotes. If you started numbering at some number other than 1, for example, entering 6 will jump you to the sixth footnote or endnote in sequence, regardless of the number that designates it in your numbering scheme.

**Going to a field.** When you pick Field in the Go To What list, the text box changes to Enter Field Name, with a drop-down list that includes every kind of field Word uses. You can choose between moving to a field of any type and moving to a specific kind of field. We'll discuss fields in Chapter 20; for now, just be aware that you can move to a specific kind of field if you know which kind you're looking for.

If you find it awkward to choose a type of item first and then move to the text box to type a specific item, note that there's a shortcut you can use instead. Choose Page in the Go To What list. Then, in the Enter Page Number text box, type a code plus a number to tell Word to go to a specific section, line, and so on. The available codes are as follows:

| Item | Code | Item | Code |
|------|------|------|------|
| Page | P | Endnote | E |
| Section | S | Table | T |
| Line | L | Graphic | G |
| Annotation | A | Any Object | O |
| Footnote | F | | |

The Go To command also provides a somewhat hidden keyboard equivalent to using the mouse and scroll bar for moving through a document. To move to the document's halfway point, for example, first choose Page in the Go To What list. Then type *50%* or *%50* and choose the Go To button. To jump to approximately three-fourths of the way through the document, type *75%* instead of *50%*, and so on. Note that Word figures the position based on number of characters, not pages. So if you have forced page breaks, for example, going to the 50% position may not take you to the middle page of your document.

# Revision Marks

NEW!

As with annotations, Word's revision marks feature is designed for documents that are reviewed and edited by more than one person. It can also be useful if you simply want to keep track of changes from one draft to the next.

When you use the revision marks feature, you will be able to edit text and see exactly what has changed. For example, if you delete text, Word will strike through that text and change its color rather than remove it from the document. And if you add text, Word will underline it and change its color. In addition, Word adds vertical bars, called revision bars, alongside the revised lines of text.

As an alternative to adding revision marks while you edit, you can tell Word to compare a revised version of a document to an original version. Word will mark the entire document.

However you add the revision markings, you can review the document to see the revisions and undo or accept them. You can make the final decision case by case, reviewing each revision individually, or you can accept or undo all revisions in one fell swoop. Here's a look at each of these possibilities, starting with marking the revisions as you make them.

## How to mark a document

To add revision marks as you revise a document, choose Tools Revisions to open the Revisions dialog box, shown in Figure 10-17 on the next page. Alternatively, you can double-click on the MRK indicator on the status bar. Check the Mark Revisions While Editing check box, and choose OK. As shown in Figure 10-18 on the next page, the MRK indicator will no longer be grayed, indicating that the revision marks feature is active.

**FIGURE 10-17**

Use the Revisions
dialog box to tell Word
to mark your revisions
as you make them.

Figure 10-18 shows some text with strikethrough formatting and some with underlining. The strikethrough indicates text that has been deleted with revision marking active; the underlining indicates text that has been added. The deleted text and the special marking for added text will show on screen only if the Show Revisions On Screen check box in the Revisions dialog box is checked. The third check box in the Revisions dialog box, Show Revisions In Printed Document, determines whether the marked revisions will be printed.

**FIGURE 10-18**

When you edit text
with Mark Revisions
While Editing turned
on, Word will strike
through any deleted
text and mark new
text in your choice
of formats—using
underlining, in
this case.

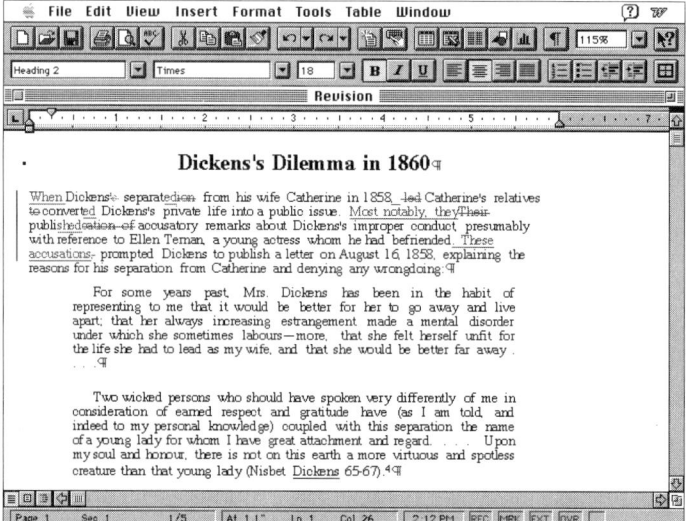

## How to change the format of inserted and deleted text

By default, Word uses the strikethrough format for deletions and uses underlining for insertions, but you can change this if you like. Although you cannot see it in Figure 10-18, the revisions are marked in color, which you also can control.

To change the format for revisions, choose the Options button in the Revisions dialog box, or choose Tools Options and then the Revisions card. Either way, the Tools Options Revisions card, shown in Figure 10-19, will open.

**FIGURE 10-19**

Use the Tools Options Revisions card to control how Word marks revisions in your document.

The Inserted Text group box includes pull-down list boxes and a Preview box to show a sample of how the current settings will affect inserted text. In the Mark box, you choose the format for new text: None, Bold, Italic, Underline, or Double Underline.

In the Color box, you can select any of 16 specific colors, Auto, or By Author. If you choose one color, Word will always use that color for inserted text. Choose Auto to use the default Macintosh text color.

By Author (the default) tells Word to use a different color for each of the first eight authors who edit the document, with authors defined by the settings on the Tools Options User Info card. The colors stand out from the original text, making it obvious who made which changes.

The choices in the Deleted Text group box work almost identically except that the only options available in the Mark pull-down list are Hidden and Strikethrough.

## How to move the revision bars

The Tools Options Revisions card also contains a group box labeled Revised Lines. This controls how Word adds the vertical revision bars alongside the text, to help you spot revisions more easily. Your options are None (no bars), Left Border (bars in the left margin), Right Border (bars in the right margin), and Outside Border. The Outside Border option tells Word to print the bars in the left margin of even-numbered pages and in the right margin of odd-numbered pages. In Normal or Outline view, the revision bars will always be displayed in the left margin; however, they will be displayed in their specified positions in Page Layout view or Print Preview, as well as on the printed page.

Any changes you make on the Tools Options Revisions card will affect the entire document, including any revisions already made with the revision marks feature active. This means that you can't change settings as a way to track different generations of edits. However, you can track different sets of changes by using the default By Author settings for colors and changing the Name entry on the Tools Options User Info card. Change the name, and Word will treat you as a different user, assigning a different color to your edits for each new name. If you use this trick, however, be sure to change the entry back to the correct name when you finish.

## How to review the revisions

At some point you have to decide whether or not to keep your revisions. Word provides tools that will let you accept or undo any revision. Accept it, and Word will delete text marked for deletion and remove the revision marks from new text. If you undo a revision, however, Word will restore text to its original form, removing the strikethrough format from text marked for deletion and deleting new text. You can accept or undo all revisions in a single step, or you can update them one at a time.

### How to accept or undo all revisions at once

To accept or undo all revisions in a document at once, choose Tools Revisions to open the Revisions dialog box. As shown in Figure 10-17, there are three buttons along the bottom of the Document Revisions group box: Review, Accept All, and Reject All.

You can accept all revisions to the document by choosing Accept All, or you can undo all of them by choosing Reject All. With either choice, Word will display a message box asking for confirmation.

If you choose Accept All or Reject All and then answer Yes by mistake, you can use Edit Undo to undo the changes. To be safe, however, you should save a copy of your marked-up document under a different filename before working on it. That way, you can always come back to the original should you change your mind later.

### How to review revisions individually

Most often you'll want to review each revision individually rather than update an entire document at once. With the cursor anywhere in the document, choose Tools Revisions to open the Revisions dialog box. Then choose the Review button in the Document Revisions group box to open the Review Revisions dialog box, shown in Figure 10-20.

Notice the two Find buttons, one with an arrow pointing left (toward the beginning of the document), and one with an arrow pointing right. Choose either button, and Word will search for and highlight the first instance of revised text it finds in the direction the arrow indicates. When it finds a revision, it will add two lines to the Description box above the Find buttons, showing what kind of change is highlighted (Inserted, Deleted, or Replaced), who made it, and the date and time the change was made. Word will do its best to display the revision where you can see it. If necessary, though, you can move the dialog box when it obstructs some of the text.

At this point, you can choose either the Accept or the Reject button to update the revised text. You can also move between the document window—to edit further—and the dialog box by pressing Control-Tab or by clicking on the window or the dialog box with the mouse. If you prefer not to make a decision for the moment, you can choose one of the Find buttons to move to the next revision.

Checking the Find Next After Accept/Reject check box tells Word to move immediately to the next revision each time you choose the Accept or the Reject button.

The Hide Marks button turns off the revision marking, showing the text as it would appear if all current revisions were accepted. This can be useful to clarify the current state of text that's cluttered with a great many revisions.

If you choose the Hide Marks button, the label changes to Show Marks. Choose Show Marks to display the revision markings again.

The Review Revisions dialog box also contains an Undo Last button. You can use this to undo any Accept or Reject choice you've made, and you can backtrack to undo all changes made since you opened the Review Revisions dialog box. However, Word will not display all the parts of the document that would let you see each Undo take place.

You can continue using the Find buttons until you reach the beginning or the end of the document. Word will then display a message asking whether you want to search the header and footer (if they exist). If you proceed, Word will ask whether you want to continue searching from the other end of the document. Choose Yes or No as appropriate.

## How to compare two versions of a document

In addition to marking revisions while editing, Word can compare two versions of a document in different files and add revision marks to indicate differences. This can be particularly handy when one of the files was revised with a word processor other than Word.

To compare two versions of a document, first open the most recent version. Next choose Tools Revisions, choose the Compare Versions button, and select the original file using the dialog box. The dialog box, shown in Figure 10-21, looks and works much like the dialog box for opening files that Word displays when you choose File Open.

After you specify the original file, choose OK to start the comparison. Word will add revision marks in the currently active document and keep you posted on progress by means of a graphic display on the status bar much like the display it uses when saving a file.

When Word finishes comparing the documents, you can review the comparisons, using the same techniques as for reviewing revisions.

**FIGURE 10-21**

The Compare Versions dialog box is similar to the dialog box for opening files.

# How to merge multiple sets of revisions

You can also merge the marked revisions from one document into another. This can be extremely useful if you've circulated the same file to several people and need to integrate all of their revisions into one document file. Note that you can merge only revisions that are already marked.

To merge revisions from a file, open the revised version of the document, choose Tools Revisions, and choose the Merge Revisions button to open the Merge Revisions dialog box. Again, this dialog box looks and works like the dialog box for opening files. Choose the original document, and then choose OK. Word will merge revisions—and annotations—into the original document. If you are combining revisions from several copies of the document, simply repeat this procedure for each copy.

The revision merging feature is much more useful if you also take advantage of Word's document protection feature before distributing the file. To do so, choose Tools Protect Document and then Revisions; you can specify a password if you want. If you choose Tools Revisions to open the Revisions dialog box while protection is applied, you'll see that the Mark Revisions While Editing check box is checked, and the option is grayed so that you can't clear it—unless you choose Tools Unprotect Document. By applying document protection before distributing the file, you are, in short, guaranteeing that all changes will come back marked as revisions.

# Topic Finder

# 11

# Building Tables

n addition to creating tabular columns with tabs, there are two other ways to create a table in Word. You can create a blank table and then fill it in, or you can convert existing text to a table. Both approaches use Word's Table menu commands. If you use tables often, or if you ever need more than the most minimal of tables, you'll find the table feature to be among Word's most useful capabilities. You can use it for anything from a simple two-column list to complex page designs for elaborate forms.

We'll start by explaining how to create a blank table and how to edit and format it. At the end of this chapter, we'll show you how to create a table from existing text.

## Creating a Table

Suppose you need to create a two-column table like the one in Figure 11-1 on the next page. Although this is a simple table, notice that the text in the second column wraps to the next line. You could create this effect using tabs, but the table feature makes this type of formatting much easier.

**FIGURE 11-1**

The Table menu commands make it easy to create tables like this one.

## How to create a table with menu commands

To create a table, place the cursor where you want the table and choose Table Insert Table. Word will open the Insert Table dialog box, shown in Figure 11-2. As you can see in the figure, Word will suggest two columns and two rows. For our sample table, two columns is the right number, but you'll need to change the Number Of Rows setting to 3.

**FIGURE 11-2**

When you choose Table Insert Table, Word will display this dialog box.

Before you choose the Table Insert Table command, be sure that you haven't highlighted any text—not even a space or a paragraph mark. If you have made a selection, Word will assume that you want to convert the selection to a table (a topic we'll discuss later in this chapter) and will create a table that will probably not be what you want.

The Insert Table dialog box also lets you specify a column width. The default setting, Auto, tells Word to determine column width by dividing the total width of the text area by the number of columns. If you're using Word's default settings, with a 6-inch width for single-column text, each column in a two-column table will be approximately 3 inches wide. For now, you can use the Auto setting. To accept the settings in the Insert Table dialog box, choose OK. Word will close the dialog box and insert a table in your document, as shown in Figure 11-3.

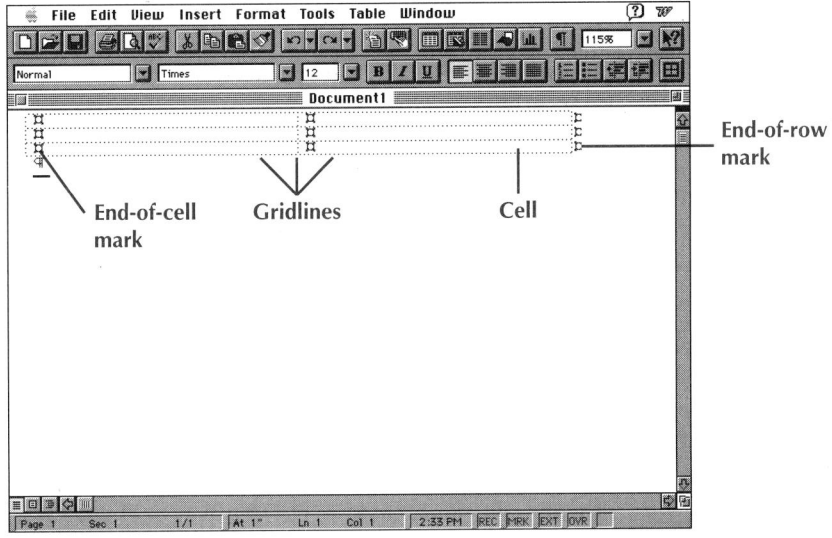

**FIGURE 11-3**

We used the Table Insert Table command to create this blank table.

If your document has a multicolumn format, Word will determine column width by dividing the width of the current text area by the number of columns in the table. For example, if you're working in a three-column document with 2-inch-wide columns and you insert a two-column table using the Auto setting, Word will insert a table with two 1-inch-wide columns.

## How to create a table with a toolbar button

Word offers another, even easier, way to insert a table. If you click on the Table button on the Standard toolbar, and hold down the mouse button, Word will display a small representation of a table, as shown in Figure 11-4.

**FIGURE 11-4**

When you click on the Table button and hold down the mouse button, Word will show you a small representation of a table.

Use the mouse to select the number of rows and columns to create. As you drag the mouse across the grid, Word will display the number of rows and columns (in RxC format) below the grid. If you need more rows or columns than Word displays in the initial grid, simply drag the pointer beyond the grid, and Word will expand it, as shown in Figure 11-5. When you release the mouse button, Word will insert the table, just as if you had chosen Table Insert Table and set Column Width to Auto. If you select two columns and three rows in the grid, the result will match the table shown in Figure 11-3.

**FIGURE 11-5**

If you need a table larger than the grid Word initially displays, simply drag the pointer beyond the grid.

## Getting your bearings

There's another way to insert a table, but it will be easier to understand certain aspects of it if we first take a look at the table we've just inserted. The blank table shown in Figure 11-3 includes *gridlines* that show the rows and columns of the table. These gridlines also define a set of boxes, or *cells*—a term borrowed from spreadsheet programs. Each cell is defined by both the row and the column that it's in.

Although you can turn the gridlines on or off, you'll most often want them on while you're working with a table. Without them, it can be difficult to visualize some important characteristics of the table, such as column width, row alignment, and row height. If your screen isn't showing these gridlines, choose Table Gridlines. (Alternatively, if you're working in Page Layout view, you can check the Text Boundaries check box on the Tools Options View card. But this option will show all text boundaries, not just the table gridlines.)

As you can see in Figure 11-3, each cell in the table contains an *end-of-cell mark*. The mark is similar in concept to a paragraph mark in that it shows how far the text in that cell extends. It's also similar in that Word will show the end-of-cell mark only if you've set the program to display paragraph marks, either by clicking on the Show/Hide ¶ button on the Standard toolbar or by choosing Tools Options View and then checking the Paragraph Marks check box. Since there is no text in the table yet, the end-of-cell mark is at the left side of the cell. There's also an identical character, the *end-of-row mark*, at the right of each row. As we'll demonstrate later in this chapter, this mark becomes important when you want to add a new column to the right edge of a table.

Word will not show a paragraph mark in a cell unless you add one by pressing Return. Nevertheless, Word will treat the text in separate cells as separate paragraphs for formatting and navigation. The end-of-cell mark, then, defines both the end of the cell and the end of the last paragraph of text in a cell.

Word will not include the gridlines, end-of-cell marks, or end-of-row marks in a printed document. However, if you want to print gridlines with a table, you can add them by adding borders. We'll show you how later in this chapter, in the section "Adding Borders and Shading in a Table" on page 377.

## How to create and format a table with the Table Wizard

The third way to create a table is with Word's Table Wizard. The wizard is an automated tool for creating tables complete with common layouts and the most frequently used row and column headings, such as years, months, or days of the week.

To use the Table Wizard, you can choose File New and choose Table Wizard as the template. Word will then open a new file and start the wizard. Most often, however, you'll want to create a table in an existing file. Simply position the cursor where you want the table, choose Table Insert Table to open the Insert Table dialog box, and then choose the Wizard button to start the wizard. Figure 11-6 on the next page shows the wizard's first dialog box.

FIGURE 11-6

The Table Wizard's
first dialog box lets you
choose a layout for the
table grid.

The Table Wizard's first dialog box can be misleading. At first glance the choices seem to be among various patterns of borders you might use in a table to group columns together. In fact, however, none of these choices adds borders. Rather, the choices determine whether the Wizard will arrange columns so two or more columns in the body of the table wind up grouped under a single cell in the table header.

Style 1 in the dialog box, for example, doesn't group columns together (and is the appropriate choice for our sample table). Style 3 groups three columns together—columns 2, 3, and 4; columns 5, 6, and 7; and so on—with each group under a single cell in the first row. You might use this layout to show monthly figures grouped by quarters, with headings in the first row specifying 1st Quarter, 2nd Quarter, and so on, and headings in the second row indicating months. Style 6 is similar to Style 3, but it groups four sets of three columns under each cell in the first row, with each trio of columns grouped under one cell in the second row. You can use this layout to indicate a year in the first row, a quarter in the second, and a month in the third. Styles 2, 4, and 5 offer the same kinds of variations for two and four columns.

The rest of the Table Wizard is self-explanatory. After you pick a style and choose the Next button to go to the next dialog box, the choices are straightforward. Briefly, you can decide:

- Whether to include column headings, with choices for months, quarters, days of the week, numbers, years, or none

- Whether to repeat column headings on each page if the table is longer than one page

- How to align column headings (left, right, or center)

- Whether to include row headings, with the same set of choices available as for column headings

- How to align row headings
- How to format cells in the body of the table (as right-aligned or decimal-aligned numbers or as left-aligned or centered text)
- Whether to print the table in portrait or in landscape mode

Note that the specific set of dialog boxes and options you'll see can vary. If you choose not to include column headings, for example, the Table Wizard will not ask you how to align them. But the point is that for all of these options, you need only move through the dialog boxes and make your choices.

To create our sample table, pick Style 1 in the Table Wizard's first dialog box. Then choose no column headings and set the number of columns to 2. Next, choose no row headings and set the number of rows to 3; specify that most table cells will be left-aligned text; and, finally, specify portrait orientation and choose Finish.

The Table Wizard will be most helpful for creating tables that can take advantage of the wizard's automatic style layouts or its ability to automatically enter such headings as quarters, months, or days of the week. If you're using Style 1 and simply entering the number of columns and rows, however, the wizard doesn't gain you much. And it takes longer to use than the Insert Table dialog box or the Table button on the Standard toolbar.

If you use a particular table layout very often—for a monthly report, for example—you might want to store it as AutoText rather than generating it from scratch each time. You can store any table as an AutoText entry, not just those you generate with the wizard. For details on Word's AutoText feature, see "Using AutoText" on page 128.

## How to use Table AutoFormat— with or without the Table Wizard

NEW!

After you finish defining a table with the Table Wizard, but before the wizard inserts the table into your document, the wizard will start Word's Table AutoFormat feature, which opens the dialog box shown in Figure 11-7 on the next page.

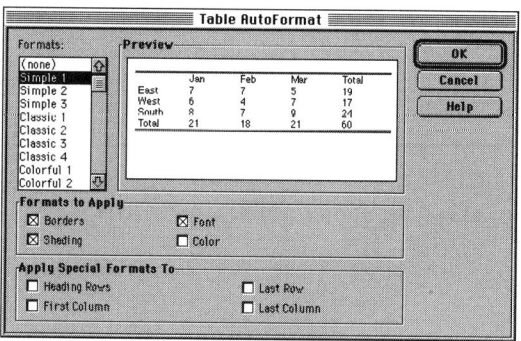

**FIGURE 11-7**

The Table AutoFormat dialog box will let you add a wide range of attractive formats to your table with minimum work.

Whether you prefer adding such formatting as borders, shading, and font enhancements to your table as a first step or as a final flourish—or whether you choose to make these additions at all—is strictly a matter of taste. Word will let you ignore the Table AutoFormat feature altogether, even when you're using the Table Wizard; simply choose Cancel to close the dialog box without adding formatting. You can also take advantage of the feature—to add, change, or remove formatting—at any time.

You can open the Table AutoFormat dialog box from the Insert Table dialog box. Simply choose the AutoFormat button. When you finish with AutoFormat, Word will return you to the Insert Table dialog box, where you can choose OK to insert the table, complete with the format you've defined. In addition, you can open the Table AutoFormat dialog box at any time by placing your cursor or selection in a table and choosing Table Table AutoFormat. When you use either of these two methods, you'll find an additional button—the AutoFit button—in the Formats To Apply group.

Using the Table AutoFormat feature is straightforward in the extreme. The Formats list box in the upper left portion of the dialog box lists 34 pre-defined formats. When you highlight a format name from the list, the Preview box will show what that choice will look like, using sample data. If you choose None, Word will format your table with no borders or shading.

You can't add custom choices to the Formats list, but you actually get far more than 34 formats since you can vary each one by using the check boxes in the bottom half of the dialog box. To give you some sense of the variety of choices, Figure 11-8 shows the Preview box for several predefined formats, with all check boxes checked. Figure 11-9 on page 340 shows the Preview box for a single format, with different combinations of check boxes checked.

**FIGURE 11-8**

These sample previews indicate the range of predefined table formats Word offers.

**FIGURE 11-9**

These sample previews
indicate the variety
available when you
check different com-
binations of check
boxes with a single
predefined table
format.

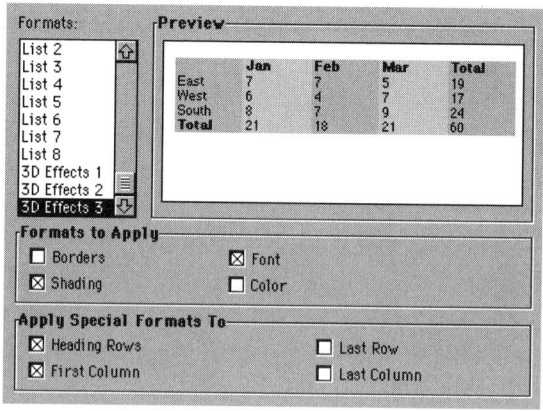

The check boxes are divided into two groups. The choices in the Apply Special Formats To group toggle formatting on or off for a specific part of the table: Heading Rows, First Column, Last Row, or Last Column. For example, if the format defines both bold and special shading for the heading rows (the rows Word identifies as part of the table heading) and you clear the Heading Rows check box, you'll turn off both the special shading and bold for the heading rows without removing shading or bold from any other part of the table.

The choices in the Formats To Apply group toggle specific kinds of formatting on or off for the entire table. The choices for Borders (meaning lines around or between cells), Shading, and Font (meaning enhancements such as bold and italic) are self-explanatory. Color is of interest only if you have a color printer.

AutoFit, which is not available if you're creating a table with the Table Wizard, adjusts column width. If there isn't much text in any cell in a given column, this option will set the column to be just wide enough for the widest line of text. If there's a great deal of text, AutoFit will adjust the column to use as few lines as possible.

The formatting you add with the Table AutoFormat feature is automatic in the sense that Word applies it automatically, but it will not automatically change as you change the table in your document. If you apply the AutoFit option, for example, and then change the text in the table, the column width will not change. However, it is easy enough to move your cursor to the table and choose Table Table AutoFormat at any time to reapply a format.

Note too that you can take advantage of AutoFit even if you don't want to add borders or shading. Simply set the Formats choice to (none), make sure the AutoFit check box is checked, and choose OK. Word will adjust table width for the current table without applying any other formats. (However, it will remove any other formats you've applied, even those you applied manually.) Alternatively, you can use the AutoFit feature by choosing Table Cell Height And Width, moving to the Column card, and choosing the AutoFit button. Be aware, however, that when you choose the AutoFit button on the Column card, Word will apply the AutoFit feature only to those cells that the cursor or selection is in, rather than the entire table.

# Using the Ruler with a Table

As you work with tables, you'll probably want to use Word's ruler. However, you'll need to know about some special features of the ruler as it applies to tables.

Figure 11-10 shows the same blank table shown in Figure 11-3, with the ruler showing and the cursor in the first cell of the first row. When you move the cursor to a table, Word will automatically set the ruler for the table, as shown in Figure 11-10.

**FIGURE 11-10**

When the cursor is in a table, the ruler marks the table and cell boundaries.

The ruler works much the same way for a table as for standard text. When you're working in a table, the ruler scale shows the width of the text area, with the left edge of the text area beginning at the zero point on the ruler and the right edge marked by a vertical line and by a change in color from white to gray. In addition, the ruler marks the boundary of each column with a cross-hatch pattern. For most columns, these boundary markers are in a small rectangular box. For the rightmost column, the marker is just to the right of the right margin boundary. For the leftmost column, the marker is just to the left of the left margin boundary and will usually be hidden in Normal view (although visible in Page Layout view) unless you scroll the page horizontally.

When you move the mouse pointer over these markers or just to the left of the leftmost boundary, the pointer will change to an arrow pointing left and right, and you can drag to change column width, as we'll discuss later. (If you drag the left-and-right arrow, the left indent marker, or the first-line indent marker to the left edge of the Word window, Word will scroll the screen to the right, so you'll be able to see the boundary marker.)

In Figure 11-10, for example, the cursor is in the first cell of the table. The text area of this cell begins at the zero point on the ruler, which is 0.075 inch from the left edge of the cell as defined by the gridlines. The marker for the

right side of the current cell is at 2.925 inches, or 0.075 inch from the beginning of the text area in the second column. This 0.075-inch offset on each side
results from Word automatically adding space to create what amounts to a
gutter between columns. We'll talk more about this space later, but for now
note that the small rectangles containing the boundary markers on the ruler
indicate the size of these gutters. Also notice that the left, right, and first-line
indent markers in Figure 11-10 indicate the text area for the cell the cursor is
located in. If you move the cursor to the second column, the ruler will show
the indent markers for the cell in that column instead.

# Entering Text in a Table

Entering text in a table is just like entering any other text: Simply move the
cursor where you want the text, and start typing. The text will appear in the
Normal style for the current document unless you've assigned a different format. (In our sample table, the Normal style calls for a 12-point Times font,
aligned flush left.)

To create the sample table shown in Figure 11-1 and again here in Figure
11-11, use the arrow keys or the mouse to move the cursor to the first cell of
the blank table and type *Dogwood*. Then move to the second cell by pressing
the Right arrow key or the Tab key or by pointing and clicking with the
mouse, and type the text for that cell. (We'll talk more about navigation techniques shortly.) To finish, simply repeat these steps until you've filled in the
table to match the sample shown in Figure 11-11.

**FIGURE 11-11**

Word will wrap text
within each cell of a
table.

If the text you enter is longer than the width of the current cell, Word will wrap the text within the cell, as you can see in Figure 11-11, and will increase the height of the cell to accommodate multiple lines of text. Notice that Word automatically increases the height of the adjacent cell in the first column as well, even though it contains only one line of text.

# Navigating in a Table

You have several choices for moving around in a table. In addition to using the mouse to click on the cell you want to work in, you can use either the Tab key or the arrow keys to move from cell to cell. If you use the Left or Right arrow key, the cursor will move through the text in each cell, going to the next cell in the same row when it reaches the beginning or end of the text in the current cell. When the cursor reaches the end of a row, it will make an extra stop at the end-of-row mark before moving to the first cell in the next row.

If you use the Up or Down arrow key, the cursor will move through the lines of text in the current cell, going to the next cell above or below after the last line of text in the current cell.

Since Word treats each end-of-cell mark as a paragraph, you can also press ⌘-Up arrow key or ⌘-Down arrow key to move between cells. If a cell contains more than one paragraph, Word will move the cursor one paragraph at a time within the cell before it moves to the next paragraph in the next cell. If each cell contains only one paragraph, the cursor will move forward or backward one cell with each keystroke. Here again, the cursor will make an extra stop at the end-of-row mark in each row, treating it as a separate paragraph.

If you use the Tab key to move forward or Shift-Tab to move backward, the cursor will move from cell to cell, highlighting all the text in the cell it moves to and skipping over the end-of-row marks when moving between the last cell in one row and the first cell in the next. When you're in a cell with se-lected text, pressing the Left arrow key will remove the highlight and leave the cursor at the beginning of the text in that cell. Pressing the Right arrow key will remove the highlight and leave the cursor at the end of the text in that cell.

If you're in the last cell of the last row of the table, pressing Tab will add a new row to the end of the table. However, if the cursor is in the first cell of the first row of the table, pressing Shift-Tab will have no effect—beyond produc-ing a beep to indicate an error.

Figure 11-12 summarizes the keyboard shortcuts for moving around in a table, including some navigation shortcuts we haven't mentioned here and some other kinds of shortcuts we'll cover later in this chapter.

| This Key Combination... | Does This... |
| --- | --- |
| Tab | Moves right one cell, *or* moves to the first cell in the next row if currently in the last cell of a row, *or* creates a new row if currently in the last cell of the last row of the table. Selects all text in the cell it moves to. |
| Shift-Tab | Moves left one cell, *or* moves to the last cell in the previous row if currently in the first cell of a row, *or* does nothing if currently in the first cell of the table. Selects all text in the cell it moves to. |
| ⌘-Up arrow key | Moves to the next cell (or the next paragraph within the current cell). |
| ⌘-Down arrow key | Moves to the previous cell (or the previous paragraph within the current cell). |
| Option-Home | Moves to the first cell in the current row. |
| Option-End | Moves to the last cell in the current row. |
| Option-Page Up | Moves to the first cell in the current column. |
| Option-Page Down | Moves to the last cell in the current column. |
| Option-Clear | Selects the entire table (Clear is located in the upper left corner of the numeric keypad). |
| ⌘-Shift-Return | Splits the table into two tables, inserting a paragraph mark above the row the cursor is currently in. |

**FIGURE 11-12**

Keyboard shortcuts for navigating in and working with tables.

## Selecting Text in a Table

In most ways, selecting text in a table is just like selecting text in any other part of a document. For example, you can use mouse techniques such as dragging to select text, double-clicking on a word, and so on. With the keyboard, you can hold down the Shift key or press F8 (Extend Selection) and then define the selection with the arrow keys.

Whenever you select text in two or more cells, Word will highlight those cells in their entirety. If you highlight the last word in a cell, for example, and extend the selection to the next cell, Word will select all the text in both cells as soon as you cross the cell boundary.

With any of these techniques, if you start and end the selection in two cells in the same column, Word will select text in that column only. If you want to select text in two or more columns, you need to start the selection in one column and end it in another. The cells you start and end with will define diagonally opposite corners for the selected block—either the upper left and lower right corners or the upper right and lower left. Word will select all text in all cells in the rectangle defined by that block.

Word also provides menu commands for selecting text in a table. With the cursor anywhere in the row or column you want to select, choose Table Select Row or Table Select Column, as appropriate. If you select several cells in a column before choosing Table Select Row, Word will select all the rows you've selected cells in. Similarly, if you select several cells in a row before choosing Table Select Column, Word will select all the columns you've selected cells in. Choose Table Select Table to select the entire table.

## Special table selection techniques for the mouse

Word also offers several special mouse techniques for selecting text in a table. These all take advantage of the same underlying feature: Each cell, row, or column in a table has its own invisible selection bar, just as each paragraph outside a table has its own invisible selection bar.

If you move the mouse pointer to the left edge of a cell, it will change to a right-arrow pointer, as shown in Figure 11-13, indicating that the pointer is in the cell's selection bar. Similarly, if you move the pointer to the left of the leftmost boundary of the table, it will also change to a right-arrow pointer, indicating that it is in the row's selection bar. If you move the pointer to the top of a column, it will change to a down-arrow pointer, as shown in Figure 11-14, indicating that it is in the column's selection bar.

**FIGURE 11-13**

You can select a row in a table by double-clicking in the selection bar for any cell in that row. The right-arrow pointer in column 2 indicates that the mouse pointer is in the cell's selection bar.

**FIGURE 11-14**

| column one ¤ | column two ¤ | column three ¤ | column four ¤ |
| column one ¤ | column two ¤ | column three ¤ | column four ¤ |
| column one ¤ | column two ¤ | column three ¤ | column four ¤ |
| column one ¤ | column two ¤ | column three ¤ | column four ¤ |

The down-arrow pointer indicates that the pointer is in the selection bar for the second column.

You can select the contents of a cell by clicking once anywhere in the cell's selection bar. To select an entire row, click once in the row selection bar, or double-click in the selection bar for any cell in that row. To select an entire column, click once in the column selection bar. To select an entire table, position the pointer in any selection bar, hold down the Option key, and double-click.

## Special table selection techniques for the keyboard

As already mentioned, when you move to a cell with the Tab key, Word will highlight the text in that cell. In addition, the standard keyboard techniques for selecting text serve well within a table, especially if you combine them with the shortcut navigation techniques for tables.

For example, to select an entire column, you can press Option-Page Up to move to the beginning of the first cell in a column, F8 to turn on the Extend Selection feature, and then Option-Page Down to highlight the entire column. Similarly, you can press Option-Home to move to the leftmost cell in a row, F8 to turn on Extend Selection, and then Option-End to select the entire row. In either case, after the row or column is selected, Extend Selection will still be turned on, so you can move left and right, or up and down, to make the selection larger or smaller. To select the entire table, press Option-Clear (on the numeric keypad) or, if NumLock is off, press Option-NumPad 5 (5 on the numeric keypad).

# Changing the Layout of a Table

After you create a table, you will often want to change its appearance by altering the width of one or more columns, changing the spacing between columns, or adding and deleting rows and columns. In fact, you may want to use a different number of columns in different parts of the table. You may also want to change the alignment of some of the rows. Word will let you make any of these changes. We'll start with a look at how to change width.

# How to adjust cell and column width

The techniques for changing the width of a cell and the width of a column are essentially the same. Changing the width of an entire column is simply a matter of changing the width of all the cells in that column.

## How to change cell or column width with the mouse

To change cell width using the mouse, first select the cell you want to change. Next move the pointer over the left or right cell boundary, as appropriate, until it changes to a vertical split pointer. Then hold down the mouse button and drag the gridline to a new position. Alternatively, you can highlight the cell, move the pointer to the cell's boundary marker on the ruler, and drag the marker to the new position. In either case, Word will ignore other cells in the column and will adjust width only for the row of the highlighted cell. What happens within that row is a bit more complicated.

If you drag to the left, you'll be able to move only to the rightmost position of the next boundary marker to the left. (Note that the rightmost position is defined by the text area of the cell rather than by the cell boundary or the gridline.) The only change in width will be for the highlighted cell and the cell to the immediate left or right of the boundary you are moving.

If you drag the left boundary to the right, you'll get much the same effect, adjusting only the single boundary. When you reach the leftmost position for the boundary marker on the right side of the highlighted cell, however, you'll find that you can move past that point. If you do, the highlighted cell will be at its minimum possible size when you stop and release the mouse button, and all the cells to the right will simply be pushed to the right, while maintaining their previous widths.

If you drag the right boundary to the right, you will once again adjust only the one boundary between two cells until you reach the leftmost position for the right side boundary marker in the cell to the right. If you drag farther, then when you stop you'll find the highlighted cell extended in width to the position where you stop, the cell to the right at its minimum possible size, and all cells farther to the right pushed to the right while maintaining their previous widths.

Figure 11-15 shows a four-column table. We've widened the first cell in the second row so that its right boundary falls just a little to the right of most of the cells in the first column. Notice that the rightmost cell in the second row is still even with most of the rest of the table. We've also widened the first cell in the fifth row so that its right boundary falls to the right of the cells in the second column. Notice that the second cell in the fifth row is at its minimum size and that the rightmost cell has been pushed to the right of the rest of the table.

If you want to change the width of two or more cells in a column, but not the width of the entire column, select the cells you want to change before you adjust the size.

**FIGURE 11-15**

When you adjust the width of a single cell, Word will reposition other cells in that row if you drag beyond the maximum position of the next cell to the right.

To adjust the width of the entire column, follow the same set of rules we just described, but select the entire column before dragging. You can also adjust column width using a slightly different set of rules if you simply drag any column boundary, with nothing selected. In this case, when you drag to the right, Word will leave the right edge of the table unchanged and will adjust all columns to the right proportionately. If you drag to the right until all the columns are at their minimum size, however, Word will then push the right edge of the table to the right as you drag still farther.

> If you've selected a column containing cells of different widths, Word will adjust all cells whose boundaries are in the same or nearly the same position as the boundary you're dragging. If you haven't selected any cells in the table, Word will adjust all cells whose boundaries are to the right of the one you move, whether the boundaries are in the same position or not.

## How to change cell or column width with the Table Cell Height And Width command

You can also adjust cell or column width with the Table Cell Height And Width command. As with many other dialog box formatting commands, this allows more precise control than dragging with the mouse.

Before choosing the Table Cell Height And Width command, you need to indicate which cells or columns to apply the settings to. If you want to adjust one column only, you can select the column or simply place the cursor in any cell in that column. If you want to adjust specific cells only or adjust more than one column, highlight the cell, cells, or columns you want to adjust. After you've indicated the cells or columns to change, choose Table Cell Height

And Width to open the dialog box shown in Figure 11-16. You can also open this dialog box by double-clicking on a boundary marker on the ruler.

FIGURE 11-16

Choose Table Cell Height And Width to open the Cell Height And Width dialog box.

As the name implies, you can adjust both height and width in this dialog box. For the moment, we're concerned only with column width, so the relevant settings are on the Column card. Notice that the first text box is labeled *Width Of Column 2*. The column number in this label will change depending on where the cursor or selection is. If you've selected cells in columns 1 and 2, for example, the label will become *Width Of Columns 1–2*.

Normally, the Width Of Column text box will show the width of the current cell or cells. However, if you've selected two or more cells of different widths, the text box will be blank.

To change the width of the column, cell, or cells you've indicated, enter a measurement in the Width Of Column text box. You can type the measurement, click on the arrows at the right of the text box, or move to the text box and press the Up or Down arrow key to change the setting in increments of 0.1 inch. When you're finished, choose OK. Not so incidentally, note that you can type the measurement in inches, centimeters, points, or picas. If you don't specify a unit of measure (by typing *in* or ", *cm*, *pt*, or *pi*), Word will use whatever unit you've chosen as your default measurement unit on the Tools Options General card.

If you choose Auto for the width, with cells in more than one column selected (but not including the last column), Word will leave the left and right boundaries of the selection in place and adjust the cells within the selection to make the cells all equal width. If the left or right boundaries vary for rows within the selection, Word will make the adjustment independently for each row. If you include cells from the last column, Word will move the right boundary of the table to the right indent for the document, if it isn't there already, and then adjust the width of the cells so that they are equal within the new boundaries.

**The AutoFit button.** The AutoFit button, just below the OK and Cancel buttons, works essentially the same way as the AutoFit button in the Table AutoFormat dialog box that we've already discussed. Briefly, if you choose this button, Word will adjust the column widths based on the contents of the cells. Note that the automatic adjustment will vary depending on how much of the table, and which parts of the table, you've selected. For consistently predictable results, we suggest that you use the AutoFit button only when you've selected the entire table.

**The Previous Column and Next Column buttons.** At the bottom of the Column card in the Cell Height And Width dialog box are two buttons labeled *Previous Column* and *Next Column*. You can use these to set the size for other columns without leaving the dialog box. When you choose the Next Column button, Word will set the width for the current column (or the currently highlighted cell or cells), move one column to the right, and show the width of the newly selected column in the Width Of Column text box. Similarly, when you choose the Previous Column button, Word will set the width for the current column (or the currently highlighted cell or cells), move the selection one column to the left, and show the width of the newly selected column.

If you have selected two or more cells in a column and you choose the Next Column or the Previous Column button, Word will select cells in the same rows when you move to the next or previous column. For example, if you've selected the second and third cells in column 2, Word will select the second and third cells in column 1 or column 3. If you select an entire column before opening the dialog box, choosing Previous Column or Next Column will select the entire neighboring column.

If you choose the Next Column button when you're in the last column of the table, Word will move to the first column of the table. Similarly, if you choose Previous Column when you're in the first column, Word will move to the last column in the table. In all cases, if you've selected less than an entire column, the selection will remain in the same row or rows.

## How to adjust the space between columns

The Column card of the Cell Height And Width dialog box contains one other text box, labeled *Space Between Columns*. As we've already mentioned, Word automatically adds some space between the text in each column of a table when you create the table. This space is indicated on your screen by the distance between the left cell boundary and the beginning of your text, or between the cell boundary and the end-of-cell mark. As you enter text, you'll see that Word also leaves blank space between the last character on each line and the right cell boundary.

Word's default spacing between columns is 0.15 inch, as you can see if you create a new table, choose Table Cell Height And Width, and then choose the Column card to see the setting in the Space Between Columns text box. This setting can be confusing, because it affects entire rows, not just the currently selected cells. And because it always affects the leftmost cell in a row, it has the effect of changing the position of the row's gridlines, as well as leaving more room between the edge of the text and the gridlines. If you increase the setting, for example, you won't see any change in the width of your table cells, but you will notice that Word shifts the cell boundaries to the left and repositions text within the cell, changing the way the text wraps.

The way Word allocates the space between columns is also a little different from what you might expect. Word divides the value in the text box between the two ends of each cell in a row. For example, if you've specified 0.5 inch as your Space Between Columns setting for a given row, Word will assign 0.25 inch to each side of each cell in that row. And you won't be able to enter text in these areas unless you change the indents for that text. (More on this later.) Note that Word inserts a 0.25-inch space at the left edge of the first cell in the row and at the right edge of the last cell. Obviously, this space will not fall between columns, despite the name of the setting.

To get a better handle on the Space Between Columns setting, look at the ruler in Figure 11-17. The four-column table in the figure contains four 1-inch-wide columns and is formatted with the default Space Between Columns setting of 0.15 inch.

**FIGURE 11-17**

This table is formatted with the default Space Between Columns setting of 0.15 inch.

As the ruler in Figure 11-17 shows, the width of the text area in the current cell is slightly less than 1 inch, extending from the zero point on the ruler to the vertical line on the ruler and the end of the white area. This width reflects the width of the cell (1.0 inch) minus the default space between columns (0.15 inch).

As Figure 11-17 also shows, the gridline marking the left boundary of the table falls to the left of the zero point on the ruler. However, the cursor (and the text in the first column of the table) is aligned with the zero point. The space between the table's left boundary line and the left edge of the text in each cell is half of the 0.15-inch setting for Space Between Columns—the space that Word has allotted to the left end of the cell.

Now consider what happens when you increase the Space Between Columns setting to 0.5 inch. If you select all the cells in one column, open the Cell Height And Width dialog box, enter .5" in the Space Between Columns text box, and choose OK, you'll get the result shown in Figure 11-18. As you can see, the left boundary of the table is shifted farther left. With the increased Space Between Columns setting, Word allocates 0.25 inch of space to each end of each cell and shifts all column boundaries to the left.

**FIGURE 11-18**

This is the same table as in Figure 11-17 after the Space Between Columns setting was increased to 0.5 inch.

When you increase the space between columns, Word does not change the relative alignment of the text in the table. Notice that the cursor and the leftmost text in the first cell are still aligned with the zero point on the ruler. Similarly, the left edge of the text in each column has retained its original alignment. However, the text area on the ruler is now only 0.5 inch wide for each cell, reflecting the 1-inch column width minus the 0.5-inch space between columns. As a result, Word had to wrap the text in each cell to a new line. Notice also how much larger the gray rectangles between columns on the ruler have become in Figure 11-18.

**Key points about table column spacing.** If you're finding this discussion of column spacing confusing, you're not alone. But if you keep just a few key points in mind, you should be able to adjust the space between columns to suit your needs:

- Remember that Word subtracts the Space Between Columns setting from the cell width. The text area is the remaining space in the cell.

- Word creates space between columns by allotting blank space at both ends of each cell in a row. This space appears at the beginning of the first cell in a row as well as at the end of the last cell in a row.

- Changing the Space Between Columns setting does not affect the horizontal alignment of text in a row. It may, however, change the way Word wraps text and breaks lines within each cell as the text area increases or decreases when you change the setting.

■ Keep in mind that the label Space Between Columns is a bit of a misnomer. In truth, the measurement you enter for this setting is not the spacing between columns but rather is twice the distance between the text and either the left or the right cell boundary.

As you'll see later in this chapter, you can use paragraph formatting to change the alignment of text within cells (and of individual paragraphs in the same cell). And by changing the paragraph indents, you can also move text into the blank area that Word allots at each end of a cell.

## How to adjust row height

As you enter text in a table, Word will automatically adjust the height of individual rows to accommodate the text. Both the size of the characters and the number of lines will affect the height of a row. In the sample table shown in both Figure 11-1 and Figure 11-11, notice how Word has adjusted the height for all the cells in each row to accommodate the second column. If you reformatted the text with a larger point size, Word would increase the row height even more.

Word also lets you increase the height of rows manually to allow more space between the text in adjacent rows. For example, to increase the height of the second row in our sample table, select either or both cells in row 2, choose Table Cell Height And Width, and choose the Row card, shown in Figure 11-19.

Notice that the Height Of Row pull-down list is labeled to indicate the row or rows that the settings will affect. If the cursor is anywhere in the table, with no selection, the settings will apply to all rows, and the label will reflect that. In our sample table, for instance, the label would read *Height Of Rows 1–3.* If you select a cell in one or more rows before opening the dialog box, the list box label will indicate those rows. Select a cell in row 2 only, for example, and the label will read *Height Of Row 2;* select cells in rows 1 and 2, and the label will read *Height Of Rows 1–2.*

When you open the Height Of Row pull-down list, you'll see three choices for specifying row height: Auto, At Least, and Exactly. Auto, the default setting, lets Word determine row height. At Least sets a minimum size that Word will not go below but also tells Word to automatically increase row height if necessary. Exactly tells Word to use the setting exactly as given, even if some of the text in the cell won't show or print.

For this example (with one or both cells in row 2 already selected), we'll use the At Least setting, enter *.75"* in the At text box, and choose OK. Figure 11-20 shows the result of the new setting for row 2. Note that you can set the height by typing the measurement, by clicking on the arrows at the right of the text box, or by moving to the text box and pressing the Up or Down arrow key to change the height in increments of 1 point. You can type any measurement that Word recognizes: *in* or " for inches, *cm* for centimeters, *pt* for points, or *pi* for picas. The next time you open the Row card, however, Word will show the setting in points.

**FIGURE 11-19**

Choose Table Cell Height And Width, and then choose the Row card to see the settings for row height.

**FIGURE 11-20**

This is our sample table of tree information after increasing the height for the second row.

When Word increases row height, it inserts the additional space below the text. If you want space above the text, use the Before setting in the Paragraph dialog box. (We'll discuss spacing later in this chapter.) Notice also that the Height Of Row setting affects all the cells in a row. Word does not allow cells of different heights in the same row. To return a row to its default height, choose Table Cell Height And Width, choose the Row card, and set Height Of Row to Auto.

### How to use the Previous Row and Next Row buttons

On the right side of the Row card in the Cell Height And Width dialog box are the Previous Row and Next Row buttons. Like the Previous Column and Next Column buttons on the Column card, these two buttons let you enter settings for additional rows without leaving the dialog box. When you choose the Next Row button, Word will set the row height or other settings for the current row or rows so that you can see the results on the screen. Word will then move down one row and display the settings for that row in the various text boxes. Similarly, when you choose the Previous Row button, Word will set the changed settings for the current row or rows and move the selection up one row.

If you choose the Next Row button when the cursor is in the bottom row of the table, Word will move to the first row. If you choose the Previous Row button when the cursor is in the top row, Word will move to the last row. If you select two or more rows before opening the Cell Height And Width dialog box, Word will select only a single row when you choose Next Row or Previous Row. After you adjust the settings, you can choose OK to accept all settings and close the dialog box. If you choose Cancel after entering a setting but before moving to a different row, Word will ignore that setting.

## NEW!  How to control whether rows can break across pages

At the bottom of the Row card in the Cell Height And Width dialog box is a check box labeled *Allow Row To Break Across Pages*. This option determines where Word will position a row if a page break falls in the middle of a row that includes multiple lines of text. If you format any given row by checking this check box, Word will break the text within the row at the page break. If you format the row without checking this check box, Word will move the entire row to the next page when a page break would otherwise fall horizontally within the row.

T
I
P
This setting affects only page breaks that fall within rows, not page breaks that fall between rows. If you want the entire table to stay together, select the table, and choose Format Paragraph. Choose the Text Flow card, and check the Keep Lines Together and Keep With Next check boxes.

# How to add rows

As we've already mentioned, you can add a new blank row to the end of a table by placing the cursor anywhere in the rightmost cell of the last row and pressing Tab. The new row will have the same formatting as the last row of the table.

To add a row in any other part of a table, use either the Table Insert Rows command or the Table Insert Cells command. The difference between inserting a row and inserting an entire row of cells is subtle but real. We'll start with the Table Insert Rows command.

## How to add rows with the Table Insert Rows command

Suppose you want to add a row between the second and third rows of the table shown in Figure 11-21. Begin by moving to the third row and either selecting nothing or selecting the entire row including the end-of-row mark. Then open the Table menu. As you can see in Figure 11-21, the Insert Rows command has now become the first item on the menu. Choose Insert Rows, and Word will add a new row above the row the cursor or selection is in. You can also add a row by clicking on the Table button on the Standard toolbar. (In fact, this button's ToolTip name changes to Insert Rows when the cursor is in a row or when a row is selected.) Still another alternative is to use the context-sensitive menu by pointing to the selected row, holding the Control key down while clicking the mouse button, and then choosing Insert Rows. Regardless of how you create a new row, Word will insert it just above the row you indicated and will give it the same formatting as that row.

**FIGURE 11-21**

If you select an entire row or simply place the cursor in a row, the Insert Rows command becomes the first item on the Table menu.

## How to add multiple rows

You can add two or more rows to a table in one step. First select as many rows as you want to insert, being careful to include the end-of-row marks. For example, if you want to insert three rows, select three. Keep in mind that Word will insert the new rows above the first row you select. After making the selection, choose Table Insert Rows, click on the Table button (whose ToolTip name is now Insert Rows), or call up the context-sensitive menu by holding down the Control key while clicking on the selection. The new rows will have the same formatting as the top row in the selection.

## How to add rows with the Table Insert Cells command

You can also add rows by inserting cells. Once again, suppose you want to add a row between the second and third rows of the table shown in Figure 11-21. This time, begin by selecting the leftmost cell in the third row. Then choose Table Insert Cells or click on the Table toolbar button (whose ToolTip name will now be Insert Cells). Word will respond with the Insert Cells dialog box, shown in Figure 11-22.

**FIGURE 11-22**

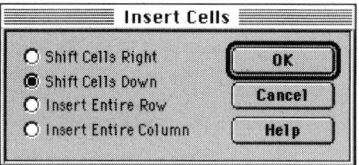

With the Insert Cells dialog box, you can shift cells right or down or insert entire rows or columns.

As you can see, the Insert Cells dialog box lets you shift cells right or down when inserting cells. You can also insert entire rows or columns. We'll cover the options of shifting right and inserting columns a little later in this chapter; for now, we'll focus on the other two options.

Choosing Insert Entire Row and then choosing OK is equivalent to choosing the Table Insert Rows command. This can be handy if you accidentally selected a partial row or rows rather than full rows, since it lets you insert rows from the Insert Cells dialog box without having to return to the table and change your selection. As before, Word will insert the new row or rows just above the top row in the selection, using the same format as that top row.

If you choose Shift Cells Down, however, and then choose OK, you will wind up with the top table shown in Figure 11-23. For comparison, the bottom table in Figure 11-23 shows the result you get if you use the Table Insert Rows command instead. If you count the rows in each table, you'll see that in both cases Word has added a new row. In the table that we've used the Insert Cell choice with, rather than Insert Entire Row, however, there are still only two rows—2 and 3—that have a different format from the rest of the rows. When you insert cells rather than rows, Word creates new rows at the *end* of the table, following the format of the last row or rows in the table. In this particular example, if you inserted three rows rather than one, Word would repeat the formats for rows 3, 4, and 5 in the new rows 6, 7, and 8.

Also notice that Word pushes all the text down by as many rows as you've just inserted—but only for those columns where you had cells selected. In the example in Figure 11-23, we had selected a cell in the first column only, so the only text Word pushed down was in the first column.

**FIGURE 11-23**

If you insert rows with Table Insert Cells and tell Word to shift cells down, as in the top table shown here, Word will add new rows at the end of the table and push the text down for columns where you had selected text.

Row·added·with·Table·Insert·Cells:¶
¶
| AAA111¤ | BBB111¤ | CCC111¤ | DDD111¤ | ¤ |
| AAA222¤ | BBB222¤ | CCC222¤ | DDD222¤ | ¤ |
| ¤ | BBB333¤ | CCC333¤ | DDD333¤ | ¤ |
| AAA333¤ | BBB444¤ | CCC444¤ | DDD444¤ | ¤ |
| AAA444¤ | BBB555¤ | CCC555¤ | DDD555¤ | ¤ |
| AAA555¤ | ¤ | ¤ | ¤ | ¤ |
¶
Row·added·with·Table·Insert·Rows:¶
¶
| AAA111¤ | BBB111¤ | CCC111¤ | DDD111¤ | ¤ |
| AAA222¤ | BBB222¤ | CCC222¤ | DDD222¤ | ¤ |
| ¤ | ¤ | ¤ | ¤ | ¤ |
| AAA333¤ | BBB333¤ | CCC333¤ | DDD333¤ | ¤ |
| AAA444¤ | BBB444¤ | CCC444¤ | DDD444¤ | ¤ |
| AAA555¤ | BBB555¤ | CCC555¤ | DDD555¤ | ¤ |

As with some other issues involved with tables, this difference between inserting rows as rows and inserting rows as cells can be confusing. Just note that in most cases you'll want to insert rows as rows so that you can match the existing rows. Also be aware that you can move and copy rows by using Word's drag-and-drop feature.

## How to delete rows

You can delete rows at the beginning, middle, or end of a table.

To delete rows at the beginning or end of a table, simply extend a selection across the top or bottom boundary line of the table into the adjacent body text, and then delete the rows with any of Word's usual deletion commands. If you start by selecting one cell in each row you want to delete, Word will automatically select entire rows as soon as you cross the top or bottom boundary line.

If you want to delete rows from elsewhere in a table, you need to use the Table Delete Rows or the Table Delete Cells command. As when inserting rows and cells, there are some differences between deleting rows and deleting cells. We'll start with the Table Delete Rows command.

## How to delete and move rows with the Table Delete Rows command

Deleting rows with the Table Delete Rows command is straightforward. Simply select the row or rows you want to delete, including the end-of-row marks, and choose Table Delete Rows. Word will delete the selection, including both the text and the cells themselves, and will move any lower rows in the table up to keep the table together.

If you accidentally delete rows that you want to keep, you can recover them with the Edit Undo command. However, be aware that Word does not put deleted rows on the Clipboard—at least, not rows that you delete through the Table Delete Rows command—so you cannot recover deleted rows by pasting them back into your document.

In contrast, if you select an entire row (by clicking on the selection bar for the row, double-clicking on the selection bar for any cell in the row, or using the Table Select Row command) and then choose Edit Cut, Word will delete the row and place it on the Clipboard. (If you don't explicitly select the row, Word will delete only the text in the row and leave the cells, even if you've selected the end-of-row mark.) After you place rows on the Clipboard, you can paste them into another section of the table, or elsewhere in your document, by choosing the Edit Paste Rows command. Note that if you select every cell in the table and then choose Edit Cut, Word will delete the entire table and place it on the Clipboard. This can be handy if you want to move a table. We'll discuss all these possibilities in more depth a little later in this chapter.

## How to delete rows with the Table Delete Cells command

The difference between Table Delete Rows and Table Delete Cells is, fortunately, less confusing than the difference between Table Insert Rows and Table Insert Cells. If you place the cursor or selection in the row or rows you want to delete and then choose Table Delete Cells, you'll see the Delete Cells dialog box, shown in Figure 11-24. If you choose Delete Entire Row and then OK, the result will be equivalent to selecting a row and choosing Table Delete Rows. Somewhat surprisingly, you can also get the same result by selecting all the cells in a row or rows without the end-of-row mark, choosing Table Delete Cells, Shift Cells Left, and then choosing OK.

There's an easier way to move rows than cutting and pasting. Place the cursor or selection anywhere in the row or rows you want to move, and press Option-Shift-Up arrow key or Option-Shift-Down arrow key. Word will select the rows and move them up or down. You can even move rows out of the table this way. Once the selected rows are at the top or bottom of the table, press the key combination one more time to move the rows past the next paragraph immediately above or below the table.

This technique for moving rows also works for moving paragraphs of body text and is related to Word's outlining feature. For this trick to work properly, Word's Outline mode must be set to view All whether you're using the Outline view or not. This is the default setting, but if you've changed it, you can reset it easily enough: Choose View Outline, and either press Control-Shift-A or click on the Show All button on the Outlining toolbar. Then return to the view you were working in.

**FIGURE 11-24**

The Delete Cells dialog box lets you tell Word to shift cells left or up or to delete entire rows or columns.

In contrast, if you select all the cells in a row or rows without the end-of-row mark, choose Table Delete Cells, Shift Cells Up, and then choose OK, Word will not delete any rows. Rather, it will delete the text in the selected cells and move all text up to fill in the now-empty cells. Figure 11-25 shows the results of using the Shift Cells Up option after highlighting the cells in row 3. Notice the newly empty row at the bottom of the table.

**FIGURE 11-25**

If you select a row (without the end-of-row mark), choose Table Delete Cells, and then choose Shift Cells Up, Word will delete the text and shift all text up by one row.

# How to insert and delete columns

Inserting and deleting columns is similar to inserting and deleting rows. In particular, just as you can add rows to the end of the table or insert them above selected rows, so too can you add columns to the right of the table or insert them before (to the left of) a selected column. We'll start with inserting columns within a table.

## How to add a column within a table or to the left side

Suppose you want to insert a new column between the AAA column and the BBB column in the sample table shown in Figure 11-26. First select the entire second column. Then open the Table menu. As Figure 11-26 shows, Word will change the first two menu items to Insert Columns and Delete Columns. Choose Insert Columns, and Word will insert a column to the left of the column you selected.

**FIGURE 11-26**

When you select one or more columns, Word will offer the choices Insert Columns and Delete Columns on the Table menu.

Alternatively, with the column selected, you can insert a new column by clicking on the Table button on the Standard toolbar. (The ToolTip name of this button will have changed to Insert Columns.) Yet another alternative is to select any part of the column (simply placing the cursor in the column won't make the proper command available), choose Table Insert Cells, Insert Entire Column, and then choose OK. All of these strategies insert a column to the left of the originally selected column, which means you can use this technique to add a column to the left side of the table by selecting the first column in the table.

Each cell in the new column will initially have the same width as the cell to its right, as shown in Figure 11-27. However, you can change the width of the cells using any of the techniques described earlier in this chapter. See "How to adjust cell and column width" on page 348.

**FIGURE 11-27**

When you insert a new column, each cell in the new column will have the same width as the cell in the same row and column that you originally highlighted.

## How to add a column to the right side of a table

To add a column to the right side of a table, select the end-of-row marks, as shown in Figure 11-28. Then choose Table Insert Columns or click on the Table button (now named Insert Columns) on the Standard toolbar. Word will add a new column on the right side of the table—or to the left of the end-of-row marks, in other words—as shown in Figure 11-29. Each cell in the column will be the same width as the cell to its immediate left.

**FIGURE 11-28**

To add a column to the right side of a table, first select the end-of-row marks.

**FIGURE 11-29**

When adding a column to the right side of a table, Word will set each new cell to the same width as the cell to its immediate left.

## How to add multiple columns

You can add multiple adjacent columns much as you add multiple rows. To add multiple columns within a table, first select the number of columns you want to add. If you want to add two new columns, for example, select two existing columns. (If you want to add more columns than you have in the current table, you can select the end-of-row marks to add an extra column.) Next choose Table Insert Columns or click on the Table (Insert Columns) button on the Standard toolbar. Word will insert the columns to the left of the leftmost column you originally selected. Each cell in the new columns will have the same width as the cell to its immediate right.

You cannot append multiple columns to the right edge of a table with a single command. However, since Word leaves the inserted column highlighted, you can get the same effect, after adding one column as already described, by repeatedly choosing Table Insert Columns or repeatedly clicking on the renamed Table button on the toolbar.

## How to delete and move columns

Deleting a column or columns is straightforward. If you want to get rid of the columns entirely, simply select them and choose Table Delete Columns. Alternatively, you can select one or more cells in the column or columns you want to delete, choose Table Delete Cells, Delete Entire Column, and then choose OK. Word will delete the selected columns and shift the remaining columns to the left to close any gaps in the table.

If you delete any columns accidentally with these techniques, you can choose Edit Undo to recover them. As with rows, Word does not place deleted columns on the Clipboard when you use these techniques, so you cannot recover the columns by pasting them back into your document. However, if you use Word's Edit Cut command to delete a column, Word will put the column on the Clipboard.

This ability to use the Clipboard comes in handy when you need to move a column to a different place in a table. For example, to move the first column in a four-column table to the third column position, select the column, choose Edit Cut, position the cursor anywhere in the first cell of what will now be the third column, and choose Edit Paste Columns. If Word's drag-and-drop feature is active, you can also select the column, drag it to the new position, and release the mouse button. You can move multiple columns with either of these methods.

# How to add and delete cells

You can use the Table Insert Cells and the Table Delete Cells commands for parts of a table that are smaller than an entire row or column. The Shift Cells Right and Shift Cells Down options in the Insert Cells dialog box and the Shift Cells Left and Shift Cells Up options in the Delete Cells dialog box tell Word how to adjust the table when you insert or delete partial rows and columns.

Consider, for example, Figure 11-30, which shows a simple four-column-by-five-row table. To delete the two cells selected in the second row, choose Table Delete Cells to open the Delete Cells dialog box, with the Shift Cells Left option already chosen. Choose OK to have the remaining cells in that row shift to the left, which will result in the table shown in Figure 11-31. If you select Shift Cells Up instead, the result will be the table shown in Figure 11-32. Notice that in this second case two blank cells appear in the fifth row of the table. Word doesn't disturb the basic shape of the table when you shift cells up.

If you start with the table shown in Figure 11-30 and you insert cells rather than delete them, shifting cells right will insert two blank cells to the left of the originally selected cells, making the second row two cells wider than the rest of the table. Shifting cells down will push the text in the first two columns down one row, leave the first two cells in the second row blank, and add a new row at the end of the table (with its last two cells blank) to handle the shifted cells.

| | |
|---|---|
| **FIGURE 11-30** | |
| We'll use this table to illustrate deleting cells. | |

| | |
|---|---|
| **FIGURE 11-31** | |
| If you Shift Cells Left when deleting the two highlighted cells shown in Figure 11-30, this table is the result. | |

| | |
|---|---|
| **FIGURE 11-32** | |
| If you Shift Cells Up when deleting the two highlighted cells shown in Figure 11-30, this table is the result. | |

## How to merge and split cells

Word will let you merge two or more cells in the same row. (You cannot merge cells in the same column.) To merge cells, simply select the cells you want to combine, and choose Table Merge Cells. Word will remove the boundaries between the selected cells and create one cell whose width is equal to the combined widths of the merged cells. For any cell that includes text, except for the last cell being merged, it will also convert the end-of-cell mark in each cell into paragraph marks and will treat each cell's text as a separate paragraph in the new cell.

A newly merged cell is treated just like any other cell. You can, for example, merge it with still other cells. If you merge the first three cells in a row and then decide that you should have merged the first four instead, you can simply merge what is now the first cell with what is now the second.

Word also offers a Table Split Cells command. If you want more cells in a given row, you can choose Table Split Cells as an alternative to the Table Insert Cells command. Simply select the cells you want to split, and choose Table Split Cells. Word will open the dialog box shown in Figure 11-33. By default, Word enters 2 in the Number Of Columns box, which means it will split each cell you've selected into two cells. You can increase this number, but if the total number of cells in the row would then exceed 31 (the maximum number of cells allowable), Word will respond with a message telling you that you have exceeded the maximum number of columns.

**FIGURE 11-33**

When you choose Table Split Cells, Word will open the Split Cells dialog box to let you specify how many cells to split each selected cell into.

## How to work with different numbers of cells in different rows

One reason for merging cells is to create a title that stretches across two or more columns in a table—as in the heading rows of the Table Wizard's layout choices, which we discussed in "How to create and format a table with the Table Wizard" on page 335.

The effect of merging two empty cells is the equivalent of deleting one cell in the row (using the Shift Cells Left option) and then resizing the remaining cells.

Figure 11-34, for example, shows two three-column tables. We produced the top table by merging the first two cells in the first row. We produced the bottom table by widening the first cell in the first row to make its right boundary even with the right boundary of the second cell in the other rows. We then

NEW!

> When you split a cell that contains text, Word will move the text into different cells based on the position of paragraph marks (if any), the number of paragraphs, and the number of cells you're creating. If the original cell contains fewer paragraphs than the final number of cells, Word will put the first paragraph in the first cell, the second in the second cell, and so on, and will leave the remaining cells empty. If the original cell contains more paragraphs than the final number of cells, Word will make an effort to divide the paragraphs evenly over the cells. Split a cell with four paragraphs into two cells, for example, and Word will put two paragraphs in each cell. Split a cell with five paragraphs in two, and Word will put three paragraphs in the first cell and two in the second.
>
> If you want all the text to stay in one cell, be sure to replace any paragraph marks with line-break characters (entered by pressing Shift-Return). (And, to make it easier to see what's happening, be sure to set Word so you can see paragraph marks. To do so, choose Tools Options View to see the View card, and check the Paragraph Marks check box.)

deleted the second cell in the top row so all rows in the table end at the same place on the ruler. In either table, if you try to select a column starting with the rightmost cell in the first row, Word will select the offset column as shown in the figure, highlighting the second cell in each row.

**FIGURE 11-34**

When you create a wide cell from a single cell or by merging two cells, Word's idea of a column will not necessarily match the way the cells line up visually, as shown in this selection of a single column.

In this table, the large cell in the first row was made by merging the cells from the first two columns.

The large cell in the first row of this column was created by changing its width and then deleting the second cell from the first row.

The offset selection of a column can make life difficult when you want to select columns to format them. For example, in Figure 11-34, you might want to select all cells in the far right column to format them with a particular shading, but there's no way to select them all at one time. To avoid this sort of problem, we recommend that when possible you create tables by approximation first, adjusting the width of any cells you plan to delete to make them as narrow as possible. Then add text and formatting so you can work with complete columns. When you're satisfied with the approximate formatting, you can merge or delete cells you don't want and adjust the final cell width as necessary. Note that if you use the Table Cell Height And Width command, Word will track columns by the position of each cell in its row. But if you adjust columns using the mouse, Word will let you move all cell borders on the same vertical line at the same time.

## Deleting an Entire Table

Occasionally you'll want to delete an entire table. Given that you can approach a table as the sum of all its rows, columns, or cells, you can use any of the techniques we've discussed for deleting rows, columns, or cells. However, we strongly advise that you get in the habit, when deleting an entire table, of using deletion techniques that put the table on the Clipboard. That way, if you delete the table accidentally, it will be available for pasting. The simplest choice for placing the table on the Clipboard is to select the entire table, with or without surrounding text, and choose Edit Cut.

## Changing Table and Row Alignment

As we've already pointed out, when you create a table, Word aligns the left edge of the text area in the first column with the left edge of your document's text column. Assuming that you're working in a single-column layout and you haven't moved the first-line or left indent marker on the ruler, the position of the left edge of the table text will correspond to the zero point on the ruler. However, the left boundary of the table itself will appear to the left of the zero point.

As you may recall, there are two settings on the Cell Height And Width dialog box Row card (shown in Figure 11-19) that we haven't discussed yet: the Indent From Left text box and the Alignment box, which offers buttons for Left, Center, and Right alignment.

The alignment setting will be noticeable only if the width of a table is less than the width of the current text column. Assuming that the table is narrower than the text, however, you can use this setting to change the alignment of the entire table or of individual rows.

The Left alignment option, which is the default, will align the left boundary of the table with the left edge of the text column. More precisely, it will align the left edge of the text in the leftmost column of the table with the left edge of the body text in the document. All the tables we've looked at in this chapter so far use left alignment.

The Center option centers the table within the document's text column. The Right option aligns the right edge of the table with the right edge of a document's text column; more precisely, with right alignment Word will align the right edge of the text area in a table's rightmost column with the right edge of the document's text column. Figure 11-35 shows three tables, each with a different alignment.

**FIGURE 11-35**

The three tables shown here demonstrate left, center, and right alignment.

In most tables, you'll want to align all the rows the same way. However, there may be times when you need a different alignment in different rows to create a special effect. For example, if you use a table to design a complex form, you may want to change the alignment of one or more rows. In these situations, you can apply the alignment to selected rows as needed. The rules for selecting rows before choosing Table Cell Height And Width and for moving through the rows with the Next Row and Previous Row buttons are the same as we discussed earlier in "How to adjust row height" on page 354.

The alignment of a table or row has nothing to do with the alignment of text within individual cells. As we'll demonstrate shortly, Word lets you change the alignment of text in a table without changing overall table alignment.

## How to indent rows

The Cell Height And Width dialog box also includes an Indent From Left setting on the Row card that can give you precise control over shifting anything—from one row to the entire table—to the left or right. For example, suppose you're using the default left alignment and you want to shift the entire table 0.5 inch to the right. You can simply place the cursor anywhere in the table (or select one or more columns), choose Table Cell Height And Width, choose the Row card, enter .5" in the Indent From Left text box, and choose OK. Word will close the dialog box and move the table 0.5 inch to the right. To shift one or more rows to the left and into the page margin, you can enter a negative number in the Indent From Left text box.

You can use the Indent From Left setting in combination with alignment settings. Any change from the default setting of 0 will shift the table or rows by the designated amount from the left, center, or right position.

### Mouse shortcuts for positioning rows

You can use the mouse to position the leftmost boundary of one or more rows in a table but not to indent the entire row in a single step. As we pointed out earlier in this chapter, if you move the mouse pointer over the left boundary marker on the ruler, the pointer will change to an arrow pointing left and right. You can then click the mouse button and drag the boundary. If you have first selected one or more cells in the first column, Word will change the leftmost position for those rows only. You'll get the same effect if you select cells in the first column, position the mouse pointer over the leftmost boundary of the table itself, and then drag when the pointer changes to the vertical split pointer.

This technique is not equivalent to indenting rows with the Table Cell Height And Width command. When you change the Indent From Left setting on the Cell Height And Width dialog box Row card, Word shifts the entire row or rows to the left or right. When you drag the left boundary, you are actually adjusting the position of the left boundary of the leftmost cell, and Word will follow the rules described earlier in this chapter for changing cell or column width. For details, see "How to change cell or column width with the mouse" on page 348.

# Entering Body Text Above or Between Table Rows

When working with tables, you may find that you need to enter some text above a table that you've inserted at the top of a new document. Or you may decide that you want to split a table in two. In either case, you need to enter a blank paragraph—above the table or between two rows.

To enter a new paragraph above a table that's at the top of a document, simply move the cursor to the beginning of the first cell in the first row, and press Return. If the table is at the very beginning of the document, Word will add a new paragraph above the table. If the table is anywhere else in the document, Word will add a new paragraph within the cell. To enter a new paragraph before a table that is not at the top of the document, of course, you need only move to the end of the paragraph immediately before the table and press Enter.

To split a table, place the cursor or selection just below the point where you want to insert the break—in the first row of what will become the bottom table—and press ⌘-Shift-Return or choose Table Split Table. Word will split the table and insert a blank paragraph just above the row the cursor or selection was in.

## How to change part of a table to text

You may sometimes want to split a table because you want to convert part of it to text. To split a table and convert rows to text at the same time, start by selecting the row or rows you want to convert. Then choose Table Convert Table To Text. Word will open the Convert Table To Text dialog box. You can then choose to separate the text that's in different cells with paragraph marks, tabs, commas, or some other symbol, as appropriate. Choose OK, and Word will convert the selected rows to normal text, splitting the table in the process. Toward the end of this chapter, we'll explain how to use this dialog box to convert an entire table to text, in "Converting All or Part of a Table to Text" on page 386.

## How to split a table vertically

Word will not let you split a table vertically between columns because you can't create two tables side by side in a single text column (unless you put one or both in a separate frame). However, you can create the same visual effect by inserting one or more new columns in the middle of a table. Choose Table Insert Columns, as we've already described, to insert a new, blank column where you want the visual split. As we'll show you later in this chapter, you can then use borders to make the result look like two separate tables. (You can also create side-by-side tables by using a two-column format and Word's section formatting features to create balanced columns. We'll cover columns in Chapter 14.)

# Working with Text in a Table

Word lets you work with the text in a table much as you would with any other document text. There are a few differences, however. We've already shown you how to select text in a table. Here are some notes on how to edit the text and format it.

## How to edit text in a table

You can use most of the same editing tools in a table as in normal document text, including all the basic editing techniques we described in Chapter 4. However, there are a few issues to keep in mind.

When you press the Return key while the cursor is in a table cell, Word will begin a new paragraph in the cell, rather than move the cursor to the next row of cells. (There is one important exception to this rule: If the table is at the very beginning of the file and the cursor is at the very beginning of the first cell of the table, pressing Return will insert a blank paragraph above the table.)

Also, when you use Word's Edit Cut, Edit Copy, and Edit Paste commands within a cell, you'll get different results depending on whether the selection you copied or cut includes an end-of-cell mark. If it does include an end-of-cell mark, the Paste command on the Edit menu will read Paste Cells, and when you paste the selection into another cell, Word will replace the entire contents of that cell. If the selection does not include an end-of-cell mark, the Paste command will simply read Paste, and Word will follow its usual behavior, inserting the selection at the cursor or replacing the current selection (assuming you have Word set to delete highlighted text when pasting).

Keep in mind that you cannot select text from two or more cells without also selecting the end-of-cell marks. If you want to paste text from two or more cells without deleting the current contents of the target cells, you must cut or copy the text from each cell separately, being careful not to include the end-of-cell mark when you select the text.

### How to select a paste area within a table

When you move or copy text from more than one cell in a table, the set of cells in the paste area will correspond to the set of cells in the area that you cut or copied—with the same number of cells across and down. However, the cells in the paste area need not be the same width or height as the cells you copied from.

For example, suppose you want to copy the text from the four cells in the bottom two rows and first two columns of the table shown in Figure 11-36 and paste it into the cells in the last two columns and first two rows of that table. First select the cells you want to copy from, as shown in the figure. Choose Edit Copy or the equivalent, using any of the copy commands you're comfortable with. Next select the target cells, as shown in Figure 11-37. Choose Edit Paste Cells, and Word will paste the text into the cells.

**FIGURE 11-36**

To copy a block of cells, first select the block to copy, and then choose Edit Copy.

**FIGURE 11-37**

To paste a block of cells, select the target cells, and then choose Edit Paste Cells.

If the block of cells you select as the paste area doesn't match the shape of the block you copied, Word will not paste the cells. Instead, it will show you a message telling you that the Paste command failed because the copy and paste areas are different shapes. Figure 11-38 on the next page shows the message Word displayed after we copied a block of two rows by two columns and then defined the paste area as two rows by three columns. If you see this message, simply choose OK, redefine the paste area, and paste the cells again.

There are exceptions to this rule. If you place the cursor or selection in a cell without selecting the end-of-cell mark, Word will treat that cell as the upper left corner of the paste area and will paste without complaint. This can be dangerous because you can accidentally overwrite more cells than you meant to. However, if you use this feature with care and check the results immediately afterward, you can always recover from mistakes by choosing Edit Undo.

You can use this feature to create new columns and rows as you paste. Consider, for example, the variations shown in Figure 11-39:

- If you place the cursor in the rightmost cell in the top row and paste the four cells, as in the second sample table in the figure, you'll overwrite the top two cells in that column and add two new cells to the right of those cells.

- If you place the cursor between the right side of the table boundary and the end-of-row mark for the first row, as in the third sample table in the figure, you'll add two new cells to each of the top two rows in the table.

- If you place the cursor in the rightmost cell on the bottom row, as in the last sample table in the figure, you'll replace the text in that cell, create a cell to the right of that cell, and add a new row. The cells to the left of the pasted cells in the new row will be blank.

**FIGURE 11-39**

Depending on the shape and size of the pasted block of cells, Word may add new rows and cells to a table.

```
Original Table ¶
AAA111¤     BBB111¤     CCC111¤     DDD111¤   ¤
AAA222¤     BBB222¤     CCC222¤     DDD222¤   ¤
AAA333¤     BBB333¤     CCC333¤     DDD333¤      ¤
AAA444¤     BBB444¤     CCC444¤     DDD444¤      ¤
AAA555¤     BBB555¤     CCC555¤     DDD555¤      ¤
Pasted with Cursor in Rightmost Cell in Top Row ¶
AAA111¤     BBB111¤     CCC111¤     AAA444¤   BBB444¤      ¤
AAA222¤     BBB222¤     CCC222¤     AAA555¤   BBB555¤      ¤
AAA333¤     BBB333¤     CCC333¤     DDD333¤      ¤
AAA444¤     BBB444¤     CCC444¤     DDD444¤      ¤
AAA555¤     BBB555¤     CCC555¤     DDD555¤      ¤
Pasted with Cursor Outside Right-Side Table Boundary in Top Row ¶
AAA111¤     BBB111¤     CCC111¤     DDD111¤   AAA444¤      BBB444¤      ¤
AAA222¤     BBB222¤     CCC222¤     DDD222¤   AAA555¤      BBB555¤      ¤
AAA333¤     BBB333¤     CCC333¤     DDD333¤      ¤
AAA444¤     BBB444¤     CCC444¤     DDD444¤      ¤
AAA555¤     BBB555¤     CCC555¤     DDD555¤      ¤
Pasted with Cursor in Rightmost Cell in Bottom Row ¶
AAA111¤     BBB111¤     CCC111¤     DDD111¤   ¤
AAA222¤     BBB222¤     CCC222¤     DDD222¤   ¤
AAA333¤     BBB333¤     CCC333¤     DDD333¤      ¤
AAA444¤     BBB444¤     CCC444¤     DDD444¤      ¤
AAA555¤     BBB555¤     CCC555¤     AAA444¤   BBB444¤      ¤
¤           ¤           ¤           AAA555¤   BBB555¤      ¤
```

### How to paste text outside a table

There is another exception to the general rule that you have to match the paste area to the area you copied from. As we mentioned earlier, you can paste copied cells anywhere outside a table to create a new table, complete with the text and cell formatting that you copied. More precisely, you will be able to paste a new table elsewhere in your document if the original selection included any end-of-cell marks. If the selection did not include an end-of-cell mark, Word will paste only the text.

If you want to create a new table this way, you must have at least one paragraph mark (or blank line, or line of text, if you prefer to think of it that way) between the original table and the cells that you paste. Otherwise, Word will simply add the newly pasted cells to the end of the current table.

## How to format text in a table

In addition to entering and editing text in a table, you'll want to format it, an issue quite separate from formatting the table itself.

Word lets you use just about any formatting feature inside a table that you can use outside of one. You can apply any combination of character and paragraph formatting; you can use styles, which we'll cover in detail in Chapter 12 (styles let you apply any combination of paragraph and character formats to a paragraph, or any combination of character formats to selected text, in a single step); and you can format each paragraph in a table independently of the others. This last feature is particularly useful, since it frees you to use different indents, alignments, line spacing, tabs, and so on for any paragraph in your table.

Among the few restrictions for formatting are that you cannot force table text to flow across a cell boundary and that you cannot create a table within a table. Also note that every cell in a table will take on the character and paragraph formatting of the text the cursor was in when you inserted the table. For example, if you insert the table while the cursor is in text formatted as 14-point Helvetica bold with centered alignment, each cell in the table will be formatted that way.

To change the format, select one or more cells, and choose the appropriate formatting commands. You can select as many cells as you like and reformat them all at one time.

To demonstrate what you can do with formatting in a table, we took a sample table that we used earlier in this chapter, added some information to it, and formatted it as shown in Figure 11-40 on the next page.

**FIGURE 11-40**

Paragraph and charac-
ter formatting can give
your tables a more
professional look.

In addition to adding boldface for the tree names, we created a title as a single merged cell across the top of the table and formatted it in 14-point bold type. We also added 8 points of space before and after the title (using the Before and After text boxes in the Paragraph dialog box), and we set the heading for each column in italics with centered alignment and with 2 points of space before and after. These are straightforward applications of formatting techniques covered in Chapter 7. Here are a few tips for less obvious ways to use standard formatting within tables.

## How to indent table text

Changing the indents of text paragraphs in a table will have an effect similar to adjusting the Space Between Columns setting on the Cell Height And Width Columns card. In either case, the text will move closer to or farther from the left and right boundaries of the cell. However, the Space Between Columns setting applies to every cell in a row, while you can change paragraph indents on a selective basis. By adjusting paragraph indents, you can effectively override the Space Between Columns setting for one or more cells.

## How to add space before and after table text

As we've already mentioned, if you choose Format Paragraph and adjust the Before and After settings in the Paragraph dialog box, you can add space between the text in a cell and the top and bottom boundaries of that cell. When you add space this way, Word will adjust the row height as necessary to accommodate the additional space. (This assumes that you haven't set the Height Of Row option to Exactly on the Cell Height And Width Row card as we discussed in "How to adjust row height" on page 354.)

In some ways, adding space before and after table text is similar to choosing Table Cell Height And Width, choosing the Row card, setting the Height Of Rows option to At Least, and then entering a row height setting that's larger than needed to show all the text. There is one important difference, however: When you adjust height on the Row card, Word adds any extra space below the text in each cell. When you adjust the Before and After settings in the Paragraph dialog box, you can specify how much space to put above the text and how much below.

### How to use tabs in a table

Given the tremendous advantages of the table feature over creating tabular columns, you might wonder why anyone would want to use tabs within a table. As it happens, there are at least two situations where using tabs makes sense. First, tabs can provide an easy way to align text within a cell. Second, and more important, decimal tabs are the easiest way to create decimal alignment for a column of numbers in a table. We covered tabs in detail in "Paragraph Formatting" on page 204.

Because the Tab key functions as a navigation key in a table, you can't use it to insert a tab in a table and move to the next tab stop. Rather, you have to move the cursor to the cell and then press Option-Tab.

# Adding Borders and Shading in a Table

As we've mentioned, the gridlines that define the rows and columns in a table on the screen don't print. But if you want a printed table to include gridlines, you can format the table with borders. When you use borders, you don't need to add lines between every row and every column. You can apply borders selectively to specific rows, columns, cells, or the entire table, to produce lots of different effects. You can also add different kinds of borders to different parts of the table.

To add a border to a table, first select the portion of the table you want to add the border to. Then choose Format Borders And Shading to open a Borders And Shading dialog box similar to the one shown in Figure 11-41 on the next page. This dialog box is essentially identical to the Paragraph Borders And Shading dialog box we discussed in Chapter 7 except that the From Text

text box is grayed out. When you are working in tables, that function is handled by the Space Between Columns setting on the Cell Height And Width Column card.

What you'll see in the Borders And Shading dialog box will vary slightly depending on the block of cells you've selected. Even the title will vary between Table Borders And Shading if you selected the entire table, and Cell Borders And Shading if you selected only part of a table. More important differences show up in the thumbnail sketch in the Border box and in the choices in the Presets box. Figure 11-41 shows the Borders card as you'll see it if you've simply placed the cursor in the table without selecting anything (in which case any changes will apply to the entire table) or you've selected a block of cells that includes at least two rows and two columns (in which case any changes will apply only to the selection). We'll discuss this version of the dialog box first.

**FIGURE 11-41**

Select the portion of the table you want to add a border to, and then choose Format Borders And Shading to open a Borders And Shading dialog box.

The thumbnail sketch of four cells in the Border box lets you define different borders (or no border at all) for the whole area you selected (the outside of the thumbnail sketch), for vertical lines between cells, and for horizontal lines between cells. The Presets choices are None, Box (adds only an outline to the selection), and Grid. In most cases, you'll want to use one of the Presets choices and choose a line style in the Style list box. However, you can also use the techniques we discussed in Chapter 7 to define a custom set of borders.

You may also want to move to the Shading card, shown in Figure 11-42, and apply shading to the selection. For details on using the Borders and Shading cards, see "Paragraph borders and shading" on page 218.

The Shading card in the Borders And Shading dialog box is identical to the Shading card for paragraphs.

If you make any changes on either the Borders or the Shading card, choose OK to close the dialog box, accept the changes, and have Word apply the new settings to the selection. Choose Cancel to close the dialog box without accepting the changes.

Figure 11-43 on the next page shows the Borders card as you'll see it when you select multiple cells in a single row, multiple cells in a single column, and a single cell.

As you can see in Figure 11-43, Word supplies thumbnail sketches that match the current selection when you choose Format Borders And Shading. If you've selected multiple cells in a single row, you can define the outline for the selection and the vertical lines between adjacent cells. If you've selected multiple cells in a single column, you can define the outline for the selection and the horizontal lines between adjacent cells. If you've selected a single cell, you can define any or all of the lines around the cell. The mechanics of defining the borders are the same in each case and, in each case, you can also move to the Shading card to define shading.

Note in passing that if you select text within a cell without including the end-of-cell mark, you can define borders for the paragraphs within the cell. These borders will not be in the same position as the borders for the cell itself.

**FIGURE 11-43**

The Border and Presets
portions of the Cell
Borders And Shading
dialog box change
depending on the
selection. These three
dialog boxes represent
what you'll see when
you've selected mul-
tiple cells in a single
row, multiple cells in
a single column, and
a single cell.

# How to define a single table to look like two tables side by side

Earlier in this chapter, we mentioned that you could not place two tables side by side in a single text area (unless you used one or more frames) but that you could get the same visual effect by creating a single table and using borders to make it look like two.

Consider, for example, Figure 11-44, which appears to show two tables side by side. The table on the left reports sales by quarter; the table on the right reports sales by region. In fact, these two apparently separate tables are one.

**FIGURE 11-44**

With careful use of borders, you can make one table look like two tables side by side.

| Sales by Quarter | |
|---|---|
| First Quarter | $16,008.96 |
| Second Quarter | $14,567.30 |
| Third Quarter | $18,301.98 |
| Fourth Quarter | $16,489.79 |

| Sales by Region | |
|---|---|
| Northeast | $12,321.32 |
| South | $6,528.12 |
| Southwest | $24,658.89 |
| West | $21,859.67 |

Figure 11-45 shows the same table before we added the borders, and with Word set to show gridlines and paragraph marks. As you can see, we've really created one table with different sections separated by a column of blank cells.

**FIGURE 11-45**

This is how the table shown in Figure 11-44 looked before we added borders.

| Sales by Quarter¤ | | ¤ | Sales by Region¤ | | ₽ |
|---|---|---|---|---|---|
| First Quarter¤ | $16,008.96¤ | ¤ | Northeast¤ | $12,321.32¤ | ₽ |
| Second Quarter¤ | $14,567.30¤ | ¤ | South¤ | $6,528.12¤ | ₽ |
| Third Quarter¤ | $18,301.98¤ | ¤ | Southwest¤ | $24,658.89¤ | ₽ |
| Fourth Quarter¤ | $16,489.79¤ | ¤ | West¤ | $21,859.67¤ | ₽ |

To create the table shown in Figure 11-45, we used several of the formatting techniques discussed earlier in this chapter. The titles for each portion of the table are in merged cells and are centered over the appropriate columns. The two columns of numbers are aligned with decimal tabs. We've added a little extra spacing above and below some of the text by choosing Format Paragraph and entering settings for Before and After. And, finally, we've formatted the titles in boldface.

To turn the table shown in Figure 11-45 into the tables in Figure 11-44, start by highlighting the bottom four rows on the left side of the table. Choose Format Borders And Shading, and then the Borders card. Select Grid in the Presets box, choose the fourth line down in the Style box, then choose OK. Word will close the dialog box. Next repeat these steps for the left side title in the first row of the table, but select Box in the Presets box. When you remove the highlight from the table, you should see a screen much like the one shown in Figure 11-46 on the next page.

FIGURE 11-46

When you return to the
document and remove
the highlight from the
table, Word will
display the border
you've just defined.

| Sales·by·Quarter¤ | | ¤ | Sales·by·Region¤ | |
|---|---|---|---|---|
| First·Quarter¤ | $16,008.96¤ | ¤ | Northeast¤ | $12,321.32¤ |
| Second·Quarter¤ | $14,567.30¤ | ¤ | South¤ | $6,528.12¤ |
| Third·Quarter¤ | $18,301.98¤ | ¤ | Southwest¤ | $24,658.89¤ |
| Fourth·Quarter¤ | $16,489.79¤ | ¤ | West¤ | $21,859.67¤ |

To add the border to the other section of the table, simply repeat these steps again, once for the body of the table and once for the title. All that remains to see the same effect on screen as in Figure 11-44 is to choose Table Gridlines to turn off the gridlines, and choose Tools Options View, then remove all checks from the check boxes in the Nonprinting Characters section of the card. But remember that the gridlines and paragraph marks won't print in any case, so you don't have to turn them off to get the side-by-side table effect on paper.

Most important, note that you can use these same techniques to build anything from a single box around a table to complicated forms complete with shaded areas and lines of different thicknesses.

## How to redefine or delete borders and shading

Deleting borders or shading from a table is a simple matter of redefining the format using the same techniques you use for adding borders and shading. Select the section you want to change, and choose Format Borders And Shading to open the dialog box. You can remove all the borders from the selection at once by selecting None in the Presets box and then choosing OK. Similarly, you can change or delete specific borders as needed. When you're satisfied with your redefinition, choose OK to close the dialog box. To redefine shading, select the section that you want to change, choose Format Borders And Shading, select the Shading card, and change the settings on the card as appropriate.

# Converting Existing Text to a Table

As we mentioned near the beginning of this chapter, Word will let you convert existing text to a table. Most often the text you'll want to convert will already be in columnar format, arranged with tabs. However, you can also convert comma-delimited text (text that's separated by commas instead of tabs), which is a common format for data that you've imported from another program, particularly a database program. (We'll discuss exchanging data with other programs in Chapter 18.)

To convert existing text to a table, select the text, and choose Table Convert Text To Table. Word will respond by opening the Convert Text To Table dialog box, shown in Figure 11-47.

**FIGURE 11-47**

The Convert Text To Table dialog box lets you tell Word how many rows and columns to use as well as what symbol designates the end of a cell.

As you can see, Word makes its best guess about the number of rows and columns the new table should contain and about which symbol should indicate the end of a cell—paragraph marks, tabs, commas, or any other single character you want to specify as a separator character. If you've followed a consistent scheme for designating each column and each row for the table (or each field and record, to use database terminology), Word's best guess will usually be right. If not, adjust the settings as necessary before choosing OK.

If you need to change any settings in the Convert Text To Table dialog box, start with the Separate Text At box because this setting will automatically adjust the Number Of Columns and Number Of Rows boxes. You can then make further changes in the two text boxes if necessary, and you can set a specific width in the Column Width box—although the Auto setting will usually provide suitable widths. You can also choose the AutoFormat button to open the Table AutoFormat dialog box, which we discussed earlier in this chapter in the section "How to use Table AutoFormat—with or without the Table Wizard" on page 337.

Once you're satisfied with the settings in the Convert Text To Table dialog box, choose OK, and Word will convert the selected text to a table. Figure 11-48 on the next page shows text in both tabular and comma-delimited formats, with the same name and address information listed in each. The tabular format represents the kind of simple column setup you might create using tabs. The comma-delimited format is a standard format that many database and spreadsheet programs use, or at least can import from and export to. Figure 11-49 on the next page shows the same document after we've converted both sets of information to tables. Word converted both of these formats to tables without our having to do anything with the Convert Text To Table dialog box beyond choosing OK.

The tabular format is representative of a simple column setup you might create with tabs. The comma-delimited format is a standard database format.

```
TABULAR FORMAT¶
LastName→FirstName → Address1    →    Address2    →    City  →  ST→Zip ¶
Girard  →  Mike   →    302 Sunshine St→              →        Redmond→WA→90201 ¶
Petrey  →  John   →    3945 Medical St→Suite 45     →        Louisville→KY →40222¶
Hambaugh→Jerry    →    893 Hoosier Ln→              →        Carmel  →  IN → 40201 ¶
¶
¶
¶
COMMA DELIMITED FORMAT¶
LastName, FirstName, Address1, Address2, City, ST, Zip ¶
Girard, Mike, 302 Sunshine Street, , Redmond, WA, 90201 ¶
Petrey, John, 3945 Medical Street, Suite 45, Louisville, KY, 40222¶
Hambaugh, Jerry, 893 Hoosier Lane, , Carmel, IN, 40201 ¶
```

Although the column widths are somewhat different in these two tables, the version converted from tabular format is otherwise identical to the version converted from comma-delimited format.

TABULAR FORMAT¶

| LastName¤ | FirstName¤ | Address1¤ | Address2¤ | City¤ | ST¤ | Zip¤ | ¤ |
|---|---|---|---|---|---|---|---|
| Girard¤ | Mike¤ | 302 Sunshine St¤ | ¤ | Redmond¤ | WA¤ | 90201¤ | ¤ |
| Petrey¤ | John¤ | 3945 Medical St¤ | Suite 45¤ | Louisville¤ | KY¤ | 40222¤ | ¤ |
| Hambaugh¤ | Jerry¤ | 893 Hoosier Ln¤ | ¤ | Carmel¤ | IN¤ | 40201¤ | ¤ |

¶
¶
¶

COMMA DELIMITED FORMAT¶

| LastName¤ | FirstName¤ | Address1¤ | Address2¤ | City¤ | ST¤ | Zip¤ | ¤ |
|---|---|---|---|---|---|---|---|
| Girard¤ | Mike¤ | 302 Sunshine Street¤ | ¤ | Redmond¤ | WA¤ | 90201¤ | ¤ |
| Petrey¤ | John¤ | 3945 Medical Street¤ | Suite 45¤ | Louisville¤ | KY¤ | 40222¤ | ¤ |
| Hambaugh¤ | Jerry¤ | 893 Hoosier Lane¤ | ¤ | Carmel¤ | IN¤ | 40201¤ | ¤ |

To get from the table shown in Figure 11-48 to the one shown in Figure 11-49, we had to convert the two sets of information separately. Word can convert text by using commas, tabs, or other symbols to indicate where each cell ends, but it can't convert using more than one separator character at a time. Word's ability to split text into cells based on only one separator character has some advantages. In particular, it means that you can use commas as part of the text in tabular columns and still convert the columns to tables.

## The rules Word uses for converting text to a table

To best use Word's conversion capabilities, it helps to understand the rules Word follows for determining settings in the Convert Text To Table dialog box:

■   When creating a table based on tabs, commas, or any symbol you've entered in the Other text box, Word will assume that you want to create a separate row in the table for each paragraph mark or each line break created with a line-break character. If a line wraps to the left side of the screen because of wordwrap, Word will still consider the line as part of the same row in the table and will continue to add cells to each row until it finds a paragraph mark or a line-break character.

This means you have to be sure that each line in the text you're converting does, in fact, end with a paragraph mark or a line-break character. It also means that any blank lines in your text will wind up in their own rows. You can use this feature to create blank rows in the table. But if you don't want a blank row at a given position, you should delete any paragraph mark or line-break character that's on a line by itself.

- Word will base the number of columns in the table on the row with the most commas, tabs, or other separator character. This means that if you have an extra comma, tab, or other separator character in one line, you could wind up with a table that's one column too long and that has the data in the one line offset from similar data in other lines. Extra commas are hard to spot in comma-delimited text, but extra tabs are relatively easy to find if you have checked the Tab Characters check box on the Tools Options View card to have Word display tab characters. If you prefer, you can adjust the table after creating it by inserting or deleting cells.

- The rules for converting text based on paragraph marks are a little different from the rules for converting text that uses other separator characters. When you tell Word to convert text to a table based only on paragraph marks, the program always suggests a single-column table, and it puts each paragraph in its own cell. If you create a table with more than one column, Word will place the paragraphs in cells from left to right, top to bottom. Converting text to a table based on paragraph marks is the least useful of the four options, but you can use it as the first step in building a table.

You can also use the Convert Text To Table dialog box to spot problems in how you've formatted the text and, optionally, to override Word's assumptions. For example, if you've created text with six rows of seven fields each and have inadvertently omitted the paragraph mark from one row because it happens to wrap at the right place, Word will enter *13* as the Number Of Columns setting, to match the longest record it finds. (In Word's count, the last field in the row with the missing paragraph mark is combined with the first field in the next row because there's no separator between them.) If you know that the number of columns should actually be 7, the setting in the dialog box should warn you that something is wrong. Choose Cancel, and look for the mistake to correct it.

Alternatively, you can change the Number Of Columns setting to 7, which will force Word to create the table you want. You'll still have to find and fix the problem rows, since Word will combine the two fields where you left out the paragraph mark, but the rest of the table will be the way you want it if—and it's a big if—you haven't made other mistakes in the way you've set up the text.

In general, you're better off finding and fixing mistakes before you convert the text to a table. That way, the settings in the Convert Text To Table dialog box are a confirmation that you located and corrected all the mistakes. However, it's usually easier to spot mistakes after the text is converted to a table, so you may decide to go ahead with the conversion in any case.

## Converting All or Part of a Table to Text

Word will also let you convert a table to text. To convert the table, begin by selecting one or more rows or selecting the entire table. (You cannot convert partial rows to text.) Next choose Table Convert Table To Text. Word will open the dialog box shown in Figure 11-50, which lets you choose whether to separate the cells in each row with paragraph marks, tabs, commas, or any other character that you enter in the Other text box. Choose Tabs for a tabular format, Commas for a comma-delimited format, Other for any other character-delimited format, or Paragraph Marks to put the information from each cell in a paragraph of its own. As when you convert text to a table, the Paragraph Marks option is generally the least useful of the four.

**FIGURE 11-50**

Word will open this dialog box when you select one or more rows and choose Table Convert Table To Text.

## Tables as Mini-Spreadsheets: Sorting and Calculating

If you've read through this entire chapter, you now have a pretty good idea of what Word's table feature can do, and you should be able to build as complex a table as you need. However, you should be aware of two other features of tables, even though we won't cover them in this chapter.

If you've ever worked with a spreadsheet program such as Microsoft Excel, you've probably noticed a more than passing resemblance between spreadsheets and the tables you can create in Word. In truth, the similarity goes further than mere resemblance; you can build a surprisingly sophisticated spreadsheet in Word. You can, for example, enter calculation fields in table cells that will automatically calculate the totals of columns. You can also use Word's sorting feature to sort tables by the entries in a column and therefore change the order of the rows. We'll cover both of these features in Chapter 23. For now, simply be aware that they are available if you need them. More immediately, we'll now turn to issues of advanced formatting and a discussion of styles.

# TOPIC FINDER

**388**

# 12

# Styles & AutoFormat

ord has any number of advanced features, such as tables, that are helpful for anyone who needs those specific capabilities. But few advanced features are as potentially helpful to as many users as styles. Styles let you define a set of formats—including font, paragraph, tab, border, language, frame, and numbering format—and apply the entire set to text all at once by applying the style. By changing the definition of a style, you can quickly reformat all text in a document that's formatted with the same style. And styles make it easy to maintain a consistent format within a document or a category of documents, when you want to maintain a corporate-wide standard, for example.

Using styles is so different from using direct formatting, however, that the concepts take a while to learn. So Word also provides an AutoFormat feature, as an easy way to get started with styles. AutoFormat can apply styles for you, even if you know nothing about styles beyond the fact that they exist. In this chapter, we'll look first at AutoFormat, which you can think of as an aid for working with styles, though it does a bit more as well. Then we'll take a look under the hood, at styles themselves.

# The AutoFormat Feature

As the name implies, AutoFormat can handle any number of formatting tasks automatically. In fact, if you simply type your text and ignore formatting, or if you import unformatted text created in another program, you'll find that you can run AutoFormat and usually wind up with a close approximation of an acceptably formatted document. If you take the time to add some clues to your text—using minimal formatting such as bold for headings, for example—AutoFormat will do an even better job of applying the right formats.

Because the feature can also add the wrong formats, Word lets you put on the brakes by giving you lots of control over the kinds of changes AutoFormat makes. As we'll discuss later, you also have the option of reviewing each change before accepting or rejecting it.

Don't confuse the AutoFormat feature with the Table AutoFormat feature. AutoFormat automatically applies styles to text. Table AutoFormat (available through the Table Table AutoFormat menu command) adds borders and shading to tables. We covered the Table AutoFormat feature in "How to use Table AutoFormat—with or without the Table Wizard" on page 337.

## How to set the AutoFormat options

To give AutoFormat its marching orders, choose Tools Options and then the AutoFormat card, shown in Figure 12-1. The AutoFormat card contains four group boxes: Preserve, Apply Styles To, Adjust, and Replace. Together, they offer 10 check boxes that give you plenty of control over the AutoFormat feature. All 10 are checked by default.

### The Preserve group box

The Preserve group box contains one option: the Previously Applied Styles check box. Checking this box tells Word to retain any styles that you have already applied to the text instead of changing them with AutoFormat. Keep in mind that Normal is the default style for any paragraph that isn't formatted with another style. When you check this check box, Word will reformat any paragraphs that are formatted as Normal, even if you have explicitly applied the Normal style.

You can get around this limitation by creating another style that is based on Normal but includes no additional formatting. (We'll explain how later in this chapter.) Give the second style an appropriate name, such as NormalToo. AutoFormat will then ignore paragraphs formatted with the NormalToo style.

**FIGURE 12-1**

The Tools Options AutoFormat card lets you control the formatting changes AutoFormat can make.

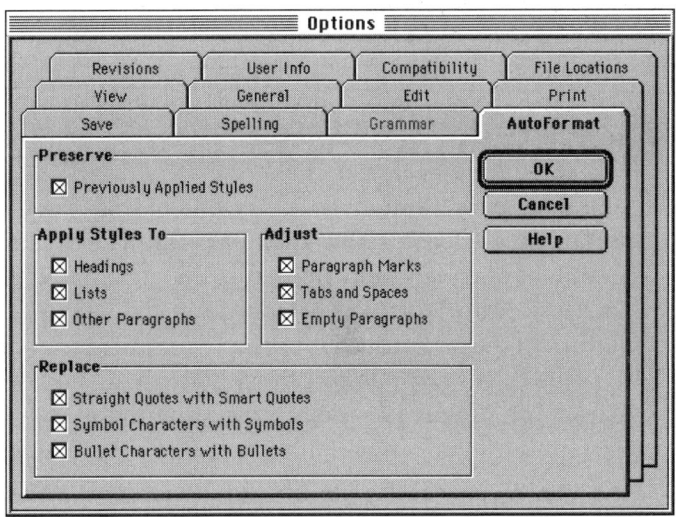

## The Apply Styles To group box

The Apply Styles To group box has three choices, representing the three categories of text that AutoFormat recognizes.

If the Headings check box is checked, Word will assign a heading level from 1 through 9 to paragraphs it identifies as headings. The program uses several rules of thumb to recognize headings. For example, if it finds a one-line paragraph that starts with a capital letter, does not end with a period, and is followed by a blank line, it will recognize the paragraph as a heading. Similarly, if Word finds headings formatted with two different size fonts, it will apply the Heading 1 style to the heading with the larger font, and Heading 2 to the one with the smaller font. In short, Word works hard to recognize headings, although you may not agree with its conclusions.

The Lists option tells Word to add appropriate list and bullet styles to any paragraphs it identifies as part of a bulleted or numbered list. Here again, Word uses rules of thumb to recognize list items. For example, it will recognize paragraphs that start with a hyphen, plus sign, or asterisk, plus a space, as bulleted paragraphs. It will also recognize numbered lists based on numbers you've typed, and it will recognize bullets and numbers you've added with Word's bullets and numbering feature.

The third option in this group box, Other Paragraphs, is a catchall. If this box is checked, Word will assign styles such as the Body Text style or the Body Text Indent style to a paragraph that it does not identify as either a heading or a list. Here again, Word uses several rules of thumb to recognize and assign particular styles.

## The Adjust group box

The options in the Adjust group box are meant to let you control the changes AutoFormat will make to several elements in your document that control spacing and line-break features.

For example, if you check the Paragraph Marks check box, Word will eliminate paragraph marks at the end of lines that should be individual lines within a paragraph rather than paragraphs by themselves. These extra paragraph marks often show up in text that originated elsewhere and that you've imported into Word. (You would get the same effect in Word by pressing Return at the end of each line you type rather than depending on wordwrap.)

The Tabs And Spaces option will strip out any extra spaces at the start of a paragraph. It will also replace spaces with tab characters where appropriate. The third option, Empty Paragraphs, tells Word to remove blank lines consisting only of paragraph marks that fall between two paragraphs formatted in the same style, and replace them with space before settings.

## The Replace group box

The fourth group box, Replace, covers a number of character replacements AutoFormat can handle.

The Replace Straight Quotes With Smart Quotes check box is reasonably self-explanatory, if you know that Smart Quotes is a commonly used term for curly quotes, meaning quotes that are curved, rather than straight up-and-down lines.

If you're familiar with Word's ability to change straight quotes to curly quotes with the AutoCorrect feature that we covered in Chapter 5, you may consider this superfluous at first glance. However, if you import a file from some other program, it is likely to have straight quotes. This option makes it easy to change them to curly quotes.

The Symbol Characters With Symbols option will replace the common typed representations of certain symbols with the actual symbol, as shown in the following list:

| If You've Typed This Text | AutoFormat Inserts This Symbol |
| --- | --- |
| (TM) *or* (tm) | ™ |
| (C) *or* (c) | © |
| (R) *or* (r) | ® |

Here again, Word can handle these replacements during typing with AutoCorrect, but the overlapping AutoFormat feature can be handy for replacing these characters after they've been typed in—particularly for documents that you've imported into Word.

The Replace Bullet Characters With Bullets option determines whether AutoFormat will replace a character such as an asterisk, a hyphen, or a plus sign with a bullet. If this check box isn't checked, Word will not replace the typed character when it detects a bulleted paragraph.

## How to use AutoFormat

To use AutoFormat, simply give the Format AutoFormat command. (We'll discuss keyboard and mouse shortcuts later.) If you want to format the entire document, you can position the cursor anywhere, without selecting text. If you want to format only a portion of the document, select that portion before choosing the command, and Word will format the selection only.

Don't worry about the possibility of ruining your document's formatting with AutoFormat. If you don't like the results of AutoFormat, you can use Word's Undo feature and return to the starting point by pressing ⌘-Z or clicking on the Undo button on the Standard toolbar. (Click on Undo twice if you chose Format AutoFormat; click once if you used the shortcuts we'll cover later.) However, it's not a bad idea to save your work before all major changes, including AutoFormat.

When you choose Format AutoFormat, Word will display the dialog box shown in Figure 12-2. If you choose the Options button, you'll go to the Tools Options AutoFormat card described in the section before this. When you're satisfied with the option settings, close the card to return to the AutoFormat dialog box in Figure 12-2. Choose OK, and Word will automatically format the document or selection.

**FIGURE 12-2**

Word will display this dialog box before it starts to automatically format a document.

AutoFormat

Word will automatically format Derby.

Afterward, you will be able to review, accept, or reject each change.

OK
Cancel
Options...
Help

After Word formats the document, it will display the AutoFormat dialog box shown in Figure 12-3. At this point, you have the choice of accepting, rejecting, modifying, or reviewing the format changes Word just made. To accept or reject all the changes, you can choose the Accept or the Reject All button, but you will usually want to review the changes first to be sure that they make sense.

**FIGURE 12-3**

After AutoFormat has finished its work, this dialog box lets you accept, reject, or modify the changes.

## How to review and modify AutoFormat changes

Word provides two approaches for reviewing and modifying the changes AutoFormat makes.

First, you can move to your document by clicking on it with the mouse or by pressing Control-Tab. You can then scroll through it, looking for format changes, modifying them, adding more formatting, or even editing the document. The AutoFormat dialog box will remain visible so you can toggle back and forth between the dialog box and the document with Control-Tab or the mouse. When you're satisfied with the result, you can choose the Accept button to accept all the changes.

The second approach is to choose the Review Changes button in the lower left corner of the dialog box. This will open the Review AutoFormat Changes dialog box, shown in Figure 12-4. This dialog box is virtually the same as the Review Revisions dialog box that we discussed in Chapter 10, except that it lacks an Accept button. In fact, the two dialog boxes are closely related, since Word treats the AutoFormat changes as revisions and will show you both inserted and deleted format information.

**FIGURE 12-4**

The Review AutoFormat Changes dialog box lets you review the changes AutoFormat made in your document.

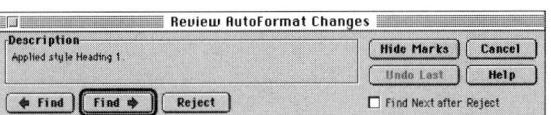

The Review AutoFormat Changes dialog box is a sophisticated tool that will help you find all the changes that AutoFormat made. The two Find buttons—one with a right-, or forward-, pointing arrow and the other with a left-, or backward-, pointing arrow—let you move forward and backward within the document. Choose either one, and Word will search in the appropriate direction for the next change.

When Word finds a change, it will highlight the affected text—highlighting a paragraph to indicate a change in paragraph style, for example. It will also use the Description box to describe the change AutoFormat made to the highlighted text. You can then choose the Reject button to return the highlighted text to its original format, or choose one of the Find buttons to continue to the next change. You can also use Control-Tab, or click with the mouse, to move between your text and the dialog box to edit or reformat the text.

If you check the Find Next After Reject check box, Word will automatically move forward to the next change whenever you choose Reject. If you change your mind about a rejection, you can choose the Undo Last button (or use Word's standard Undo command) to undo the rejection.

When you first open the Review AutoFormat Changes dialog box, Word will modify your document to show all changes on screen. It will also add revision bars in the left margin to indicate lines where AutoFormat has changed the format. And it will show paragraph marks even if you've set Word not to show them. If you have set Word to show paragraph marks, style changes will show as two paragraph marks (one deleted, one inserted).

If seeing both the insertions and deletions at the same time makes it difficult to judge whether you want to keep a given change, you can choose the Hide Marks button. Word will show you the text as it will appear if you accept the changed format. Word will also change the Hide Marks button name to Show Marks, and gray out the Find and Reject buttons. To continue reviewing the changes, choose Show Marks.

When you first open the dialog box, the upper right button will be labeled Cancel. As soon as you reject a change or use the Hide Marks button, however, Word will change the name to Close. In either case, it performs the same function: Use it to close the Review AutoFormat Changes dialog box and return to the AutoFormat dialog box.

There is also one other way to modify AutoFormat changes: by using the Style Gallery button in the AutoFormat dialog box to open the Style Gallery dialog box. However, you can get exactly the same results by choosing Format Style Gallery from the document itself, so we'll ignore this choice until we've discussed a bit more about styles. We'll cover it later in the chapter, in the section "Using the Style Gallery" on page 399.

If you choose the Accept button in the AutoFormat dialog box and then immediately spot something in your document that makes you want to review the changes after all, you have another alternative for reviewing AutoFormat changes. You can give the Undo command once—by pressing ⌘-Z, choosing Edit Undo, or clicking on the Undo button on the Standard toolbar. You can then choose Tools Revisions and click on the Review button to open the Review Revisions dialog box and work your way through the document in essentially the same way as with the Review AutoFormat Changes dialog box. In this case, however, you'll have to choose the Accept button for each item rather than accepting all items at once. For a long document, this trick can save a great deal of time compared to choosing Undo twice to undo all the formatting and then running AutoFormat again just so you can reopen the Review AutoFormat Changes dialog box.

## How to use AutoFormat shortcuts

As we mentioned earlier, Word also provides shortcuts for using the AutoFormat feature. Specifically, you can press ⌘-K, or you can click on the AutoFormat button, which is just to the right of the Redo button on the Standard toolbar. (The AutoFormat button icon looks a bit like a page with a star sparkle in the upper left corner.)

If you use either of the shortcuts, Word will automatically format your document—but without going through the AutoFormat dialog boxes, without giving you a chance to change the options, and without giving you a chance to review the changes. While this makes the process more automatic, it also gives the feature the chance to run amok. And although you can undo all the changes with the Undo command, you have to undo everything in a single step instead of giving the Undo command once and then using Word's revision features to review the changes. Given all these drawbacks, we recommend that you not use these shortcuts until you're extremely familiar with AutoFormat and are satisfied that it does what you want it to do. Even then, be sure to look over the formatted result before you accept it as final.

# A Closer Look at Styles

As we've already suggested, you can use AutoFormat without knowing much about styles beyond the fact that they exist. But you can take better advantage of AutoFormat if you understand a little about them. And as you learn more about styles, you'll find that you can go well beyond AutoFormat's capabilities.

Briefly, a style is a set of formatting instructions. Apply the style, and you apply all the formatting defined by that style in a single step. For example, you might create a style called Indented Quotes with all the formatting features you want to apply to each quote in your document. The style might switch the font to italic, change left and right indents, and even change font size. After you define the style, you can format each quote as you create it simply by applying the style. In essence, it's that simple.

Although formatting a paragraph with one command instead of three is an obvious timesaver, the real beauty of styles is that they make it much easier to modify the format later on a wholesale basis. Once you've formatted text with styles, you can, in a single step, change the format of all the text formatted with any given style throughout your document—changing every figure caption, for example, from 10-point Helvetica italic type to 12-point Times bold.

One actual example should make the case for how useful styles can be. In writing this book, we set the Normal style to single spacing. That lets us see as much text as possible on screen at once, a valuable feature when writing and editing. When we print, however, we need double-spaced output to make the text easier to read on paper. To get the format we need, we simply change the Normal style to double spacing. It takes about 10 seconds to give the commands that change the style, and it sets every paragraph throughout the file to double spacing simultaneously. When we finish printing, we reset the Normal style to single spacing so we can continue working with greatest efficiency.

Styles can get pretty complex if you want to learn all their nuances. But you can work with them in useful ways even if you learn only a little about them. And you'll find that the time they save makes them well worth mastering. In fact, they are one of the most valuable features in Word.

## Types of styles

There are several ways to categorize styles. One difference, for example, is between paragraph and character styles. Another is between built-in and custom styles. And yet another is between automatic and manually applied styles. Here's a look at each.

### Paragraph and character styles

The difference between paragraph and character styles is the same as the difference between paragraph-level and character-level formatting. Paragraph styles can define font, indents, tabs, borders, language, frames, and numbering. But regardless of the format, the style applies to the paragraph as a whole. All paragraphs in a Word document are formatted with a paragraph style, even if you never go anywhere near styles or the AutoFormat feature. The default paragraph style for most text in your document, for example, is Normal. And you can change the default settings for font, paragraph indent, and so on by changing the definition of the Normal style.

Character styles are limited to font and language options, but they can apply to any arbitrary selection of text. Word comes with several predefined character styles, including, for example, a style that it automatically applies to footnote references. Character styles let you define a format for a given type of text to be different from the rest of the paragraph, without having to resort to direct formatting.

### Built-in and custom styles

As the name implies, a built-in style is one that Word supplies by default; it is literally built into the program. A custom style is one that you define, using a different name than any of the style names that Word provides. For the most part, Word treats built-in styles and custom styles the same way, and you won't see any differences between them when you use them or redefine them. However, you can't delete a built-in style such as Normal. You can redefine it—essentially overlaying it with a custom style of the same name—but you can't get rid of it.

### Automatic and manually applied styles

You can apply any style manually, using techniques we'll discuss later in this chapter. But Word also applies certain styles automatically. Insert a footnote, for example, and Word will automatically format the footnote with the Footnote Text style and the footnote reference with the Footnote Reference style. As you might expect, all of the automatic styles are also built-in styles. However, not all built-in styles are automatic. In general, you'll find automatic styles for most of the common elements in a document—such as headers, footers, footnotes, and annotations—that Word can identify unambiguously when you enter the text.

## Where styles are stored

One of the most critical issues for understanding styles is knowing how they're stored. Briefly, Word stores styles in templates—the same templates that you attach to a file when you give the File New command and choose a template in the New dialog box. However, Word does not store styles in templates only.

Most important—and this is the tricky part—once you create a document, Word does not directly use the styles as stored in the template. Rather, the templates serve as a kind of reservoir for the styles. When you first create a document and tell Word which template to base it on, Word adds all the style information to the document for the entire set of styles in that template. But the document only stores the information as it exists at that moment. If you attach a different template or make changes to the original template—adding new styles or redefining old ones—the document styles won't change unless you specifically update them. And, in fact, you can update the styles in the document based on the styles in *any* template.

# Using the Style Gallery

NEW!

The Format Style Gallery command lets you update all the style definitions in the current document at one time, copying the updated definitions from a template to the current document. You can use the Style Gallery feature at any time, but you'll find it most useful if you've already added styles to your document, either with the AutoFormat feature or by applying the styles manually.

To use the Style Gallery, you can choose Format Style Gallery from within your document, or you can choose the Style Gallery button in the AutoFormat dialog box. Either way, you'll see the Style Gallery dialog box, shown in Figure 12-5.

**FIGURE 12-5**

The Style Gallery dialog box lets you import a new set of styles into a document.

On the left side of the Style Gallery dialog box is the Template text box, with a list box containing a list of available templates. Figure 12-5 shows only the templates that come with Word, but if you've created your own templates, those will be available as well. By far the largest part of the dialog box is the Preview Of box to the right. This preview box shows the effects of the styles stored in the template currently entered in the Template text box.

Just below the list of templates is the Preview group box with three options. Choose Document to see how your document will look if you import the styles from the currently highlighted template to replace styles of the same name currently in your document. Choose Example if you'd rather see the effects of the template on a sample document. Choose Style Samples if you want to see an alphabetical list of all the styles in the template, along with samples of the format for each. Note that not all templates have examples or samples. In particular, these two choices will have no effect with templates you've created yourself.

If you've already applied styles to your document and want to see how the styles in a different template will affect it, the Document option is the obvious choice. But to get the most from this option, you have to use the same names for the same functions in all templates. For example, if you have a style for paragraph-length quotes in the template you used to create your document, and the style is named Long Quotes, Word will look for a Long Quotes style in the template you're using for the preview and will apply that style. This is easy with Word's built-in styles, since all templates must share the same names for the same built-in styles. But the benefit of using identical names for equivalent styles is something you should keep in mind when you create your own styles.

You can look through the templates until you find a set of styles you want to use, or decide to keep the set you started with. Then choose OK to import styles from the currently highlighted template, or choose Cancel to close the dialog box without changing the styles in the current document. The Browse button opens a dialog box that works much like the Open dialog box, and will let you move to a different folder to look for a particular template file.

When you are looking for the right template to use, it may help to know that Word comes with several templates designed for various purposes. The categories include brochures, directories, fax cover sheets, invoices, letters, manuals, manuscripts, memos, presentations, press releases, purchase orders, reports, resumes, theses, and a weekly time sheet. The names of the template files themselves are similar to these category names.

In addition, Word designates so-called families of templates. Whatever the purpose of a given template, 1 at the end of its name indicates that it is using Word's classic set of styles, 2 indicates the contemporary set, 3 indicates the typewriter set (meaning these styles make text look as if it were created on a typewriter), and 4 indicates the elegant set. Once you know which families you like, you can ignore the ones you don't like. You may also want to follow this same numbering scheme, or add to it, when you create your own templates.

It will also help to know what gets changed in your document when you use the Style Gallery command. Briefly, any styles in your document that have the same name as styles in the template you're copying from will be replaced by new definitions copied from the template. Any styles in the template that have different names from styles in your document will be added. And any styles in your document that have different names from styles in the template will remain unchanged.

If you change the template a document is based on after you create the document, you can use the Style Gallery dialog box to update the document to match the current styles in the template. Simply open the document, choose Format Style Gallery, enter the template name in the Template text box, and choose OK.

# Working with Styles

As we've already suggested, there is a lot more to learn about styles. We'll start by focusing on how to use styles within a single document, which is the way you'll usually work with them.

You can create as many styles for a document as you care to add, with each one formatted in any way that meets your needs. You might, for example, have styles for figure captions, indented quotes, bulleted lists, and so on. And keep in mind that you can create either paragraph styles or character styles.

Character styles open the possibility of creating such things as an Emphasis style. You could, for example, define the Emphasis style as bold and use it for selected text within paragraphs scattered throughout your document. If you later change your mind and decide you want to use italic for emphasis instead, you can then redefine the style and change all the isolated emphasized text throughout your document at once.

## How to see a list of styles in your document

If you want to see the list of styles that Word considers actively in use for a document, you can open the Style list on the Formatting toolbar as a pull-down list, as shown in Figure 12-6, by clicking on the down arrow next to the box, or as a drop-down list by pressing ⌘-Shift-S and then the Down arrow key. Alternatively, you can choose Format Style (or press ⌘-Shift-S twice) to open the Style dialog box, then set the List box to Styles In Use, to have Word list the active styles in the Styles box, as shown in Figure 12-7. (Note that although these two lists will generally match, there is one slight difference between them. The list on the Formatting toolbar will always include the Heading 1, Heading 2, and Heading 3 styles, even if you haven't used them in your document. The Styles In Use setting will include these choices in the list of active styles only if you've actually used these styles in your document.)

**FIGURE 12-6**

To see the list of available styles for a document, you can open the Style list on the Formatting Toolbar.

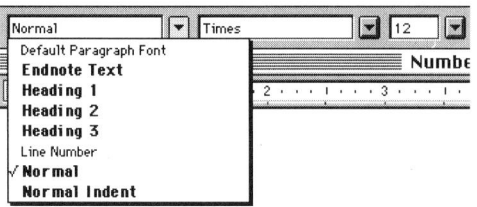

**FIGURE 12-7**

To see the styles currently in use, choose Format Style to open the Style dialog box, and set the List box to Styles In Use.

You can use either of these lists to apply styles to the current paragraph or paragraphs in your document—by which we mean the paragraph or paragraphs your cursor or selection is in. If you're using the list on the Formatting toolbar as a pull-down list, highlight the name of the style you want to use and release the mouse button. If you're using it as a drop-down list, highlight the name and press Return. If you're using the Style dialog box, double-click on the name or highlight it and choose the Apply button. As you can see in Figures 12-6 and 12-7, Word shows paragraph styles, but not character styles, in bold, so you can easily see which category a given style falls into. Note too in Figure 12-7 that Word puts a check mark next to the paragraph and character styles of the current selection or cursor location. If the selection includes more than one style of either category, Word will not add the check mark.

One advantage of using the Style dialog box instead of the list on the Formatting toolbar is that you can easily move to an expanded list of styles. The toolbar list is limited to the same styles you'll see in the Style dialog box when you select Styles In Use, plus Heading 1, Heading 2, and Heading 3 even if those styles aren't already in your document.

If you're using the Normal template, haven't added or redefined any styles, and haven't yet added any text to your document, the styles in use will consist of the Normal paragraph style and the Default Paragraph Font character style. The list will also include any custom styles you've defined, any built-in styles you've redefined, and any other styles you've used in the document.

Clearly, most styles do not, by default, show up on the Styles In Use list. However, you can see them and easily apply them to your text if you choose All Styles in the List box at the bottom left of the Style dialog box. The third choice for this box, User-Defined Styles, is handy when you want to see a list of just those styles you've created or modified.

Unless told otherwise, Word will use the Normal style to format the main body text in a document. In fact, you can think of the Normal style as defining a document's default format. And you can modify that format to taste. For example, although the original default font will vary depending on the printer you have installed, it will be 12-point Times, or something similar, for most laser printers.

As we've already suggested, Word actually provides several methods for applying styles. Before we discuss the various choices, we'll show you how to create alternative styles so you'll have more styles to apply. We'll also take a closer look at what a style is and show you how to change the default Normal style. Along the way, we'll touch on some of the methods you can use to take advantage of styles.

## How to view a style definition

Another advantage of choosing the Format Style command to see the list of styles is that Word will show you a definition in the Description box for the style currently highlighted in the list box, as shown in Figure 12-7. You can also see a preview of the paragraph-level formatting in the Paragraph Preview box and character-level formatting in the Character Preview box. Together, these features make it easy to find the style you want even if you're not sure of its name.

In addition to the Styles list and the List, Description, and Preview boxes, the Style dialog box has seven buttons: Apply, Cancel, New, Modify, Delete, Organizer, and Help. If you choose Apply, Word will apply the currently highlighted style to the current paragraph or paragraphs and will close the dialog box. If you choose Cancel, Word will close the dialog box without applying a style. The rest of the buttons need a little more explanation.

## How to define a new style or modify an existing one

As you might guess, you can choose New in the Style dialog box to define a new style or choose Modify to redefine an existing style. In fact, the two procedures are almost identical. In this discussion, we'll work through the choices for defining a new style, but keep in mind that all of these comments also apply to modifying an existing style. We'll start with some general considerations, and save the mechanics for a little later in this chapter, in the section "How to create and change styles" on page 411.

To define a new style, choose the New button to open the New Style dialog box, shown in Figure 12-8.

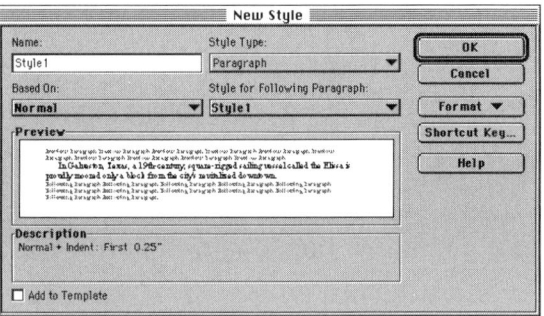

**FIGURE 12-8**

Choose the New button in the Style dialog box to open the New Style dialog box.

The New Style dialog box includes Description and Preview boxes that serve the same purpose as the Description and Paragraph Preview boxes in the Style dialog box. It also includes the Name text box, three boxes with pull-down lists, and two buttons besides the usual OK, Cancel, and Help.

The Name text box lets you enter a name for the style. By default, Word suggests Style1, Style2, and so on, but if you don't use a descriptive name, odds are you'll soon forget what the style is for. You can simply type in the name you want to use.

You can also make use of mixed uppercase and lowercase letters to make style names easier to read. Note too that you can include letters, spaces, numbers, and any punctuation in a style name except a backslash (\), a semicolon (;), or curly brackets ({}). Names can be up to 253 characters, but we recommend keeping them short enough to fit completely in the Styles list box on the Style dialog box. Otherwise you won't be able to read the name easily.

NEW!

Each style must have a unique name. Because Word distinguishes between uppercase and lowercase letters, you can create two style names that differ only in case. In general, you will want to avoid that. However, you might consider taking advantage of this feature if you're disciplined enough to follow a clear convention, such as capitalizing the first letter of all paragraph styles and using all lowercase for character styles. You can then create, say, an *Emphasis* paragraph style that adds bold, italic, and a border to paragraphs, plus an *emphasis* character style that adds bold and italic to shorter selections. If you take this route, however, we recommend that you use it sparingly and that, to avoid confusion, you follow whatever convention you choose as strictly as possible.

In general, you'll want to use names that will help you remember the purpose of each style, and you'll want the names to describe the kind of text the style is meant for, rather than the formatting, in case you decide to change the formatting later. In short, function-related names such as Long Quote and Emphasis are preferable to format-related names such as Indented Italic and Bold Italic Caps. Using functional descriptions will make it easier to change your mind about the formats you want to use.

The Style Type pull-down list offers two choices: Paragraph and Character. As you would expect, you should choose Paragraph to define a paragraph style and Character to define a character style. We'll come back to the other two pull-down lists a little later.

Notice also the Add To Template check box in the lower left corner of the dialog box. You can check it when you want to tell Word to store a new style in a template as well as in the document you're currently working in. We'll cover this feature later in this chapter; for the moment, however, we'll ignore it, since we are focusing on working within a single document.

## Style formatting choices

If you click on the Format button, you'll open a pull-down menu with seven choices: Font, Paragraph, Tabs, Border, Language, Frame, and Numbering. Each choice opens an additional dialog box. These closely resemble the dialog boxes Word opens when you choose the menu items of the same, or similar, names on the Format and Tools menus. The only important difference is that the definitions apply to the style you're defining rather than to a specific selection of text.

> If you click on the Format button when you're defining a character style, the only two choices available will be Font and Language. All the other choices will be grayed out because they are all paragraph-level formatting features.

Some options in these dialog boxes will not be available when you open them through the New Style dialog box. The Default Tab Stops text box, for example, is missing from the Tabs dialog box. Similarly, the Default buttons in the Font and Language dialog boxes will be grayed out. None of these options would make much sense when you're defining a style. Remember that when you redefine the Normal style, you are in fact defining the default for the document, so there's no need to define defaults when defining other styles as well. Note too that you'll find two cards, rather than three, in the Bullets And Numbering dialog box. (The multilevel card is missing.)

If you need details on how to use any of these dialog boxes, you'll find the Font, Paragraph, Tabs, and Border dialog boxes covered in Chapter 7, the Bullets And Numbering dialog box in Chapter 13, and the Frame dialog box in Chapter 14. We touched on the Language dialog box in Chapter 6 when discussing the spelling checker, but it's worth taking a quick look at it here as well.

Figure 12-9 shows the Language dialog box. Its most prominent feature is the Mark Selected Text As list box, which lists a number of languages, including a choice at the start of the list labeled (no proofing), which isn't visible in the figure. As the text at the bottom of the dialog box says, the spelling checker and Word's other proofing tools automatically use the dictionary for the language that's highlighted in the list box, if that dictionary is available.

**FIGURE 12-9**

Use the Language dialog box to choose the language for Word's proofing tools to use.

For obvious reasons, most users in the United States will want to format most of their text with the English (US) choice. However, if you include some paragraphs written in another language—and if you have the dictionary and other proofing tools for that language—you will likely want to format that text for the other language. Similarly, if your document includes a list of trademarks, proper names, or other unusual text, you may want to format it with the (no proofing) choice.

You can format such text directly, of course, but you can create special "no proofing" or foreign language styles as well. We highly recommend using a style rather than direct formatting, since you can then easily change the language format throughout your document by changing the style. You might, for example, format trademarks and proper names as (no proofing) until your final pass. That will tell Word to ignore them most of the time when proofing but will let you proof them easily when you want to simply by changing the Language setting in the style.

## How to specify the next style

The two pull-down lists just above the Preview box in the New Style dialog box are labeled Based On and Style For Following Paragraph. If you open either one, you'll see a list of all styles available in the document, including all built-in styles, whether you're using them in the document or not. (Note, however, that if you're modifying the Normal style, you can't open the Based On list box, since the Normal style can't be based on any other style.)

The Style For Following Paragraph list box applies only to paragraph styles and will be grayed out if you're defining a character style. This list box lets you tell Word what style to use immediately after the style you're currently defining. When you enter a section heading, for example, you'll almost always want the next paragraph to be body text, formatted with the Normal style. By specifying Normal as the next style, you're telling Word that when you press Return to start the next paragraph after a section heading, that paragraph should be formatted as Normal.

This ability to define a style for the following paragraph is a nice touch. It saves you from having to give a separate command to format a paragraph when you know that a given style will always (or almost always) follow some other specific style.

For Word to change styles for the next paragraph as instructed, the cursor must be located just before the paragraph mark when you press return. Otherwise, the new paragraph will keep the same style as the preceding one. You can take advantage of this behavior to split a paragraph and keep the same style in both the resulting paragraphs. You can also use it if, for some reason, you don't want to change styles in a given situation. Simply type an extra space and move one character to the left before pressing Return.

There is one constraint to keep in mind when you specify the next style: You must pick the style name from a list of existing styles. This can be a problem if you haven't yet created the style you want to use as the next style. For example, if you are about to create a list of names and telephone numbers, and you want to move automatically from a bold Name style to an italic Phone style and back to the bold Name style, you can't fully define either style until you've defined the other. In this case, you might define either one first, starting with Name, say, and entering Normal in the Style For Following Paragraph box. Then define the Phone style, entering Name as the next style. Finally, redefine Name and enter Phone as the next style.

In a longer repetitive list, you'll want to define the styles in reverse order. In other words, the first style you define should be the last style you need in the sequence. When you've defined the entire sequence, you can redefine the last style to use the first one as the next style.

## How to base one style on another

The Based On pull-down list in the New Style dialog box lets you define formatting characteristics for one style, and then use those characteristics as the starting point for other styles. That, in turn, lets you redefine whole groups of styles by redefining a single style.

For example, suppose you define the Normal style for a document as single-spaced text in 10-point Helvetica font and you then define all your other styles as based on Normal. Heading 1, for example, might be Normal plus bold and 12-point text. Later you decide you want to use double-spaced text in Times throughout your document. If all your styles are based on Normal, you need only change these settings in the Normal style definition. All the text formatted in the other styles will adopt the new font and spacing automatically. If you haven't used the based-on feature, you'll have to redefine the settings in each individual style.

When you base one style on another, the description for the style you're defining begins with the name of the style you've based it on. In addition, the description will show only those characteristics that differ from the style it's based on.

In much the same way, if you look at the description of the Normal style shown in Figure 12-7, you'll see that the definition doesn't spell out every formatting characteristic. For example, the Normal style uses no indents, but this is not specifically stated in the definition. Except for the font, font size, paragraph alignment, line spacing, widow/orphan control, and language for proofing, the definition of any style that isn't based on another style will specify only those formatting characteristics that differ from Word's defaults.

As shipped, Word defines some styles with different fonts than the Normal style, even though these styles are otherwise based on the Normal style. If you want a style to follow any font changes you make in Normal, you'll first need to modify that style to use the same font as Normal. Your first step must be to modify the style to match Normal even if you plan to change Normal to match the style's current font. If you change Normal to match the style instead, and you then change Normal again, you'll find that the other style stays with its original font. The general rule is: if you want a style to follow changes in a style that it's based on, change the format in the first style to match the format in the based-on style before making other changes.

## Styles based on styles that are based on styles

You can also base a style on another style that is itself based on another style. In other words, you can link styles in multiple steps.

Suppose, for example, that you've created a character style called Emphasis that's based on the Default Paragraph Font style and adds bold. You can then create another character style called Serious Emphasis that's based on Emphasis and adds double underlining and all caps. Figure 12-10 shows examples of these two styles. Each is applied to some text within a paragraph that's formatted as Normal, with Normal defined as 12-point Times. If you change the font in the Normal style to Helvetica, the change will affect the font in the Emphasis and Serious Emphasis styles as well, as shown in Figure 12-11 on the next page. Similarly, if you change the Emphasis style to bold plus italic, you'll also get bold plus italic when you format with the Serious Emphasis style, as shown in Figure 12-12 on the next page.

**FIGURE 12-10**

This paragraph includes text formatted with the Emphasis character style as well as text formatted with the Serious Emphasis style, which is based on the Emphasis style.

This sentence is formatted using only the Normal paragraph style, which is defined as 12-point Times. A portion of this sentence has been assigned **the Emphasis character style, which is based on Normal and adds the Bold attribute.** And a portion of this sentence has been assigned <u>THE SERIOUS EMPHASIS CHARACTER STYLE WHICH IS BASED ON THE EMPHASIS CHARACTER STYLE AND ADDS ALL CAPS AND UNDERLINE ATTRIBUTES.</u> This last sentence is again formatted only with Normal.

**FIGURE 12-11**

This is the same document as in Figure 12-10 after we've changed the Normal style from Times to Helvetica.

**FIGURE 12-12**

This is the same document as in Figure 12-11 after we've changed the Emphasis style from bold to bold plus italic.

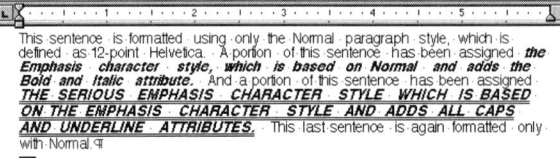

All this boils down to one simple rule: If there are any differences between the current style and the style you've based it on, the definition for the current style will always take priority. If you keep this rule in mind, you can design your styles so that if you decide to change styles—standardizing on a different font, for example—the change will require minimal work. There is more to be said about based-on styles; we'll come back to this subject after we finish discussing how to create and change styles, in "How to use based-on styles when defining by example" on page 420 and in "Notes about based-on styles" on page 421.

## Special considerations for character styles

The only character style that Word always treats as in use is Default Paragraph Font. If you highlight this style in the Style dialog box, you'll see that it's defined as using the font of the underlying paragraph style. Note too that the Modify button in the dialog box will be grayed out, making this the only built-in style that you can't modify.

All of Word's other built-in character styles are based on the Default Paragraph Font style. Since you can't modify this style, that's equivalent to saying that each of these styles is defined as matching the underlying paragraph style, plus whatever modifications you add. Note too that when you define your own character styles, you'll also find a choice called (underlying properties) in the Based On pull-down list. Given that Default Paragraph Font is defined as following (underlying properties), these two choices are fully equivalent.

Somewhat confusingly, the Character Preview box in the Style dialog box will display the default paragraph font as Times (or the equivalent font for the printer you have installed) regardless of the actual font for the paragraph or paragraphs the cursor or selection is in. This remains true even if you don't have a single paragraph style in the document defined to use Times. In fact, Word will show all character styles in Times in the Character Preview box, unless you specifically define them otherwise. Don't let this throw you. Word simply uses Times—or the equivalent for your printer—as a sample font. When you apply the style to text, you'll get the correct font (meaning the font of the underlying paragraph style) unless you've defined the style otherwise.

## How to create and change styles

At this point, you know almost everything you need to about creating and modifying styles, except for the actual mechanics of the process. There are actually two approaches. We'll start with the more straightforward one.

### How to add a style

To add, or create, a style, choose Format Style, then choose the New button to open the New Style dialog box, and type a name for the style in the Name text box. For this example, we'll create the Emphasis character style we just discussed when talking about based-on styles. Type *Emphasis* in the text box, as shown in Figure 12-13.

**FIGURE 12-13**

To create a new style, open the New Style dialog box.

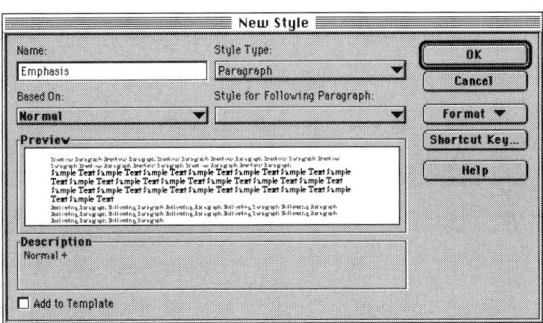

As you can see in Figure 12-13, Word assumes that you want to create a paragraph style and that you want to base the new style on the style the current paragraph was formatted with when you opened the Style dialog box—Normal in this example. In this case, however, you want to create a character style instead. If you choose Character in the Style Type box, as shown in Figure 12-14, Word will automatically change the entry in the Based On box.

**FIGURE 12-14**

When you change the style type to Character, Word will enter an appropriate style in the Based On box.

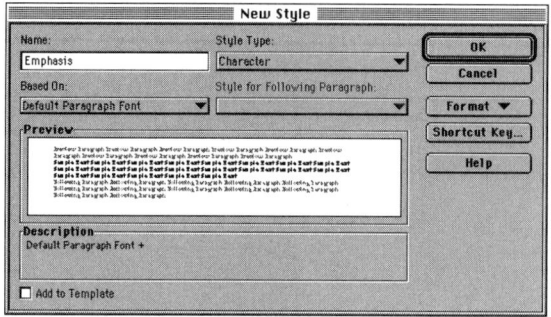

If, when you gave the Format Style command, the cursor or selection was located in text that was formatted with a character style, Word will enter that style in the Based On box when you set the style type to Character. Otherwise, it will enter Default Paragraph Font, as in Figure 12-14, which happens to be the choice you want in this case. If you want to base the new style on a different style, you can open the Based On pull-down list and choose the appropriate style. Note that when you set the style type to Character, Word will gray out the Style For Following Paragraph choice, since the option is meaningless for character styles.

Next, use the menu available through the Format button to define the format for the new style. Remember that when you define a character style, the only choices available will be Font and Language. (If you were defining a paragraph style, you could open additional dialog boxes for paragraph-level formatting such as indents or tabs.) For this example, choose the Format button, then Font to open the Font dialog box. Highlight Bold in the Font Style list, and choose OK. Then choose OK again to return to the Style dialog box.

At this point, you can choose Apply to apply the style to currently selected text, or you can choose Close to return to your document. In either case, Word will add the style to the Style list on the Formatting toolbar and to the list of styles in use in the Style dialog box.

## How to modify a style

As we've already mentioned, the procedure for modifying a style is nearly identical to the procedure for creating one. Suppose, for example, that you've created a second style called Emphasis 2 and you want to change it to match the Serious Emphasis style of our earlier example. To keep the steps simple, we'll assume that you've defined Emphasis 2 as the Default Paragraph Font style plus italic.

To modify Emphasis 2, choose Format Style, highlight Emphasis 2 in the Styles list, and choose the Modify button to open the Modify Style dialog box, shown in Figure 12-15.

**FIGURE 12-15**

To change a style, open the Modify Style dialog box.

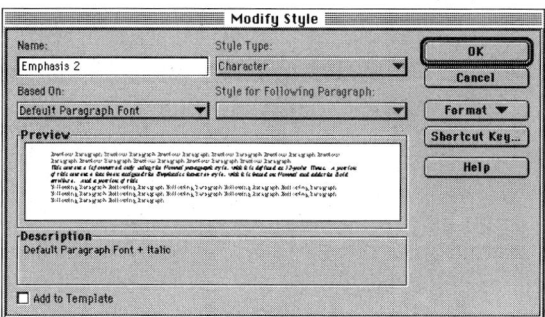

The Modify Style dialog box is almost identical to the New Style dialog box, but with one important difference: When you open the Modify Style dialog box, Word will limit you to changing the style that was highlighted in the Style dialog box when you chose the Modify button. If you change the name in the Name text box, for example, you will rename the style rather than create a new style. Note too that Word will gray out the Style Type box; you cannot change one kind of style to the other. (In Figure 12-15, Word has also grayed out the Style For Following Paragraph box, but that's because Emphasis 2 is a character style. When you modify a paragraph style, you can change the entry in the Style For Following Paragraph box.)

The Modify Style dialog box works essentially the same way as the New Style dialog box. To eliminate italic from the Emphasis 2 definition and add the all-caps and double-underline attributes, choose the Format button, then Font to open the Font dialog box. Next, delete the Italic entry, or choose Regular, in the Font Style box on the Font card, check the All Caps check box, and choose Double from the Underline pull-down list. Then choose OK to return to the Modify Style dialog box. Note that in the original shipping version of the program, when you open the Font dialog box, Word may show the Font Style as Regular, even though you've defined it as italic and Word shows the definition as including italic. Be aware that if you accept the initial, incorrect entry of Regular, and choose OK, Word will *not* remove Italic from the definition. To remove the Italic attribute, choose Italic first, then delete it from the text box or replace it with Regular. (If the style definition includes Bold or Bold Italic, Word will show the appropriate setting in the Font Style box to begin with.)

The description for Emphasis 2 should now read *Default Paragraph Font + Double Underline, All Caps.* If you then choose Emphasis from the Based On list, the description will change to *Emphasis + Double Underline, All Caps.* If you choose OK at this point, Word will close the Modify Style box, redefine the style, and return to the Style dialog box. Alternatively, you can choose Cancel to return to the Style dialog box without accepting the redefinition.

 Keep in mind that if you accept the new definition of the style, Word will reformat not only text that you apply the changed style to but also any other text in the document already formatted with that style.

Be aware, finally, that there are no important differences between working with paragraph styles and working with character styles. The only differences in procedure are those that we've already mentioned. And, as we've pointed out, the main difference is that when creating or modifying paragraph styles, you can define a style for the following paragraph.

## How to rename a style

To rename a style, choose Format Style, highlight the name in the Style dialog box, choose the Modify button, and enter the new name in the Name text box. To continue with the example we've been working with, you might rename the Emphasis 2 style to Serious Emphasis. After you change the name and make any other necessary changes, choose OK. Word will accept the new name and will update it in the Styles list and wherever else it appears.

You can give a style more than one name by using Word's alias feature. If you enter two or more names in the Name text box, separated by commas, Word will treat them all as valid names for that style. This can be useful if you want a fully descriptive name for a style, such as Serious Emphasis, but also want the ability to designate it by typing a shortcut term, such as *SE*, in the Style box on the Formatting toolbar.

## How to modify Normal and other built-in styles

Changing a built-in style such as Normal is essentially identical to changing a custom style except that you can't rename a built-in style. If you try, Word will simply add the new text as an alias for the existing style name. If you try to change Normal to Norm, for example, Word will show the style name as Normal,Norm, treating the new name as an alias.

## How to save style changes

It's important to realize that when you change a style, Word is saving your changes to memory only, not on disk. However, Word will automatically save the style changes the next time you save the document.

Remember that the Normal style is special, in that redefining it effectively redefines the default format settings for your document. Note too that if you open a template file and redefine the Normal settings in the template, the result will define the default format settings for all new files based on that template (but not for existing files, unless you specifically copy the new definition to each existing file).

### How to delete a style

The Style dialog box offers a Delete button, which you can use to delete custom styles. Simply highlight the style that you want to delete in the Styles list, and choose Delete. Word will stop and ask for confirmation. If you choose Yes, it will both delete the style from the list and remove the style formatting from any text that was formatted with that style.

# More About Built-In and Automatic Styles

Word offers roughly 75 built-in styles in the Normal template: about a half-dozen character styles and the rest paragraph styles. Of these, a little under half are automatic styles as well, meaning that Word will automatically apply them when you use certain features. When you insert a footnote, for example, Word will automatically apply the Footnote Text and Footnote Reference styles. There are some additional styles, such as the Heading styles or even the Normal style, that Word doesn't classify as automatic but that it applies automatically in some situations. We've already covered the Normal style, which defines the default settings for text in your document, and we've shown how to change it. Here's a closer look at the other built-in styles.

## Built-in styles other than Normal

Although most of Word's automatic styles won't show up in a document's active style list until you add the type of text element that the style applies to or until you manually apply the style, it's helpful to know what the automatic styles are so you aren't surprised by them. Figure 12-16 on the next page lists the name and purpose of each automatic style. Figure 12-17 on the next page lists the additional built-in styles that Word doesn't classify as automatic. Note also that many of Word's templates include custom styles defined within those templates.

| Word Uses This Style | To Automatically Format This Element |
|---|---|
| Annotation Reference | The annotation reference mark that appears in a document (a character style) |
| Annotation Text | Text in an annotation |
| Caption | Captions inserted by the Insert Caption command |
| Default Paragraph Font | Matches the default font setting of the paragraph style (a character style) |
| Endnote Reference | The endnote reference that appears in the document (a character style) |
| Endnote Text | Text in an endnote |
| Footer | Text in a footer |
| Footnote Reference | The footnote reference mark that appears in a document (a character style) |
| Footnote Text | Text in a footnote |
| Header | Text in a header |
| Index 1–Index 9 | Levels of entries in an index |
| Line Number | Automatic line numbers (a character style) |
| Macro Text | Text of a WordBasic macro |
| Page Number | Automatic page numbers (a character style) |
| Table of Authorities | Entries in a table of authorities |
| Table of Figures | Entries in a table of figures |
| TOC 1–TOC 9 | Entries in a table of contents |

**FIGURE 12-16**

Word's automatic styles.

| Word Provides This Style | To Format This Element |
|---|---|
| Body Text | Body text in documents |
| Body Text Indent | Based on the Normal style; for text that you want formatted the same way as Body Text but with a left indent |
| Closing | The closing of a letter, above the signature |

**FIGURE 12-17**

Word's additional built-in styles.

(continued)

**FIGURE 12-17** *continued*

| Word Provides This Style | To Format This Element |
|---|---|
| Envelope Address | The address on an envelope |
| Envelope Return | The return address on an envelope |
| Heading 1–Heading 9 | Heading levels for section headings and for Outline view |
| Index Heading | Heading separators in an index |
| List and List 2–5 | List items with a hanging indent; by default, lower levels (higher numbers) indicate larger left indents for the entire paragraph |
| List Bullet and List Bullet 2–5 | List items with bullets; by default, lower levels (higher numbers) indicate larger left indents for the entire paragraph |
| List Continue and List Continue 2–5 | Additional paragraphs in a numbered or bulleted list item; by default, lower levels (higher numbers) indicate larger left indents for the entire paragraph |
| List Number and List Number 2–5 | List items with numbering; by default, lower levels (higher numbers) indicate larger left indents for the entire paragraph |
| Normal | All text not assigned another style (the default format) |
| Normal Indent | Based on the Normal style; for text that you want formatted the same way as Normal but with a left indent |
| Signature | The signature on a letter |
| Subtitle | A subtitle within a document |
| Title | The title of a document |
| TOA Heading | Table of authorities heading |

## How to add an automatic style to a document manually

As we've already pointed out, Word will add automatic styles to a document whenever you add the appropriate text elements to that document. For example, when you add a footnote, Word will automatically format the footnote and add two styles to the list of styles in use: Footnote Reference, to format the number or symbol you use as a footnote reference mark; and Footnote Text, to format the footnote itself.

If you want to use an automatic style for some other element in a document, keep in mind that you can see a list of all styles—not just those in use—by choosing Format Style and setting the List box to All Styles. You can then apply the style. Once you've applied a style, Word will recognize it as in use and will add it to the pull-down list on the Formatting toolbar and to the list in the Style dialog box when the dialog box is set to show styles in use.

## The relationship between Normal and other built-in styles

Except for the macro text style, all of Word's built-in styles (in the Normal template, at least) are defined by default as based on the Normal style—or based on another style that's based on Normal. This has two important consequences.

First, the format specified by each built-in style will use all the characteristics of the Normal style except those that are explicitly defined otherwise.

Second, as we've already pointed out in discussing based-on styles in general, any change you make to the Normal style will affect the other built-in styles. For example, if you change the font for the Normal style from Times to Helvetica, most of the other built-in styles will use Helvetica as well. The whole point of the based-on link is to help you maintain consistency among the different parts of a document.

We suggest that whenever you need to make wholesale changes to a document, you start by adjusting the Normal style as appropriate. This is another variation on a top-down formatting strategy; it will minimize the number of changes you have to make in styles that are based on Normal.

This is an important enough point to be worth belaboring a bit. For example, suppose you create a document and directly format the main body text as 12-point Helvetica, rather than modifying the definition of the Normal style. Then suppose you decide to add a header to the document.

Since you formatted the body text with direct formatting, the header, which is based on the Normal style, will still use the default 12-point Times font rather than the 12-point Helvetica you're using for body text. So if you want the font in the header to be consistent with the rest of the document, you'll have to either manually reformat the header text, modify the header style, or modify the Normal style—which is what you should have done in the first place. You'll face the same choice if you add a footer, a footnote, or any other element that Word supplies an automatic style for.

You can avoid this problem entirely by applying styles instead of direct formatting. It's far easier to redefine the Normal style for a document than to reformat each element or each automatic style as it shows up.

# More About Custom Styles

Earlier in this chapter, when we explained how to create a new custom style by defining it from scratch, we also mentioned that there is another way to create and modify styles. This second approach involves formatting some text the way you want it first, and then telling Word to use the formatted text as an example for the style.

## How to create and modify styles by example

To create a custom style by example, place the cursor or selection in the formatted text that you want to use as a model. Then move to the Style box on the Formatting toolbar by clicking on it with the mouse or pressing ⌘-Shift-S. Alternatively, choose Format Style, choose the New button to open the New Style dialog box, and go to the Name text box. In either case, type the new style name in the text box, and press Return. Word will create a new style using the format of the currently selected text or the text the cursor is in. (Note that if the Formatting toolbar isn't showing, pressing ⌘-Shift-S will open the Style dialog box.)

If you use the Style box on the toolbar to create a style, Word will always create it as a paragraph style. If you use the New Style dialog box, you can define the new style as either a paragraph style or a character style.

To modify a style by example, start by formatting some text with the style you want to change and then reformat the text with direct formatting. Next, with the cursor or selection still in the text, either open the pull-down list and click on the style name, or move to the Style box on the Formatting toolbar with ⌘-Shift-S, then open the list by pressing the Down arrow key, make sure the style name is highlighted, and press Return. Word will respond with a dialog box asking whether you want to redefine the style using the selection as an example, or whether you want to change the selection to match the style. Choose the appropriate option and then OK to return to the document window. Choose Cancel to return to the document without making any changes.

Note that you cannot use the style-by-example approach to modify a style with the Format Style command.

### Advantages and disadvantages of creating a style by example

The main difference between creating a style by defining it in the New Style dialog box and creating it by example is that when you create by example, you define the format before you name the style. One advantage of this approach is that you can see the effects of your formatting before you actually create the style. This is particularly helpful with a complicated format that requires fine-tuning to get exactly the result you want.

In addition, creating a style by example can come in handy when you've manually formatted a paragraph and then decide after the fact that you want to use the same format in other locations in your document. Rather than manually reformatting the other text, you can use the first paragraph as an example to define a new style and then apply the style to all the paragraphs you want to format the same way.

Creating a style by example also has at least one disadvantage. When you create a style by example, Word assumes that the style for the following paragraph should be the same as the style you just created. Since that will often not be what you want, you'll have to choose Format Style, then the Modify button, and set the Style For Following Paragraph to match your needs.

Note that when using the style-by-example approach, you may get unexpected results if you accidentally extend the selection to include more than one format. When you use this technique, be sure to confine the selection to text that uses the formatting you actually want. Better yet, simply place the cursor in appropriately formatted text.

## How to use based-on styles when defining by example

Whenever you define a new style, Word will assume that you want it to be based on an existing style. In particular, if you define a new paragraph style by example using the Format Style command and the New Style dialog box, Word will automatically set the Based On box to the style the paragraph was formatted with before you gave the Format Style command. Similarly, when you define a new character style by example, Word will automatically set the Based On box to the character style the text was formatted with before you gave the Format Style command. If the text wasn't explicitly formatted with a character style, Word will set the Based On box to Default Paragraph Font. This means it's a good idea to decide which style you want to use as your based-on style before you begin to define a new style by example. You can then use that style as your starting point.

For example, suppose you want to create a new paragraph style with all the characteristics of the Normal style except that the first line of each paragraph will be indented ¾ inch. Since this new style is so similar to Normal, it would make sense to start with a paragraph that's formatted with the Normal style. Not only will this save work in formatting the new style, but Word will automatically make Normal the based-on style. If necessary, however, you can change the based-on style later.

## Notes about based-on styles

Because specifying a new based-on style changes the foundation of a style, it can drastically change the attributes of the current style. Suppose, for example, that the document you're working with contains styles named Normal, Style1, and Style2. The Normal style uses 12-point Times type with flush-left alignment and no indents. Style1 is based on Normal, and its definition reads *Normal + Bold, Italic, Indent: Left 0.5" Right 0.5" Justified, Space Before 10 pt*. Style2 is based on Style1 and is identical to Style1 except that it uses 14-point type. Figure 12-18 shows the definition and previews for Style2.

**FIGURE 12-18**

Style2 is identical to Style1 (its based-on style) except for font size.

Suppose you want to change the based-on style for Style2 to Normal. Choose Format Style, highlight Style2 in the Styles list, and choose the Modify button to open the Modify Style dialog box. Then enter *Normal* in the Based On box. The result should match Figure 12-19.

**FIGURE 12-19**

If you replace a based-on style, the current style will lose all the formatting characteristics defined in the previous based-on style.

With Style2 now based on the Normal style, as shown in Figure 12-19, the formatting instructions for Style2 build only on the Normal style, without the instructions you had added to Style1. As a result, text formatted with Style2 will look similar to text formatted with Normal, rather than text formatted with Style1, except that it will have 14-point rather than 12-point characters.

It's best to avoid basing styles on unrelated styles. Consider, for example, what might happen if you've based an Indented Quote style on one of your heading styles because the two happen to be similar. You might then decide to change your headings to another format, but you might not want the change to affect the Indented Quote style. In that case, you'll need to redefine the Indented Quote style, basing it on another style. If you base your styles on related styles, in contrast, you're more likely to avoid this sort of situation.

Keep in mind that when you change a style that serves as the based-on style for other styles, most of your changes will affect those other styles. For example, as we mentioned earlier, if you change the font for the Normal style, you will change the font for most styles based on Normal. The only exceptions will be those styles that have a different font defined as part of the style or as part of an intermediate based-on style. The moral is simple: Be careful with changes, and watch out for a cascading effect.

## How to create a style that is not based on any other style

If you want to create a style that's completely independent of the other styles in your document, you can enter the (no style) choice in the Based On box. The resulting style description will consist of Word's default settings, plus any changes you've defined in the style, as with the Normal style.

Just because you *can* create a style that's independent of any other style doesn't necessarily mean you should. In fact, it's generally a bad idea. Remember that one of the biggest advantages of using based-on styles is precisely that you can change a feature in an underlying style, such as Normal, and have that change automatically show up in all styles that are based on that style. This avoids the hassle of having to make the same change in each style if you change the font in the Normal style, for example, or change the line spacing.

In short, don't create an independent style unless you have good reason to. Typically, that means you want to ensure that its format remains unchanged no matter what changes you make to other styles in your document.

### Notes about related styles

A style can be directly based on only one style, but any given style can be indirectly related to several styles, through a chain of based-on styles—as in our earlier example, with Style2 based on Style1, which was in turn based on Normal. In that example, Style2 was indirectly related to Normal, but directly related to Style1.

Word will not let you create circular style references. For example, suppose you create a Style3 and base it on Style2. If you then try to redefine Style1 to base it on Style3, Word will refuse to make the change and will respond with the message *This style has a circular Based On list*. You can then choose OK in the message box and enter a different based-on style.

Word will also refuse to let you create more than 11 levels of based-on styles (with 10 connections). For example, you can create a set of styles with Style10 based on Style9, which is based on Style8, and so forth, through Style1, based on Normal. But if you then try to create a Style11 and base it on Style10, Word will not accept it and will respond with the message *The style you want to create is based on too many styles*. Fortunately, it's unlikely that you'll need even 11 levels for your styles.

# Applying Styles

Most of this chapter up to now has been concerned with creating and modifying styles. However, we've mentioned only a few techniques for applying styles. In fact, we've purposely skipped over one of the most important techniques: attaching styles to shortcut keys. Once you've assigned shortcut keys, you'll find that they're the quickest way to apply styles to any text in your document.

### How to assign shortcut keys to a style

You can attach styles to shortcut keys by way of the Customize Keyboard card. You can reach the card by choosing Tools Customize, then Keyboard, or by choosing the Shortcut Key button that's available in both the New Style and Modify Style dialog boxes. The Tools Customize command will give you full access to all of Word's keyboard customization features. If you choose Format Styles, in contrast, then choose Modify or New, and then the Shortcut Key button, you'll have the more restricted ability to add shortcuts only for the one style you're currently defining. We'll cover the full-blown use of the

Customize Keyboard card in Chapter 28, "Customizing Menus, Keys, & Templates," starting on page 903. For now, we'll look only at the more restricted capability available though the Modify Styles and New Styles dialog boxes.

When you open the Customize dialog box this way, Word will automatically take you to the Keyboard card, as shown in Figure 12-20. It will not let you move to the other cards or even pick another style to assign a key to. Quite the contrary, in fact; the only item you'll be able to assign a key to is the style you were defining before you chose the Shortcut Key button. That style—Normal in this case—will show in the Commands list box as the only choice in that list.

**FIGURE 12-20**

Choose the Shortcut Key button on the Modify Style or New Style dialog box to open the Customize dialog box with the Keyboard card showing.

For the moment, the only two items you need be concerned with on this card are the Press New Shortcut Key text box and the Current Keys list box. The Current Keys list box will list any shortcut keys currently assigned to the style you're working with. (As you'll see, you can assign more than one key combination.) The Press New Shortcut Key box is where you enter the key combination to use.

Word will let you assign shortcut keys that use two keystrokes rather than one. This makes it far easier to use mnemonics rather than arbitrary combinations of easily forgotten keys. However, there is a dizzying array of choices for the keys to use. The first keystroke can be a combination of Control, ⌘, Control-Shift, ⌘-Shift, Option-Control, ⌘-Control, ⌘-Option, Option-Control-Shift, ⌘-Control-Shift, ⌘-Option-Shift,⌘-Option-Control, or ⌘-Option-Control-Shift with nearly any alphanumeric, punctuation, or function key on the keyboard. The second keystroke can be any of the allowable alphanumeric, punctuation, or function keys by itself or in combination with the Shift key.

When you first open the dialog box, Word will place the cursor in the Press New Shortcut Key box. To enter the shortcut key combination, simply press the appropriate keys. If you want a two-keystroke shortcut consisting of Control-Shift-P followed by N, for example, simply press Control-Shift-P and then press N. Word will show this in the Press New Shortcut Key box as Control+Shift+P,N. It will also add a note below the box that will either read

*Currently Assigned to (unassigned)* or will show the name of the command, macro, style, or other item that the keystroke is currently assigned to. If you want to change the shortcut key definition, you can press Delete to back up and start again.

As soon as you enter anything in the Press New Shortcut Key box, Word will make the Assign button available. Choose it to assign the shortcut key or keys to the style, and Word will add the shortcut to the Current Keys list, even if it was previously assigned to another item. Word will also gray out the Assign button and wait. Figure 12-21 shows the Keyboard card after we've defined the Normal style as Control-Shift-P,N.

**FIGURE 12-21**

After you define a keyboard shortcut for a style, Word will wait to let you define additional shortcuts.

Once you've defined a shortcut key combination, you can choose Close to close the dialog box, or you can define additional shortcuts. The ability to define additional shortcuts can be handy if more than one person works on your system and each prefers a different set of shortcuts. You can also delete shortcut keys by moving to the Current Keys list, highlighting the shortcut you want to delete, and choosing the Remove button. When you've finished assigning shortcut keys, choose Close to close the dialog box and return to the Modify Style or New Style dialog box.

We strongly recommend that you take advantage of Word's two-keystroke capability and that you divide shortcut key mnemonics into groups to make them even easier to remember. You might, for example, use Control-Shift for all style-related shortcut keys, with Control-Shift-P for paragraph styles and Control-Shift-C for character styles. Alternatively, if you depend heavily on styles and on shortcut keys, you might use a scheme such as ⌘-Shift for paragraph styles and ⌘-Control for character styles. This would free you to use such mnemonics as ⌘-Shift-H,1 for the Heading 1 style, ⌘-Shift-H,2 for the Heading 2 style, ⌘-Shift-E,A for the Envelope Address style, and so on.

## How to apply a style with shortcut keys

Once you've attached a shortcut key to a style, applying the style is simple. To apply a paragraph style, place the cursor or selection in the paragraph or paragraphs you want to apply the style to and press the shortcut key. To apply a character style to any arbitrary selection of text, and just that selection even if it stops in the middle of a word, select the text and press the shortcut key. To apply the style to a word, place the cursor anywhere in the word and press the shortcut key. To apply the style to text you are about to type, place the cursor where you want to insert the text—being careful to make sure it is not within a word—press the shortcut key, and start typing.

## How to use a list or a text box to apply a style

If you don't like using shortcut keys, or if you find you can't remember the keys for styles you use infrequently, you can take advantage of any of several other methods Word offers for applying styles. Most of these let you choose the style name from a list. All assume that you've already positioned the cursor or selected the text you want to format, following the same rules we just described for applying a style with shortcut keys. Since that's a universal requirement, we won't bother mentioning that step for the rest of this discussion.

### How to apply a style from the Formatting toolbar

If you can recognize the name of the style you want, and if the style is already in use in the document, one of the simplest options is one we've already mentioned—using the Formatting toolbar. Assuming that the toolbar is already showing on screen, open the Style list with the mouse, or by pressing ⌘-Shift-S and then the Down arrow key. If you're using the mouse to pull down the list, scroll through the list to highlight the name of the style you want to use, and then release the mouse button. If you used the keyboard to open the list as a drop-down list, you can either click on the name with the mouse or highlight it with arrow keys and press Return.

Alternatively, if you already know the style name, you can simply move to the Style box with ⌘-Shift-S, type the name, and press Return. You can also type part of the name and press the Down arrow key to have Word jump to the first style name in the list that matches the letters you typed. For example, typing *in* and then pressing the Down arrow key might move the highlight to Indented Quote or Index 1, if either name is in the list.

With any of these methods, when you designate the style, Word will immediately apply it to the current paragraph or paragraphs if it's a paragraph style, or the current word, selected text, or cursor position if it's a character style.

### How to apply a style from the Style dialog box

If the Formatting toolbar is not showing when you press ⌘-Shift-S, Word will take you to the Style dialog box, just as if you had chosen Format Style. You can set the List option to All Styles, Styles In Use, or User-Defined Styles as appropriate, and then scroll through the Styles list, reading the description for each style as you highlight it, until you see the style you want. Once you find it, highlight it in the Styles list. Then choose Apply, or double-click on the style name, to apply the style and close the dialog box.

# Displaying the Style Area

As you become more comfortable with using styles, you'll find that it's often useful to know the style for the paragraphs you're currently looking at. Although the Style box on the Formatting toolbar always shows the name of the current style for the text the cursor is in, that style will sometimes be the current character style rather than the paragraph style.

In any case, it's even more helpful to see the style names for all the paragraphs on screen. You can see the names by opening the style area, which runs vertically along the left edge of the document window. When you open the style area, Word will show the name of the style for each paragraph alongside the first line of each paragraph. (And note that you can open the Style dialog box quickly by double-clicking anywhere in the style area.)

Word will show the style area only when you're in Normal, Outline, or Master Document view. To see the area, first make sure you are not in Page Layout view. Next, choose Tools Options, then the View card, and enter a setting between 0.1 and 4.43 inches in the Style Area Width box. For this discussion, we'll use a setting of 0.6 inch. You can type the number in, or you can click on the arrows at the right of the box to change the setting in 0.1-inch increments. When you're done, choose OK to accept the new setting and close the dialog box.

Your screen should now look similar to the one shown in Figure 12-22 on the next page, assuming you have some text on your screen. Word will separate the style area from the text area with a vertical line and will show the style names for each paragraph in the style area.

**FIGURE 12-22**

When you open the style area, Word will show you the style for each paragraph, putting the style name to the left of the first line of each paragraph.

When you pick a size for the style area, your first thought will probably be to make it wide enough to show the longest style name in your document. If you make the style area too wide, however, your text may run off the right side of your screen, so you may have to compromise. In Figure 12-22, for example, the Normal Indent style name is cut off by the vertical line between the style area and the text area, and the body text still runs off the screen on the right side. If you can recognize the style name even when it's cut off, there's no reason why you shouldn't make the style area narrower than your longest style name.

## How to resize the style area

You can resize the style area at any time by choosing Tools Options View and changing the setting in the Style Area Width box. Alternatively, you can use the mouse at any time to move the vertical line that separates the style area from the text area. If you move the mouse pointer over the style area split bar (the vertical line at the right edge of the style area), the pointer will change to a vertical split pointer, as shown in Figure 12-23. When the pointer changes shape, press the mouse button, drag the split bar to its new location, and release the button.

**FIGURE 12-23**

**FIGURE 12-23**

The pointer will change shape when you move it over the style area split bar.

## How to close the style area

After you open the style area in a document, Word will show you a style area in each new document until you close the style area. To close it, use the mouse to drag the style area split bar to the left edge of the document window. Alternatively, you can choose Tools Options View, change the setting in the Style Area Width box to 0, and choose OK.

# Printing Lists of Styles and Shortcut Keys

NEW!

You'll find it easier to maintain consistency among style names in different documents if you have a printed list of the styles and a list of all the shortcut keys. That way, you can refer to the lists as you work on each document. You can easily print either list by choosing File Print, opening the Print pull-down list, and choosing Styles or Key Assignments from the list, as appropriate. Figure 12-24 shows the pull-down list. Simply specify the item you want and choose OK to print it.

**FIGURE 12-24**

Among its print options, Word offers choices for printing a list of styles and a list of key assignments.

# Using Styles and Direct Formatting Together

As you format a document, you can combine direct formatting changes with style formatting. In most cases, Word will simply add your direct formatting changes to the formatting features specified by the styles.

For example, suppose your document includes a paragraph style named Style1 that specifies 12-point bold Courier type. If you select some text that's formatted with this style and then use direct formatting to add italic, the paragraph will show with italic formatting in addition to the bold and other features specified by Style1. Similarly, you can change the paragraph, tabs, border, and language format. In each case, the direct formatting changes will override the style formats, but Word will continue to show the style name in the style area and in the Style box on the Formatting toolbar, and it will continue to highlight the name in the Styles list in the Style dialog box.

This ability to override styles with direct formatting is essential in Word. Without it, you wouldn't be able to use direct formatting at all, given that Word assigns a style to every paragraph. And note that you can override both paragraph and character styles.

As a general rule, we strongly recommend that you use styles whenever possible. The reason is simple: If you format large amounts of text directly, you lose much of the benefit of styles, since you can no longer make wholesale changes in your document simply by redefining a style.

Consider: Direct formatting overrides style formats. That's why it works. So when you change the underlying style, the new style format will still be overridden by any direct formatting commands you've added. For example, if the Normal style is defined as Times, and if you've used direct formatting to change several paragraphs to Helvetica, those paragraphs will stay in Helvetica even if you change the Normal style definition to, say, Chicago.

For real confusion, consider what would happen if you made your changes with a mix of styles and direct formatting. For example, suppose that after you defined one or more paragraphs as Helvetica with direct formatting, you then changed the definition of the Normal style to Helvetica. Later, you decide to change the Normal style to Chicago font. Before you redefine the Normal style, all the paragraphs with that style will look the same, since all will be set to Helvetica. But after you redefine it, any paragraphs that were originally formatted in Helvetica with direct formatting will still be in Helvetica, while any that were formatted with styles only will change to Chicago. And there is no easy way to tell beforehand which paragraphs will change and which won't.

Adding still more possibility for confusion is that some formatting commands act as toggles. For example, suppose you've formatted one sentence within a paragraph as italic for emphasis. If you then redefine the style for that paragraph as italic, Word will automatically toggle the emphasized sentence to nonitalic. This makes good sense, since it automatically maintains the emphasis. However, if you've directly formatted an entire paragraph in italic—to indicate a long quote, for example—and you then redefine the style as italic, you'll find that the italic text changes to nonitalic in that situation too. Once again, the best way to avoid confusion is to use styles whenever possible.

This same effect, with a formatting command acting like a toggle, can also crop up when you use character styles. But you are not likely to have formatted an entire paragraph with a character style, since the handiest tool in that case would be a paragraph style.

When you're first learning about styles, it's hard to use them as consistently as you might, if only because you have to define a new style every time you need a new format. This can create problems when you return to work on a document after learning more about styles or when you work on a document created by someone who hasn't taken advantage of styles. Fortunately, Word provides some shortcuts to make it easier to work with documents that are already formatted with a mix of styles and direct formatting. These shortcuts help remove the direct formatting and reset the text to the format defined in the underlying style.

## Removing direct formatting

To understand how the reset commands work, you first have to understand how Word uses its two levels of formatting: character and paragraph. Character-level formatting is similar to, but not exactly the same as, the set of formatting choices that are available when you choose Format Font or the equivalent formatting shortcuts. Paragraph-level formatting is similar to the set of formatting choices available when you choose Format Paragraph or the equivalent shortcuts.

Character-level formatting includes any formatting that applies to individual characters—font, font size, bold, and italic, for example. It also includes the Language setting, which is available through the Tools Language command. Paragraph-level formatting applies to entire paragraphs and includes such formatting as indents, line spacing, space before and after, borders, and tabs. Word provides a simple reset command for each of these two levels.

The shortcut for removing paragraph-level formatting is ResetPara, a built-in command that, by default, isn't on any menu but is assigned to the shortcut key ⌘-Option-Q. To use the command, simply place the cursor or selection in the paragraph or paragraphs you want to reset, and press ⌘-Option-Q.

Removing character-level direct formatting with the ResetChar command is similarly straightforward. Select the text you want to reset and press ⌘-Spacebar or ⌘-Shift-Z. Word will remove all character-level direct formatting.

You can reset a selection of any size, from one character to your entire document. If you want to reset the text for your whole document, press ⌘-A to highlight the entire document, and then press ⌘-Option-Q, then ⌘-Spacebar.

# NEW!   Merging Styles from Another Document

Early in this chapter, we showed how to use Word's Style Gallery feature to copy all the styles from any template to the document you're working with. But Word lets you copy styles from other documents as well as from templates, and it also lets you copy only one or a few styles at a time. This ability to copy styles can save you from having to redefine styles in more than one document.

## How to copy one style

The most straightforward way to copy a style from one document to another is to copy a paragraph or some text formatted in that style. More precisely, to copy a paragraph style, you can copy a paragraph mark from a paragraph formatted in that style, and to copy a character style, you can copy a character formatted in that style. Although the technique works for either kind of style, we'll use paragraph styles for this example.

Suppose you've created the style Long Quote in a document called *Chapter One* and you want to copy the style to the document *Chapter Two*. Start by formatting a paragraph in *Chapter One* with the Long Quote style. Next select the paragraph mark at the end of that paragraph, by itself or with text, and choose the Edit Cut or Edit Copy command to place the formatted paragraph mark on the Clipboard. If you've set Word so it's not showing paragraph marks, you can still select the paragraph mark and copy it to the Clipboard. Move the cursor to the immediate right of the last character in the paragraph and then select from that position as far to the right as possible, using the mouse or the keyboard. If you then choose the Edit Cut or Edit Copy command, Word will place what amounts to an invisible paragraph mark on the Clipboard. For the rest of this discussion, we'll simply refer to a *paragraph*, by which we mean a paragraph mark or the equivalent, with or without text.

Once the paragraph is on the Clipboard, you can open *Chapter Two* (or move to that document window if it is already open) and paste the paragraph into the document. When you paste it, Word will automatically add the style name and definition to that document's list of styles.

When you copy a style this way, watch out for duplicate style names. If you try to copy a style into a document that contains a style with the same name, Word will not redefine the style in the target document to match the format in the document you're trying to copy from. Rather, the paragraph will take on the format of the already defined style in the current document.

If the style definition you're copying includes an entry for a based-on style, Word may modify the formatting instructions when you paste the paragraph into the destination document—but only if the modification is needed to maintain the formatting.

For example, suppose you are working in a document that contains styles named Sub1 and Sub2. The formatting instructions for Sub1 specify 14-point Helvetica type. Sub2, based on Sub1, specifies 12-point Helvetica type, so its definition reads *Sub1 + Font: 12 pt*. If you copy a paragraph formatted as Sub2 into a document that doesn't have a Sub1 style and whose Normal style is defined with 12-point Times, Word will add the Sub2 style using the formatting instructions *Normal + Font: Helvetica*.

Similarly, if the destination document has a Sub1 style that's formatted with 10-point Times, bold, and double spacing, Word will retain Sub1 as the based-on style but will change the Sub2 definition to read *Sub1 + Font: Helvetica, 12 pt, Not Bold, Line Spacing Single*. In both cases, Word will maintain the format of Sub2 in the destination document to match the format it had in the source document.

The best way to avoid uncertainty about the effect of copying a style from one document to another is to make sure you don't have duplicate style names—which may mean deleting a style of the same name in the destination document before copying. Of course, you can't avoid having a Normal style or other built-in styles in each document. And that means you can't copy and paste built-in styles between documents. One of your first steps in setting up a new document should be to set the Normal style to suit that particular document. Then, if you copy any styles based on Normal from one document to another, you'll need to watch carefully for unwanted format changes and make adjustments as necessary.

# How to import styles with Word's Organizer

In addition to letting you copy individual styles by copying text and letting you copy sets of styles with the Format Style Gallery feature, Word also offers a far more elegant tool that will let you copy a single style, a designated subset of styles, or an entire set of styles, between documents, between templates, or between a document and a template. The feature is Word's Organizer. We'll cover it fully in Chapter 27, "Templates," starting on page 883, after we've discussed templates further. For the moment, however, we'll take a brief look at it, since you should at least be aware it exists.

To open the Organizer dialog box, shown in Figure 12-25, choose Format Style, then choose the Organizer button.

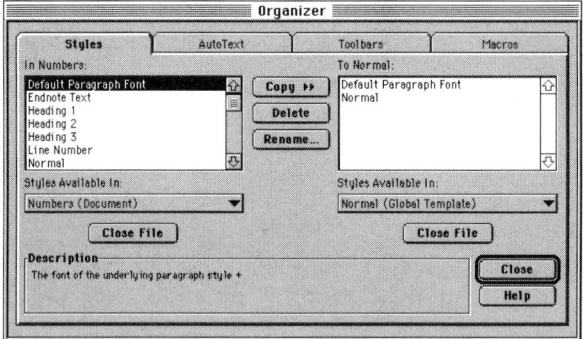

**FIGURE 12-25**

To manage Word's styles, choose Format Style and then the Organizer button to open the Organizer dialog box.

The Organizer dialog box offers several cards. The only one we're interested in at the moment is the Styles card. The left and right sides of the card are essentially identical to each other, with two sets of a list box, a pull-down list, and a button. If you choose the Close File button on either side of the card, Word will erase all information from the boxes above the button and will change the button to Open File. If you then choose Open File, you'll see a dialog box that's similar to the dialog box you see when you choose File Open.

You can use the dialog box to choose a file—meaning any Word-format document or template file—for either the left or right side of the card. As you can see in Figure 12-25, Word will list the styles available in that file in the top box on that side and will enter the filename in the Styles Available In box. You can then highlight one or more styles on either side of the card and copy them to the file on the other side of the card by choosing the Copy button. You can also highlight styles to delete them or rename them, using the Delete and Rename buttons. For more details on using the Organizer, see "The Organizer dialog box" on page 897.

# Changing Defaults

If you create some styles that you may need to use in virtually any document, you'll want to add them to the Normal template so they'll be available to each new document you create. Similarly, if you prefer different default formats than Word provides for Normal or other built-in styles, you'll want to change the definition of those styles in the Normal template. Otherwise, you'll have to change them in every new document you create. Fortunately, changing styles in the Normal template is no more complicated than changing styles in a document.

## The effect of changing a style in a template

Before we discuss how to change a style in a template, it's important to understand the effect of making a change. Some changes to a template apply to all documents that have the modified template attached, no matter when those files were created. Other changes apply only to files that you create after making the changes.

Changes in styles fall into the second category. That means that if you want to make changes to styles in already existing documents, you have to import the changed styles, using any of the techniques we've just discussed. It also means that you're free to change styles in a template without worrying about making inadvertent changes to existing documents.

## How to modify styles in the Normal template from a document

One way to add styles to the Normal template—or any other template, for that matter—is to open the template and define the styles the same way you would in a document file. In fact, you can open, edit, and change a template just as you can any other Word document. But there are other choices as well, starting with the Organizer feature we discussed earlier.

Suppose you have a document that has only the Normal template attached and already has style definitions that you want to add to the Normal template. Start by opening the document and choosing Format Style. Then choose the Organizer button to open the Organizer dialog box. One side of the Styles card should be labeled with the document name; the other side should simply be labeled Normal. To copy styles to the Normal template, highlight the styles you want to copy in the list box on the document side of the card, and choose Copy. When you're done, choose Close to close the dialog box. That's all there is to it.

You can also create or modify document styles and Normal template styles at the same time. In the lower left corner of the New Style and Modify Style dialog boxes is a check box we've ignored until now. The check box is labeled Add To Template. If you check this box, Word will add the style you're currently modifying or creating to the template that's attached to the document as well as to the document itself. Note that whenever you open either dialog box, the check box starts out blank to protect you from modifying a style in the template by accident.

These techniques work exactly the same way for copying styles to any other template. Simply start by opening a document that contains the styles you want to copy and is attached to the supplementary template you want to copy the styles to. For details on templates, see Chapter 27, "Templates," starting on page 883.

Depending on the current settings on the Tools Options Save card, Word may or may not prompt you for permission to save changes to the Normal template. If it does, simply answer Yes to complete the save. Much the same comment applies to saving styles in other templates. When you finish your changes, choose File Save All to ensure that the changes are saved.

## How to return to Word's original default settings

If you've changed the default styles in the Normal template and you later decide you want to restore the styles to their original form, you can simply erase the Normal template file, Normal, from your hard disk. The next time you start Word, the program will revert to its default settings for the Normal template. You can delete the file by going to the appropriate folder, using the Finder, and dragging the file to the trash. Note that if you erase the Normal template, however, you'll also lose any other changes you've made to the template, including AutoText entries, macros, and other advanced customizations that we'll discuss in Part Five. A more selective approach is to open the Normal template and modify the list of styles only, using the techniques discussed in this chapter. We'll look at editing templates in Chapter 27; for now, in the next two chapters, we'll move on to other advanced formatting issues.

# TOPIC FINDER

438

# 13

# Bullets, Numbering, & Sections

n Chapter 7, we explained the basics of formatting Word documents. In Chapter 12, we covered styles. In this chapter and the two that follow, we'll cover some of Word's more complex formatting features (meaning features for complex formatting, not features that are hard to use). In this chapter, we'll cover automatic numbering, and we'll also explore sections, a topic that we've mentioned in earlier chapters but not looked at in detail.

Word's numbering features break down into two categories: by line and by paragraph. Numbering by paragraph can be further broken down into numbering that affects all paragraphs regardless of style (a category that includes bullets as well as numbers) and numbering that affects only paragraphs formatted with certain styles. We'll start with the most detailed level of numbering—lines—and work our way through the other categories.

For most of the examples in this chapter, we'll use the text in Figure 13-1 on the next page. What makes this sample text appropriate for illustrating the concepts we'll discuss is that it's representative of many real-world documents, with several levels of headings separating paragraphs of body text.

439

**FIGURE 13-1**

We will use this
sample text in our
examples of the
different numbering
options.

# Numbering Lines

Some people need to create documents with numbered lines. The numbers
may have to show up next to each line of text, next to every fifth line, or tenth
line, or at some other interval. Word not only makes it easy to add numbering,
it automatically updates the line numbers to reflect changes as you revise the
document.

To create line numbers in your documents, choose File Document Layout
and then choose Layout to open the Layout card, shown in Figure 13-2. We'll
discuss this card in detail later in this chapter. For now, we're interested only
in the Line Numbers button on the left side of the card near the bottom, and
the Apply To box just under it.

**FIGURE 13-2**

The Document Layout
card lets you choose
line numbering for
your document.

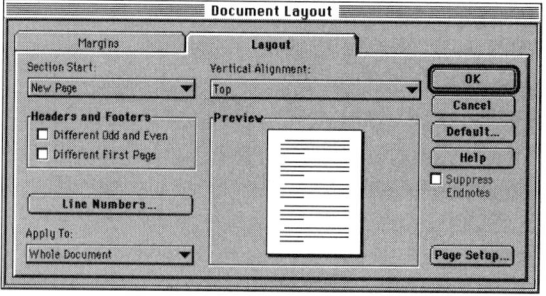

The choices in the Apply To pull-down list will vary depending on your document, but Whole Document will always be one of the choices. There will also always be a second choice, which will either be This Point Forward if you haven't selected any text in the document, or Selected Text if you have. If the document includes more than one section, you'll see a third choice as well: either This Section if you haven't selected any text in the document, or Selected Sections if you have. (But note that if your selection extends to more than one section, you won't see Selected Text as a choice.) To add line numbers, choose the appropriate Apply To option, and then choose the Line Numbers button to open the Line Numbers dialog box, shown in Figure 13-3.

**FIGURE 13-3**

The Line Numbers dialog box provides options for numbering lines of text.

When you first open the Line Numbers dialog box, most of the choices will be grayed out. To make them available and turn on line numbering, check the Add Line Numbering check box.

The Start At text box tells Word what number to use as the starting number for the first line. This is a useful feature if you've broken a long document into several files and want to maintain continuous numbering. The default is 1, but you can enter any number from 1 through 32,767.

Even with 60 lines per page, the maximum starting number of 32,767 allows nearly 550 pages before you run out of acceptable starting numbers. But note that although you can't enter a larger starting number, Word is quite willing to continue numbering lines past this point.

The From Text box lets you specify the distance between the right edge of the line numbers and the left edge of your text. The default setting is Auto, which will serve most needs. However, you can set this to as high as 22 inches if you like. This is farther from your text than you'll ever need, however, since

22 inches is also Word's maximum page width. Note that if you click on the arrows to the right of the box, Word will change the setting in increments of 0.1 inch, but you can use the keyboard to enter other increments, such as 0.25 or 0.27 inch.

The Count By option specifies how often the line numbers will appear. The default is every line, but you can set any number of lines that you like. For example, if you set Count By to 5, Word will number every fifth line, so the numbers will appear as 5, 10, 15, and so on.

The Numbering options tell Word whether and when to restart counting, starting with the setting you've entered as the Start At number. You can tell Word to restart the numbering at the beginning of every new page or every new section, or you can choose Continuous for continuous numbering. The default setting is Restart Each Page.

## How to view line numbers

For now, we'll accept all the default values, choose OK, and then choose OK again on the Layout card. If Word is in Normal or Outline view, you may be surprised to see that the document is unchanged.

To see the line numbers, you have to set Word for either Page Layout view or Print Preview, or print the document. Figure 13-4 shows our sample document in Page Layout view, complete with line numbers. Note that Word adds the numbers in the margin of the document. If we reformat the document to have two columns, it will add the numbers to the left of each column of text, as in Figure 13-5. (We'll discuss multicolumn formatting in Chapter 14.)

**FIGURE 13-4**

Word adds line numbers to the left of your text.

**FIGURE 13-5**

If your document is formatted with multiple columns, Word adds line numbers to the left of each column. In this example, the Count By option is set to 5.

As you can see in these examples, Word counts every line. In fact, if your document contains a blank line that you created by pressing Return, Word will count that line as well. If you've formatted a paragraph to have extra space between lines, however, or between paragraphs, Word will not number that space, as you can see by the space between lines 1 and 2 in Figure 13-4. Figure 13-5 shows how a Count By setting of 5 affects the line numbering.

## How to remove line numbers

If you want to get rid of all the line numbers, choose File Document Layout, then Layout, then the Line Numbers button, and clear the X from the Add Line Numbering check box.

There might be times, however, when you want to selectively remove line numbers from your document. For example, you might want to number only the body text and leave the headings out of the count. To remove numbering from selected paragraphs, place the cursor or selection in the paragraph or paragraphs you don't want numbered, choose Format Paragraph, and then choose Text Flow to see the Text Flow card, shown in Figure 13-6 on the next page. To exclude the paragraph or paragraphs from line numbering, check the Suppress Line Numbers check box on the left side of the card.

FIGURE 13-6

The Paragraph Text
Flow card includes the
Suppress Line Numbers
check box, which lets
you exclude a para-
graph from line
numbering.

Figure 13-7 shows our sample document with the Suppress Line Numbers option active for the headings, leaving line numbers next to body text
only. As you can see, the Suppress Line Numbers option not only tells Word
not to show numbers for these paragraphs, it leaves the headings out of the
count altogether.

**FIGURE 13-7**

In this sample, the
Suppress Line Numbers
option is active for all
the headings, so only
the body text lines are
numbered.

You can automatically skip line numbering for headings by formatting your heading paragraphs with styles and defining the heading
styles with the Suppress Line Numbers option. For more details on
paragraph formats in styles, see "Working with Styles" on page 401.

# Numbering Paragraphs and Creating Lists

For those who need to number paragraphs rather than lines, Word offers a paragraph-numbering feature also. More precisely, Word will let you use numbers, letters, or typographical bullets to mark paragraphs. It even provides outline formats that mix letters and numbers. For this discussion, we'll use *numbering* as a generic term for adding Arabic or Roman numerals, letters in alphabetical order, or any combination of these.

A difference between Word's line-numbering and paragraph-numbering features is that paragraph numbering is not an all-or-nothing proposition that you turn on for the entire document and then have to make specific exceptions for. Rather, you select just those paragraphs that you want numbered and then give the command to number them. Another difference is that you can see the results of paragraph numbering in all views, not just in Page Layout view, in Print Preview, and on the printed page.

There are two ways to number paragraphs in a document. You can number each one in sequence, as in a list, or you can number them according to different levels, as in an outline. Word can easily manage either choice and will automatically update numbers as you add, move, or delete paragraphs. We'll start with numbering in sequence.

## How to number paragraphs in sequence

Certain kinds of documents—particularly certain kinds of legal documents—typically number individual paragraphs. But most people are most likely to use Word's paragraph-numbering feature for lists. In either case, you can add the numbering before or after you've created the text. If you're just starting the first paragraph you want numbered, simply press Return to create the paragraph, and with the cursor in the new paragraph, choose Format Bullets And Numbering. Then choose Numbered to go to the Numbered card, shown in Figure 13-8 on the next page. If you've already created the text (in one or more paragraphs), highlight it first and then give the command.

The Numbered card contains six thumbnail sketches of predefined numbering formats. To use one, simply click on the one you want and choose OK. The Hanging Indent check box in the lower right corner lets you format the paragraphs so that all lines after the first line in each paragraph are indented, with the numbers in a column to the left of the text.

To create your own format for numbering, first choose the predefined format that's closest to what you want, and then choose the Modify button to open the Modify Numbered List dialog box, shown in Figure 13-9 on the next page.

The Numbered card in the Bullets And Numbering dialog box offers settings for numbering paragraphs.

The Modify Numbered List dialog box lets you define the format for numbering.

The Modify Numbered List dialog box contains two group boxes and a Preview box that shows the effects of your choices. The Number Format group box has three text boxes, a pull-down list, and a button. The Text Before and Text After boxes let you specify text and punctuation to use with each number (with a limit of 32 characters in the Text Before and Text After boxes combined).

The Number box has a pull-down list that shows the available choices for format. You can number your paragraphs using any of these (or none if you prefer):

| | |
|---|---|
| 1, 2, 3, 4 | a, b, c, d |
| I, II, III, IV | 1st, 2nd, 3rd, 4th |
| i, ii, iii, iv | One, Two, Three, Four |
| A, B, C, D | First, Second, Third, Fourth |

The Start At box tells Word the starting number to use in its count. As with line numbering, the maximum value you can start with for a number format is 32,767, but Word will continue numbering paragraphs with values higher than that if you are using Arabic numerals or a numbering format based on spelled-out numbers. If you are using Roman numerals, the highest number you can start with is MMMCMXCIX (3999), but the numbering will stop there and the next paragraph will be numbered I. For letters, the highest starting number is 780 (30 Zs in a row), and the next paragraph will be marked with an *A*.

The Font button opens the Font dialog box, where you can specify font formatting for the numbers. We covered the Font dialog box in "The Font dialog box" starting on page 228.

The choices in the Number Position group box control the placement of the numbers. The first choice, Alignment Of List Text, lets you align the numbering as Left, Right, or Centered in the space between the first-line indent and the left indent for the text in the first line of the paragraph. The Distance From Indent To Text setting lets you control the amount of that indent, while Distance From Number To Text lets you further control spacing between the numbering and the text. The Hanging Indent check box lets you specify that the rest of the paragraph be indented by the same amount as the text in the first line, so the numbers are to the left of the text, with all text starting at the same indent.

Figure 13-10 shows our sample document after we created a numbered list using default settings. Notice how the hanging indents place the numbers to the left of the text.

**FIGURE 13-10**

This document was numbered using the Format Bullets And Numbering command.

You can also number paragraphs by placing the cursor or selection in the paragraph or paragraphs you want to number and then clicking on the Numbering button on the Formatting toolbar—the fifth button from the right. When you use the Numbering button, Word will generally use the current default numbering format, meaning the current settings for numbering. If the paragraph immediately before or after the selection is already formatted as numbered, however, Word will use the same formatting as the already numbered paragraph.

Note too that if you select a single blank paragraph and choose the Numbering command, Word will add a number. If you select more than one paragraph, however, Word will indent, but not add numbers to, any blank paragraphs. Rather, Word will assume that you want a single, continuous numbering system throughout the selection and that you also want to skip the blank lines.

## How to remove numbering

Word will automatically add numbering to paragraphs that you create by pressing Return while the cursor is in a numbered paragraph. When you finish entering the last paragraph in a list and you press Return to start a new paragraph that you don't want numbered, you'll need to remove the numbering from the new paragraph. To remove numbering from one or more paragraphs at the beginning or end of a sequence, place the cursor or selection in the appropriate paragraph or paragraphs, and then either choose Format Bullets And Numbering and choose the Remove button from any of the cards in the dialog box or click on the Numbering button on the Formatting toolbar. Be aware, however, that the Numbering button will sometimes produce unexpected results if you have selected more than one blank paragraph.

Another way to skip a paragraph but keep the numbering sequence intact is to place the cursor or selection in the paragraph or paragraphs you want to skip, and with the mouse pointer on line with any of the paragraphs in the sequence, hold the Control key down and click the mouse button to bring up a context-sensitive pop-up menu. Choose Skip Numbering to remove the numbering from the selected paragraph or paragraphs while continuing the numbering sequence with the next paragraph. The pop-up menu also offers two other items related to numbering: Stop Numbering and Bullets And Numbering. Stop Numbering removes numbering from the paragraph or paragraphs the cursor or selection is in and restarts the numbering sequence in the next paragraph. The Bullets And Numbering choice opens the Bullets And Numbering dialog box. These three choices will not be available if the selection includes a paragraph formatted with a Heading style.

There may also be times when you want to remove numbering from paragraphs that are in the middle of a group of numbered paragraphs. To remove numbering, select the appropriate paragraph or paragraphs, and either choose Format Bullets And Numbering and then choose the Remove button or click on the Numbering button on the Formatting toolbar.

Be aware that there is an important difference between these two choices. If you use the Format Bullets And Numbering command, you'll find that Word will break the list in two, so that the numbering starts over again when it picks up after newly unnumbered paragraphs. If you want to maintain a single sequence, use the Numbering button on the Formatting toolbar; Word will change the remaining numbers to maintain a single sequence and will indent the unnumbered paragraph or paragraphs to match the rest of the paragraphs.

## Bullets

In addition to the Numbered card in the Bullets And Numbering dialog box, there is also a Bulleted card, which works much the same way. A bullet is a symbol—typically a dot—that marks each item in a list that might otherwise be numbered. Almost any symbol can be a bullet, including a square, a diamond, or a box. And lists that use bullets are generally called bulleted lists. The Bulleted card is shown in Figure 13-11.

**FIGURE 13-11**

The Bulleted card in the Bullets And Numbering dialog box lets you add bullets to a list of paragraphs.

As with the Numbered card, you can either choose from the six thumbnail sketches of predefined bulleted formats, or define your own format. To define a format, choose the Modify button to open the Modify Bulleted List dialog box, shown in Figure 13-12 on the next page.

**FIGURE 13-12**

The Modify Bulleted
List dialog box lets you
define a format for
bulleted lists.

The dialog box offers six predefined bullet characters, as well as Point Size and Color boxes that let you modify the character you choose. In addition, you can choose the Bullet button to open the Symbol dialog box and choose any character you want. This is the same dialog box you'll see if you choose Insert Symbol. We covered it in "The Insert Symbol command" on page 144.

The options in the Bullet Position group box are essentially identical to the equivalent options for numbers in the Modify Numbered List dialog box, and they work the same way.

In fact, almost all of the bullet-related features work much the same way as the equivalent features for numbering paragraphs. You can, for example, use the Bullets button on the Formatting toolbar to add or remove bullets from paragraphs. As with the Numbering button, the feature will generally indent, but not add bullets to, blank paragraphs when you have more than one paragraph selected. You can even hold the Control key down and click the mouse button to bring up the same context-sensitive menu for bulleted paragraphs as for numbered paragraphs. The bullet and number features are so closely related, in fact, that the choices on the menu still say Skip Numbering and Stop Numbering. Choose Skip Numbering to remove a bullet but keep the indent. Choose Stop Numbering to remove both a bullet and the indent.

Figure 13-13 shows our sample text with bullets added to the second and third paragraphs after the second heading. To get this result, we selected both paragraphs and used the default bullet settings in the Format Bullets And Numbering dialog box.

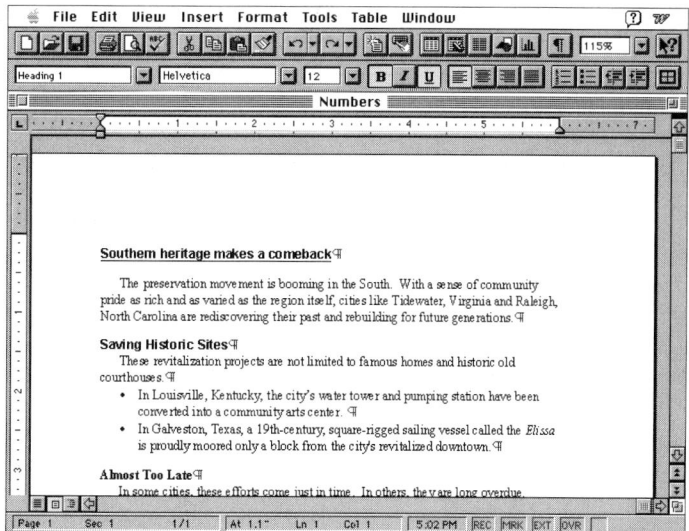

**FIGURE 13-13**

Word's bullet feature helps you set off lists from the rest of your text, making them easier to read.

## Multilevel numbered paragraphs: Classic outlines

You can think of Word's multilevel numbered paragraphs as a tool for producing classic outlines—the kind you probably learned in high school—with each paragraph numbered appropriately, depending on how it's indented. Don't confuse this feature with Word's View Outline feature, which is a collapsible outliner for working with documents in outline form. (We'll cover the collapsible outline feature in Chapter 19.) The multilevel-numbering feature is a tool for producing an outline format in which the outline itself is the final product. For purposes of this discussion, we'll call this an *outline list* or a *multilevel list*, to distinguish it from Word's collapsible outliner.

To create an outline, or multilevel, list, start by placing the cursor or selection in the paragraph where you want numbering to start or in the paragraphs you want to add numbering to. Then choose Format Bullets And Numbering and choose the Multilevel card, as shown in Figure 13-14.

**FIGURE 13-14**

The Multilevel card in the Bullets And Numbering dialog box gives you control over paragraph numbering in outlines.

As with the other two cards in this dialog box, the Multilevel card offers six thumbnail sketches of predefined formats. Since the predefined formats rely on hanging indents, there is no check box for hanging indents on the card. The Modify button takes you to the Modify Multilevel List dialog box. This is nearly identical to the Modify Numbered List dialog box, but with three notable exceptions.

First, because multilevel numbering offers nine levels and because you can format each level separately, you'll find a scrollable Level box that lets you choose which level to format. Second, instead of a Number box, you'll find a Bullet Or Number pull-down list. The options in the list let you pick a predefined number format, *or* pick a predefined bullet, *or* choose New Bullet to open the Symbol dialog box and pick any symbol you like for the bullet—as we've just described for the Modify Bulleted List box.

Third, the Modify Multilevel List dialog box adds the Include From Previous Level option. This lets you define the current level to include the numbers, the numbers and position, or nothing from the previous (next highest) level. Choose the Numbers option if you want the number format to include the full numbering scheme, as in *1.2.2.* Choose Numbers And Position if you want each number in the sequence to be under the corresponding number from the previous, higher level (as shown in the list at the right in Figure 13-15). Note that the Preview box shows the current settings for all nine levels. Figure 13-15 shows a document with three short outline lists, showing the effect of each choice available in the Previous Level box.

**FIGURE 13-15**

These three outline lists show the effect of each of the three choices in the Previous Level box.

When you're satisfied with the numbering format definition, choose OK to close the Modify Multilevel List box. As with the other numbered paragraph options, Word will not number any paragraphs that lack text.

You can use the Increase Indent and Decrease Indent buttons on the Formatting toolbar to promote or demote paragraphs to different levels, or you can use the Option-Shift-Right arrow and Option-Shift-Left arrow shortcut keys, or the Promote and Demote commands on the pop-up menu. In all cases, Word will automatically renumber the paragraphs and change the indents appropriately. To produce the outline list shown in Figure 13-15, for example, we entered some paragraphs, applied multilevel numbering, added more paragraphs, and either demoted or promoted each paragraph to its appropriate level as we worked with them.

As with the other approaches to numbering paragraphs, you can use the Control key and mouse button to call up a pop-up menu to either skip or stop numbering.

# Numbering Headings

NEW!

There is an alternative for producing outlines that's related to the collapsible outline feature. You'll generally find it the more efficient approach when you want an outline of the entire document and you want to include unnumbered text paragraphs within the outline. This second approach takes advantage of heading styles.

As we discussed in Chapter 12, Word comes with a variety of built-in style definitions, including nine levels of heading styles, named Heading 1, Heading 2, Heading 3, and so on. If you've defined paragraphs with these styles, you can tell Word to number them automatically. If you use this feature, Word will number only those paragraphs that use heading styles 1 through 9, in contrast to multilevel numbering, which creates an outline list that numbers all paragraphs that include text.

The feature is called *heading numbering*, and it's an all-or-nothing proposition—you turn it on or off for the entire document. Figure 13-16 on the next page shows our sample document with heading numbering turned on. The style area in the figure shows the style for each paragraph.

To turn on heading numbering and define the format to use, choose Format Heading Numbering to open the Heading Numbering dialog box, shown in Figure 13-17 on the next page.

This sample document shows the effect of the Format Heading Numbering command. Note that Word numbers only those paragraphs that are formatted with a heading style.

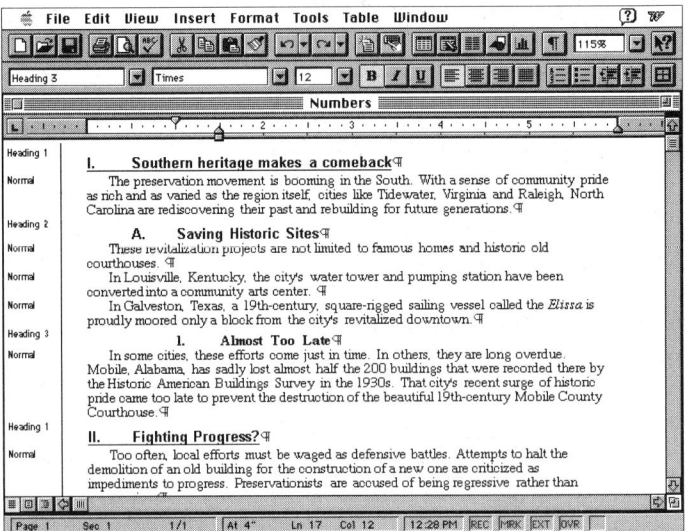

The Heading Number-ing dialog box is similar to the Multi-level card in the Bullets And Numbering dialog box.

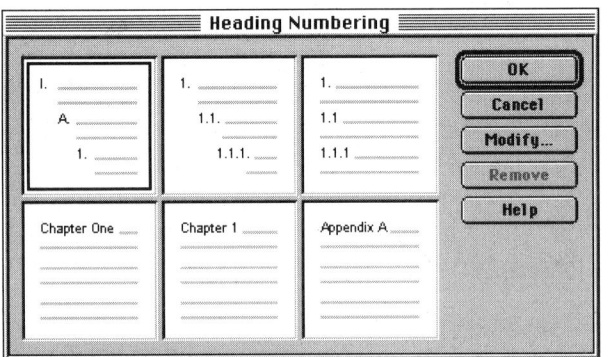

This dialog box is similar to the Multilevel card, described in the section just before this, and it works the same way. You can choose one of the six thumbnail sketches of predefined formats, or you can choose the Modify but-ton to define your own. The Modify Heading Numbering dialog box is nearly identical to the equivalent dialog box for multilevel numbering, except that it also has a check box labeled Restart Numbering At Each New Section. This check box lets you start each chapter in a document as a separate section and have Word automatically number the chapter for you.

# Multisection Documents

In all our discussions of formatting up to this point, we've treated each document as a single large chunk of text consisting only of paragraphs, words, and characters. As we've mentioned several times, however, there is another level of organization: the section. And by taking advantage of sections, you can open up a whole new range of formatting options.

For example, we mentioned section headers and footers when we discussed headers and footers. You might use these when you have a long document broken into separate chapters that you want to keep in one file. Define each chapter as a section, and you can create a different header and footer for each.

Sections have a place in shorter documents as well. For example, if you want to vary the number of columns, you'll need to create sections. We'll discuss how to use columns in "Multicolumn Formatting" starting on page 469.

In fact, you will need to use multiple sections whenever you want to change any of the following in your document:

- Margins
- Paper size or orientation
- Paper source
- Line numbering
- Contents and position of headers or footers
- Number of text columns
- Page numbering
- Numbering and formatting of footnotes or endnotes

When you create a new section, it inherits the formatting for all these features from the section you created the new section from. This means that if you split up a document into sections, they will all start out with the same settings. You can then make formatting changes to the individual sections without affecting the whole document. If you want to change a format for one section only—to switch the page orientation for a single page, for example—you can save some steps by creating two new sections (so you have a total of three) and then moving to the first new section to make your changes. When you go to the second new section, it will still have the original format.

# How to divide a document into sections

Every new Word document initially consists of one section. If you want to create a new section, place the cursor where you want the section to begin, and choose Insert Break to open the Break dialog box, as shown in Figure 13-18. As you can see, the dialog box includes option buttons for Page Break and Column Break, plus four options in the Section Breaks box labeled Next Page, Continuous, Even Page, and Odd Page. For the moment, we're concerned only with the four section break options.

**FIGURE 13-18**

The Break dialog box lets you insert four kinds of section breaks into your document.

| Break |
| --- |
| **Insert** |
| ● Page Break    ○ Column Break |
| **Section Breaks** |
| ○ Next Page    ○ Even Page |
| ○ Continuous    ○ Odd Page |
| OK |
| Cancel |
| Help |

Any of the options in the Section Breaks box will insert a section break, but they differ in how Word will treat that section break.

If you choose the Continuous option, Word will start the new section without starting a new page. This is especially useful when you want to mix different column layouts on a single page.

If you choose the Next Page option, Word will immediately begin a new page and a new section. The first paragraph in the new section will be printed at the top of a new page, which means that part of the previous page may be left blank.

If you choose the Even Page or Odd Page option, Word will not only start the new section at the top of a new page, but will make sure that the page is even numbered (left) or odd numbered (right), as appropriate. If necessary, Word will insert a blank page to force the new section to start on the even-numbered or odd-numbered page.

You might want to use the Even Page or Odd Page choice in a long report that you plan to hand out in a binder. In books, for example, it's a common practice to begin each chapter on an odd-numbered page. Similarly, if your report contains charts and descriptions, you might want to ensure that all the charts appear on even pages and their descriptions appear on odd pages.

After you specify the kind of section break you want, choose OK to close the dialog box. If you are in Normal view or Outline view, Word will mark the section break on your screen with a horizontal line and the label *End of Section*, as shown in Figure 13-19. The markers will not show in Print Preview mode or on a printed document. They will show in Page Layout view, but not on their own line and only if Word is set to show all nonprinting characters on the Tools Options View card, or with the Show/Hide ¶ Toolbar button.

**FIGURE 13-19**

Word marks section breaks on your screen with a horizontal line.

After you divide a document into two or more sections, Word will use the Sec indicator in the status bar to indicate the section the cursor is currently in. For example, notice that the status bar in Figure 13-19 shows *Page 2 Sec 2*. This tells you that the cursor is on page number 2 in the second section of the document.

Note that this page is not necessarily the second page in the document. If you are using continuous numbering, it will be, but if you've used the Insert Page Numbers Format Start At option to number each section separately starting with page 1, the second page in section 2 will be page number 2, no matter how many pages are in section 1. To see the difference, look to the right of the Sec indicator. In Figure 13-19, you'll see *7/8*, which means you're on the seventh page of an 8-page document, with 5 pages in section 1 and with page 1 of section 2 starting on the sixth page.

## The Document Layout dialog box

Many of the options for section-level formatting are available in the Document Layout dialog box, which we touched on briefly at the start of this chapter and which is shown in Figure 13-20 on the next page. To open this dialog box, choose File Document Layout.

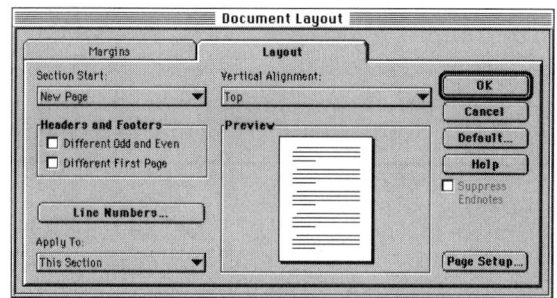

**FIGURE 13-20**

The Document Layout dialog box lets you vary certain characteristics from section to section.

The cards in this dialog box let you specify settings for margins and layout. We have already covered most of these settings elsewhere in this book.

At the bottom of each card in the Document Layout dialog box, you'll see an Apply To box with a pull-down list. If you haven't selected any text before opening the dialog box, the choices in this list will always include This Point Forward and Whole Document. If the document includes at least two sections, you'll also see This Section. Whole Document and This Section are self-explanatory. Less obvious is that if you choose This Point Forward, Word will insert a section break and apply whatever format change you've just defined to the new section only.

If you selected some text before opening the Document Layout dialog box, Word will add the choice Selected Sections if the selection includes more than one section and both Selected Sections and Selected Text if the selection is limited to part of one section. Here again, the Selected Sections choice is self-explanatory. If you choose Selected Text, Word will insert section breaks before and after that text to make it a separate section.

## How to change the type of section break

There are a few additional options on the Layout card that deserve mention here.

The Section Start pull-down list lets you change the type of section break without having to delete the current section break and insert another. Figure 13-21 shows the options available in the list. Four of these match the options available in the Break dialog box when you insert a section break. The fifth, New Column, tells Word to start the new section at the start of a new column and applies only to multicolumn formats.

**FIGURE 13-21**

Word offers five Section Start options in the Document Layout dialog box.

If you need to change the type of section break, keep in mind that the change will apply to the section the cursor or selection is currently in. For example, if you originally inserted a section break that starts section 2 on a new page and you want to change the break to Continuous, position the cursor in section 2 before choosing Format Section Layout.

## How to set vertical alignment

The Vertical Alignment option on the Layout card lets you tell Word how to position text between the page's top and bottom margins. Figure 13-22 on the next page shows how each of the Vertical Alignment options affects a sample printed page.

By default, Word uses the Top option, which tells Word to place the first line on each page just below the top margin. If there are not enough lines of text to fill the entire text area between the top and bottom margins, Word leaves all the blank space at the bottom of the page.

The Center option spaces the text evenly between the top and bottom margins. If there are not enough lines to fill a page—either because it's the last page of a section or because of a manual page break—Word will center the text vertically on the page. This option is handy for creating a title page.

The Justified option tells Word to insert an equal amount of space between the paragraphs on each page. (This option does not affect the spacing between the lines within each paragraph.) As with the Center option, this makes a difference only when there aren't enough lines to fill the page. The amount of space inserted between paragraphs depends on how much extra space there is on the page. If two pages have 20 lines of text, but one page has only two paragraphs of 10 lines each and the other has five paragraphs of 4 lines each, the spacing between paragraphs on the two pages will be very different.

Be aware that you can't see the effects of the Vertical Alignment options except in Page Layout view, in Print Preview, or on a printed page. Also, the Preview box on the Layout card looks the same no matter which setting you choose because the preview assumes an entire page of text.

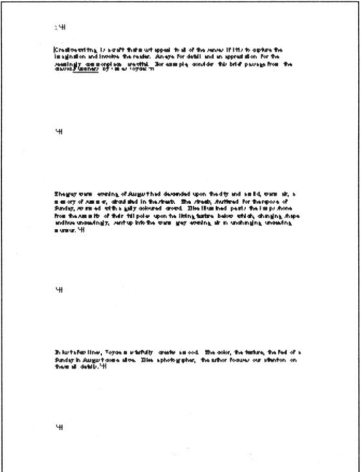

**FIGURE 13-22**

The Vertical Alignment options (Top, Center, and Justified) in the Page Setup dialog box let you control the vertical position of the text on a page.

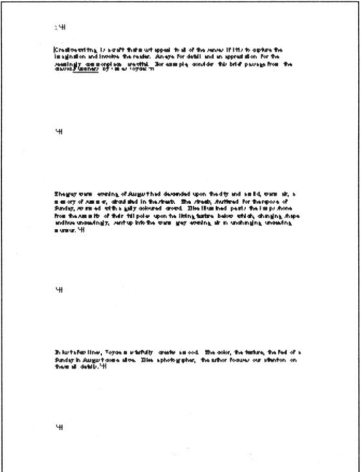

## NEW!   How to change paper size and orientation from one section to another

If you choose File Page Setup, Word will open a dialog box, similar to the one shown in Figure 13-23, for setting paper size and orientation. We covered most of the features in this dialog box in "Document Formatting" on page 193. For the moment we are interested only in the Apply Size And Orientation To pull-down list in the lower left corner of the dialog box.

**FIGURE 13-23**

You can make changes
to the page size and
orientation for indi-
vidual sections within
a document.

This list offers the same choices as the Apply To list in the Document Layout dialog box. More important, it works the same way for defining paper
size and orientation settings for different sections of your document. This
ability to change size and orientation can come in handy. A typical use is for a
chart or other graphic that you want to print in landscape orientation within a
document that's otherwise designed for portrait orientation. Simply add section breaks before and after the chart with each break defined as starting a
new page. Then define the one page with landscape orientation.

## How to change page numbering from one section to another

In Chapter 5, we explained how to number pages by inserting a page number
in a header or footer or by using the Insert Page Numbers command. We also
introduced the five numbering formats for pages and explained how to position page numbers in the header. As we mentioned, you can optionally restart
numbering with each new section. You can also use different numbering
schemes and entirely different headers and footers in each section.

For this discussion, we'll assume that you already have a header or footer
in your document and that you need to change the page numbering for one or
more sections. Because the commands for headers and footers are essentially
identical, we'll follow the same convention we used in Chapter 5 and talk primarily about headers. Except where explicitly stated otherwise, however,
these comments apply to both headers and footers.

Whether you have numbered your pages by using Insert Page Numbers
or by inserting a field in a header or footer, you can change the numbering by
choosing Insert Page Numbers and then choosing the Format button to open
the Page Number Format dialog box, shown in Figure 13-24 on the next page.

Changing the numbering for pages is straightforward in the extreme. First be certain that the cursor or selection is in the section that you want to change. Keep in mind that it may be in some other part of the document than is currently showing on your screen; use the position information in the status bar to check the current section. If the selection crosses section boundaries, the status bar will show the position for the end of the selection, but the changes will affect all sections the selection is in.

**FIGURE 13-24**

Word's Page Number Format dialog box lets you control page numbering section by section.

Page Number Format

| | | |
|---|---|---|
| Number Format: | 1, 2, 3, ... ▼ | OK |
| ☐ Include Chapter Number | | Cancel |
| Chapter Starts with Style | Heading 1 ▼ | Help |
| Use Separator: | - (hyphen) ▼ | |
| Examples: 1-1, 1-A | | |

Page Numbering
○ Continue from Previous Section
● Start At:     1    ⬍

## How to number sections separately

The Number Format box in the Page Number Format dialog box lists five numbering systems.

The Page Numbering box has two option buttons that let you determine the starting value for the section's page numbering. The Continue From Previous Section option does just what it says: It takes whatever number was used last by the previous section and uses the next consecutive number as its starting point. This is Word's default setting.

If you choose the Start At option, you can then specify what to use as the section's first number or letter. Word uses the existing number format unless you tell it otherwise. If you enter *1* here, Word will use *A, a, I,* or *i,* depending on the format. However, you can also enter the starting number in the appropriate format—letters or Roman numerals. You can specify any number from 0 through 32,767 as the Start At value for the *1, 2, 3...* format, 1 through 780 for the letter formats, or 1 through 3999 for the Roman numeral formats. But if you're restarting numbering for a new section, you'll typically want to restart with 1.

After you make your changes, choose OK to close the Page Number Format dialog box, and OK again to close the Page Numbers dialog box and return to your document. Word will show the numbering change and the number format change in both the status bar and in the header or footer page numbers.

The ability to use different number formats and to restart the numbering is particularly useful for long documents with a preface or an introduction that you want to number differently from the main portion of the text. One common numbering scheme is to make the front matter one section and to number it using the lowercase Roman numerals: i, ii, iii, iv, and so on. The rest of the text would be a second section, using Arabic numerals: 1, 2, 3, 4, and so on. You would assign the format separately to each section and start the numbering over at page 1 for the first page of the first chapter.

## Section headers and footers

In Chapter 5, we showed how to create, position, and format headers and footers and how to create a special header or footer for the first page of a document. As we've already suggested, these settings are also tied to sections, so you can vary the headers and footers from one section to another. The most likely situation for using this feature is when your section breaks correspond to major document divisions, such as chapters. You can, for example, vary the headers to include the chapter number or title for each section. But note too that you can change headers and footers at any point, if you like, by adding a section break. For the rest of this discussion, we'll give examples using headers only, but be aware that all of these comments apply to footers as well.

It's important to understand how Word handles headers for a multisection document. If you simply create a header anywhere in a document, the header will show up in all sections of the document. This holds true whether you created the header before or after you inserted the section breaks and regardless of which section you were in when you created the header. If you then change the header while in any section in the document, the change will carry over to all the other headers unless you specifically break the link between headers in different sections. For example, if you change the header in section 2 of a three-section document, you'll see the change in sections 1 and 3 as well unless you break the link first, as we'll describe in the section after this one.

To vary the text or format of the header for a particular section, first make sure that the cursor or selection is in the section that you want to change. Then choose View Header And Footer, or, if you're in Page Layout view or Print Preview, double-click on the header you want to change. Word will show you the header, which will look much like the sample in Figure 13-25.

**FIGURE 13-25**

The top of the header area shows the section number for that header.

## How to break or reestablish a link between section headers or footers

As you can see in Figure 13-25, Word adds two pieces of identification at the top of the header. One, on the left side, identifies the particular header you're working with, in this case labeled *Header Section 3*. The other, *Same As Previous*, on the right side, identifies this header as being the same as the header in the previous section. As long as the headers from two or more sections are linked so that each one after the first shows this *Same As Previous* message, any changes you make to any header in the linked group will apply to all the headers in that group.

Note that the fourth button on the Header toolbar, which is also shown in Figure 13-25, is named Same As Previous. You can choose this button to break the link between the header in the current section and the previous one or to reestablish it later. When the header of the current section is already linked to the previous section, this button will appear to be depressed. (The button will never appear depressed for the first section in a document, because the first section of a document has no previous section.)

When you choose the Same As Previous button to reestablish a link, Word will ask for confirmation. Choose Yes, and not only will Word change the header to match the previous section, but the change will cascade forward to any headers in later sections that are linked to the current section.

 Word does not ship with a shortcut key to let you break or reestablish links from the keyboard. However, you can easily add one, using the techniques we'll describe in Chapter 28, "Custom Menus, Keys, and Templates." The one additional piece of information you'll need is the name of the command to attach the shortcut key to, since it's less than obvious. The command is ToggleHeaderFooterLink.

### The Different First Page option

In Chapter 5, we explained how to use the Different First Page option on the Layout card in the Document Layout dialog box. Briefly, the option lets you create a separate header for the first page of a document or effectively eliminate the header from the first page by creating a blank header. This same option lets you create separate headers for the first page of each section. (Keep in mind that, here again, all comments about headers also apply to footers.)

Unless told otherwise, Word will link the first-page header of any given section to the first-page header of the section before. If you want the first-page header in a particular section to be different from the first-page header of the section before, place your cursor in the appropriate section, choose File Document Layout, choose Layout, and be sure the Different First Page check box is checked. Then return to the document, choose View Header And Footer or double-click on the header if you're in Page Layout view, and choose the Same As Previous toolbar button to break the link to the previous header. Finally, make whatever changes you like to the header.

## How to combine two document sections

If you want to combine two adjacent document sections, simply delete the section-break marker between them by selecting the marker, or moving the cursor to it, and pressing the Del key. If the two sections have different settings, the new, merged section will retain the settings from the second section. (This is similar to what happens when you merge two paragraphs by deleting the paragraph mark at the end of the first one. The merged paragraph will retain the format of the second paragraph, whose paragraph mark—with its associated formatting information—wasn't deleted.)

> If you want to merge two sections but use the settings for the first section, cut the section marker to the Clipboard. Then move the cursor to the end of the second section, insert the first marker before the second one, and delete the second marker.

We're not quite finished with sections, but to discuss them further, we need to look at them in the context of other features. Until now, we have dealt mostly with text that flows smoothly from the top of a page to the bottom and then to the top of the next page. At times, you'll want to create more complex documents, with multiple columns, pictures, graphs, or other items that make the final product more visually interesting. Some of these items work hand in glove with sections—occasionally, at least. In the next chapter, we'll look at how to add these other elements to your document and how to use them with sections when appropriate.

# TOPIC FINDER

# 14

## Columns, Frames, & Pictures

s we've already pointed out, although Word for the Macintosh is not a desktop publishing program, it will let you produce highly sophisticated layouts with ease. You can easily create and control multicolumn layouts, and you can position charts, drawings, tables, and other images in your documents. Word will even let you insert information from other Windows-based applications easily. In this chapter and the next, we'll look at all of these features, starting with multicolumn formats.

## Multicolumn Formatting

Almost every one of our sample documents to this point has been formatted as a single stream of text, flowing from the top of one page to the bottom and then continuing at the top of the next page. The only notable exceptions were in Chapter 11, where we covered tables. Tables format text in columns, but even tables are based on the concept that the text area goes from the left margin of the page all the way across to the right margin, and from top to bottom.

There may be times when you'll want to format a page into narrower columns that flow from the bottom of one column to the top of the next, as in a newspaper. This layout is often called *snaking columns, newspaper-style columns,* or simply *columns.* All these terms are interchangeable. For our purposes, we will usually refer to some variation of columns, text columns, or multiple columns. The Standard toolbar button that goes with the feature is called the Columns button.

## Why use multiple columns?

Before microcomputers and laser printers, the vast majority of American business documents were produced on typewriters, using monospaced fonts. (Monospaced fonts use the same amount of horizontal space for each character, as opposed to proportional fonts, which use more horizontal space for wide characters such as *m* and *w* than for narrow characters such as *i* and *l*.) Most often the font was Courier at 10 characters to the inch, also called *10-pitch* or *Pica spacing*. To squeeze more information on a page, some people used a Prestige font at 12-pitch, or Elite spacing, but most people feel that with letter-size paper, 12-pitch text with 1-inch margins is harder to read than 10-pitch text.

There is a typographical rule of thumb that explains why most people prefer 10-pitch over 12-pitch for letter-size documents. In general, the most readable formats contain one and a half to two alphabets' worth of characters—39 to 52 characters—per line. One-inch margins on a letter-size page yield 65 characters per line for Pica spacing or 78 characters for Elite spacing. A line that contains 65 characters is a bit longer than ideal but still acceptable. A 78-character line is long enough to make it hard to read.

When the laser printer and proportional fonts such as Times Roman arrived on the scene, computer users began to move away from typewriter-style monospaced fonts. Proportional fonts allow more characters on a line. This is both good news and bad. The good news is that you can get more text on a page; the bad news is that more characters per line make the pages more difficult to read.

This is where multiple columns come in. If you take the text within the 1-inch margins, carve it into thinner vertical strips, and put some space between the strips, you end up with almost the same amount of text per page but with shorter lines, which are much easier to read. This isn't enough reason to format a business letter with an unconventional two or three columns, but it's a strong argument for formatting other kinds of documents that way—a newsletter for clients, for example.

## How to add column formatting with the Columns button

You can quickly transform any document into a multiple-column format. Word allows one column definition per section, which is another way of saying that columns are a section-level formatting feature. If you want to apply the format to just the current section or selected sections, the easiest way is with the Columns button on the Standard toolbar.

When you click on this button and hold the mouse button down, Word will show you a thumbnail sketch of a multiple-column format, with four columns, as in Figure 14-1. You can then drag the mouse pointer across these columns, left to right. Word will highlight the columns and use the area below the columns to report the number of columns it will create. If you need more than four, continue dragging to the right. The thumbnail sketch will expand, to a maximum of six columns.

If you highlight two of the four columns, as in Figure 14-1, and then release the mouse button, Word will reformat the document as in Figure 14-2 on the next page (which is set to Normal view). Note that when you create multiple columns using the Columns button, Word will use its current settings for the amount of space between the columns and for whether it will add a line between the columns. (We will cover both of these shortly.)

**FIGURE 14-1**

The Columns button on the Standard toolbar lets you quickly create columns.

**FIGURE 14-2**

In Normal view, multiple columns appear as a single column on screen. The ruler shows the column width and tab settings.

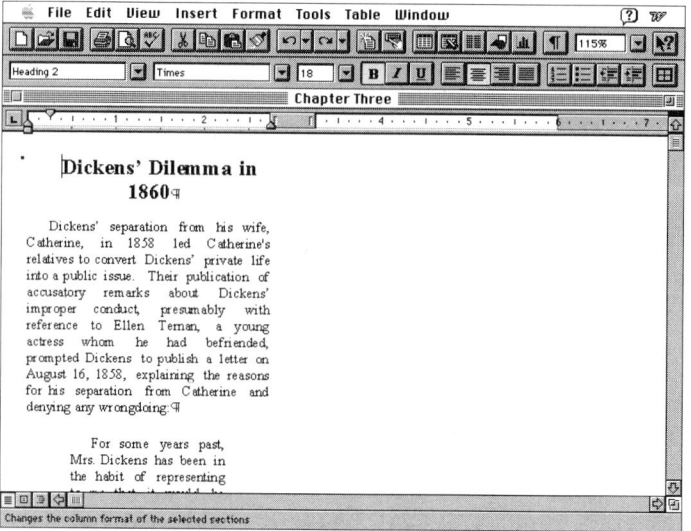

Since Figure 14-2 shows the document in Normal view, it shows only one column on the screen. Note that the ruler shows the new column width and tab settings and also indicates a second column on the right side, even though it doesn't show any text there. To see the columns on screen as they will print, choose View Page Layout to switch to Page Layout view, shown in Figure 14-3.

**FIGURE 14-3**

In Page Layout view, multiple columns show side by side, as they will look on the printed page.

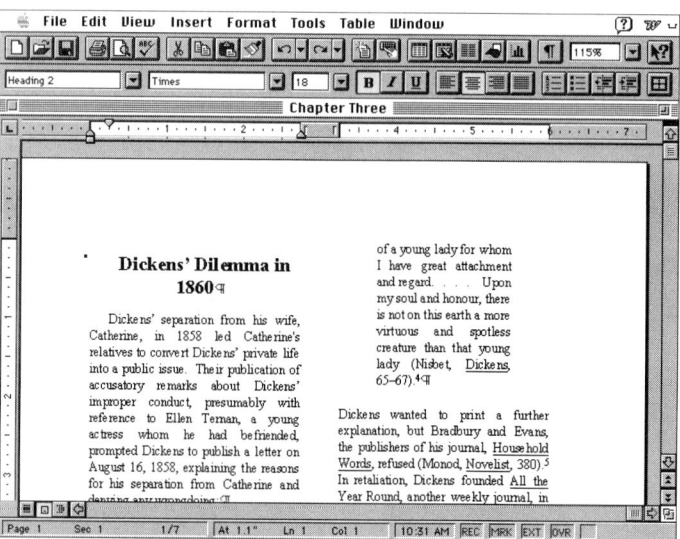

In Page Layout view, you can see how Word automatically formats the document so that a predefined amount of space appears between the two text columns. Note that the headline on the page in Figure 14-3 is formatted to fit into one column rather than spread across the entire width of the page. Word will let you change both the amount of space between columns and the format for the headline, as we'll discuss shortly.

To use the Columns button to add columns to only a portion of your text, select the text before clicking on the button. Word will then add section breaks before and after the selection and will apply the column formatting to the selection only.

## How to remove column formatting with the Columns button

If you want to remove column formatting immediately after adding it, you can use the Edit Undo command. You can also revise the number of columns for the current section at any time with the Columns button. To return to a single column of text, simply click on the Columns button and then drag to the leftmost column in the thumbnail sketch.

## How to control column formatting with the Format Columns command

You can also create columns, but with more control over the format, by using the Format Columns menu command instead of the toolbar button. Choose Format Columns to open the Columns dialog box, shown in Figure 14-4.

**FIGURE 14-4**

The Columns dialog box lets you control the formatting of text columns.

| Columns |
|---|
| **Presets** |
| One  Two  Three  Left  Right |
| OK |
| Cancel |
| Help |
| Number of Columns: 2 |
| □ Line Between |
| **Width and Spacing** |
| Col #: Width: Spacing: |
| 1: 2.75"  0.5" |
| 2: 2.75" |
| ☒ Equal Column Width |
| **Preview** |
| Apply To: Whole Document |
| □ Start New Column |

As with most of Word's formatting dialog boxes, the Columns box includes a Preview box with a thumbnail sketch of how the page will look. As you make changes to the settings, the sketch in this box will change to reflect your choices.

**NEW!** Word provides five predefined column formats in the Presets group box. You can choose a one-column, two-column, or three-column format with equal column widths, or two columns of unequal widths with the thinner column to the left or to the right.

The Number Of Columns text box accepts whole numbers starting with 1, but the upper limit depends on the paper size, orientation, and margin settings defined in the dialog boxes available through the File Document Layout and File Page Setup menu commands. Word insists on a minimum 0.5 inch per column, so on an 8.5-by-11-inch page in portrait orientation, with 1.25-inch margins, you can have up to 12 columns. The maximum number of columns is 44, which requires a 22-inch-wide page with no margins. In any case, the number of columns available is greater than you're likely to need.

If you check the Line Between check box, Word will print a vertical line centered between the columns. The line will be as long as the longest column to either side. Note that you won't see these lines on the screen unless you choose Page Layout view or Print Preview mode.

**NEW!** The Width And Spacing group box lets you define the width of each column and the space between columns. As you can see in Figure 14-4, the group box has three sets of text boxes for width and spacing. If you've set the number of columns to more than three, Word will add a scroll bar at the left of the group box so you can scroll to see the settings for the other columns. If you want all the columns the same width, check the Equal Column Width check box. Word will then gray out everything in the Col #, Width, and Spacing columns except the first row. The logic here is that all columns will have the same settings, so you need to define the width and spacing only once. If you don't check the Equal Column Width box, you can define different widths and spacing for each column.

**NEW!** When you change almost any setting in the Columns dialog box, Word will automatically adjust other settings to match. If you choose Two in the Presets box, for example, Word will check the Equal Column Width box and, assuming default page size and margins, set Width to 2.75 inches. If you change the settings in the Number Of Columns box to 3, Word will change the Presets setting to Three and set the column widths to 1.67 inches. In short, Word tries hard to make sure that everything will fit properly on the page, but its automatic changes may not match what you want—particularly if you accidentally made the wrong choice somewhere along the line. So be sure to double-check the settings when you've finished.

To minimize the number of iterations you have to go through when adjusting settings for unequal columns, start with the first column width, adjust spacing, go on to the second column width, and so on. Word makes its automatic changes to the subsequent column width settings in each case—unless you change the last column's width setting, at which point Word will make equal changes to all previous Spacing settings.

## Columns and sections

The Apply To list box determines what part of your document Word will apply the column specification to. If you didn't have any text selected when you chose Format Columns, this list will offer a minimum of two choices: Whole Document and This Point Forward. In addition, if the document includes more than one section, you'll find the choice This Section. (We'll discuss the choices you'll see with text selected in a moment.) The rest of this discussion assumes you're at least vaguely familiar with sections, which we covered in Chapter 13. If you're not, take a look at "Multisection Documents" starting on page 455.

If you choose This Section in the Apply To box, the settings you specify will apply only to the current section (the section where the cursor was located when you opened the dialog box). If you choose Whole Document, the settings will apply to all sections (whether your document consists of one or more sections). If you select This Point Forward, Word will insert a new section break at the cursor location and will apply the formatting to that new section and all later sections.

In some cases, you will want to restrict the new column format more than these three options easily allow. For example, you might want to create a three-column section for part of a page that is otherwise formatted as a single column. You can manage that easily enough by highlighting the text you want to apply the format to before choosing Format Columns.

## How to add columns only to selected text

If you select some text before opening the Columns dialog box, you'll find a slightly different set of options in the Apply To box. You'll still find the Whole Document option. But if the selection is confined to a single section (whether you have one section in the document or more), you'll find the option Selected Text. And if the document already has more than one section, still another choice will be Selected Sections, whether the selection extends into multiple sections or not.

As the name implies, the Selected Sections option applies the new settings to any sections the selection was in when you opened the dialog box. (If the selection was in only one section, this option is equivalent to choosing This Section.)

More interesting is the Selected Text option, since it will do several things at once. If you apply a column format to selected text, Word will insert a section break both at the beginning and at the end of the selection, and it will format only the newly defined section. This is how we created the three-column section in Figure 14-5, with single-column text before and after. This choice lets you create the new sections and apply the format to the selected text in a single step.

**FIGURE 14-5**

If you highlight text before choosing Format Columns to open the Columns dialog box and you then choose the Apply To Selected Text option, you can insert section breaks and format the text as a new section at the same time.

When you choose the Apply To Selected Text option, Word applies the column format only to the selected text even if the selection starts or ends in the middle of a paragraph or even a word, so be careful to select all the text you want to format.

The Start New Column check box causes affected section breaks to be formatted as New Column. Word treats these section breaks as column breaks, which forces the text following each section break to start a new column at the top of the page. If there is no room to start a new column on the current page, the column will start on the next page. The Apply To box controls which section breaks are affected. Figure 14-6 summarizes the effect of the option with the different choices.

| When You Apply It To This... | Start New Column Has This Effect... |
| --- | --- |
| Whole Document | Forces each section in the document to start a new column. |
| This Section | Forces a new column at the beginning of the current section. Other sections are not affected. |
| This Point Forward | Inserts a section break at the current cursor location and forces the new section (and any later sections) to start with a new column. |
| Selected Text | Inserts section breaks before and after the selected text and forces both of the new sections to start new columns. |
| Selected Sections | Forces a new column at the beginning of all selected sections. |

**FIGURE 14-6**

The choices available for the Start New Column option, and their effects.

## How to control column breaks

Word provides several ways to control column breaks. For example, you can use the Keep Lines Together option in the Paragraph dialog box to prevent Word from splitting a paragraph between two columns. Similarly, you can use the Keep With Next option to ensure that a given paragraph, such as a section heading, is in the same column as the next paragraph.

Word also lets you force the start of a new column by inserting a column break. Simply place the cursor where you want the column break, choose Insert Break, and then choose the Column Break option. Alternatively, place the cursor where you want the column break, and press the shortcut key combination ⌘-Shift-Return.

In Normal view, Word shows a column break as a dotted line labeled *Column Break*. In Page Layout view, it simply moves the text to the top of the next column. If you want to see the dotted line indicating a column break even in Page Layout view, set Word to show all nonprinting characters on the Tools Options View card, or click on the Show/Hide ¶ button on the Standard toolbar.

# How to format with both single and multiple columns

Each section in a document can have only one setting for columns. To change the column format for some of your text but not all, you must create a new section. We mentioned earlier that you can combine different column formats. Here's a closer look at the process.

Consider the sample document we've been using in this chapter. When we formatted it as two columns, the title text wrapped to two lines, as shown in Figure 14-7. Since the title's paragraph is formatted as centered, the title remains centered in the one column, not centered on the page.

**FIGURE 14-7**

The title in this document has wrapped to a second line in this two-column format.

You can easily change this document so that the headline remains on one line, centered across the entire width of the page. The trick is to put the headline in a section of its own and define that section as one column.

To create a new section, simply place the cursor before the first character of the first paragraph after the title, and insert a section break with the Insert Break command; use the Continuous option here since you want the title on the same page as the rest of the text.

After you insert this new section break, the status bar will indicate that the first paragraph of body text is in section 2 rather than section 1. If you move the cursor to the title, the status bar will show that the current section is 1.

With the cursor in the section that contains the title, reformat that section as a single column using the Format Columns command or the Columns button on the Standard toolbar. Figure 14-8 shows the result, as seen in Page Layout view, with the title centered above two columns of text.

You can enter the section break and reformat the first section in a single step. Start by selecting the title paragraph. Then choose Format Columns to open the Columns dialog box, set Number Of Columns to 1, choose Selected Text in the Apply To box, and then choose OK. Alternatively, after selecting the text, click on the Columns toolbar button and drag to define the number of columns as one.

**FIGURE 14-8**

Page Layout view
shows the title centered
over two columns.

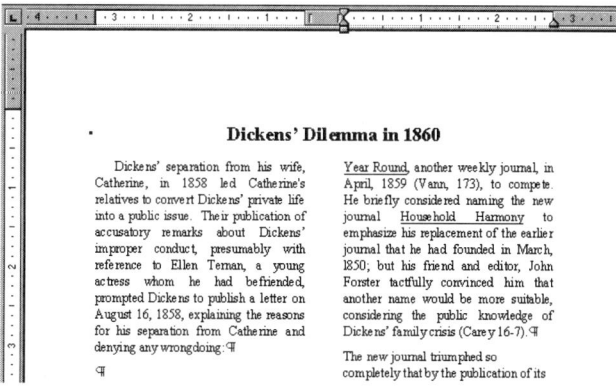

**Dickens' Dilemma in 1860**

Dickens' separation from his wife, Catherine, in 1858 led Catherine's relatives to convert Dickens' private life into a public issue. Their publication of accusatory remarks about Dickens' improper conduct, presumably with reference to Ellen Ternan, a young actress whom he had befriended, prompted Dickens to publish a letter on August 16, 1858, explaining the reasons for his separation from Catherine and denying any wrongdoing.

Year Round, another weekly journal, in April, 1859 (Vann, 173), to compete. He briefly considered naming the new journal Household Harmony to emphasize his replacement of the earlier journal that he had founded in March, 1850; but his friend and editor, John Forster tactfully convinced him that another name would be more suitable, considering the public knowledge of Dickens' family crisis (Carey 16-7).

The new journal triumphed so completely that by the publication of its

You can use this technique to position two tables side by side on a page that is otherwise using a one-column format. Simply add a two-column section to the page, with the section starting immediately before the first table and ending immediately after the second.

## How to create columns of equal length

You can also use section breaks to create columns of equal length. For example, suppose you're writing a newsletter and you have two stories on the same page, each of which takes half a page. If you format the page as a single section with three text columns, the first story will run from the top of the first column to the middle of the second column, and the second will run from the middle of the second column to the end of the third. A more sophisticated layout would place the first story in three columns on the top half of the page and the second in three columns on the bottom half. You can create this layout by entering a section break at the end of the first story.

Whenever a page contains one or more sections with multicolumn formatting, Word will break the columns at the section boundaries and wrap the columnar text within the sections. In other words, inserting a continuous section break tells Word to wrap the columns within each section separately from the other sections. That means you can use section breaks to determine the depth of the columns within each section.

You can also use this technique to balance columns at the end of a section. For example, Figure 14-9 shows the Page Layout view of the last page of our sample document, which doesn't have enough text to fill the page. Instead of having most of the text on one side of the page, you might prefer to have two equal-length columns at the top of the page.

**FIGURE 14-9**

Page Layout mode shows that there is not enough text in this example to fill the page.

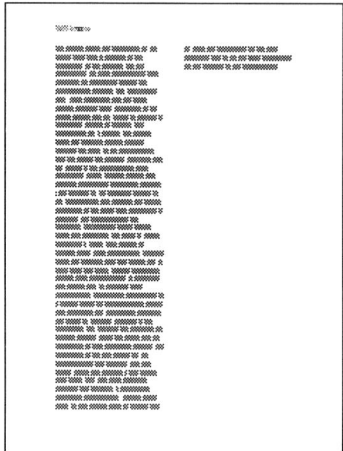

To create two equal-length columns, simply insert a section break, defined with the Continuous option, at the end of the text. Word will automatically reformat the two columns to equal length, as shown in Figure 14-10.

**FIGURE 14-10**

If you insert a new section break at the end of the text, Word will reformat the text from Figure 14-9 into two balanced columns.

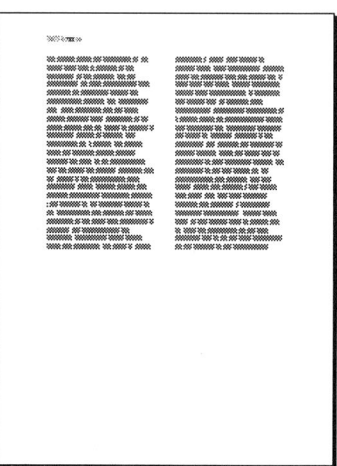

The combination of section breaks and column formatting gives you a great deal of control over mixing column formats within a document and even within a page. However, there are times when you need even more control over the placement of elements on the page. For that, you need frames.

# Frames: Positioning Text and Graphics on the Page

In all of our discussion of formatting so far, we've treated a Word document almost entirely as a linear sequence of text, with each line following the one before it. Among the few exceptions to this rule are headers, footers, and footnotes. But these are set off in their own reserved text areas. All the body text for a document is still in a linear sequence.

There will likely be times when you won't want a linear sequence. For example, you may want to place a box filled with text or a graphic at a specific position on a page and have other text flow around the box as you enter or edit the text.

That, in part, is what frames are for. Frames let you place whatever you want wherever you want it. We'll start with examples that use text, but keep in mind that you can also insert other items into frames: pictures, tables, graphs, and even objects from other Windows applications. We'll cover these other items in the next chapter. For now, we'll concentrate on the concept of frames.

Frames are close relatives, in both behavior and capabilities, of two other Word features—text boxes and callouts. These are both among Word's drawing capabilities. We'll save the discussion of text boxes and callouts for later in this chapter, but be aware that much of this discussion—including virtually all of the concepts and many of the details—applies to text boxes and callouts as well.

## Frames in different views

First, it's important to realize that frames and their contents look different, depending on which view Word is in. Figure 14-11 on the next page shows a sample document, complete with a frame, as it appears in Page Layout view.

The figure shows a two-column format and a headline (in its own section) that spans both columns. It also shows a box in the middle of the page that includes a quote. (In publishing circles, this is referred to as a *readout* or a *pull quote*.) Notice how the text in the columns flows around the box, and notice that the text in the box can't readily be described as coming either before or after any particular paragraph of text in the columns.

This document has a frame that contains some text; you can see its position in Page Layout view.

## Frames in Normal view

Figure 14-12 shows the same document in Normal view. As you can see, it looks very different from Figure 14-11: The body text appears as a single column, the section break appears below the headline, and the readout box and text have a specific linear placement relative to the column of text, namely, between the first and second paragraphs.

The same document as in Figure 14-11 in Normal view shows the frame's linear position in relation to the text in the document, not its position on the page.

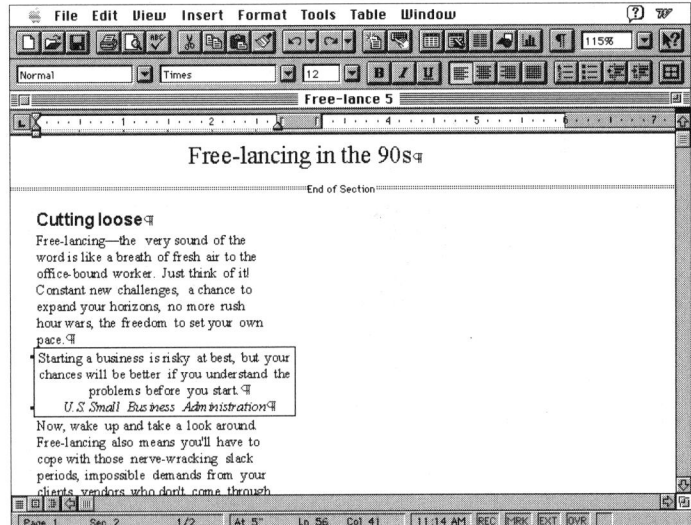

Note also that in Normal view, Word adds small squares to the left of the first line of each paragraph in the box. These squares (which are visible only if you have Word set to show paragraph marks) are markers indicating that these paragraphs are contained within a frame. The box around the text is simply a border around the paragraphs in the frame. You can get rid of the box if you want, as we'll discuss a little later. And if you choose to get rid of the border, the squares become important as a way to identify text that's within the frame.

## Frames in Outline view

As shown in Figure 14-13, Word does not mark a frame at all in Outline view. In fact, Word will not show a frame's border in Outline view, even if the frame is defined to have a border.

**FIGURE 14-13**

In Outline view, Word does not mark frames at all.

## The importance of using Page Layout view

In general, you will want to set Word to Page Layout view when you are working with frames. Not only will you be able to see the actual layout, but you'll be able to easily edit, resize, and move the frame on the page, and see the results immediately.

Page Layout view is so central to working with frames that Word even offers to switch to Page Layout view if you try to add a frame while in Normal view. All of this brings us to the mechanics of adding a frame.

## How to add a frame

Word lets you add an empty frame or add one around an existing part of your document. The only difference between the two choices is whether you highlight some text (or other items) before choosing the Insert Frame command. If you start by selecting some text, Word will place the selection inside the frame and automatically set the frame size to match the existing text. You can then move and resize the frame. If you don't select the text first, Word will wait for you to define a position and size for the frame. You can then enter text in the frame by typing it in or by copying already existing text using Word's Cut, Copy, and Paste commands. In this example, we'll start with an empty frame and create the sample document we've been using for the frames discussion.

As we just pointed out, you'll usually want to be in Page Layout view to work with frames. In fact, if you choose Insert Frame while in Normal view, Word will display a message box asking whether you want to switch to Page Layout view. If you choose No, Word will return you to your document without inserting a frame (unless you selected some text first). If you choose Yes, Word will switch to Page Layout view, where you can insert the frame. For purposes of this example, we'll assume you started out in Page Layout view.

NEW! When you choose Insert Frame, the mouse pointer will change to a crosshair, and Word will display a prompt on the status line that says *Click and drag to insert a frame.* Use the mouse to position the pointer where you want one corner of the frame, and then anchor that corner by pressing and holding down the mouse button. Drag with the mouse to enlarge the frame to the size you want.

When you release the mouse button, Word will create an empty frame, as shown in Figure 14-14. (The figure uses Word's default settings for frames. We will discuss the settings in detail shortly.) Note that the frame includes a paragraph symbol inside a border (because Word is set to show paragraph marks). Note too the blank space between the border and the surrounding columns of text, and the diagonal lines around the frame. The diagonal lines indicate the actual borders of the frame. The fact that you can see them indicates that the cursor is inside the frame.

At this point, you can add text. With the cursor inside the frame, simply type the text and format it if you like. When you're done, the result should look something like Figure 14-15. In the figure, we've also formatted the last line in italics and formatted the paragraphs as centered.

**FIGURE 14-14**

Word's default settings for frames include wrapping surrounding text and adding a thin border. The pattern of diagonal lines surrounding the frame indicates that the cursor is inside the frame.

**FIGURE 14-15**

You can format the text within a frame.

# How to add a frame to existing text

You can also add a frame to existing text—from a word to a group of paragraphs. Select the text you want to put in a frame, and choose the Insert Frame command. Word will add the frame around the text.

Because you don't have to define a frame with the crosshair pointer when you use the Insert Frame command, you can create a frame with the keyboard as easily as with the mouse using this technique. Note too that this technique lets you define a frame without switching to Page Layout view.

## How to move the cursor to a frame

Although Word's default settings for frames will often serve your needs, there may be times when you'll want to change those settings. The first step in making any changes to a frame—including editing or formatting the text in the frame—is to move the cursor inside the frame.

In most cases, it's easier to move to a frame with the mouse than with the keyboard. If the cursor isn't already in the frame, simply position the mouse pointer anywhere within the frame and click. Word will move the cursor to the frame and show you the frame's border.

You can use the keyboard to move the cursor to a frame in either of two ways. First you can move the cursor to the point in the document where the frame is located linearly (as Word will show it in Normal view). In Normal view, this is easy enough, but in Page Layout view, this position does not necessarily bear any relation to where the frame appears on the page. Word treats the start of the frame as the start of a paragraph, but it can show another paragraph (or several paragraphs if the frame spans more than one column) wrapping around the frame.

If you're in Page Layout view, you can also move to a frame by starting from a line of text that appears directly above or below the frame, and using the Down or Up arrow key to move into the frame. You cannot move into a frame from text that is adjacent horizontally.

## Anchors

If you are in Page Layout view and you want to find out where the frame is located linearly within the document, you can move the cursor inside the frame using any of the above methods and then press the Right arrow key repeatedly until the cursor leaves the frame. When the cursor leaves the frame, it will go to the position immediately after the point where the frame is located within the text. However, there's another, more elegant, way to find out where the frame is located.

Word keeps track of frames by anchoring each to the paragraph that follows it in linear sequence—meaning the paragraph that comes immediately after the frame in Normal view. While you are in Page Layout view, you can see which paragraph your frame is anchored to. Starting from Page Layout view, if you choose Tools Options View, you'll find an Object Anchors check box in the Show box. Check Object Anchors, and whenever you highlight a frame Word will indicate the anchor paragraph with a small anchor to the left of the first line of the paragraph, as in Figure 14-16. If you drag the frame to a new position, and the new position changes the frame's linear position in the document, Word will move the anchor on the screen. (You can also toggle the anchor symbols on and off with the other nonprinting characters by clicking on the Show/Hide ¶ button on the Standard toolbar.)

**FIGURE 14-16**

Word can display an anchor symbol to indicate the paragraph a frame is anchored to.

 Word will sometimes align the left edge of the text on the left edge of your display so that you can't see the anchor symbols, which Word generally places in the margin. To be sure you can see the anchors, either scroll the display to the left or adjust the Zoom setting so that you can see the left margin.

The anchor symbol can help prevent accidental deletion of a frame when you're working in Page Layout view. If you delete a selection that includes the paragraph before the anchor, plus any part of the anchor paragraph, you will delete the frame and its contents as well. Since the frame may be positioned where you can't see it when editing the anchor paragraph, you might not notice it becoming selected along with the text you want to delete. If you select the frame before working in the area around the frame, you can locate the anchor symbol so you'll know where the frame is. In general, however, if you're about to do substantial editing anywhere near a frame, it's safest to switch to Normal view.

## How to select a frame to change its shape, size, or position

To change the shape or size of a frame by dragging with the mouse, you need to select it first. To select a frame, move to the frame so you can see the shaded border. Then move the mouse pointer over the border. When the pointer is at the proper position, it will change to a left-pointing arrow with a four-headed arrow below it. At this point, you can click and hold the mouse button down to move the frame by dragging, or you can simply click on the frame to select it. (In truth, you can select the frame even without the border showing. When you move the mouse pointer over the proper position, the pointer will change whether you can see the border or not. However, it's easier to point to the border if you can see it, so we recommend moving to the frame first.)

When you click on the frame, Word will add eight square boxes around the edge of the frame, as shown in Figure 14-17. These boxes, called *handles*, indicate that you've selected the frame.

As we'll discuss shortly, you can use the mouse to grab the handles and resize the frame by dragging. Note that there is no way to select the frame or use the handles with the keyboard. Be aware, however, that if you have the Typing Replaces Selection option on and the frame selected, Word will delete all text in the frame if you type anything.

## How to adjust frame settings

Frame settings fall into two categories. One consists of settings specific to frames, such as size or position. The other consists of paragraph-level formatting. Most of the settings in the second category are straightforward applications of formatting techniques you can use on any text. For example, you can center text within a frame by formatting the paragraphs as centered. One setting in this second category is worth special mention, however, since you'll often apply it to the frame as a whole. The setting is for borders and shading.

### Borders and shading

The default setting for a new frame includes a single-line border. To change the border, first either select the frame or place the cursor inside the frame. Then choose Format Borders And Shading to open the Paragraph Borders And Shading dialog box.

Be careful not to highlight any text or objects within the frame before you choose Format Borders And Shading, or else the settings you choose will affect only the selected paragraph or object, rather than the whole frame. One way to be certain your choices will apply to the frame and not just to some of its contents is to click on the frame to select it.

We discussed this dialog box in detail in Chapter 7. All the options we discussed there apply here as well, including all the shading options. For this discussion, we'll simply stay with the default settings. Keep in mind, however, that you can use this dialog box to define lines for some sides of the frame but not others. You can also choose the Shading card to create effects that will make readouts and other framed items stand out visually from the rest of your text. For details on using these features, see "Paragraph borders and shading" starting on page 218.

## How to move and size the frame with the mouse

Among the features specific to frames are the commands for moving and resizing them. Word lets you move and resize either by dragging with the mouse or by entering settings in a dialog box. Each approach has its advantages.

Dragging with the mouse is more natural because you're working with a visual representation of the page. When you click and drag, you can see the results of the changes almost immediately (depending on the speed of your system). The dialog box offers more precision, but it loses the immediate visual feedback. We recommend that you use dragging techniques for broad changes—moving a frame to the approximate position, for example—and then shift to the dialog box to make fine adjustments.

As we've already mentioned, when you click on a frame, you'll see eight handles appear around the edge of the frame. If you then move the mouse pointer over the frame, you'll find that it changes shape depending on where it is in respect to the frame and the handles. If you place it directly over one of the handles, it will turn into a two-headed arrow—pointing left and right if it's on one of the two side handles, up and down if it's on the top or bottom handle, or diagonally if it's on a corner handle. When the pointer changes to any of these shapes, you can click and drag to resize the frame in the directions indicated by the arrows. (The diagonal arrows let you change height and width simultaneously.)

We used this click-and-drag technique to modify our frame to the one shown in Figure 14-18, making the frame wider than it was originally and not as tall. Note how Word automatically reformatted the text to fit the frame, so it fits on four lines in Figure 14-18 instead of five.

If you hold down the Control and Option keys as you click and drag to resize a frame, Word will change the position for the current and the opposite side of the frame simultaneously—meaning top and bottom, left and right, or diagonally opposite corners. This lets you change the size and shape of a frame while keeping it centered on its current position. If you hold down the Shift key while dragging a corner handle, Word will keep the proportions the same as it resizes the frame. Note too that if you hold down both the Shift and the Control key while dragging a corner handle, Word will keep the proportions the same while also keeping the center of the frame at the same position.

**FIGURE 14-18**

We used the frame's handles to change its size.

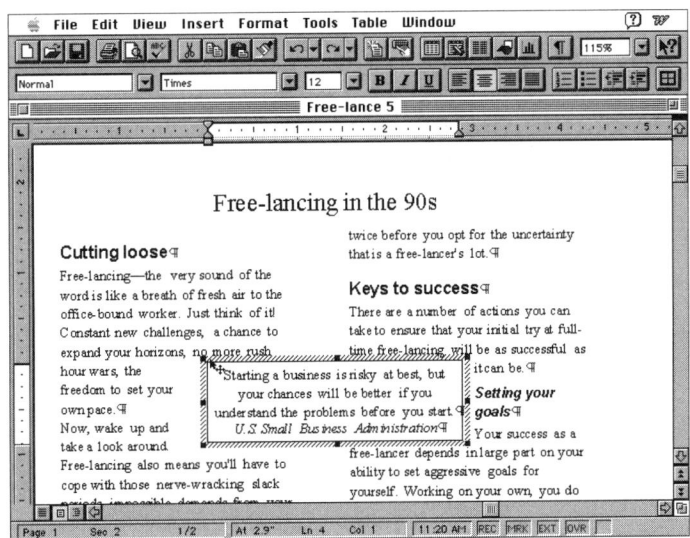

The mouse pointer in Figure 14-18 is near the upper left corner of the frame, between two of the handles. The arrow with a four-headed arrow pointer indicates that you can use it to drag the frame to a new location.

In this case, it's a good idea to move the frame down a bit since it's forcing the heading *Setting your goals* into two lines. By clicking on the frame and dragging it down, we can get the heading to appear on its own line, as shown in Figure 14-19 on the next page.

**FIGURE 14-19**

Word will reformat the document around the frame when you move the frame to a new position.

# The Frame dialog box

The next step in this example is to center the frame between the two columns. You could use the mouse to drag the frame and wind up reasonably close to the right position. But this is the sort of fine adjustment that's better handled through the Frame dialog box.

To open the dialog box, you can move to or select the frame you want to adjust and then double-click on the edge of the frame or choose Format Frame. Word will respond with a dialog box like the one in Figure 14-20. All of the settings will match the current settings for the frame.

**FIGURE 14-20**

The Frame dialog box gives you precise control over frame settings.

## How to flow text around a frame

The upper left group box in the Frame dialog box is labeled Text Wrapping. This defaults to the Around setting, as shown. As indicated in the thumbnail sketch, the setting tells Word to wrap text around the frame, as we've shown in our sample document up to now. If you change Text Wrapping to None, Word will not print any text on the lines level with the frame. Figure 14-21 shows the result for our sample document. Regardless of the setting for Text Wrapping, Word will not flow text into an area that is 1 inch wide or less.

**FIGURE 14-21**

If you set Text Wrapping to None, Word will format the document so that no text prints on the lines level with the frame.

## Frame size

The Size box lets you specify width and height for the frame. As you can see in Figure 14-20, there are pull-down lists for both Width and Height, and each is paired with its own At text box, where you can enter a dimension. The Width list offers two choices: Auto and Exactly (the default). The Height list box offers the same two options, plus a third: At Least. This is the default setting. The Auto setting in each case tells Word to enlarge or shrink the frame's size based on its contents. The Exactly settings let you specify a precise size that Word won't change, regardless of contents. The At Least setting for height lets you specify a minimum height for the frame, but it tells Word to automatically enlarge the height beyond that minimum if necessary, based on the frame's contents.

## How to align frames

The two group boxes on the right side of the Frame dialog box are Horizontal and Vertical. The settings in these boxes let you precisely position the frame on the page, and they let you specify a distance from other text. They also let you tell Word to determine the frame's position relative to some other element on the page. These positioning features are worth examining in detail.

### Horizontal alignment

The Horizontal box offers three items to set: Position, Relative To, and Distance From Text.

When you first create a frame or drag it with the mouse, Word determines the horizontal position as a specific location, and it shows the location for the left edge of the frame as a specific measurement in the Position box, as shown in Figure 14-20. (The number matches the edge's position as measured by Word's ruler.) Since we want to center the frame horizontally on the page, we could calculate the correct position based on page width and frame width and then enter the result in the Position box. But it's much easier to let Word do the work.

If you open the drop-down list attached to the Position box, you will see five choices: Left, Right, Center, Inside, and Outside. If you choose Center, Word will automatically center the frame, as in the centered frame in Figure 14-22. As long as the frame is defined as centered, Word will keep it centered, even if you change the width of the frame. (Note that the precise effect of choosing Center for horizontal position depends on the setting in the Relative To box. In Figure 14-22, the frame is defined as centered relative to the page. We'll come back to this issue in a moment.)

**FIGURE 14-22**

Word will automatically position a frame if you choose the Left, Center, or Right option for the horizontal position setting.

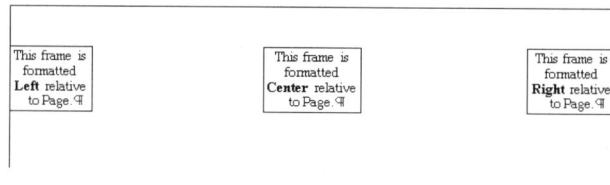

The other four settings for horizontal position also let you automatically place a frame in a specified location. The Left and Right options move the frame to the left or right edge of the page, placing it in the margin, as also shown in Figure 14-22. (Here again, this assumes the position is defined as relative to the page. In Figure 14-22, we've set the View Zoom setting to show both edges of the page.)

The Inside and Outside settings are similar to the Left and Right settings except they let you choose the correct position when you've defined Mirror Margins on the File Document Layout Margins card. The Mirror Margins feature, which we discussed in Chapter 7, is useful when you want to print a document on both sides of each page, with a center binding. The Inside setting places the frame all the way to the right on even-numbered pages and all the way to the left on odd-numbered pages so the frame is always to the inside of the page, next to the binding. The Outside setting is just the opposite, placing the frame on the outside of the page.

The Relative To list box offers two choices in addition to the Page choice: Margin and Column. The default setting is Page, which is why we've used it until now. The other two choices produce slightly different results.

As shown in Figure 14-22, setting the horizontal position to the left or to the right relative to the page moves the frame to the extreme edge of the page. This may not print correctly, since many printers cannot print to the edge of the page. Also, although there are times when you might want to place a frame in the margin (as we'll discuss a little later in this chapter), more often you'll want to place a frame within the text area. By positioning the frame left or right relative to the margins, you can automatically line up the edge of the frame with the edge of the text area. Similarly, if you're using a multiple-column format, and you position a frame relative to the column, you can automatically line up the frame with the left or the right edge or in the center of the column.

The Distance From Text text box lets you enter the amount of blank space for Word to put between the outside of the frame and any adjacent text to the left or right. The default setting of 0.13 inch will usually provide an attractive layout, but you can change it if you prefer.

## Vertical alignment

The settings in the Vertical box are similar to those in the Horizontal box. In particular, the vertical alignment Position box settings, in addition to a measured position on the page, are Top, Bottom, and Center. The choices in the Relative To box are Page, Margin, and Paragraph (the default setting). The Distance From Text text box works the same way as the Distance From Text box for horizontal placement, but it determines the distance for text above and below the frame. The default setting is 0, or no space.

In our sample document, the frame is positioned a specific distance relative to the upper left corner of the closest paragraph. Note that the Relative To Paragraph setting is not relative to the paragraph closest to the frame's linear position as seen in Normal view; rather, it is based on the frame's visual proximity to the nearest paragraph in Page Layout view.

Figure 14-23 shows how Word positions frames set for Top, Center, and Bottom relative to the page.

Keep in mind that the warning we gave about placing a frame in the nonprintable region for any given printer applies to vertical as well as horizontal placement.

**FIGURE 14-23**

Word has settings that let you automatically position a frame at the top, center, or bottom of a page.

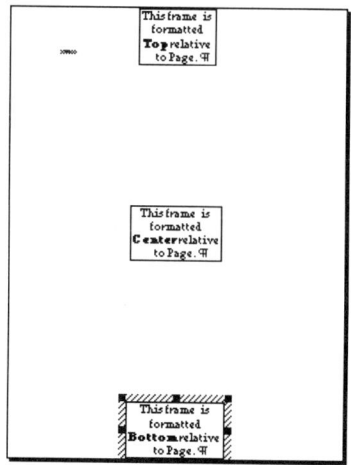

## How to position with text

There are two more items in the Vertical box: Move With Text and Lock Anchor. We discussed anchors earlier in this chapter when we pointed out that Word keeps track of frames by anchoring them to the paragraph that comes immediately after them in the linear sequence you see in Normal view.

Move With Text tells Word to move the frame with the paragraph it's anchored to when you edit or format that paragraph. If you define a frame to move with the text, however, Word may change the anchor paragraph automatically if you move the frame on the page. The Lock Anchor option ensures that the frame will remain anchored to the same paragraph it is currently anchored to, which means it will always be on the same page as that paragraph. You'll still be able to move the frame, but the anchor will not move. We discussed anchors, and how to see which paragraph a frame is anchored to, in "Anchors," starting on page 486.

### How to remove a frame

There are several ways to remove a frame from your document. One choice is to move to or select the frame, open the Frame dialog box by choosing Format Frame, and then choose the Remove Frame button. This will remove the frame itself without deleting the contents of the frame.

To remove a frame along with its contents, highlight the frame so that its eight handles show, and choose the Edit Cut command to copy the frame to the Clipboard or choose Edit Clear to delete the frame and contents altogether.

## Text Boxes and Callouts

As we pointed out earlier, frames are close relatives of text boxes and callouts, two of Word's drawing tools. In fact, you can think of text boxes as a variation on frames.

The key difference between frames and text boxes is that while frames force text to either wrap around them or break the text so there is no text on a horizontal line with the frame, text boxes let body text print over the text box. With text boxes, in fact, there's no way to prevent the overprinting. Note too that unlike frames, text boxes will not automatically grow in size vertically as you add more text. Callouts are a special kind of text box that includes an attached line you can use to point to a particular item. Callouts are most often used within graphics as a way to label parts of the graphic.

Be aware that the term *text box* is a bit of a misnomer since you can add pictures and other graphic objects inside a text box just as you can add them inside a frame. *Text box,* however, is the term Word uses for the appropriate toolbar button. Be aware too that unlike frames, which Word shows in Normal view, you cannot see text boxes at all in Normal view—or in Outline or Master Document view, for that matter.

Because text boxes are so much like frames, we'll take a look at them here, independent of the rest of Word's drawing tools. And because they are so much like frames, we'll refer to many text box features as working the same way as the same features for frames. The rest of this discussion assumes that you're already familiar with frames.

## How to insert a text box

To insert a text box, click on the Drawing button in the Standard toolbar—three buttons to the left of the zoom percentage text box—or choose View Toolbars and check the Drawing check box. Word will add the Drawing toolbar, shown in Figure 14-24. By default, Word will place the Toolbar at the bottom of the Word window.

**FIGURE 14-24**

By default, Word will add the Drawing toolbar at the bottom of the Word window when you click on the Drawing button.

The Text Box button is sixth from the left on the Drawing toolbar. To insert a text box, click on the button, and then define the box with the mouse pointer, just as you would define a frame. As Figure 14-25 shows, the text box, unlike a frame, does not force text to wrap around it or break. Instead, the text simply prints over the same area as the text box. (Unlike a frame, you cannot add a text box around existing text. More precisely, you can add a text box to the same area as existing text, but the text will not be part of the text box's contents.)

**FIGURE 14-25**

When you add a text box, such as the top rectangle here, Word does not alter the layout of the body text in any way. With a frame, Word does alter the layout, as you can see by the middle and bottom rectangles.

## How to adjust text box settings

Among the more important features that text boxes share with frames are the ways you enter and format both text and graphics objects within the frame or text box. Text boxes also let you use the mouse the same way you use it with frames. You can move the text box or select the text box and then drag a handle to resize the box. As with a frame, you can delete a text box and its contents by highlighting the text box so that its eight handles appear and then choosing Edit Cut or Edit Clear. Unlike frames, you can't remove the text box and leave its contents.

Text boxes have some advantages over frames. You can move text boxes with more precision from the keyboard than you can with the mouse. Simply select the text box, and then use the arrow keys to move the box up, down, left, or right. To move in even more precise increments, hold the Control key down as you press the arrow keys. If you have more than one text box or other drawing object (such as a line) created with Word's other drawing tools on the current page, and one of the objects is already selected, you can use the Tab key to cycle through the objects, selecting another object each time you press Tab.

Another, more critical, difference between text boxes and frames is the way you move to a text box to work with the contents of the text box, rather than with the body text that shares the same area on the page. Although you can use the same mouse technique as with a frame—clicking on the text box—there is no way to move into the text box from adjacent text. As with frames, however, when you move into a text box, Word will outline the border of the box with a shaded border to give visual confirmation that you're working in the box.

## The Drawing Object dialog box

As with a frame, you can control size and positioning of a text box through a dialog box, specifically, the Drawing Object dialog box, shown in Figure 14-26 on the next page. To open the dialog box, move to or select a text box and then choose Format Drawing Object or double-click on the border.

**FIGURE 14-26**

The Drawing Object dialog box lets you control the size and position of text boxes, as well as other drawing-related objects.

The Drawing Object dialog box offers three cards: Fill, Line, and Size And Position. The Size And Position card, shown in Figure 14-26, is analogous to the Format Frame card we've already discussed, and it even offers many of the same settings.

Most of the available settings are self-explanatory. In the Position group box, for example, the Horizontal and Vertical settings let you specify where to place the box. Unlike the equivalent choices for frames, you're limited to entering an actual measurement, but like the choices for frames, the From boxes let you specify Margin, Page, or Column for the horizontal position or Margin, Page, or Paragraph for the vertical position.

The Lock Anchor check box has the same function here as in the dialog box for frames. If you check Lock Anchor, the text box will stay anchored to the paragraph it's currently anchored to, which means it will always be on the same page as that paragraph.

The Height and Width boxes in the Size group box simply control the height and width of the text box, as their names imply. The Internal Margin setting determines how much space you'll have between the border of the box and the text inside the box. Think of it as a margin setting. The Callout button will be grayed out unless you've selected a text box you created as a callout— a subject we'll come back to later.

## The Line and Fill cards: Borders and shading

You can use the Format Borders And Shading command with text boxes much as you can with frames, but text boxes offer an alternative, and in some ways more flexible, approach to borders and shading through the Fill card, shown in Figure 14-27, and the Line card, shown in Figure 14-28.

FIGURE 14-27

The Fill card in the Drawing Object dialog box lets you control the color and pattern of the background for a text box.

The Fill card lets you choose a background color for the text box, a pattern to overlay the color, and a color for the pattern overlay.

FIGURE 14-28

The Line card in the Drawing Object dialog box lets you control the format for a text box's line border.

The Line card lets you specify no line for the text box border or define a custom line, using any of several patterns (including a solid line or dashes) and your choice of colors and line weight. You can also add a shadow effect or rounded corners, with the two check boxes on the card. The Arrowhead group box is grayed out in Figure 14-28, since the feature doesn't apply to a standard text box. Note, however, that it would apply for a callout box, which has a line you can use to point to a particular item. The Preview box on both cards lets you see the effect of your choices.

# Callouts

As we've already said, a callout is a variation on a text box that includes an attached line you can use to point to or from a particular item. Figure 14-29 shows three sample callouts, one with an arrow pointing from the item to the callout, one with an arrow pointing from the callout to the item, and one with a line that lacks an arrowhead.

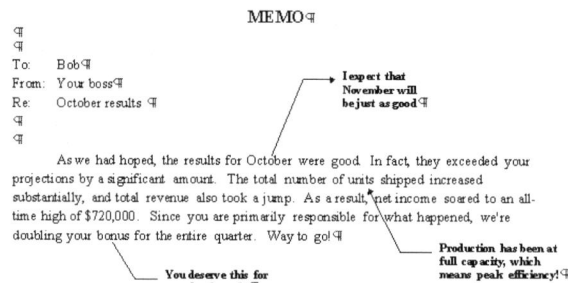

**FIGURE 14-29**

Callouts are variations on text boxes, with lines attached to let you tie the callouts to other items.

To insert a callout, you follow the same procedure as for inserting a text box except that you use the Callout button, which is immediately to the right of the Text Box button on the Drawing toolbar. When you select a callout, you'll find that the attached line includes its own handle or handles, which you can drag to change the position and length of the line. (The number of handles depends on the style of the line.)

If you move to or select a callout and then choose Format Drawing Object, you'll see the same set of cards as for standard text boxes. One difference will be that the Arrowhead group box on the Line card will be available, so you can define the width and length of the arrowhead and the style. And note that the choices in style include the direction the arrow is pointing: to the box, from the box, in both directions, or none—meaning no arrowhead on either side.

The only other difference from using a standard text box is that if you move to the Size And Position card, you'll find that the Callout button is available. Choose it to open the Format Callout box, shown in Figure 14-30.

The Format Callout dialog box lets you define the format for the attached line, including how many handles are available within the line, the gap between the callout line and the text, whether the line is parallel to or pointing to the callout text, and so on. After specifying the settings, choose OK to close the dialog box and set the new format. You can also open this dialog box by moving to or selecting the callout and clicking on the Format Callout button, immediately to the right of the Callout button.

**FIGURE 14-30**

The Format Callout dialog box lets you define the format for the line attached to the callout box.

## When to use frames, and when to use text boxes or callouts

You can use frames and text boxes more or less interchangeably in any situation where there is no possibility of conflicting with body text in the same area. If you're adding a graphic or text in the margin, for example, you can generally use either choice.

If you want text to flow around an object, however, as you might with a graphic you're referring to within your text, you must use a frame. If you want text to print over an object, to produce a watermark effect, such as the word *DRAFT* written across a page of text, you will generally want to use a text box. (You can also use a frame for a watermark, as we'll discuss later, but the text box is the more straightforward choice.)

If you want an arrow pointing to or from some object, a callout is usually the preferred choice. But if you need text to wrap around the box, you can use a frame and then use Word's other drawing tools, which we'll cover in the next chapter, to create a line or an arrow between the box and the item you want to connect to. Callouts are usually the most useful way to label parts of graphics.

## Some Formatting Tricks with Frames and Text Boxes

You can use frames or text boxes to create highly sophisticated formats for your documents. Before we move on to another subject, it may be helpful to look at some ways you can take advantage of frames and text boxes. Specifically, here's a look at how to create scholar's margins, repeat text or graphics on multiple pages, and create watermarks such as *DRAFT*, *CONFIDENTIAL*, or *TOP SECRET* to print across each page.

# How to create scholar's margins

The sample document in Figure 14-31 shows a layout that is often called *scholar's margins*. The layout leaves ample white space beside the text so readers can write notes. This layout also provides a convenient place to put section headings and subheads to help guide the reader through the material. We created the headings and subheads in the figure by using frames.

The page in Figure 14-31 is formatted with a 2.3-inch left margin. The subheads are in frames and are horizontally positioned with paragraph formatting to indent them by 0.3 inch from the left and the right; this indention ensures that the text does not fall outside the printer's printable region at the edge of the page. The vertical position is specified as 0 inches relative to the paragraph, which automatically aligns each subhead with its associated paragraph. The frames are formatted with a Distance From Text setting of 0 inches since the paragraph indenting will suffice to keep the frame away from the text.

**FIGURE 14-31**

This document uses frames to put the text headings in the margin. Because the frames are defined to move with the text, their vertical positions will change as text is added to or deleted from the document.

### Southern heritage makes a comeback¶

The preservation movement is booming in the South. With a sense of community pride as rich and as varied as the region itself, cities like Tidewater, Virginia and Raleigh, North Carolina are rediscovering their past and rebuilding for future generations.¶

**Saving Historic Sites**¶

These revitalization projects are not limited to famous homes and historic old courthouses.¶
In Louisville, Kentucky, the city's water tower and pumping station have been converted into a community arts center. ¶
In Galveston, Texas, a 19th-century, square-rigged sailing vessel called the *Elissa* is proudly moored only a block from the city's revitalized downtown. ¶

**Almost Too Late**¶

In some cities, these efforts come just in time. In others, they are long overdue. Mobile, Alabama, has sadly lost almost half the 200 buildings that were recorded there by the Historic American Buildings Survey in the 1930s. That city's recent surge of historic pride came too late to prevent the destruction of the beautiful 19th-century Mobile County Courthouse.¶

**Fighting Progress?**¶

Too often, local efforts must be waged as defensive battles. Attempts to halt the demolition of an old building for the construction of a new one are criticized as impediments to progress. Preservationists are accused of being regressive rather than progressive.¶

If you create this sort of layout, check the Move With Text and Lock Anchor check boxes to ensure that the headings stay with their paragraphs. In a finished design, you would probably want to remove the borders that Word automatically adds to frames, but we left them in our sample since borders make the frames easier to see.

If you're printing on both sides of each page, use the Mirror Margins choice in the File Document Layout Margins card so the 2.3-inch margin in Figure 14-31 is defined as an outside margin rather than a left margin. Then format the frames to have a horizontal position of Outside relative to the page so the headings will always appear in the outside margins. Figure 14-32 shows how this page looks as a right-hand page. Notice that the wide margins and the headings both fall to the right of the text. (Notice also that you can't use text boxes for this since you cannot define text box position as inside or outside.)

**FIGURE 14-32**

If you choose Mirror Margins and then use the Outside horizontal position setting for the headings in frames, the headings will automatically stay in the outside margin even if reformatting shifts them to another page.

**Southern heritage makes a comeback**

The preservation movement is booming in the South. With a sense of community pride as rich and as varied as the region itself, cities like Tidewater, Virginia and Raleigh, North Carolina are rediscovering their past and rebuilding for future generations.

These revitalization projects are not limited to famous homes and historic old courthouses.

In Louisville, Kentucky, the city's water tower and pumping station have been converted into a community arts center.

In Galveston, Texas, a 19th-century, square-rigged sailing vessel called the *Elissa* is proudly moored only a block from the city's revitalized downtown.

In some cities, these efforts come just in time. In others, they are long overdue. Mobile, Alabama, has sadly lost almost half the 200 buildings that were recorded there by the Historic American Buildings Survey in the 1930s. That city's recent surge of historic pride came too late to prevent the destruction of the beautiful 19th-century Mobile County Courthouse.

Too often, local efforts must be waged as defensive battles. Attempts to halt the demolition of an old building for the construction of a new one are criticized as impediments to progress. Preservationists are accused of being regressive rather than progressive.

Saving Historic Sites

Almost Too Late

Fighting Progress?

The beauty of all this is that once you create them, you do not need to manually place any of the headers—Word will place them for you. If you edit your text so it changes, the headings will move freely with their adjacent paragraphs, falling to the left or the right automatically, depending only on whether they are on a left-hand or a right-hand page.

## How to repeat a frame or a text box on every page

You can also use frames and text boxes in headers and footers. Any frame or text box that's part of a header or footer will print on every page where that header or footer appears. Given the flexible positioning for frames and text boxes, you can place either one anywhere on the page, even outside the header or footer area. What's more, since frames and text boxes can hold pictures as well as text, you can use a frame in a header or footer to place a logo or other repeating illustration on every page of a document—in the top or bottom margin, in a corner, centered horizontally and vertically in the middle of the page, or printed as a watermark, such as *DRAFT* or *TOP SECRET*, across the text.

It's worth noting in this context that when you use the Insert Page Numbers command, Word puts the page number in a frame in the header or footer. Here, then, is an example of how to insert a frame in a header. But note that the procedure is exactly the same for both frames and text boxes and for both headers and footers.

To add a frame to a header, first be sure you're in Page Layout view. Then choose View Header And Footer, and, if necessary, use the Switch Between Header And Footer button on the Header And Footer toolbar to move to the header. Next add the frame, placing it anywhere on the page; it does not have to be within the header or footer area. Figure 14-33 on the next page shows a page with both frames and text boxes inserted in the header, but placed both in the margins of the page and in the body text area.

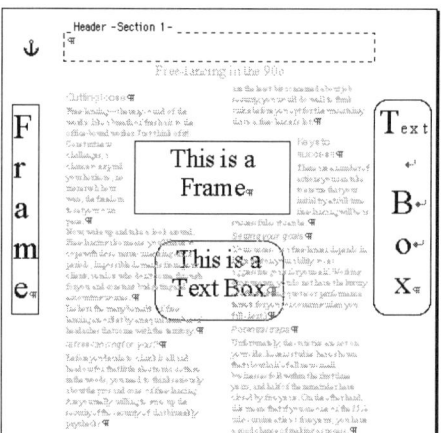

**FIGURE 14-33**

This page includes two text boxes and two frames. All four were added in the header, even though they show elsewhere on the page.

> Regardless of where you put the frame, if you've set Word to show object anchors and then you move to or select the frame, you'll see that the anchor is attached to a paragraph in the header area, as shown in Figure 14-33.

Remember that you can change header and footer contents by dividing your document into sections, as we discussed in Chapter 13. You can use sections to turn the repeating frames on and off or change their contents at different points in your document. Remember too that you can use the Document Layout Layout card to specify different headers and footers for first pages, and for odd and even pages, so you can, for example, create different repeating headers for odd and even pages and leave the repeating header off the first page.

## How to create a watermark

Although the heading for this section is "How to create a watermark," in truth we've already shown how. A watermark in Word is any text or object that is printed in the same place as other text. It can consist of a word, such as *DRAFT*, across a page, or a graphic image that you print text over. So whenever you create a text box in the area of the page where body text goes, you have, in fact, created a watermark. If you put the text box in the header, the watermark will be repeated on every page. The text box in Figure 14-33 that says *This is a text box* is also a watermark.

You can use any font available on your system formatted any way you like to produce a more interesting-looking text watermark. Most important, you can use color to have the watermark print in light gray, rather than solid black, so you can read the text the watermark overprints. In fact, one of the colors available for fonts on the Format Font Font card is light gray.

Remember that whether your printer will actually print the text in light gray depends on your printer. We recommend that you print a test page using text of different colors to see how your particular printer reproduces them on the page.

Keep in mind that you can insert a graphic in the frame in addition to or instead of text. That means you can use not only graphics but fancy text formats, such as those you can produce with the WordArt mini-application that we'll discuss in the next chapter.

If, for whatever reason, you would prefer to use a frame to create a watermark rather than use a text box, you can. The trick is to define the top margin in the File Document Layout Margins card with a negative number. Briefly, if you use a positive measurement, such as 2", Word will start the text at that point—in this case, 2 inches down from the top of the page. If you then add more lines to the header, Word will push the text farther down automatically. And if you insert a frame when you are using a positive measurement, Word will wrap body text around the frame, as in Figure 14-33.

If you use a negative measurement, however, such as –2", Word will *always* start the body text at the designated point and will expand the header to fill the entire page. If you add more lines to the header than will fit in the 2 inches, the additional lines will overprint the body text. And if you insert a frame when you are using a negative measurement, the frame will overprint the body text as well. This technique can be particularly handy when you want to take advantage of the additional positioning features available only with frames.

## Pictures

Our discussion of frames and text boxes so far has centered on text. However, both features work just as well for positioning pictures. And we'd argue that one of Word's strongest features for producing attractive output is that it will let you add pictures and other graphic objects. Word provides several tools for manipulating pictures within a document, letting you size, crop, and position a picture as needed. Word also offers ways to modify a picture or even create a new one from scratch, as we'll discuss in Chapter 15.

Although you can insert a picture into a document by itself, it's best to place your pictures in a frame or a text box—and preferably a frame, unless you are creating a watermark. Either a text box or a frame will let you position the pictures with a minimum of effort. In addition, a frame will let you easily format text to flow around the pictures. For the rest of this section, we'll concentrate on using pictures with frames, but you can apply much of this discussion to text boxes as well.

## How to insert a picture

For now we'll focus on using an existing picture that you've created in another program. In truth, Word offers support for so many types of graphics files, and offers so many ways to bring them into your documents, that this subject can be overwhelming. For example, if you are working in another application, you can cut or copy an image to the Clipboard and then paste it into your document. You can also insert picture files stored in a variety of file formats by importing them directly into a document. (We will cover the different formats that Word supports in Chapter 18, when we look at importing and exporting files.)

To simplify this discussion, we'll limit ourselves to the graphics files that come as part of the Word package. If you used the Setup program to install the complete version of Word, you should have a folder named Clip Art in your Word program folder, and it should contain a number of images, as well as another folder called EPS Clip Art.

There are two major classes of graphic images—bitmapped and object-oriented. Bitmapped images define individual dots that make up the picture; object-oriented images are based on combinations of shapes such as lines, polygons, and circles. Popular bitmapped image formats include TIFF and PICT formats. (We will discuss these formats and some of the programs that generate them in Chapter 18.) Bitmapped images offer the advantage of being able to handle mixed colors and subtle shadings more easily than object-oriented images, but they have the disadvantage of often losing picture quality when resized. If you have a choice of which type to use, keep this difference in mind.

We will insert a picture into the sample document that we used for our discussion of frames. The original document is shown in Page Layout view in Figure 14-34.

Note that the cursor is at the start of the second paragraph of text in the document. This is the position where we'll insert the picture. You can either create an empty frame first and then place a picture in the frame or create the picture first and then add the frame. In this example, we'll import the picture first. We'll then add the frame and use the frame to position the picture between the two columns of text, just as we did with the text example earlier in this chapter.

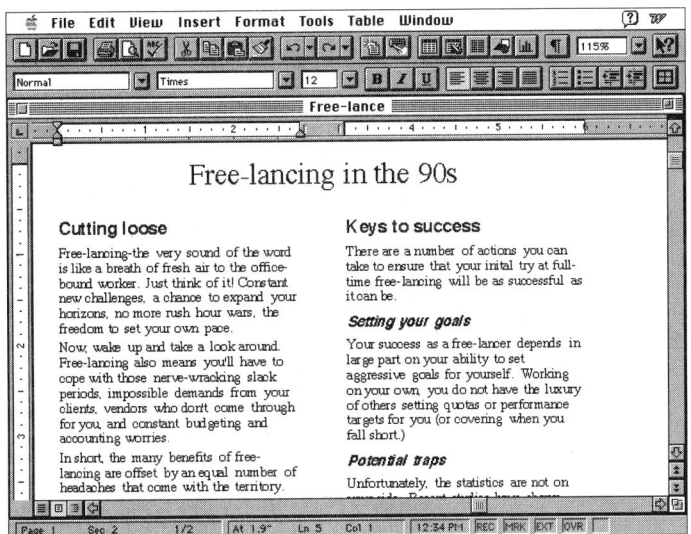

**FIGURE 14-34**

We will add a picture to this document using the clip art files that come with Word for the Macintosh.

## The Picture dialog box

Since this document is an article about free-lance work, and since this topic appeals to people's desire for fun and freedom, we want to add a picture that has something to do with these issues. Start by looking at the clip art Word has to offer. While in Page Layout view and with the cursor at the start of the second paragraph, choose Insert Picture to open the dialog box for inserting pictures, which is shown in Figure 14-35 on the next page. Note that the box that shows the current folder indicates that we've already moved to the EPS Clip Art folder in the Clip Art folder in the Word program folder.

**FIGURE 14-35**

You can use this dialog box to choose an image and insert it into your document.

This dialog box should look familiar since it's similar to the dialog boxes for saving, opening, and inserting files. The various pull-down lists, buttons, and boxes are essentially identical to the equivalent items in dialog boxes for saving and opening files, and they work the same way. The Find File button even takes you to the same Search and Find File dialog boxes that you can open by choosing File Find File.

One difference in detail between this dialog box and similar dialog boxes is that the List Files Of Type list box lists picture-format file types rather than text-format file types. The list includes an entry for each image-file import filter you've installed for your copy of Word.

There are four items in this dialog box that you won't find in the dialog boxes for opening or saving files: the Preview box and the Preview Picture, Link To File, and Save Picture In Document check boxes.

The Preview box lets you see a picture from a file before you bring it into your document. This makes it easy to browse through the clip art on your disk to look for the right file.

The Preview Picture check box lets you turn the preview feature on and off. For example, in Figure 14-35, the Flyace.eps filename is highlighted in the list of filenames and the picture appears in the Preview box. If you remove the check from the check box, the picture will disappear from the Preview box. But as long as there's a check mark in the check box, Word will preview each file as you highlight the name. If you have a relatively slow system, you may want to turn this feature off and then turn it back on again only after you highlight the name of a likely-sounding candidate file.

The Link To File check box tells Word to enter a field in your document that creates a link to the picture file on disk. You'll still be able to see the image in your document, however, as long as you set Word to show field results rather than field codes. Remember, you can toggle this setting with the Field Codes check box on the Tools Options View card.

One advantage of using a link is that if you change the image on the disk, you can update the image in the document without having to go through all the steps of importing the image again. If you don't use a link, the image is stored only as part of the document itself, as a duplicate of the original image, and completely divorced from it.

A second advantage of using a link is that you then have the option of saving the picture in the document or not, using the Save Picture In Document check box. If this box is checked, Word will store a copy of the image as part of your document. Storing a copy in your document will let Word load the file faster. Choosing not to store a copy of the picture in your document means Word will take longer to load the file, since it will have to update the image based on the link to the original. But it will also make the file substantially smaller.

After you've made your choices in the Insert Picture dialog box and chosen OK, Word will return to the document and insert the picture, as shown in Figure 14-36.

**FIGURE 14-36**

Word will insert the picture so you can see it in your document, shown here in Page Layout view.

## How to size a picture

Note how the picture in Figure 14-36 is aligned with the left margin. As our next step, we can either adjust the picture's size and then add a frame so we can adjust the picture's position, or we can add a frame and then adjust both size and position by adjusting the frame.

In this example, we'll adjust the size first and then add a frame, but note that most of the sizing techniques work the same way in either case. Note too that when you select a picture and then insert a frame, you'll find that you cannot resize the frame—or even select the frame—independently of the picture unless you choose Format Frame and change the frame size through the dialog box. This also holds true if you create the frame first and then take care to insert only a picture. If you create a frame that includes any additional elements besides the one picture, however, even a single-space character, you'll find that Word treats the frame and picture as separate elements. In general, working with pictures in frames is much easier if Word treats them as a single element, and the easiest way to ensure that will happen is to insert the picture into your document, select the picture, and choose Insert Frame either before or after changing the picture size. Note too that these comments apply to text boxes as well.

To size a picture, first select the picture by clicking on it with the mouse or by moving to its immediate left or right and using the same keyboard selection techniques you would use to select an individual character. Word will indicate the selection by adding a box with eight handles around the picture, so the picture will look much like a selected frame, but without the frame border with diagonal lines.

You can use the mouse either to scale or to crop the picture. Scaling changes the picture's dimensions—along the horizontal dimension, the vertical dimension, or both at once. Cropping lets you cut pieces off the edges as you might with a photograph. In the case of the picture of the airplane and banner that we've been using, we want to make the picture a little larger rather than shrink or cut it, but any of these modifications are easy to make. Figure 14-37 shows three versions of the same picture. The version at the top was simply inserted into a Word document. The middle version was proportionally scaled to half its size. The bottom one is in the original proportions but is cropped to eliminate unwanted parts.

You can scale and crop by using the mouse to drag the handles located around the selected picture (or frame or text box), or you can enter a specification for the changes in a dialog box. As with frames, the mouse techniques provide interactive control with immediate visual feedback, which is useful for broad changes. The dialog box provides precise control for finer adjustments. You will often be best off using both methods, making broad changes with the mouse before making final changes with the keyboard. We'll start with the mouse in this example as well.

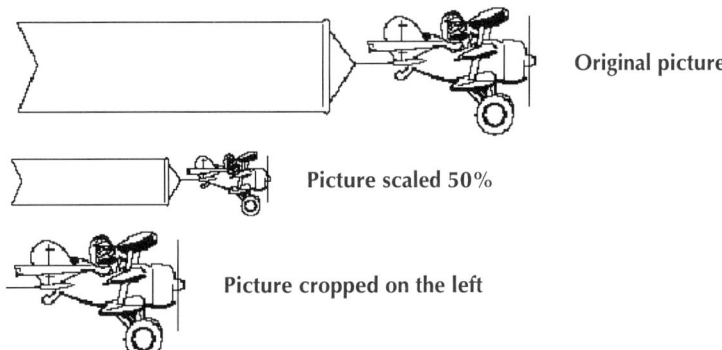

**FIGURE 14-37**

These three images show the difference between resizing a picture by scaling and by cropping.

Original picture

Picture scaled 50%

Picture cropped on the left

## How to scale and crop by dragging with the mouse

You can scale a picture simply by moving the mouse pointer to one of the eight handles around a selected picture, and then clicking and dragging the handle to a new position. However, which handle you grab makes a difference in the kind of change you can make.

If you use any of the four corner handles, the mouse pointer will turn into a two-headed diagonal arrow pointer. This pointer will maintain the picture's current proportions as you change the size of the picture. In other words, you'll be able to make the picture half as tall only if you also make it half as wide. Note too that the operative phrase here is *current proportions*: If you've already changed the picture from its original proportions, Word will maintain that change when you scale the picture this way.

Note that this does not work the same way as when you are resizing frames. With frames, the diagonal double arrow does not force you to maintain the same proportions.

If you use the handles on the sides, top, or bottom of the picture, you will change the scale along one dimension only: vertical or horizontal. Be careful when making this sort of change; it can yield an image that looks stretched or squashed. Although this will not be a problem for some images and can even result in an interesting visual effect for others, the result can look strange indeed if you distort a face or some other recognizable subject.

Fortunately, it's easy to restore a picture to its original proportions. Whenever you're dragging a handle, Word puts a message in the status bar showing the scaling proportions for whatever dimension or dimensions you're currently adjusting. If you're dragging a corner handle, Word will show the current scaling factors for both height and width. If you're dragging a top, bottom, or side handle, it will show the scaling factor for just height or width, as appropriate. Scaling factors are given in terms of the original picture, so if both height and width show the same scaling factor, the picture has its original proportions.

To crop a picture, just hold down the Shift key before you click on a handle. When you move the pointer over the handle, the pointer shape will change to a square whose lines overshoot two of the corners with a thin diagonal line through the square. If you then drag the edge or corner handle to make the picture smaller, Word will cut off any part of the original image outside the edge or edges. However, the full image will still be available to Word, so if you crop too much, you can drag the handle out again to restore some or all of the picture. (You can also drag the handle away from the original, complete, picture, to add blank space around the picture.) As with scaling, Word will display a message at the bottom of the screen showing how much you have cropped the picture—showing the measurement in this case rather than the proportions. In general, you will probably want to crop just one side at a time, using the left, right, top, or bottom handle. If you use one of the corner handles, Word will maintain the overall picture's proportions and will crop two sides at once.

## How to scale and crop with the Picture dialog box

As we've already mentioned, Word provides a dialog box for formatting pictures. Like the Frame dialog box, the Picture dialog box lets you make changes with mouse or keyboard and it has the advantage of greater precision than dragging with the mouse. And like the Frame dialog box also, the Picture dialog box has the disadvantage of not letting you see the effect of your changes until you close the dialog box. To open the Picture dialog box, select a picture and choose Format Picture. Word will respond with the dialog box shown in Figure 14-38, with settings taken from the currently selected picture.

**FIGURE 14-38**

The Picture dialog box lets you scale and crop a picture with precision.

The entries in the Picture dialog box are all straightforward. However, it's important to understand how they interact with each other.

The Crop From box has four text boxes, one for each side of the picture. These text boxes have default settings of 0. To crop part of a picture, simply enter a positive number for the appropriate edge. To add white space around the image, enter a negative number. Note that when you enter a setting for cropping the picture, it will affect the height or width of the picture. That, in turn, changes the entry in the Height or Width text box in the Size box. If you start with a 4-inch-wide picture, for example, and crop 1 inch on the left side, Word will automatically change the width entry in the Size box to 3 inches.

In much the same way, the Width and Height text boxes in the Scaling and Size boxes are also related to each other. Change either width setting, and Word will automatically change the other. Similarly, if you change either height setting, Word will automatically change the other. For example, suppose the Crop From text boxes are all set at 0 for a 4-inch-wide picture, and you change the scaling width to 50 percent. Word will change the setting in the Size Width box to 2 inches.

If you want to maintain (or regain) the original proportions for the picture, simply make sure that the Width and Height scaling factors are set to the same value. If you want to return to the original values, choose the Reset button. Notice also that Word shows the picture's original dimensions in the Original Size box at the bottom of the dialog box.

## How to add a frame to a picture

One other item in the Picture dialog box that's worth mention is the Frame button, which is grayed out in Figure 14-38. If the picture were already in a frame, the Frame button would be available. Choosing the button would then open the Frame dialog box and would be equivalent to selecting the frame with the picture and then choosing Format Frame.

One reason for putting a picture in a frame is so you can change its position on the page. Another reason is to let text wrap around it, with text on the same horizontal lines as the picture. To add a frame, either select the picture, and choose Insert Frame, or bring up the context-sensitive menu by holding the Control key down while clicking on the picture, and choose Frame Picture. Word will add the frame, which you'll see as shaded border around the picture when you have the picture selected. In contrast to empty frames or frames you add around text, when you add a frame around a picture, Word will, by default, not include a border.

### How to position a picture

With the frame in place around the picture, you can move the picture just as you can move a frame filled with text. Figure 14-39 on the next page shows our sample document after we resized the picture, inserted a frame, and moved the frame to its new position, centered horizontally relative to the page.

Adding a frame to a picture lets you place the picture anywhere on the page.

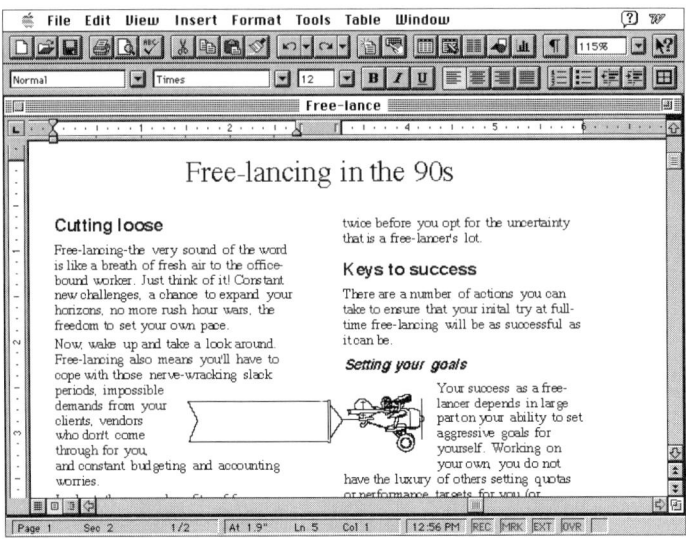

## NEW! How to add a caption or other text to a picture

The one thing still missing from our picture is a caption that will stay with the picture rather than stay with the body text if we later move the picture again or edit or reformat the document. In addition, the picture we're using includes a banner where we can add some text, such as *Take Off on Your Own!*, to make the picture better match the document content. You can easily add either or both of these items with a text box, using a slight modification of the techniques we described earlier in this chapter.

The easiest, most reliable way to add a text box and have it stay with the picture is to add it as part of the picture itself. Start by double-clicking on the picture. Depending upon the original file format, you may see a dialog box about converting the picture. If so, click on OK to use the copy of the picture shown. Word will open the Word Picture editing window, with the picture loaded. The screen will still look much like the Word document-editing screen, but all your text will disappear. In addition, you'll see the Drawing toolbar, whether it was visible before or not, along with the Picture toolbar, which includes the Close Picture button, and the Reset Picture Boundary button, which looks like a tic-tac-toe grid.

To add text, simply click on the Text Box button, define the text box inside the banner, and enter and format the text you want to use. Then repeat the procedure for the caption. The result should look much like Figure 14-40.

**FIGURE 14-40**

The picture-editing window looks much like a document-editing environment. Note that the caption's text box lies partly outside the picture boundary lines.

In Figure 14-40, the text box with the caption, which is immediately below the picture, lies partly outside the four lines that designate the picture boundaries. If you choose Close Picture at this point, the part of the text box that lies outside the boundaries will not show up in the picture when you return to the document. To include the entire text box in the picture, click on the Picture Boundary button. Word will reposition the boundaries to include the entire picture. If you then choose Close Picture, you should see the entire picture, including the full caption, as in Figure 14-41.

**FIGURE 14-41**

If you add a caption as part of the picture, the picture and caption will always stay together.

# How to place a border around a picture

In many cases, you'll want to add a border around your picture. If the picture includes a caption, you have two basic choices: You can select the entire frame and define a border for it, or you can double-click on the picture, to open Microsoft Word 6.0 Picture, and define a rectangle around the picture—by choosing the rectangle button and defining a rectangle much as you would define a text box. You can also define one border for the frame and one for the picture itself. To define a border for the frame, select the frame, choose Format Borders And Shading to open the Picture Borders And Shading dialog box, and define the border just as you would for any paragraph. You can use the same technique for a text box, or you can use the alternative we described earlier in this chapter, in "The Drawing Object dialog box." Figure 14-42 shows the frame formatted with a border.

**FIGURE 14-42**

If you add a frame to a picture, you can add a border to the frame, to the picture, or to both.

# How to position a picture in a table

Be aware also that there is another way to control the positioning of a picture. Rather than using a frame, you can insert a picture into a cell of a table. This technique does not give you the positioning features and ability to wrap text around the graphic that you get with a frame, but it offers a quick and easy way to arrange pictures and text side by side. You might prefer using a table rather than a frame for a simple layout.

As much as we've covered in this chapter, we've barely begun to look at Word's capabilities for inserting and manipulating graphics. In fact, Word comes with a set of applications for drawing, creating graphs, creating fancy text for titles, and more. Word will also let you insert data created in other programs. We'll take a look at these features in the next chapter.

# TOPIC FINDER

# 15

# Drawing, Graphics, & Other Objects

hapter 14 explained how to add pictures to your documents using the clip-art images that come with Microsoft Word. As we mentioned then, however, you are by no means limited to clip art. You can also import pictures from other sources, as we'll discuss in Chapter 18, or insert such objects as a Microsoft Excel worksheet or chart, as we'll briefly explain at the end of this chapter.

What's more, you can create your own images by using Word's built-in drawing features or any of three tools that come with Word: Microsoft WordArt, Microsoft Graph, and Microsoft Equation Editor. We'll cover Equation Editor in Chapter 23 because it serves as a mathematics editing tool rather than a graphics program. But all three of these programs are mini-applications. Although we do not stress the point in Chapter 23, Equation Editor actually inserts an image of your equations, which is why you can scale the equations after you add them to your document, just as you can any other picture. The other two mini-applications work much the same way: You use them to create an image and then embed it in your document.

Unfortunately, the very sophistication of the Word drawing tools and the mini-applications leads to a problem: Trying to cover them in depth would demand many more pages than we can justify by their importance to most users. Our aim in this chapter, then, is to introduce and provide an overview of the drawing tools and two of the programs. But keep in mind that we are merely opening a door on the subject. It's as if we were writing a book about the United States and had to explain football, baseball, and basketball in one chapter. We can cover most of the rules, but we won't get anywhere near describing the nuances of each game.

# Using Word's Drawing Tools

Word's drawing tools differ from its mini-applications in that the tools are part of Word itself. If you click on the Drawing button on the Standard toolbar (third to the left of the Zoom button), Word will add the Drawing toolbar, shown in Figure 15-1. By default, this toolbar is displayed at the bottom of the Word window, and Word switches to Page Layout view.

**FIGURE 15-1**

When you click on the Drawing button, Word positions the Drawing toolbar at the bottom of the Word window by default.

We introduced the Drawing toolbar in Chapter 14, where we showed you how to use its Text Box and Callout buttons to insert text boxes in your document. Text boxes are actually drawing objects. For this discussion, we'll assume that you're familiar with text boxes and the related features and concepts explained in Chapter 14. If you're not, we suggest that before you proceed here, you read "Frames: Positioning Text and Graphics on the Page" on page 481, and that you pay particular attention to "Text Boxes and Callouts" on page 497.

In addition to creating text boxes, you can use the Drawing toolbar to draw other objects directly in your document—including lines, arrows, rectangles, ellipses, and freeform shapes. Figures 15-2 and 15-3 list the toolbar buttons and their purposes. If you know how to work with text boxes, many, if not most, of these buttons should be self-explanatory; others will be familiar to users of nearly any object-based drawing program.

| Button | Tool Name | Lets You Click and Drag to Insert This Kind of Drawing Object |
|---|---|---|
| **Tools for inserting lines and shapes** | | |
| | Line | Straight lines |
| | Rectangle | Rectangles, including squares |
| | Ellipse | Ellipses, including circles |
| | Arc | Arcs |
| | Freeform | Freehand polygons and other shapes |
| **Text box tools** | | |
| | Text Box | Text boxes |
| | Callout | Callout text boxes |

**FIGURE 15-2**

The Drawing toolbar buttons for inserting objects.

 Many of the buttons in Figure 15-3 on the next page are equivalent to choosing the Format Drawing Object command and setting options on the Fill, Line, or Size And Position card in the Drawing Object dialog box. Figure 15-3 mentions the equivalent dialog box options where appropriate, including the card in the Drawing Object dialog box on which the options can be found. We looked at these options in Chapter 14, where we discussed text boxes.

| Button | Tool Name | Purpose |
|---|---|---|
| **Formatting tools** | | |
| | Format Callout | Opens the Format Callout dialog box for formatting all selected callouts; equivalent to choosing the Callout button on the Size And Position card |
| | Fill Color | Opens a grid of colors plus shades of gray to change the fill color of all selected objects; equivalent to the Color grid on the Fill card |
| | Line Color | Opens a grid of colors plus shades of gray to change the line color of all selected objects; equivalent to the Color list on the Line card |
| | Line Style | Opens a list of various line styles and weights, with and without arrowheads, to change the line style of all selected objects; equivalent to the Arrowhead group box and the Style and Weight options in the Line group box on the Line card |
| | Select Drawing Objects | Lets you click and drag to create a rectangle designating the objects that will be affected by formatting or other subsequent commands |
| | Bring To Front | Positions the selected objects in front of others so that the selected objects hide, or partially hide, the objects in back |
| | Send To Back | Positions the selected objects behind others so that the selected objects are hidden, or partially hidden, by the objects in front |
| | Bring In Front Of Text | Similar to Bring To Front, except that it positions the selected objects to hide text in the same area of the page |
| | Send Behind Text | Similar to Send To Back, except that it positions the selected objects to be overwritten by text in the same area of the page |
| | Group | Groups all currently selected objects into one object |

**FIGURE 15-3**                                            *(continued)*

The Drawing toolbar buttons for formatting and other tasks.

**FIGURE 15-3** *continued*

| Button | Tool Name | Purpose |
|---|---|---|
| | Ungroup | Breaks a set of grouped objects into individual objects so that you can format them individually |
| | Flip Horizontal | Flips all the selected items in a horizontal plane; if more than one item is selected, the items flip as a group |
| | Flip Vertical | Flips all the selected items in a vertical plane; if more than one item is selected, the items flip as a group |
| | Rotate Right | Rotates all the selected items 90 degrees clockwise; if more than one item is selected, the items rotate as a group |
| | Reshape | Shows all available handles on a freeform object so that you can click and drag to reshape the object |
| | Snap To Grid | Opens the Snap To Grid dialog box shown in Figure 15-4 |
| | Align Drawing Objects | Opens the Align dialog box shown in Figure 15-5 |
| **Other tools** | | |
| | Create Picture | Opens a window for creating a picture if no objects are selected; converts any selected drawing objects to a single picture object |
| | Insert Frame | Equivalent to choosing the Insert Frame menu command |

## A closer look at the drawing tools

Word's drawing features are object-oriented—that is, all the images you create with the drawing tools are composed of either individual lines or filled objects. The objects are defined by straight and curved lines, which are themselves defined by a set of points.

To use the tools that create lines and shapes, you simply click on the appropriate button on the Drawing toolbar. Then click on a spot in your document to anchor one end of a line or one corner handle of a shape, hold down the mouse button, and drag to draw the line or shape. Release the button to finish creating the line or shape.

For shapes—such as rectangles and ellipses—Word will fill the inside of the shape using the current fill settings for drawing objects, and it will create a line defining the outside of the shape using the current line settings. If you've set the line format to include an arrowhead, the arrowhead will appear on any lines you draw, but not on closed shapes such as rectangles and ellipses.

After you create an object, you can move it. You can also reshape it, by moving the points that define its lines. To get a sense of how this works, think of the lines—whether curved or straight—as rubber bands that are tacked down in some places and attached to invisible wires in others. If you pull on the invisible wires or move the tacked-down points, the rubber bands will change shape, size, or both. Word also lets you change the color of an object, as well as such details as the weight and color of the outside line, by changing the settings for the fill and the line.

It's important to note that although you can resize and reshape objects, you can work with them only as complete objects. You cannot, for example, erase part of a line; instead you must resize it. This approach differs from the one you'll find in bitmap-oriented programs, such as MacPaint, in which you create images with a group of dots, or bits. Bitmapped images are more like paintings on canvas, in which you define shapes by where you put the paint. To change shapes in bitmapped images, you must change the position of the bits. When you change color, you change the color of each individual dot. And, unlike the way you work with drawing objects, you can erase part of a bitmapped line by erasing only certain bits.

Another important feature of drawing objects allows you to group objects together or break a group of objects apart. You can also select one or more objects and move them either in front of or behind other objects. The objects in back will be partly or completely hidden by the objects in front.

If these concepts seem a bit difficult, we suggest that you experiment with the drawing tools a bit to see how they work on the screen and then come back and read these sections again. We'll also offer some notes on specific tools in the following section, covering important aspects of those tools that may not be immediately obvious.

If you click on one of the Drawing toolbar buttons to draw a line or a shape, Word will deactivate the button as soon as you finish drawing one object. If you initially double-click on the button, however, Word will keep it active until you click on it again or click on another button. As long as the button is active, you can create as many objects with that tool as you need. Like all toolbar buttons, when the button is active, it will look as if it has been pressed.

## How to control movement of objects

In practice, you'll find that it's hard to move an object or a handle in an exact vertical, horizontal, or diagonal direction. To make the task easier, hold down the Shift key as you drag. When you do so, you will be able to move the object only in a precisely vertical or horizontal direction. If you are resizing an object (by moving the handles), each handle will move only in a specific direction—side handles move horizontally, top and bottom handles move vertically, and corner handles move diagonally. When you are moving an object, the object can move only horizontally or vertically. If you drag the object diagonally, it will move only in one or the other direction. If your diagonal dragging is uneven, the object may appear to jump from being moved horizontally to being moved vertically.

## How to use the Shift, Control, and Option keys

If you're creating an ellipse, holding down the Shift key as you drag will draw a circle (rather than an oval). Similarly, if you're creating a rectangle, you can hold down Shift to draw a square. If you're drawing a straight line and holding down Shift, Word will draw only a vertical line, a horizontal line, or a line at a 30-, 45-, or 60-degree angle to the vertical or horizontal. If you're extending an existing line, holding down the Shift key will maintain the current angle—that is, you can only extend the line, not rotate it.

To resize an object around its center point, hold down the Control and Option keys. Word will then adjust all appropriate parts of the object as you drag. You can hold down Control-Shift to combine effects when resizing using a corner handle so that the object retains its proportions. If you hold down Control-Option when you create an ellipse or a rectangle, the first click will anchor the center of the shape rather than a corner handle. Holding down Control-Shift will also anchor the center and draw a circle or a square.

## The Freeform button

The freeform tool has two modes of operation. If you click on the Freeform button, click in one position on the screen, and then click in another, you'll get a straight line between the two points. If you move the pointer and click a third time, you'll get a second line between the second click position and the third. You can create a closed freeform object consisting of straight lines by adding as many lines as you need and then positioning the end of one line at the starting point of the first line. (Note that you can zoom in on the image with Word's zoom feature, for precise placement.)

To use the second freeform drawing mode, hold down the mouse button and drag. You'll get a line that follows the pointer's movement, as if you were using a pen or pencil. When you release the mouse button, the pointer will stop drawing this way and will return to the first mode.

If you create a closed polygon, the freeform tool will recognize when the object is finished and will turn off automatically. To turn off the tool manually at any point in drawing a line, press Esc or double-click.

## The Reshape button

Freeform objects can display two sets of handles. The first set consists of eight handles arranged around the object along a rectangular outline. The second set consists of a variable number of handles, which lie on the line that defines the object, at places where the direction of the line changes. To go back to our rubber-band analogy, the first set of handles acts as the points to which the invisible wires are attached, allowing you to resize the object as a whole. The second set of handles, available only on freeform objects, represents the points where the rubber bands are tacked down. You can move these handles to alter the shape. To toggle between the first and second set of handles, select a freeform object and click on the Reshape button.

## The Snap To Grid button

The Snap To Grid button opens the Snap To Grid dialog box, shown in Figure 15-4. If you're familiar with graphics programs, you probably already know that the concept *snap to grid* constrains movement to discrete increments. This makes it easier to control position, size, and shape, since you can drag objects only in increments defined by the grid.

**FIGURE 15-4**

By default, the Snap To Grid increments are 0.1 inch.

As you can see in Figure 15-4, the default Snap To Grid settings are 0.1 inch. You can use this dialog box to change the settings for horizontal and vertical movement—or to turn the feature on or off, by checking or clearing the Snap To Grid check box. The Horizontal Origin and Vertical Origin boxes let you shift the position of the grid on the page.

> If the Snap To Grid feature is turned on and you hold down the ⌘ key as you start to drag with the mouse to either draw or position an object, Word turns off the Snap To Grid feature. This can be useful if the grid increments are too large to let you position an object where you want it to appear, saving you the effort of turning the feature off and then on again. On the other hand, if the Snap To Grid feature is turned off, holding down the ⌘ key as you drag will turn the feature on.

## The Align Drawing button

The Align Drawing button opens the Align dialog box, shown in Figure 15-5. The dialog box choices enable you to align the currently selected object or objects relative to the page or to one another, in both horizontal (Left, Center, Right, or None) and vertical (Top, Center, Bottom, or None) directions. If you only have one object selected, you can only align it with respect to the page, but if you select multiple objects, you can align them with each other or the page.

**FIGURE 15-5**

The Align dialog box lets you quickly align selected objects with one another or in relation to the page.

This alignment feature can be quite helpful. If you want to create several concentric circles, for example, you can create the circles quickly, without worrying about their positions. You can then use the Select Drawing Objects button to select them all, click on the Align Drawing button, set the dialog box options to center the circles horizontally and vertically relative to one another, and choose OK.

## The Create Picture button

If you select at least one drawing object before clicking on the Create Picture button, Word will convert the object to a Word picture object, which we'll discuss in a moment. If you select more than one object first, Word will join them and convert them to a single picture object. Generally, you will want to convert a drawing object (or group of objects) to a single picture object so that you can place it as a picture within your document (rather than as separate drawing objects). You can then work with the new picture using the techniques described in the previous chapter. If you simply want to work with a group of objects as a single drawing object temporarily, use the Group button instead. You can use the Ungroup button to break a group of drawing objects back into individual objects. There is no way to convert a picture object to a drawing object.

Joining multiple objects into a single picture object makes it impossible to get at the individual parts. However, you can still modify parts of the picture if you open a Word picture editing window (which we touched on briefly in Chapter 14). To open a picture editing window to modify a picture object, simply double-click on the picture object. Alternatively, you can select the object, choose the Edit Picture Object command, and then choose Open. (The Object command on the Edit menu is usually grayed. When you select an appropriate object, however, such as a picture object, the command name changes to match the selected object and the command becomes available.) You can also open a blank picture editing window by clicking on the Create Picture button with no drawing object selected.

## How to use Word's picture editing window

As we mentioned in Chapter 14, a picture editing window is a special kind of window Word provides for editing picture objects. Figure 15-6 shows a picture editing window that was opened by double-clicking on a set of concentric circles we created with Word's drawing tools and then converted to a picture object.

**FIGURE 15-6**

Word's picture editing window is similar to a document window in Page Layout view.

As you can see in Figure 15-6, the picture editing window is quite similar to a document window in Page Layout view. You can, for example, still use most of Word's menu commands and toolbar buttons. But the only item you can edit is the picture object itself. Notice that the title bar in Figure 15-6 is labeled *Picture in Document1*. That's precisely what you'll see: the single picture you are currently editing.

When you open a picture editing window, Word will add the Drawing toolbar (if it isn't already displayed) and the Picture toolbar. The Drawing toolbar and all the drawing tools work the same way in a picture editing window as they do in a document window. The Picture toolbar contains two buttons. The Reset Picture Boundary button expands or shrinks the boundary that defines which part of the picture Word will insert in your document. If you edit the picture so that it no longer matches the original boundary, click on Reset Picture Boundary to ensure that the entire picture is inserted in your document. (The current boundary is represented in the window by a rectangle that is formed by thin lines and delineated with crop marks—two short lines at right angles—at each corner.) The Close Picture button closes the picture editing window and returns you to the document window with the modified or newly created picture inserted.

You can use Word's drawing tools either to annotate text (for example, with a callout) or to create an image. When you annotate text, obviously you'll want to enter the drawing objects directly in your document, where you can see the text. But if you want to create a complex illustration, and particularly if you want to ensure that you won't accidentally change its elements later while working in the document, you'll be better off working in a picture editing window.

You can also use a picture editing window to edit images imported from other sources. For most bitmapped images, such as TIFF or MacPaint files, Word can only resize or reproportion the image. With object-oriented images, you can generally do more.

## Working with Word's Mini-Applications

Unlike Word's drawing tools, which are integrated into the program, the mini-applications that come with Word stand somewhat apart from Word. To use them, you must first place the cursor in your document where you want to add the new element and then choose Insert Object. (Word provides an Insert Chart button on the Standard toolbar, but we'll ignore that for the moment.) Word will open an Object dialog box similar to the one shown in Figure 15-7 on the next page.

**FIGURE 15-7**

The Object dialog box
lists different object
types that you can
insert.

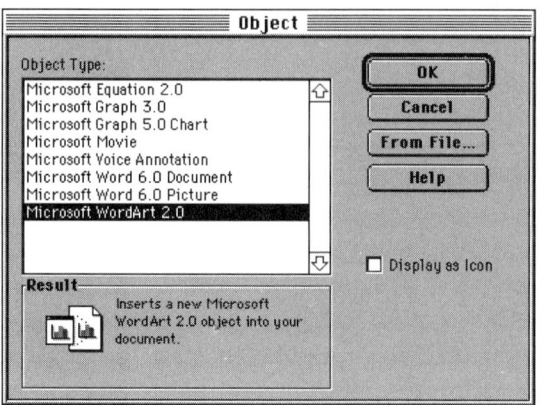

The list you see in the Object Type list box on your screen can differ from the one shown in Figure 15-7. What you'll see depends on how you installed Word and what other applications you have installed. For example, if you have installed Microsoft Excel, you'll see the Microsoft Excel Worksheet option. At the moment, however, we're concerned only with Microsoft WordArt 2.0, which comes with Word and should be available on your system. If it's not, you can install it from the original Word disks (or a backup copy) by running the Setup program again.

## NEW! How to use the Object dialog box

As you can see in Figure 15-7, there is a From File button; choose this to open a dialog box similar to the one used by the Insert File command. You can use this dialog box for files created in other programs, such as Microsoft Excel, to insert the contents from an existing file into Word. You can then edit the file later in the original application. We'll cover the Insert File command in Chapter 18, "Sharing Data with Other Programs," starting on page 587.

The Object dialog box lets you create an object and insert it at the same time. The Object Type list shows all available types of objects. You can use the Display As Icon check box, which you'll find on both this dialog box and the dialog box that appears when you use the From File button, to insert the object into your document as an icon. To see the object's contents, you can then double-click on the icon in your document to call on the application in which the object was created.

If you check the Display As Icon check box, the Object dialog box will display the icon that Word will use.

When you create an object such as a spreadsheet, a graph, or another document whose contents need to be visible in your Word document both on screen and in printed form, be sure that you do not check the Display As Icon check box. When you want to create a hypertextlike link that will open another application so that you can see and edit an item in that application, you should check this check box.

## Creating Font Effects with Microsoft WordArt

NEW!

Of Word's three mini-applications, WordArt 2.0 is likely to be of most interest to most people.

Simply put, WordArt lets you create a rich variety of special font effects using a wide range of typestyles. As is the case for any fancy effect, you won't want to overdo it, but you'll find this program a fun and flexible way to add some visual pizzazz to your documents, from memos to newsletters. To give you a flavor of what WordArt can do, Figure 15-8 presents some sample WordArt images.

As you can do with any image, you can place a WordArt image in a frame so that you can control its placement on the printed page. See Chapter 14, "Columns, Frames, & Pictures," starting on page 469.

**FIGURE 15-8**

WordArt offers many font effects that you can use to dress up your printed pages.

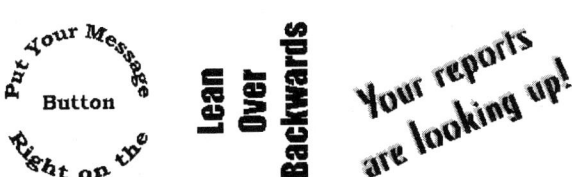

Suppose, for example, that you want to add a fancy title to the newsletter shown in Figure 15-9 on the next page. Because you'll want the WordArt image to span all three columns, after you've created the image you'll want to place it in a frame and then resize the frame to fill the top of the page.

We will use WordArt
to add a title at the top
of this sample news-
letter.

Be sure that the cursor is at the top of the document. To insert the WordArt
object, choose Insert Object, highlight Microsoft WordArt 2.0 in the Object
Type list box, and choose OK to start WordArt. The WordArt window will appear, as shown in Figure 15-10.

The WordArt window
lets you create and
modify WordArt
objects.

The title for this newsletter is *Stone & Poor's WordArt Tips*. Start by typing
this title in the text box at the top of the window. You can press Return to create separate lines, if you want. You can then choose the Update Display button to update the text displayed in the WordArt image, although WordArt
will automatically update the text when you choose another option in the
window.

After entering the text, you'll need to tell WordArt how to format it. You can add the formatting in any order.

The first formatting choice in the window is the Choose A Shape pull-down list. If you open the pull-down list, you'll see the grid shown in Figure 15-11. Each shape on this grid represents a different pattern for laying out the text. As you'll see in a moment, you can modify these further. Figure 15-11 shows some samples of how our newsletter title would look with some of the choices in this grid. For our example, we'll use Curve Up, which is the fourth item down in the left column of the grid.

**FIGURE 15-11**

These sample WordArt images differ only in the Choose A Shape box setting.

The next choices down in the window are the Font and the Size pull-down lists. The Font list is a list of all of the fonts installed on your system. For our example, we'll use Arial Rounded MT Bold. (If you have not installed Word's TrueType fonts on your system, you may not have this font available.) For Font Size, you can choose Best Fit or specify a size. We'll stay with Best Fit.

The next formatting choice is the Alignment box and its pull-down list. Although we won't use this button, it requires a bit of explanation. The pull-down list offers six choices: Center, Left, Right, Stretch Justify, Letter Justify, and Word Justify. The best way to understand the differences among these settings is to try each one. Before you can see the differences, however, you'll have to turn off the Stretch To Frame feature and make the frame larger than the text. We'll show you how to make the frame larger a little later as part of this example.

To the right of the Alignment box is the Color box, where you can choose the color for your WordArt text.

Along the bottom of the window there are three sets of buttons, labeled Fill, Effects, and Stretch. We'll cover each group in turn.

## The Fill buttons

The first button in the Fill group is the Shadow button. If you click on the Shadow toolbar button, WordArt will open the grid shown in Figure 15-12. You can then choose a shadow to complement your text. As you can see, the dialog box will let you pick not only a type of shadow but also a shadow color. For our example, we'll stay with silver for the color, pick the rightmost shadow type, and then choose OK to close the dialog box.

**FIGURE 15-12**

Choose the Shadow button to open the Shadow dialog box.

The second button in the Fill group is the Shading button. If you click on it, WordArt will open the Shading dialog box, shown in Figure 15-13. This lets you define the fill for the characters in the WordArt text. You can pick a pattern in the Style box and select foreground and background colors. The Sample box will show you the effect of your settings. For our example, we'll use a solid pattern, with a black foreground.

**FIGURE 15-13**

The Shading dialog box lets you adjust the fill pattern for the text characters.

The third button in the Fill group is the Border button. If you click on it, WordArt will open the Border dialog box, shown in Figure 15-14. You can pick both a line thickness and a line color in the Border dialog box. We won't use this effect in our example.

FIGURE 15-14

The Border dialog box lets you set the thickness and color for a line that appears around each WordArt character.

If you add a border, it appears around each individual character, and not around the WordArt image as a whole. If you have a color printer, this feature can produce a striking outline effect. If you want to add a border around the entire object, you must return to Word, select the object, and use Word's Format Borders And Shading command to add the border.

## The Effects buttons

The first two of the three Effects buttons are the Bold and Italic buttons. These act as toggles, turning that formatting feature on and off. The third one is called the Even Height button, and it raises all the letters—both uppercase and lowercase—so that they are the same height.

## The Stretch buttons

The first button in the Stretch group is the Stretch button. Choose this button to have WordArt set the text so that it will stretch to fill the frame around the object.

The second button is the Flip button. This causes each letter to rotate 90 degrees to the left but remain in its position. Used in conjunction with the Rotation button, it can be a handy way to create a vertical label that reads from top to bottom.

The third button in the Stretch group is the Rotation button. When you click on it, you'll open the Special Effects dialog box, shown in Figure 15-15 on the next page. The settings in the Special Effects dialog box will vary depending on the shape you selected in the Choose A Shape pull-down list. For now, we'll look only at the options that go with the Curve Up choice.

**FIGURE 15-15**

You can rotate text and adjust the relative size of characters with the Special Effects dialog box.

The Rotation setting in the Special Effects dialog box lets you control the rotation for the WordArt text as a whole. Rotate a straight horizontal line of text by 90 degrees, for example, and the text will be vertical but on its side. You can then use the Flip button to rotate each letter and wind up with text that reads from top to bottom. Again, the best way to see how these features interact is to experiment with them a bit. For purposes of this example, we'll leave the Rotation setting at 0 degrees.

The Slider setting determines whether the size of the text grows from left to right. If this setting is 0, the text will be the same height across. By default, the Curve Up shape uses a setting of 50 percent. To exaggerate this effect, we'll use a setting of 100 percent.

The last button in the Stretch group is the Spacing Between Characters button, with a short double-headed arrow underneath the letters *AV*. If you click on it, you'll open the Spacing Between Characters dialog box, shown in Figure 15-16. As you can see, you can set the spacing of the characters in pre-set levels ranging from Very Tight to Very Loose, or you can set a custom spacing. Check the Automatic Kern Character Pairs check box if you want WordArt to automatically adjust spacing between pairs of characters.

**FIGURE 15-16**

You can control character spacing in WordArt with the Spacing Between Characters dialog box.

Once you've defined the WordArt object the way you want it, you can re-turn to Word's editing window by choosing OK in the WordArt dialog box. If you then click on the object in your document, you'll see a rectangle that frames the object, along with the usual eight handles that you can drag to change size and proportions. Use these handles to stretch the rectangle to the right margin. If you've followed all the steps in our example precisely, the result should look much like the sample shown in Figure 15-17.

If you want to move a WordArt object on your page, add a frame by selecting the object and choosing Insert Frame. You'll then be able to move it around like any other object in a frame, using the techniques described in Chapter 14, "Columns, Frames, & Pictures," starting on page 469.

## How to create a dropped capital letter

WordArt isn't limited to creating dramatic effects. Figure 15-18 shows a report that uses what is called a dropped capital letter, or "drop cap," in the opening paragraph. This popular typographic effect is easy to create using WordArt, even with a shadow, as shown in this example. Word also has a menu command for creating drop caps, but WordArt can create more visually interesting variations.

**May is Derby month**

The first Saturday in May may yield the most the weeks before Derby day are filled with e least two weeks before the Derby, Louisville races, concerts, and other special activities.

The annual balloon race draws record crowd from across the nation gather to compete in the colo

## How to create a drop cap with Word's Format Drop Cap command

Certainly the quickest way to create a drop cap is with Word's built-in Format Drop Cap command. Start by placing the cursor in the paragraph where you want the drop cap. Then remove any first-line indent, and choose Format Drop Cap to open the Drop Cap dialog box, shown in Figure 15-19.

**FIGURE 15-19**

Word's Format Drop Cap command lets you define a drop cap using this dialog box.

As you can see in Figure 15-19, the Drop Cap dialog box offers three choices for position: None, Dropped, and In Margin. You can also pick a font, define the number of lines for the drop cap, and set the distance from the text. We'll use the Dropped position and we'll accept the defaults of a 3-line drop and 0 distance from the text. You can see the result in Figure 15-20.

**FIGURE 15-20**

This drop cap was produced by Word's built-in drop cap feature.

May is Derby month

The first Saturday in May may yield the most t weeks before Derby day are filled with equall two weeks before the Derby. Louisville is bri concerts, and other special activities.
   The annual balloon race draws record crowd from across the nation gather to compete in the colo rather keep your feet more firmly planted on the gro marathon and bike race to vie for your attention. Or,

## How to create a drop cap with WordArt

While there's nothing wrong with the drop cap shown in Figure 15-20, it just doesn't have the extra zip of the version you saw in Figure 15-18. To create the drop cap shown in Figure 15-18, start by deleting the first letter of the paragraph. Then, with the cursor at the leftmost position in the paragraph, choose the Insert Object command and start WordArt 2.0.

Figure 15-21 shows the finished WordArt image. The only text is a single capital T in the Times font. We also specified Best Fit in the Font Size box. We selected Plain Text in the Choose A Shape pull-down list because of the simple horizontal orientation of the image. The image is also defined with solid black shading and with a shadow option that creates a drop shadow.

After you define the WordArt image, choose OK to return to editing in Word, select the image, and choose Insert Frame to add a frame around it. You can then use the Word commands discussed in Chapter 14 to resize and reposition the character as needed. Also be sure that the frame is anchored to the paragraph that contains the drop cap. (You can use the mouse to drag the anchor to that paragraph.) We covered frames in detail in Chapter 14; for more details on anchoring in particular, see "Anchors" on page 486.

**FIGURE 15-21**

When inserted into a document and sized appropriately, this WordArt image will yield the drop cap shown in Figure 15-18.

To finish the drop cap in the example, select the frame, choose Format Frame, set the Width and Height to Auto, set Distance From Text to 0.03 inch, and check the Move With Text and Lock Anchor check boxes so that the drop cap will move with the appropriate paragraph if you edit the page or change the page's formatting. Then choose OK.

It takes only a minute or so to create a drop cap with this method, and the extra visual appeal is well worth the effort. Note too that you can use WordArt (but not Word's built-in feature) to create a raised cap (a large first letter that reaches above the first line of text) as well as a raised and dropped cap (a large first letter that reaches both above and below the first line of text).

# Creating Charts with Microsoft Graph

We're about to jump to a completely different subject: Microsoft Graph. Just about the only thing that Microsoft WordArt and Microsoft Graph have in common is that both are mini-applications that come with Word. Not only are they completely different kinds of applications, but they don't even work the same way: WordArt opens a separate window to work in and returns you to your document only when you finish working with the object, whereas Graph lets you work with a graph in the context of the Word document that will contain the object.

With that difference in mind, we'll also add a warning: Having taken a fairly complete look at WordArt, to give you a sense of the complexity of the mini-applications that come with Word, we'll take a much less detailed look at Microsoft Graph.

When you have a mass of numbers, it's usually far easier to make sense of them by looking at a chart than by looking at the numbers themselves. That's why spreadsheet programs such as Microsoft Excel include graphing features. Word will let you import charts from any program that supports OLE— the Object Linking and Embedding standard. But you might not own such a program. And even if you do, you may occasionally have a document with a set of numbers that needs to be converted to chart form.

Microsoft Graph lets you create attractive charts in short order. You start Graph in much the same way you start WordArt. Position your cursor where you want the graph to appear in your document. Then click on the Insert Chart button on the Standard toolbar or choose Insert Object, choose Microsoft Graph 5.0 Chart from the Object Type list box, and choose OK. Figure 15-22 shows the Word screen after you give the command to insert a Microsoft Graph.

**FIGURE 15-22**

Microsoft Graph will let you prepare attractive business graphs and charts quickly and easily.

As you can see in Figure 15-22, Graph opens a window on top of the document window, replaces the toolbars with its own, and changes the menu commands. The Datasheet window, in the lower half of the figure, looks like a spreadsheet made up of rows and columns. The image of the graph—as defined by Graph's current settings—appears in the document window. Figure 15-22 shows the default data and settings Graph uses when it first starts.

If you select an existing chart and then choose Edit Chart Object Open, or if you have Word set to show Field Codes (on the View card of the Tools Options dialog box), the graph will appear in its own window, and not in the document window. In that case, the File menu will have only two commands—Update and Quit & Return To Document—and there will be no Window menu. We'll discuss Graph assuming you are working with the chart in Word's document window.

The fundamental concept of Graph is that you arrange your data in the datasheet and then select the rows and columns you want to use to create the chart. As you make changes in the Datasheet window, the Chart will automatically reflect those changes. You can also change the settings that define the format of the chart itself.

## How to use the Graph menus

Graph's menu commands include a number of sophisticated features. Figure 15-23 shows the menus; we'll take a quick look at each. Note that you can use Graph's toolbars to access many of these commands; we'll cover the toolbar buttons after running through the menus.

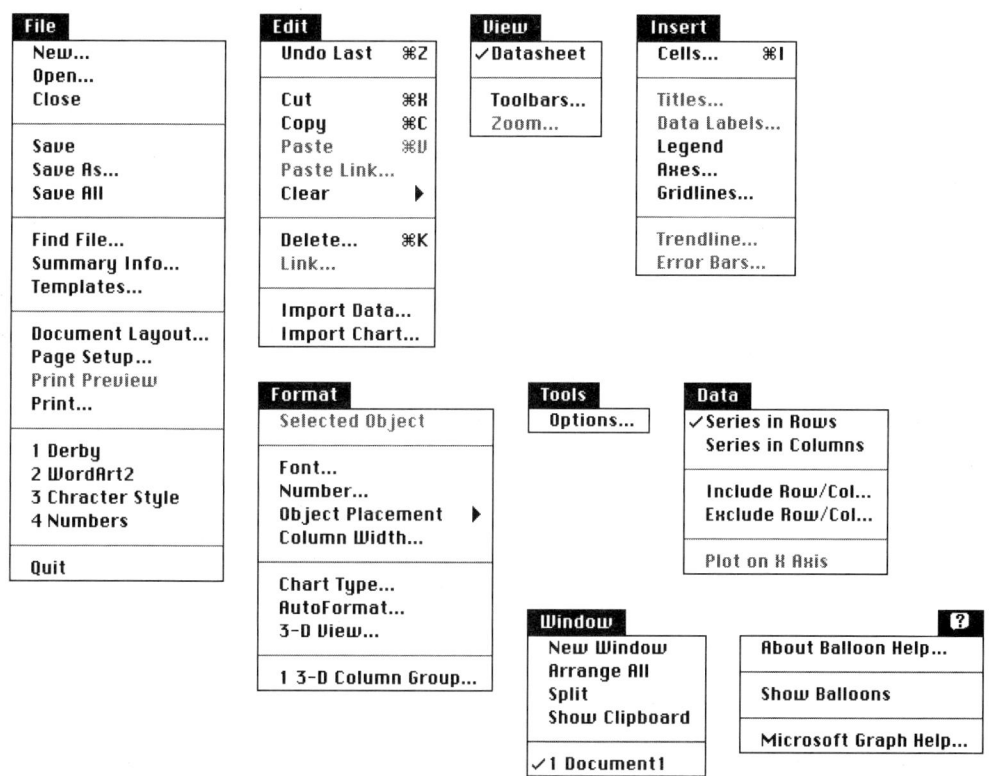

**FIGURE 15-23**

Graph's menus offer a wide range of commands that provide control over your charts.

You can use the keyboard to access the menu commands within Graph, but only by pressing F10 to activate the menu. If you press ⌘-Tab to activate the menu, the Word menu will be activated and not the Graph menu.

## The File menu

The File menu is unchanged by Graph; in fact, it remains under Word's control. If you choose any of the commands from this menu, control will switch back to Word while the command is executed, and then will return to Graph when the command is complete.

## The Edit menu

Most of the Edit menu commands are the same as those on Word's Edit menu. They are particularly useful in setting up the data you want to graph. You can enter and edit data in Graph's Datasheet window manually. Alternatively, if the data is available in tab-delimited or table form, you can copy and paste it into the window.

If the data has already been entered in some other application, it is usually faster, easier, and more accurate to import the data directly from that application with the File Import Data command. (This command will be grayed unless the Datasheet window is open.) You can import up to 4000 rows and 256 columns of data this way. Note that labels and legend keys must be in the first row and column of the imported data, as they are in the sample datasheet displayed when you open Graph. When you choose this command, you will see a dialog box that is similar to the dialog box for opening files in Word. The dialog box also includes an Options button, and when you choose this, you can specify whether you want the entire file or just a range of data imported. You can use the range feature to specify a specific block of cells from an Excel spreadsheet.

The last option on the Edit menu will let you insert a Microsoft Excel chart.

## The View menu

The first item on the View menu is Datasheet. This will have a check mark next to it if the Datasheet window is displayed. You can close the Datasheet window either by choosing this item on the menu or clicking on the graph in the document window.

The View menu also has a Toolbars item. This opens a Toolbars window that lists three toolbars: Standard (which is the standard Graph toolbar, not the Word toolbar), Drawing, and Formatting. We will discuss the contents of these three toolbars after we cover the menu options.

The last item on the View menu is Zoom, which you can use to enlarge or reduce the view of your graph.

## The Insert menu

The commands on the Insert menu affect the appearance of the chart in various ways, letting you define titles, labels, gridlines, and so on. All but one of these commands open dialog boxes that offer further choices.

The Insert Cells command lets you add new cells to an existing Datasheet. If the Datasheet is not displayed, this option will be grayed out. If only a single cell in the Datasheet is highlighted, then choosing this command will open a dialog box that will let you choose whether to insert a single cell or an entire row or column. (This works much the same as the Table Insert Cell command in Word; see Chapter 11, "Building Tables," starting on page 331, for more information on working with Word's table feature.) If you have an entire row or column highlighted when you choose this command, Graph will automatically insert a new row above a highlighted row, or a new column to the left of a highlighted column.

The Legend, Axes, and Gridlines commands will be the only other available commands on this menu if the Datasheet is displayed. The Legend command will toggle the display of a legend on your chart, showing the different data series used in the graph. The Axes and Gridlines commands open dialog boxes that you can use to specify which axes to display in the chart and which gridlines to display.

If the Datasheet window is not open and the chart itself is active, the Titles and Data Labels commands will be available as well. The commands open dialog boxes that let you specify whether or not you want to add text to your chart, and whether you want Graph to automatically show the values, labels, or both for data points on your chart. The Trendline command will open a dialog box where you can specify the kind of regression analysis you want to use to create a trendline for the selected data series on your chart. The Error Bars command lets you define how to calculate the measurement error—fixed value, percentage, standard deviation, or standard error—and the type of error bar to be used.

## The Format menu

The first command on the Format menu is Selected Object, though the "Object" will be replaced with a different term depending on which object in the chart you have highlighted before opening the Format menu. This command offers a wide range of formatting controls, which will vary depending on the type of object. For example, if you were to highlight a set of bars in a bar chart, this command would open a dialog box with a series of tabbed cards, including

Patterns and Data Labels. If you highlight an axis instead, the dialog box cards will be Patterns, Scale, Font, Number, and Alignment. We recommend that you explore some of these options on your own, since there is a rich range of choices available.

You can open the format dialog box for any object in a chart by double-clicking on the object.

The other choices on the Format menu open dialog boxes or provide other choices. If you have an object in the chart highlighted, some choices will be grayed out, and when you select others, you will see the same dialog box as with the Selected Object that we just described. If the Datasheet window is open, you may see different dialog boxes.

The Font, Number, and Column Width commands are all fairly self-explanatory. The Object Placement command allows you to choose among Bring To Front, Send To Back, and Group (or Ungroup); this works only with drawn objects that you add to a chart, which we will describe shortly.

The Chart Type command opens a dialog box that lets you choose among a variety of two- and three-dimensional chart formats. Figure 15-24 shows the main groups of three-dimensional formats that you can use. For each group, you can also choose additional options, such as the width of the columns and the spacing between them on a column chart.

**FIGURE 15-24**

The Format Chart Type command lets you choose from a wide range of two- and three-dimensional chart formats.

The AutoFormat command lets you apply a predefined format to a set of data. If you have a format you have created that you want to use repeatedly in the future to create new charts, you can store a custom format using the AutoFormat feature. This is especially helpful when you want to make a series of charts look similar, as you might in a report or for a newsletter or other publication.

The 3-D View command deserves special comment. Like the other dialog boxes available through the Format menu, this one will vary somewhat depending on the type of chart, but the variations share key features. Figure 15-25 shows one example of what the Format 3-D View dialog box can look like.

You can create a dizzying range of alternatives with this dialog box, rotating charts about their axes. But keep in mind that although it's fun to spin the charts around, the effect is often more dramatic than it is useful. If your intention is to give a broad overall view, 3-D charts shown at dramatic angles may be appropriate. But if you expect the reader to make studied judgments based on the data in the chart, be aware that these perspective views can often clutter the message more than they clarify it.

The last command on the Format menu will be for the format options for the type of chart used by the current chart. It is the same dialog box that you can reach by using the Format Chart Type command and then choosing Options as described earlier.

## The Tools menu

There is only one command on the Tools menu, Options, which opens a dialog box with three tabbed cards. The Datasheet options card lets you enable drag and drop for cell contents and automatic advance to the next cell down when you press Return. The Chart card includes a setting that lets you pick the default chart format and another that tells Graph how to deal with empty cells in data ranges. And the Color card lets you set the different colors to be used for various data sets and chart components; you can create custom palettes to match colors for specific presentations, if you want.

## The Data menu

The Data menu lets you tell Graph how to treat the rows and columns that you've selected to use in the chart. Include Row/Col and Exclude Row/Col let you designate rows or columns in the datasheet that will or will not be included in the chart. Series In Rows and Series In Columns are mutually exclusive choices you can toggle between, telling Graph whether to treat each row or each column as a data series. Graph puts a check mark next to the choice that's currently active.

The last menu command, Plot On X Axis, is available only for XY charts (also known as scatter plots). You can use this to tell Graph which row or column to use for the tick-mark labels along the *x*-axis of your chart. You must first select the row or column and then the command.

### The Window and Help menus

Graph also has Window and Help menus, which work much as they do from Word's menu.

### Context-sensitive menus

As in Word, you can hold down the Control key as you click on an object or the Datasheet within Graph. A context-sensitive menu will be displayed, and its commands will vary depending on the object.

## The Graph toolbars

As we mentioned earlier in this chapter, Graph displays its own Standard toolbar in place of the Word toolbars. There are also two other toolbars that you can choose to display and, if you are working with the chart in its own window, you can customize the toolbars or create new ones. We'll start by looking at the Standard toolbar.

### The Standard toolbar

Most—but not all—of Graph's Standard toolbar buttons duplicate commands that are available on Graph's menus, which we described in the preceding section of this chapter. Figure 15-26 shows the Graph Standard toolbar. As with Word's toolbars, you can use the ToolTips feature to see the name of each button; you can turn the ToolTips feature on and off in the View Toolbars dialog box, just as you can with Word.

 **FIGURE 15-26**

The Standard toolbar
in Microsoft Graph.

The first two buttons from the left are Import Data and Import Chart, which correspond to the same commands on the Edit menu. The third button is View Datasheet, and it will appear as if it had been pressed while the Datasheet window is displayed.

The next three buttons are the same as on the Word Standard toolbar: Cut, Copy, and Paste. The next button is the Undo button; there is no pull-down list of commands to undo as there is on the Word Standard toolbar.

The seventh and eighth buttons are By Row and By Column, and they correspond to the Data menu Series In Rows and Series In Columns commands; whichever command has a check mark next to it in the Data menu will have the corresponding button on the toolbar appear as if pressed.

The next button is Chart Type, and the arrow opens a pull-down list of chart types. The next two buttons, Vertical Gridlines and Horizontal Gridlines, correspond to the Major Gridlines options on the dialog box that opens with the Insert Gridlines command.

The thirteenth button is Legend, and toggles between including a legend with the chart or removing it. The button will appear to be pressed when the legend is included.

The next two buttons provide access to features that are not directly available on any Graph menu. The Text Box lets you add a text box as an annotation for your chart. (For more information on text boxes, see "Text Boxes and Callouts" on page 497.) The Drawing button opens the Drawing toolbar.

The next two buttons are Color and Pattern. Use the arrow to pull down a palette of options, then click on the button itself to apply the option to a highlighted object. These correspond to the pattern and color features available through the Format Selected Object menu command.

The last button on the Standard toolbar is Help, which provides point-and-click access to context-sensitive help for any aspect of Graph, just as it does in Word.

## Graph's other toolbars

As already mentioned, Graph has a Drawing toolbar that is very similar to the one offered in Word. There is also a Formatting toolbar that can be displayed using the View Toolbars command. The Formatting toolbar, shown in Figure 15-27, lets you change the formatting for a highlighted object (or cell in the Datasheet). Like the Formatting toolbar in Word, Graph's toolbar offers both a Font and a Font Size pull-down list along with Bold, Italic, Underline, Align Left, Center, and Align Right buttons.

 **FIGURE 15-27**

The Formatting toolbar in Microsoft Graph.

Graph's Formatting toolbar has five additional buttons that you can use to format numeric data in the Datasheet. These provide quick access to options that are also available through the Graph menu's Format Number command. The Currency Style adds a dollar sign to the number, and the Percent Style converts the data to a percentage. The Comma Style button applies a standard numeric style with commas. The last two buttons, Increase Decimal and Decrease Decimal, increase and decrease the number of digits to the right of the decimal point, one digit at a time.

If you open the chart in its own window, you can also customize these toolbars or create your own, using the Customize and New buttons in the Toolbars dialog box (which opens when you give the View Toolbars command). This feature works the same as in Word; for more information on customizing toolbars, see "Customizing Toolbars" on page 288.

## Where to go from here

We've just taken a quick romp through a complex program, but it should be enough to get you started. The best way to become familiar with the program is simply to experiment with it. Even if this is the first graphing program you've used, it won't be long before you'll be creating sophisticated charts with minimal effort.

# Inserting Other Objects

As we mentioned earlier in this chapter, you can insert other objects in your documents. The available choices will depend on the applications installed on your system. If you choose to insert one of these other objects, keep in mind that if you follow the techniques described in this chapter, the object will be available only through your document, not as a separate file that exists outside the document. If you want to make any changes to the object, you must open the document and either double-click on the object or select it and choose the Edit Object command.

For example, if Microsoft Excel is installed on your system, Word will let you insert Microsoft Excel worksheets and charts in your Word documents. If you choose Insert Object and then choose Microsoft Excel Chart or Microsoft Excel Worksheet, Word will load Microsoft Excel so that you can create or edit the data. And when you leave Microsoft Excel, Word will embed the object at the cursor location in your Word document, where it will be printed as if you had created it within Word. Choosing Edit Excel Chart Object or double-clicking on the object will load Microsoft Excel again, allowing you to edit the information further. For more information about the various ways you can embed and link to objects, see Chapter 18, "Sharing Data with Other Programs," starting on page 587.

# TOPIC FINDER

552

# 16

# Advanced Printing & Formatting

n Chapter 7, we explained the basics of formatting in Word. We described how to determine the layout of pages, format individual paragraphs, and apply character formatting such as fonts and font size. In this chapter, we'll cover Word's more complex formatting features.

One of the tasks that many Word users find baffling is trying to get the screen to accurately predict the final printed page. To help minimize the confusion, we'll cover some of the fundamentals of screen and printer fonts. We'll also delve a bit further into how to set up different right and left page layouts. And we'll wrap up the chapter with a look at how to create long documents from two or more shorter documents.

## Understanding Screen Fonts and Printer Fonts

One reason many people are drawn to the Macintosh in general, and to Word in particular, is the WYSIWYG (What You See Is What You Get) display. But many users are disappointed to find that the reality falls a little short of the promise and that what they see on the screen is sometimes different from what they get at the printer—in some cases, very different.

To understand why this happens and how to minimize the differences, you have to understand the relationship between screen fonts and printer fonts. The most important point to understand is that these are two entirely different sets of fonts.

Once you have that distinction firmly in mind, you also need to understand the difference between bitmapped fonts and scalable fonts. More important, your choice of a bitmapped or a scalable font affects how well the screen and the printer will match. We'll take a look at these issues and how they relate to each other.

## TrueType

At the risk of jumping ahead of ourselves a bit, it's worth pointing out that the problems with matching the screen display and the printed result with the Macintosh have been greatly simplified with System 7 and the introduction of TrueType fonts. These are scalable fonts that can both appear on screen and print on any printer that uses a driver that supports graphics. (We'll explain what a scalable font is in a moment.) Figure 16-1 shows an example of a TrueType font included with Word 6.0. If you limit your font selections to TrueType fonts and set your printer driver to use TrueType fonts, your printed output will match your screen displays fairly closely.

**FIGURE 16-1**

Word 6.0 adds a number of TrueType fonts to your system.

This advice to limit your font selections to TrueType need not constrain your creativity, since Word 6.0 comes with an assortment of TrueType fonts, as do other programs that you might have on your system. Also, you can obtain additional TrueType fonts from Microsoft and other sources.

## Bitmapped and scalable fonts

You can think of bitmapped fonts as pictures of individual characters, with a different picture for every size of every character you want to use. Scalable fonts, in contrast, consist of a set of rules that describe characters. The Macintosh can use either kind of font for screen fonts.

The advantage of bitmapped fonts is that you can get finely tailored images. The disadvantage is that all those individual pictures take up a lot of storage space.

With scalable fonts, when the computer calls for a 10-point Helvetica lowercase *a*, all the printer needs to have on hand are the rules for Helvetica characters so that it can create the letter in the size the computer requests. And if the printer lacks the rules for the particular font, the Macintosh can create the character instead and send it to the printer.

Although scalable fonts take less storage space than bitmapped fonts, they make greater demands on the processor—either in the printer's controller or in the computer, depending on which is generating the fonts. That, in turn, can slow printing speed.

## Resident printer fonts

Macintosh-compatible printers fall into two large categories: PostScript and non-PostScript.

If you have a PostScript printer (such as the LaserWriter IINT), the system software will try to use the PostScript fonts that are resident in the printer when printing. If the required font is not available, it will try to find a matching PostScript font on the Macintosh's hard disk. If it can't find a PostScript font, it will use a TrueType font. And if there is no TrueType font, it will use a bitmapped font, reduced or magnified if necessary to approximate the desired size.

If you do not have a PostScript printer (such as a Personal LaserWriter SC), the system software will first use a matching bitmapped font, then a TrueType font, then a resized bitmapped font.

In general, you will get best results most easily if you use TrueType fonts in your Word documents.

# Setting Up Right and Left Pages

If you plan to print a document on both sides of each sheet of paper, you will probably want to take advantage of Word's ability to create different odd and even (or right and left) page layouts. This type of page layout is sometimes called facing pages, or mirror margins (because the left and right margins of facing pages mirror each other). This layout is especially useful for bound documents, making it easier to read pages that are bound along one edge. We've already covered many of these issues in earlier chapters, but here's a quick recap and a few additional pointers.

There are a couple of ways to create different formats on right and left pages. For example, instead of specifying left and right margins, you can specify inside and outside margins, with the inside margin on the binding edge of your paper. Standard practice is to start numbering with the page that faces you as you open a book, which means a page on the right-hand side. Odd-numbered pages will then fall on the right half of a two-page spread, and even-numbered pages on the left.

Generally, you'll want to make the inside margin wider than the outside to allow room for binding. Word lets you do this either by defining different sizes for inside and outside margins or by using equal margins and then adding a page gutter on the binding edge of a page. On odd-numbered pages, the page gutter is on the left; on even-numbered pages, it's on the right. If you use this second method, the space on the binding edge of each page will consist of the inside margin plus the gutter. Note that with either approach you'll need to check the Mirror Margins check box on the Margins card of the Document Layout dialog box.

To specify a setting for page gutter, inside and outside margins, or both, choose File Document Layout to open the Document Layout dialog box, and select the Margins card. For details on using the cards in the Document Layout dialog box, see "Margins" on page 196.

## How to add right and left headers and footers

If you're using a mirror margin layout, you may also want headers and footers to be different on opposite pages.

As we mentioned briefly in Chapter 5, the Layout card in the Document Layout dialog box contains a Different Odd And Even check box for headers and footers, which lets you create different headers and footers for right and left pages. You may have noticed that books often use this type of layout, placing the book title at the top of even-numbered pages and the chapter title at the top of odd-numbered pages. Even when the text is the same on both right and left pages, it may vary in position. For example, in some magazines you might see page numbers on the outside edge, the name of the magazine in the center, and the date on the inside edge of each page.

The Different Odd And Even option on the Document Layout Layout card is independent of the Mirror Margins and the Gutter settings on the Document Layout Margins card. This means that you can vary your headers and footers for right and left pages even if you're not using a page gutter or inside and outside margins.

When you check the Different Odd And Even check box, Word will add Even or Odd to the label on the header and footer areas displayed in Page Layout view. Figure 16-2, for example, shows even and odd headers and footers. Notice that Word also displays the Header And Footer toolbar.

**FIGURE 16-2**

By zooming to two pages in Page Layout view, you can see the headers and footers for both even-numbered and odd-numbered pages of a book.

## How to link right and left headers and footers

In our discussion of multisection documents in Chapter 13, we described how headers and footers for each section are linked to later sections. When you are using even and odd headers or footers in a multisection document, the situation remains essentially the same except that each kind of header or footer maintains a separate link to other sections.

For example, if you're working with a single-section document with different odd and even headers and with a different first-page header, you'll see one header on all odd pages, another on all even pages, and another on the first page only.

Now suppose you split your document into three sections. Initially, the even, odd, and first-page headers in the second and third sections will have the same text as the equivalent headers in the first section. If you change one of the headers in the second section—for instance, changing the even header to *Chapter 2*—the equivalent headers in the other two sections will also change unless you break the link to the previous section first.

When a header is linked to the corresponding header (even, odd, or first-page) in the section before it, the Same As Previous button on the Header And Footer toolbar will look as if it has been pressed. To break the link, simply click on the button. If you then change the even header in the second section, the even header in the first section will remain unchanged, but the change will cascade forward to headers in later sections. If you want to prevent this, move to the third section and break its link with the previous (second) section before you change the even header in the second section. To reestablish the link between the even headers for the second and first sections, you need only go to the even header in the second section and click on the Same As Previous button again. The current header will be replaced by the one from the previous section.

In short, when you have different even, odd, and first-page headers or footers, the rules for linking between sections are the same as those used when you have a single header or footer for each section. The only difference is that each of the three kinds of headers and footers maintains a separate set of links, allowing you to link or unlink each one independently of the others.

## How to format facing pages using frames

Remember that you can use frames to place objects inside or outside paragraphs, as you saw in the example of scholar's margins in "How to create scholar's margins" on page 504. You can also use this feature to place other items, such as pictures, on the inside or outside of each page. The key to this technique is to position the frame inside or outside relative to the page or the margin. You can also use Word's drawing tools to set off areas with lines or boxes. See the section "Frames: Positioning Text and Graphics on the Page" on page 481 for more information on frames.

# Defining the Position of a Header or Footer

We haven't yet covered two items on the Document Layout Margins card: the Header and Footer settings in the From Edge group box. To see the card, choose File Document Layout, and then select the Margins card.

The From Edge settings work much as you would expect. Enter *0.75"* in the Header box, for example, and Word will start the first line of the header 0.75 inch from the top edge of the paper. Enter *0.75"* in the Footer box, and Word will position the last line of the footer 0.75 inch from the bottom edge of the paper.

There is a little more to these settings, however. Both interact with—and can override—the top and bottom margin settings. If you set the top margin to 1 inch and set the header to appear 3 inches from the edge, the header will push down the top margin (and of course the text) so that the margin will be 3 inches deep instead of 1 inch. Similarly, if you set the footer's distance from the edge to be larger than the bottom margin, the footer will push up into the body text area, leaving less room for body text. Note, however, that the header or footer will intrude into the body text area only when you add text to the header or footer.

Word will automatically adjust the margins by pushing the text up or down whenever you create a header or footer that's too large to fit into the space Word allots by default. You can, however, override this feature. As we mentioned in Chapter 15, if you enter the margin settings as minus numbers, Word will always follow the margin setting exactly for defining the body text area on the page. If your headers or footers in this case are larger than their allotted space, Word will simply print both body text and header or footer at the same place on the page—usually an undesirable result, for obvious reasons. Occasionally, however, you might actually want to overlay a header on a page; see the discussion of watermarks in "How to create a watermark" on page 506.

## Working with Long Documents

Although the length of Word documents is limited only by disk space, you'll find that it often makes sense to break long documents into shorter pieces. The longer the document, the longer it will take to move through the document, save it, and load it. The loss of performance depends on many factors, including the speed of your computer's processor and disk drive and the complexity of the document. But even if speed is not an issue, you may sometimes find it more convenient to work with different sections separately—when working with the chapters of a book, for example.

Unfortunately, breaking a long document into several files also presents problems. For example, you'll probably want to maintain continuous page numbering across files. And if you want to generate a table of contents or an index, you'll want a single table of contents or index for all files. In Word 6.0, you can handle these tasks quite easily by creating a Master Document to link the files.

There are actually two ways to create a Master Document with Word. One involves cobbling files together with fields, which can be a bit tedious. Easier by far is using Word's Master Document feature, which provides a simple tool for assembling a long document from separate files.

## NEW!    How to use Master Document view

Word's Master Document feature builds on Word's Master Document view, which is similar to Outline view. In fact, both views use the same Outlining toolbar. The difference is that Outline view works with a single document file, whereas Master Document view lets you assemble the parts of a long document to view them in outline form. The outline features make it easier to organize and change the sequence of the pieces. Because Master Document view is so similar to Outline view, we'll ignore the outline features here. For a thorough discussion of outline features, take a look at Chapter 19, "Outlining," starting on page 615.

### How to create a Master Document

You can create a Master Document by converting a normal text document, by adding existing documents to your Master Document as subdocuments, or with some combination of the two methods, as we'll show here. Assume, for example, that you want to combine a few files that you already have on disk but that you also want to put them in the context of a larger outline. You can start by opening a new file and entering the outline.

If you're writing a book, for example, and you've already written the first three chapters, you might enter an outline that starts with Chapter 4. If you want Word to recognize different sections as subdocuments, choose a heading style to mark the starting points. Assuming you've reserved Heading 1 for the book title, you might mark each chapter title with the Heading 2 style.

Once you've entered the outline, choose View Master Document. Word will switch to an outline format and will add the Outlining toolbar and the Master Document toolbar on the same line at the top of the Word window, by default.

For purposes of this discussion, we'll ignore the Outlining toolbar here. Be aware, however, that the Outlining toolbar is useful for organizing your document and for controlling how much detail you can see—Word lets you collapse the outline to display only specified levels of headings. We'll cover the Outlining toolbar in depth in Chapter 19, "Outlining," starting on page 615.

Figure 16-3 lists the buttons on the Master Document toolbar. This toolbar provides not only easy access to Word's Master Document functions but also a handy reference for what those functions are.

The first toolbar button on the left is Create Subdocument. You can use this button to convert selected text in the Master Document to a subdocument file. For instance, after entering text and assigning heading levels in your outline, you can select the parts of the outline containing the sections to be subdocuments, starting with the first heading level that marks the first section of text you want to place in its own subdocument. If you then click on the Create Subdocument button, Word will add an end-of-section marker just before each heading level that it recognizes as the start of a new subdocument and another at the end of each new subdocument. It will also surround each section of text with a box to delineate each subdocument and will add an icon in the upper left corner, as shown in Figure 16-4 on the next page. The next time you choose File Save, Word will create new files using names based on the first 31 characters of each section of text. If a file with that name already exists, Word will change one or more of the last characters to digits in order to create a unique name.

| Button | Button Name | Action |
|--------|-------------|--------|
| | Create Subdocument | Converts selected portions of an existing Master Document to subdocuments based on a heading style |
| | Remove Subdocument | Converts a subdocument to text in the Master Document |
| | Insert Subdocument | Inserts the contents of an existing file as a subdocument |
| | Merge Subdocument | Converts selected subdocuments to a single subdocument |
| | Split Subdocument | Splits an existing subdocument into two separate subdocuments |
| | Lock Document | Locks or unlocks a subdocument; no changes can be made to a locked subdocument |

**FIGURE 16-3**

The Master Document toolbar buttons.

Once you've divided your text into subdocuments, you can work on each individual subdocument directly, opening it from the Master Document. Simply double-click on the icon in the upper left corner of the subdocument, and Word will open the subdocument file in its own window. By opening individual subdocument files this way, you can work with more manageable portions of your text. (Note that you can also edit directly in Master Document view if you prefer.) You can use the Window menu to move between open subdocuments and the Master Document.

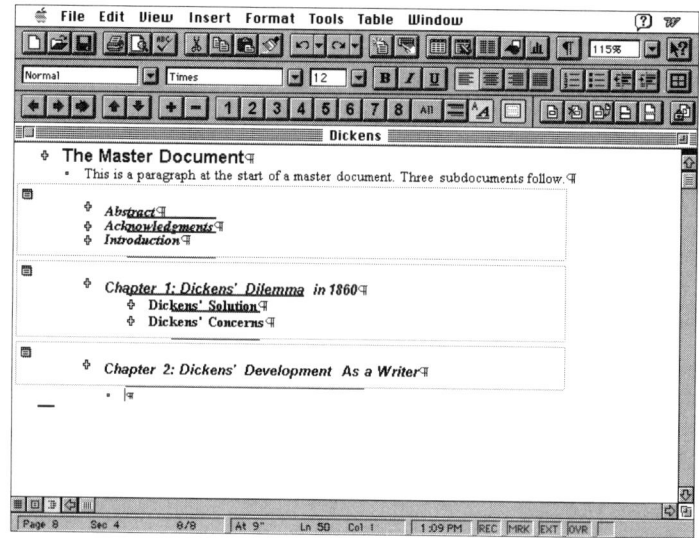

**FIGURE 16-4**

In Master Document view, Word surrounds subdocuments with a box and adds an icon in the upper left corner, which will let you open the subdocument file.

You can display a Master Document in Word's other views. Normal view is convenient for overall editing. You can use Page Layout view to see how your pages will look when they are printed. You can also use Print Preview to see the formatted pages.

## How to add existing files to a Master Document

If you want to add existing files as subdocuments in a Master Document, choose the Insert Subdocument button (third from the left on the Master Document toolbar). Word will open a dialog box, which looks and works like the dialog box for opening files. Find the file you want to add, and choose OK. Word will insert the file as a subdocument, in its own section, starting at the cursor's current position.

You can insert a subdocument inside another subdocument if you position the cursor inside a subdocument before clicking on the Insert Subdocument button, but we recommend against it. Once you insert a second-level subdocument, it will show up as part of the higher-level subdocument whenever you edit that higher-level document. This defeats the main purpose of using a Master Document, which is to keep long documents broken into smaller, more manageable pieces. It's much better to use only one level of subdocuments.

## How to lock subdocuments

You can control a subdocument's locked status using the button on the right end of the Master Document toolbar: Lock Document. If the cursor or selection is in a subdocument that's locked, this button will look as if it has been pressed. Click on the Lock Document button to toggle the status between locked and unlocked.

When you open a locked subdocument by double-clicking on its icon in Master Document view, Word will open it as read-only. Word indicates the locked status with a small padlock icon below the subdocument's icon in Master Document view. When you open a subdocument, that section will be locked in the Master Document.

The Master Document locking feature differs from the other protection features covered elsewhere in this book, but it also interacts with those features. If you protect a document for revisions using Tools Protect Document, for example, you may not be able to unlock that protection using the Master Document's locking feature. More precisely, if you try to remove the lock, you'll see a message telling you that the operation cannot be completed because the subdocument has a higher protection rating than the Master Document. If you add the same protection to the Master Document, however, you'll be able to remove the lock and edit the subdocument.

## How to use other Master Document toolbar buttons

Let's look at the other three buttons on the Master Document toolbar. Second from the left is the Remove Subdocument button. The name is a little misleading, since clicking on this button doesn't remove the subdocument's text from the Master Document. Instead, it keeps the subdocument's contents in the Master Document but breaks the link to the file that contained the subdocument. To actually delete a subdocument and its contents, first unlock the subdocument if it is locked. Then click on the subdocument's icon to highlight the entire subdocument contents, and press the Del key.

The fourth button from the left is Merge Subdocument, which will let you join two adjacent subdocuments. To merge the two subdocuments, first highlight them both. (The easy way is to hold down the Shift key and click on each subdocument icon.) Then click on the Merge Subdocument button. The next time you choose File Save, Word will save both merged subdocuments in the file that previously held the first subdocument. The file that previously held the second subdocument remains on your disk, but you can erase it if you don't need it.

The fifth button—Split Subdocument—does just what it says. Click on the button, and Word will split a subdocument into two subdocuments, starting at the current cursor position. The cursor must be positioned at the start of a paragraph.

## Format considerations for Master Documents

Word relies on paragraph styles to determine the structure of a Master Document. If you want to view your document as an outline, you must use Word's built-in heading styles: Heading 1, Heading 2, Heading 3, and so on.

When you look at a subdocument while in a Master Document, Word will use the style definitions stored in the Master Document. If you open the subdocument in its own window, however, Word will use the style definitions stored in the subdocument. If the two sets of styles differ, you'll find that the subdocument formats differently. For information about how to copy style definitions from one document to another to ensure consistency, see "Merging Styles from Another Document" on page 432.

Since Word places each subdocument of a Master Document in its own section, you can also control the contents of headers and footers and other section-dependent formatting. If you want a setting to apply to all parts of the Master Document, set it in the Master Document itself rather than repeating it in each subdocument. On the other hand, if you want a different setting for each subdocument, you can define the setting in each one. See "Multisection Documents" on page 455 for more about section-dependent formatting.

When Word creates a section break between subdocuments, it may not create the kind of break you want. If you want a subdocument to start on a new page (as a new chapter in a book would do), you would not want a Continuous section break. You can change the type of break by choosing File Document Layout and selecting the Layout card. See "How to divide a document into sections" on page 456 for more information about section breaks.

## How to create a table of contents or an index in a Master Document

Using a Master Document makes it easy to create a table of contents or an index for a long document. You add these features as part of the Master Document itself rather than making them part of any subdocument. This means you don't have to do anything special to have continuous numbering—or a continuous table of contents or index. You can simply create the index or the table of contents while in the Master Document file, just as you would in a single document file. For details on tables of contents and indexes, see Chapter 22, "Tables of Contents & Indexes," starting on page 723.

# Using Special Fields for Formatting and Printing

Word has a number of special fields that you can use in formatting and printing your documents. We will cover the topic of fields in depth in Chapter 20, and you can look there for more information on how to insert fields. For now, you can simply choose the Insert Field command and insert a field from the Field Names list in the dialog box.

## The BARCODE field

The BARCODE field lets you insert a postal bar code in your document. This is the same field used to put bar codes on envelopes with Word's envelope printing feature. See "How to create an envelope" on page 257.

This field uses the format

```
{BARCODE "text" [switches]}
```

where text is used to create the content of the barcode. It may be a ZIP code, or it may be the name of a bookmark that contains a ZIP code. If *text* is a bookmark, you must use the \b switch with the field. You can also use the switch

```
\f "letter"
```

where *letter* is either A or C. A produces a courtesy reply mark, and C produces a business reply mark.

Another switch that you can use with the BARCODE field is the \u switch, which signifies that you are using a United States postal address.

## The ADVANCE field

The ADVANCE field offsets your document up or down or to the right or left. Any text that is moved beyond the margins or to a subsequent page will not be printed.

You can control the position of the text by using switches, each of which is followed by a number that represents a distance, measured in points. The \d switch moves the text down the specified number of points; the \u switch moves the text up. Similarly, the \l switch moves the text to the left, and the \r switch moves it to the right. The \x switch starts the text at a specified number of points from the left margin, and the \y switch starts the text at a specified distance from the top of the page.

## The SECTION and SECTIONPAGES fields

These two fields do not use extra text or switches. Their results are numbers, based on your document. The SECTION field will return the number of the current section. The SECTIONPAGES field returns the total number of pages in the section. You may find it convenient to use these fields in conjunction with the PAGE field in a document header or footer—for example, *Page {PAGE} of Section {SECTION}* or *Page {PAGE} of {SECTIONPAGES}*.

# TOPIC FINDER

# 17

# Advanced File Handling

f you've worked your way through all or most of the preceding chapters, by now you should be familiar with the basic techniques for opening, closing, and saving files. You should certainly be aware that you can manage most of your file-handling needs through choices on the File menu. The one clear exception is file deletion. As we discussed in Chapter 2, "File Handling," to delete a file from within Word, you can open the Find File dialog box—by choosing File Find File or by choosing File Open and then Find File—locate the file, choose the Commands button, and then choose Delete.

In this chapter, we'll look at Word's most sophisticated file-handling features, all of which are available through the Find File dialog box. Among these are the ability to search for files in more than one directory, preview files, and sort lists of files in various ways. Before we look at the mechanics of advanced file handling, however, we'll discuss some strategies that will make it easier for you to keep track of your files.

# Managing Files

After you've worked with Word for a while, your hard disk will likely contain dozens (possibly hundreds) of document files, including old memos, letters, reports, and so on. Of course, the more document files on your disk, the more of a challenge it is to find a particular file. You can make the process considerably easier by taking a little time to organize your files into logical groupings.

A common oversight among computer users is to pay little attention to the filing system for data files. Many users create a single data folder for each program—dumping all their Word documents, for example, into one folder. Worse yet, some users save files with no regard to where the files are located.

An even more common mistake is to store all Word document files in the Microsoft Word folder. Unfortunately, Word makes this an easy trap to fall into. By default, every time you load Word, the folder for opening and saving files is the Microsoft Word folder.

The problem with all of these strategies—or lack of strategy—is that it quickly becomes exceedingly difficult to find any particular file. Consider: You probably wouldn't take all your paper files and store them in a file cabinet without any divisions, logical groupings, or order. Dumping all your document files into a single folder on your hard disk amounts to the same approach.

Computer files are similar to paper files in some very important respects. Each contains information that you'll want to be able to find again. More important, being able to find the information requires some sort of filing system. And if you're not following a clearly defined system, the odds are good that you'll lose your files with appalling regularity.

There is nothing mysterious about creating a filing system on your disk. The same principles apply to a computer filing system as to a paper filing system. Only the mechanics are different. With a filing cabinet, you use file folders, file drawers, and file drawer separators to group information. With a disk drive, you use metaphorical folders, and you put folders within other folders.

We'll discuss the mechanics of creating folders in a moment. But far more important is the issue of deciding *how* to group your files. There are no hard-and-fast rules. The trick is to create divisions that make sense to you and make sense for the way you work.

For example, you might create one folder for letters, one for memos, one for reports, and so on. Or you might create a different folder for each client or each project. Or you might mix these concepts, using a folder for each client, for example, and additional folders within each client folder for each project.

Some filing systems will meet your needs better than others, and it's worth putting some effort into devising a system that's right for you. But any system is better than none, and the main point is to devise a system and use it. If you come up with a better idea later, you can change the way your files are organized, just as you can reorganize a file cabinet.

In an earlier chapter, we suggested a simple approach to organizing data files, and we explained the mechanics of changing the default Documents folder on the File Locations card. Briefly, we suggested setting the default Documents folder to a main data folder that contains nothing but additional folders that hold the actual data. You can then start from the main data folder the first time you choose the File Open command in any given session, and you can easily move to the folder you actually want. You can put the main data folder anywhere—even at the desktop level along with your hard disk. For more details on both our suggestion and on setting default locations, see "The File Locations card" starting on page 286.

As files accumulate within any given data folder, you can create new folders and move files appropriately. For example, you might start with a single folder for a given project and later create additional folders within the project folder for letters, memos, and reports. As a rule of thumb, you should consider creating new folders when the number of files in any given folder grows too large to scroll through quickly in various dialog box file lists.

Another strategy is to use separate folders for files you've finished working with. For example, if you're still working on both a letter and a report for a given project, leave both in the active project folder. But when you've finished with them, move each to an appropriate inactive folder. Alternatively, you might choose to handle such housekeeping functions only when you notice that a folder is getting cluttered.

Unfortunately, Word does not offer a simple command for moving files. But, as we mentioned in Chapter 2, you can get the same effect by saving a file in the new folder and deleting the original. Even better, you can copy a file to a new folder without opening it first. We'll show you how at the end of this chapter.

# Folders

If you're already familiar with Macintosh folders and how to create them, you can skip this section and go to the discussion of retrieving documents. If you're not familiar with folders, however, here's a quick overview.

Although any file you store goes physically on the disk, the Macintosh provides a metaphorical desktop that it treats as one organizational step higher than the disk. In fact, when you're working in the Finder, you'll find that your disk goes on the desktop, and you can store files or folders on the desktop as well—at the same organizational level as the disk.

Starting from the desktop, without any windows open, you can open the window for the metaphorical hard disk (in sharp contrast to the actual hard disk) by double-clicking on the hard disk icon. Here again, you can store files at this level or you can create folders in the hard disk window, and store your files inside the folders.

All folders that aren't on the desktop or in the hard disk window are within other folders. For example, if you installed Word with the default settings, you'll find that the installation program created a Microsoft Word folder on the hard disk, with Setup, Macros, Templates, Clip Art, Tutorial, and Word Extensions folders within the Word folder. The install routine should have also created a Microsoft folder on the hard disk (if you didn't have one there already) to hold Equation Editor, WordArt, the spelling dictionary, and other files that Word can share with other Microsoft programs, such as Microsoft Excel.

You can organize files by putting folders within folders to any number of levels. You can also create aliases—the file management equivalent to cross-references in text. If you want a given file available in two different folders, for example, you can create an alias for the file and move the alias to the second folder. You can also create aliases for folders and even for shared disk drives on a network if you like.

Note that an alias is not a copy of the original. It simply points to the original, so you can open the same original file—or folder or disk—by using the alias. Using an alias has two advantages over creating a copy of the original. First, it saves precious disk space, since you haven't duplicated any information. And second, it means that any changes you make in the file, folder, or disk will automatically show up no matter where you open the item from. If you created multiple copies, you would have to make changes in each individual copy.

One particularly useful aspect of aliases is that they will let you maintain a highly organized filing system for files and folders, and still keep the items you use most frequently near at hand. If you spend a great deal of time word processing, for example, you might like to create an alias for Word and put the alias on the Desktop, so you can start Word from the desktop. Similarly, if you divide your files into project folders, you might like to create aliases for each active project folder, and put those on the desktop too. That way, you won't have to navigate through multiple levels of folders to find the files you're looking for.

## How to create folders and aliases

Creating a folder or an alias is simple. You'll find both choices on the Finder's File menu. Suppose, for example, that you want to create the folder Data within the Microsoft Word folder. First open the Microsoft Word folder while in the Finder, and choose File New Folder. The Finder will immediately add a new folder to the Microsoft Word window, label it *untitled folder*, and select the label so you can change it. Simply type *Data* or any other label you want to use. And that's it. You're done.

To create an alias, first highlight the file or folder you want to create the alias for. Then choose File Make Alias. The Finder will immediately add a new item to the window with the same name as the one you had highlighted, but with the word *alias* added. You can then use the mouse to drag the alias to the desktop or to the folder you want the alias in. If you like, you can also change the name to remove the word *alias*. You can still spot aliases, even without the word, because the Macintosh will use italics for the alias name.

Note in passing that you will also find choices in some dialog boxes in Word for creating new folders. We won't delve into those here, however, since we cover them in the context of the appropriate dialog boxes.

# Retrieving Documents

Storing your document files in multiple folders divided into logical groups makes it easier to find a given file. As a first step, you can go to the folder and limit your search to just that folder. Unfortunately, no matter how organized you are, you will occasionally store a file in the wrong place. And even if you've stored the file in the right place, you still need to find the right file.

Word provides document-retrieval tools to help. To take full advantage of these retrieval tools, you need to fill out the Summary Info dialog box for each file. As we discussed in Chapter 2, this dialog box contains information such as title, subject, and author, as well as keywords and any comments you care to add. If you take the time to enter the information the first time you save each file, you can use Word's retrieval tools to find files using any of these criteria. But even if you don't fill in the information, you can still search for files by author, creation date, and last date saved, among other choices.

To find one or more specific files on your disk, choose File Find File or File Open and then the Find File button. The first time you choose File Find File, and any time you choose File Open and then Find File, you'll see the Search dialog box, shown in Figure 17-1.

**FIGURE 17-1**

The Search dialog box lets you specify the files to search for.

## How to define a basic file search

The Search dialog box lets you give Word some basic search information or choose a more complicated search that you've previously defined and saved. We'll start with the basics: filename, file type, and location.

If you can remember any part of the filename, you can enter it in the File Name text box. If you are looking for a letter and you always start letters with *Letter to*, or end them with *letter*, for example, you can enter the filename as *letter*. Word will find all filenames that include the word *letter*.

Note that the file type is set to Word Document by default, so you generally won't need to make any changes. If you want to find a different file type, however, you can change the setting with the File Type pull-down list. The other choices on the list will vary depending on the programs you have installed on your system.

Below the File Type pull-down list is the Location pull-down list, which shows the drives available to search.

If you want to define a search from scratch, use the Clear button at the bottom of the dialog box to delete anything in the File Name text box and set the File Type to Word Documents.

Use the Rebuild File List check box when you want to be sure that Word will create a new list of files when you choose OK. Otherwise, if you opened the Search dialog box from the Find File dialog box (which we'll describe a little later in this chapter) and haven't made any changes in the search criteria, Word will, under some conditions, simply use the previously compiled, and possibly incomplete, list of files.

# How to define an advanced file search

A basic search may be all you need in many cases, but sometimes you'll need Word's more sophisticated search capabilities. To use those features, choose the Advanced Search button at the bottom of the Search dialog box. Word will open the Advanced Search dialog box, shown in Figure 17-2.

The Advanced Search dialog box lets you narrow or widen your search based on almost anything you can remember about the file you're looking for. As you can see in Figure 17-2, it offers three cards: Location, Summary, and Timestamp. We'll start with the Location card.

## How to specify drives and folders to search using the Location card

The Location card lets you specify locations to search—meaning specific folders or disks. The File Name text box and File Type pull-down list are identical to the items with the same names in the Search dialog box. Any entries you made in these boxes while in the Search dialog box will be carried over here. And any entries you make in these boxes while on the Location card will be carried over to the Search dialog box.

**FIGURE 17-2**

The Advanced Search dialog box lets you set advanced criteria for finding files.

The Include Subfolders check box, below the Add, Remove, and Remove All buttons, lets you tell Word whether to confine the search to the specific locations you enter in the Search In box or to search all subfolders—meaning all folders that are within the folders or disks you've specified. For example, if you don't check this box and you enter *Macintosh HD* as the location, Word will look only for files that are in the hard disk window. If you check the Include Subfolders box, however, Word will search the entire disk.

The Include Subfolders check box is an all-or-nothing choice. For example, you cannot add two folders to search on the Location card and tell Word to include Subfolders for one but not for the other.

To define a location to search, choose the Add button. Word will open a dialog box that looks and works much like the dialog box for opening files. Use it to find the folders or drives you want to include in the search. As you navigate through your disk, you'll see the Select button at the bottom of the dialog box change to match the currently designated item. When the Select button shows the name of a folder that you want to add to the search list, click on the button. Word will close the dialog box, and add the folder name to the Search In list. If you want to add another folder to search in, simply choose the Add button again.

### How to delete folders from the search

As soon as you add at least one folder or disk to search, the Remove and Remove All buttons will become available. If you want to remove a single item from the Search In list, simply highlight the name and choose the Remove button. If you want to delete the entire list so you can create a new definition from scratch, choose the Remove All button.

### How to search by title, author, keywords, or subject using the Summary card

The middle tab in the Advanced Search dialog box is for the Summary card, shown in Figure 17-3.

**FIGURE 17-3**

The Summary card lets you set search criteria based on a document's Summary Info.

**Advanced Search**

| Location | Summary | Timestamp |

Title:

Author:

Keywords:

Subject:

Options:   Create New List   ☐ Match Case

Containing Text

☐ Use Pattern Matching   Special

OK   Cancel   Help

As we mentioned earlier, to take full advantage of the Find File feature, you should fill in the Summary Info dialog box for each file you create. This card is why. As you can see in Figure 17-3, the first four text boxes on the Summary card match entries for the Summary Info dialog box: Title, Author, Keywords, and Subject. If you can remember any of these entries for the file or files you're searching for, simply enter them in the appropriate box or boxes, and Word will look for matches in the Summary Info entries.

Keep in mind that even if you don't normally fill in the Summary Info box, Word will fill in the Author entry for you (although you can override the entry if you like). This automatic entry can help you find files in any case.

When Word searches for Summary Info entries, it also finds files that contain a superset of the search text. You can use this to your advantage when you're not sure what you're looking for. If you're looking for files by M. David Stone, for example, and you don't know how the name is entered in User Info, you can enter *Dav* in the Author field. This will find any files with the author name stored as *M. David Stone*, *David Stone*, or *Dave Stone*. Of course, it will also find files by authors *David Poor* and *Alfred Davies*, so you need to use this trick with care.

Note that filling in more than one text box tells Word to find matches for all the filled-in boxes, so the more text boxes you fill in, the narrower the search. Try to make your search criteria as specific as possible without excluding any of the documents you want to find.

## Special characters for searching by Summary Info fields

Word provides seven special search characters that let you further fine-tune your search. Figure 17-4 on the next page lists all seven characters and their functions. All of these work for any Summary Info field.

The question mark (?) and asterisk (*) are called wildcard characters. Use the question mark to take the place of any single character within a word. Use the asterisk to take the place of multiple characters. For example, to find all files with *John Smith* or *Jerry Smith*, but not *Bob Smith*, as the author, you could specify *J * Smith* in the Author text box.

The backslash (\) lets you use any of the special characters as literal characters. You'll most often use this feature with commas, question marks, or ampersands. For example, if you rarely use a question mark in your titles and you want to search for the title *Are You Ready?*, you can simply enter \? as the title in the Title text box. The quotation marks (" ") let you join words into phrases. Normally, the space works the same way as the ampersand; if you enter *David Stone* as the author you'll turn up all documents by David Poor or by Alfred Stone, as well as all files by David Stone. To find only those documents by David Stone, you can enter the name as *"David Stone"*—and Word will search for an exact match, including the space.

The comma (,) lets you search for more than one possible match for an item. To search for all documents that include the phrase *Artificial Intelligence* or the phrase *Expert Systems* as keywords, for example, enter *Artificial Intelligence,Expert Systems* in the Keywords text box.

The ampersand (&) or a space lets you search for files that match more than one criterion for a particular text box. To search for documents that include both the phrase *Artificial Intelligence* and the phrase *Expert Systems* as keywords, enter *"Artificial Intelligence"&"Expert Systems"* in the Keywords text box.

Finally, the tilde (~) lets you search for files that don't match the stated criterion. For example, if you want to search for all files that do not have the word *Chapter* as part of the title, you could enter *~Chapter* in the Title text box.

| This Character... | Tells Word to Do This... |
| --- | --- |
| ? (question mark) | Match any single character. |
| * (asterisk) | Match a group of characters. |
| " " (quotation marks) | Treat all the characters in quotes, including any special characters, as literal characters. Also treat everything within the quotes as a single item requiring an exact match—including spaces and punctuation marks. |
| \ (backslash) | Treat the following special character as a normal text character. |
| , (comma) | Accept a file as a match if its summary information matches any or all items in the text box that are separated by commas. (This is a logical OR.) |
| & (ampersand) or a space | Accept a file as a match if its summary information matches the items on both sides of the ampersand or space. (This is a logical AND.) |
| ~ (tilde) | Select a file if its summary information does not match the item in the text box. (This is a logical NOT.) |

**FIGURE 17-4**

Special characters you can use in searches using the Summary Info fields.

# How to search for any text

In many ways, the Containing Text text box is the most useful option for defining a search. It lets you enter any word, phrase, or other text to tell Word to search the full text of each document to look for matches. (For obvious reasons, this works only with documents Word can open and read.) This comes in handy when the document you're looking for contains a keyword or phrase that you didn't enter as a keyword, or when you're looking for all documents relating to a specific project. For example, suppose you're writing a book, with each chapter in its own file, and you want to find every mention of a given topic throughout the book. If all the chapters are in one folder, you can search the full text of every file in the folder and list all files that contain mention of the topic.

The drawback to a full text search, as you might expect, is that it takes Word a relatively long time. As a result, you'll want to use this feature sparingly or as a last resort. You'll also want to include as many other search criteria as possible to keep the list of files to a minimum. In addition, you'll want to use the other search criteria first and then run the full text search on only those files, using the choices in the Options box that we'll describe a little later in this chapter. But it's certainly the best choice for ensuring that you find all documents relating to a specific subject.

## Special characters for searching for any text

In addition to the special characters for use with the Summary Info fields, Word provides a set of nine characters specifically for full text searches. To use them, you must first check the Use Pattern Matching check box.

Figure 17-5 on the next page shows the list of special pattern-matching characters that you'll see if you choose the Special button to open the Special pull-down list. These are the same pattern-matching characters that you can use for searching or replacing in Word. You can use the Special button to add these characters to the Containing Text text box, or if you know the special characters you want to use, you can type them in directly. For details on how these pattern-matching characters work, see "How to use pattern matching" on page 100.

| Special ▼ |
|-----------|
| Any Character |
| Character Range |
| Beginning of Word |
| End of Word |
| Expression |
| Not |
| Num Occurrences |
| Previous 1 or More |
| 0 or More Characters |

If you choose the Special button, Word will show you this list of pattern-matching characters.

### Matching case

Another way to narrow the search is to check the Match Case check box just above the Containing Text box, on the right side of the dialog box. As the name implies, this option tells Word to search on uppercase or lowercase letters exactly as you've entered them.

## How to cast a wider or narrower net using the Options box

There's one other item on the Summary card: the Options box. The choices in the pull-down list let you widen or narrow a search, as appropriate.

If you have hundreds of document files on your disk, you may find that the list Word comes up with is overwhelming. At other times, if you're searching for several related files, you may find that Word hasn't found all the files you need. In both cases, the Options setting lets you modify the list of filenames, either by adding to it to cast a wider net or by trimming it to narrow the net.

To modify a list of filenames after running a search, you first need to return to the Summary card in the Advanced Search dialog box by choosing Search from the Find File dialog box and then choosing Advanced Search. After you make the appropriate changes to the search criteria for the next search (including changes on the Timestamp card, which we haven't covered yet), you can open the Options pull-down list. The default choice for the Options box is Create New List, which creates a new list from scratch. If you want to add matches from the second search to the files you've already found, choose the Add Matches To List option. If you want to trim the list, choose Search Only In List. This choice speeds the process since Word will look at only the files already in the list. You can then restart the search, using the techniques we'll discuss shortly, to modify the original list.

## How to search by date using the Timestamp card

The rightmost tab in the Advanced Search dialog box is for the Timestamp card, shown in Figure 17-6.

**FIGURE 17-6**

The Timestamp card lets you set search criteria based on who created and last saved the file and when.

The Last Saved and Created group boxes on the Timestamp card each include From, To, and By text boxes. The first two boxes in each group box let you specify a date or range of dates to look for.

Suppose, for example, that you created a document yesterday, but you can't find it on your disk. One way to search for it is to look for files created after the day before yesterday and before today by entering the appropriate From and To dates in the Created box. This search will find only those documents that were created yesterday. Similarly, if you created the file some weeks ago, but you worked on it yesterday, you could enter the same dates in the From and To text boxes in the Last Saved box.

The By text box in the Created group box is equivalent to the Author box on the Summary card. In fact, if you enter or change information in either of these two text boxes, the change will show up in the equivalent text box on the other card.

## How to search by the last person who saved the file

Word not only keeps track of the author and the creation date of each file, it also keeps track of the last person who saved the file. To search for files last saved by a particular person, enter that person's name in the Last Saved By box. If you're not sure how Word has recorded the person's name, you can open his or her installation of the program, choose Tools Options, and then choose User Info to see the name. This feature is useful when you're searching on a network for a document that someone else has edited.

NEW!
## How to store a search definition for future use

After you define the advanced search criteria, choose OK to return to the Search dialog box. At this point, you'll see the search criteria detailed in the Search For group box. As before, you'll only be able to edit the File Name box and choose options from the File Type and Location boxes, but Word will show you each of the other criteria , so you can easily see the search you've defined.

Having defined a search, you can save the definition so you can use it again as needed. Simply choose the Save Search As button. Word will open the Save Search As dialog box, where you can enter a name and choose OK to save it. The search name will now be available in the pull-down list above the Save Search As button. To tell Word to use it, simply open the list and choose the name. You can delete a search definition at any time by selecting the name from the list and choosing the Delete Search button.

## How to search for a file

Of course, the whole point of entering search criteria is to get the list of files. After defining a search, choose OK in the Search dialog box to start the search. Then stand back while Word does all the hard work. Word will immediately close the Search dialog box and will display a message box labeled *Building File List*.

The message box reports current status, showing the number of matches found at any time. It also includes a Cancel button, so you can stop the search. When Word finishes the search, it will open (or return you to) the Find File dialog box, shown in Figure 17-7.

**FIGURE 17-7**

The Find File dialog box offers a variety of document-retrieval functions.

# The Find File dialog box

The Find File dialog box provides features for opening, managing, and printing one or more documents. The dialog box consists of three areas. The Listed Files box on the left shows a list of all files that meet the current search criteria. On the right is an area that changes depending on which option you've chosen in the View box for the information to show along with the files. In Figure 17-7, the View box is set to Preview, this area is labeled *Preview Of*, and it shows the contents of the file currently selected in the Listed Files box. We'll discuss this area and the other choices for filling it a little later.

At the bottom of the screen are five buttons and a pull-down list. The pull-down list lets you change the View setting. The five buttons let you open the Search dialog box, give commands for managing and printing files, open one or more files, close the dialog box, and ask for help.

## How to select files

In Chapter 2, we discussed how to highlight filenames in the File Name list box so you could delete the files. The same techniques apply when highlighting filenames to open, print, or copy files. To highlight a name with the mouse, simply click on the name. To highlight more than one adjacent file, either hold down the mouse button as you extend the highlight or click on the first filename you want to include and then hold down the Shift key as you click on the last one. Word will automatically highlight all the filenames between the two extremes. To select nonadjacent filenames with the mouse, hold down the ⌘ key while you click on filenames.

To highlight a filename with the keyboard, use the arrow keys to move the highlight to the name. To highlight several adjacent files, hold down the Shift key as you extend the highlight with the arrow keys.

## How to sort the list of files

After you've used Word's search features to find a list of files, you still have to find the right file or files in the list. Word provides several options to help ease this task as well, including the ability to change the sort order of the listed files. If you choose the Commands button to open the pull-down Commands menu and then choose Sorting from the menu, Word will open the Options dialog box, shown in Figure 17-8 on the next page.

FIGURE 17-8

The Options dialog box lets you choose the order for sorting filenames.

NEW!

You can tell Word to sort the filenames by author, by filename, by size, by the date the file was created or last saved, or by the name of the person who last saved the document. Word will remember the most recent setting and continue to use it until you change it again.

To sort the filenames by any of these sort keys, choose the appropriate option in the Sort Files By box. When you close the Options dialog box by choosing OK, Word will sort the files in the specified order.

NEW!

NOTE

The second group box in the Options dialog box is List Files By, with File Name and Title as the only choices. If you choose Title, Word will list the titles if it finds them. For those files that lack titles, however, Word will list the filename set off with hyphens, so you don't have to worry about overlooking a file that doesn't happen to have a title. Note too the Show Folders check box, which is checked by default. Leave this checked if you want to see the files listed within each folder. Remove the check mark if you don't want to see the folder names.

## How to choose the information to display for each file

As already mentioned, Word will let you specify the information to show on the right side of the Find File dialog box as you highlight each filename. The three choices are Preview, which will show you the actual contents of any file that Word can read; Summary, which will show you the Summary Info and statistical information stored with any Word file; and File Info, which will show you information such as filename, size, and author in columnar format, with one file per row. All three choices are available on the pull-down list in the View box at the bottom left of the Find File dialog box.

NEW!

The precise information you'll see when View is set to File Info will vary somewhat, depending on the sort order of the listed files. If you sort by the person who last saved the file, for example, you'll see columns labeled *File Name*, *Size*, *Last Saved By*, and *Last Saved*. If you sort by author, the last two columns will be labeled *Author* and *Last Saved*. If you sort by creation date, the last column will be labeled *Created*.

When set to Preview, Word will show the contents of all documents it can read, changing the Preview image each time you highlight a different filename in the Listed Files list. If you have a relatively slow machine, moving through a list of files that include graphics will likely be tedious. If you need to use the preview feature on a slow machine, you might try using the File Info or Summary setting to find what seems like the likely file that you're looking for and then move to that file in the list before setting View to Preview. If it's not the right file, reset the View to one of the other choices before moving on.

## How to change summary information

Another choice on the menu that opens when you choose the Commands button is Summary. If you choose Summary while you have a file highlighted that Word can read, you'll open the same Summary Info dialog box that you can reach from a document window by choosing File Summary Info.

The Summary command provides a convenient way to change summary information without opening a file. You may find this particularly useful if you haven't been filling in the summary information and decide to fill it in for all your older files at once.

## How to open one or more documents

You can open any one file in the Listed Files list by double-clicking on the filename or by highlighting the filename and choosing the Open button. To open more than one file with a single command, simply highlight the files you want open, using the techniques we described earlier in this chapter, and choose the Open button.

You can also open one or more files as read-only by highlighting the names, opening the Commands pull-down menu from the Commands button, and then choosing Open Read Only from the menu.

## How to print, delete, or copy one or more documents

Three other choices on the Commands button pull-down menu that opens when you choose the Command button are Print, Delete, and Copy. In each case, the command applies to all files you've selected before choosing the Command button. Here are some points to remember for each of the three commands.

## The Print command

Choosing Print opens the same dialog box you reach by choosing File Print from a document window. The only difference is that when you open the dialog box from the Find File dialog box, you can print all the files you currently have highlighted. We covered the Print dialog box in "Using the File Print command" on page 240.

## The Delete command

We covered file deletion in Chapter 2. Briefly, when you choose Delete, Word will respond with a message box asking you to confirm the deletion of all the files. Choose Yes or No, as appropriate. As we pointed out in Chapter 2, you need to be careful when deleting multiple files: It's easy to highlight and delete an extra name. Pay careful attention when you highlight, and be sure to read the filenames in the message box when Word asks you to confirm a deletion. Note also that you can delete any file with the Delete button, not just Word document files.

## The Copy command

The Copy command lets you copy one or more files to another folder; it also lets you create a second copy of one file in the same folder and give the new file a different name than the original.

To copy one or more files to another folder, highlight the file or files, choose Commands, and then choose Copy. Word will respond with the dialog box shown in Figure 17-9. You can then select the appropriate folder, using the pull-down list and scrollable list on the left side of the dialog box. Alternatively, you can choose the New button to create a new folder to copy the file or files to. If you are copying multiple files, the bottom of the dialog box will include a Copy To button. If you are copying only one file, there will be a text box in its place where you can optionally type a new name for the file. When you finish entering the target folder, filename, or both, choose OK to tell Word to copy the file or files.

**FIGURE 17-9**

Word's Copy dialog box lets you specify the drive and directory to copy files to, but it won't let you specify a new filename.

## How to rename and move files

Missing from Word's built-in file-management features are commands for re-naming files and for moving files to another directory. One way to rename files from within Word is to open each file, save it under the new name with the Save As command, and then delete the old file. The Find File dialog box offers a somewhat easier approach, since you can move files by copying them to the new folder and then deleting them from the old folder. First highlight the name or names of the files you want to move, and then choose Copy from the Command button's pull-down menu. When Word finishes copying, it will leave the filenames highlighted so you can delete them simply by choosing the Delete command.

# TOPIC FINDER

# 18

# Sharing Data with Other Programs

 ord can share information with other programs in a variety of ways. The most straightforward is to convert a file from one format to another—either importing the file into Word format when you open the file or exporting it to some other format by specifying that format when you save the file.

Word can also share data in more sophisticated ways. Topping the list is that you can insert information from another program into a Word document in a way that lets you use the other program to edit the information. We've already covered some of these capabilities, since several of the tools that come with Word depend on them—including, for example, WordArt, which we discussed in Chapter 15. The variations on these more sophisticated data-sharing features are called *linking* and *embedding*. You can make use of Word's linking and embedding features to share data with any other Macintosh program that supports these features, including, for example, Microsoft Excel.

In this chapter, we'll look at both Word's file conversion features and its linking and embedding features.

# Some Thoughts on Exchanging Data

Before we look at the mechanics of exchanging files with other word processing programs, it's important to understand some limitations of the process. First, and most important, although Word makes it reasonably painless to import files from and export them to a wide range of other word processor formats, the translation is not perfect. In fact, it's impossible for any program to convert documents to and from all of the major word processing formats with complete accuracy.

One of the key limitations for conversions involves character formatting, particularly the choice of fonts. If you move a document to a computer that has different fonts available, the printed output may vary even if you use the same program. Word has no way to know which fonts to use when importing a file created with fonts that are not on your computer.

Other conversion problems relate to differences in capabilities. For example, if a word processor is limited to one-line headers, a Word document with multiple-line headers cannot possibly translate correctly to that format. And Word contains any number of other features—including hidden text, frames, embedded objects, and fields—that are handled differently in other programs or are not supported at all.

The moral of all this is simple: Keep your expectations low. If you convert a document to another format, don't be surprised if you lose some of the formatting in the process. In fact, complex formatting may well create problems, leaving you with a difficult clean-up job at the other end. Often your best bet is to simplify the source file as much as you can and then put back the formatting after you move the text to the other program. If you can afford the luxury of making a dry run, you can try a test conversion first to see which formatting features convert well and which create problems.

For detailed information about limitations on converting files between Word and other specific programs, use the Search feature in the Word help system to search for the word *readme*, and choose the File Conversion topic.

With these warnings in mind, we can take a look at how to exchange documents with other programs, starting with the process of importing files stored in other formats.

# Opening Documents Stored in Other Formats

Word makes it easy to open or save a document that isn't saved in Word 6.0 for the Macintosh format, although the list of recognized formats will depend on how you installed Word. The Setup program can install file converters for a variety of word processing and graphics file formats. If you don't see as many options on your system as we'll discuss here (or if you don't see any at all), you may want to rerun Setup to add the file converters.

## How to import document files into Word

To import a foreign-format document file (by which we mean a file in any format other than Word 6.0 for the Macintosh format), start by choosing File Open. Then use the options in the Open dialog box to specify the drive, folder, and file to open, just as if you were opening a document that had been created in Word.

By default, the entry in the List Files Of Type text box tells Word to list all readable files. As we discussed in Chapter 2, however, you can easily list files created specifically by Word, or by other applications. Figure 18-1 shows some of the types of files that you can specify.

**FIGURE 18-1**

The List Files Of Type box lets you limit the kind of files displayed in the Open dialog box.

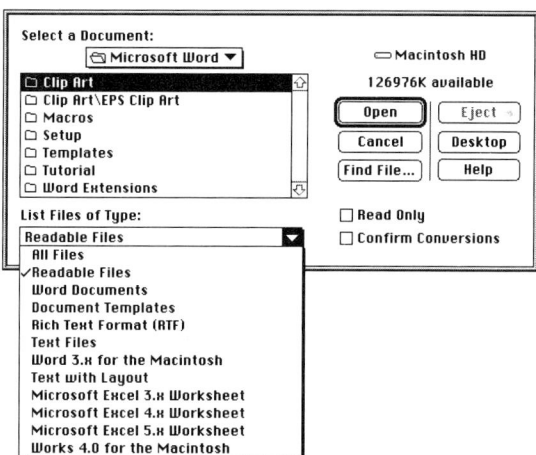

You can open a file by highlighting the filename and choosing OK. Notice the Confirm Conversions check box in the lower right corner of the Open dialog box. If this box isn't checked and Word recognizes the format of the file you have selected, it will simply convert the file and load it. If the box is checked or if Word can't recognize the format, the program will display the Convert File dialog box, shown in Figure 18-2, and will wait for you to specify the format of the file. Simply highlight the appropriate format and choose OK.

**FIGURE 18-2**

Word can open documents stored in various formats.

You can monitor the progress of the conversion by watching the status bar, which displays a visual gauge in the form of a line of blocks to indicate the proportion of the file that has been converted. When Word finishes the conversion, it will put the document in a new document window, using the original filename.

> If you set Word to show hidden text in a document that you've converted from another format, you may see Word's PRIVATE field, which is displayed as the word *PRIVATE* surrounded by curly brackets. (To see hidden text, click on the Show/Hide ¶ button on the Standard toolbar to toggle all nonprinting characters on.) The PRIVATE field has no effect on the document while you're working with the document in Word. Rather, this field stores information that Word needs for converting the document back to its original form as closely as possible. If you plan to return the document to its original format, make sure you know where the PRIVATE field is so that you don't accidentally delete it.

## Text file formatting issues

Most word processing programs, including Word, can save documents on disk as pure text files, with all formatting instructions stripped out. In addition, nearly every word processing program (and many spreadsheet and database programs) can read pure text files. This text file format is often called *ASCII format* or *ASCII text format* because all MS-DOS–based computers (and most others) use the ASCII (American Standard Code for Information Interchange) system to represent characters, including numbers, letters, punctuation, and other symbols.

As we mentioned at the start of this chapter, many of the problems you'll run into when converting files from one word processing format to another grow from differences in formatting features. Because files in ASCII format consist only of text, with no formatting, ASCII serves as a basic, and the simplest, format for all word processing documents. And ASCII text format is certainly the safest choice when you want to move text and don't care about formatting. Even ASCII files, however, allow some variation.

ASCII uses values from 0 through 127 to represent characters. For example, your computer knows the letter *e* as ASCII value 101. However, because of the way microcomputers store their information, it is more convenient to use a system that has 256 choices. ASCII defines characters only for the values 0 through 127, leaving 128 unused values. To take advantage of these values, many computer and software manufacturers, as well as the American National Standards Institute (ANSI), define their own sets of characters for the values 128 through 255. These characters are referred to as the *extended character set* or the *high-order characters*. When this set is combined with the ASCII set, the two together are often referred to as *extended ASCII*. Unfortunately, various manufacturers use different characters for these values, which means that many printers and programs interpret these characters differently.

Word offers several options for exporting documents in text file format, with variations for each of two categories: Text and MS-DOS Text. If your text consists of numbers, standard punctuation such as periods and commas, and the English alphabet (with no foreign-language characters), it doesn't matter whether you use the Text options or the MS-DOS Text options. They are identical for all characters with ASCII values of 127 and below. If you're using foreign-language characters or unusual symbols, however, the difference is important.

The Text options are meant for exchanging files with other Macintosh applications or Windows-based applications. The MS-DOS Text options are meant for exchanging files with MS-DOS–based applications. The two categories differ in how they deal with high-order characters. The Text options follow the ANSI high-order character set. The MS-DOS Text options follow the character set used by MS-DOS (sometimes called the *OEM character set* or the *IBM extended character set*).

For importing text files, Word offers two options: Text Files and Text With Layout. The Text Files option is absolutely literal about converting the source text file. If Word encounters a carriage return, it puts an end-of-paragraph mark at that point in the document. Unfortunately, some programs produce text files that have a carriage return at the end of each line rather than at the end of each paragraph. This can cause problems when you use the Text Files option because Word will then treat each line of the file as a separate paragraph, and it won't wrap the text properly if you edit or reformat it.

If the file you're importing has a carriage return at the end of each line, you will probably want to use the Text With Layout option. With this choice, Word will try to identify each paragraph in the source file and format it as a paragraph. For example, it will recognize two carriage returns (indicating a blank line between paragraphs), a carriage return followed by a tab (indicating an indent at the beginning of a paragraph), or a carriage return followed by spaces (also indicating an indent) as indicating the start of a new paragraph, and it will format the text accordingly.

When you are importing files that do not include a carriage return at the end of each line, the Text With Layout option will often guess wrong—and will create extra work, since you'll need to clean up the incorrect guesses. It's best to avoid this option with files that don't have extra carriage returns.

For files that do include a carriage return at the end of each line, Text With Layout will generally work well, especially if the document contains nothing but paragraphs of body text. But if the source file includes tables or lists, you may be better off importing the file twice, once without layout and once with layout. You can then use Edit Cut and Edit Paste to combine the properly formatted parts of each document.

# Importing Data

In addition to importing information by opening a file and converting it, Word offers three other methods for importing information: the Clipboard, the Insert File command, and the Insert Database command.

## How to import data using the Clipboard

In many cases, the simplest way to move information to Word will be to copy and paste, or cut and paste, by way of the Clipboard (which we discussed in Chapter 4). Of course, it's easier to use the Clipboard if you have both Word and the other program running simultaneously. But even if your system doesn't have enough memory to load more than one program at a time, you can still transfer data using the Clipboard.

First open the file containing the graphic, worksheet, or other information you want to copy into Word. Select the information you want to transfer, and choose Edit Copy or Edit Cut to have the application put a copy of the selection on the Clipboard. Next load Word or switch to the Word window, open the document that you want to paste the information into, and place the cursor where you want to insert the information. Then choose either the Edit Paste or the Edit Paste Special command to insert the contents of the Clipboard into your document.

If you choose Edit Paste, Word will insert the data either as text or as a graphic image, depending on what you originally cut or copied. If you're pasting information that started out in a Microsoft Excel worksheet, for example, the Edit Paste command will paste the text into your document as a table. The Edit Paste Special command lets you insert the item as a linked object, as we will discuss later in this chapter.

## How to import data using the Insert File command

If you want to insert information from another program or another Word file directly into your document, you can use the Insert File command, which can read and convert all the same file formats as the File Open command. When you choose Insert File, Word will display a dialog box that is nearly identical to the dialog box for opening files, right down to the Confirm Conversions check box. However, it has two important additions: the Range text box and the Link To File check box. There is one missing element: the Read Only check box.

If you highlight a file in the Select A File To Insert box and choose Insert, Word will insert the contents of the entire file into your document, just as if you had typed or pasted it. If you prefer, however, you can specify a portion of the file in the Range text box. The type of range you can specify depends on the type of file you're inserting. For example, if you've defined a section of text with a bookmark in a Word document, you can insert only that section of text by specifying the bookmark. Similarly, you can specify a named range of cells when inserting from a Microsoft Excel worksheet file.

If you check the Link To File check box before choosing OK, Word will insert the contents of the file as a linked field, which we'll cover later in this chapter.

## How to import data using the Insert Database command

Database files create special challenges for importing data. Instead of simply translating the data into Word format, you may want to import only some of the information from the database, and you may need it sorted in a particular order.

A quick lesson in database jargon will help here: Databases store information as *records*, with each record consisting of related information such as a name and an address. They also divide records into *fields*, with each field consisting of a specific kind of information, such as first name, state, or zip code. Each field has a *field name* (such as FIRST, STATE, or ZIP), used to refer to the contents of that field across records. When you import database files into Word, you may want to import, or select (to use the proper jargon), only certain records. And you may want to import information from some of the fields but not from others. Word's Insert Database command provides tools for importing, selecting, and sorting all at one time, as well as for specifying which fields to include from each record. When Word imports the data, it will place it in a table, creating one row for each record and one column for each field.

You might need to import data from a database file for any number of reasons, ranging from creating a simple table in your document to using Word as a sophisticated report generator for your database program. But one of the most important reasons for importing data is to use it for mail merges. The Insert Database command, with its ability to sort and select as it imports data, makes it easy to maintain a database in Microsoft Excel or in most database programs and then import the data into a Word table only when you need it for mail merging form letters, labels, and the like. For details on mail merging with Word, see Chapter 21 starting on page 679.

To import data from a database file, start by positioning the cursor where you want to insert the data in your Word document. Then choose Insert Database to open the Database dialog box, shown in Figure 18-3.

**FIGURE 18-3**

Use the Database dialog box to import, select, and sort data from a database file.

| Database |
| --- |
| Data Source: |
| Get Data... |
| Data: Mailing List Info |
| Data Options: |
| Query Options...    Table AutoFormat... |
| Insert the Data into the Document: |
| Insert Data... |
| Cancel |
| Help |

From the Database dialog box, choose the Get Data button in the section labeled Data Source. Word will display the dialog box for selecting a data file, which is identical to the dialog box for opening files except that the List Files Of Type pull-down list includes choices of files that can contain information organized as a database (or as a table in the case of Word or text options). You can use the same techniques you use in the dialog box for opening files to move to the appropriate folder and designate the file that contains the data you want to insert. Choose Open, and Word will return to the Database dialog box, which now displays the path and name of the chosen file below the Get Data button, as shown in Figure 18-3. (Note that some files may display an intermediate dialog window asking you to pick either the whole database or a range of records before returning you to the Database dialog box shown here.)

## How to define the database import options

Once you've specified the file to use, the two buttons in the Data Options section of the Database dialog box and the Insert Data button at the bottom of the dialog box will become available. Since you'll generally want to retrieve a subset of information from the database file, your next step will usually be choosing the Query Options button to open the Query Options dialog box, shown in Figure 18-4.

**FIGURE 18-4**

The Filter Records card in the Query Options dialog box lets you specify which records to import.

Figure 18-4 shows the Filter Records card, which lets you set the criteria for the records to select. Suppose, for example, that the database includes the names and addresses of your clients and that you want to include the records for all clients except those in New York and New Jersey.

As you can see in Figure 18-4, the dialog box contains four columns of text boxes, with only three boxes in the first row. The three columns labeled Field, Comparison, and Compare To let you define the filter, or selection criteria. Each row lets you define a criterion based on the information in one field of each record. The additional text boxes in the unlabeled column let you specify how to link the criteria: with *And* (the record must meet the earlier criteria *and* the criterion in this row), or with *Or* (the record must meet the earlier criteria *or* this one). When Word inserts the data, it will filter out the records that don't meet the criteria—to use the common database jargon, it will *select* those records that meet the criteria.

In Figure 18-4, the filter is defined to include all records in which the REGION field is not equal to NY and is not equal to NJ. To set the criteria, start by opening the Field pull-down list in the first row. The list will include all the fields in the database file. Highlight the field name *REGION* and release the mouse button to enter it in the text box. Next use the same techniques to enter Not Equal To in the Comparison box in the first row. Then move to the Compare To box and type *NY*. (This example assumes that the database uses two-character abbreviations for states.)

Use the same techniques to fill in the text boxes in the second row. If you decide you want to start over at any point, you can choose the Clear All button at the bottom of the card.

You can also tell Word how to sort the records, using the Sort Records card, shown in Figure 18-5.

The Sort Records card in the Query Options dialog box lets you specify a sort order for the imported records.

The Sort Records card will let you specify up to three levels of sorting. You might, for example, want a list of clients grouped together by region, by city within each region, and alphabetically by name within each city. To generate the list, you would sort first by region, then by city, and then by last name. To designate the field for each level of the sort, open the pull-down list for the appropriate text box and use the mouse or keyboard to choose from the list. The Ascending and Descending option buttons for each text box let you specify the direction for that level of the sort (ascending or descending order for numbers, and alphabetic or reverse alphabetic order for text). If necessary, you can choose the Clear All button to remove all entries.

The third and last card in the Query Options dialog box is the Select Fields card, shown in Figure 18-6. This card lets you tell Word to import only those fields that you want in your document. It also lets you specify the order for the fields.

The Select Fields card includes two lists of fields. The Fields In Data Source list, on the left, includes all fields in the data file. The Selected Fields list, on the right, shows the fields Word will import, in the order in which it will import them.

**FIGURE 18-6**

The Select Fields card lets you specify which fields to import and in what order.

When the highlight is in the Fields In Data Source list, the two buttons between the lists are labeled Select and Select All. When the highlight is in the Selected Fields list, the buttons will change to Remove and Remove All. Choosing the Select button will add the currently highlighted field name or names to the Selected Fields list, while choosing the Remove button will delete the currently highlighted field name or names from the list. Similarly, choosing the Select All button will add all the field names in the database file to the Selected Fields list, while choosing the Remove All button will delete all the field names.

When you first open the Select Fields card while defining query options for a database file, the list of selected fields will include all fields in the database file, in the same order as they appear in the database file. To change the list, highlight the field names and choose the Remove button as appropriate to take out those fields that you don't want to include or that are in the wrong order. To change the order of the fields, simply add the field names back in the new order.

To create the list shown in Figure 18-6, for example, we first chose Remove All to clear the Selected Fields list. Next we highlighted CONTACT and chose Select and then highlighted all the fields from COMPANY through ZIP_CODE and chose Select again. At that point, we had added two unwanted entries: CON_TITLE and a second entry for CONTACT. To get rid of them, we simply highlighted them in the Selected Fields list and chose Remove.

The last item on the Select Fields card, just below the Selected Fields list, is the Include Field Names check box. If you want to include the field names in the table Word creates from the database, make sure this box is checked. If you don't want the field names included, make sure the box isn't checked.

When you're finished with the Query Options choices, choose OK to return to the Database dialog box.

## How to define a format for the imported database data

In the Data Options section of the Database dialog box, you'll find the Table AutoFormat button. You can choose this button to open the Table AutoFormat dialog box and define a format for the table that Word will insert. This is the same dialog box you'll see if you choose the Table AutoFormat command. For details about this dialog box, see "How to use Table AutoFormat—with or without the Table Wizard" on page 337.

## How to insert the database data

Once you've specified a data source and have (optionally) defined a query and/or a format, you can choose the Insert Data button in the Database dialog box to open the Insert Data dialog box, shown in Figure 18-7.

**FIGURE 18-7**

The Insert Data dialog box lets you specify whether to insert all records that meet your criteria or only certain records.

```
═══════════════ Insert Data ═══════════════
┌─Insert Records───────────────┐  ┌──────────┐
│  ○ All                       │  │    OK    │
│  ● From: [1]     To: [3]      │  ├──────────┤
│                              │  │  Cancel  │
│  □ Insert Data as Field      │  ├──────────┤
└──────────────────────────────┘  │   Help   │
                                   └──────────┘
```

The Insert Data dialog box lets you specify whether to import all records that meet the criteria you've defined or whether to import a range of records. Enter 1 in the From text box and 3 in the To text box, for example, and you'll import only the first three records that meet your criteria.

Limiting the import to a range of records can be useful if you want to test a query definition. A quick test run will let you see whether the query does in fact retrieve the appropriate set of records in the format you want. To make a test run even faster, be sure not to include a sort definition.

If you check the Insert Data As Field check box in the Insert Data dialog box before choosing OK, Word will insert the contents of the file as a DATA-BASE field, which maintains a link to the database. We'll explain links later in this chapter; see "Linking and Embedding" starting on page 603.

# Moving Word Documents to Other Programs

So far in this chapter, we've concentrated on moving data into Word files. But you will probably need to move data in the other direction as well: from Word format to other applications. Word provides plenty of options for that too.

## How to save Word documents in other formats

You can save a Word document in a foreign file format just as easily as you can load a document that's in a foreign format. Start by loading the document in Word. Then choose File Save As to display the Save As dialog box. We covered this dialog box in Chapter 2, and you should be familiar with most of its options. Here we're interested in the Save File As Type pull-down list. When you open this list, you'll see a list like the one shown in Figure 18-8.

The Save File As Type list offers a range of file formats for your document.

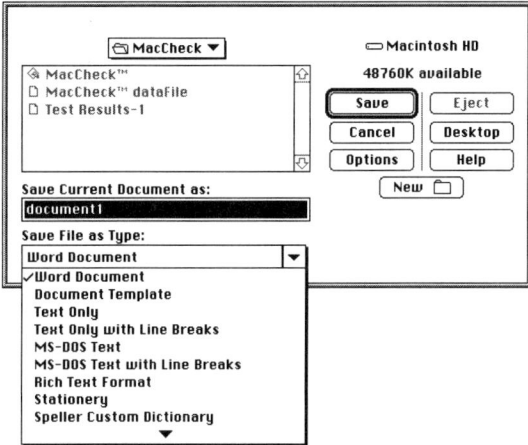

This list is similar to the one Word offers for confirming the format when you open a file that's already in a foreign format. Recall that if you have checked the Confirm Conversions check box in the Open dialog box, Word will pause and let you confirm the format before opening the file. In that case, Word shows you the list of file formats in a separate dialog box (Convert File) after you choose OK in the Open dialog box. In contrast, when you save a file, you must designate the format before you choose OK.

There is another difference as well. In addition to the text file formats discussed earlier, you'll find two more in the Save As dialog box: Text Only With Line Breaks and MS-DOS Text With Line Breaks. If you choose either of these line-break formats, Word will save the file as ASCII text without trying to preserve the layout, but it will end each line with a carriage return. This contrasts with the Text Only and MS-DOS Text options, which put a carriage return at the end of each paragraph only (wherever Word has an end-of-paragraph mark).

If you're saving a document in text format to be edited in another program, you will probably want to use either the Text Only or the MS-DOS Text option so that you will not have to remove all the extra carriage returns when you import the file into the other program. If you intend to send the file as a message over an electronic mail system, however, you will probably want to use one of the With Line Breaks options to add a carriage return at the end of each line. Since most electronic mail systems can't handle lines of text longer than 80 characters, this will make the file more palatable to the system.

Remember that, aside from the text options, your list of available file formats may not match the lists that appear in our illustrations. The list you see will depend on the conversion filters you have installed. You can install and remove conversion filters using the Microsoft Word Setup utility program.

## How to use the Clipboard

You can also move data from Word documents to other applications with the Clipboard. Simply copy or cut the portion of the document that you want to move, and then switch to the other application.

# Customizing the Conversion Process

As we've discussed, word processing files can contain complex formatting information, and it can be difficult to reliably convert the formatting from one file format to another. While we recommend that you put as little formatting as possible into any document that you intend to convert, we also recognize that you can't always get away with minimal formatting. You may, for example, need to exchange files with a client or co-worker who uses a different word processor. For those occasions when you must import or export heavily formatted files, Word provides an impressive array of features to let you fine-tune the way it converts and displays files.

## How to use the Tools Options Compatibility card

One of the more sophisticated and easier-to-use features for working with heavily formatted imported files is the set of options on the Tools Options Compatibility card, shown in Figure 18-9.

**FIGURE 18-9**

The Tools Options Compatibility card controls how Word displays documents on screen.

The settings on this card do not affect in any way the information stored in the file. Rather, they affect how Word interprets that information to format the document on screen and on paper. You can use these settings to tell Word to treat certain kinds of formatting information the same way as another specific program treats it, to have Word more closely match the way the other program displays the file.

For example, the second item in the Options list is Don't Add Automatic Tab Stop For Hanging Indent. Ordinarily, when you create a paragraph with a hanging indent (also known as an "outdent" in earlier versions of Word), Word will automatically define a tab stop so that the first tab on the first line of the paragraph is lined up vertically with the first character of the second and later lines. Other programs don't provide that convenience. As a result, if you have a 1-inch hanging indent in a paragraph in Word and one tab at the beginning of the first line, the text will start 1 inch from the left of the beginning of the first line. In Word for MS-DOS, in contrast, the same tab character will indent the first line by only 0.5 inch, since Word for MS-DOS leaves its default tab stops untouched. To tell Word 6.0 for the Macintosh to display the paragraph with the same indents and tab stops that you would see in Word for MS-DOS, you need to turn off the automatic tab stop by making sure to check the Don't Add Automatic Tab Stop For Hanging Indent check box.

Word has several predefined sets of options for the Compatibility card, each designed to make Word mimic the behavior of some other specific program. The predefined choices, which will set all the Compatibility options at one time, turning them on or off as appropriate, are available in the Recommended Options For pull-down list, along with a choice for a custom definition. You can use these predefined sets or create a custom definition to set the options as needed. More important, Word stores the settings separately for each file, so you can save a different set of options for each file.

 Word will normally use the recommended option settings for Microsoft Word 6.0 as its default (with none of the check boxes in the Options list checked). Most users will want this as the default. If you work with a lot of files from another program, however, and you want your default settings to match the other program's formatting, you can set the options in the Options list the way you want them and then choose the Default button to make that set of options the new default for all documents based on the Normal template.

## Font conversions

One potentially troublesome issue in converting file formats is finding the right fonts to use. Word provides help for that aspect of file conversion as well. Choose the Font Substitution button on the Compatibility card, and if your current document uses a font that is not installed on your system, Word will open the Font Substitution dialog box shown in Figure 18-10.

**FIGURE 18-10**

The Font Substitution dialog box lets you substitute fonts in a document, on either a temporary or a permanent basis.

 If all the fonts specified in the converted document are available to Word, you will not be able to open the Font Substitution dialog box. Instead, when you choose the Font Substitution button, you will see a message box stating that no font substitution is necessary.

The Font Substitutions list box, which takes up the top half of the dialog box, consists of two columns. The Missing Document Font column lists any fonts specified in the converted document that are not available within Word. The Substituted Font column shows what Word is using instead—which either will be a specific font, if you've defined one to use, or will simply be listed as Default.

If you highlight an entry in the Font Substitutions list, Word will display the appropriate parts of that entry in the Missing Document Font and Substituted Font text boxes. It will also display a message below the text boxes indicating the font it's using as a substitute. If you've chosen a specific font, the message will simply repeat the information that appears in the Font Substitutions list and in the two text boxes. If the substituted font is set to Default, the message will state what the default font is. If you want to change the setting, open the Substituted Font pull-down list to choose a different font from the list of fonts available on your system.

The substitutions listed in the Font Substitution dialog box affect only the way Word works with the file. The original font information is still stored in the file, and if you convert the file back to its original format, the original fonts remain. If you want to change the original fonts to the substituted fonts permanently, choose the Convert Permanently button.

# Linking and Embedding

NEW!

All the features we've covered in this chapter so far deal with importing data into Word or exporting data from Word on an essentially permanent basis. What you wind up with in either case is a snapshot of the file's original contents. If you import data into a Word document with File Insert (and without checking Link To File), for example, later changes to the original file will not appear in the copy that's in the Word document. And if you want to change some imported data, you have to make the changes with Word.

At times, these limitations will be precisely what you want, either because you don't want changes in the source data to affect your Word document or because you want to make changes within the Word document without affecting the source. But there will also be times when you'll want the two applications to share information. If you've inserted a section of a worksheet into a Word document, for example, you might want the convenience of being able to make changes once, in the worksheet, and have them appear in the Word document as well.

In addition, you'll find that it's more convenient to edit certain kinds of data—such as spreadsheet data, for example—using the application that created it in the first place. This can be important whether you want to share the data between Word and another program or simply want the convenience of using the more appropriate tool for the task. For these needs, Word provides linking and embedding features.

Linking and embedding can be confusing topics. Part of the problem is that Word handles both features through fields, a subject we'll discuss in Chapter 20. Trying to learn all the different fields, along with the variations for each, can be overwhelming. However, Word will insert the fields for you automatically if you choose the appropriate menu commands, which means that you can take advantage of linking and embedding without knowing anything about fields.

For purposes of this discussion, we'll largely ignore fields, although we'll mention which commands create which fields, and we'll talk about moving the cursor or selection to a given field—by which we mean placing the cursor or selection in the imported text, graphic, or other data. (As we'll discuss in Chapter 20, Word can also display codes for the fields rather than the data itself.) We'll focus here on using the menu commands, which include Insert Object, Edit Paste Special, Insert Picture, Insert File, and Insert Database.

## Different kinds of links

Any time you establish a connection between two data files in a way that lets them share data, you've established a link. But how that link behaves can vary a great deal—depending on what kind of field the link is based on and what settings, or switches, the field is using.

Some kinds of links will automatically update the data in Word if you change the original, or source, file. Other links require that you give a command to update the data. Similarly, some kinds of links will let you import text into Word and edit the text in Word just as if it were normal text—although you'll lose your edits if you update the field. Other kinds of links will let you edit the text only by calling the program the text was created in and using that program to edit. All links, in short, are not created equal. It's important to keep that in mind.

Earlier we discussed the Insert File command and pointed out the Link To File check box. If you check this box before choosing OK in the File dialog box, Word will create an INCLUDETEXT field. This inserts the text in a way that lets you either edit the text within Word or edit it by opening the source program and loading the source file.

When you create a link with the Insert File command, however, Word will not automatically update the text in one place when you edit in the other. Rather, once you've edited the source file, you can give a manual command to update the inserted text in the Word document. To update, place the cursor or selection in the field and press F9. Alternatively, you can move the mouse pointer to the field, hold down Control as you click the mouse button, and choose Update Field from the context-sensitive menu. In either case, Word will reimport the text from the linked file, and you'll lose any changes you've made to the text you previously imported into Word.

You can establish a similar kind of link with the Insert Database command, which we also discussed earlier in this chapter. In this case, the equivalent check box is labeled Insert Data As Field. If you check it before choosing OK in the Insert Data dialog box, Word will create a DATABASE field. The DATABASE field differs from the INCLUDETEXT field in detail, but it behaves in much the same way. Here again, you can edit the text within Word or in the original file. You can use F9 or Update Field to update the field in Word; and if you update it, you'll lose any changes you made to the imported version of the data.

The Insert Picture dialog box includes a Link To File check box that serves much the same purpose for pictures. If you insert a picture without checking this check box, Word will insert the picture itself. If you check the box, Word will use an INCLUDEPICTURE field; you can edit the picture by using the source application, as you can edit text added with the INCLUDETEXT field or the DATABASE field, and you can then update it in Word with F9 or the Update Field command. For details on using the Insert Picture command, see "How to insert a picture" starting on page 508.

A more sophisticated kind of link is one that takes advantage of a feature called OLE and uses Word's LINK field. OLE links are generally preferable to other kinds of links, although you can't always use them because not all programs support OLE. If you choose Insert Object, you will see an Object Types list that lists all the programs that have been installed on your system that support OLE. In some cases, you'll see more than one entry for a program; for Microsoft Excel, for example, the list includes both Microsoft Excel Worksheet and Microsoft Excel Chart. We'll talk about how to use the Insert Object dialog box later in the chapter.

With OLE, Word inserts an image of the text, graphic, or other item in your document. This is called an *object* because you can't work with the data directly using Word commands, regardless of the kind of data. You can work only with the object as a whole, moving it, resizing it, or otherwise modifying it as a complete object.

To edit the data in a linked object, you can edit the original file by loading the source application and then loading the data file. More interesting is that you can also open the source application and automatically load the data file from within your Word document simply by double-clicking on the object in the Word document or by selecting the object and choosing the Edit Object command. (The precise name for the Object command on the Edit menu will vary depending on the kind of object you've selected.)

When you choose Edit Object, Word will use the OLE feature to open the appropriate program, load the appropriate file, and let you edit the data. In some cases, the source program will run separately and display the data in an editing window, much as if you had opened the program directly. WordArt as described in Chapter 15 is an example of a program that works this way. In other cases, the Word menu and toolbars will be replaced with the equivalents from the source program but will continue to display the Word document so that you can see the object in context. Microsoft Chart, also described in Chapter 15, is an example of a program that works this way.

## Linking vs. embedding

The difference between linking and embedding is subtle but straightforward. In both cases, if you're working in Word, you can double-click on the object (or choose Edit Object) to edit the object in the source application. With a linked object, the data exists in a file outside your Word document: You can open it directly by loading the source application and then opening the file. With an embedded object, however, the data exists only in the Word document: There is no way to work with the data without first loading Word and the appropriate Word document. Some programs—WordArt 2.0, for example—will let you create embedded objects only; there is no way to save those objects as stand-alone files.

Use embedding when you don't need to share the data with another file (not even with another Word document). Embedding is often more convenient than linking because all the data is stored in the Word document file. This means that you don't have to keep track of extra files, and you still have quick access to the source application when you want to edit the data.

If you need to share information among files, however, linking will let you update the information in one place and make the update easily available to all linked files. It will also let you edit the linked data by loading the source application and opening the data file directly. When linking files, you'll generally be better off using OLE links rather than the less sophisticated kinds of links we discussed earlier (such as using the Insert File command)—unless, of course, you're linking to data created by programs that don't support OLE. In that case, you can use the less sophisticated kinds of links as a fallback.

# How to embed data with the Insert Object command

The easiest way to embed an object in Word is with the Insert Object command, which opens the Object dialog box. As we explained in Chapter 15 when discussing WordArt 2.0, you can create new objects and embed them at the same time by using this dialog box. For details on using this dialog box, see "How to use the Object dialog box," page 532.

You can also embed the contents of existing files using the From File button in the Object dialog box, which opens the dialog box for selecting a document shown in Figure 18-11.

**FIGURE 18-11**

Use the dialog box for selecting a document to embed the contents of an existing file.

As shown in Figure 18-11, the dialog box is similar to Word's dialog box for opening files and lets you specify a file the same way. The Display As Icon check box lets you tell Word to display an icon instead of the object's contents. The Link To File check box lets you create an OLE link to a file rather than inserting its contents as an embedded object. (We'll cover this possibility in a moment.) To embed the contents of an existing file, leave this check box cleared.

When you select a file in the dialog box and choose Open, Word creates an EMBED field, which, in essence, creates a copy of the file as an embedded object. Because an embedded object is associated with a particular application, you can edit the object by double-clicking on it or by selecting the object and choosing the Edit Object command. Word will automatically open the associated application.

Figure 18-12 on the next page shows a Word document that contains an embedded Microsoft Excel 5.0 worksheet. This figure lets you see how the worksheet normally appears in the document. Figure 18-13 on the next page shows how a Microsoft Excel 5.0 worksheet looks when it's open for editing. Notice that the menus and toolbars shown in Figure 18-13 are Excel menus and toolbars.

This is how an embedded Microsoft Excel 5.0 worksheet normally looks in a Word document.

Here you can see the visual effect of editing a Microsoft Excel 5.0 worksheet embedded in a Word document.

## How to link data with the Insert Object command

The easiest way to create a linked object is to use the Insert Object command to link to an already existing file. However, make sure you've checked the Link To File check box in the dialog box for selecting a document before choosing OK. Word will then create a LINK field rather than an EMBED field and will set it to automatically update the data in the Word document if you change the data in the source file.

## How to use the Edit Paste Special command to embed or link data

You can also embed or link data using Word's Edit Paste Special command. Start by loading the source application, opening the appropriate file, and using that program's Edit Copy command to copy the data to the Clipboard. Then open your document file in Word, and choose the Edit Paste Special command to open the Paste Special dialog box, shown in Figure 18-14.

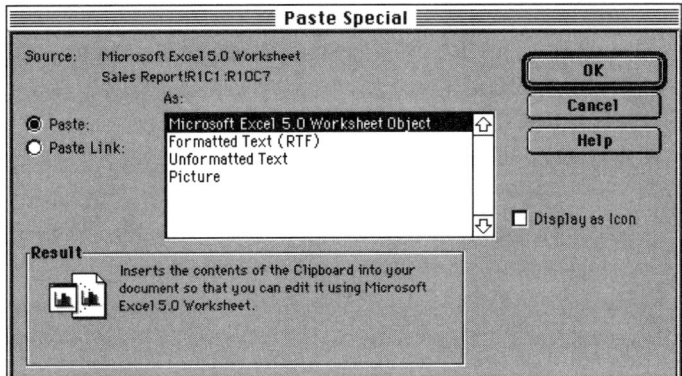

**FIGURE 18-14**

You can embed or link data from other applications using the Clipboard and the Edit Paste Special command.

The Paste Special dialog box shows the source of the data that is currently on the Clipboard. It also provides option buttons that let you choose whether to paste or "paste link" the data. If you choose the Paste option button, choosing an item from the As list that is described as an object—such as Microsoft Excel 5.0 Worksheet Object—will result in an embedded object. Other choices from the As list, such as Formatted Text (RTF), Unformatted Text, and Picture, will add data you can edit directly, either as text or as a picture.

If you choose the Paste Link option button, choosing any item in the As list will result in a linked object, although the behavior and appearance of the object will vary because Word will insert the LINK field with different settings depending on the choice. Using Paste Link with an object results in an OLE link.

If you are unsure about how a given choice from the list will be inserted, you can choose the Paste or Paste Link button and then highlight the item in the list. In the Result section of the dialog box, Word will display a short explanation of how the choice will be inserted.

## How to update and maintain linked data

If your document includes links to other files using any of several fields—including LINK, INCLUDETEXT, and INCLUDEPICTURE—you can easily change the link settings with the Links dialog box, shown in Figure 18-15. To open the dialog box, choose the Edit Links command, with the cursor or selection located anywhere in the document. (If you haven't defined any links, the Links command on the Edit menu will be grayed.)

**FIGURE 18-15**

You can use the Links dialog box to maintain the links between objects in a Word document and their source applications.

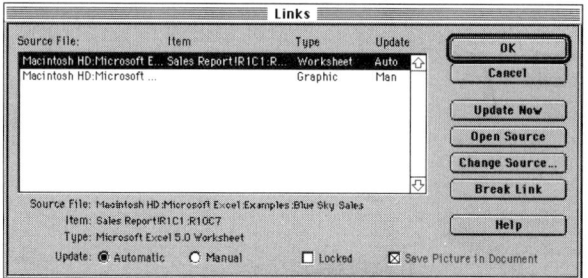

The Links dialog box lists all the links currently defined for your document. For each link, it shows the source file, the item (an identification such as a cell range), the type of link (indicating the name or the type of the source application the item was created in), and whether the link is set for manual or automatic update or is locked, which prevents any update.

You can modify the links by highlighting one or more entries in the list and then setting the appropriate options in the dialog box. To highlight a link, simply click on it or move the highlight to it with the arrow keys. You can highlight multiple links by using the standard keyboard or mouse techniques.

After you highlight the links you want to change, you can set the Update option. To keep Word from updating the linked information under any conditions, be sure to check the Locked check box at the bottom of the dialog box. When this check box is checked, Word will gray the Automatic and Manual option buttons. If the box isn't checked, these two option buttons will be available, and you can set the link for either automatic or manual updates, as appropriate.

The Update Now button will update all highlighted links, based on the current version of the source file or files. (There is no reason to choose this button for links that are set for automatic update.) The Open Source button will be available only if you have highlighted a single link. Choose this button to activate or load the source application and to either load the source file or activate the window the source file is already loaded in.

The Break Link button will break the highlighted link. (When you break a link, Word will convert linked text to text and a linked picture to a picture.) If you choose the Change Source button, Word will open the Change Source dialog box, which is similar to Word's dialog box for opening files. You can use this dialog box to specify a different source file for a link. You can also use the Item text box at the bottom of the dialog box to specify which portion of the linked file to use, such as a range of cells in a Microsoft Excel worksheet.

## A quick look at fields for embedding and linking

Although we purposely haven't discussed fields much here, since we'll cover the subject in Chapter 20, one or two additional details demand mention. In particular, you should be aware that you can toggle between seeing field results—such as an embedded object—and seeing field codes by placing your cursor or selection in the field code or field result and either pressing Shift-F9 or checking the Field Codes check box on the Tools Options View card. Figure 18-16, for example, shows both an embedded object and the field code that produces it.

**FIGURE 18-16**

This figure shows an embedded object—the result of a field—and the field code that produces the field result.

You can create or modify LINK and EMBED fields directly if you like. As we mentioned earlier, you can use a number of optional settings, or switches, with the LINK and EMBED fields. Word's default settings, which it adds when you create these fields with the menu commands, will serve in most cases, but you may want to explore the available choices more closely. To see the list of switches and other information about the field type, use one of the techniques just described to set Word to show the field code, place the cursor in the field, and press Help to see the Word Help screen for that field.

Many programs that don't support OLE do support a feature called *dynamic data exchange,* or DDE, which is an older, less sophisticated technique for sharing data among programs. Word supplies two fields that take advantage of DDE: DDE and DDEAUTO. Because more and more programs support OLE, odds are that you'll never need to know anything about the DDE fields. But if you do need to use them, you should be aware that these fields are not available on the Insert Field list that we'll discuss in Chapter 20. However, you can still insert them manually by pressing ⌘-F9 to create Word's field characters and then typing the field code directly into your document. (We'll cover this procedure fully in Chapter 20.)

Both fields use the same format:

{FieldName AppName FileName PlaceReference}

*FieldName* is either DDE or DDEAUTO, depending on which one you want to use. The DDE field must be updated manually with the F9 key or the Update Field command, while the DDEAUTO field automatically updates the field based on changes in the source file. *AppName* is the name of the source application, such as Microsoft Excel. *FileName* is the name of the source file. *PlaceReference* is optional, but you can use it to specify a portion of the source file, such as a range of cells in a Microsoft Excel worksheet.

# How to create links in other programs

Keep in mind that other applications can embed and link objects created in Word, just as Word can embed and link objects created in other programs. Look for commands named Paste Special or Paste Link on the Edit menus of other programs; these are the most common choices for implementing these features. You might also want to check the programs' manuals.

# Power Tools

# TOPIC FINDER

# 19

# Outlining

utlining is one of those subjects that often seems like a religious issue. Some people swear by outlines as a way to help them organize their thoughts, and they wouldn't write anything without one. Others swear *at* outlines as a constraint to creativity and have no idea what the outline for a given piece of writing should look like until after they've finished writing.

If you fall into the first group, you'll find Word's outlining feature a tremendous help, and you'll probably use it whenever you can.

If you fall into the second group, you may be pleasantly surprised to find that the outlining feature can help the way you work as well. Even if you never create an outline to organize your thoughts before writing, you can use the feature after the fact. If your documents include headings of any sort, you can format those headings with Word's heading styles and then use the outline feature to quickly move sections around when you want to change the organization. You can also use the outlining feature to move quickly through a document. Or you can simply use it to look at the current organization while you decide what to write about next.

The basis of Word's outlining feature is the Outline view. Working in combination with several of Word's other features, the Outline view provides a sophisticated, fully integrated collapsible outliner. By *collapsible,* we mean that you can collapse the outline to show just the headings or just certain levels of headings. And because you can easily move from Normal or Page Layout view to Outline view and back, you can use the outline as an aid to organization even while you write.

Do not confuse Word's outline feature with Word's ability to produce outline-style lists. The collapsible outline feature lets you work with large text documents, collapsing them to show only headings so that you can better grasp the organization of the full document. It also gives you a convenient way to reorganize your document: Move a heading, and all of the collapsed text under that heading moves with it.

In contrast, an outline-style list is simply that: a list that follows an outline format like the one you probably learned in high school. Outline-style lists, which Word calls *multilevel lists,* serve a different purpose than a collapsible outliner. Because a multilevel list is, in essence, a numbered list rather than an outline in the sense of Word's outline feature, we'll cover it with other numbered lists. For details on creating and using multilevel lists, see "Multilevel numbered paragraphs: Classic outlines" starting on page 451.

To switch to Outline view, choose View Outline or click on the Outline View button at the left of the horizontal scroll bar. Word will add the Outlining toolbar below the Standard and Formatting toolbars if they are showing, replacing the ruler if it is showing. Figure 19-1 shows the buttons on the Outlining toolbar. To leave Outline view, choose View Normal or View Page Layout.

The Outlining toolbar contains a set of buttons you can use to assign heading levels to paragraphs in your document, to expand and collapse your view of the document, to move text, and also to adjust what Word shows in the document. We'll look at each of these buttons as we discuss how to use Outline view.

| Button | Button Name | Action |
|---|---|---|
| | Promote | Changes the heading style or styles to the next higher level, or changes body text to match the heading level of the nearest heading before it. |
| | Demote | Changes the heading style or styles to the next lower level, or changes body text to a heading one level lower than the nearest heading before it. |
| | Demote To Body Text | Changes the heading or headings to body text. |
| | Move Up | Moves the paragraph or paragraphs the cursor or selection is in up one paragraph. |
| | Move Down | Moves the paragraph or paragraphs the cursor or selection is in down one paragraph. |
| | Expand | Reveals the next level of text—from heading levels 1–9 plus body text—below the heading the cursor or selection is in, or, if the selection includes the paragraph marker at the end of the heading paragraph, reveals the lowest level of text included in the selection. (Note that slightly different rules apply if you select the text by clicking on the plus sign to the left of the text.) |
| | Collapse | Hides the lowest level of text—from heading levels 1–9 plus body text—currently showing after the heading the cursor or selection is in, or, if the selection includes the paragraph marker at the end of the heading paragraph, hides all levels lower than the level of the first paragraph of the selection. (Note that slightly different rules apply if you select the text by clicking on the plus sign to the left of the text.) |
| | Show Heading 1 through Show Heading 8 | Specifies the lowest level of headings to show. All higher-level headings also show. |
| | Show All | Shows all text. |
| | Show First Line Only | Displays only the first line of each paragraph of body text. |
| | Show Formatting | Toggles between showing the headings and text with and without character formatting. |
| | Master Document View | Switches Word to Master Document view, and adds the Master Document toolbar to the screen. |

**FIGURE 19-1**

The Outlining toolbar buttons.

# Headings and Body Text

Outline view recognizes two categories of text: headings and body text. Each heading is assigned a level, labeled Heading 1 through Heading 9. Everything that's not a heading is body text. You enter headings as you would any other text, usually as single-line paragraphs. You then identify these paragraphs as headings and assign a heading level at the same time, either by directly applying the appropriate heading style or by switching to Outline view and using the appropriate buttons on the Outlining toolbar to apply the style.

The nine heading levels represent categories and subcategories in an outline. For example, in writing this book we've used Heading 1 for section titles; Heading 2 for chapter titles; and Heading 3, Heading 4, and Heading 5 for three levels of headings within each chapter. You can use all of these entries as headings in your finished document, as we have, or you can hide them from view after you finish writing and editing by formatting the heading paragraphs as hidden.

Word helps you visualize the relationships between different parts of your outline by indenting the different levels when you're in Outline view. The headings for main topics—meaning those headings formatted with Heading 1 styles—start at the left margin. Heading 2 entries are indented ½ inch, Heading 3 entries are indented 1 inch, and so on, with each new level indented an additional ½ inch. Body text for any level is indented an additional ¼ inch from the heading itself. (More precisely, the amount of indention for each level matches the default tab setting for the document. To see the current default setting for any given document, choose Format Tabs. If you change this setting, Word will change the amount of indention for each level in the outline.)

# Building an Outline

The easiest way to become familiar with Outline view is to create a sample document. To illustrate, we'll create the article about free-lancing that we used in Chapter 14 to work with multiple text columns. We'll take the approach of someone who likes to use an outline to help organize ideas and then build on the outline to create a finished document. To follow the example, open a new document and choose View Outline to switch to Outline view.

Figure 19-2 shows a portion of our sample article's outline. To create this outline, start by typing the first heading, *Cutting loose,* and then pressing Return to start a new paragraph. Whenever you begin a new outline, Word assumes that your first paragraph will be a Heading 1 entry. It also assumes that each subsequent paragraph will be the same level as the previous entry unless you indicate otherwise.

**FIGURE 19-2**

We'll start by entering headings in Outline view and assigning levels to them.

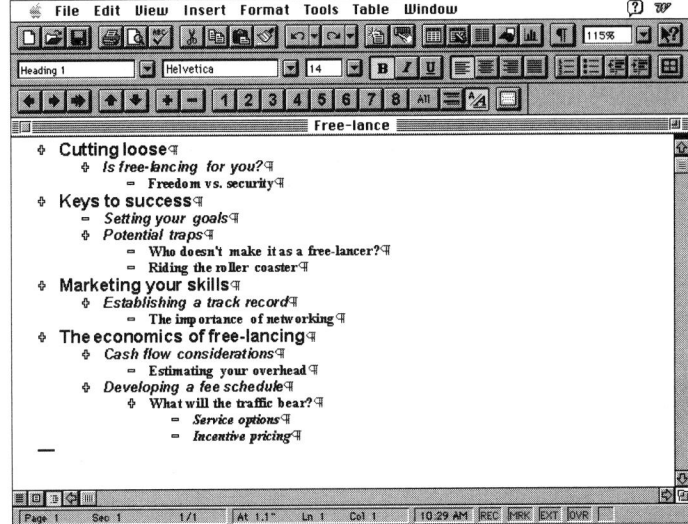

To create a second-level heading on the second line of the sample outline, you can click on the Demote button on the Outlining toolbar or press Option-Shift-Right arrow, or you can apply the Heading 2 style by choosing the Format Style command or using the Style drop-down list on the formatting toolbar. Any of these choices will assign both the Heading 2 style and the Heading 2 level to the paragraph.

You can type the text for the paragraph before or after assigning the heading level. Type the phrase *Is free-lancing for you?* As you type the text, notice that in demoting the second paragraph to Heading 2 level, Word has automatically indented the paragraph ½ inch. And note that you can see the heading levels by specifying a non-zero setting in the Style Area Width box on the Tools Options View card and using the mouse to adjust the width of the style area as needed. (We covered styles and how to set the Style Area Width in Chapter 12.)

Press Return again to begin the third paragraph; set the heading to level 3 by clicking on the Demote button, pressing Option-Shift-Right arrow, or applying the Heading 3 style. Then type the text for this heading as well: *Freedom vs. security.*

In addition to the various levels of indention, notice in Figure 19-2 that Word has assigned different character formats to the heading levels. The formats for each heading are defined in the document or its template. If you prefer not to see these formats, you can click on the Show Formatting button or make sure Num Lock is off—by pressing Shift and the Clear key, if necessary—and press the slash key on the numeric keypad. (These are toggles, so you can easily switch back and forth between seeing the character formatting and not seeing it.) Seeing the text without the formatting, as in Figure 19-3, may make it easier to interpret the structure of your document.

Note also that if you have numbered your outline headings with Format Heading Numbering, the font formatting for the numbers will not change when you use the Show Formatting button to turn off the character formatting of the headings themselves.

**FIGURE 19-3**

You can click on the Show Formatting button or press the slash key on the numeric keypad to suppress character formatting in Outline view.

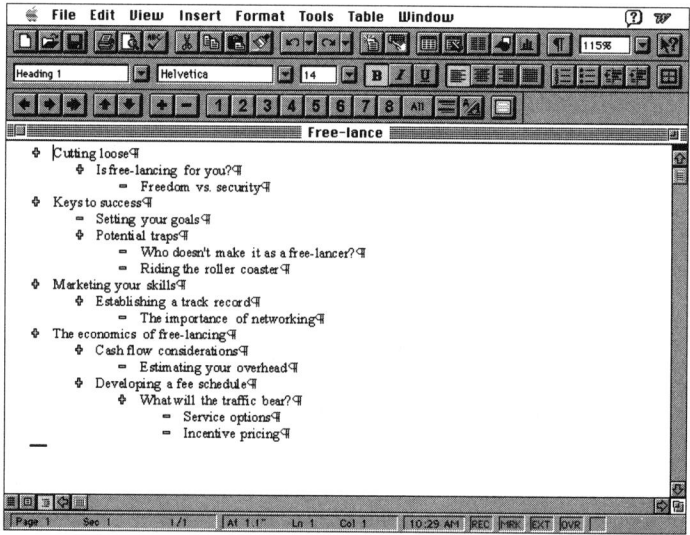

After you type the text for the third heading, you're ready for the next major topic: *Keys to success.* You'll want this paragraph to use the same heading level as the first heading in Figure 19-2. When you press Return at the end of the third paragraph, however, Word assumes that you want this new paragraph to be at Heading 3 level. You'll need to promote the paragraph to Heading 1 level by clicking on the Promote button twice, pressing Option-Shift-Left arrow twice, or applying the Heading 1 style.

To complete the outline, continue typing the sample text shown in Figures 19-2 and 19-3. Adjust the heading levels as appropriate by clicking on the Promote and Demote buttons, pressing Option-Shift-Left arrow and Option-Shift-Right arrow, or assigning the styles directly. Although our sample outline uses only four heading levels, you can create as many as nine. Note that if you're using Word's default styles, there won't be a Heading 4 style in your Formatting toolbar's drop-down Style list until you've created a Heading 4 level by using either of the first two techniques for assigning headings or by typing the style name in the Style text box.

We'll discuss this issue in more detail in a moment. But before we go any further, you should be sure you're familiar with the icons Word uses for headings and body text. You'll see these icons to the left of the paragraphs in Outline view. A small square icon indicates a paragraph of body text. A plus sign indicates a heading with subordinate text or subordinate headings. A minus sign indicates a heading without subordinate text or subordinate headings. (By *subordinate text* and *subordinate headings,* we mean all the headings and body text between the current heading and the next heading of an equal or higher level.)

## How to view an outline in Normal view

As you enter the outline text, keep in mind that Outline view is really just another type of document view. Any actions you take in Outline view will also affect what you see in other views. For example, if you return to Normal view after typing the sample outline shown in Figure 19-2, your screen will look like the one in Figure 19-4. As you can see, Word's default style formats still make it easy to identify the relationships among the headings.

**FIGURE 19-4**

If you switch back to Normal view, the document's text will look like this.

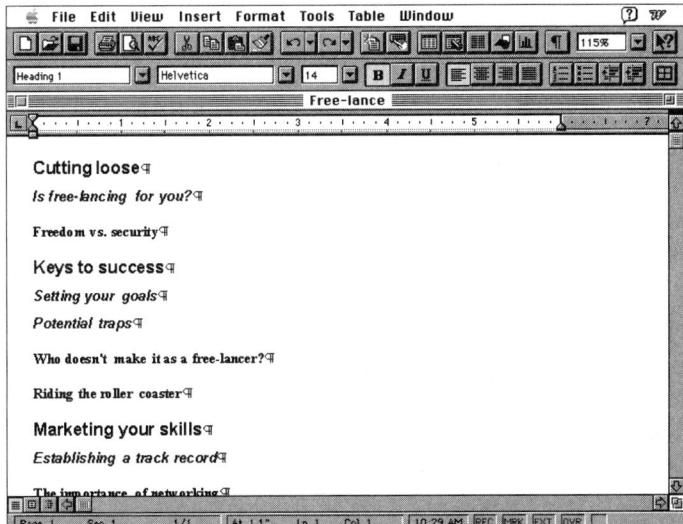

When you return to Normal view, you'll see that each heading level carries different character and paragraph formats. If you keep your eye on the Style box on the Formatting toolbar as you move the cursor through your text (or if you set the style area to a non-zero value, as we've already suggested), you'll see the heading style assigned to each paragraph.

When you create an outline, Word assigns styles behind the scenes, even if you don't explicitly assign styles yourself. As we discussed in Chapter 12, Word's default is to offer the styles Heading 1, Heading 2, and Heading 3 in every document's drop-down Style list. If you need more than that for any given document, you can create the added styles as we've indicated, by demoting a paragraph in Outline view to create a heading at one of the additional levels (through Heading 9). And, of course, you can modify the style definitions to change the format for different heading levels. We'll come back to this idea later in this chapter. First, however, we'll add some body text and explore techniques for editing a document in Outline view.

## How to add body text

You can add body text to a document while in Outline view, but you'll generally want to use Normal view instead. In Normal view, you can see more text on screen at once, without the indents on each line to indicate outline level. If you're following our example and you're ready to add some body text, switch to Normal view, if you're not there already, by choosing View Normal. Next, place the cursor immediately before the paragraph mark at the end of the first paragraph, and press Return to create a new paragraph. Word will automatically format the paragraph as Normal, applying the Normal style as defined in your document, as shown in Figure 19-5.

**FIGURE 19-5**

In Normal or Page Layout view, when you position the cursor after the last character in a heading paragraph and press Return, Word will automatically assign the Normal style to the next paragraph.

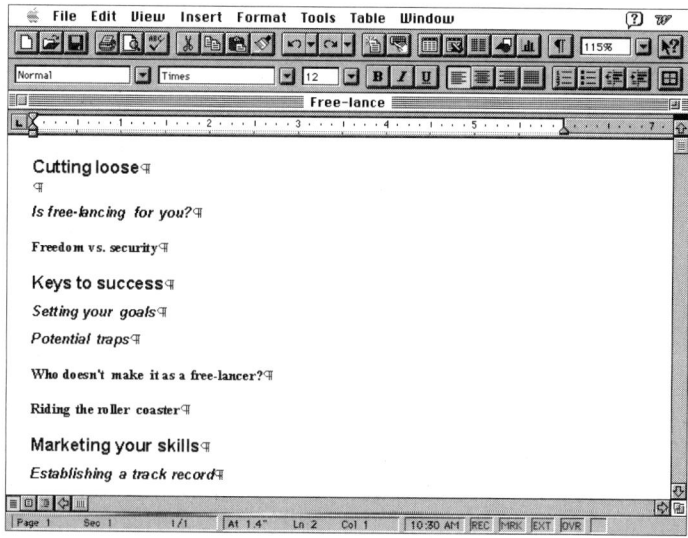

After typing some body text, toggle back to Outline view and notice what happens to the outline. As Figure 19-6 shows, Word redisplays the indentions to show the relationships between headings. Also notice that each body-text paragraph is indented ¼ inch more than the heading it falls under, providing another visual clue to the document's organization.

**FIGURE 19-6**

When you return to Outline view, you'll see that each body-text paragraph is indented ¼ inch to the right of the heading it falls under.

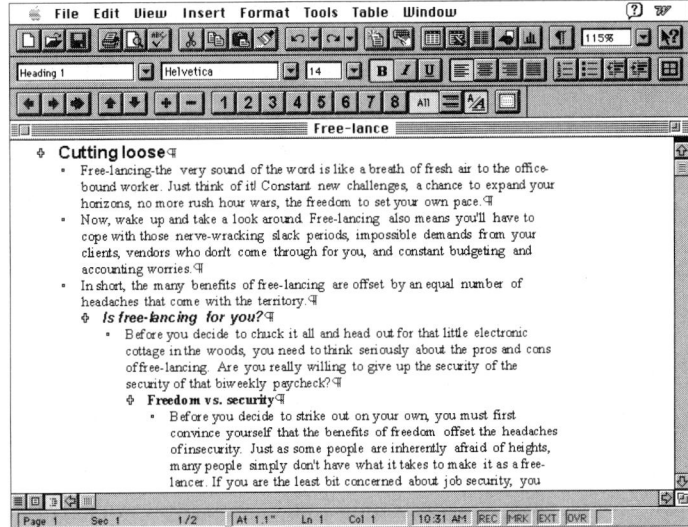

## How to simplify Outline view

To help reduce clutter in Outline view and see the structure of your document better, you can toggle between seeing all of the body text and seeing just the first line of each paragraph by clicking on the Show First Line Only button on the Outlining toolbar—the third button from the right—or by pressing the equivalent shortcut keys. By default, the shortcut key is Control-Shift-L. Press Control-Shift-L or click on the button once and, as shown in Figure 19-7 on the next page, you'll see just enough text for each paragraph to help remind you of the topic. When you condense the body text this way, Word will place ellipses at the end of each line to indicate that there's more in the paragraph. If you want to view the full text again, press Control-Shift-L or click on the Show First Line Only button a second time.

## If you don't like writing from outlines

So far we've assumed that you'll start by creating an outline before filling in the text. But even if you don't, you can get to this same point by a different route. If you prefer writing without an outline (or keeping the outline in your head), simply write the text as you usually would, but be sure to assign the appropriate heading and body styles to each paragraph, as we described in Chapter 12. Even if you never switch to Outline view, you'll want to assign the heading styles to the heading levels just for their formatting capabilities. As we'll discuss shortly, however, you can make good use of Outline view for other purposes.

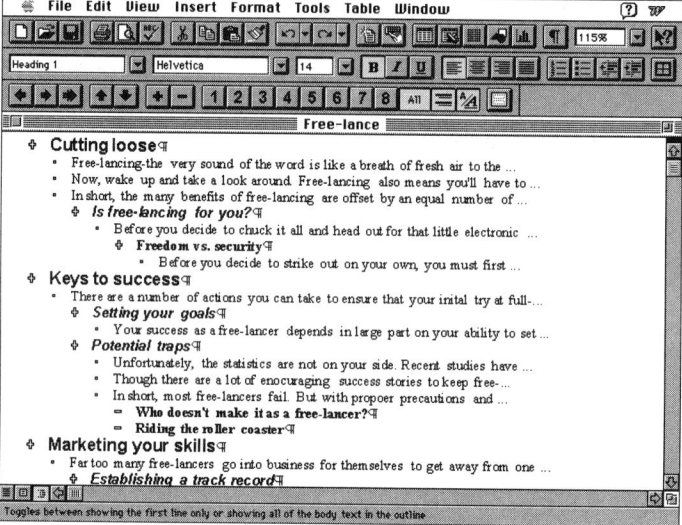

**FIGURE 19-7**

To simplify your view of the document, press Control-Shift-L to show only the first line of each paragraph of body text.

## Selection Techniques

After you've entered some or all of the headings and body text for your first draft, you'll probably need to make some changes in your text and reorganize it a bit. At this point, it doesn't matter whether you started with an outline or not, as long as you've used the heading styles for your headings.

Word offers several shortcuts for editing a document in Outline view. As in Normal view, you must select the text before you can edit it. More important, Word provides selection techniques that work in Outline view only.

When you're working within a single paragraph of an outline, you can use Word's standard selection techniques (described in Chapter 3) to select the text to work with. For example, to select an entire word, you can double-click on that word, or place the cursor anywhere in the word and press F8 twice. To select an entire sentence, press the ⌘ key and click on that sentence, or place the cursor anywhere in the sentence and press F8 three times.

In Normal view, you can select an entire paragraph by double-clicking in the selection bar next to that paragraph or by placing the cursor in the paragraph and pressing F8 four times. In Outline view, F8 works the same way; however, selection with the mouse works a little differently. You need to click only once in the selection bar to select an entire paragraph, whether it is a heading or body text. You can also select an entire heading by placing the cursor anywhere in the heading and then holding down the Shift key while clicking on the heading's icon. (The pointer will change to the four-headed arrow shape when it is on the icon.)

If you double-click in the selection bar next to a heading or click on a heading's icon without pressing the Shift key, you will highlight not only the heading next to the pointer, but also all the subordinate text and headings below that heading.

For example, if you click once in the selection bar next to the Heading 1 entry *Cutting loose* at the top of the outline in Figure 19-7, you will highlight that entire paragraph. If you double-click in the selection bar next to this heading, however, or if you click on the heading icon next to this heading once, your screen will look like the one shown in Figure 19-8. As you can see, Word highlights the paragraph containing the text *Cutting loose* as well as the subordinate text up to the next Heading 1 paragraph.

**FIGURE 19-8**

To highlight a heading and all its subordinate text and headings, double-click in the selection bar next to the heading or click on the heading icon once.

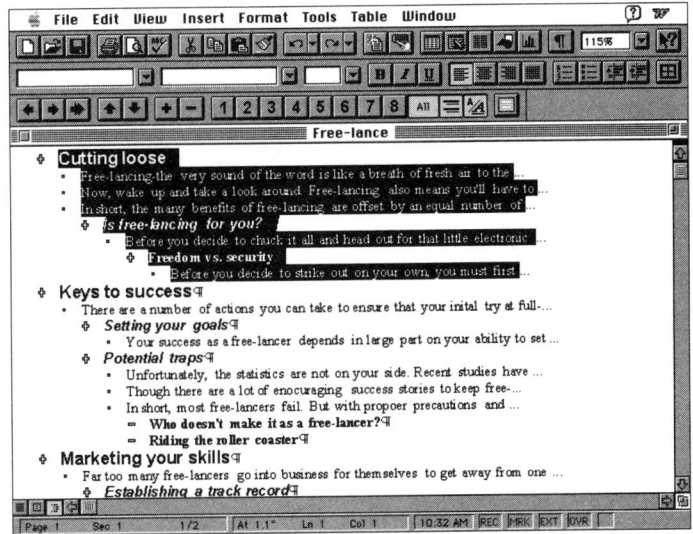

# Collapsing and Expanding an Outline

Even if you've set Word to show only the first line of each paragraph of body text, the outline can get pretty lengthy after you've created several levels of headings and inserted body text under each. If you lose the sense of the document's organization, you can eliminate some of the clutter by collapsing the outline to hide the body text and one or more levels of headings.

For example, suppose you want to see only the Heading 1 entries in your outline. To collapse the outline, click on the Show Heading 1 button (labeled 1) on the Outlining toolbar, or press Control-Shift-1. As shown in Figure 19-9, Word will hide all body text and subheadings below the level 1 headings. In addition, Word will place a faint underline under any headings that have subordinate text or headings hidden from view.

**FIGURE 19-9**

When you click on the Show Heading 1 button or press Control-Shift-1, Word will collapse your outline to show only Heading 1 entries.

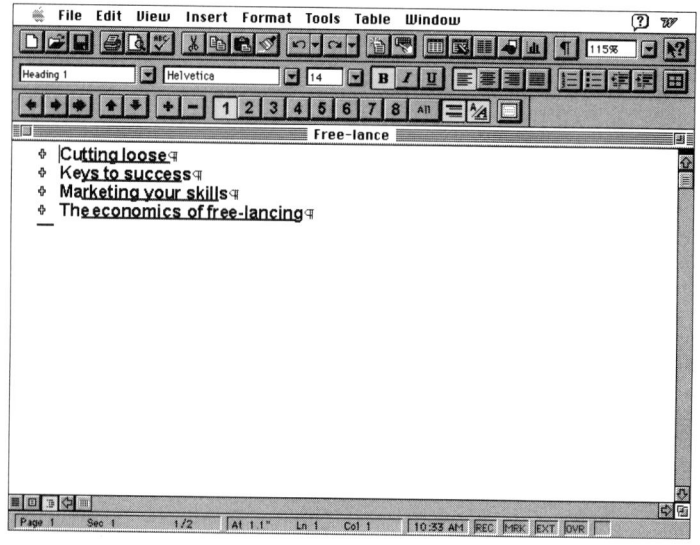

To expand the outline again, click on another Show button to indicate the highest-numbered level you want to see, or press the equivalent Control-Shift key combination. For example, if you click on the Show Heading 3 button or press Control-Shift-3, Word will expand the outline to display all Heading 1, Heading 2, and Heading 3 entries, with body text still hidden from view.

The Show buttons affect the display of the entire outline; however, the Expand and Collapse buttons—indicated with a plus for the Expand button and a minus for the Collapse button—affect only the currently selected portions of an outline. You can also use the plus and minus keys on your numeric keypad as Expand and Collapse keys by themselves, or use the plus and hyphen keys in the top row of your keyboard in combination with Control-Shift. Note that you have to turn Num Lock off to use the shortcut keys on the numeric keypad. For the rest of this discussion we'll simply assume that Num Lock is off rather than mentioning it each time.

To bring all of the headings and the body text back into view, click the All button, press Control-Shift-A, or press the asterisk key (*) on the numeric keypad. (Note that there is no Show button for level 9 headings. You must use the keyboard shortcut, Control-Shift-9, to show heading level 9.)

For example, suppose you want to collapse only the headings and body text below the second Heading 1 entry (*Keys to success*) in the document shown in Figure 19-8. Position the cursor in the heading and then click on the Collapse button, press the minus-sign key on your numeric keypad, or press Control-Shift-hyphen. As shown in Figure 19-10, Word will collapse all of the body text that originally appeared under that heading. If you use the collapse feature again, Word will collapse all Heading 3 entries below that heading; if you use it a third time, Word will collapse all Heading 2 entries. To reverse this process, place the cursor in the heading and then click on the Expand button, press the plus key on the numeric keypad, or press Control-Shift-Plus.

**FIGURE 19-10**

You can use the Collapse button, the minus key on your numeric keypad, or Control-Shift-hyphen to collapse selected portions of the outline.

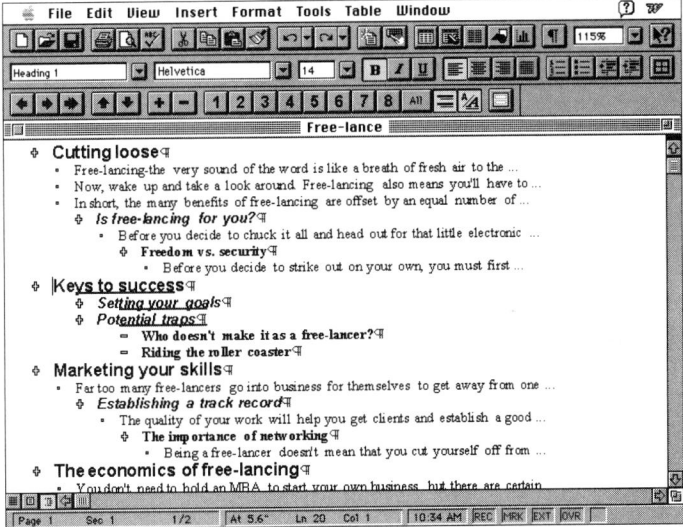

As you can see in Figure 19-10, when you use these expand and collapse techniques, Word will act on only the text that falls between the current heading and the next heading of an equal or higher level. In our example, Word collapsed only the text between the second and third Heading 1 entries. You could also move the cursor to a Heading 2 entry to collapse all text between that heading and the next heading of the same or a higher level.

To collapse all subordinate text and headings below a particular heading in one step, first select the entire heading paragraph and then give the collapse command with the Collapse button or the equivalent shortcut keys. (Do not select the text by clicking on the plus sign, or Word will collapse only one level at a time.)

Selecting the heading with the keyboard can be a little tricky because the part you really need to select is the paragraph mark. If paragraph marks are showing, simply select the paragraph mark and Word will automatically highlight the rest of the heading. If the paragraph marks are not showing, however, you can start with the cursor near the end of the heading and extend the selection toward the end of the paragraph. You will eventually select the invisible paragraph mark, and Word will automatically select the rest of the heading paragraph. You can then use the collapse or expand feature. When collapsing text, you can extend the selection into the next paragraph without changing the way the collapse feature will work. When expanding text, however, be sure to select only those headings you want to expand.

## A navigation tip

When you are working with a long document that contains headings and you want to move to a particular section, you can use Outline view to quickly move to the section you want to go to. Switch to Outline view, and collapse the outline to the level appropriate for seeing the heading you want to look for. Next, move the cursor to that heading, and switch back to Normal view. At this point, Word will show you the part of the document you want to see.

# Editing in Outline View

You can use any of Word's usual editing techniques to edit text while in Outline view. However, be aware that if you use the Edit Find or Edit Replace command, Word will not search through collapsed text—whether body text or headings.

If you want to search all text in your document, you'll usually find it easier to choose the Edit Search or Edit Replace command in Normal or Page Layout view. However, if you want to search only through text that appears in headings, you may be able to streamline the search or search-and-replace procedure by working in Outline view, set to see the appropriate level of headings.

In addition to the standard editing techniques, Word offers a number of special editing features for use in Outline view only. These include commands for changing heading levels and for adding, deleting, and moving headings.

## How to change a heading level

You can change the level of a heading at any time, using the commands we discussed in the context of creating the outline. Place the cursor or selection in the paragraph or paragraphs you want to change. Then apply the appropriate style to the paragraph, click on the Promote button or the Demote button, or press Option-Shift-Left arrow to promote the heading one level or Option-Shift-Right arrow to demote it.

When you use the promote or demote feature to change a heading level, Word will immediately assign the new heading level to the paragraph, change the indention of the paragraph to reflect its new level, and adjust the indention of any body text immediately below the heading. Unless you tell it to, however, Word will not change the levels of subordinate headings in the outline or body text under those headings.

If you want to promote or demote a heading and all of its subordinate text and headings, you must first select the subordinate text and headings along with the heading. You can then click on the Promote or Demote button or use the appropriate keyboard commands to change all the heading levels at the same time.

After you've selected a heading and all of its subordinate text and headings, you can press Option-Shift-Left arrow or Option-Shift-Right arrow to promote or demote the entire block at once. (Don't apply styles, because a style would apply to all of the selected text.) Alternatively, you can drag the heading icon for the highest-level heading to the left or right. The mouse pointer will take the shape of a double-headed arrow as you drag, and Word will display a vertical line to indicate where the heading will move to when you release the mouse button. The line will move in ½-inch increments, snapping to each possible level.

For example, let's say that you click on the heading icon next to *Keys to success* in Figure 19-7 (or double-click in the selection bar), to select the heading and its subordinate text, and then click on the Demote button. Your outline will look like the one shown in Figure 19-11 on the next page. It will also look like Figure 19-11 if you drag the heading icon one level to the right. If you're using the keyboard, place the cursor before the word *Keys* in the Heading 1 entry and use the Shift-arrow key combinations to select all subordinate headings and body text down to the next Heading 1 entry. Then, to demote the highlighted text, press Option-Shift-Right arrow.

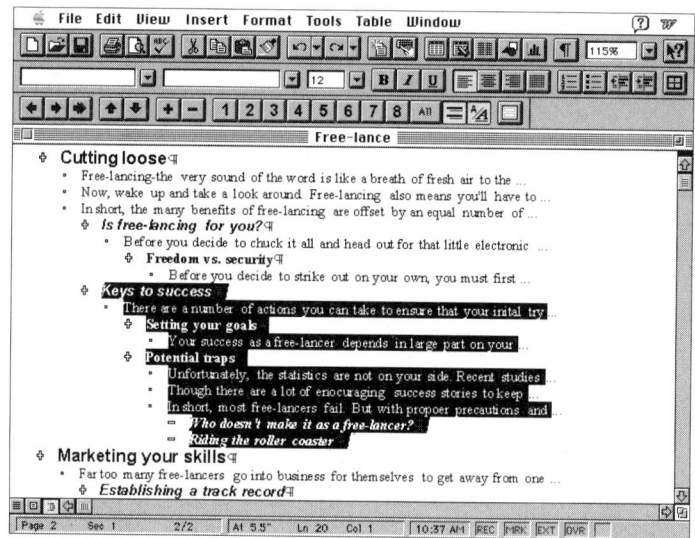

To demote a heading and its subordinate text and headings, first select everything you want to demote, and then use the demote feature.

Whichever route you choose, Figure 19-11 shows how Word will demote all subordinate headings and body text between the *Keys to success* heading and the next Heading 1 entry. The *Keys to success* heading and its subordinate text now fall under the first Heading 1 entry, *Cutting loose*.

## How to convert body text to a heading

You can convert body text to a heading with the same commands you use for changing heading levels. If you place the cursor in a body-text paragraph while in Outline view and then click on the Promote button, press Option-Shift-Left arrow, or drag the body-text icon to the left, Word will convert that body text to the same level as the closest previous heading. For example, if you move the cursor to the body-text paragraph that begins *Free-lancing—the very sound* in the second line of our sample outline and then click on the Promote button, Word will promote the entire paragraph to a level 1 heading. If you click on the Demote button instead, Word will convert the body text to a heading one level below the closest previous heading. As Figure 19-12 shows, when you convert the paragraph to a heading, Word will show you the entire contents of that heading rather than only the first line, even if you've toggled the program to show first lines only.

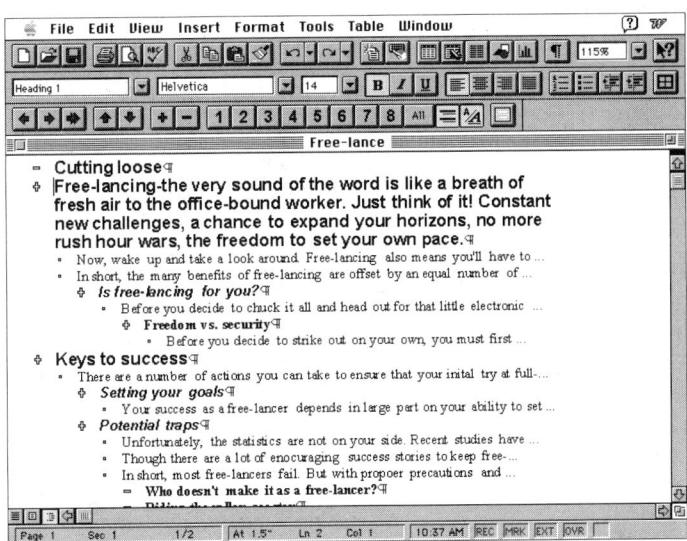

**FIGURE 19-12**

When you convert body text to a heading, Word will show the full paragraph.

## How to convert a heading to body text

To convert a heading to body text, place the cursor in the heading and then click on the Demote To Body Text button or press ⌘-Shift-N.

When you convert a heading to body text, Word will change the indention of that paragraph and any subordinate body text immediately below it so that it is ¼ inch to the right of the heading immediately preceding it. In short, the paragraph and any body text between it and the next heading become part of the subordinate body text for the preceding heading.

For example, if you start with our sample document as it appears in Figure 19-10, move the cursor to the Heading 2 entry *Is free-lancing for you?*, and click on the Demote To Body Text button, your screen will look like the one shown in Figure 19-13 on the next page. Notice that the body text formerly attached to the Heading 2 level now shows the same indention as the rest of the body text for the Heading 1 entry *Cutting loose*. As you can see, however, Word did not change the Heading 3 entry *Freedom vs. security* below the converted Heading 2 entry.

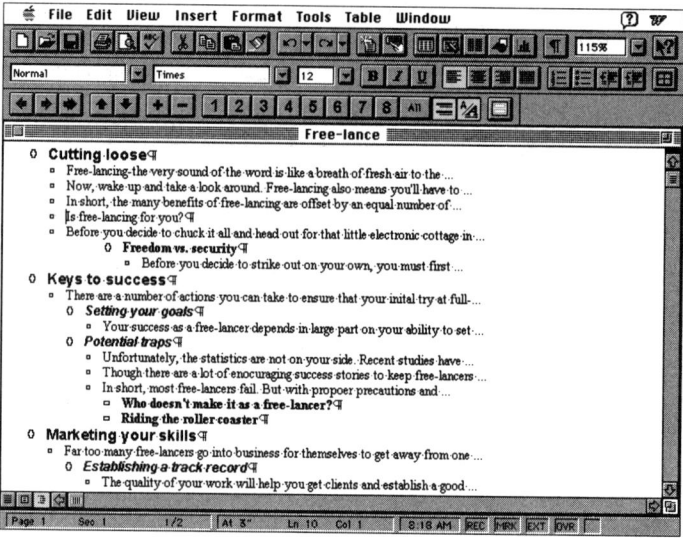

**FIGURE 19-13**

You can use the Demote To Body Text button or ⌘-Shift-N to convert a heading to body text.

## How to insert a new heading

Inserting a new heading into an outline is no different from inserting any other kind of text. Place the cursor where you want the heading, press Return and enter the text, and then use any of the techniques we've discussed to set the appropriate heading level.

## How to delete a heading

Just as you can insert a heading like any other text, so too can you delete a heading like any other text. Be careful, though. Before you delete a heading, you should be sure to expand the outline or switch to Normal or Page Layout view. Otherwise, you may inadvertently delete all subordinate text for the heading as well.

It's important to realize that when you select a heading in a collapsed outline, you also select the subordinate text for that heading. For example, if you select the Heading 1 entry *Cutting loose* as shown in Figure 19-9 and then expand the outline, you'll see that Word has selected all of the subordinate text between the first level 1 heading and the second one. In short, any changes you make to a heading while the outline is collapsed will affect all subordinate text and headings below that heading.

# How to move text and headings

There are four ways to move blocks of text while in Outline view. The first is the standard cut-and-paste procedure. Select the heading and any subordinate text you want to move, choose Edit Cut, move the cursor to the spot where you want to place the text, and choose Edit Paste. Similarly, you can use Word's drag-and-drop technique (assuming the option is active) to drag any text selection from one place to another in the document. Word also provides several methods of moving text that are meant primarily for Outline view: the Move Up and Move Down buttons, the equivalent keyboard commands Option-Shift-Up arrow and Option-Shift-Down arrow, and a click-and-drag technique in which you click on a heading or body-text icon and drag the text.

When you use the Edit Cut command to delete or move text while in Outline view, your changes may affect more text than you can currently see on your screen. Keep in mind that selecting a heading that includes collapsed subordinate headings and body text automatically selects the collapsed text as well.

If you do not want Word to move the subordinate text along with the selected heading, you'll need to expand the outline before you select the heading and choose the Edit Cut command. However, if you want Word to include the subordinate text in your selection, you may find it easier to collapse the outline before you begin the cut-and-paste procedure. (The same comments apply to copying text.) Similarly, when you select your paste area, you may want to expand any collapsed text in that area to ensure that you're inserting the text exactly where you mean to.

Note that these comments about moving selected text, including collapsed subordinate text and headings, apply to all techniques for moving text or headings in Outline view. In fact, this is one of the strengths of Outline view—it gives you the ability to reorganize a document, including all the text in each section, simply by collapsing the document and moving the headings. You can then rewrite as necessary to maintain logical transitions between the sections.

You can use the Move Up and Move Down buttons to move selected text without cutting it first. To use the buttons, place the cursor or selection in the paragraph you want to move, or extend the selection into the paragraphs you want to move. Then click on the Move Up button to move the text up one paragraph, or the Move Down button to move the text down one paragraph. If you've selected only part of a paragraph, Word will extend the selection to include the entire paragraph, and any collapsed subordinate text and headings, before it moves the text. The shortcut keys for this function are Option-Shift-Up arrow (move up) and Option-Shift-Down arrow (move down).

When you move text up or down by one paragraph, you'll move the text by paragraphs that currently show on screen, skipping any collapsed text. If you need to move the text a long distance, you can save time by collapsing some or all of the outline text before you begin.

Finally, one of the most convenient ways to move text is by clicking and dragging. Just as you can drag text to the left and right to promote and demote paragraphs, you can point to a heading icon or a body-text icon, hold down the mouse button, and drag the icon—and the text it represents, including any subordinate text—up or down to reposition it in your document. If you click on a heading icon, you'll automatically select all subordinate body text and headings and move those too, even if that section of the outline isn't collapsed. If you click on a body-text icon, you'll select only the one paragraph. When you drag an icon, Word displays a line across the Word window to indicate where the text will be inserted.

You can use Option-Shift-Up arrow and Option-Shift-Down arrow to move text in Normal or Page Layout view also. Place the cursor in the paragraph you want to move, or extend the selection to include any other paragraphs you want to move, and then press Option-Shift-Up arrow or Option-Shift-Down arrow, as appropriate. Word will select the entire paragraph or paragraphs and move them up or down by one paragraph for each keystroke.

This can be a handy trick for moving text around. But if you use it in Normal or Page Layout view, be careful. The selection that Word automatically makes in the text to decide how much text to move up or down depends on the setting for the Show buttons in Outline view. If the setting in Outline view is Show All, then Word will highlight and move just the paragraph or paragraphs that the cursor or selection is in. If Show is set to any other level, however, Word may highlight more text than you intend. If it's set to Show Heading 1, for example, and you press Option-Shift-Up arrow in Normal view, Word will highlight all text between the cursor and the next paragraph formatted as Heading level 1. Word will then proceed to move the entire selection.

Note, too, that several other outline shortcut keys will work in Normal mode as well. Option-Shift-Right arrow and Option-Shift-Left arrow will promote and demote selected paragraphs, and ⌘-Shift-N will convert the paragraph the cursor or selection is in to Normal style. This last shortcut, in particular, can be handy when you're reformatting your documents.

# Outline View and Styles

As we've mentioned, Word's Outline view works in conjunction with styles. When you edit a document in Outline view, Word assumes you will want to use each topic in the outline as a heading in your document, and it assigns each level of heading an automatic style named for that level—Heading 1, Heading 2, and so on.

In Chapter 12, we pointed out that Word has nine automatic heading styles corresponding to nine heading levels. By default, Word supplies three of these in the Formatting toolbar's Style drop-down list. It automatically adds the others as needed when you create the first heading in any document at level 4, level 5, or beyond.

In addition to giving you a head start by providing automatic styles, Word provides some clear differences in the formatting for these styles. Figure 19-14 shows the default definitions for each.

| Style Name | Default Definition |
| --- | --- |
| Heading 1 | Normal + Font: Helvetica, 14 Point, Bold, Kern at 14 pt, Space Before 12 pt After 3 pt, Keep With Next |
| Heading 2 | Normal + Font: Helvetica, Bold, Italic, Space Before 12 pt After 3 pt, Keep With Next |
| Heading 3 | Normal + Font: Bold, Space Before 12 pt After 3 pt, Keep With Next |
| Heading 4 | Normal + Font: Bold, Italic, Space Before 12 pt After 3 pt, Keep With Next |
| Heading 5 | Normal + Font: Helvetica, 11 Point, Space Before 12 pt After 3 pt |
| Heading 6 | Normal + Font: Helvetica, 11 Point, Italic, Space Before 12 pt After 3 pt |
| Heading 7 | Normal + Font: Helvetica, 10 Point, Space Before 12 pt After 3 pt |
| Heading 8 | Normal + Font: Helvetica, 10 Point, Italic, Space Before 12 pt After 3 pt |
| Heading 9 | Normal + Font: Helvetica, 9 Point, Italic, Space Before 12 pt After 3 pt |

**FIGURE 19-14**

Heading styles and their default definitions.

You can easily change these style definitions. First, because they are all based on the Normal style, start by modifying the Normal style to suit the document, using the techniques we described in Chapter 12. You can then make additional changes to the definitions for each heading style.

To modify each style, simply follow the procedures we described in Chapter 12. Choose Format Style to open the Style dialog box, choose the name of the style you want to modify, and then choose Modify to open the Modify Style dialog box. Next specify the character and paragraph formats for that heading level. When you're satisfied with your changes, choose OK to return to the Style dialog box, and repeat the process for the next style you want to change. When you're done, choose Close to close the dialog box, and Word will apply the specified formats to the headings in your document.

If you don't want the text from a particular heading level to show up in your finished document, simply format the style for that heading level as Hidden. Then choose Tools Options and choose the Print card to make sure that the check box for printing hidden text is cleared.

If you change the definitions for the heading styles, you may want to change the Based On styles as well. You can base each heading style on the next-highest heading style instead of Normal. You might want to leave Heading 1 based on Normal but base Heading 2 on Heading 1, base Heading 3 on Heading 2, and so on. That way, if you make format changes to the Heading 1 style—new indention settings, for example—those changes will automatically affect all heading levels for the document.

# Printing an Outline

To print an outline, simply switch to Outline view, if you're not there already, and choose File Print. You can control which levels will print by expanding or collapsing the outline. In general, what you see on the screen is what will be printed, with one exception: Even if you've set Word to show only the first lines of body-text paragraphs, Word will print all paragraphs in their entirety.

In the printed outline, Word will ignore paragraph formatting for the text, using the indentions you see on the screen in Outline view instead; however, it will apply the character formatting, as well as any headers, footers, section breaks, or manual page breaks you've added to the document. Figure 19-15 shows the printed version of the outline for our sample document, collapsed to show heading levels 1, 2, and 3.

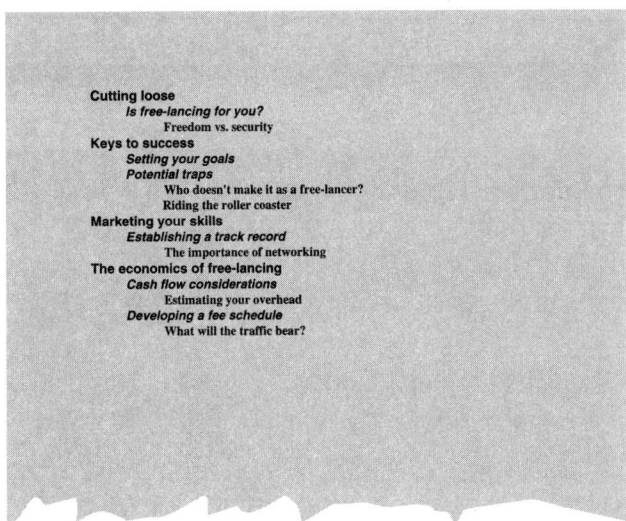

**FIGURE 19-15**

You can use the File Print command to print a copy of your outline.

# Outline Numbering

After you have created an outline, you can use Word's automatic numbering feature to number some or all of the outline's headings and body text. Choose Format Heading Numbering, and then choose the numbering system you want to use. We covered automatic numbering in detail in Chapter 13, "Bullets, Numbering, & Sections," page 439.

# Master Documents

There is one button on the Outlining toolbar that we have not discussed: the far right button, Master Document View, which switches between Outline and Master Document views. Master Document view is similar to Outline view in that both use the Outlining toolbar. And knowing how to work in Outline view is important for working with a master document. Because Master Document view is intended for working with long documents, however, it's more appropriate to discuss it along with other features for working with long documents. We'll cover master documents in "How to use Master Document view" starting on page 560.

# TOPIC FINDER

**638**

# 20

# Fields

n this chapter, we'll look at one of Word's most notable strengths: fields. We've mentioned fields elsewhere, including Chapters 5, 16, and 18. In this chapter, we'll look at how to display and recalculate a field's result, how to edit a field, and how to change the format of a field result. We'll also look at some specific fields in depth—including Word's DATE and TIME fields—and we'll look at several categories of fields, including document information, user information, and document automation fields.

## What Is a Field?

A field is a special code that you can enter in a document. You can use fields for something as straightforward as adding a date to a header or as complex as building an index. Fields give Word tremendous flexibility and broaden the range of what you can do with a word processor. Word offers approximately 70 fields that can be divided into three categories: result fields, marker fields, and action fields.

## Result fields

Most of the fields you'll use frequently are result fields. Result fields retrieve a particular piece of information and place it in the document. When you enter the DATE field, for example, it retrieves the current date from your computer's system clock and enters that date at the field position. Similarly, the AUTHOR field retrieves the name of the document's author and places that information at the field position.

## Marker fields

A marker field does not return a result. Rather, it supplies information to Word. For example, you can use the XE (Index Entry) field to mark entries for an index. The Index Entry field does not return a result; it merely provides the information that Word uses to compile the index.

## Action fields

Unlike result and marker fields, action fields tell Word to perform an action. For example, the FILLIN field tells Word to prompt the user for information and to store that information in the document. Some action fields tell Word to perform the action only when you update the fields; others tell Word to perform the action automatically.

# The Format for Fields

All fields share a similar format. All have names, and all are enclosed in field characters. In addition, many fields have one or more arguments, or instructions. The arguments may tell the field what to act on, or they may control the way the field displays its result. For example, in the field {DATE \@ "MMM-yy"}, the field name is DATE, the field characters are { and }, and the arguments are \@ and MMM-yy. This field tells Word to retrieve the current date from your computer's system clock and display it in the MMM-yy format, as in Jan-95.

## Field types

A *field type* is a short, descriptive word or phrase that helps identify what the field does. For example, the DATE field returns the current date, the TIME field returns the current time, and the FILLIN field prompts the user to fill in a blank in the document. In most cases, the field type and the field name are the same; in some, however, the field name is an abbreviation for the field type. For example, the field name for the Index Entry field is XE. That is, Index Entry is the field type; however, you must use the field name, XE, when inserting the field into a document.

# Field characters

Field names are always enclosed in the field characters { and }. Word will treat the enclosed text as a field. You cannot generate these characters by typing curly brackets from your keyboard. You enter them by either pressing ⌘-F9 or choosing the Insert Field command. We'll show you how shortly.

# Arguments

Most of Word's fields allow *arguments*; some require them. An argument tells Word either what to operate on or how to show the field's result.

The argument in the field {INCLUDETEXT "Budget"} is the document name Budget. The INCLUDETEXT field tells Word to insert the contents of another document into the current document. The Budget argument tells Word which document file to insert.

Notice that we've enclosed this argument in quotation marks. Word requires quotation marks only around multiple-word arguments, to indicate that all the words are part of a single argument. However, it generally does no harm to add the quotation marks, and we recommend getting in the habit of adding them in every case to make sure they're there when needed.

When a field requires more than one argument, you must either enclose each argument in quotation marks or separate the arguments by a space. As we discussed in Chapter 15, you can mark part of a document file with a bookmark and then use the INCLUDETEXT field to include just the bookmark. The field would have two arguments and would take the form {INCLUDETEXT Budget FirstQuarter} or {INCLUDETEXT "Budget""FirstQuarter"}. You could also add a space between the two arguments in quotation marks.

If you need to use a literal quotation mark within an argument, precede it with a backslash (\). To include a backslash as part of an argument you must type two backslashes (\\).

Field arguments can include literal text, formulas, bookmarks, identifiers, switches, or other fields. Here's a brief look at each type of argument.

## Literal text

Some field arguments consist of literal text, as with the INCLUDETEXT field. To place the contents of the document Budget in the current document, you type the actual name of the document file so that the field reads {INCLUDETEXT "Budget"}.

## Formulas

Other field arguments consist of mathematical formulas, or expressions. The = (Formula) field, for example, takes a mathematical formula and calculates the result, so that the field {= 2+2} would return the result 4. Note that the = (Formula) field does not accept quotation marks around its argument.

## Bookmarks

As we discussed in Chapter 10, a bookmark is a name you've assigned to selected text in a document. You can use a bookmark as an argument in several different kinds of fields. The field {INCLUDETEXT "Budget" "FirstQuarter"}, which we've already discussed in our earlier example of using multiple arguments, will return the text defined by the bookmark FirstQuarter in the Budget document. The field {PAGEREF "FirstQuarter"} will return the page number where you'll find the FirstQuarter bookmark in the current document. You can find out more about the PAGEREF field by looking in the Word Help system.

## Identifiers

Some fields require an *identifier* argument. This is simply a name that identifies a series of terms in a group. For example, you can use the SEQ (Sequence) field to label a specific series of items—such as figures, tables, or illustrations—for automatic numbering. Because you'll sometimes need to label two separately numbered series, such as tables and figures, in a document, you can optionally supply an identifier in the field to tell Word which sequence the field is part of.

For example, you could number each figure as Figure {SEQ "figure"} and each table as Table {SEQ "table"}. Word will maintain separate numeric sequences for the two sets of items. We recommend using identifiers that describe the items you are numbering, since they will be easier to remember.

## Switches

Fields can also use *switches* as arguments. A switch consists of a backslash (\) followed by a single character. Some switches are followed by an additional argument. A switch changes the way a field works or the way it formats its result. Without a switch, the field {TIME} will return the current time in h:m AM/PM format. If you want a field that uses 24-hour format with a leading zero, add the switch \@ HH:mm so that the field becomes {TIME \@ "HH:mm"}. We'll discuss this and other switches for the TIME field later in this chapter.

# Inserting Fields

As we've already mentioned, you cannot type the curly brackets that serve as the beginning and end markers for a field definition. However, Word provides more than one way to enter these brackets: by themselves, in combination with field names, or as part of a complete field definition.

## How to insert fields with the Insert Field command

It may take you a while to learn each of the fields that you'll use regularly, and you may never learn the format for fields that you use only occasionally. The Insert Field command is usually the easiest way to insert those fields you're not familiar with.

Place the cursor where you want to insert a field, and then choose Insert Field to open the Field dialog box shown in Figure 20-1. You can define the field completely from within this dialog box.

**FIGURE 20-1**

The Field dialog box is usually the simplest way to enter fields when you don't know the field names and arguments.

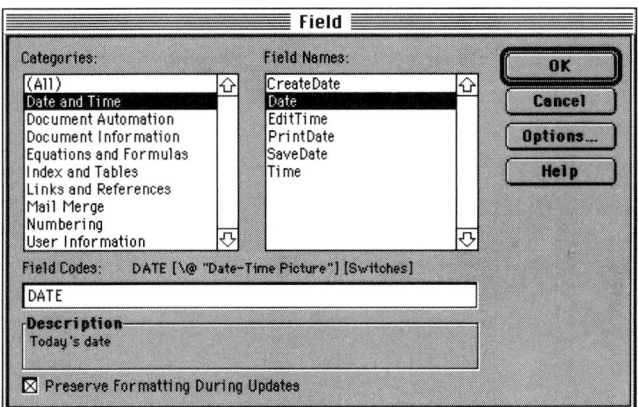

Word gives you two ways to find and choose a field. You can accept the default (All) choice in the Categories list box, and then look for the field you want in the list of all fields that Word will put in the Field Names list box. Alternatively, you can choose any specific category in the Categories list box to tell Word to list only those fields from the chosen category.

As a rule of thumb, if you know the exact name of the field you want, you can usually find it most quickly by choosing (All) in the Categories list box, then moving to the Field Names list box and pressing the key corresponding to the first character of the field name as many times as necessary to highlight the name. If you don't know the exact field name, you can usually find it most quickly by choosing the appropriate category and then browsing through the shorter list in the Field Names list box. If necessary, you can move through the Field Names list box with the Up and Down arrow keys. As you highlight each name, Word will show you a description of that field in the Description box near the bottom of the dialog box.

To insert a field, highlight the name in the Field Names list box. If you scroll through the list, you'll notice that Word will automatically place the highlighted field name in the Field Codes text box below the Categories list box, and will place a short description of the field in the Description box just below that. Word will also add the syntax for the field to the right of the title for the Field Codes text box. You can use the syntax reminder as a guide for your own entry.

In Figure 20-1, we've highlighted the Date And Time category and the field name Date. Word automatically entered DATE in the Field Codes text box, added the syntax, DATE [\@ "Date-Time Picture"][Switches], above the text box, and added the comment *Today's date* in the Description box.

After you highlight the field name, you can simply choose OK, and Word will insert the field name in your document, enclosed in field characters. If you want to add any arguments, you can then type them in. Alternatively, you can type the arguments directly in the Field Codes text box, using the syntax above the text box as your model. When you're finished, choose OK. Word will insert the field name, argument, and field characters into your document.

By default, Word will add the format switch with the MergeFormat argument to fields you define with the Field dialog box so that, once formatted, the field will keep its formatting if you update it later. If you don't want this switch, clear the Preserve Formatting During Updates check box at the bottom of the Field dialog box. Alternatively, you can delete the switch from the field after Word inserts it into your document. For more about the format switch, see "Formatting Field Results" on page 654.

If you need more details for filling in the arguments—such as detailed information about the Date-Time Picture or Switches argument in Figure 20-1— choose the Options button. Word will open the Field Options dialog box, which contains cards similar to the ones shown in Figure 20-2.

**FIGURE 20-2**

The Field Options dialog box will help you fill in specific arguments for fields.

The specifics of the Field Options dialog box will vary, depending on the field you've specified in the Field dialog box. In some cases, the Options button will be grayed and the dialog box unavailable. But if the field allows arguments, you'll generally be able to choose the Options button and use the Field Options dialog box.

In Figure 20-2, the list box on the left side of the General Switches card, labeled Date-Time, contains format choices for the Date-Time Picture switch. We'll discuss these later in this chapter. For the moment, simply note that you can highlight the format you want and then choose the Add To Field button; Word will add the argument to the Field Codes text box. (Notice that the text box still appears at the bottom of the Field Options dialog box.) Once you've added an argument, the Undo Add button will become active, and you can remove the argument by choosing the button.

As you can see in Figure 20-2, the Field Options dialog box for the DATE field includes two cards, labeled General Switches and Field Specific Switches. These represent the two bracketed sets of arguments indicated in the syntax definition, [\@ "Date-Time Picture"] and [Switches]. The number of tabbed cards, if any, and the labels on the tabs will vary with the field. With the AUTHOR field, for example, you'll find only one card in the dialog box.

As you can see in the Field Codes text box in Figures 20-1 and 20-2, Word enters field names in all uppercase letters, and we'll continue using all uppercase letters in this book to make the field names easy to identify. If you enter the names yourself by typing them in, however, you don't have to worry about case.

## How to insert fields with the Insert Field key (⌘-F9)

For fields you're already familiar with, it will usually be faster to insert the field name and arguments by typing them. Word provides a function-key command to make this easy. Move the cursor to the appropriate place in the document, press ⌘-F9, and Word will insert a paired set of field characters around the cursor. You can then type the appropriate field name and arguments. For example, suppose you want to insert the field {AUTHOR}. Simply press ⌘-F9 and type *AUTHOR*. Then press F9 to calculate the field result. Alternatively, you can type the text for the field first, select it, and then press ⌘-F9. Word will add the field characters around the selected text.

Word must be set to Insert mode when you insert a field by typing text within the field markers. If Word is set for Overtype mode, it will not expand the space between the field characters { and } to let you add text.

## How to insert fields with other menu commands

Be aware that some menu commands automatically insert fields for you. For example, if you select some text and then choose Insert Index And Tables, Mark Entry, and then Mark, Word will insert an Index Entry field for you. If you prefer, you can insert these fields with the Insert Field command or by typing them manually. But for fields that Word provides specialized menu commands for, it's usually easier to use the menu commands and let Word insert the fields automatically. One menu choice worth special note is the Insert Date And Time command, which we'll discuss later in this chapter. It's limited to inserting fields that will produce the date, the time, or both.

# Field Results vs. Field Codes

After you insert one or more fields in a document, you'll generally want to see the field results. At times, however, you'll want to see the fields themselves—to delete them, change them, or simply check that you've entered a particular item as a field rather than as regular text. You can toggle between seeing the field codes and seeing the field results.

## How to change the Tools Options View Field Codes setting

If you're not sure whether Word is currently set to show field codes or field results, you can find out by choosing Tools Options and then selecting the View card. If the Field Codes check box is checked, Word is set to show field codes. If the check box is cleared, Word is set to show field results. You can change to the other setting by simply checking or clearing the box.

You can also see your text in both views at once, as shown in Figure 20-3. Open the file in two windows, or split a single window into two panes. Then set one to show field codes and the other to show field results. Figure 20-3 shows a single document split into two panes, with the top pane showing the field results and the bottom pane showing the field codes.

**FIGURE 20-3**

The Field Codes check box on the Tools Options View card toggles between showing field results, as in the top pane, and showing field codes, as in the bottom pane.

## How to toggle between codes and results
## for selected fields or for the whole document

In addition to toggling the Field Codes setting by using the Tools Options View card, you can toggle it on and off with the shortcut key Option-F9. If you prefer, you can toggle a single field or selected fields, rather than all fields in the document. Place the cursor in the field you want to toggle, or extend the selection to more than one field, and then press Shift-F9. Word will toggle the display of just the selected field or fields, as shown in Figure 20-4. If you toggle the view for a field that appears in multiple panes or windows, Word will toggle the setting in all open panes, as shown in the figure.

**FIGURE 20-4**

You can use Shift-F9 to toggle selected fields between showing field codes and showing results. If the field is displayed in more than one pane or window, the field will toggle in all open panes.

## How to set field shading to indicate fields

In some circumstances, it's not necessary to see the actual field codes, as long as you can tell where the fields are. For example, you may want to know whether a date or time is entered as a field code or as text, without needing to see the details of the code itself.

You can easily add shading to fields, so you can spot fields at a glance. To set field shading, choose Tools Options and then the View card. As shown in Figure 20-5, the Field Shading option is in the Show group box on the View card, near the center of the dialog box.

**FIGURE 20-5**

You can use the Field Shading option on the Tools Options View card to identify fields by adding shading.

The Field Shading pull-down list contains three choices: Never, Always, and When Selected. If you choose Never, Word won't add shading to fields under any conditions. Choose Always, and Word will always add shading. Choose When Selected, and Word will add shading only when you move your cursor or selection into a field.

Both Always and When Selected apply whether you are showing field codes or field results. We recommend that you choose one of the shading options because it can serve to warn you if you are about to delete or edit a field code, mistaking it for normal text. The choice between the two settings is largely a matter of personal preference.

## How to update a field's result (F9)

In some situations, you'll see field codes even when Word is set to show field results and you haven't changed individual fields. In particular, if you insert a field by pressing ⌘-F9 and then typing the field name, Word will initially display the field code even if it is set to show field results, as shown in Figure 20-6 on the next page. If you move your cursor or selection to the field and press Shift-F9 to show field codes, Word will show nothing for the date, as in Figure 20-7 on the next page.

FIGURE 20-6

If you insert a field
by pressing ⌘-F9 and
typing the field name,
Word will initially
show the field code as
you typed it, even if
the program is set to
show field results.

FIGURE 20-7

If you insert the field as
shown in Figure 20-6
and then press Shift-F9,
Word will show
nothing for the result
of the DATE field. (We
created a second pane
so that you can see the
field codes.)

The reason Word doesn't show a date in this situation is simply that you
haven't told it to calculate the field result. If you place the cursor or selection
in the field and give the field update command by pressing F9, however,
Word will immediately calculate the field and show the result. In contrast,
when you insert a field with the Insert Field command, Word will handle this
step automatically.

You also need to update most result fields whenever the results would change.
For example, if you're inserting another document by using the INCLUDETEXT

field and you make changes to the source file of the included document, you'll need to update the field if you want to include the revised document.

Word provides an option that will automatically recalculate result fields whenever you choose the Tools Mail Merge or File Print command. To set the option, choose Tools Options and then the Print card; then make sure there's a check in the Update Fields check box in the Printing Options box. Regardless of how this option is set, however, you can use the F9 key at any time to update one or more fields. Simply place the cursor in the field you want to update, or extend the selection to include the fields you want to update, and press F9.

Note that if you have fields nested within fields (a situation we'll discuss later in this chapter), updating a field automatically updates all of its nested fields. However, pressing F9 will not update some marker and action fields. Also note that if you update a field accidentally, you can choose Edit Undo to restore the field's previous result.

## How to update a source for an INCLUDETEXT field (⌘-Shift-F7)

As we've just mentioned, if you make a change in another document that has been included in the current document with an INCLUDETEXT field, you have to update the field to update the change. Word also provides a command that will let you copy changes you make in the INCLUDETEXT field result from the INCLUDETEXT field to the source document. (Note that this update source feature works for INCLUDETEXT fields only and only if the included document is a Word file.) To update the source, press ⌘-Shift-F7.

## How to lock a field (⌘-F11 or ⌘-3)

If you need to, you can lock one or more fields to keep Word from updating the field results. Simply place the cursor in the field you want to lock, or extend the selection to include all fields you want to lock, and press ⌘-F11 or ⌘-3. Unfortunately, locked fields don't look any different from unlocked fields; the only way to tell whether a field is locked is to place the cursor or selection in it and press F9 to update the field. If the field is locked, Word won't update the field, and your computer will beep to alert you.

## How to lock a field that's part of a BOOKMARK, an INCLUDETEXT, or a REF field result

You should also be aware of how field locking applies to BOOKMARK, INCLUDETEXT, and REF fields or, more precisely, how it applies to any fields that are part of the result of a BOOKMARK, an INCLUDETEXT, or a REF field.

Suppose you're using an INCLUDETEXT field to insert several paragraphs from another document. In the source document, you have the NUMPAGES field (which returns the number of pages in a document). Unless you tell Word otherwise, updating the INCLUDETEXT field will also update the result for the NUMPAGES field *for the current document*. If you want the result to show the number of pages in the included document instead, you need to lock the fields inserted with the included text so that Word won't update them.

To lock the fields in the result, add the lock result switch \! at the end of the field code. The INCLUDETEXT field, then, would take the following form: {INCLUDETEXT "filename" \!}.

## How to unlock a field (⌘-Shift-F11 or ⌘-4)

To unlock one or more fields locked with ⌘-F11 or ⌘-3, place the cursor in the field or extend the selection to include all of the fields, and then press ⌘-Shift-F11 or ⌘-4. Here again, you can't tell that (or whether) the field is unlocked unless you try to update it.

Note that these shortcut keys have no effect on the results of fields that are locked with the lock result switch added. To change a BOOKMARK, an INCLUDETEXT, or a REF field so the results of included fields are no longer locked, you have to remove the lock result switch, as we'll describe in a moment.

## How to unlink a field (⌘-Shift-F9)

Although you can lock a field to prevent Word from changing a field's result, you'll sometimes want to unlink the field for the same effect. When you place the cursor or selection in a field or fields and press ⌘-Shift-F9, Word will replace the selected fields with their most recent results. If the selected fields have no result, pressing ⌘-Shift-F9 will delete them. When you want to guarantee that you'll never accidentally unlock a field, unlink the field rather than locking it. Note that if you unlink a field accidentally, you can restore the field with the Edit Undo command.

## How to move to a field (F11, Shift-F11)

Word also provides keyboard commands for moving to the next or previous field in a document. To move to and select the next field, press F11. To move to and select the previous field, press Shift-F11.

If you've formatted any fields in your document as hidden text—other than fields, such as the Index Entry field, that Word normally inserts as hidden—

and Word is set not to show hidden text, there are a couple of rules you'll need to keep in mind when moving to fields this way. If you press F11 or Shift-F11 and the next field forward or back is hidden, Word will move the cursor to the field, even though you can't see it. However, it will move to the next field the next time you press F11 or Shift-F11. Note too that Word will skip over any marker fields that are automatically formatted as hidden (such as the Index Entry field)—even if Word is currently set to show hidden text. To move to a marker field, set Word to show hidden text, and use the Edit Find command to search for the field name.

# Editing Fields

After you insert a field in your document, you can edit the text just as you edit any other text. The only requirement is that you must be in Insert mode to add text between the field characters { and }. If you are in Overtype mode, you can type over characters that are already in the field, but you can't type additional characters. In Insert mode, however, you can edit any part of a field except the field characters, and you can add text as needed. For example, if you have the field {DATE \@ "d-MMM-yy"} and you want to change the argument to "MMMM, yy", you can simply change the text using any of Word's standard editing techniques.

If you're viewing field results rather than field codes, you can edit the text returned by result fields just like any other text as well. If you make changes to a field result and then update that field, however, Word will replace the changes with the new field result. In general, therefore, you won't want to modify a field result unless you also lock or unlink the field.

## How to delete or copy a field

All of Word's standard cutting, copying, and pasting features work on fields themselves as well as the text within a field. To delete a field, for example, you can select the entire field and press the Delete key or Del key. If the field codes are currently showing, you can select the entire field by selecting either the { or } character. If field results are showing, you can select an entire field result by selecting its first or last character. (Note that if the field result ends with a paragraph mark, the paragraph mark itself counts as the last character. )

To cut or copy a field, select the field or result and choose the Edit Cut or Edit Copy command. Then move the cursor where you want to insert the field, and choose the Edit Paste command.

# Formatting Field Results

You can format a field result just like any other text. You can also define character formatting—by which we mean some combination of font, paragraph, and style formatting—for an entire field result. And you can easily control case and numeric formatting in field results.

## How to set character formatting for a field result

For some fields—such as the DATE field, which can specify the field result without additional arguments—you can define character formatting for the result by formatting the first character in the field name. The next time you update the field, Word will show the result in the new format.

For example, suppose you want the result of a DATE field to appear in boldface. You can format the result as boldface, or you can format the letter D in the field name, using Word's direct font-formatting commands, and then press F9 to update the field. You can format other characters in the field name too, but the format of the first character is the only one that determines the format of the field.

### How to set character formatting with CharFormat and the format switch

The character-formatting technique just described won't work with fields, such as the INCLUDETEXT field, that import data specified in arguments rather than by the field name itself. To apply character formatting in these cases, you have to add arguments to the fields, using the format switch.

The format switch \* lets you control character formatting, case, and numeric formatting for a field result. The syntax for the format switch is \* *FormatName*, where *FormatName* is the argument that defines the special formatting you want to apply. The argument for applying character formatting to an entire field result is CharFormat.

When you add the format switch and the CharFormat argument to a field that uses an argument to specify the result, you can then format the entire field by formatting the first letter of the field name. For example, suppose you want to import the document file Short, and you want all the imported text formatted in italic. Simply enter the field as:

{INCLUDETEXT "short" \* charformat}

Next, format the I in INCLUDETEXT and press F9 to update the field. Word will format the entire field in italic letters.

Not so incidentally, be aware that if the source document has mixed character formatting, all formatting will be replaced with the formatting specified by the CharFormat argument.

## How to set character formatting for part of a field result

At times you'll want to format only part of a field result. As we've already mentioned, you can format the text in the result directly, but unless you tell Word otherwise, it will reset that format the next time it updates the field.

If you use the MergeFormat argument, however, Word will retain any added formatting on a word-for-word basis when it updates the field. For example, assume that you're using the INCLUDETEXT field to import a few paragraphs from another document file and you've formatted the second sentence in the result as italic. Assume that the first sentence is five words long and the second, eight. At some later time you make changes to the source document and then update the field. If you've defined the INCLUDETEXT field as

{INCLUDETEXT "any doc" \* mergeformat}

Word will reimport the text and format the sixth through the thirteenth words as italic.

You have to be careful with this approach. If you've made changes to text that follows the formatted text, the updated field will maintain the formatting you want. But if you've made changes to the first and second sentences, the formatting won't necessarily show up where you want it. For example, if you delete the first sentence, the italics will start with the sixth word of the sentence you want italicized and will spill over into the next sentence. In short, you'll want to use this feature only when the position of the formatted text isn't likely to change.

# How to control case

Word offers four arguments to control the case for a field result: Upper, Lower, FirstCap, and Caps. The Upper argument formats all characters in uppercase; Lower formats them in lowercase. The FirstCap argument formats the first character of the first word in the result in uppercase, without affecting the remaining characters. Caps formats the first character of each word in uppercase and the remaining characters in lowercase. Figure 20-8 on the next page shows the effect of each argument on the same text in the field result, using the AUTHOR field. The authors, as entered in the Summary Info dialog box for the document, are *M. David Stone & Alfred Poor*.

| Field Code | Sample Result |
|---|---|
| {AUTHOR} | M. David Stone & Alfred Poor |
| {AUTHOR \* Upper} | M. DAVID STONE & ALFRED POOR |
| {AUTHOR \* Lower} | m. david stone & alfred poor |
| {AUTHOR \* FirstCap} | M. david stone & alfred poor |
| {AUTHOR \* Caps} | M. David Stone & Alfred Poor |

**FIGURE 20-8**

Field codes and sample results, using the AUTHOR field with different arguments.

## How to control numeric formats

The format switch recognizes eight arguments for numeric formats, or what Word calls its *number conversion category*. Figure 20-9 shows the complete field code and sample results for each, using the NUMPAGES field, which returns the number of pages in the current document.

| Format Code, Including Argument | Sample Result |
|---|---|
| {NUMPAGES} | 11 |
| {NUMPAGES \*arabic} | 11 |
| {NUMPAGES \*ordinal} | 11th |
| {NUMPAGES \*roman} | xi |
| {NUMPAGES \*Roman} | XI |
| {NUMPAGES \*alphabetic} | k |
| {NUMPAGES \*Alphabetic} | K |
| {NUMPAGES \*cardtext} | Eleven |
| {NUMPAGES \*ordtext} | Eleventh |
| {NUMPAGES \*hex} | B |
| {NUMPAGES \*dollartext} | Eleven and 00/100 |

**FIGURE 20-9**

Field codes and sample results, using the NUMPAGES field, for numeric formats recognized by the format switch.

Most of the arguments are self-explanatory. The one possible exception is hex. Hex is short for hexadecimal, a numbering system often used to translate between the decimal system that people use and the binary system that computers are based on; the hexadecimal system uses a base of 16, rather than 10 as in the decimal system. The first 16 numbers in the hexadecimal system (not including 0) are 1, 2, 3, 4, 5, 6, 7, 8, 9, A, B, C, D, E, F, 10.

As Figure 20-9 shows, the first letter of the roman and alphabetic arguments controls the case of the result. For example, *Roman* or *ROMAN* would produce *XI*, but *roman* would produce *xi*. You can control the case of arguments that produce a text result (CardText, OrdText, and DollarText) by using the case arguments already discussed (Upper, Lower, FirstCap, and Caps). In fact, you can control the case of both Roman and Alphabetic by either method.

## How to use the numeric picture switch

As you will discover, many fields return a numeric result. For example, the NUMCHARS field returns the number of characters in the current document, and the EDITTIME field returns the number of minutes the current document has been open.

Unless you specify otherwise, Word will always display numeric results in a general numeric format, without special characters such as commas or percent signs, and it will display as many digits as necessary after the decimal point. If you prefer, you can use the numeric picture switch \# to define a format. For example, if a field returns the value 1234.1, you can tell Word to show the result as 1,234.10 or as $1234.10.

Figure 20-10, starting on the next page, shows the characters available for creating a model, or *numeric picture*. You can redefine the decimal separator character and the thousands separator character by opening the Macintosh Control Panels folder, choosing Numbers, and then setting the decimal and thousands separators as appropriate. For this discussion, we'll assume you've accepted the default decimal separator character (a period) and the default thousands separator character (a comma). Note that if you include the numeric picture switch in a field that does not return a numeric value, the switch will not affect the field's result.

| Argument | Name and Function |
|---|---|
| 0 | **Zero (digit placeholder).** If the result has fewer digits than there are zeros in the numeric picture, Word adds zeros. If there are more digits to the right of the decimal point than in the numeric picture, Word rounds the number. (The format \# "$000.00" applied to 12.4 yields $012.40. The same format applied to 0.4 yields $000.40.) |
| # | **Number sign (digit placeholder).** If the result has fewer digits than there are number signs in the numeric picture, Word adds spaces rather than zeros to the left or right of the decimal point. If there are more digits to the right of the decimal point than are included in the numeric picture, Word rounds the number. (The format \# "$###.##" applied to 12.456 yields $ 12.46. The same format applied to 0.4 yields $ .4.) |
| x | **x (truncating digit placeholder).** If x is the leftmost character in the numeric picture and the result has more digits to the left, those digits are truncated. If x is the rightmost character after the decimal point, Word rounds the number. (The format \# "x##.#x" applied to 123456.348 yields 456.35.) |
| . | **Period (decimal separator character).** Defines the position of the decimal point, as shown in many of the examples in this table. (The decimal separator character and the thousands separator character match the decimal point and thousands separator characters defined in your system settings.) |
| , | **Comma (thousands separator character).** If the result includes more than three digits to the left of the decimal point and you've included the separator character in the numeric picture, Word will add a comma separator character. (The format \# "#,###.#" applied to 123456.3 yields 123,456.3. Applied to 1123456.3, it yields 1,123,456.3.) |
| – | **Minus (negative) sign.** If the result is negative, Word will add a minus sign before the number, which is the default in any case. If the result is positive, Word will add a space before the number. (The format \# "–###.##" applied to –123.23 yields –123.23. Applied to 123.23, it yields 123.23, with an extra space in front of the number.) |
| + | **Plus (positive) sign.** If the result is negative, Word will display a minus sign before the number. If the result is positive, Word will display a plus sign. (For example, the format \# "+###.##" applied to –123.23 yields –123.23. Applied to 123.23, it yields +123.23.) |

**FIGURE 20-10**

(continued)

Characters available for creating a numeric picture.

**FIGURE 20-10** *continued*

| Argument | Name and Function |
|----------|-------------------|
| ; | **Semicolon.** Lets you define two or three variants, to provide different formats for positive, negative, and zero results. If you have two numeric pictures separated by a semicolon, the first will apply to positive results and zero, the second to negative results. If you have three numeric pictures separated by semicolons, the first will apply to positive results, the second to negative results, and the third to results of zero. (The format \# "$0.00;($0.00);0" applied to 123.23 yields $123.23. Applied to −123.23, it yields ($123.23). Applied to 0, it yields 0. Do not add spaces before the semicolons since Word will add the space to the result. If you add quotation marks, use a single set of quotation marks around the entire numeric picture.) |
| 'text' | **Any text (literal text).** Adds text to the result, using exactly the same characters as defined in the numeric picture. (The format "###.## 'tax'" applied to 123.23 yields 123.23 tax. Note the quotation marks around the full argument and the single quotation marks around the literal text.) |
| ` | **Sequence.** Returns the value of a sequence, such as the current table number. (The format " 'The grand total of Table' `table` 'is' ###.00" applied to Table 4 with a total of 123.23 yields The grand total of Table 4 is 123.23. |
| Other | **All other characters.** To include other characters, such as a dollar sign, or parentheses to indicate a negative number, simply type the character(s) in the appropriate place, as in the examples earlier in this table. |

## The Date-Time Picture switch

Word offers several fields that will return dates or times: DATE, TIME, CREATEDATE, PRINTDATE, SAVEDATE, and EDITTIME.

You can specify a format, rather than simply accepting the default, by using the Date-Time Picture switch \@. As with the numeric picture switch, the Date-Time Picture switch lets you create a picture, or model, for Word to follow. For example, if a field returns the date 3/31/98, you can use the Date-Time Picture switch to display the resulting date as March 31, 1998, or Mar-31, 1998, or any other form you like.

If you include the Date-Time Picture switch in a field that does not return a date or time, the switch will not affect the field's result. We'll take a closer look at this switch shortly, in the section "DATE and TIME Fields."

# Nesting Fields

Occasionally, you'll want to use a field as an argument in another field. For example, you might use FILLIN fields as arguments in an INFO field:

{INFO {FILLIN "Which item?"}{FILLIN "New entry"}}

As we've mentioned, a FILLIN field prompts the user to enter information. An INFO field returns information taken from a document's Summary Info dialog box and lets you change it. By combining the two, you can create a field that prompts the user to type some information and then changes the entries in the Summary Info dialog box.

The FILLIN fields in this example collect input from the user and return that input as arguments in the INFO field. Note that Word always evaluates the innermost field first and the outermost field last.

# DATE and TIME Fields

For the rest of this chapter, we'll look at specific fields and how to use them. We'll start with the two fields you're likely to use most often, the DATE and TIME fields.

## How to insert a date or a time

The DATE field returns the current date, as given by your computer's system clock. The form of this field is simply {DATE}. You can, however, display the date in any other format by adding the Date-Time Picture switch. The field will then take the form

{DATE \@ "Date-Time Picture"}

The TIME field returns the current time, from your computer's system clock. The form for this field is simply {TIME}. As with the DATE field, you can display the time in another format by adding the Date-Time Picture switch. The field will then take the form

{TIME \@ "Date-Time Picture"}

Although the default results for the DATE and TIME fields differ, you can use either field to display the date, the time, or both. Add the Date-Time Picture switch with any format to either field, and you'll get the same result.

One of the most common places to display a date or time is in a header or footer. As explained in Chapter 5, Word provides buttons on the Header And

Footer toolbar to let you insert the DATE or TIME field. However, if you want to display either the date or the time in some format other than the default, you'll have to modify the field or insert it some other way—by pressing ⌘-F9 and typing in the field code, by choosing Insert Field, or by choosing Insert Date And Time.

For most purposes, choosing Insert Date And Time is the fastest way to insert the date or time and specify a format simultaneously. Figure 20-11 shows the Date And Time dialog box.

**FIGURE 20-11**

The Date And Time dialog box offers a total of 13 formats for a date, a time, or both.

The dialog box offers 13 formats for a date, a time, or both. Each choice shows the current date, time, or both, in a specific format. To insert the field with this dialog box, place the cursor where you want the date or time, choose Insert Date And Time, and highlight the format you prefer. Be sure the Insert As Field check box is checked, and choose OK.

> The Insert As Field check box is easy to miss, but important. If the box is not checked, Word will insert the date or time as text rather than as a field. Inserting the field as text will be the preferred choice if you don't want the date or time to change—as with a date and time stamp on a note, for example, where the whole point of adding a date and time is to document when you wrote the note.

If you insert any of these variations of the date or time and then view the field code, you'll see a representation of the format. Figure 20-12 on the next page shows each of the samples from Figure 20-11, with the Date-Time Picture switch that defines the formats. If you look at the field codes, you'll find that Word uses the TIME field in each case.

| This Form of the Date-Time Picture Switch... | Yields This Format... |
| --- | --- |
| \@ "M/d/yy" | 8/3/98 |
| \@ "dddd, MMMM dd, yyyy" | Monday, August 03, 1998 |
| \@ "d MMMM, yyyy" | 3 August, 1998 |
| \@ "MMMM d, yyyy" | August 3, 1998 |
| \@ "d-MMM-yy" | 3-Aug-98 |
| \@ "MMMM, yy" | August, 98 |
| \@ "MMM-yy" | Aug-98 |
| \@ "M/d/yy h:mm AM/PM" | 8/3/98 5:02 PM |
| \@ "M/d/yy h:mm:ss AM/PM" | 8/3/98 5:02:12 PM |
| \@ "h:mm AM/PM" | 5:02 PM |
| \@ "h:mm:ss AM/PM" | 5:02:12 PM |
| \@ "H:mm" | 17:02 |
| \@ "H:mm:ss" | 17:02:12 |

**FIGURE 20-12**

Date-Time Picture switches and sample results.

You can also insert the TIME or DATE field by choosing Insert Field. Highlight either (All) or Date And Time in the Categories list box, and select TIME or DATE in the Field Names list box. If you then choose the Options button, you'll find that Word offers the same format choices as in Figure 20-12, plus one more: \@ "dd MMMM yyyy" (which gives the date in the form 03 August 1998). To insert the DATE or TIME field after choosing the Insert Field command, highlight either field in the Field Names list box. Then optionally add a Date-Time picture, and choose OK. Alternatively, after selecting the field, choose Options, highlight a Date-Time Picture in the Date-Time list box, and choose the Add To Field button. Then choose OK to close the Field Options dialog box, and choose OK again to insert the field into your document.

## How to define custom date and time formats

In addition to the built-in formats Word supplies, you can define a custom format for any DATE or TIME field. That way, you can create fields that return the day of the week as well as the date, month, and year. You can also create combinations of dates and times in the same field.

To create a custom format, type the Date-Time Picture switch along with the abbreviations and literal text that define the format you want. You can create the field from scratch by using ⌘-F9 to insert the field characters and then typing the field name, the \@ Date-Time Picture switch, and the format in the form

{DATE \@ "Date-Time Picture"}

Alternatively, you can insert the field with any technique we've already described and then modify the format as needed. Figure 20-13 lists all date and time abbreviations that Word recognizes. If you add any literal text in the Date-Time Picture switch, including commas or spaces, Word will include that text in the field result.

| Abbreviation | Description | Sample Result |
|---|---|---|
| M | Number of month | 1 through 12 |
| MM | Number of month with leading zeros | 01 through 12 |
| MMM | Three-letter month abbreviation | Oct |
| MMMM | Full month name | October |
| yy | Year as two digits | 98 |
| yyyy | Year as four digits | 1998 |
| d | Date as one or two digits | 1 through 31 |
| dd | Two-digit date with leading zeros | 01 through 31 |
| ddd | Three-letter day of the week | Wed |
| dddd | Full day of the week | Wednesday |
| h | Hours on a 12-hour clock | 1 through 12 |
| hh | Hours on a 12-hour clock with leading zeros | 01 through 12 |
| H | Hours on a 24-hour clock | 1 through 24 |
| HH | Hours on a 24-hour clock with leading zeros | 01 through 24 |
| m | Minutes | 1 through 59 |
| mm | Minutes with leading zeros | 01 through 59 |
| AM/PM | Uppercase AM or PM | 9 AM, 5 PM |
| am/pm | Lowercase am or pm | 9 am, 5 pm |
| A/P | Uppercase A or P | 9A, 5P |
| a/p | Lowercase a or p | 9a, 5p |

**FIGURE 20-13**

Date-time abbreviations Word recognizes, with descriptions and sample results.

## How to combine date and time

As we've already pointed out, the DATE and TIME fields will return the same result when you include a Date-Time Picture switch. This means you can use any combination of the abbreviations listed in Figure 20-13 to create a field that displays both date and time. For example, to insert a field that returns date and time in the format

Oct-15, 1995 at 5:30 PM

you can create either of the following two fields:

{DATE \@ "MMM-d, yyyy 'at' h:mm AM/PM"}
{TIME \@ "MMM-d, yyyy 'at' h:mm AM/PM"}

# Summary Information Fields

Word offers six fields that return information stored in the Summary Info dialog box: TITLE, SUBJECT, AUTHOR, KEYWORDS, COMMENTS, and INFO. These are listed in the Field dialog box under the Document Information category. Figure 20-14 uses a split screen to show how the first five fields appear in a document. The top pane shows the field codes; the bottom pane, the field results.

**FIGURE 20-14**

Summary information fields retrieve information from the Summary Info dialog box.

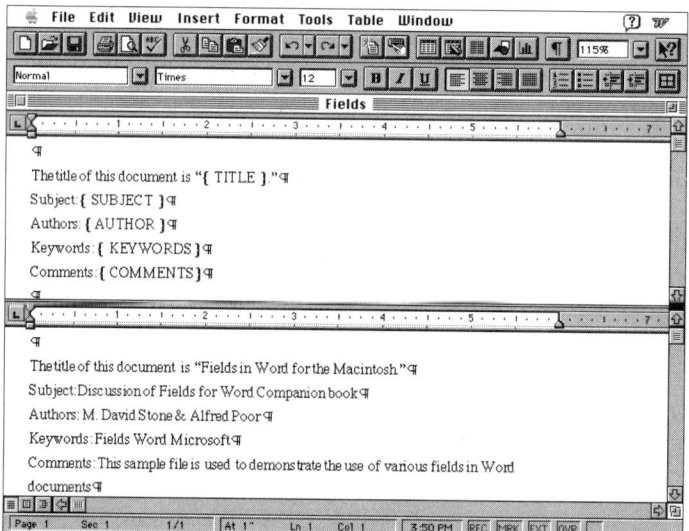

All summary information fields work essentially the same way. In each case, the field can take one of two forms: {FIELDNAME} or {FIELDNAME "NewEntry"}. If you use the first form, as in Figure 20-14, the field will simply return the current information stored in the Summary Info dialog box:

The TITLE field will return the current title, the SUBJECT field the current subject, and so on. If you use the second form, Word will replace the information in the dialog box with the new entry you've added as an argument. It will then return that new entry as the result for the field. To make this a little more concrete, we'll give a specific example, using the TITLE field.

## The TITLE field

The TITLE field returns the title stored in the current document's Summary Info dialog box. The two forms for this field are

{TITLE}

{TITLE "NewTitle"}

The first form returns the entry stored in the Title text box in the Summary Info dialog box. For example, line 1 of the example document shown in Figure 20-14 contains the text

The title of this document is "{TITLE}."

If the current file is entitled *Fields in Word for the Macintosh,* Word will return this title as the result when it updates the field, as shown in the lower pane of Figure 20-14.

The second form of the TITLE field changes the entry in the Summary Info dialog box to whatever new title you've entered as the *NewTitle* argument. If the title consists of more than one word, it must be enclosed in quotation marks. For example, if you insert and update the field

{TITLE "Chapter 20: Field of Fields"}

Word will change the Title entry in the Summary Info dialog box to *Chapter 20: Field of Fields* and return that entry as the field result.

## The SUBJECT, AUTHOR, KEYWORDS, and COMMENTS fields

The other summary information fields work essentially the same way as the TITLE field.

The SUBJECT field returns the entry stored in the Subject text box in the Summary Info dialog box. The forms of this field are

{SUBJECT}

{SUBJECT "NewSubject"}

The AUTHOR field returns the name stored in the Author text box in the Summary Info dialog box. The forms of this field are

{AUTHOR}

{AUTHOR "NewAuthorName"}

The KEYWORDS field returns the entry stored in the Keywords text box in the Summary Info dialog box. The forms of this field are

{KEYWORDS}

{KEYWORDS "NewKeywords"}

The COMMENTS field returns the comments stored in the Comments text box in the Summary Info dialog box. The forms of this field are

{COMMENTS}

{COMMENTS "NewComments"}

In each of these cases, the first form of the field retrieves the appropriate entry from the Summary Info dialog box. The second form lets you change the entry to whatever new text you've entered as the argument.

## The INFO field

The last summary information field is the INFO field. This field lets you define which entry to retrieve from or update in the Summary Info dialog box. Otherwise, INFO works the same way as the other fields. The forms are

{INFO InfoType}

{INFO InfoType "NewEntry"}

*InfoType* can be any of the other five fields we've just discussed. For example, if you insert the field {INFO TITLE}, you will get the same result as if you insert the field {TITLE}. If you insert the field {INFO TITLE "NewTitle"}, you will get the same result as for {TITLE "NewTitle"}.

At first glance, the INFO field appears redundant; however, it can be handy under some conditions. For example, you can use it in combination with the FILLIN field to prompt for information and then change any of the summary information fields. You can create the nested field

{INFO {FILLIN "Change which info item?"}{FILLIN "Change to what?"}}

When you update this field, Word will open a dialog box asking, "Change which info item?" You would respond with one of the summary information field names and choose OK. Word will then ask, "Change to what?" When you type a new entry and choose OK, the INFO field will change the appropriate item.

# Statistical Fields

Word also offers 12 fields that will return statistical information about the current document: CREATEDATE, EDITTIME, FILENAME, FILESIZE, LASTSAVEDBY, NUMCHARS, NUMPAGES, NUMWORDS, PRINTDATE,

REVNUM, SAVEDATE, and TEMPLATE. All of these fields return information that you can otherwise see by choosing File Summary Info and then the Statistics button. Word lists some of these in the Field dialog box as part of the Document Information category and others as part of the Date And Time category. (REVNUM is under Numbering.) Figure 20-15 shows Word's statistical fields in two panes, with Word set to show field codes in one pane and field results in the other.

**FIGURE 20-15**

Word's statistical fields retrieve the same information you can see by choosing File Summary Info and then choosing the Statistics button.

Many of these fields recognize one or more field-specific switches for modifying the field results; we'll cover these switches along with each field. But note too that you can control the format for many of these fields with the format, numeric picture, and date-time switches discussed earlier in this chapter. For details on using these switches, see the section "Formatting Field Results" starting on page 654.

Here's a look at each of the fields, in the same order as they appear in Figure 20-15.

## The CREATEDATE field

The CREATEDATE field returns the date and time the document was created. The form of this field is simply

{CREATEDATE}

You can specify the format with the Date-Time Picture switch.

## The EDITTIME field

The EDITTIME field returns the total number of minutes the document has been open since it was created, as of the moment you update the field. The form of this field is

{EDITTIME}

The EDITTIME field recognizes the numeric picture switch and the format switch options for controlling numeric format.

## The FILENAME field

The FILENAME field returns the filename of the current document. The form of this field is

{FILENAME}

The FILENAME field recognizes the \p switch, which will add the full path to the filename. In addition, it recognizes the format switch options for controlling case.

## The FILESIZE field

The FILESIZE field returns the size of the current document file. The form of this field is

{FILESIZE}

The FILESIZE field recognizes the \k switch, for displaying the result in kilobytes, and the \m switch, for displaying the result in megabytes. In addition, the FILESIZE field recognizes the numeric picture switch and the format switch options for controlling numeric format. By default, the FILESIZE field returns file size in bytes.

## The LASTSAVEDBY field

The LASTSAVEDBY field returns the name of the person who last saved the document, as of the moment you update the field. The form of this field is

{LASTSAVEDBY}

The LASTSAVEDBY field recognizes the format switch options for controlling case.

## The NUMCHARS field

The NUMCHARS field returns the number of characters in the document, as of the moment you update the field. The form of this field is

{NUMCHARS}

The NUMCHARS field recognizes the numeric picture switch and the format switch options for controlling numeric format.

## The NUMPAGES field

The NUMPAGES field returns the total number of pages in the document, as of the moment you update the field. If you've divided the document into sections, Word totals the number of pages in all sections. The form of this field is

{NUMPAGES}

The NUMPAGES field recognizes the numeric picture switch and the format switch options for controlling numeric format.

## The NUMWORDS field

The NUMWORDS field returns the number of words in the document as stored in the Statistics dialog box, as of the moment you update the field. The form of this field is

{NUMWORDS}

The NUMWORDS field recognizes the numeric picture switch and the format switch options for controlling numeric format.

## The PRINTDATE field

The PRINTDATE field returns the date and time the document was last printed. The form of this field is

{PRINTDATE}

If you've never printed the document, the date and time will be 0/00/00 0:00 AM, as shown in Figure 20-15. You can use the Date-Time Picture switch to specify the format.

## The REVNUM field

Each time you create a new document, Word assigns it revision number 1. Each time you save the document, Word increments the revision number by one. The REVNUM field returns the revision number of the current document, as of the moment the field is updated. The form of the field is

{REVNUM}

The REVNUM field recognizes the numeric picture switch and the format switch options for controlling numeric format.

## The SAVEDATE field

The SAVEDATE field returns the date and time the document was last saved, as of the moment you update the field. The form of this field is

{SAVEDATE}

You can use the Date-Time Picture switch to specify the format.

## The TEMPLATE field

The TEMPLATE field returns the name of the document's template file, as of the moment you update the field. The form of this field is

{TEMPLATE}

By default, the result takes the form Normal. However, you can add a path to the filename by using the \p switch. The TEMPLATE field also recognizes the format switch options for controlling case.

## Using the INFO field instead of statistical fields

Just as the INFO field can use any of the summary information field names as its *InfoType* argument, it can also use any of the statistical field names. With the statistical fields, however, you can only get information with the INFO field; you cannot change it. The only form of the INFO field for statistical information is

{INFO InfoType}

where *InfoType* is the field name for the particular statistical field. There is really no good reason for using the INFO field this way, since the field merely duplicates the result for the equivalent statistical field.

# User Information Fields

Word offers three user information fields. These normally return information stored on the Tools Options User Info card, although you can also override the information. The three fields are USERADDRESS, USERINITIALS, and USERNAME. The first field returns the user's mailing address; the second, the user's initials; and the third, the user's name. The forms for the three fields are

{USERADDRESS ["OverrideAddress"]}

{USERINITIALS ["OverrideInitials"]}

{USERNAME ["OverrideName"]}

*OverrideAddress, OverrideInitials,* and *OverrideName* are optional arguments you can add to override the information stored on the User Info card. Unlike the *NewEntry* arguments for the INFO field, these arguments do not replace the information on the User Info card; they only override it when inserting the information into the document for the particular field.

# Action Fields

We said early in this chapter that, to some extent, fields redefine what a word processor can do. Action fields provide the basis for that statement. And it's worth taking a look at some action fields to get a sense of what they are. Here, then, is a look at the MACROBUTTON and GOTOBUTTON fields.

## The MACROBUTTON field

A macro is essentially a set of instructions you've written or recorded to give commands to Word. For example, if you often print just the page you're working on, you could record a macro as you give the commands to print the current page. You can then assign the macro to a shortcut key, a toolbar button, or—as we're about to discuss—to a MACROBUTTON field. Once you've assigned the macro to any of these possibilities, you can print the current page by simply pressing the shortcut key, clicking on the toolbar button, or double-clicking on the MACROBUTTON field. We'll cover macros in Part Five of this book, "Customizing Word." For the moment, simply note that macros will let you create what amount to new commands that can be highly customized for particular tasks.

The MACROBUTTON field lets you create a button in your document similar in concept to the buttons on Word's toolbars. After you create the button, you can double-click on it to run a macro or a command. The MACROBUTTON field takes the form

{MACROBUTTON "MacroOrCommandName" DisplayLabel}

where *MacroOrCommandName* is the name of the macro or command you want the button to run, and *DisplayLabel* is the text or graphic that will serve as the button in the document.

If you use text for *DisplayLabel,* you should not enclose it within quotation marks. If you do, the quotes will appear as part of the button text. Note also that Word's online Help calls the first argument *MacroName.* This is slightly misleading because a MACROBUTTON field can also run built-in commands. If you create the macro using the Insert Field dialog box, you can choose one of Word's built-in commands or a macro by choosing Options and then choosing the command or macro in the (misnamed) Macro Name list box.

When Word shows the result of the MACROBUTTON field, you'll see the button, meaning either the text or the graphic you've specified as the *DisplayLabel* argument. Word will automatically update the field result any time you edit the argument. Note that if you create the field code by pressing ⌘-F9 and then typing the field code, you'll have to toggle the field (with the cursor in the field, press Shift-F9) to display the result. Simply pressing F9 won't do anything, even if Word is currently set to show results.

Once created, you can use a MACROBUTTON by double-clicking on the text or graphic returned by the field. If you prefer using the keyboard, select the button with the usual keyboard commands and press Option-Shift-F9.

The ability to run macros or commands with a button you've placed in a document expands what you can do with a word processor. For example, suppose you have a monthly report that stays much the same from month to month except for some changes in the numbers and names that make up the report. Assume that you've automated the updating process with a macro that imports information from other files, asks the user to enter other details, reformats the report, and prints five copies.

If you assign a shortcut key to this macro, you may have trouble remembering it because you use it only once a month. Similarly, there is little point in taking up space on a toolbar for a button you'll use only once a month.

If you add a MACROBUTTON field to the top of the document, however, and you use UPDATE as the display text, you will have the benefit of automating the task without any risk of forgetting how to run the macro. Figure 20-16 shows a simple example, using a macro named UpdateMacro and the text *UPDATE* for the *DisplayLabel* argument.

Assuming the name of the macro you want to run is UpdateMacro, you can produce a button like the one shown in Figure 20-16 with the field

{MACROBUTTON "UpdateMacro" *UPDATE*}

Make sure the field is in a paragraph of its own. Then place the cursor or selection in that paragraph, choose Format Borders And Shading, and define a border. (Defining a border is not necessary, but it helps set off the button.) Finally, adjust the paragraph indents so that the border is no wider than the word it's surrounding.

You can also create a fancier button if you want to. Figure 20-17 shows a MACROBUTTON field that uses a WordArt graphic for the *DisplayLabel* argument. For information about using WordArt, see "Creating Font Effects with Microsoft WordArt" on page 533.

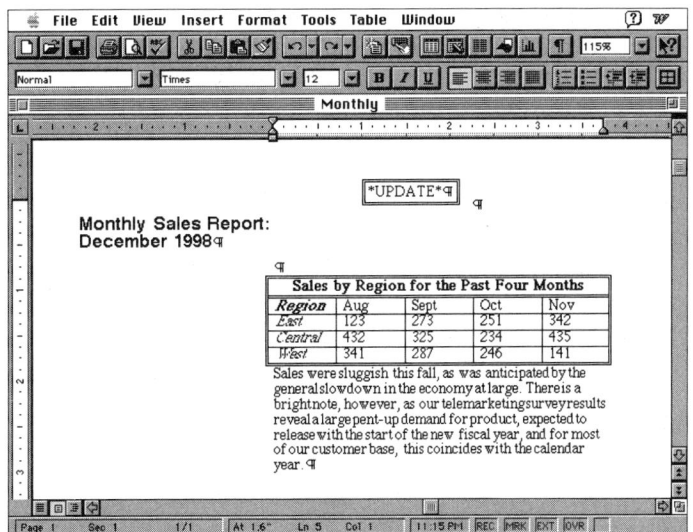

**FIGURE 20-16**

By adding a MACROBUTTON field, as with the button labeled *UPDATE* in this document, you can run a macro or command simply by double-clicking on the field or placing the cursor on it and pressing Option-Shift-F9.

The field code for the MACROBUTTON field shown in Figure 20-17 is

{MACROBUTTON "UpdateMacro" {EMBED WordArt \s \* mergeformat}}

The nested EMBED field is automatically added by Word when you use the Insert Object command, choose Microsoft WordArt 2.0, and then define the image. We also added a frame with a border to the WordArt object. Note that by putting the border around the frame rather than around the paragraph, we've avoided having to adjust the paragraph indents.

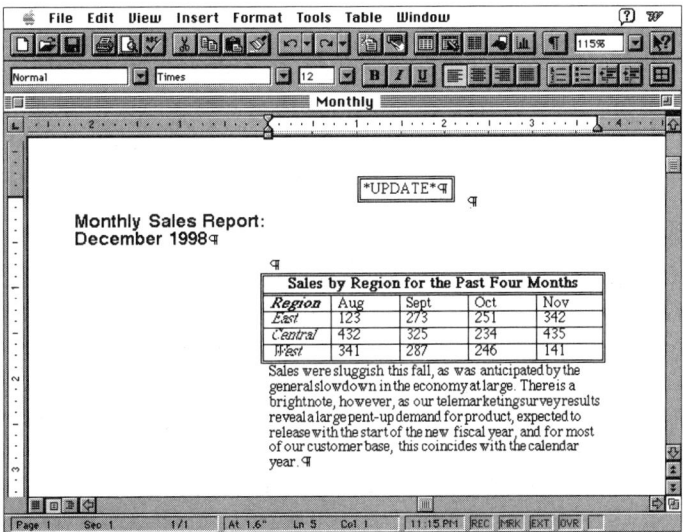

**FIGURE 20-17**

The MACROBUTTON field shown here is identical to the one shown in Figure 20-16, except that it uses a WordArt graphic as the *DisplayLabel* argument.

# The GOTOBUTTON field

As with the MACROBUTTON field, the GOTOBUTTON field will let you create a button in your document. In this case, however, choosing the button will take you to a specified destination in the document. The field takes the form

{GOTOBUTTON "GoToInstruction" DisplayLabel}

where *GoToInstruction* is any destination you can type or select in the Go To dialog box, and *DisplayLabel* is the text or picture you want to display as the button. As with *DisplayLabel* in the MACROBUTTON field, you should not enclose the *DisplayLabel* argument in quotation marks.

The GOTOBUTTON field is similar to the MACROBUTTON field in several other ways as well. When you look at the result of a GOTOBUTTON field, you'll see the text or picture you've specified in the *DisplayLabel* argument. If you like, you can apply some character formatting to the *DisplayLabel* argument to distinguish the button text from the surrounding text. And as it does with the MACROBUTTON field, Word will update the result of the GOTOBUTTON field whenever you edit the field code. And as with the MACROBUTTON field, you use a GOTOBUTTON field by double-clicking on it with the mouse or by moving the cursor to the button and pressing Option-Shift-F9.

The GOTOBUTTON field lets you create something very much like hypertext. Hypertext is simply text that's been extensively cross-referenced and that takes advantage of a computer's capabilities to jump quickly and easily among referenced areas. Word's Help system is an example of hypertext, with its ability to let you jump to related subjects or see a definition of selected terms that are mentioned on any given screen. Quite simply, the GOTOBUTTON field lets you create hypertext buttons in your document, which you can use to jump to other locations in the document.

For example, suppose you've created the document shown in Figure 20-18. The text discusses technology in the automotive industry. Elsewhere in the document, you've included some definitions for many of the specialized terms you've used, including the term *Multivalve Engine,* which we've highlighted in the figure. If your readers will be reading this file on a computer while running Word, you might want to provide a way to jump to the term's definition. To add that capability, you need only mark the definition later in the document with a bookmark and replace the term with a GOTOBUTTON field. The reader can then choose the button to see the definition.

To set up the button, first define a bookmark named Multivalve at the beginning of the definition for *Multivalve Engine.* Next return to the text shown in Figure 20-18, and replace the phrase *Multivalve Engine* with the field

{GOTOBUTTON "Multivalve" Multivalve Engine}

as we have in Figure 20-19. When you view the result of this field, you'll see the text *Multivalve Engine,* as shown in Figure 20-20 on the next page. Notice that we've formatted this text in boldface to give a visual clue that it is a GOTOBUTTON field. (You might want to define the font in a different color as well.) To view the definition, the reader can simply double-click on the term or move the cursor to the term and press Option-Shift-F9. Word will immediately move the cursor to the Multivalve bookmark.

**FIGURE 20-18**

We'll use a GOTOBUTTON field in place of the term *Multivalve Engine* to let the reader jump to that term's definition.

**FIGURE 20-19**

Word will show the formatting you've applied to the *DisplayLabel* argument in this field code when it displays the field result.

**FIGURE 20-20**

With the GOTOBUTTON field defined, a reader can jump to the definition of *Multivalve Engine.*

# Other Fields and Where to Find Them in This Book

We've covered about 30 fields in this chapter, out of approximately 70 that Word provides. The remaining fields are either covered elsewhere in this book as part of another subject or are automatically inserted by Word so that you'll rarely, if ever, need to know about them.

# TOPIC FINDER

# 21

# Form Letters, Labels, & Forms

f you're like most Word users, you often need to say the same thing, in slightly different ways, to a large group of recipients such as clients or customers. One of the benefits of word processing in general is that it can automate such tasks. The good news is that Word 6.0 goes further than most word processing programs, with features that even help automate the process of producing the files you need.

Word calls this capability *mail merge*. Briefly, mail merge lets you combine two files to create customized documents. One file stores standard text, such as a form letter. The other stores information that will vary, such as names and addresses. When you merge these two files, Word creates merge documents, using the standard text from the first file and customizing each document with the variable information from the second file.

The mail merge feature depends heavily on fields. To best understand this chapter, you should first make sure you're familiar with the concepts of fields, discussed in Chapter 20.

# Benefits of Using Mail Merge

If you've ever dealt with a cantankerous word processor that makes your form letters look like glued-together bomb threats from an illiterate terrorist, you may have doubts about the usefulness of mail merging. Even if you haven't used the feature, you've probably received computer-generated form letters with your name either truncated because it's too long or floating in the middle of white space because it's too short. For example, the name Catherine Hammerschmidt can come out as *Catherine Hammers*.

In truth, such awkward mail merge results are all too common. But Word's mail merge feature is among the best, with sophisticated capabilities that avoid these problems. Word will automatically adjust the text to format each document properly, with no gaping holes.

Of course, Word's mail merge also provides all the advantages of any mail merge feature. Because you create only one copy of the form letter (or other standard text), and one data file for the variable information, you save disk space and time when creating the files. And you save more time when printing because one command prints all the documents.

Still another advantage is that you need to create any given main document (the standard text) or any data file only once. You can, for example, send monthly mailings to your entire client list using the same data file each time. Similarly, you can use one main document with any number of data files; for instance, you can create a letter introducing your services and mail it to different groups of people at different times. This ability to reuse information not only saves time but also minimizes errors. Get the information right once, and you don't have to worry about getting it right again.

# Preliminaries: Database Definitions

As you'll see shortly, Word's automation features will let you use mail merge without having to know much about the details. However, it will be easier to talk about mail merging if you understand some core terms.

A *record* consists of all the specific information meant for a single merge document. For example, if you're including a name, address, and salutation in each merge document, a single record will include one specific name, address, and salutation.

A *field* in the data file consists of the information that fills in one blank, or field, in the main document. These two uses for *field* are obviously different from each other, but having two meanings for one term isn't a problem. The type of field we're talking about at any time will usually be obvious from the context, but we'll sometimes talk about *merge fields* in a document to distinguish them from fields in a data file.

Note also that these two kinds of fields are related. If you have one field in the main document for an entire name and a second field for an entire address, for example, you need to divide each record in the data file into two fields—one for the name and one for the address. On the other hand, if you have fields in the main document for first name, last name, street address, city, state, and zip code, you'll need six fields in each record in the data file to match the six in the main document.

> For maximum flexibility in using the data in a data file, you should divide each record into the maximum number of fields you're ever likely to need. For example, even if you're creating a form letter that will use full names only, you should create separate fields for first and last names. That way, if you ever need to use the same data in a letter that will use either the first or last name by itself, you won't have to retype all the names. Before you create the data file, invest some time considering how you might use that data, and decide how many fields to use.

A *field name* refers to a given field in every record. For example, if you create a field for first names, you might identify it with the field name FirstName. When you create merge fields in the main document, the field names indicate which information goes in which merge field.

A *variable* is the data that varies from one record to the next, such as names and addresses in a data file.

A *value* is the actual data for a given field within a record. If the state for a specific record is California, for example, then CA is the value of the State field for that record.

A *variable name* is the name for the variable that goes in a given field. The field name and the variable name are always the same; for example, the State field holds the State variable.

## Using the Tools Mail Merge Command

As we've already mentioned, mail merging needs at least two files: a main document, or main file; and a data file. (You can also use additional files, as we'll discuss later.) The main file contains the text to print in each document. The data file contains the text that will vary from one document to the next. Word combines the information from both files to create customized merge documents. (For purposes of this discussion, the terms *main document, main file*, and *main document file* are interchangeable. Similarly, *data file, data document, data document file*, and *data source* are interchangeable.)

You can create the main file and the data file manually. However, the easiest way to use (or learn) mail merge is to take advantage of Word's ability to partially automate the task of creating the files. For most of this discussion, we'll assume that's what you're doing.

**NEW!**   The starting point for mail merging is the Tools Mail Merge command, which opens the Mail Merge Helper dialog box shown in Figure 21-1. The choices in the dialog box function as a checklist for the most important steps in creating the files you need. We'll start with an example of using the Mail Merge Helper to create a form letter.

**FIGURE 21-1**

The Mail Merge Helper dialog box is the starting point for automating many of the tasks involved in creating and using files for mail merging.

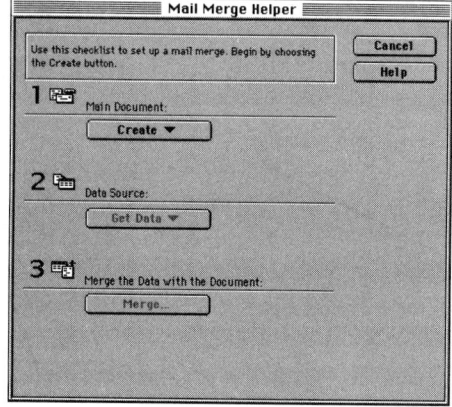

## NEW!   How to designate the main document

The first step in setting up a mail merge, as indicated by the number 1 in the dialog box, is designating which main document to use. Click on the Create button in the Mail Merge Helper dialog box, and hold the mouse button down, to open the pull-down menu shown in Figure 21-2.

**FIGURE 21-2**

Click on the Create button in the Mail Merge Helper dialog box to see this menu, which lets you designate the kind of main document to use.

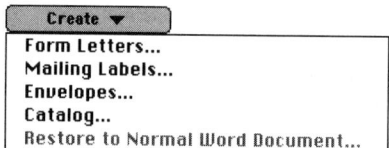

The Create menu offers several choices for the type of main document. For this example, you can choose Form Letters to see the message box shown in Figure 21-3.

**FIGURE 21-3**

When you choose Form Letters from the Create menu, Word will show you this message box.

The message box lets you choose whether to use the document in the active window to create the form letters or open a new document window. After you choose the appropriate button, Word will return to the Mail Merge Helper, as shown in Figure 21-4.

**FIGURE 21-4**

After you specify which main document to use, Word will return you to the Mail Merge Helper dialog box.

Notice that when you return to the dialog box, as shown in Figure 21-4, Word will have added several items in the Main Document section of the dialog box. Two new lines under the Create button show the merge type (Form Letters, in this case) and the name and location of the main document (Main File, in this case). You'll also find an Edit button added to the right of the Create button. And note that the Get Data button is no longer grayed out.

## How to create a data file with Word's help

**NEW!**

Once you've designated the main document, you can choose the Edit button, but you'll be limited in what you can do since you haven't specified a data file yet. In most cases, you should click on Get Data next, which will open a pull-down menu with three choices: Create Data Source, Open Data Source, and

Header Options. We'll discuss each in turn. For the moment, however, we're concerned only with the Create Data Source item. Choose it, and Word will open the Create Data Source dialog box, shown in Figure 21-5.

**FIGURE 21-5**

The Create Data Source dialog box prompts you for the field names to use in the data file.

The Create Data Source dialog box makes it easy to name the fields in the data file you're about to create. When you first open the dialog box, you'll find a number of field names in the Field Names In Header Row list box. (The *header row* is the first row in the data file; it contains the names of the fields.) You can browse through the list and delete any fields you don't want by highlighting the field name and choosing Remove Field Name.

To add a field name, type it in the Field Name text box, and choose Add Field Name. Word will always add a field name at the end of the list. To change a name's position, highlight the name in the list, and choose the up or down arrow button to the right of the list box.

Once you've defined the field names, choose OK. Word will open a dialog box that looks and works just like the dialog box for saving document files. Designate a folder and filename, then choose Save to create the file.

After saving the file, Word will show you a message box which points out that the new data file contains no records and that you can either add new records at this point or add merge fields to your main document. The message box offers three buttons in addition to Help: Edit Data Source, Edit Main Document, and Cancel. The first two are self-explanatory. Choosing the Cancel button will return you to the Mail Merge Helper dialog box, as shown in Figure 21-6. As you can see in the figure, after you've defined a data file, Word will add an Edit button to the dialog box just to the right of the Get Data button.

**FIGURE 21-6**

After you create a data file, Word will give you the choice of editing the main document, editing the data file, or closing the Mail Merge Helper dialog box.

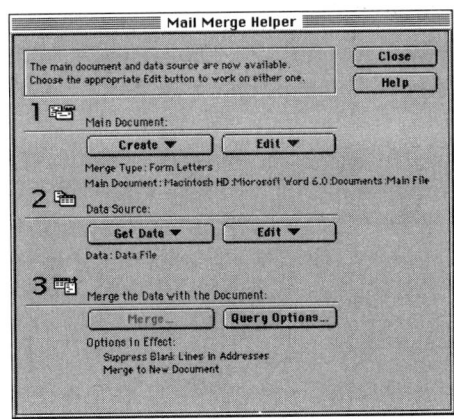

If you click on the Edit button in the Main Document section of the Mail Merge Helper dialog box, and hold the mouse button down, Word will open a one-item, pull-down menu showing the filename of the main document. You can then highlight the choice and release the button to edit the main document. Similarly, if you click on the Edit button in the Data Source section of the dialog box, Word will open a one-item, pull-down menu showing the name of the data file. And you can simply highlight the choice and release the mouse button to edit the data file.

## How to enter and search records with the Data Form dialog box

For this example, we'll assume you want to add some records to the data file at this point. Click on the Edit button in the Data Source section of the dialog box, and choose the data file from the one-item menu. Word will open a Data Form dialog box like the one shown in Figure 21-7.

**FIGURE 21-7**

The Data Form dialog box lets you add, delete, and find records in a data file.

The Data Form dialog box includes a list of the field names in the data file, with a text box for each field. Word provides a scroll bar to the right of the fields so you can scroll through the list if necessary. You can enter the data for each record by typing it in the appropriate text boxes. Then choose the Add

New button (or press Return while in the last text box in the record) to save the current record and start a new one.

Just below the list of field names is the Record text box, with arrow buttons on either side. The text box shows the number of the record you're currently viewing. If you know the number of a record you want to move to, you can type that number in the text box and press Tab or Return to move to that record. Alternatively, you can click on the arrow button to the right of the text box to move to the next record in the data file or the button farther to the right to move to the last record in the file. Similarly, you can click on the equivalent buttons to the left of the text box to move back one record or to the first record in the file. Each time you move to another record, you'll save any changes you made in the previous record.

> You can also use the Data Form dialog box to manage data. When any given record is showing in the dialog box, you can delete the record by choosing Delete, or you can modify it by editing the entry. When you move to another record, Word will automatically save the changes. If you make a mistake and need to return to the original text for a record before saving the changes, choose the Restore button.

You can also find records by searching for specific entries. If you choose the Find button in the Data Form dialog box, Word will open the Find In Field dialog box, shown in Figure 21-8.

**FIGURE 21-8**

Use the Find In Field dialog box to search for a record in a data file.

To search for a record, open the In Field pull-down list and choose the field to search through. Then, in the Find What text box, enter the value to search for. If you're searching for a Texas address, for example, you would choose the State field and type the value *TX* in the Find What box. Then choose Find First to find the first record with a TX entry. The Find First button will change to Find Next so that you can use it to find the next record with a TX entry. Once you find the record you're looking for, you can modify it or delete it as appropriate.

## How to view the data file

By using the Data Form dialog box, you can enter and modify the records for mail merging without ever seeing the data file itself. If you choose the View Source button, however, Word will close the dialog box and show you the data file.

As you can see in Figure 21-9, Word stores the data in a table, using one row for each record and one column for each field.

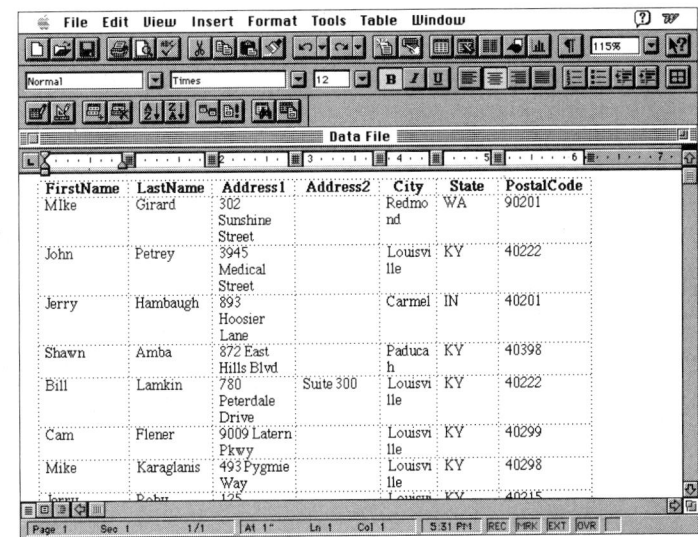

The top row in the table—the header record—consists of the field names. Unless you tell Word otherwise, it will always treat the first record in a data file as the header record and will use those entries to define the field names for the data file and the main file. This approach will always be the most convenient choice when you create the data file with Word's help. In some cases, however, it's more convenient to keep the header record in a separate file. For example, if you maintain the data with a database program and routinely import the data into Word format for monthly mailings, you can create the header record once and keep it in a separate file. We'll discuss this option later in this chapter.

## How to work in the data file

You can edit the table in the data file directly, using the table features we discussed in Chapter 11. More interesting is that you can manipulate the data in various ways using the Database toolbar, which Word automatically provides when you're working in the data file. You can see the Database toolbar just above the ruler in Figure 21-9. Figure 21-10 on the next page lists the 10 buttons on the Database toolbar and their functions.

| Button | Button Name | Action |
|---|---|---|
| | Data Form | Opens the Data Form dialog box |
| | Manage Fields | Opens the Manage Fields dialog box, which lets you add, delete, or rename fields |
| | Add New Record | Adds a new record as a blank row at the end of the table |
| | Delete Record | Deletes records by deleting the row or rows that the cursor or selection is in |
| | Sort Ascending | Sorts the records in ascending order using the column the cursor or selection is in |
| | Sort Descending | Sorts the records in descending order using the column the cursor or selection is in |
| | Insert Database | Lets you update the database from another source |
| | Update Fields | Updates any Word field (such as a TIME field) that the cursor or selection is in |
| | Find Record | Opens the Find In Field dialog box to let you search for a match within a specific field |
| | Mail Merge Main Document | Switches from the data file to the main document |

**FIGURE 21-10**

The Database toolbar buttons.

The leftmost toolbar button is the Data Form button, which opens the Data Form dialog box. Next on the toolbar is the Manage Fields button, which opens the Manage Fields dialog box, shown in Figure 21-11. If you enter a name in the Field Name text box and choose the Add button in this dialog box, Word will add a field, in the form of a column, at the end of the table. You can also delete a field from the table by highlighting a name in the dialog box list and choosing Remove. If you highlight a name and choose Rename, Word will open another dialog box that will let you enter the new field name. Word will automatically apply any of these changes to the table in the data file.

**FIGURE 21-11**

The Manage Fields dialog box lets you add, remove, or rename fields in your data file.

The next two buttons on the Database toolbar are the Add New Record button and the Delete Record button. Choose Add New Record, and Word will add a record, as a blank row, at the end of the table. Choose Delete Record, and Word will delete the row or rows that the cursor or selection is currently in.

Next come the Sort Ascending and Sort Descending buttons. To use either of these, place the cursor or selection in one column of the table and click on the button. Word will select the entire column and sort the table based on that column, in either ascending or descending order, depending on which button you choose.

Next is the Insert Database button. Choosing this button is equivalent to choosing the Insert Database menu command, which we covered in Chapter 18. We'll explain why you might want to use this command shortly. For details on the Insert Database command, see "How to import data using the Insert Database command" starting on page 593.

To the right of the Insert Database button is the Update Fields button, which will update any fields that the cursor or selection is in. This is equivalent to pressing the F9 shortcut key for updating fields.

The next button on the toolbar is the Find Record button. It will open the Find In Field dialog box described earlier. The rightmost button is the Mail Merge Main Document button, which will return you to the main document.

## Other choices for creating a data file

In addition to creating a data file with Word's help, you can also create a data file manually, by building the table from scratch; or you can import data from another file format, such as a Microsoft Excel spreadsheet. (We discussed importing data in Chapter 18.) Word will also let you organize the data without using a table. In fact, if you have more than 31 fields in each record, you must use a different organization, since 31 columns is the maximum a table allows. Figure 21-12 on the next page shows a data file, complete with a header record, that we created manually.

**FIGURE 21-12**

Word also recognizes this alternative data file format, with each record in a single paragraph and fields separated by tabs.

In Figure 21-12, each record is in its own paragraph, with fields separated by tabs. It's not important that each record fit on a single line, although that makes the data easier to read. The important detail is that you must use a paragraph mark after each record.

You can separate the fields with other separators besides tabs. The most common choice for a separator other than a tab is a comma, for what's known as *comma-delimited variable format* or *comma-separated variable format*—often abbreviated to CSV. CSV format is a popular choice for exporting data from database programs. However, data is somewhat difficult to read in this format.

If you choose to create your data files manually, remember that you can put the field names in a separate header file. See "Header files" on page 700.

## How to use a data file created without Word's help

To use a data file created without help from Word, start by creating the file and saving it to disk. You can then open a file for the main document, choose Tools Mail Merge, and designate the open file as the main document. Next, in the Mail Merge Helper dialog box, open the Get Data pull-down menu and choose Open Data Source.

Word will respond with a dialog box that looks and acts like the dialog box for opening document files. Specify the data file you want to use, and choose Open. Word will show you a message box stating that Word found no merge fields in your main document. You can then choose Edit Main Document or choose Cancel to return to the Mail Merge Helper dialog box, where you can choose any of the options we've described.

## How to enter tabs, commas, paragraph marks, and quotes as data

Because Word interprets tabs and commas as field delimiters and recognizes paragraph marks as indicating the end of a record, you may be wondering how to enter literal tabs, commas, and paragraph marks in your data. If the data file uses the table format, this isn't a problem, since Word recognizes each cell (the intersection of a column and a row) as a field, regardless of what the cell contains. If the data is in tabular (fields separated by tabs) format or comma-delimited (fields separated by commas) format, however, you must enclose the entire field in quotation marks if it includes a tab, comma, or paragraph mark.

For example, you would enter the company name MegaCorp, Inc., as *"MegaCorp, Inc."* The quotation marks around the entry tell Word to interpret the contents—including the comma—literally.

To include quotation marks as part of the data, enter two sets of quotation marks. For example, suppose you have a client who insists on calling himself Jim "Pop" Stallone. You would enter the name in the data file as *Jim ""Pop""Stallone*. Word will interpret this as one set of literal quotation marks around the word *Pop*.

**NEW!**

If you're using a tabular or comma-delimited format and you enter data with the Data Form dialog box, Word will add the quotation marks automatically for all these cases.

**NEW!**

# How to edit the main document

So far in this chapter, we've largely ignored the main document—and for good reason. Although you can create a main document and even add text to it at any time, it's difficult to add merge fields until after you've defined the field names in the data file. Once you've defined the field names, however, creating the main document is straightforward.

To move to the main document from the Mail Merge Helper, choose Edit in the Main Document section of the dialog box. To move to the main document from the data file, click on the Mail Merge Main Document button on the Database toolbar. You can also press ⌘-F6, or choose the document name from the Window menu.

## How to insert a merge field

When you move to or open the main document, Word will add a new toolbar, called the Mail Merge toolbar, just above the document window's title bar, as shown in Figure 21-13 on the next page. As you can see in the figure, we've added some text. In fact, we've added all the text we want to include in every merged document. However, the document does not yet include any merge fields.

When working in a
mail merge main
document Word adds
the Mail Merge
toolbar, shown here
just above the docu-
ment window title bar.

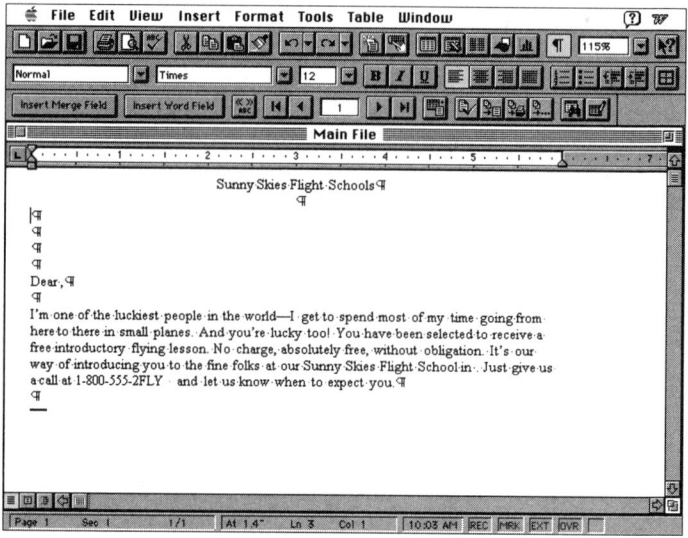

Among other useful features, the Mail Merge toolbar can help automate
the process of adding merge fields. The first button on the left is labeled Insert
Merge Field. To use it, place the cursor where you want to add a field, and
click and hold down the mouse button. In Figure 21-13, for example, the cursor is immediately to the left of the first left-justified paragraph mark in the
letter, which is where we want the address to start.

Figure 21-14 shows the pull-down menu that opens when you click on the
Insert Merge Field button and hold down the mouse button. This menu lists
all the field names as they appear in the header record. To insert a merge field
from the menu, you can simply highlight the field name and release the
mouse button. Word will insert the field at the cursor location.

The Insert Merge Field
menu makes it easy to
insert mail merge fields
into a main document.

If you prefer using the keyboard rather than the mouse, you can ignore
the Insert Merge Field button and press Control-Shift-F instead. Word will
open the Insert Merge Field dialog box, shown in Figure 21-15.

**FIGURE 21-15**

You can use the Insert Merge Field dialog box to insert mail merge fields into a main document.

The Insert Merge Field dialog box contains two list boxes: the Mail Merge Fields list box and the Word Fields list box. The Mail Merge Fields list contains the same field names as the Insert Merge Field menu. To insert a merge field, highlight a field name in this list, and choose OK.

The Word Fields list box offers essentially the same list of fields you'll see if you choose the Insert Word Field button on the Mail Merge toolbar. In either form, this list offers advanced control over merging. We'll discuss these fields later in this chapter in the section "Using Special Fields for Mail Merging" on page 700.

Figure 21-16 shows the main document after we've inserted the FirstName field. To make it easier to follow these comments, we've opened two panes in the figure, one showing the field code and one showing the field result. (You can toggle between seeing field codes and field results by placing the cursor or selection in the field and pressing Shift-F9.)

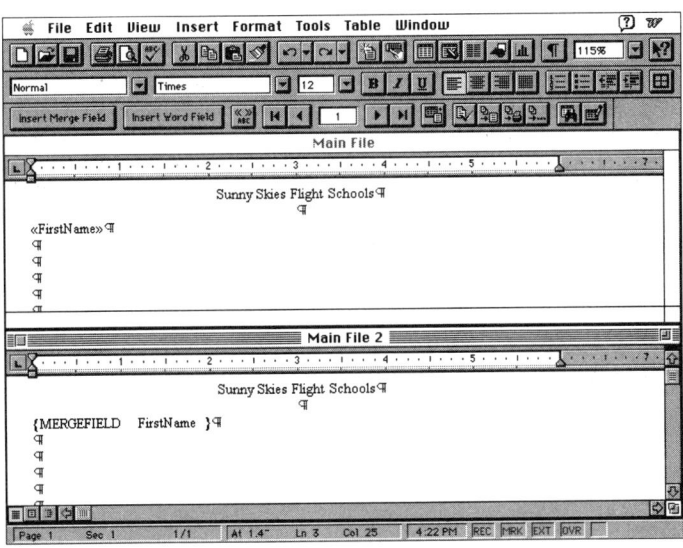

**FIGURE 21-16**

These two views of the mail merge field show that the field name FirstName (in the top pane) is the result of a Word MERGEFIELD using the field name FirstName (in the bottom pane).

As Figure 21-16 shows, if Word is set to show field results, you will normally see the field result as the field name, or variable name, surrounded by what are sometimes called chevrons (« and »). If Word is set to show field codes, however, you can see that the field code consists of the MERGEFIELD field plus the variable name.

Figure 21-17 shows the sample main document with all the mail merge fields inserted and Word set to show field results. Note that we've used the FirstName field twice—once in the address and once in the salutation. You can use a field name as many times as you like in a main document. You can also choose not to use some fields from the data file. Note that if you apply direct character formatting to merge fields, the merged result will retain the formatting.

The finished sample form letter includes the merge fields inserted at the appropriate locations.

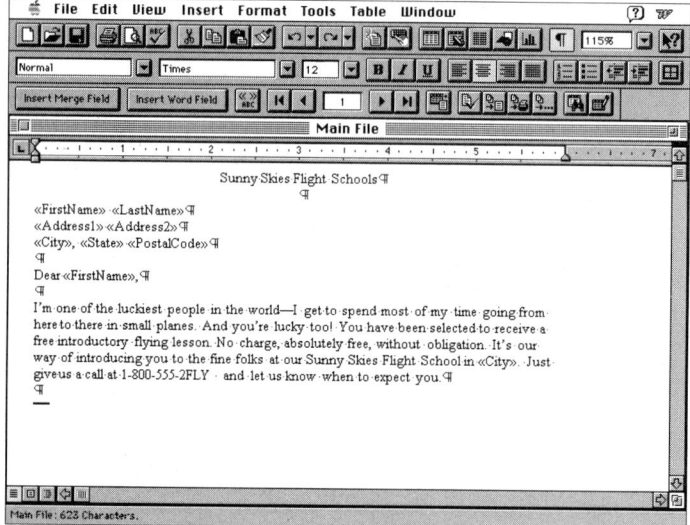

## How to view data from the main document

When you run the mail merge, Word will replace each merge field in the main document with data from the data file, using successive records for each copy of the main document.

If you like, however, you can have Word show actual data in the main document on screen before you run the mail merge: Simply click on the View Merged Data button, the third from the left on the Mail Merge toolbar. By default, Word will display the data from the first record in your data file. However, you can specify another record or browse through the data one record at a time using the set of four buttons and a text box to the right of the View Merged Data button.

These toolbar items are identical to the text box and arrow buttons in the Data Form dialog box, and they work the same way. To move through the data records, click on the First Record, Previous Record, Next Record, or Last Record button, as appropriate, or enter a number in the Go To Record text box to move directly to a specific record.

Being able to see the data on screen before you run the merge can save a lot of wasted effort, since it will give you a preview of how your merged documents will look. You'll often find that your data file includes variations you hadn't thought of: names with *Esq.* at the end instead of a title such as *Mr.* or *Ms.* at the beginning, for example. By browsing through the records, you may spot complications in spacing or punctuation that you can easily fix, before you print the merged documents.

If you prefer the keyboard to the mouse, you will be disappointed to find that Word has no built-in keystrokes that let you see the data or change the current record. However, you can use the techniques we'll cover in Chapter 28 to add most of the relevant commands to menus or to attach them to your choice of shortcut keys. The Word commands that you'll need in order to define the menu items or shortcut keys are MailMergeViewData, MailMergeFirstRecord, MailMergePrevRecord, MailMergeNextRecord, and MailMergeLastRecord.

The two buttons at the far right end of the Mail Merge toolbar are also concerned with viewing or working with data. Second from the right is the Find Record button, which will open the Find In Field dialog box we discussed earlier. The rightmost button is the Edit Data Source button, which will open the Data Form dialog box.

Figure 21-18 lists all the Mail Merge toolbar buttons, including some that we'll cover in the next section.

| Button | Button Name | Action |
|---|---|---|
| Insert Merge Field | Insert Merge Field | Inserts a mail merge field into the main document |
| Insert Word Field | Insert Word Field | Inserts one of Word's special merge-related fields into the main document |
| « » ABC | View Merged Data | Replaces the merge fields in the main document, as they show on screen, with the appropriate data from the current record in the data file |
| ◄ | First Record | Moves to the first record in the data file |

*(continued)*

**FIGURE 21-18**

The Mail Merge toolbar buttons.

**FIGURE 21-18** *continued*

| Button | Button Name | Action |
|--------|-------------|--------|
| ◀ | Previous Record | Moves to the previous record in the data file |
| 1 | Go to Record | Lets you specify the record to go to in the data file |
| ▶ | Next Record | Moves to the next record in the data file |
| ▶❙ | Last Record | Moves to the last record in the data file |
| | Mail Merge Helper | Opens the Mail Merge Helper dialog box |
| | Check For Errors | Opens the Checking And Reporting Errors dialog box, which lets you either simulate or perform the mail merge and have Word either report errors as they occur or create a list of error messages |
| | Merge To New Document | Starts the actual mail merge and sends the result to a new document |
| | Merge To Printer | Starts the actual mail merge and sends the result to the printer |
| | Mail Merge | Opens the Merge dialog box, which lets you control the record selection and the output for a mail merge |
| | Find Record | Opens the Find In Field dialog box, which lets you search the data file for a match within a specific field |
| | Edit Data Source | Opens the Data Form dialog box |

## NEW!   How to use toolbar buttons to start a merge

There are several buttons on the Mail Merge toolbar that we skipped over. Just to the right of the Last Record button on the Mail Merge toolbar, you'll see the Mail Merge Helper button. Clicking on this button is equivalent to choosing the Tools Mail Merge menu command; both open the Mail Merge Helper dialog box.

Next comes a group of four buttons that are all concerned with giving the command to run a merge. We'll start with the rightmost of these, the Mail Merge button, and work our way left. When you click on the Mail Merge button, Word opens the Merge dialog box, which we'll discuss shortly. Choosing this button is equivalent to choosing Tools Mail Merge and then choosing the Merge button in the Mail Merge Helper dialog box.

The two buttons to the left of the Mail Merge button are shortcuts for starting a merge without going through the dialog box. The Merge To New Document button gives the command to run the mail merge and place the results in a single new document, with each individual merge document in its own section. The Merge To Printer button sends the merge documents directly to the printer.

The leftmost button in this group is the Check For Errors button. Click on it, or press Control-Shift-K, to open the Checking And Reporting Errors dialog box shown in Figure 21-19.

**FIGURE 21-19**

The Checking And Reporting Errors dialog box lets you check your data files for errors in form.

As you can see in the figure, Word gives you three choices for checking for errors in form—such as an extra comma in a comma-delimited file, which Word will see as indicating one too many fields in the record. You can choose to simulate the merge and have Word report errors in a new document, to actually run the merge and have Word pause to report each error it finds, or to run the merge without stopping but have Word report any errors in a new document.

If you have any doubts about your data having exactly the right format—as you might, for example, if you entered a great deal of data—you should use one of these options. Which one you choose is a matter of taste and of how much confidence you have in your data. Note that if you use either of the options that actually run the merge, Word will not stop to ask whether to merge to a new file or directly to a printer. Rather, it will use whichever choice is currently set in the Merge dialog box (to a new document, by default).

## Merge options

Once you've designated a data file to use and created the main document, complete with mail merge fields, you can start the mail merge by choosing any of the four toolbar buttons we've just mentioned or by choosing Tools Mail Merge and then choosing the Merge button in the Mail Merge Helper dialog box. If you choose the Mail Merge Helper's Merge button (or the Mail Merge button on the toolbar), you'll open the Merge dialog box, shown in Figure 21-20.

**FIGURE 21-20**

The Merge dialog box provides control over the mail merge output.

The Merge To pull-down list in the dialog box offers a minimum of two options: New Document and Printer. The New Document option creates a new document file with each individual merged document in its own section. This can be useful if you want to review the merged data before printing.

The Records To Be Merged section lets you merge all records in the data file or merge a range of records based on their positions in the data file (such as records 1 through 10). You can specify the range in the From and To boxes.

Keep in mind that you can use the sorting feature on the Database toolbar to arrange a data file so that all the records you want to merge are together in a group. You can then specify the group as a range of records.

The two option buttons in the When Merging Records section let you specify how to treat blank lines that result from empty fields. Consider a mailing list with some addresses that need only three lines and others that need a fourth line—for a company name, for example. You'll need to include a field for the company name in your main document. But when the address doesn't include a company name, you'll want to avoid printing a blank line between the name and the street address. The option button labeled Don't Print Blank Lines When Data Fields Are Empty, which is the default setting, tells Word not to print these blank lines. The Print Blank Lines When Data Fields Are Empty button tells Word to print them.

If you like, you can also define a query for a mail merge, to select a subset of records from the data file and sort them in a particular order. To define a query, choose the Query Options button to open the Query Options dialog box, shown in Figure 21-21. (You'll also find a Query Options button in the Mail Merge Helper dialog box.)

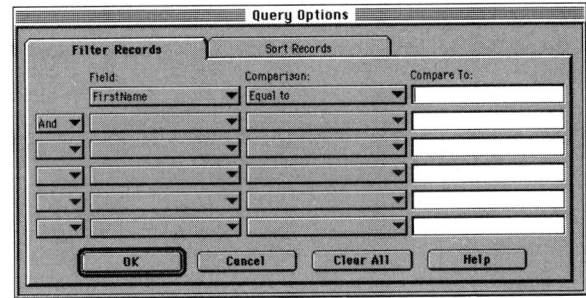

The Query Options dialog box lets you tell Word to select only those records that match a filter you define and to sort them in a specified order.

This is the same Query Options dialog box that we discussed in Chapter 18 in the context of importing data with the Insert Database command. Briefly, you use the Field and Comparison pull-down lists on the Filter Records card to specify the fields to base the selection on and the comparison to use. You then enter the field value for that comparison in the Compare To box for the appropriate row. The first box in all rows but the first lets you tie the criteria together with AND or OR. The other card in the dialog box, Sort Records, lets you choose up to three fields to sort by and lets you specify whether to use ascending or descending order for each. For more details on how to use the Query Options dialog box, see "How to define the database import options" on page 595.

After you finish defining a query, choose OK to close the Query Options dialog box and return to the Merge dialog box. At this point you may want to choose the Check Errors button. This will open the Checking And Reporting Errors dialog box, which we discussed in the preceding section, and it will give you a chance to check the effect of your settings.

The ability to define a query to select records is highly useful, but it can also be confusing at first. We strongly recommend that you test a new query definition by merging a relatively few records and sending the results to a new document, rather than risk wasting time and paper merging an entire data file and sending the results to the printer.

When you're satisfied with all your settings, choose Merge, and Word will run the merge, sending the output to your printer or to a new file. If you've chosen to merge to your printer, Word will open the Print dialog box before printing to let you set print options.

NEW!  ## Header files

The only time you'll need a header file is when your data file does not include the field names as headings in the first row. In those cases, you'll need to create a separate file that contains only the field headings. (Note that if you do attach a header file, the first row in your data file will be treated as data even if it actually contains headings.) Header files are useful if you routinely use data files in which the structure of the data files remains the same from one mail merge to the next, with data imported from other programs that cannot conveniently add headings as the first row.

Since the sample data file we used earlier included headings in the first row, we didn't need a header file. If you need one, the easiest way to create it is with the Mail Merge Helper dialog box. Choose Get Data, and then choose Header Options from the Get Data menu. In the Header Options dialog box, choose Create. Word will open the Create Header Source dialog box, which works the same way as the Create Data Source dialog box. You can use the same procedures we described for creating a data file to create the header file.

# Using Special Fields for Mail Merging

Word offers a number of special merge-related fields, including fields that insert text from other Word documents, fields that let you update specific information manually each time you merge a given main document, and fields that let you create logical criteria for printing selected portions of the main document.

You can enter these fields in your main document using any of the techniques described in Chapter 20. When you're working in a main document that's already attached to a data file or a header file, however, Word provides an easier way—two ways in fact—to enter many of these fields. One choice is to click on the Insert Word Field button on the Mail Merge toolbar to open a pull-down menu of these fields. Alternatively, you can press Control-Shift-F to open the Insert Merge Field dialog box, shown in Figure 21-22, which also offers a list of these fields.

**FIGURE 21-22**

The Insert Merge Field dialog box has a list of merge-related Word fields that you can use in a main document.

Insert Merge Field

| Mail Merge Fields: | Word Fields: | |
|---|---|---|
| FirstName | Ask... | OK |
| LastName | Fill-in... | Cancel |
| Address1 | If...Then | Help |
| Address2 | If...Then...Else | |
| City | Merge Record # | |
| State | Next Record | |
| PostalCode | Next Record If | |

The Insert Word Field pull-down menu is slightly different from the Word Fields list in the Insert Merge Field dialog box. In particular, the Merge Sequence # choice (for the MERGESEQ field) is available only on the pull-down menu, and the Quote choice (for the QUOTE field) is available only from the Word Fields list.

There's another difference between using the Insert Word Field pull-down menu and the Insert Merge Field dialog box. Some fields require more than just a field name. The FILLIN field, for example, requires a prompt that asks the user for information to fill in. When you insert one of these fields from the pull-down menu, Word will provide a dialog box with appropriately labeled text boxes for you to fill in the information. After you enter the required information and choose OK, Word will create the field for you and insert it into the text.

In contrast, when you insert the same field from the list in the Insert Merge Field dialog box, Word will not open a dialog box for the field. Instead, it will immediately insert the field, complete with reminders that show the form each field takes. To complete the field, you'll need to substitute the actual information for the reminders. In short, you get the same reminders for what to add, but in a less elegant form.

For purposes of this discussion, we'll ignore the Insert Word Field pull-down menu and assume that you're using the Insert Merge Field dialog box. If you understand the fields well enough to replace the reminders with the appropriate text, however, you should have no trouble with the dialog boxes you'll see if you use the pull-down menu. Here, then, is a look at each choice in the Word Fields list box.

 Because some of Word's terminology is a bit arcane, we'll occasionally use different terms than those Word uses, to aid understanding. When we use different terminology, however, we'll also mention the terms that Word uses.

## Ask

The first choice in the Word Fields list box is Ask, which will enter an ASK field in the main document. The most common reason for using the ASK field is to let you enter information in the main document by typing that information from the keyboard during the merge.

For example, suppose you want to create personalized letters, using the recipient's first name in some cases and a more formal form of address in others. You could enter the information as a field in the data file. But if several people in your office generate letters using the same file, the appropriate salutation may change depending on whose signature goes on the letter. In that case, you may want to enter the salutation with the ASK field.

As we discussed in Chapter 20, you can enter a field by pressing ⌘-F9 to enter the field characters { and } and then typing the text for the field inside the field characters. If you enter a bookmark name between the field characters, the result for the field will be the text defined by the bookmark. In this particular case, you'll define the bookmark text with the ASK field.

Start by creating a field using the bookmark name Salutation so that the appropriate line of your main document reads

Dear {Salutation}:

Now that you've designated where you want the information to go, you can enter the ASK field. We recommend placing all ASK fields at the beginning of the main document to make them easier to find if you need to modify them. The basic form of the ASK field is

{ASK Bookmark "Prompt"}

In this example, the bookmark is Salutation, and the prompt is the text you want Word to use to prompt users so that they will know what data to enter.

When Word comes across an ASK field during a mail merge, it will display the prompt as part of a dialog box and will wait for the user to type a response in the dialog box's text box. The response will define the bookmark text to use in the appropriate bookmark field or fields. For example, in this case you might define the ASK field as

{ASK Salutation "What greeting do you want for {MERGEFIELD FirstName} {MERGEFIELD LastName}?"}

This field will produce the dialog box shown in Figure 21-23. The prompt includes the results of the FirstName and LastName fields so that you can see the full name of the addressee. Without those fields, it would be difficult to know who the addressee was for each letter or what the salutation should be.

**FIGURE 21-23**

You can use mail merge fields in your ASK fields to make it easy to see which record is being processed.

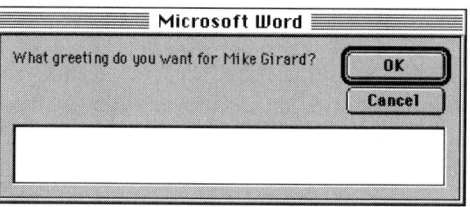

After you enter a response in the text box and choose OK, Word will treat your response much as it treats any other data, assigning it to the appropriate bookmark name. As with merge fields, you can use the same bookmark name in more than one place in the main document.

### How to create a default response to an ASK field

The ASK field has two option switches. You can create a default response with the \d switch, using the form

> {ASK Bookmark "Prompt" \d "Default"}

\d is the default switch. The text you enter as the default, following the switch, will appear automatically in the text box of the dialog box Word displays when it encounters the ASK field (for example, the dialog box shown in Figure 21-23).

### How to enter a response for all merged documents at one time

The other switch is \o, which tells Word to prompt for a response to an ASK field once at the beginning of a mail merge and use that response for all the merged documents, rather than prompt for each individual document. This is handy when you create many batches of documents from the same main document but want to be able to change one item for all the documents in each batch—such as the sender's name.

## Fill-In

The Fill-In choice in the Word Fields list box inserts a FILLIN field, which is similar to an ASK field in that it tells Word to prompt for a response that Word then uses in the merged document. The main difference is that the FILLIN field does not define a bookmark that you can then enter in any number of places within the document. Instead, the field itself marks the location for the data you're entering. The field takes the form

> {FILLIN "Prompt"}

As with the ASK field, you can include merge fields as part of the prompt. You can also use the same switches you use for the ASK field: \d for a default response and \o to prompt one time at the start of a mail merge, with the response used in all the merged documents.

## If...Then and If...Then...Else

The next two choices in the list box both insert an IF field. In either variation, the IF field provides great flexibility for personalizing merged documents. You can use it to have Word make decisions about what to include in each document, based on information in each data record.

The If...Then choice inserts a field in the form

> {IF ConditionalTest "TrueResult"}

The If…Then…Else choice inserts a field in the form

{IF ConditionalTest "TrueResult" "FalseResult"}

(Note that Word uses different terminology when it inserts this field, as we'll discuss in a moment.)

The first item, *ConditionalTest*, is an expression that Word can evaluate as either true or false. If *ConditionalTest* is true, the field will return *TrueResult*. If *ConditionalTest* is false, the field will return *FalseResult* for the If…Then…Else choice or nothing for the If…Then choice.

When Word inserts an IF field, it uses the term *Exp Op Exp* rather than *ConditionalTest*. *Exp Op Exp* is an abbreviation for *Expression1 Operator Expression2*, which is a literal representation of the format, as opposed to the descriptive *ConditionalTest*. Briefly, *ConditionalTest* compares two expressions using one of the conditional operators shown in Figure 21-24.

| Operator | Definition |
|----------|------------|
| > | Greater than |
| < | Less than |
| = | Equal to |
| >= | Greater than or equal to |
| <= | Less than or equal to |
| <> | Not equal to |

**FIGURE 21-24**

The operators available to an IF field.

You can use any of these operators with both text and numeric entries. With text entries, Word will use the ASCII value of the text to perform the test. For example, all of the following expressions are conditional tests:

{MStatus}="Single"

{NumItems}>100

{Spouse}<>""

Any expression that uses one of the conditional operators must be either true or false. Consider the conditional test {*NumItems*}>100. If the value of the *NumItems* variable in the current record is 100 or less, the result is false. If the value is greater than 100, the result is true.

Note also that Word uses the terms *TextIfTrue* and *TextIfFalse* when inserting the fields rather than the terms *TrueResult* and *FalseResult*. (However, the Help screen for the IF field refers to *TrueText* and *FalseText*.) But *TextIfTrue* and

*TextIfFalse* are somewhat misleading since these results need not be limited to text. They can, in fact, be fields, including ASK fields or nested IF fields. (The SET and INCLUDE fields, which we'll discuss later in this chapter, can be particularly useful as a result of an IF field.)

The actual text for the *TrueResult* or *FalseResult* returned by an IF field can be any length and can contain page-break markers and section-break markers. If the item consists of either a single word or a single merge field, you don't need to enclose it in quotation marks. In most situations, however, you'll probably use more than one word, so we recommend that you get in the habit of always using quotation marks. You can use the IF field anywhere in the main document.

One common use of the IF field is to determine whether a particular field in the current record contains an entry. For example, suppose your data file stores names in three fields: F, MI, and L (for first name, middle initial, and last name). If you want to include a person's full name in your main document, you might use the merge fields

{MERGEFIELD F} {IF {MI}<>"" "{MERGEFIELD MI} "}{MERGEFIELD L}

Notice that the conditional test *{MI}<>""* tests for the presence of an entry in the MI field of the data file. If there's an entry for the field, the result of the conditional test is true (the MI field is not empty), and the IF field will use whatever you've defined as *TrueResult*—in this case, the MI field plus a space. If the MI field is empty, the result of the test is false, and the IF field will use whatever you've defined as *FalseResult*. Since we didn't specify *FalseResult*, Word will print nothing, and you won't wind up with an extra space between the first and last names.

You can also use the IF field to print text that isn't part of your data file. For example, assume your data file has a field named Spouse that contains the name of each customer's spouse—if he or she has one. You can use this information to personalize a message, using a field like this:

{IF {Spouse}<>"" "Of course, we'd also be thrilled if {Spouse} could accompany you! The more, the merrier!" "Please feel free to invite a guest to help us celebrate!"}

If any given record includes a spouse's name, Word will print the first sentence in the merged letter, including the spouse's name. If the Spouse field is empty, the test condition will be false, and Word will print the second sentence, inviting the customer to bring a guest.

You can also combine IF fields to create more sophisticated conditional tests. For example, to create an AND condition, nest IF fields so that the second field is the *TrueResult* of the first. Consider the following IF field:

{IF State="CA" {IF Married="Y" "We have a special rate in our California office for married couples."}}

In this case, both conditions must be true for Word to include the sentence in the merge document. If the state is California, the first IF condition is satisfied, but its *TrueResult* is another IF field. If the Married field is Y, the second IF field is also true, and Word will print the sentence. But because neither IF statement includes a *FalseResult*, Word will print nothing if either condition is false.

The easiest way to create an OR condition is to use two separate IF fields with the same *TrueResult*, such as

{IF State="CA" "We have special rates for California and Washington residents."} {IF State="WA" "We have special rates for California and Washington residents."}

Word will test each field separately and will print the message if either condition is true.

You can also use nested IF fields to take full advantage of If...Then...Else logic. For example, suppose you have two discount rates—one for California residents and one for married couples—and suppose you want to mention the California discount only to California residents and the married-couple discount only to married couples outside California. In that case, you would enter the fields as:

{IF State="CA" "We have special rates for California residents." {IF Married="Y" "We have special rates for married couples."}}

## Merge Record #

The Merge Record # choice inserts a MERGEREC field. The form of the field is simply {MERGEREC}. When Word comes across a MERGEREC field during a merge, it places the number of the current mail merge record in the merge document, using 1 for the first record in the data file, 2 for the second record, and so on. The most common use for the MERGEREC field is as a debugging tool when you are creating and testing main documents, especially those that use the Next Record, Next Record If, and Skip Record If fields.

## Next Record and Next Record If

When you set mail merge to send output directly to the printer, Word will start each merged document on a new page. Similarly, when you set it to send output to a new document, Word will put each merge document in its own section, with the section break defined to start a new page.

In most cases, this approach will be exactly what you want—starting a new page for each copy of a form letter, for example. However, in some situations you'll want data from more than one record on the same page. In those cases, you can choose Next Record or Next Record If from the Word Fields list box to enter the NEXT field or the NEXTIF field in your main document. Either field will prevent Word from automatically starting a new page for each record.

### The NEXT field

The NEXT field tells Word to move to the next record in the data file and fill the remaining MERGEFIELD fields in the main document, without starting a new page. The form of the field is simply *{NEXT}*.

For example, suppose you want to create a list of client names, with 10 names on each page. If you simply create a main document with the fields

{MERGEFIELD FirstName} {MERGEFIELD LastName}

Word will print one client name on each page. If you repeat the line 10 times, Word will print the same name 10 times.

To print 10 different names on each page, use the NEXT field in front of each line except the first. Lines 2 through 10 will read:

{NEXT}{MERGEFIELD FirstName} {MERGEFIELD LastName}

Each time Word reaches a NEXT field, it will move to the next record in the data file and use the entries for that record until it reaches another NEXT field or reaches the end of the main document.

### The NEXTIF field

The NEXTIF field is equivalent to a NEXT field placed inside an IF field, using the form

{IF ConditionalTest "{NEXT}"}

Instead, you can use the simpler form

{NEXTIF ConditionalTest}

to get exactly the same effect.

The NEXTIF field produces either of two effects, depending on the result of the conditional test. If the result is false, the NEXTIF field will have no effect whatsoever. If the result is true, the field will act like a NEXT field, telling Word to read the next record of the data document and use the entries for that record until it reaches another NEXT or NEXTIF field or the end of the main document. You'll note that Word uses the term *Expression* rather than *ConditionalTest* when it inserts the NEXTIF field into your document. This is inconsistent with the terminology the program uses for the IF field, however, since the actual format for *ConditionalTest* is *Expression1 Operator Expression2* (which, oddly enough, is the format Word uses in the NEXTIF Help screen).

## Quote

The Quote choice in the Word Fields list box inserts the QUOTE field into a main document. The QUOTE field, which inserts literal text, takes the form

{QUOTE "LiteralText"}

where *LiteralText* is the text (enclosed in quotation marks) that you want to insert into the document. Word will update the QUOTE field as soon as you modify its field code. The most likely reason for using the QUOTE field is to specify an ANSI character as an ANSI code. Simply put the code outside the quotation marks that enclose *LiteralText*.

For example, if you enter the field

{QUOTE "This Book, c 1995"}

in a document, the field result will be *This Book, c 1995.* If you enter the field

{QUOTE "This Book,  " 169 "1995"}

the field result will be *This Book, ©1995.* Note that the code 169 appears outside two separate sets of quotation marks, not inside quotation marks. And because 169 appears outside the quotation marks, Word substitutes ANSI character 169 (the copyright symbol).

## Set Bookmark

The Set Bookmark choice inserts a SET field, which takes the form

{SET Bookmark "text"}

(Word uses the term *data* rather than *text*, but to avoid confusion, we prefer reserving the term *data* for information stored in the data file.)

The SET field serves much the same function as an ASK field using the \o switch. By entering the bookmark name in one or more fields in the main document (using ⌘-F9 to enter the field characters around the bookmark name) and then defining the text for the bookmark with the SET field, you can enter the text for that bookmark one time, and Word will use the same text for every copy of the merged document.

The main difference between defining the bookmark text with an ASK field and defining it with a SET field is that with an ASK field Word prompts you for the text when you start the mail merge. With a SET field you enter the text directly in the main document. Another difference is that with the ASK field you must enter the text each time you run a merge. With the SET field the text remains stored in the document until you change it.

Because the SET field and the ASK field with the \o switch are so similar in function, they are almost interchangeable. However, the SET field is the preferred choice when you want to use the same text repeatedly and change it only occasionally. The ASK field with the \o switch is the preferred choice when the text rarely remains the same from one merge run to the next or when you want to ensure that you enter the correct text each time.

T
I
P

We recommend placing SET fields at the beginning of the main document so you can find them easily if you need to change them.

## Skip Record If

The Skip Record If choice enters a SKIPIF field in your main document. Like the NEXTIF field, SKIPIF is a variation on the IF field. The form of the field is

{SKIPIF ConditionalTest}

The effect of the field depends on the result of the conditional test. If the result is false, the field has no effect. If the result is true, however, SKIPIF tells Word to skip the current record, move to the next record in the data file, and start a new page, starting at the beginning of the main document. The actual format for *ConditionalTest* is *Expression1 Operator Expression2*, as with the IF field, although Word enters the SKIPIF field as *{SKIPIF Expression}*.

## Merge Sequence #

As we mentioned earlier, the menu attached to the Insert Word Field button on the Mail Merge toolbar offers one choice that isn't in the Insert Merge Field dialog box: Merge Sequence #. If you choose this from the Insert Word Field menu, Word will insert a MERGESEQ field at the cursor position. The form of the field is simply *{MERGESEQ}*.

MERGESEQ is similar to the MERGEREC field in that when Word comes across a MERGESEQ field during a merge, it places a number in the merge document to represent the current record. However, the number for the MERGESEQ field is based on the order of the mail merge, not on the position of the record in the data file. If you're merging record numbers 50 through 100, for example, the MERGEREC field will return the numbers from 50 through 100, whereas the MERGESEQ field will return numbers from 1 through 50. This can come in handy when you want to create a sequential set of numbers, such as invoice numbers or serial numbers.

## The INCLUDETEXT field

Although it is not available through the Insert Merge Field dialog box, one other field can be especially useful for mail merging and is generally considered a merge-related field: the INCLUDETEXT field. Since it is not in the Word Fields list box, you'll need to insert it using one of the techniques we discussed in Chapter 20, such as the Insert Field command.

The INCLUDETEXT field lets you take large sections of text from another Word document file and insert them into your merge documents. The field takes one of the two forms

{INCLUDETEXT "Filename"}

{INCLUDETEXT "Filename" Bookmark}

where *Filename* is the name of the file containing the text you want to insert and *Bookmark* is a selection of text that you've defined as a bookmark in that file.

There are at least two situations in which you might want to use the INCLUDETEXT field to place text in your merge documents rather than simply entering that text in the main document. First, you can use the field to include text from the same file in any number of main documents, saving the time, effort, and disk space required to enter the text in each of several files. Second, you can use the conditional fields discussed in this chapter to insert different INCLUDETEXT fields in different merged documents. This makes it easy to provide different versions of the merged document with large sections of text that vary, yet still have the variations automatically controlled by some aspect of the merged record.

# Mail Merging Envelopes, Mailing Labels, and Catalogs

There are four types of main documents that Word automatically recognizes. If you choose Tools Mail Merge and then click on the Create button in the Mail Merge Helper dialog box, you'll see choices for Envelopes, Mailing Labels, and Catalog in addition to the choice for Form Letters. You can choose any of these when you first specify a main document. You can also change the document type at any time by reopening the dialog box, choosing the Create button, and choosing a different type of main document from the menu. If you started from an existing main document, Word will ask you whether you want to change the document type or create a new main document. Simply choose the appropriate answer to continue.

## Envelopes and labels

If you designate a main document as a Mailing Label or Envelope type, Word will add a Setup button rather than an Edit button to the Main Document section of the Mail Merge Helper dialog box. After designating your data source, choose Setup. Word will open either the Label Options dialog box, shown in Figure 21-25, or the Envelope Options dialog box, shown in Figure 21-26, as appropriate.

You can use the dialog box options to set the envelope or label format. We explored both of these dialog boxes in Chapter 8; for details on how to use them, see "Envelopes and Labels" starting on page 256.

When you finish with the Label Options or the Envelope Options dialog box, choose OK. Word will close the dialog box and open either the Create Labels dialog box or the Envelope Address dialog box. The options in both dialog boxes will be essentially the same, with a text box, an Insert Merge Field button, and an Insert Postal Bar Code button, as shown in Figure 21-27.

**FIGURE 21-25**

If you designate the main document as a Mailing Labels type, Word will provide a Setup button that opens the Label Options dialog box.

**FIGURE 21-26**

If you designate the main document as an Envelopes type, Word will provide a Setup button that opens the Envelope Options dialog box.

**FIGURE 21-27**

When you finish with the Label Options or the Envelope Options dialog box, Word will open a dialog box like this one.

You can use the buttons to create an address format in the text box. To insert a field in the address, place the cursor where you want the field, click on the Insert Merge Field button and hold down the mouse button to see a menu of all the fields in the attached data file, and then choose a field from the menu.

To insert a postal bar code, choose the Insert Postal Bar Code button. Word will open a dialog box that will let you specify which merge field represents the zip code and which represents the street address. You'll also find a check box to add a FIM code to an envelope if you need to. (If you don't know what a FIM code is, you almost certainly don't need it.)

 When you first return to your document, you may get a text message about invalid zip codes. Don't worry. This message will be replaced with the proper symbols when you view your data or merge the document.

When you choose OK to close the Create Labels or Create Envelope Address dialog box, Word will format the main document either as an envelope or as mailing label stock. Word will also add the merge fields to the document, return you to the Mail Merge Helper dialog box, and change the Setup button to an Edit button. Figures 21-28 and 21-29 show sample main documents for labels and envelopes.

**FIGURE 21-28**

The Mail Merge Helper automated much of the work in creating this main document for merging labels.

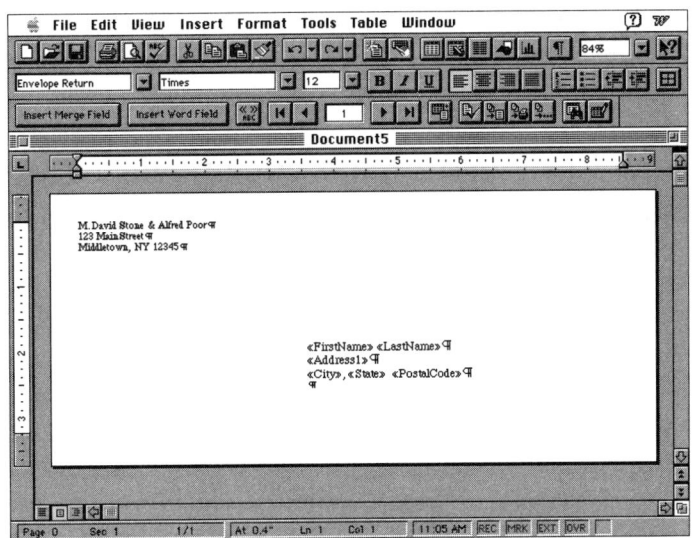

Although formatting a main document for envelopes takes less work than formatting one for labels, the Mail Merge Helper automates the job to make it even easier.

Once you have created the main document, mail merging envelopes or labels is much the same as mail merging form letters. However, we recommend that you take a look at Chapter 8 for details about Word's envelope and label features.

## Catalogs

The fourth, and last, type of main document Word recognizes is the Catalog type. This choice is meant for producing repetitive information such as you'd find in a catalog, a directory, or even a simple list.

When you define a main document as a Catalog type, Word does not start a new page for the merge documents each time it comes to the end of the main document. Rather, it continues on the same page, using the next record. The result is equivalent to defining a main document that repeats itself as many times as there are records in the data file and starts each repetition with a NEXT field, to prevent starting a new page. Use the Catalog choice when you want to print a continuous list of data, fitting as many repetitions of the merged information on each page as possible.

## How to change to a different data file and main document type

As we've indicated, you can change the main document type at any time by opening the Mail Merge Helper dialog box, choosing the Create button, and choosing any of the main document types from the Create menu. You can also choose a different data file for a main document at any time. Simply open the

Mail Merge Helper dialog box, choose Get Data, and then choose either Create Data Source or Open Data Source. You can then specify or create a different data file, using any of the techniques we've already discussed.

## How to change a main document back to a normal Word document

The Create menu in the Mail Merge Helper dialog box also offers the choice Restore To Normal Word Document. If you decide, for whatever reason, that you don't want to use a given file as a main mail merge document anymore, you can change it back to a normal document file simply by opening the Mail Merge Helper dialog box and choosing Restore To Normal Word Document from the Create menu. Then choose Yes when Word asks for confirmation. When you return to the document, you'll find that Word will no longer show the Mail Merge toolbar in the document window.

# Creating Forms

Although forms are not a mail merge feature, they provide a similar capability, making it easy to create documents combining information that remains the same on all copies of the form with information that varies from one document to the next. They are also similar in that you fill in fields to add the variable information. Instead of using a main document, however, you store the form as a template and use the template to create a new document when you want to fill in a form.

We'll cover templates in detail in Chapters 27 and 28. For the moment, you only need to know that creating a template is just like creating any other document except that you save it as a template instead of as a document. After you save a template, however, you can open new documents based on the template. Word will automatically insert text, fields, and other items it finds in the template into the new document. You can then edit the new document without disturbing the template.

The basic building blocks of a Word form are the FORMCHECKBOX, FORMDROPDOWN, and FORMTEXT fields. However, these form fields are not ordinary fields. If you try to enter them with the techniques described in Chapter 20, you'll find that Word doesn't recognize them. Instead, you must enter them from a menu, using the techniques we'll explain here.

As a simple example, we'll create a standard phone message form. To create the form, start by choosing File New. Choose the Template option in the

New section of the dialog box, accept Normal as the template to base the new template on, and then choose OK to open a new, untitled template.

Next fill in the text, lines, and other non-varying features that you want in the form, including a heading, labels for fields, and so on. If you like, you can create a table to define a grid for entering text and fields and use the Format Borders And Shading command to build lines or boxes with the techniques discussed in Chapter 11.

If you prefer, you can use Word's drawing tools to add lines and boxes. To make the drawing tools available, choose View Toolbars, check the Drawing check box, and choose OK to return to the document, with the Drawing toolbar showing. For more details, see "Using Word's Drawing Tools" starting on page 522.

Once you've entered the background text, your screen should look something like the one shown in Figure 21-30. At this point, you can enter the form fields.

**FIGURE 21-30**

Starting with this phone message format, we'll create a phone message form.

## How to enter a drop-down form field

To enter the first form field, move the cursor to where you want the field—in this case, just after the To: label on the first line below the heading. Then choose Insert Form Field to open the Form Field dialog box, shown in Figure 21-31 on the next page.

FIGURE 21-31

To insert a form field, start with the Form Field dialog box.

As you can see in the figure, there are three types of form fields to choose from: text, check box, and drop-down. An Options button lets you set options for each individual form field. For our example, we'll assume you have a limited number of people in your office, which means it makes sense to create a drop-down list for the To: field. Choose the Drop-Down type, and then choose the Options button to open the Drop-Down Form Field Options dialog box, shown in Figure 21-32.

**FIGURE 21-32**

The Drop-Down Form Field Options dialog box lets you customize each drop-down form field.

The dialog box shown in Figure 21-32 offers a number of features that we'll merely mention in passing. For example, the two pull-down lists in the Run Macro On section give you the option of telling Word to automatically run a macro when you either move to or leave the field. The text box in the Field Settings box lets you define a bookmark name, so a macro can refer to the field. The check box lets you enable the drop-down list so users can open it when they're filling in the form. Also notice the Add Help Text button. This button opens a dialog box you can use to add Help messages that will show in the status bar or in response to pressing Help when the cursor is in the form field.

To create the drop-down list, enter each item for the list in the Drop-Down Item text box, then choose Add. If you make a mistake, you can delete the item by highlighting it and choosing Remove. If you want to move an item to a different position in the list, highlight it and choose the up or down arrow button to the right of the list box. When you're done, choose OK to return to the editing screen, with the form field entered at the cursor position.

## How to enter a text form field

Most of the other fields in the Phone Memo form will be text form fields, which you will use to type in some text when you fill in the form. To enter a text form field, position the cursor where you want the field. Then choose Insert Form Field, choose Text type, and choose Options. Word will open the Text Form Field Options dialog box, shown in Figure 21-33.

Many of the options in this dialog box are the same as for the drop-down form field. For this example, we're interested only in the options that are specific to the text form field.

**FIGURE 21-33**

The Text Form Field Options dialog box lets you customize each text field.

The text field-specific options start with the Type pull-down list. The list includes six choices: Regular Text, Number (the field will accept numbers only), Date (the field will accept dates only), Current Date (the field will automatically enter the current date), Current Time (the field will automatically enter the current time), and Calculation (lets you enter an = (Formula) field within the form field to calculate a result).

For the phone memo form we're creating, you would want to use Regular Text form fields for the fields that go with the From:, Of:, and Message: labels. For the Time: label, you'd probably want to add both a Current Date and a Current Time form field after the label.

Other options that you can set for a text form field include a maximum length and a default entry. For regular text, you can also choose a capitalization format from the Text Format drop-down list: Uppercase, Lowercase, First Capital (the first character of the entry is capitalized), or Title Case (the first character of each word is capitalized). With the possible exception of setting a maximum length, however, these other options are irrelevant for our sample form. To finish entering each field after you set the options, choose OK. (Note in passing that for dates, times, and numbers, you'll be able to choose from an appropriate set of formatting options as well.)

## How to enter a check box form field

All that remains in our sample form is to create two check boxes for the Will Call Back and Please Call items on the form. To enter a check box form field, position the cursor where you want the field. Choose Insert Form Field, then Check Box, and choose the Options button to open the Check Box Form Field Options dialog box, shown in Figure 21-34.

**FIGURE 21-34**

The Check Box Form Field Options dialog box lets you customize each check box form field.

Here again, most of the choices in this dialog box are similar to the ones we mentioned briefly when discussing the drop-down field options. Only four items are specific to the check box form field. The choices in the Default Value box let you specify whether the check box should be checked as a default. For this form, we'll choose Not Checked for both boxes. The Check Box Size options let you define a size for the check box, or let Word automatically determine the size. We'll use the Auto choice for both check boxes. When you're finished with the dialog box, choose OK to close it and insert the check box form field.

## Finishing touches

Once you've finished entering the form fields, you can add any finishing touches you like to the form: color, shading, lines, boxes, and so forth.

When the form is finished, you must choose Tools Protect Document, choose the Forms option in the Protect Document dialog box, and then choose OK. If you don't set this option, users will be able to move anywhere within the document when they fill in the form and can accidentally change the supposedly static text. If you set the protection feature, users will be limited to moving to the fields and won't be able to change the form itself. After you've set the protection feature, you can save the form and close the file.

Word also provides a Forms toolbar that you may find convenient to use. You can add the toolbar to the screen by choosing Insert Form Field and then choosing the Show Toolbar button. You'll see buttons on the toolbar for inserting each of the three kinds of form fields and for opening the appropriate Options dialog box for a currently selected field. You'll also find buttons for inserting a table, inserting a frame, adding or removing shading, and turning on the form protection feature. Figure 21-35 shows each of the toolbar buttons and describes their function.

| Button | Button Name | Action |
|---|---|---|
| | Text Form Field | Inserts a default text form field |
| | Check Box Form Field | Inserts a default check box form field |
| | Drop-Down Form Field | Inserts a default drop-down form field |
| | Form Field Options | Opens the appropriate Options dialog box for the currently selected form field |
| | Insert Table | Same as the Insert Table button on the Standard toolbar. Inserts a table or lets you modify an existing one |
| | Insert Frame | Inserts a new empty frame or adds a frame around the current selection |
| | Form Field Shading | Turns form field shading on or off throughout the document (form fields are shaded by default) |
| | Protect Form | Protects the current document as a form so that changes can be made only to the contents of form fields |

**FIGURE 21-35**

The Form Field toolbar.

## How to fill in a form on your computer

Once you've created a form as a template, you can use it whenever you like. For example, choose File New and specify the form you just created as the template to use. The new file should look much like the one shown in Figure 21-36.

**FIGURE 21-36**

If you open a new file using the form template, you'll see a finished phone message form like this one.

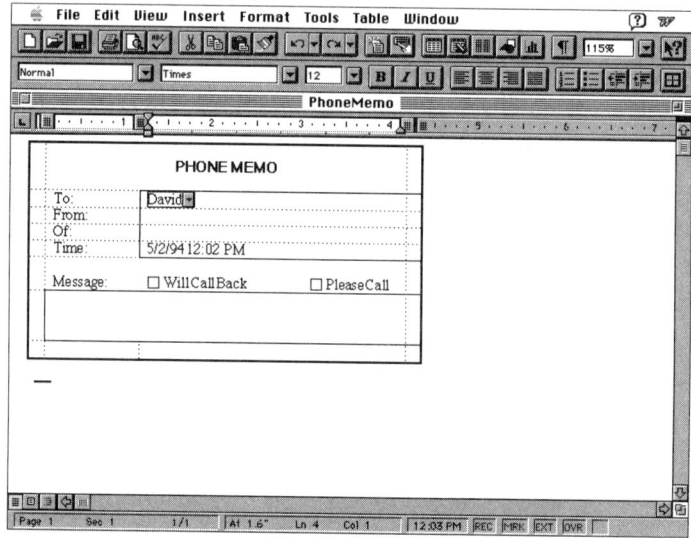

When you create the new file based on the form template, Word will automatically fill in the current date and time in the appropriate fields. You can fill in the rest of the form in much the same way that you make choices in a dialog box—tabbing or clicking to move from field to field, entering text, checking a check box, and selecting from a drop-down list. In fact, with the form protection feature on, you'll find that you can't move anywhere outside of the fields, so that filling in the form is almost identical to working in a dialog box. You can even toggle the checks in the check boxes on and off by moving to a check box and pressing the Spacebar.

# Topic Finder

# 22

# Tables of Contents & Indexes

O ne of the most time-consuming tasks involved in creating a document is developing a reference aid such as an index, a table of contents, a table of figures, or a table of authorities. Word takes much of the tedium out of this chore with its index and table features.

The steps for creating an index and for creating various kinds of tables are similar. In all cases, you enter markers in the body of your document to flag the entries you want to include. The markers can be fields for indexes or tables, or, for tables of contents and tables of figures, they can be your choice of paragraph styles. In all cases also, you use the Insert Index And Tables command to enter a field that compiles the final result.

We'll cover the basics of creating tables and indexes first, and then look at how to create them for large documents broken into several files. Because Word's indexing and table features are based on fields, you should make sure you're familiar with the concepts we presented in Chapter 20 before you read this chapter.

# A Note on Index-Related and Table-Related Fields

If you're familiar with Word's fields, you can create all the index-related and table-related fields in Word using any of the techniques covered in Chapter 20. Most users, however, will find that the special tools Word provides for creating these particular fields are far easier to use than the tools for creating fields in general.

For one thing, if you choose your options from a dialog box, you don't have to worry about learning the codes, or switches, Word uses to change settings for the various fields. To the contrary, Word will enter them for you automatically, along with the rest of the field. Even if you're a longtime Word user who has memorized the switches for each index- and table-related field, you'll find that many of these more specialized tools will save you work. For example, the Mark Index Entry dialog box includes an option that will mark all occurrences of a given word or phrase throughout your document with a single command. (The technical term for features like this is "Pretty slick.")

Because you don't need to learn all the details of how each field operates, we won't look at the fields themselves in much detail in this chapter. But we will explain them well enough to show you how to change the text entry for each marker field, or otherwise modify the field, without having to delete the field and redefine it.

If you're the sort of person who wants to know what's going on under the hood, you can easily learn more about any field discussed in this chapter, including the details of the various switches for that field. Start by creating the field using the tools we'll discuss here. Next, for those fields that show field results in the form of an index or a table, toggle the view to show the field code by placing the cursor or selection in the field result and pressing Shift-F9. Then press the Help key to bring up the Help screen that explains the switches for that field.

# Creating a Table of Contents

Word gives you a choice for marking entries for a table of contents. If you've used the outline feature (discussed in Chapter 19) or styles (discussed in Chapters 12 and 19) in your document, you can tell Word to create a table of contents directly from the headings in your text. Alternatively, you can enter TC fields to indicate entries for the table of contents. We'll cover both techniques, starting with styles. But first there's one issue you need to consider before you create a table of contents—or any other table, for that matter: the effect of the table on page numbers.

## How to number pages in a table of contents

Normally you'll want to put the table of contents at the beginning of your document. If you simply add it there, however, it will change the pagination for the rest of your text, pushing the text forward by as many lines as the table uses. You'll then usually want to add a page break after the table, but that will also change pagination, so you'll have to generate a new table of contents. Add more front matter, such as a table of figures, and you'll change the pagination once again.

The elegant solution to this problem is the one that most books use: Create a separate numbering scheme for your table of contents pages, along with any other front matter such as the title page and the acknowledgments page. A common scheme is to use lowercase Roman numerals (i, ii, iii, and so on) for this part of the document.

Word can manage this trick easily. To number the front matter pages separately from the rest of the document, first make sure the table of contents is in its own section, with other front matter if appropriate. (You can insert a section break by choosing Insert Break, specifying any of the section-break options, and then choosing OK. In this case, you'll probably want to use the Next Page option. We discussed section-break options as they apply to multi-section documents in "Multisection Documents" on page 455.)

Next place the cursor anywhere in the section containing the table of contents. If you want to use page numbers only, without additional text in the header or footer, you can choose Insert Page Numbers and then choose the Format button to open the Page Number Format dialog box. Open the Number Format pull-down list, highlight the format you want to use, and then choose OK to close the dialog box and return to the Page Numbers dialog box.

To finish, open the Position pull-down list, and choose either the Top Of Page (Header) or the Bottom Of Page (Footer) option. Then open the Alignment pull-down list, choose an alignment option, and choose OK. Repeat the process in the next section of the document, choosing an appropriate format in the Page Number Format dialog box and setting the numbering to start at 1 by entering the number 1 in the Start At text box.

If you want to add text to the header or footer, you'll need to use the View Header And Footer command. For details on creating a header or footer, see "Creating headers and footers" starting on page 153 and "How to change page numbering from one section to another" starting on page 461.

If you created the table of contents before you put it in its own section, be sure to update it after you've adjusted all the page numbers: Simply place the cursor or selection anywhere in the table and press F9.

# How to build a table of contents from styles

In Chapter 19, we discussed how to assign a special set of style names to a document's headings. Major headings use the Heading 1 style; subheadings use Heading 2, Heading 3, and so on, up to as many as nine levels of headings. For documents that use headings, these styles provide the easiest way to create a table of contents. If you haven't already assigned heading styles to the document, you can assign them using any of the techniques we covered in Chapters 12 and 19.

Word will also let you use any paragraph style or styles to flag paragraphs that you want to include as entries in the table of contents. In most cases, however, heading styles will be the preferred choice, since the paragraphs you'll want to include in a table of contents will almost always be section headings. For this discussion, then, we'll assume that you'll normally be using heading styles when creating a table of contents from styles.

## How to compile a table of contents using heading styles

After you create a document that includes heading styles, you can compile the table of contents by moving the cursor to the position where you want the table—usually the beginning of the document. Then choose the Insert Index And Tables command. Word will open the Index And Tables dialog box, shown in Figure 22-1. The dialog box offers four tabbed cards, including the Table Of Contents card.

**FIGURE 22-1**

To compile a table of contents, first choose Insert Index And Tables to open the Index And Tables dialog box, and then choose the Table Of Contents card.

Most of the options on the Table Of Contents card are concerned with defining the format for the table—a subject we'll return to later. For the moment, we only want to choose the Options button to open the Table Of Contents Options dialog box, shown in Figure 22-2.

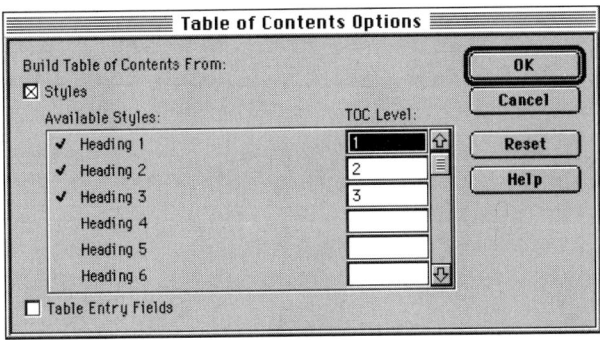

**FIGURE 22-2**

To tell Word how to compile a table of contents, choose Options from the Table Of Contents card to open this dialog box.

The Table Of Contents Options dialog box offers two check boxes that let you tell Word whether to use styles, table entry fields, or both. By default, Word checks the Styles check box. You can then specify which styles to use.

When you compile a table of contents from paragraphs formatted with specific styles, Word will look for the paragraphs with those styles and use the text from those paragraphs in the table of contents. As you can see in Figure 22-2, the Available Styles section of the dialog box includes a list of the heading styles, plus a TOC Level text box for each. The text boxes let you specify whether to include each style and, if so, at what level.

By default, Word will include the first three levels of heading styles. Paragraphs formatted with the Heading 1 style will become first-level entries, paragraphs formatted with the Heading 2 style will become second-level entries, and paragraphs formatted with the Heading 3 style will become third-level entries. You can easily change this, however. For example, if you've used Heading 1 for a book title and Heading 2 for your chapter titles, you can tell Word not to include Heading 1 paragraphs in the table of contents and to treat Heading 2 paragraphs as first-level entries. Simply delete the number from the TOC Level text box for Heading 1, enter *1* in the text box for Heading 2, and adjust the TOC Level boxes for the other heading levels accordingly. You can also set the same level for two or more styles. If you've made changes and then decide that you want to return to the default, choose the Reset button.

After you've specified the appropriate levels for the styles, choose OK to accept the settings and return to the Table Of Contents card. Then choose OK again to compile the table.

Word will start by looking to see whether a table of contents already exists in the document. If it finds one, it will highlight the table and ask whether you want to replace the existing table of contents. Choose Yes, No (to add a second table), or Cancel, as appropriate. If the cursor or selection was in a table of contents when you gave the command, the No option won't be available and your choices will be OK and Cancel.

Word can find a table of contents easily because the table is actually a TOC field, not ordinary text. To toggle between seeing the table of contents, which is the TOC field result, and seeing the field code, place your cursor or selection in the field, and press Shift-F9.

If you don't already have a table of contents in the document, or if you chose Yes or OK in response to Word's question, Word will repaginate the document, search for the heading styles, and compile the table of contents, complete with page numbers. Word will finish by inserting the table at the cursor position—or at the same position as the previous table of contents if you've chosen to replace an existing table.

Note that when compiling a table of contents, Word will ignore hidden text. Note too that if you need to interrupt the compilation for any reason, you can press Esc.

Figure 22-3 shows a sample table of contents. Each entry contains the table of contents text, followed by a tab with dot leaders, the page number, and a paragraph mark to end the entry. Note that when Word creates a table of contents, it adds a set of TOC styles to the document's list of styles. If you look at the Style drop-down list on the Formatting toolbar or choose Format Style and look at the list of styles in use, you'll see that the list now includes the style names TOC 1, TOC 2, and so on through TOC 9. Later in this chapter, we'll discuss how to change the table's format by modifying these styles.

**FIGURE 22-3**

When Word compiles a table of contents, it adds styles to the document's list of styles and applies those styles to the table of contents entries.

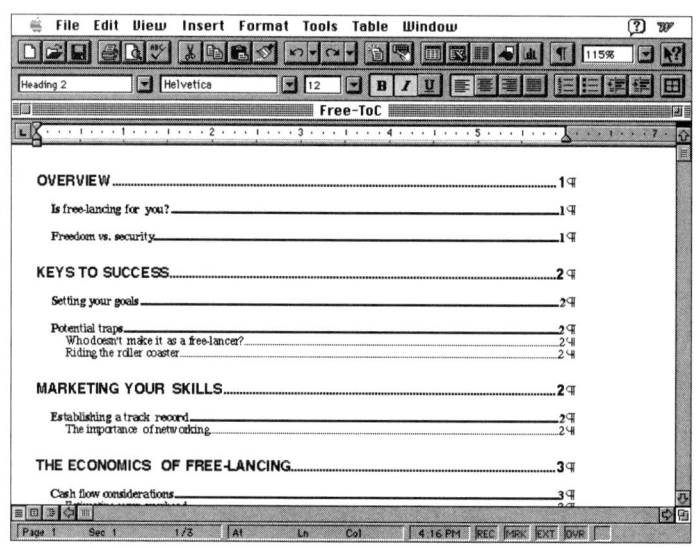

## How to update a table of contents

To update a document's table of contents, use the Insert Index And Tables command, or place the cursor or selection anywhere in the table and press F9 to update the field. If you use F9, Word will respond with a dialog box that lets you choose to update the entire table or to update the page numbers only. (The second choice is useful if you've applied direct formatting to the table and you want Word to leave the formatting alone.) Choose the appropriate setting, and then choose OK to update the table.

The best time to compile or update a table of contents is immediately before you print the document. If you edit or reorganize the document after updating, the page numbers may change, and the table will no longer be accurate.

## How to build a table of contents from fields

If you don't want to use headings as table of contents entries, or if you need more entries than you have headings, you can use TC fields to create the entries—either instead of or in addition to using paragraphs formatted with particular styles.

The TC field takes the form

{TC "text" [switches]}

where *text* is the text you want to appear in the table of contents. Figure 22-4 on the next page shows an example of a document where TC fields can come in handy. The first TC field in Figure 22-4 is at the beginning of the text. The second, {TC "Is free-lancing for you?"}, is near the bottom of the screen. The first field defines a table of contents entry for a section of text that doesn't have its own heading. The second field repeats text that's functioning as a heading but is part of the same paragraph as body text, so you can't format the heading with its own paragraph style.

Note that when you use TC fields, you must specify the full entry for the table of contents, even if the text is already in your document. (Don't worry about the switches in these examples just yet. Word will enter them for you.)

Note too that a TC field's sole purpose is to mark table entries (including entries for other kinds of tables, as we'll discuss later in this chapter). There are no field results, so you won't see a difference if you toggle between viewing field codes and viewing field results. When you enter the field, however, Word will format it as hidden. If you want to see it, either choose the Show/Hide ¶ button on the Standard toolbar or choose Tools Options, choose the View card, and check the Hidden Text check box.

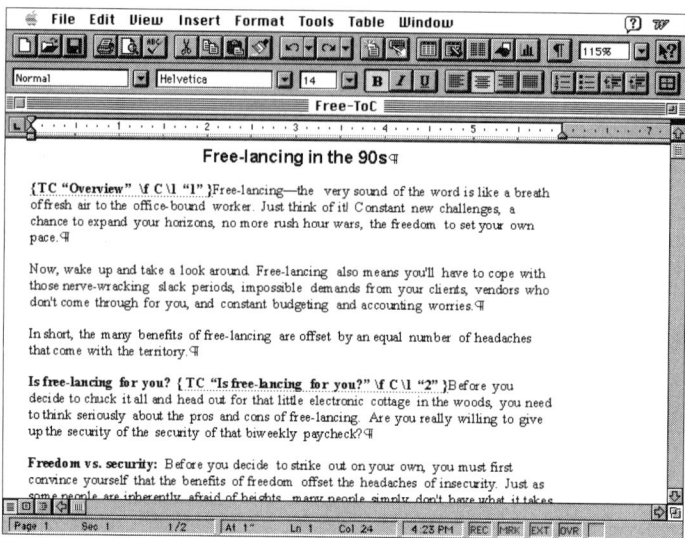

FIGURE 22-4

This sample document includes two TC fields.

## How to enter a TC field

The easiest way to enter a TC field, by far, is with the Mark Table Of Contents Entry dialog box, shown in Figure 22-5.

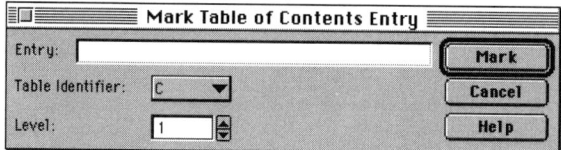

**FIGURE 22-5**

This dialog box makes it easy to enter a TC field.

To use the dialog box, first position the cursor where you want the field. Alternatively, if all or part of the text you want to use for the table of contents entry is already in your document at the position where you want the field, select the text. Then press ⌘-Option-Shift-O to open the Mark Table Of Contents Entry dialog box.

Next enter the text for the table of contents entry in the Entry text box. If you didn't select any text before opening the dialog box, the text box will be blank. If you selected text first, Word will have inserted the selection for you, although you can modify it if you like. For now, we'll ignore the Table Identifier pull-down list except to say that the default entry C is the right choice for a table of contents entry. The Level box lets you set a level for the entry, from 1 through 9.

Choose the Mark button, and Word will insert the TC field into your document at the cursor position or immediately after the selection if you have selected text. Word will not close the dialog box, however. In fact, once you've opened the dialog box, you can use it to create as many TC fields as you like.

To move between the dialog box and your document, point and click with the mouse or press Control-Tab. While in the document, you can position your cursor for the next TC field and even select text for automatic entry in the dialog box. You can then move back to the dialog box, add or change the entry and the level as appropriate, and choose Mark to enter the next TC field. When you've finished, choose Close to close the dialog box.

### How to compile a table of contents using TC fields

Compiling a table of contents from TC fields is much like compiling one from headings. After you've entered all the fields, position the cursor where you want the table of contents. Next choose Insert Index And Tables, and choose the Table Of Contents card. Choose the Options button to open the Table Of Contents Options dialog box, shown in Figure 22-2. In this case, you'll want to make sure that the Table Entry Fields check box is checked. You can also check the Styles check box or not, as appropriate.

When you choose OK to close the Table Of Contents Options dialog box and then choose OK again to create the table of contents, Word will follow the same procedure we described earlier. It will check to see whether a table of contents already exists, ask whether to replace the table if it finds one, repaginate the document, search for TC fields (and for styles if you checked the Styles check box), compile the table, and insert the TOC field at the cursor position or at the position of the TOC field it's replacing.

# How to restrict a table of contents to a portion of a document

You can tell Word to compile a table of contents for only part of a document. This can come in handy if your document is divided into sections or chapters and you want a separate table of contents for each section or chapter.

First define a bookmark indicating the part of the document you want to compile the table for. Then create the TOC field, using the techniques we've already described, and edit the field to add the switch

\B "bookmark"

where *bookmark* is the name of the bookmark you've defined. If the field started out as

{TOC \F}

for example, you would edit it to read

{TOC \F \B "bookmark"}

(You don't have to know anything about the \F switch to add the \B switch, but in case you're wondering, the \F tells Word to compile the table of contents using TC fields.) After you make the change, update the field's result to generate the table.

## NEW!  How to format a table of contents

Until now, we've largely ignored the Table Of Contents card in the Index And Tables dialog box, rushing past it on the way to the Table Of Contents Options dialog box. But if you're concerned with how your table of contents looks, you'll want to take advantage of the formatting options on this card. To see the card, shown in Figure 22-6, choose Insert Index And Tables, and then choose the Table Of Contents card.

**FIGURE 22-6**

To format a table of contents, choose Insert Index And Tables, and then choose the Table Of Contents card.

As you can see in Figure 22-6, the Formats list box offers six predefined formats, plus one custom style. The Preview box shows a sample of the highlighted format with the current settings, so you can browse through the list of formats and see what each will look like.

Below the Formats list box is the Show Page Numbers check box. By default, this box is checked for each format choice, but you can eliminate page numbers by clearing the check box. When this box is checked, you can optionally check the Right Align Page Numbers check box. And when the Right Align Page Numbers box is checked, you can optionally define a tab leader. The choices in the Tab Leader pull-down list are no leaders, solid lines, dashed lines, and dotted lines. The default settings for right-aligned page numbers and for tab leaders vary depending on the predefined format.

If you highlight the Custom Style format, you can choose the Modify button to open the Style dialog box. This is essentially the same dialog box you'll see if you choose Format Style. When you open it from the Index And Tables dialog box, however, the only choices available will be for the TOC styles. You can then modify any of the TOC styles to suit your custom table of contents, using the techniques discussed in Chapter 12. When you finish, choose Close in the Style dialog box. Word will apply the new settings to all paragraphs formatted with that style.

Before you change the formatting instructions for one or more TOC styles, you might want to change the based-on style. Instead of using Normal in each case, you may prefer to base each TOC style on the next-highest TOC style. For example, you can base TOC 3 on TOC 2, which would be based on TOC 1, which would be based on Normal. With this approach, you can change the TOC 1 style, and the change will affect all other TOC styles. That makes it easier to maintain consistency throughout the various levels in a table of contents.

# Creating a Table of Figures

You can use the Index And Tables dialog box to compile other types of tables, such as a table of figures. As with a table of contents, you can use styles, fields, or both to build these tables. You can also use captions that you've entered with the Insert Caption command. In fact, using caption entries will usually be the preferred choice, assuming you've taken advantage of the Insert Caption feature. Because the procedures for using styles or fields are nearly identical to the equivalent features that we've already covered for tables of contents, however, we'll cover those two choices first.

## How to build a table of figures using styles

Creating a table of figures is similar in both concept and mechanics to creating a table of contents—aside from the captions feature that we're ignoring for the moment. You can, for example, use a paragraph style to mark text in your document simply by formatting the text with the appropriate style. You can even give the style a descriptive name, such as *For Table of Figures.*

Once you've formatted the text with the appropriate style, move the cursor to the point in your document where you want the table. Then choose Insert Index And Tables, choose the Table Of Figures Card, and choose Options to open the Table Of Figures Options dialog box, shown in Figure 22-7.

**FIGURE 22-7**

To create a table of figures, choose Insert Index And Tables, go to the Table Of Figures card, and choose Options to open this dialog box.

**Table of Figures Options**

Build Table of Figures From:

☐ Style: Caption

☐ Table Entry Fields
   Table Identifier: F

OK
Cancel
Help

The Table Of Figures Options dialog box resembles the Table Of Contents Options dialog box, but it is simpler because you can use only one style for any given table of figures. Here, too, the dialog box offers two check boxes that let you tell Word whether to use a style, table entry fields, or both to compile the table.

If you want to use a style only, make sure the Table Entry Fields check box isn't checked. Then open the Style pull-down list, and choose the style to use. (When you choose a style from the list, Word will automatically check the Style check box, if it isn't checked already.) Because a table of figures can have only one level of entry, Word lets you pick only one style from the list. When you've made your choice, choose OK to return to the Table Of Figures card, and then choose OK again to compile the table.

If the cursor is in a table of figures when you give the command to compile a table, Word will ask whether you want to replace the existing table of figures. Answer OK or Cancel, as appropriate. If you choose OK, Word will repaginate the document, search for the appropriate style, compile the table of figures, and insert the table at the cursor position. If you toggle the field to show the field code, you'll see that it's a TOC field.

## How to build a table of figures using fields

If you prefer, you can use TC fields to define the entries in a table of figures. To use a TC field, you must add an identifier to distinguish these fields from entries that are meant for the table of contents or for other tables.

To insert a TC field with the appropriate identifier, press ⌘-Option-Shift-O to open the Mark Table Of Contents Entry dialog box, shown earlier in Figure 22-5. This is the same dialog box we've already described for creating TC fields for a table of contents. The only difference is that you'll need to take advantage of the Table Identifier pull-down list.

As we mentioned earlier, the C identifier is the correct choice for marking an entry for the Table Of Contents. However, you can choose any other letter of the alphabet for the identifier. And you can choose any letter other than C for each table of figures you want to create.

To make the identifier easy to remember, you might want to use the first letter of the table name. For a table of equations, for example, you might use E, and for a table of illustrations, you might use I. It doesn't matter what letter you use, however, as long as you're consistent.

After you insert the TC fields in your document using the techniques described earlier in this chapter, you can compile the table of figures. Choose Insert Index And Tables, choose the Table Of Figures card, and choose Options. Check the Table Entry Fields check box, and set the Table Identifier box to match the identifier you used in the TC fields. Unless you want to compile the table using both TC fields and a style, be sure to clear the Style check box. Then choose OK to return to the Table Of Figures card, and choose OK again to compile the table.

## How to build a table of figures using captions

As we've already suggested, the preferred choice for creating a table of figures takes advantage of captions you've entered with the Insert Caption command, which we cover in detail in "Numbering Items in Sequence" on page 784.

Briefly, you can use the Insert Caption feature to maintain separate sets of captions for figures, equations, tables, and any other category you care to define. Word will format each of these captions with the same style, and will insert the same field for each—specifically an SEQ, or Sequence, field.

The Sequence field lets Word keep track of each table, equation, or other item you've labeled with a caption, and automatically renumber the captions as you add, delete, or move them. Even better, when you insert the fields with the Insert Caption command, Word also adds identifiers to the fields so that it can number each type of caption independently.

The identifier also lets Word use the Sequence fields the same way it can use TC fields—to find the captions for each item in a given sequence and generate a table of figures for that sequence, meaning a table of tables, table of figures, table of equations, and so on.

To specify the type of caption to include in a table, first decide whether you want to use only captions to identify the entries for the table, or use captions plus styles, TC fields, or both. Then choose Insert Index And Tables and go to the Table Of Figures card, shown in Figure 22-8.

**FIGURE 22-8**

To create a table of figures based on captions, choose the type of caption from the Caption Label list.

Next choose the Options button to open the Table of Figures Options dialog box that we've already discussed, and make sure the Style and Table Entry Fields check boxes are checked or not, as appropriate. Then choose OK to return to the Table Of Figures card, and choose the caption type from the Caption Label list. Note that the list will always include at least four entries: Equation, Figure, Table, and None. In addition, you'll find any other caption types you've defined through the Caption dialog box, which you can open by choosing Insert Caption. When you've finished specifying the entries to use in the table, choose OK, and Word will generate the table.

## How to format a table of figures

Creating a table of figures is similar to creating a table of contents in one other important way: You can control the format for the table with the Table Of Figures card in the Index And Tables dialog box. To see the card, choose Insert Index And Tables and then choose the Table Of Figures card, shown in Figure 22-8.

The Table Of Figures card is similar to the Table Of Contents card, with a list of predefined formats (including a Custom Style option) and a Preview box to show the effect of current settings. Other shared features include check boxes that let you choose whether to show page numbers and whether to right-align the page numbers. You'll also find the Tab Leader pull-down list that lets you specify a dotted, dashed, or solid line, or no tab leader for right-aligned page numbers. All of these features work the same way as on the Table Of Contents card, as already described in the section "How to format a table of contents" on page 732.

The Table Of Figures card also includes two items that aren't on the Table Of Contents card: the Caption label list box that we covered in the section just before this, and the Include Label And Number check box. The check box applies only to tables based on captions. If the box is checked, Word will include the caption identifier, such as *Figure 1* or *Table 3*, in the table. If the box is not checked, Word will include only the actual caption.

As with the Table Of Contents card, the Table Of Figures card includes a Custom Style choice in the Formats list box. And in this case too, if you choose the Custom Style format, Word will make the Modify button available. Choose Modify to open the Style dialog box.

The only style you'll be able to modify when you open the Style dialog box this way is the Table Of Figures style, which Word uses for formatting the tables of figures, and which the program will add to your document automatically when you first create a table of figures. As with TOC styles, you can modify the Table Of Figures style however you like, using the techniques we discussed in Chapter 12. When you choose OK in the Style dialog box, Word will apply the new instructions to all the paragraphs that are formatted with that style.

# Creating an Index

Creating an index is similar in many ways to creating a table of contents or a table of figures from TC fields. To define index entries, you use an XE (Index Entry) field. The compiled index is the field result of an INDEX field. You can enter the INDEX field with the Insert Index And Tables command, the same way you can enter a TOC field for a table of contents or figures. You can also insert the XE field automatically.

We'll explore each of Word's indexing features, but it will be helpful to start with a simple example to put the more complex features in context.

## A quick example

Suppose you've created the document shown in Figure 22-9 and you want to define the heading *Division of Parts* as an index entry. (In this example, and for most of this discussion, we'll assume that Word is set to show hidden text and to show field results rather than field codes.)

**FIGURE 22-9**

We'll use this document to demonstrate Word's indexing capabilities.

To define the entry, select it, and then press ⌘-Option-Shift-X to open the Mark Index Entry dialog box, shown in Figure 22-10 on the next page.

You can also open the Mark Index Entry dialog box by choosing Insert Index And Tables, choosing the Index card, and choosing the Mark Entry button. The ⌘-Option-Shift-X shortcut is much faster, however.

The easiest way to
define index entries in
your document is with
the Mark Index Entry
dialog box.

As you can see in Figure 22-10, Word will automatically place the text
you've selected in the Main Entry text box. If you like, you can edit the entry
at this point. When you're done, choose the Mark button. Word will insert an
XE field after the text you selected, as shown in Figure 22-11. This field, which
defines the index entry, is {XE "Division of Parts"}. Notice that the field appears with a dotted underline, indicating that it's formatted as hidden text.

The Mark Index Entry
dialog box inserts an
XE field immediately
after the text you
selected.

The Mark Index Entry dialog box will remain open so you can make further
entries. You can use the dialog box to define all the index entries for your document, moving between the document and the dialog box by pointing and clicking with the mouse or by pressing Control-Tab. Close the dialog box when you're
done. When you're ready to compile the index, move the cursor to where you
want the index—typically, at the end of the document. Then choose Insert Index
And Tables, and go to the Index card, shown in Figure 22-12.

**FIGURE 22-12**

To compile an index, choose Insert Index And Tables, go to the Index card, and choose OK.

To keep this example as simple as possible, we'll ignore the options on the Index card for now. Choose OK to accept the default options. Word will repaginate your document, search for index entries, and insert an index like the one shown in Figure 22-13, complete with section breaks before and after the index.

**FIGURE 22-13**

This sample index, shown in Page Layout view, uses Word's default index settings.

That's all there is to it. Of course, this example illustrates only the basics of creating an index. Word offers other indexing features that you will likely want to take advantage of.

## How to define index entries

For anything but the simplest index, your first step before you define an index entry is to decide whether you want to create a term entry or a topic entry. A *term entry* always refers to a single page, such as 49 or 156. A *topic entry* can refer to a range of pages, such as 49–51 or 156–62. After you decide which type of entry you want to create, you can define the entry.

## How to define term entries

To create an index entry for a particular word or phrase in your document, start by highlighting that word or phrase. Then press ⌘-Option-Shift-X to open the Mark Index Entry dialog box, shown in Figure 22-10. As we've already pointed out, Word will place the text you highlighted in the Main Entry text box. If you like, you can then edit the entry in the text box.

If you need to insert a colon, make sure that you precede it with a backslash (\), or you won't get the results you expect. (Word uses the colon character to create multiple-level headings, as we'll explain in a moment.) If the original highlighted text included a colon, Word will automatically insert the backslash for you.

To create the index entry as a term entry, make sure that the Options section of the dialog box is set for Current Page before you choose Mark to enter the XE field.

## How to define topic entries

Creating a topic entry is somewhat different from creating a term entry. Before you can create a topic entry, you have to assign a bookmark to the block of text the entry will refer to. For example, to create the index entry *getting started* that refers to the first 12 paragraphs in your document, you'll need to highlight those paragraphs, choose Edit Bookmark, type an appropriate name such as *GettingStarted* in the Bookmark Name text box, and choose Add.

After you've assigned a bookmark name to the block of text, press ⌘-Option-Shift-X to open the Mark Index Entry dialog box. Then enter the text for the index entry—*getting started*, in this case—in the Main Entry text box. Next open the Bookmark drop-down list in the Options section of the dialog box, and highlight the bookmark name for the entry—*GettingStarted*, in this example. Finally, choose the Page Range option button, and choose the Mark button to enter the XE field.

Although you can enter the XE field for a topic entry anywhere in your document, we suggest you enter it immediately before or immediately after the bookmark it refers to so that you'll know where to find it later if you want to change or delete it.

## How to define multilevel entries

Word also lets you create multilevel index entries, which are important when you need to break a topic into subtopics. For example, you might want to create a group of entries like this:

printing

    envelopes, 326–29

    graphics, 325

    legal-size paper, 329–30

To create multilevel entries, simply use the first-level entry as the main entry for all the related entries. Enter the first-level entry in the Main Entry text box, and enter each second-level entry in the Subentry text box when you define the entry.

For example, to create the sample group of entries under *printing*, you would enter three fields at the appropriate places in your document, using *printing* as the main entry in each case, but using *envelopes, graphics,* and *legal-size paper* as the subentries. When Word inserts the XE field, it will separate the main entry and the subentry by a colon.

## How to refer to other entries

Sometimes you'll want to create an index entry that refers to another entry instead of a page number. For example, you might want to create the entry

Word. *See* Microsoft Word

To create such entries, press ⌘-Option-Shift-X to open the Mark Index Entry dialog box, and enter text in the Main Entry text box and optionally in the Subentry text box, as already described. Then choose Cross-Reference in the Options section of the dialog box, and enter the cross-reference in the text box to the right of the option button. Word already provides the word *See* in the text box, so you need only type the reference itself. Here again, choose the Mark button to enter the XE field.

As with fields that define topic entries, fields that refer to other entries can appear anywhere in a document. However, we recommend that you enter these fields at the end of the document, just before the INDEX field that compiles the entries, so that you can find them easily if you want to change or delete them.

## How to format page numbers

Two check boxes at the bottom of the Mark Index Entry dialog box let you set the format for page numbers. The boxes are labeled *Bold* and *Italic*. If you want the page number reference for the index entry printed in bold, italic, or both, be sure to check the appropriate check box or boxes. This feature is available for all types of entries.

## How to mark a word or phrase throughout a document with Mark All

Near the beginning of this chapter, we mentioned that Word will let you mark all occurrences of a given word or phrase throughout your document with a single command. That feature is also in the Mark Index Entry dialog box: the Mark All button.

The Mark All button is available only when you are defining term entries— meaning that you're using the Current Page option—and only when you've selected some text in your document. But it can be quite useful, nonetheless.

To take advantage of this feature, start by selecting some text and then opening or returning to the Mark Index Entry dialog box. If you then choose Mark All, Word will mark all occurrences of the selected text throughout your document. If you like, you can change the main entry text, add subentry text, or do both before choosing Mark All. Word will still find all occurrences of the selected text and mark them with the main entry text and subentry text that you've defined.

## How to mark a word or phrase throughout a document with AutoMark

Word offers another choice for marking a word or phrase throughout a document. To take advantage of it, you first have to create a second file, called a *concordance file*. Start by creating a new Word document file and creating a two-column table. Enter a word or phrase that you want to index in the left column of each table row, and enter the index entry to use for that word or phrase in the right column. When you finish entering the information, save the file. (We discussed how to work with tables in "Building Tables," starting on page 331.)

Once you've created the concordance file, open the file you want to index, and choose Insert Index And Tables. Next, choose the Index card, and then the AutoMark button. Word will open a dialog box that's similar to the dialog box for opening files and works the same way. Use it to designate the concordance file, just as you would designate a file to open, and choose OK. Word will then work its way through your file, finding all matches to the words and phrases in the first column of the concordance file and entering XE fields using the text in the second column.

# How to choose a format for the index

Once you've defined the index entries in a document, you can create the index. As we've already discussed, you can compile the index by choosing Insert Index And Tables, choosing the Index card, and then choosing OK. What we haven't discussed yet are the settings on the Index card that affect the format of the index.

## Indented vs. run-in format

The Type section of the Index card lets you choose between two kinds of indexes: indented and run-in. If you choose the Indented option (the default), Word will indent each subentry on a new line under the main entry, as shown in the Preview box in Figure 22-12. If you choose the Run-In option, Word will include each subentry in the same paragraph as the main entry, as shown in Figure 22-14, with a colon after the main entry, and with each subentry separated from the other subentries by a semicolon.

**FIGURE 22-14**

The Run-In option tells Word to include each subentry in the same paragraph as its main entry.

## Other format choices for indexes

In addition to choosing an index type, you can specify how many columns to use for the index in the Columns box just below the Preview box. And if you've chosen to use an indented format, you can specify right-aligned page numbers, using the Right Align Page Numbers check box. You can also use the Tab Leader pull-down list to define the tab leader as a solid, dashed, or dotted line or to specify no leader.

The Index card has two other features in common with the Table Of Contents and Table Of Figures cards. Here, too, you can browse through a list of predefined formats and see the effect of each in the Preview box. And here again you'll find the Custom Style choice in the list of formats. If you highlight Custom Style, the Modify button will become available, and you can then choose it to open the Style dialog box and modify the index styles that Word automatically adds to the document. In this case, the styles are for nine levels of index entries, from Index 1 through Index 9.

### How to compile an index for a portion of a document

In this discussion, we've assumed that Word is set to display field results rather than field codes. If you place the cursor or selection in the index and press Shift-F9 to toggle the view, you'll find that the index, like a table of contents, is actually the result of a field—in this case, the INDEX field. The form of the field is simply {INDEX [switches]}.

You can compile an index for a portion of your document using essentially the same technique we described earlier for compiling a table of contents for only part of a document. First create a bookmark that defines the part you want to index. Then add the \b switch and the bookmark name in the INDEX field. For example, if you've created a 50-page document and you want to compile an index for pages 1 through 25, highlight the first 25 pages, choose Edit Bookmark, and assign a name to those pages. If you name the bookmark *FirstHalf,* for example, you could compile an index for those pages only, by adding the switch

\b "FirstHalf"

to the index field.

## How to break up an index

If you create an index that contains a few thousand entries, your computer may run out of memory (or run slowly) when it compiles the index. Fortunately, Word offers a switch that lets you break the process into smaller pieces.

To compile part of an index, edit the INDEX field to include the \p switch followed by a starting letter and an ending letter. For example, if you want to divide an index into two parts, you can use the INDEX fields

{INDEX \p a-m}

{INDEX \p n-z}

When you compile the index, simply update each INDEX field individually. You can also break the index into still smaller parts by adding more INDEX fields with a smaller range in each field.

## How to update an index

To update a document's index, you can use the Insert Index And Tables command to replace the current index, or you can simply place the cursor or selection anywhere in the index and press F9. As with a table of contents, the best time to compile an index is just before you print the final version of a document. If you edit or reorganize the document after compiling the index, the page numbers may change, so the index will no longer be correct. As with a table of contents also, you may want to put the index in its own section and number it separately, using the same techniques we discussed earlier in this chapter for the table of contents.

# Creating a Table of Authorities

Tables of authorities are a reference aid that lawyers often need. If you don't know what they are, you don't need them. If you need them, however, Word's table of authorities feature can be invaluable.

Although the final result of this feature is called a table, the feature really has more in common with indexing. It lets you select some text and open a dialog box that lets you create the citation by editing a copy of the selected text. It then inserts a TA field that takes the form

{TA \l "LongCitationText" \s "ShortCitationText" [switches]}

After you finish entering the TA fields in your document, you can use the Insert Index And Tables command to compile the fields into a table. We'll take a closer look at each of these steps, starting with marking the entries in your document.

## How to define table of authorities entries

To create a table of authorities entry, start by selecting the text you want the table to refer to. Then press ⌘-Option-Shift-I to open the Mark Citation dialog box, shown in Figure 22-15 on the next page.

You can also open the Mark Citation dialog box by choosing Insert Index And Tables, choosing the Table Of Authorities card, and then choosing the Mark Citation button. The ⌘-Option-Shift-I keyboard shortcut is more direct, however.

When you open the dialog box, Word will insert two copies of the text you selected—one in the Selected Text box and one in the Short Citation box. You can edit both copies of the text, if you like, without affecting the text in your document. The edited copy in the Selected Text box will serve as the long citation, and Word will show it in the Long Citation text box at the bottom of the dialog box once you've entered the TA field. The edited copy in the Short Citation text box will serve as the short citation for the field.

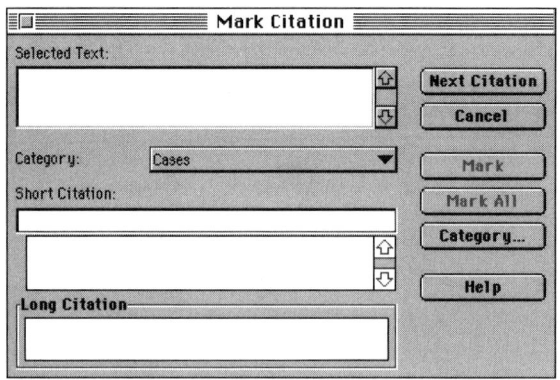

**FIGURE 22-15**

To enter the marker fields for a table of authorities, open the Mark Citation dialog box.

You can also designate a category for each entry. Open the pull-down Category list box for a list of 16 categories to choose from. (You can also rename any of these categories by choosing the Category button to open the Edit Category dialog box.) When you're finished, choose Mark to insert the TA field for the highlighted text only, or choose Mark All to insert TA fields for all occurrences of the short citation.

After Word inserts the TA field or fields, it will leave the Mark Citation dialog box open so you can mark additional citations. As with the equivalent dialog boxes for marking entries for an index or other kinds of tables, you can move between the dialog box and your document by pointing and clicking with the mouse or by pressing Control-Tab.

The Next Citation button will take you to the next TA field in the document and show you the short and long citations as well as the category for that field. It will also help you find text that looks as though it should be marked as a citation, stopping at anything that reads *In Re*.

## How to format and create a table of authorities

Once you've finished entering the TA fields, you can generate the table of authorities. Position your cursor where you want the table. Then choose Insert Index And Tables, and choose the Table Of Authorities card, shown in Figure 22-16.

**FIGURE 22-16**

To format and generate a table of authorities, go to the Table Of Authorities card in the Index And Tables dialog box.

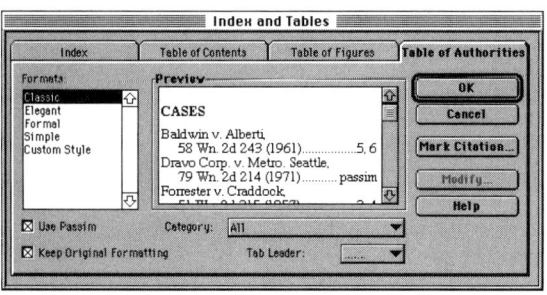

The Table Of Authorities card is similar to the other cards in the dialog box, with a Formats list that offers a set of predefined formats, a Preview box that shows the effect of the current settings, and a Tab Leader pull-down list that lets you choose whether to include a tab leader, and if so whether to make it a dotted, dashed, or solid line. Here, too, if you choose Custom Style in the Formats list, Word will make the Modify button available so you can easily open the Style dialog box and modify the styles related to the table of authorities—in this case, the Table Of Authorities and TOA Heading styles.

There are three options on the card that are specific to the table of authorities feature. The Use Passim check box, when checked, tells Word to use the word *passim* rather than individual page references if there are five or more references to the same authority. The Keep Original Formatting check box tells Word to use the same character formatting that the original text had in your document. The Category box lets you tell Word to include all TA fields or only those for a specific category.

When you finish setting the options on the card, choose OK to have Word generate the table of authorities. Word will repaginate the document, compile the TA entries, and insert the table of authorities as the field result of a TOA field.

# Working with Long Documents

Historically, the chore of creating a research aid such as an index or one of the tables we've discussed in this chapter was exceeded only by the major headache involved in creating the same research aids in a document shared among multiple files. The tricks involved in cobbling together the data from several files to produce a single, integrated index or table often seemed like more trouble than they were worth. So it's no small matter to say that creating an index or a table in Word version 6.0 is no different for a document spread out over multiple files than for one that's fully contained in a single file.

To use on multiple files any of the features that we've discussed in this chapter, first create a master document that includes all the separate files as subdocuments. Then open the master document, choose View Normal, and use the index, table of contents, table of figures, and table of authority features exactly as you would use them on any other document. It's that simple. For more information on using the master document feature, see the section in Chapter 16 titled "Working with Long Documents," starting on page 559.

# 23

## Assorted Goodies

ost of the features we've discussed in the last few chapters, such as mail merge and tables of contents, are potentially critical to those who need them. But Word offers an assortment of other features—small touches that are rarely critical but that can help you work more efficiently. In this chapter, we'll cover a number of these, including Word's ability to sort, perform mathematical calculations, create equations to use within body text, create references, and send commands directly to a printer. Here, then, is a potpourri of Word's more specialized features.

## Sorting

Word's Table Sort command can rearrange paragraphs of body text, tabular lists (text separated by tabs), comma-delimited lists (text separated by commas), and Word tables. (Note that the exact wording of the Sort item on the Table menu and the name of the Sort dialog box will vary depending on the selection that you're sorting, but we'll use the names *Table Sort* and *the Sort dialog box* throughout this discussion.) When you choose Table Sort, Word will open the Sort dialog box, shown in Figure 23-1 on the next page. Choose the Options button to open the Sort Options dialog box, shown in Figure 23-2 on the next page.

**FIGURE 23-1**

Word will open this
dialog box when you
choose the Table Sort
command.

**FIGURE 23-2**

Choose the Options
button from the Sort
dialog box to open this
dialog box.

If you're sorting paragraphs of standard text, the only choice in the Sort Options dialog box that matters is the Case Sensitive check box. If it's checked, words containing uppercase letters will come before the same words containing lowercase letters. If you're sorting a list that's in tabular, comma-delimited, or similar format, with each row broken into what are called *fields*, you can set the proper separator character in the Separate Fields At box. The Sort Column Only check box will be available only if you are sorting text in a Word table or in tabular columns. Choose Sort Column Only when you want to sort only the currently selected column or columns.

Incidentally, the Help file (in the original shipping version of the program at least) will reliably misinform you that the Sort Column Only check box will be available for newspaper-style columns. Ignore it. The Help file is wrong.

After you finish with the sort options, choose OK to close the dialog box and return to the Sort dialog box. As you can see in Figure 23-1, you can use this box to define up to three sort levels. For each one, you can set the type—text, number, or date—and choose whether to sort in ascending or descending order. The My List Has box lets you tell Word whether a table, tabular list, or comma-delimited list includes a header row. If you indicate that it has one, Word will use the items in the first row as the names for the fields, and it won't include that row in the sort.

If you don't select any text before choosing Table Sort, Word will automatically highlight the entire document—unless the cursor or selection is in a Word table, in which case it will highlight the table. (In this context, a Word table is a table created with Word's table feature, as distinguished from a list created with tabs.) By default, Word sorts all the paragraphs in your document by the first character in each paragraph. If two or more paragraphs begin with the same character, Word will compare the second characters, then the third, and so on, until it finds a variation to base the sort on or until it reaches the end of identical paragraphs.

As an example, suppose you've created the list of used cars shown in Figure 23-3, and you want to sort the list in alphabetic order based on the manufacturer's name and then the model name, the first two items in each row. Since you want to sort only the paragraphs that are part of the list, start by selecting those paragraphs. Next choose the Table Sort command, and choose OK to accept the default settings. Word will sort the selected paragraphs as shown in Figure 23-4 on the next page.

**FIGURE 23-3**

This is the list of used cars before sorting.

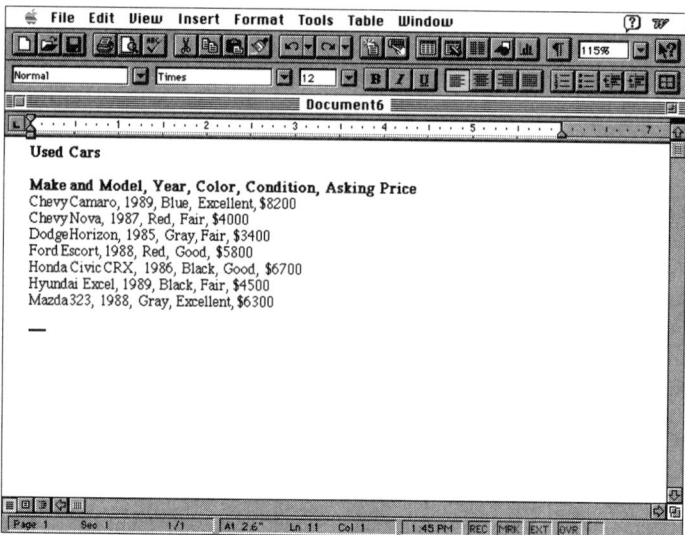

FIGURE 23-4

This is the same list as in Figure 23-3 after alphabetic sorting.

When sorting paragraphs, Word sorts the entire document as one unit, without regard to section boundaries. If you want to sort only part of a document, be sure to select the text to sort before you choose Table Sort. Also note that you can undo a sort with the Edit Undo command.

## Alphanumeric sorts

Word will usually recognize the type of data in the selection and automatically set the Type in the Sort By section of the dialog box to Text, Number, or Date, as appropriate. If Type is set to Text, Word will sort in alphanumeric order, which specifies a sort order for letters of the alphabet, numbers, and all other printable characters. The ascending sort order starts with punctuation marks and other symbols, goes on to numbers, and ends with letters.

If a paragraph begins with an indent, a tab, or a space, Word will ignore the blank space and sort the paragraph according to the first character after the white space. Blank paragraphs—that is, paragraphs that consist of a paragraph mark with no text—precede nonblank paragraphs in an ascending sort.

By default, Word will ignore case when sorting letters. For example, in an ascending sort, a paragraph that begins with *able* will come before a paragraph that begins with *Apple* because *b* comes before *p* in the alphabet. If you check the Case Sensitive check box in the Sort Options dialog box, however, a paragraph that begins with *Apple* will precede one that begins with *able* because *Apple* begins with an uppercase *A*.

## Numeric sorts

If you set Type to Number, Word will look at the actual value of each number it's sorting, rather than comparing the numbers character by character, left to right. If you set Type to Text, for example, to sort 6 and 10, Word will compare the 6 to the 1 and decide that 10 should come first in an ascending sort. But if you set Type to Number, Word will compare the value 6 to the value 10 and decide that 6 should come first. The Number setting also recognizes negative numbers, so –6 is treated as less than 0, and –23 is treated as less than –6. Note too that you can format the numbers with commas or with a dollar sign.

If a paragraph contains more than one number, and Type is set to Number, Word will evaluate that paragraph as an equation: A paragraph that reads *2 + 3* will be treated as *5*, and a paragraph that reads *3 – 2* will be treated as *1*. If the paragraph contains more than one number but doesn't include an actual equation, Word will add the numbers together. For example, it will treat a paragraph that reads *14 gibberish 6* as *20*. If Word finds any paragraphs that lack numbers during a numeric sort, it will treat them as less than the lowest number it finds in the sort, even if that number is negative. Note, however, that it will treat all such paragraphs the same way, without any attempt to sort them alphabetically.

## Date sorts

In addition to alphanumeric and numeric sorts, Word can sort dates. Figure 23-5 on the next page shows the date formats that Word recognizes.

Word will use all the information included in your date values when it sorts. For example, if you sort *Dec-92*, *Nov-92*, and *Jan-93*, Word will arrange the paragraphs in the order *Nov-92*, *Dec-92*, and *Jan-93*. But if you include a day and time, Word will sort by time for all entries on a given date. When you use numbers, as with the m/d/yy format, you can optionally include the zero for single-digit months or days, using the form *01/08/95*.

| Date Format | Example |
|---|---|
| MMM d | Jan 8 |
| MMM-yy | Jan-95 |
| MMM d, yyyy | Jan 8, 1995 |
| MMMM d, yyyy | January 8, 1995 |
| M/d/yy | 1/8/95 |
| M d y | 1 8 95 |
| M-d-yy | 1-8-95 |
| d-MMM-yy | 8-Jan-95 |
| M/d/yy h:mm AM/PM | 1/8/95 3:30 PM |

**FIGURE 23-5**

Acceptable date formats.

## How to sort in Outline view

You can also sort while in Outline view, in which case Word will base the sort on the highest-level paragraphs in the selection. For example, Figure 23-6 and Figure 23-7 show the same file before and after sorting, based on the second-highest-level paragraphs shown in the figures. Notice that Word moved the third-level sections along with the second-level headings, without changing the order of the third-level sections.

## How to sort tabular lists

Word's ability to sort tabular lists is similar to the sort features in many simple database programs. Assume, for example, that you've created a tab-delimited list, with information in columns that are aligned at tab stops and with each row consisting of one paragraph. To use database terminology, each column represents one field, with the fields separated by tabs. Each paragraph is a separate record. (Note that you can replace the tabs with commas, and that a paragraph can include as many lines as needed to hold all its fields. But, for the moment, we'll stay with the simplest possibility—a tabular list with one line in each paragraph—to make the examples easier to follow.)

This figure shows a file in Outline view before sorting. Note that the selection does not include the highest-level paragraph in the figure, but it includes all others.

When you sort in Outline view, Word keeps subordinate paragraphs under the same headings they started with, without sorting the subordinate paragraphs.

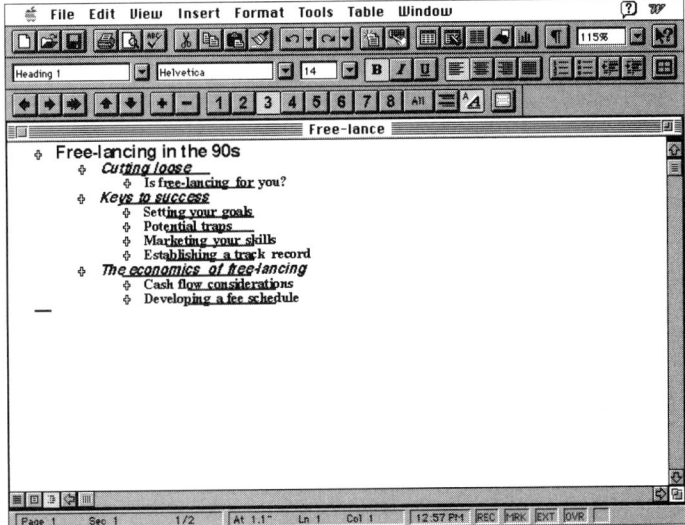

## How to sort a tabular list by key column

By default, Word will sort a tabular list based on the first column, or field, of each paragraph, or record. However, you can sort the list based on any field. Suppose, for example, that you've created a document that includes the list shown in Figure 23-8 on the next page. You want the most recently hired employees to be at the top of the list, which means you need to sort this information in descending order by year hired.

**FIGURE 23-8**

You can use Word to sort a tabular list like this one.

If there is anything in the file besides the list, you'll want to start by selecting the list so you won't sort other paragraphs as well. For this example, however, we'll assume there's nothing else in the file. Start by choosing Table Sort to open the Sort dialog box and automatically select the entire file. Then choose the Header Row option to indicate that the selection contains a header row, and choose the Options button to open the Sort Options box. Be sure that the Separate Fields At box is set to Tabs. Then choose OK to return to the Sort Text box.

Because you want the sort to be based on the Year Hired column, move to the Sort By drop-down list, and choose Year Hired from the list. Next, in the Sort By section of the dialog box, choose the Descending sort order option, and set Type to Number. (When you are working with a year in this format, you can set Type to either Number or Text, but not to Date. Word does not recognize a year by itself as a date.) To also sort by department within each year (to help show patterns for each department), open the first Then By drop-down list, which will now be available, choose Department from the list, and be sure that Type is set to Text and that the sort order is set to Ascending.

If you also want to sort by a third column, you can enter the appropriate settings in the second Then By section of the dialog box, which will now be available. To sort by salary within department, for example, choose Salary from the second Then By drop-down list, and be sure that Type is set to Number and the sort order is set to Ascending. Finally, choose OK. Word will sort the list as shown in Figure 23-9.

**FIGURE 23-9**

When you sort the tabular list shown in Figure 23-8, you can sort it by any combination of up to three columns. In this case, we've specified sorting by year, then by department, and then by salary.

## How to sort data in a single column

In addition to letting you sort rows based on the entries in a column, Word can also sort a single column without disturbing other columns. This type of sort can be useful when you're organizing a document that includes unrelated columns. For example, Figure 23-10 shows a list of contributors, with individual contributors in the left column and corporate contributors in the right column. You might want to sort each column independently of the other.

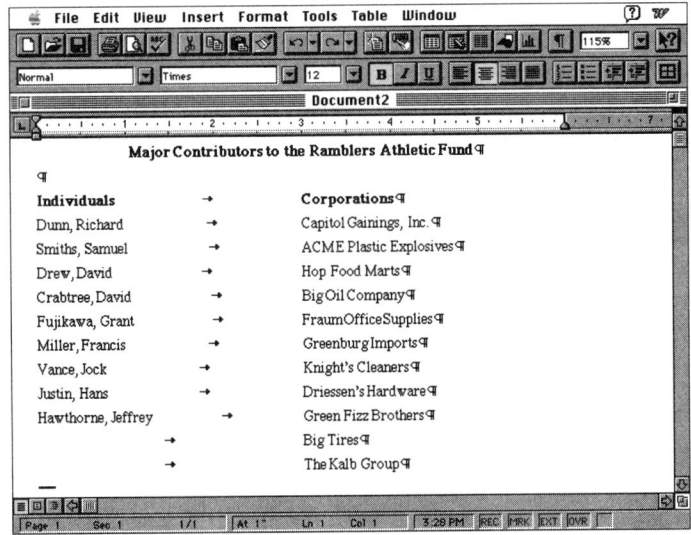

**FIGURE 23-10**

When you have unrelated columns of data, it's often useful to sort the columns independently.

To sort a single column, first select the column to sort. To use the mouse, hold down the Option key as you extend the selection. To use the keyboard, place the cursor at one corner of the area you want to select, press ⌘-Shift-F8, and then use the cursor control keys (including the arrow keys, End, and Home) to define the selection. With the column selected, choose Table Sort, choose Options to open the Sort Options dialog box, check the Sort Column Only check box, and choose OK. Then make any other appropriate settings in the Sort Text box, and choose OK. Word will sort the entries in the selected column only.

 When you set the options in the Sort Text box, be sure the Sort By entry is set either to Paragraphs or to the first field (either Field 1 or the name of the field as shown in the header row). This is essential, even if you are sorting a column other than the first. Although it would seem to make more sense to set the Sort By entry to match the field number or the name of the column you're sorting, Word will not sort the column if you set it that way.

## How to sort comma-delimited lists

As we've already mentioned, Word can also sort paragraphs that contain entries separated by commas. In fact, sorting comma-delimited lists is identical to sorting tabular lists. However, because the entries are separated by commas, you will need to specify the comma separator option in the Sort Options dialog box.

For example, Figure 23-11 shows the list of used cars that we started with at the beginning of this discussion on sorting. Notice that each paragraph, or record, includes a set of fields for one car. Note too that each paragraph has the same number of fields arranged in the same order, starting with the manufacturer and model of the car, followed by the year, color, condition, and price.

Suppose you want to sort this list in ascending order based on the year of each car—which happens to be the second entry, or field, in each record. First select all the paragraphs in the list, excluding the title and blank line at the top of the document but including the header row. Then choose Table Sort, and make sure the My List Has option is set to Header Row to indicate that you've included a header row. Next choose the Options button, make sure the options are set to Separate Fields At Commas, and choose OK to return to the Sort Text dialog box.

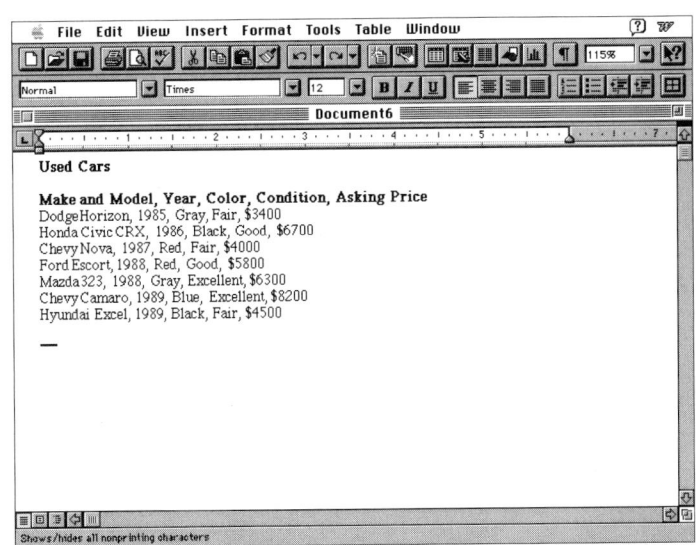

**FIGURE 23-11**

Word can also sort a comma-delimited list like this one.

To finish up, choose Year from the Sort By drop-down list, choose Number for Type, and choose Ascending for the sort order. (As we pointed out earlier, you need to use Number or Text rather than Date for Type because Word will not recognize a year by itself as a valid date format.) When you choose OK, Word will sort the list.

## How to sort a Word table

Sorting a Word table (a table built with Word's table feature) is similar in many ways to sorting a tabular list or a comma-delimited list. With a Word table, however, the contents of each field is in its own cell (the intersection of a row and column), each column is a field, and each record is a separate row in the table. In determining how to sort a table, Word looks at the first character, or characters, in each cell. If a cell contains more than one paragraph, sorting the table will not affect the order of paragraphs within the cell.

As we've already mentioned, if you want to confine a sort to a table, you don't have to specifically select the table before choosing Table Sort. If the cursor is in the table when you choose the command, Word will automatically select only the table, rather than selecting the entire document. In every other way, sorting a table is essentially identical to sorting a tabular list or a comma-delimited list, except that you don't have to specify either a comma or a tab separator. In fact, the Separator choice isn't available in this case.

Suppose, for example, that you've created the table shown in Figure 23-12. (The table has the same information as the one in Figure 23-11.) Suppose also that you now want to sort the information alphabetically by condition.

**FIGURE 23-12**

This table has the same data as in Figure 23-11, but in table format.

To sort the table by condition, first place the cursor anywhere in the table. Choose Table Sort, set the options appropriately, and then choose OK to tell Word to sort.

Most of the sort options work the same way for tables as for tabular or comma-delimited lists. However, note that if you don't have a header row when sorting tables, the choices in the Sort By drop-down list will refer to columns rather than fields.

As with tabular lists, you can easily sort a single column without changing the order of other columns by highlighting the one column and checking the Sort Column Only check box. The one important difference is that Word will automatically put the selected column number (or name from the header row) in the Sort By box and it won't give you any other choices in the Sort By drop-down list.

# NEW! Performing Mathematical Calculations

We're not quite done with tables, although we've finished our discussion of sorting in tables. As we mentioned when discussing sorting, Word will automatically evaluate basic mathematical expressions while performing a numeric sort. But Word's ability to perform mathematical calculations is a specialized feature by itself, independent of sorting. Word can add, subtract, divide, multiply, and more. It can also enter the results in your documents automatically.

For example, suppose you've created a table of cash receipts, as in Figure 23-13, and you want to compute the total receipts for the week. Simply move the cursor to the cell where you want the total, just to the right of the cell with the word *Totals*, and choose Table Formula to open the Formula dialog box, shown in Figure 23-14.

**FIGURE 23-13**

Word can add a column of numbers such as the cash receipts in this table.

**FIGURE 23-14**

Choose Table Formula to open the Formula dialog box and add a formula to your tables.

Word supplies the formula = SUM(ABOVE) as a default entry in this case. As you might guess, this formula returns the sum of all numbers in all cells above the current cell. Since this is exactly the formula you want to enter, choose OK to let Word enter it in the cell. Figure 23-15 on the next page shows the result in two panes, one showing the $6,125.09 total and the other showing the formula that produces the total.

**FIGURE 23-15**

After you enter the = (Formula) field (shown in the bottom pane), Word calculates the total (as shown in the top pane).

The field we just used to calculate a total in a Word table is one form of Word's = (Formula) field. You can use any of the techniques we discussed in Chapter 20 to insert formula fields in your document. Keep in mind that the Formula dialog box, available through the Table Formula command, helps automate the task and is generally the preferred choice unless you have all the variations for the field memorized. Most important, be clear that despite the location of the Formula choice on the Table menu, you can use the Table Formula command to enter the = (Formula) field anywhere in your document.

There's more to be said about using the = (Formula) field in tables, but we need to take a look at the field itself first.

## Word's = (Formula) field

Word's = (Formula) field offers a straightforward approach for performing mathematical calculations in your document. The form of this field is

{= Formula}

where Formula is the mathematical formula you want to evaluate.

The simplest variation on the = (Formula) field uses numbers and common mathematical operators, such as a plus sign (+) and a minus sign (–) to specify the formula. For example, {= 2+2} would have a field result of 4, while {= 10–8} would have a field result of 2.

In addition to recognizing the plus sign (+) for addition and the minus sign (–) for subtraction, the = (Formula) field recognizes the asterisk (*) for multiplication, the slash (/) for division, the percent sign (%) for calculating a percentage, and the caret (^) for calculating the power or root of a number. Figure 23-16 summarizes these six operators.

| Character | Operation |
|-----------|-----------|
| + | Addition |
| – | Subtraction |
| * | Multiplication |
| / | Division |
| % | Percentage (divides the number by 100 and then uses the result) |
| ^ | Power (if the number following is greater than or equal to 1) or root (if the number following is between 0 and 1) |

**FIGURE 23-16**

Word's mathematical operators.

Arithmetic expressions in Word follow much the same rules you would use to calculate results with pencil and paper. You enter the +, –, *, or / operators to the left of the number you want to add, subtract, multiply by, or divide by. For calculating percentage, enter the % sign directly after a number, as a substitute for dividing the number by 100. To calculate 18 percent of 70, for example, you could enter the = (Formula) field {= 18%*70}, which will give you the same result as the field {= 0.18*70}.

## Operator precedence

When a formula includes more than one operator, Word follows the same rules of precedence that you may remember from school. This order is summarized in Figure 23-17 on the next page. Unless you've entered parentheses to indicate otherwise, Word will first calculate any power or root in the formula. It will then go on to multiplication and division and finish with addition and subtraction. Given the field {= 5+10*4}, for example, Word will first multiply 10 by 4 and then add 5, yielding 45.

| Operator | Precedence |
|----------|------------|
| ^ and % | 1 |
| * and / | 2 |
| + and – | 3 |

**FIGURE 23-17**

The order of precedence for mathematical operations.

You can indicate a different order of precedence with parentheses. Here again, Word follows basic mathematical rules, evaluating anything inside the parentheses before evaluating anything outside the parentheses. Given the field {= (5+10)*4}, Word will first add 5 and 10 (yielding *15*), and then it will multiply by 4, yielding a field result of *60* rather than the *45* it would return without the parentheses.

In addition to recognizing mathematical operators, the = (Formula) field recognizes several logical operators that you can use as part of logical expressions (as distinguished from mathematical formulas). You might want to use a logical expression as part of a formula that first tests a condition and then takes a particular action, depending on the result. We'll discuss this a bit more when we talk about the IF function later in this chapter. Figure 23-18 lists the logical operators.

| Operator | Description | Operator | Description |
|----------|-------------|----------|-------------|
| = | Equal to | <= | Less than or equal to |
| < | Less than | >= | Greater than or cqual to |
| > | Greater than | <> | Not equal to |

**FIGURE 23-18**

Word's logical operators.

Keep in mind that the = (Formula) field behaves much like any other Word field. In particular, Word will update the field result only when you place the cursor within the field and press F9, or when you print the file. (This assumes that Word is set to update fields when it prints. To confirm that this option is set, choose Tools Options, then choose Print, and make sure the Update Fields check box is checked.) Before you take any results from the = (Formula) field too seriously, make sure you update the field—and before you update the field, make sure you update any fields that the field depends on.

## How to use bookmarks in an = (Formula) field

One way to automate calculations is to use bookmarks to define numbers and then use bookmark names in the formula as operands. For example, suppose you've assigned the bookmark name *SALES* to the number 1000 and the bookmark name *COGS* to the number 700. To calculate the value of SALES minus COGS, you can insert the field *{= SALES – COGS}* in the document, which will yield the field result *300*.

Defining an = (Formula) field this way has no advantage for a one-time-only calculation. But it can be extremely useful as part of a regular report. For example, suppose you have to calculate the total of SALES minus COGS at the end of each week to include in a letter to the home office. After you define the bookmarks and formula once, you need only change the numbers each week, highlight the = (Formula) field (or the whole document), and press F9 to update the result.

## Functions

In addition to using operators and bookmark names in an = (Formula) field, you can use a set of built-in functions as well. Figure 23-19 on the next page lists all the functions. We'll briefly discuss each one.

### The ABS function

The ABS function returns the absolute (positive) value of a number or formula. The form of this function is

ABS(Formula)

where *Formula* is the number or formula whose absolute value you want to determine. For example, both *{= ABS(−5)}* and *{= ABS(5)}* return the value *5*.

| Function | Result |
|----------|--------|
| ABS | The absolute value of a number |
| AND | 1 if both arguments are true; 0 if either argument is false |
| AVERAGE | The average of a list of values |
| COUNT | The number of values in a list |
| DEFINED | 1 if the expression can be calculated without error; 0 if the expression cannot be calculated without error |
| FALSE | 0 (see the discussion of the IF function) |
| IF | One of two user-specified values, depending on the outcome of a conditional test |
| INT | The integer portion of the number (the part to the left of the decimal) |
| MAX | The highest value in a list |
| MIN | The lowest value in a list |
| MOD | The remainder of a division operation |
| NOT | The inverse of a logical value |
| OR | 1 if either argument is true; 0 if both arguments are false |
| PRODUCT | The product of a list of values |
| ROUND | The rounded value of a number |
| SIGN | The sign of a value (−1, 1, or 0) |
| SUM | The sum of a list of values |
| TRUE | 1 (see the discussion of the IF function) |

**FIGURE 23-19**

Word's built-in functions.

## The AND function

You can use the AND function to join two logical expressions to form a single complex expression. The form of this function is

AND(Logical1,Logical2)

where *Logical1* and *Logical2* are the two logical expressions you want to test.

If both *Logical1* and *Logical2* are true, this function will return the value *1* (true); if either is false, it will return the value *0* (false). For example, the field *{= AND(1<2,3<4)}* returns the value *1*, and the field *{= AND(1<2,3>4)}* returns the value *0*.

## The AVERAGE function

The AVERAGE function returns the average (arithmetic mean) of a list of values. The form of this function is

AVERAGE(Value1,Value2,...ValueN)

where *Value1*, *Value2*, and so forth are either the values you want to average or the formulas whose results you want to average. For example, the field *{= AVERAGE(2,4,6)}* returns the average of 2, 4, and 6, which is *4*.

## The COUNT function

The COUNT function counts the number of items in a list. The form of this function is

COUNT(Value1,Value2,...ValueN)

where *Value1*, *Value2*, and so forth are the values or formulas you want to count. For example, the field *{= COUNT(3,49,10.8)}* returns the value *3*.

## The DEFINED function

The DEFINED function determines whether an expression can be calculated without error. The form of this function is

DEFINED(Expression)

where *Expression* is the expression you want to check. If *Expression* can be calculated without error, the function will return the value *1* (true). If the expression cannot be calculated without an error, the function will return the value *0* (false). For example, the field *{= DEFINED(5/0)}* returns the value *0*; the field *{= DEFINED(5/1)}* returns the value *1*.

## The IF function

The IF function returns either of two user-specified values based on the result of a conditional test. The form of this function is

IF(ConditionalTest,TrueResult,FalseResult)

Word will evaluate *ConditionalTest* as either true or false. If *ConditionalTest* is true, the function will return the value you entered as *TrueResult*. If *ConditionalTest* is false, the function will return the value you entered as *FalseResult*. For example, the field *{= IF(2<3,1,0)}* evaluates the conditional test 2<3. Because 2<3 is true, the function returns the value *1* defined as the *TrueResult*.

Note that *TrueResult* and *FalseResult* normally are numeric values and that you'll most often want to use *1* for *TrueResult* and *0* for *FalseResult*, simply because Word, like most programs, uses the number *1* to represent the value *True* and the number *0* to represent the value *False* when it evaluates logical

statements. If you prefer, however, you can define both *TrueResult* and
*FalseResult* with any number, any formula that evaluates to a numeric value,
or any bookmark that represents a numeric value. In each case, Word will return the specified value. Also note that Word recognizes the word *True* as
equivalent to *1* and the word *False* as equivalent to *0* without your having to
define the words as bookmarks.

## The INT function

The INT function returns the integer portion of a specified value or formula
(the numbers to the left of the decimal). The form of this function is

　　　INT(Formula)

where *Formula* is the formula or value whose integer portion you want to
truncate. For example, the field *{= INT(7/4)}* returns the value *1*.

## The MAX and MIN functions

The MAX and MIN functions let you find the highest or lowest values in a list.
The forms of these functions are

　　　MAX(Value1,Value2,...ValueN)

　　　MIN(Value1,Value2,...ValueN)

where *Value1*, *Value2*, and so forth can be either values or formulas whose results you want to evaluate. For example, to find the highest value in the list
32, 19, 7, 2*40, 78, 34, you can use the field *{= MAX(32,19,7,2*40,78,34)}*,
which returns the value *80*. To find the lowest value in the list, you can use the
field *{= MIN(32,19,7,2*40,78,34)}*, which returns the value *7*.

## The MOD function

The MOD function computes the modulus (remainder) that results from dividing one value by another a whole number of times. The form of this function is

　　　MOD(Dividend,Divisor)

The result of this function is the remainder that results from dividing *Dividend* by *Divisor*. For example, the field *{= MOD(3+2,2)}* returns the value *1* because 5 divided by 2 equals 2 with a remainder of 1.

## The NOT function

The NOT function inverts a logical value so that NOT applied to a true result
evaluates to 0 (false) and NOT applied to a false result evaluates to 1 (true).
The form of this function is

　　　NOT(Logical)

where *Logical* is the logical value or expression you want to invert. For example, the field {= *NOT(2+2=5)*} returns the value *1* (true) because the formula 2 plus 2 equals 5 is false.

## The OR function

You can use the OR function to join two logical expressions to form a single complex expression. The form of this function is

OR(Logical1,Logical2)

where *Logical1* and *Logical2* are the logical expressions you want to test. If either *Logical1* or *Logical2* is true or if both are true, this function will return the value *1* (true); if both *Logical1* and *Logical2* are false, the OR function will return the value *0* (false). For example, the field {= *OR(1<2,3>4)*} returns the value *1*; the field {= *OR(1>2,3>4)*} returns the value *0*.

## The PRODUCT function

The PRODUCT function multiplies all of its arguments and returns their product. The form of this function is

PRODUCT(Value1,Value2,...ValueN)

where *Value1*, *Value2*, and so forth can be either values or formulas. For example, if you want to multiply the numbers 3, 4, 5, and 6 and the result of the formula 3+4, you can use the field {= *PRODUCT(3,4,5,6,3+4)*}, which returns the value *2520*.

## The ROUND function

The ROUND function rounds the value of a number or the result of a formula to a specified number of decimal places. The form of this function is

ROUND(Value,NumPlaces)

where *NumPlaces* specifies the number of decimal places to use when rounding. For example, the field {= *ROUND(2*3.14159,3)*} will return the result *6.283*—the value that results from multiplying 3.14159 by 2 and then rounding to three decimal places.

## The SIGN function

The SIGN function returns the sign of a specified value or result. The form of this function is

SIGN(Value)

If *Value* is positive, the function will return *1*; if *Value* is negative, the function will return *–1*; if *Value* is *0*, the function will return *0*. For example, the field {= *SIGN(16/–32)*} returns the value *–1* because the formula results in a negative number.

### The SUM function

The SUM function adds a list of values. The form of the SUM function is

SUM(Value1,Value2,...ValueN)

where *Value1*, *Value2*, and so forth can be either values or formulas. For example, to add the numbers 3, 4, 5, and 6 and the result of the formula 2∗3+1, you can use the field *{= SUM(3,4,5,6,2 ∗3+1)}*, which returns the value *25*.

## The Formula dialog box

The Formula dialog box, which we've already touched on, is simply an aid to entering the = (Formula) field, using the functions and mathematical operators we've just described. To enter an = (Formula) field using the dialog box, choose Table Formula. Word will open the dialog box shown in Figure 23-20.

**FIGURE 23-20**

Choose Table Formula to open the Formula dialog box.

The Formula text box at the top of the dialog box is where you enter the formula for the field. Note in Figure 23-20 that Word has supplied only the equal sign to start the formula, since we're inserting the field outside of a table. When you choose the Table Formula command and the cursor is in a table, Word looks for clues in the table and makes its best guess for the formula you want to enter, as in the example we gave earlier.

You can enter a formula by typing it in the Formula text box. This can be particularly handy when you simply want the equivalent of a pocket calculator to come up with an answer. If you need the total of 349.34 plus 282.98, for example, you can start with the equal sign that Word supplies, type *349.34+282.98*, and choose OK. Word will insert the field in your document and show you the total, *632.32*. Having Word calculate a result has an advantage over using a pocket calculator, however—you can look at the field (by moving the cursor to it and pressing Shift-F9) to check your entries.

You can type any formula, including functions and bookmarks, in the Formula text box, or you can have Word paste the functions and bookmark names for you by using the Paste Function and Paste Bookmark pull-down lists. Simply open either list, and choose an item from it. Figure 23-21, for example, shows the dialog box after we've pasted in the AVERAGE function and then reopened the Paste Function list to paste additional functions that we want the AVERAGE function to evaluate.

When you paste in a function, Word will add the parentheses, if the function needs them. In this case, we want to calculate the average of the absolute value of two bookmarks, which we'll simply call One and Two. The finished formula will read = *AVERAGE(ABS(One),ABS(Two))*.

**FIGURE 23-21**

You can paste functions and bookmarks into the Formula text box by choosing them from the Paste Functions and Paste Bookmark pull-down lists.

The third drop-down list in the Formula dialog box is the Number Format list. If you open the list, you'll see a number of predefined formats to choose from, as shown in Figure 23-22 on the next page. If you choose a format from this list, Word will add it to the end of the field, in the proper position for a number format—along with the required \# switch to indicate a number format.

When you've finished entering the formula, choose OK to enter the field in your document. For information about using number formats, see "How to use the numeric picture switch" on page 657.

**FIGURE 23-22**

The Number Format drop-down list makes it easy to add a number format to an = (Formula) field.

You can also use the Formula dialog box to modify an existing = (Formula) field. Simply place your cursor in the field, and choose Table Formula. Word will open the Formula dialog box and place the field's formula in the Formula text box and the number format, if any, in the Number Format box. You can then modify it as appropriate.

# Setting Up a Spreadsheet with a Table

If you've ever worked with a spreadsheet application such as Microsoft Excel, you've probably noticed more than a few similarities between spreadsheets and Word tables. Sorting a Word table, for example, is much like sorting a spreadsheet. In truth, the similarities go even deeper.

Although Word cannot perform the more complex tasks that spreadsheet programs handle as a matter of course, you can use Word's tables along with Word's calculation features to set up a surprisingly capable spreadsheet within a document. In this discussion, we'll assume you're familiar with all the details about tables that we covered in Chapter 11. In particular, we'll assume you already know how to edit a table and how to make text and numeric entries. We'll also assume that you're familiar with the concepts of fields we discussed in Chapter 20, with the = (Formula) field we have just looked at in detail, and with the concept of a cell as the intersection of a row and a column.

## How to refer to cells

To set up a table as a spreadsheet, you need to enter formulas that refer to other cells in the table. The first step is to understand how to refer to those cells.

All cell references take the form

ColumnRow

where *Column* is given as a letter and *Row* as a number. The upper left corner of the table is A1. The cells to the right in the first row are B1, C1, D1, and so on. The cells down the first column are A1, A2, A3, and so on.

If you're familiar with almost any spreadsheet program, these labels will be familiar, since this system is essentially identical to the way most spreadsheet programs designate cells.

You can also designate a range of cells—a rectangular group of adjacent cells—using the same shorthand as most spreadsheet programs use. For example, if you want to designate a range of cells that includes the first two columns (A and B) and the first three rows (1 through 3), you would enter *A1:B3*—specifying the upper left and lower right cells in the range, with a colon between them. You can use this in an = (Formula) field, along with a function, so the field result of *{= SUM(A1:B3)}* would be the sum of all values in all cells in the range. Note too that you can designate a complete column or row, so that *{= SUM(B:B)}* will return the sum of all values in column B and *{= SUM(1:1)}* will return the sum of all values in row 1.

You can, in short, build formulas in tables, using cell references the same way you would in a spreadsheet program. There are six functions that can accept references to table cells: AVERAGE, COUNT, MIN, MAX, PRODUCT, and SUM. And, in addition to using cell references along with functions, you can use cell references by themselves in an = (Formula) field. For example, the field *{= B2+B6}* will return the sum of the value currently in cell B2 plus the value currently in B6.

When you enter a formula in a table, the SUM function allows four variations that will often eliminate the need to enter specific cell references. The variations are ABOVE, BELOW, RIGHT, and LEFT. ABOVE, used earlier in this chapter in the field *{= SUM(ABOVE)}*, tells Word to calculate the total of all values in the cells above the current cell and below the first cell containing text (or the start of the table). As we've mentioned, when you enter an = (Formula) field in a table with the Table Formula command, Word often suggests one of these forms of the SUM function, if it seems appropriate for the data that's already in the table.

# Equation Editor

In addition to Word's calculation feature, which lets you perform calculations, Word comes with an application called Equation Editor, which lets you insert virtually any equation into your document. Equations created with

Equation Editor do not calculate results. Rather, they let you use equations as illustrations—for scientific and technical papers, for example.

Equation Editor is a separate program, similar in many respects to WordArt, which we discussed in Chapter 15. As with WordArt, you can call on Equation Editor to embed an object in your document. Word treats objects as graphics, so you can place, scale, and crop them as with any other picture.

More than that, Equation Editor is a sophisticated program in its own right—so much so that we could easily spend several chapters exploring it. We'll cover it here only in enough depth to get you started.

What you see on screen when you start Equation Editor will vary. If you've set Word to show field codes, Equation Editor will open in its own window. If you can still see enough of the document at that point, you may be able to see the EMBED field code that represents the Equation Editor object. If you've set Word to show field results, you'll be able to take advantage of the OLE ability to show you the equation object in the context of the document itself. Unfortunately, you'll also find that many of Equation Editor's shortcut keys don't work because Word treats them as commands to Word instead of passing them on to Equation Editor. For this example, then, we'll assume that Word is set to show field codes. To set it, choose Tools Options, then choose View, and make sure the Field Codes check box is checked.

Be aware also that there are some slight differences in the menus available on the menu bar, depending on whether Equation Editor is running in its own window. Most important, Word will keep its own File menu and Window menu on its menu bar if you're editing the equation in the context of the document. If you're in a separate Equation Editor window, the File menu will be limited to four choices, as we'll discuss shortly, and you won't see a Window item on the menu.

There is one other point it's important to understand. The equations you build in Equation Editor are made up of separate characters and symbols. After you bring an equation into your Word document, however, you'll find it's been converted to a graphics image (an embedded object, to be precise). You can perform all the formatting and resizing tasks on it that you can on other images, but you will not be able to change any individual element in the equation while in Word. You can double-click on the equation, however, or select the object and choose Edit Equation Object and then Edit to return to Equation Editor. When you're back in Equation Editor, the equation will once again be a collection of separate components that you can edit.

To open Equation Editor to create a new equation, choose Insert Object. Word will open a dialog box similar to the one in Figure 23-23. Highlight Microsoft Equation 2.0 in the Object Type list and choose OK to start the program. You will then see a screen similar to the one in Figure 23-24 or the one in Figure 23-25 on the next page.

**FIGURE 23-23**

The Object dialog box lists the programs on your system that support OLE.

**FIGURE 23-24**

When Equation Editor starts, it either replaces the Word menu bar and toolbar, as shown here, or runs in its own window, as in Figure 23-25, depending on the current settings in Word.

Note that in Figure 23-24 Equation Editor has replaced the Word menu bar with one that's similar to Word's but not identical. Similarly, it has replaced Word's toolbars with Equation Editor's floating toolbar. Note too that the position where the cursor was located when you gave the Insert Object command is now surrounded by a crosshatched box. The box is the Equation Editor editing area. Inside the editing area is a dashed outline of a smaller box. The dashed outline indicates both the insertion point and the size of the next character you'll enter in the equation. Figure 23-25 shows Equation Editor in its own window, as we'll be using it in this example. Here again, the Equation Editor menu bar has replaced the Word menu bar, and the Word toolbar is gone from the screen. But Equation Editor's toolbar is at the top of the Equation Editor window.

Before we look at an example of how to use Equation Editor, we'll take a look at the program's menus, toolbars, and shortcut keys.

**FIGURE 23-25**

Equation Editor running in its own window.

## The Equation Editor menus

In many ways, the Equation Editor menus are similar to Word's menus. In fact, many of the commands and options are the same. But there are also notable differences, which are a direct result of the program's different purpose. Figure 23-26 shows the program menus.

### The File menu

As already mentioned, if you're working with Equation Editor in the context of the document, Word will keep its own File menu. The File menu in Figure 23-26 is the one you'll see if you're running Equation Editor in its own window. The menu has only four options, none of which appear to have anything to do with saving your work. The commands are File New, File Close, File Update, and File Quit.

**FIGURE 23-26**

The Equation Editor
menus offer a full set of
editing and formatting
features.

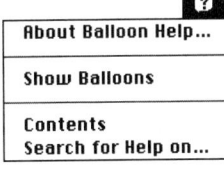

The File New command opens an additional Equation Editor window. This can be useful if part of the equation needs to be repeated several times. You can create that repeated section in its own window, and then paste it into the original equation window wherever you need that section repeated.

The File Close, File Update, and File Quit commands all automatically place a copy of the equation, as it currently appears in Equation Editor, in your document. File Close and File Quit both close the current Equation Editor window; if that is the only window, they will both exit the program as well. If there is more than one open window, File Quit will close all of the windows and exit. File Update lets you continue editing in the Equation Editor window.

Note that you don't need any of these commands when you're working with the equation in the context of the document. If you want to create a second equation for cutting and pasting, you can simply insert one nearby in the document, so there's no need for a File New command. And there's nothing to update or close. Any changes you make are already in the document; and when you leave the Equation Editor object to move to the portion of the document that Word controls, OLE automatically cleans up behind itself, removing the Equation Editor menus and toolbar from the screen and returning the Word menus and toolbars. To leave Equation Editor when working in the context of the document, you need only click on any other part of the document.

## The Edit menu

The Edit menu commands are Undo, Cut, Copy, Paste, Clear, and Select All. (Select All in this case selects all the items in Equation Editor's window or edit area.) Note that the Edit Cut and Edit Copy commands place the selected items on the Clipboard, which makes the image available to most programs.

## The View menu

The View menu offers commands for three magnifications—100%, 200%, and 400%—plus a Zoom command. However, these choices are not available when you're working with Equation Editor in the context of a Word document. Rather, the current Zoom settings for Word control the size of the image. If you want to change the Zoom setting, leave Equation Editor and change the setting in Word. All four choices are available when you're working in a separate Equation Editor window, with the Zoom command opening a dialog box that lets you specify a custom Zoom setting.

The Toolbar command toggles the display of the toolbar on and off. The Redraw command repaints the current window, which is useful if the display becomes cluttered. The Show All command displays all of the nonprinting characters.

## The Format menu

The Format menu commands let you align multiple lines of equations in different formats, including left, center, and right options, similar to Word's paragraph alignment choices. There are also two other alignment options: Align At = (which aligns equations at their equal signs) and Align At . (which aligns at the rightmost decimal point).

The Format Matrix command lets you modify a previously created matrix and gives you the same options that were available when the matrix was first created. (If you don't know what a matrix is, don't worry about it; you almost certainly won't need the feature.) The Format Spacing command opens a dialog box that lets you control automatic spacing options such as line spacing, superscript height, and subscript depth. Figure 23-27 shows the Define Spacing dialog box.

**FIGURE 23-27**

Equation Editor's Define Spacing dialog box lets you control the automatic spacing for your equations.

## The Style menu

The Style menu choices let you apply several predefined font settings to the various elements of your equations. You can change these predefined settings with the Style Define command, and you can override any of the settings with the Style Other command. The Style menu commands also control such issues as whether you see Greek characters or the standard alphabetic characters when you type at the keyboard. (Choose Style Greek, for example, to type Greek characters.)

### The Size menu

The Size menu commands let you apply text sizes to the various elements of an equation. You can change those settings with the Size Define command, or you can override them with the Size Other command. The Size Define command opens the Define Sizes dialog box, shown in Figure 23-28.

**FIGURE 23-28**

The Define Sizes dialog box lets you change the sizes of the various equation elements.

### The Help menu

Equation Editor Help on the Help menu is a valuable source of information while you learn to use Equation Editor.

### The Window menu

As we mentioned earlier, Equation Editor has no Window menu of its own. If you're editing an equation in the context of a document, however, you'll see Word's usual Window menu as one of the choices in the menu bar.

## How to use the template and symbol icons

In addition to the various menu commands, Equation Editor also offers 19 icons on the Equation toolbar, arranged in two rows. These icons are actually more like menus than they are like Word's toolbar buttons. If you move the mouse pointer to an icon and press the mouse button, you'll open what amounts to a pull-down menu; Equation Editor calls these *palettes*. The palettes come in two varieties: Symbol palettes on the top row and Template palettes on the bottom row. Each Symbol palette has a set of symbols. Each Template palette provides a set of templates—essentially a fill-in-the-blanks format that you can plug specific characters or symbols into. For example, the first icon on the left in the top row refers to various relational symbols. You can click on this icon to pull down a palette of 11 symbols. The palette attached to the second icon from the left in the second row, in contrast, offers 9 templates for representing division (or fractions) and root formulas.

The rest of the icons provide a wide range of symbols, embellishments, and formula templates. We encourage you to browse though the choices to see what's available. As you highlight each icon, Equation Editor will show you a short explanation of it in the status bar. In general, however, if you need any of these symbols you'll probably already know what they mean. If you don't know what a given symbol means, you probably won't need it.

To insert a symbol or a template into your equation, first pull down the appropriate palette by clicking on it and holding the mouse button down. Then highlight the specific item you want to insert, and release the mouse button to insert it.

## Keyboard shortcuts

You can also insert the symbols and templates with keyboard shortcuts. Figure 23-29 lists the shortcuts available within Equation Editor as well as the keystrokes for inserting spaces, applying embellishments (such as a tilde over a character), and repositioning elements of an equation. Note, however, that many of the shortcuts for inserting symbols and templates will work reliably only if you're working with Equation Editor in its own window. They will not work if you're editing the equation in the context of your document, taking advantage of OLE. Most keystrokes for inserting spaces, applying embellishments, and repositioning will work in either case.

### For inserting symbols

| Symbol | Description | Press ⌘-K Followed by This Key |
|--------|-------------|-------------------------------|
| ∞ | Infinity | I |
| → | Arrow | A |
| ∂ | Derivative (partial) | D |
| ≤ | Less than or equal to | < or , |
| ≥ | Greater than or equal to | > or . |
| × | Times | T |
| ∈ | Element of | E |
| ∉ | Not an element of | Shift-E |
| ⊂ | Contained in | C |
| ⊄ | Not contained in | Shift-C |

**FIGURE 23-29**

*(continued)*

Equation Editor keyboard shortcuts.

**FIGURE 23-29** *continued*

## For inserting common templates

| Template | Description | Keystrokes |
|---|---|---|
| (▯) | Parentheses | ⌘-9 or ⌘-0 |
| [▯] | Brackets | ⌘-[ or ⌘-] |
| {▯} | Braces | ⌘-{ or ⌘-} |
| ▯ | Fraction | ⌘-F |
| ▯/▯ | Slash fraction | ⌘-/ |
| ▯ | Superscript (high) | ⌘-H |
| ▯ | Subscript (low) | ⌘-L |
| ▯ | Joint sub/superscript | ⌘-J |
| √▯ | Square root | ⌘-R |
| ∫▯ | Integral | ⌘-I |

## For inserting other templates

| Template | Description | Press ⌘-T Followed by This Key |
|---|---|---|
| (▯) | Parentheses | ( or ) |
| [▯] | Brackets | [ or ] |
| {▯} | Braces | { or } |
| \|▯\| | Absolute value | \| (vertical bar) |
| ▯ | Fraction | F |
| ▯/▯ | Slash fraction | / |
| ▯ | Superscript (high) | H |
| ▯ | Subscript (low) | L |
| ▯ | Joint sub/superscript | J |
| √▯ | Square root | R |
| ∜▯ | Nth root | N |
| Σ▯ | Summation | S |
| ∏▯ | Product | P |
| ∫▯ | Integral | I |
| ▦ | Matrix template (3x3) | M |
| ▯ | Underscript (limit) | U |

*(continued)*

**FIGURE 23-29** *continued*

## For inserting spaces

| Icon | Description | Keystrokes |
|------|-------------|------------|
| ⌷b | Zero space | Shift-Spacebar |
| a b | Thin space | ⌘-Spacebar |
| a b | Thick space | ⌘-Shift-Spacebar |

## For applying embellishments

| Icon | Description | Type the Character to Embellish, Then This Key |
|------|-------------|-----------------------------------------------|
| ⊼ | Over-bar | ⌘-Shift-Hyphen |
| ⊼ | Tilde | ⌘-Tilde (~) |
| ⊼ | Arrow (vector) | ⌘-Option-Hyphen |
| ⊼ | Single prime | ⌘-Option-Apostrophe (') |
| ⊼ | Double prime | ⌘-Quote (") |
| ⊼ | Single dot | ⌘-Option-Period (.) |

## For repositioning the elements of an equation

| Description | Select the Elements and Then Press This Key Combination |
|-------------|---------------------------------------------------------|
| Left one pixel | ⌘-Left arrow |
| Right one pixel | ⌘-Right arrow |
| Down one pixel | ⌘-Down arrow |
| Up one pixel | ⌘-Up arrow |

# An example

To give you a feel for how to use Equation Editor, here's a simple example showing how to build two statements of the Pythagorean theorem. Figure 23-30 shows the final result.

**FIGURE 23-30**

You can use Equation Editor for relatively simple equations such as these or for far more complex statements.

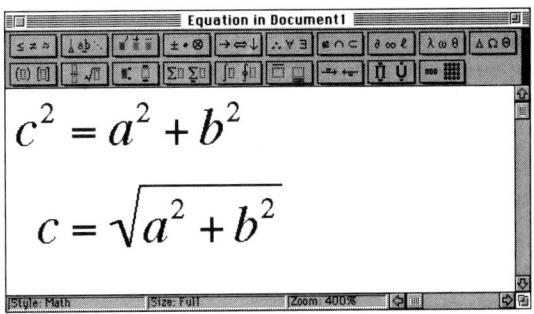

Starting with a blank screen in Equation Editor, type a lowercase letter $c$. The box outline will disappear, and the $c$ will appear where the box outline was, while a blinking cursor similar to the Word cursor will appear just to the right of the $c$. Next enter the superscripted 2. To use the mouse, click on the icon in the bottom row, third from the left of the toolbar, point to the choice in the upper left corner, and release the button. To use the keyboard, press ⌘-H. Either method will produce a superscripted box, as shown in Figure 23-31, and will place the cursor there. You can then type a 2.

**FIGURE 23-31**

When you indicate that the next character should be super-scripted, Equation Editor will use the box outline to show you the superscripted position.

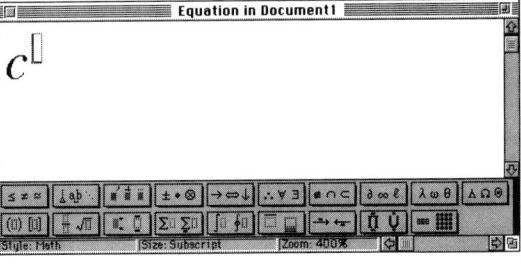

Next press the Right arrow key once to restore the full-size cursor, and then type an equal sign and a lowercase $a$. Add a superscript 2 to the $a$, as already described, and then add a plus sign and a lowercase $b$ with a superscript 2. You've now finished the first formula.

Press the Right arrow key to restore the full-size cursor; then press Return to move to the next line and start the second formula. Type $c=$ and then use the mouse or keyboard to enter the radical (square root) symbol. To use the mouse, pull down the Template menus attached to the second icon on the bottom row of the toolbar, and choose the fourth box down on the left side. To use the keyboard, press ⌘-R.

With the radical template in place, enter the remaining characters—a lowercase $a$, a superscript 2, a plus sign, a lowercase $b$, and a superscript 2—using the same techniques that you used for the first formula. Notice that the radical symbol automatically grows as you add characters below it.

The final step is to align the two statements. Simply select both equations (either by dragging with the mouse or by holding down the Shift key and using the arrow keys, as you would in Word). Then choose the command Format Align At =. Your screen should now look like the example shown in Figure 23-30.

## NEW!   Numbering Items in Sequence

Depending on the kind of documents you produce, you may need to number items in sequence—as with the figures in this book, for example. Depending on taste or house style, you may need a single numbering sequence for all kinds of items, or you may need a separate sequence for each kind—such as tables, equations, and illustrations.

One of the annoyances of numbering in sequence is the chore of having to figure out the next number to use. Even more annoying is having to renumber when you add or delete one of the items—especially if you have more than one set of numbered items. Word's SEQ field turns both of these annoyances into nonissues by automatically supplying the numbers, and by renumbering as necessary if you add, delete, or move a numbered item.

Note that the renumbering is not always fully automatic, in the sense of automatic updating of the numbers as you make each editing change. Rather, Word does not, in general, update anything until you manually update the fields (by selecting the fields and pressing F9) or until you print. The automated part of the update is the calculation that determines the correct number without any input from you.

You can enter the SEQ field manually, using any of the techniques we discussed in Chapter 20. But having to enter the field can be a bother, especially if you haven't memorized the various switches. To make this feature as painless as possible, Word provides a special tool for the field that doesn't require you to know anything about fields. The tool is the Caption dialog box, shown in Figure 23-33. You can get to it simply by choosing Insert Caption. And note that if you use the Caption dialog box rather than inserting the fields manually, Word will, in some circumstances, automatically update the numbers for you as well, each time you insert a new field.

Because you don't need to know anything about the field codes to use the dialog box, we'll largely ignore the field code it produces for now (although we'll come back to the code itself at the end of this discussion). We'll assume, therefore, that you have Word set to show field results rather than field codes. To check the setting, choose Tools Options, then View, and make sure the Field Codes check box isn't checked.

# The Caption dialog box

The easiest way to explain using the Caption dialog box is with an example. Suppose you're creating a document that has three tables, as in the sample document in Figure 23-32. You can label these literally as *Table 1*, *Table 2*, and *Table 3*, or you can use the Caption dialog box to insert the label, or caption, for each.

**FIGURE 23-32**

We want to insert a label, or caption, for each of these tables.

To insert the caption for the first table, start by selecting the entire table. Then choose Insert Caption to open the dialog box shown in Figure 23-33.

**FIGURE 23-33**

The Caption dialog box can insert fields for you that automatically keep numbered items—such as tables—numbered correctly.

The Caption dialog box offers one text box, labeled Caption, and two pull-down lists, for label and position. The Label list offers three predefined names for captions—Equation, Figure, and Table. You can also add other names by choosing the New Label button, entering a name in the New Label dialog box, and choosing OK. Similarly, you can delete any label name that you've added to the list by highlighting it on the Label list and choosing Delete Label. You can't delete the predefined choices.

The Position list offers two choices: Above Selected Item and Below Selected Item. If you didn't select anything before opening the dialog box, the Position box will be grayed out, and Word will insert the caption at the cursor position.

In this example, we'll label all three tables as *Table* and put the caption above each table, so we'll choose Table for Label and Above Selected Item for Position. Since this is the first table in the file, Word will enter the text *Table 1* in the Caption text box, as shown in Figure 23-33. You can't delete this part of the entry, but you can add punctuation and a more descriptive caption, such as *Sample Phone List*. Then choose OK to enter the caption in your document.

Next select the second table and repeat the process, adding the description *Sample Scores* to the Caption text box before choosing OK. Finally, repeat the process with the third table, adding the text *Sample Room List*. The result should look like the sample document in Figure 23-34. Note how Word automatically numbered the captions when it inserted them.

**FIGURE 23-34**

When you enter captions with the Insert Caption command, Word automatically numbers them in sequence.

## How to change the label for an item in a sequence

One of the Insert Caption command's most valuable features is its ability to renumber the items in a sequence automatically when you make a change that affects the numbering. Just as important is its ability to maintain more than one numbering sequence in the same document.

Suppose, for example, that you decide you want to make the second table part of a different sequence, which we'll call Illustrations. To change the caption, first select the part of the caption with the label and number—*Table 2* in this case—and choose Edit Clear. Then select the descriptive part of the caption and choose Edit Cut to put the text on the Clipboard. Next, select the table. (Selecting the table tells Word to format the caption paragraph using the Keep With Next option. That, in turn, will ensure the caption won't fall on a separate page from the table.)

Next choose Insert Caption to open the Captions dialog box, and paste the Clipboard contents into the Caption text box by using the ⌘-V keyboard shortcut. At this point, you can choose Illustration from the Label list if it already exists. Otherwise, you'll have to create the label—by choosing the New Label button, entering the word *Illustration*, and choosing OK. Word will add Illustration to the Label list, show it as the current label in the Label box, and add it to the beginning of the Caption text box, in front of the rest of the text for the caption, along with the appropriate number. To enter the revised caption in your document, choose OK. Word will insert the new caption. At this point, the captions will be, in order, *Table 1*, *Illustration 1*, and *Table 3*.

To update the numbers automatically, select all the fields. (The easy way is to select the entire document by choosing Edit Select All or pressing ⌘-A.) Then press F9 to update the numbering. Word will recalculate the numbers so the captions will be *Table 1*, *Illustration 1*, and *Table 2*, shown in Figure 23-35.

**FIGURE 23-35**

Word can also number more than one kind of item in separate sequences.

## How to change the label for an entire sequence

You can also change the label for an entire sequence at once. Suppose, for example, that after you've changed one Table item to an Illustration item, you decide to change all of the Table items to Illustration items. Start by selecting the label and number for any of the Table items. Then choose Insert Caption to open the Captions dialog box. Word will automatically insert the Table choice in the Label and Caption boxes. Choose Illustration from the label list, and Word will replace Table with Illustration in the Caption text box as well.

When you choose OK, Word will replace all the Table items with Illustration items. It will also update the numbering in the process, so the captions will read *Illustration 1, Illustration 2,* and *Illustration 3.*

## How to define the number format

When you create or redefine a caption, you can specify number formats other than the default Arabic numbers. To change the format, choose the Numbering button at the bottom of the Caption dialog box to open the Caption Numbering dialog box, shown in Figure 23-36.

**FIGURE 23-36**

You can set a number format with the Caption Numbering dialog box.

The Caption Numbering dialog box offers a pull-down list box containing several choices for the number format: Arabic numerals (1, 2, 3...), uppercase and lowercase letters (A, B, C... or a, b, c...), and uppercase and lowercase Roman numerals (I, II, III... or i, ii, iii).

The dialog box also offers an Include Chapter Numbering check box. If you want to restart the numbering sequence at 1 at the beginning of each chapter and you want to include the chapter number as part of the item number (as with the figures in this book), make sure this box is checked. You can then specify the style that indicates the start of a new chapter by using the Chapter Starts With Style list, and you can indicate the separator between the chapter number and item number.

To include the chapter number, you also have to number the chapters with the Format Heading Numbering command. Otherwise, Word will use a 0 (zero) for the chapter number in each caption. For details on how to number chapters, see "Numbering Headings" starting on page 453.

## How to insert captions automatically

If some or all of the items that need sequential numbering are Word tables or objects that will be created in other programs and inserted in the document using OLE, you can use Word's AutoCaption feature to add the captions automatically. (We discussed OLE and importing data in Chapter 18.) To define the labels and numbering format for automatic captions, choose Insert Caption and then the AutoCaption button to open the AutoCaption dialog box, shown in Figure 23-37.

The choices you see in the Add Caption When Inserting list depend on which programs you've installed on your system that support OLE. The Microsoft Word 6.0 Table option is always available and refers to tables created within Word. To tell Word to add a caption for any of the items in the list, first check the item's check box and highlight the item, using the mouse or keyboard. Then choose a label for the highlighted item in the Use Label pull-down list and a position from the Position pull-down list. Note that you can use different labels and other settings for each item in the list or use the same label for more than one type of item.

Note too the New Label button, which you can choose to open a dialog box that lets you define a new label, just as you can from the Caption dialog box. Similarly, you can choose the Numbering button to open the Caption Numbering dialog box and specify a numbering scheme. When you're finished with the AutoCaption dialog box, choose OK to close it and return to your document.

## The SEQ field

We've been carefully ignoring the SEQ field so far. However, there are some things you can't do with the Caption dialog box, so we can't completely avoid rolling up our sleeves and looking under the hood. To see the actual fields that the dialog box commands insert, choose Tools Options, then View, add a check to the Field Codes check box, and choose OK. Your document should now look much like the one in Figure 23-38 on the next page.

**FIGURE 23-38**

If you set Word to show field codes, you can see the SEQ fields Word uses to keep track of sequence numbers.

As you can see in Figure 23-38, when Word inserts a caption, it inserts part of it as text and part as a SEQ field. The format for the field is

{SEQ Identifier Switches}

where *Identifier* is the label you've chosen to identify the type of item, and *Switches* represents whatever additional options you've added. The only switch in Figure 23-38 is the format switch, \* ARABIC, which tells Word to use Arabic numbers. There are other switches you may want to add manually. If you choose to add them, you can insert the entire field manually, using any of the techniques we discussed in Chapter 20, or you can use the Insert Caption command, set Word to show the fields, and edit the field. Finish by resetting Word to show field results and then updating the field you changed.

## How to repeat the previous sequence number: \c

If you want a SEQ field to return the same number as the previous SEQ field, use the \c switch. For example, if you've used {SEQ Table \* ARABIC} to generate a table number and you need to generate the same table number again—so you can refer to that table by number in your text, for example—enter the second instance as {SEQ table \* ARABIC \c}.

## How to reset the sequence number: \r

If you want to reset the sequence number to a particular value, use the \r switch followed by the value you want to reset to. For example, to reset the sequence number to 1 for the first table in a new chapter, without having to include the chapter number, enter the field as {SEQ Table \* ARABIC \r 1}.

### How to create a placeholder SEQ field: \h

At times you'll want to set the sequence number without inserting the field result in your document. To create this kind of placeholder, enter the \h switch after any other switches in the field code. For example, if the current file contains the second half of a document that has 14 tables in the first half, you might want to enter the field *{SEQ table \r 14 \h}* at the beginning of the file. This ensures that Word will number the first table in the file as *15*, even if you later delete or move the table that you originally created as the first table in the file.

### How to use bookmarks in a SEQ field

If you've used earlier, Windows-based versions of Word, you may know that you can use bookmarks in SEQ fields to let you automatically update references to sequential items. We mention this here only to point out that although Word still recognizes cross-references created with this technique, it's no longer necessary. In fact, Word now provides a much simpler way to create cross-references of all kinds, as we'll discuss next.

# Creating Cross-References

NEW!

Depending on the kind of documents you create, you may find that you need to refer to something—such as a chart, a detailed discussion, a chapter title, or a footnote—that appears pages away from the reference to that item. Finding the right page, item number, or title to refer to is always a bother. Keeping references up to date after you edit your text or change formatting can be a time-consuming chore.

The good news is that Word can automatically *update* cross-references. (As with the caption numbers we've just discussed, *automatic* in this context refers to calculating the right number. You still have to choose the command manually to update the field.) The better news is that Word also makes it easy to *create* cross-references, and that the feature works the same way for cross-referencing any type of item in your document.

## The Insert Cross-Reference command

Word's Insert Cross-Reference command makes entering cross-references as easy as you could possibly hope for. Suppose, for example, that you're working with the file shown in Figure 23-39 on the next page.

**FIGURE 23-39**

We want to add a cross-reference to the partial sentence at the bottom of this document.

The text in Figure 23-39 ends in the middle of a sentence that begins *As we discussed in*.

Suppose you want to add a reference to a section name and give a page number for that section as well (a format we use in this book, for example). To insert the reference, leave the cursor at the position where you want the reference, and choose the Insert Cross-Reference command. Word will open the Cross-Reference dialog box, shown in Figure 23-40.

**FIGURE 23-40**

The Cross-Reference dialog box makes it easy to insert a cross-reference to any kind of item.

As you can see in Figure 23-40, Word lists all the available reference types in the document in the Reference Type list box. These include all the standard types, such as headings, bookmarks, footnotes, endnotes, equations, figures, and tables, plus any types that you've defined by defining labels for the Insert Caption command. The Illustration choice in Figure 23-40, for example, is one that we defined.

For whichever type you've highlighted in the Reference Type list, Word will provide a complete list of those items in the For Which list and will change the name of the list as appropriate. In Figure 23-40, we've highlighted the Heading type, and Word has labeled the For Which box as *For Which Heading*. The choices include all the paragraphs marked as headings in the current document: *Cutting Loose, Is free-lancing for you?, Freedom vs. security*, and so on.

The Insert Reference To box lets you specify the kind of reference to insert. The choice of kinds varies with your choice of reference type. For the Heading type, for example, the choices are Heading Text, Page Number, and Heading Number. For the Footnote type, in contrast, the choices are Footnote Number and Page Number. The important point is that the choice is always appropriate to the type of item.

In this example, we want to refer to the section *Cutting Loose*, followed by the page number. To insert the reference, highlight *Heading* in the Reference Type box, highlight *Cutting Loose* in the For Which Heading list, highlight *Heading Text* in the Insert Reference To list, and choose Insert. Then highlight *Page Number* in the Insert Reference To list, choose Insert again, and then choose Close to return to the document.

Assuming the heading was on page 1, Word will enter the reference as *Cutting Loose1*. To finish, move the cursor to just before the *1* and then type a comma, a space, the text *starting on page*, and another space. You then need to add a period at the end of the sentence. The finished result, shown in Figure 23-41, is *as we discussed in Cutting Loose, starting on page 1.*

**FIGURE 23-41**

The finished cross-reference shown here inserts both the heading name and the page number.

And that's all there is to it. When you want to update the references after further editing, simply select the field, and give the Update command by pressing F9 or by holding the Control key down and clicking the mouse button with the mouse pointer in the field and choosing Update Field from the context-sensitive menu.

The Insert Cross-Reference command uses the reference fields, as you can see if you insert a reference and then set Word to show field codes. Instead of using names, however, Word's Insert Cross-Reference command uses numeric references that take the form RefXXXXXXXX, where the Xs represent a number that Word automatically assigns. Be aware that you should not edit these references. If you change them, Word will give you an error message if you then update the field.

Word will update changes to the heading text as well as changes to the page number. But if you change a heading, be careful to modify what's there rather than deleting all the text and starting again. If you delete the heading entirely, Word won't know that the new heading is a substitute for the old, and you'll get an error message when you try to update the field. Fortunately, if you make this mistake, you can define a new cross-reference easily enough.

## NEW! The STYLEREF Field

The STYLEREF field is a specialized reference field designed to let you add information to a header or footer automatically. For example, if you're creating a glossary, you can use the STYLEREF field to show the first and last glossary words on each page automatically—the same format you'll find in a dictionary. You can also use the STYLEREF field to insert the current chapter name on each page automatically as part of a header or footer. The form of this field is

{STYLEREF "StyleName"}

{STYLEREF "StyleName" Switches}

where *StyleName* is the name of the style assigned to the text you want to return as the field result. To search for one of Word's built-in heading styles (such as Heading 1, Heading 2, and so on), you would enter the style name. (Note that the name must be enclosed in quotes.) Word will search for the nearest paragraph formatted with that style, such as the chapter title, and return the text in that paragraph as the result for the field.

To use the STYLEREF field effectively, you need to understand how Word determines which paragraph is the nearest. That determination depends on where the STYLEREF field is and on whether you've included the \l switch (the letter L). Note that the \l switch is available only in headers and footers. The switch tells Word to search from the bottom of the page, which means it lets you retrieve the text from the last paragraph of the specified style on the page. Figure 23-42 summarizes all the possibilities for the STYLEREF field.

| If STYLEREF Is In | Word Will Search |
|---|---|
| Body text | From the field code to the beginning of the document and then from the field code to the end of the document |
| Footnotes or annotations | From the reference mark in the body text to the beginning of the document, and then from the reference mark to the end of the document |
| Headers or footers | From the beginning of the current page to the end of that page, then from the end of the previous page to the beginning of the document, and then from the beginning of the following page to the end of the document |
| With \l switch (available only in headers or footers) | From the end of the current page to the beginning of the document, and then from the beginning of the following page to the end of the document |

**FIGURE 23-42**

How Word searches with STYLEREF.

Since the STYLEREF field is most often used in headers and footers, we'll confine this discussion to examples using headers and footers.

Figure 23-43 on the next page demonstrates the way you're most likely to use the STYLEREF field. In this document, we've assigned the Heading 1 style to all section headings and the Title style to the document title, and we've entered the header

{STYLEREF "Title"} - {STYLEREF "Heading 1"}

When Word updates the fields, as shown in Figure 23-43, and shows the field results, it will insert the document's title along with the nearest appropriate section heading that's formatted in the Heading 1 style, as shown in Figure 23-44 on the next page.

Figure 23-45 on page 797 demonstrates how you can use the STYLEREF field to create dictionary-style headers. The document in this case is a glossary. Each glossary term is in its own paragraph, and each is assigned the Heading 2 style. In this case, the header fields take the form

{STYLEREF "Heading 2"} - {STYLEREF "Heading 2" \l}

This header is designed to show the first and last terms on each page to provide a set of keywords at the top of each page.

**FIGURE 23-43**

**FIGURE 23-43**

The STYLEREF field in the header of this document retrieves the first section header on the current page or the nearest header before the current page.

**FIGURE 23-44**

This is how the document shown in Figure 23-43 will look after you update the fields, assuming Word is set to show field results.

The first field in this header retrieves the glossary term that appears nearest the top of the page. The second field contains an \l switch, which retrieves the glossary term nearest the bottom of the page. Figure 23-46 shows how the document will appear after you update and display the field results.

FIGURE 23-45

The STYLEREF fields in the header of this document yield dictionary-style headings.

FIGURE 23-46

This is how the document shown in Figure 23-45 will look after you update the fields, assuming Word is set to show field results.

Note that the STYLEREF field also recognizes the \n switch, which inserts any paragraph numbering from the referenced paragraph.

# Customizing Word

# Topic Finder

# NEW! 24

# Recording Macros

s you use Word, you'll find yourself repeating some tasks far more often than others. For example, you may often want to delete or move a word, sentence, or line; enter a time stamp with the current date and time; and so on. Instead of handling these tasks manually, you can record them in macros. That way, you can give the command with one or two keystrokes using shortcut keys, with a menu command, or with a toolbar button. We'll explain how to assign already existing macros to keystrokes and menus in Chapter 28, "Customizing Menus, Keys, & Templates," starting on page 903. You can find details on assigning already-existing macros to toolbars in "Customizing Toolbars" on page 288.

There are, in general, two kinds of macro features available in the entire universe of computer programs: keyboard macros and programmed macros. A keyboard macro records keystrokes and then, when you run it, plays the keystrokes back just as if you had typed them yourself. A programmed macro may also include keystrokes or even be limited to replicating keystrokes, but the essence of a programmed-macro feature is that it offers you the tools to let you add programming logic. For example, a programmed macro might stop to ask a question by way of a dialog box and then perform one task or another, depending on your answer. Word's macro feature falls in the second category. In fact, Word's macro language actually is a programming language, called WordBasic.

Don't let the idea of macros as programs scare you. Word will still let you record macros, much as you can with a keyboard macro feature. However, because Word records commands rather than keystrokes, the results may sometimes surprise you—a point we'll come back to in Chapter 25.

In this chapter, we'll look at how to record macros, how to modify their properties—such as their names and descriptions—and how to edit them. In the two chapters after this, we'll look at how to write macros from scratch and how to use the Dialog Editor to help create dialog boxes for your macros.

# Recording a Macro

Word's Record Macro feature, also called a learn mode, lets you create a macro by telling Word to record a procedure as you perform it manually. Suppose, for example, that you want the ability to quickly and easily delete a word at a time with the option to reinsert the word elsewhere—a useful editing capability that Word doesn't happen to supply as a built-in feature. Word will let you delete the word to the immediate right of the cursor by pressing ⌘-Del or ⌘-Option-G, or the word to the left by pressing ⌘-Delete, but neither of these actions puts the deleted word on the Clipboard for pasting later. However, you can record the steps in a macro, assign the macro to a shortcut key, and add what amounts to a new feature to Word—one that allows you to delete a word with the Edit Cut command and put it in the Clipboard with a single keystroke.

## How to record a macro

The first step in creating a macro is to decide exactly what you want the macro to do. This isn't to say that you can't change it later. As we'll describe in the final section of this chapter, you can edit the macro as needed after you've created it. However, you can eliminate lots of work, and lots of false starts, by giving some thought beforehand to what you want to accomplish.

Assume that you want the macro to cut from the current cursor position to the end of the current word, including any space that follows the word. The standard keystrokes in Word for manually performing this task are ⌘-Shift-Right arrow followed by either ⌘-X or F2. This puts the deleted text on the Clipboard so that you can paste it elsewhere with ⌘-V or F4.

To record the macro, you should first type a few words on the screen so you'll be able to see the effect of your actions as you perform them. Place the cursor in a word, or just in front of one, and choose the Tools Macro command. Then choose Record to bring up the Record Macro dialog box, shown in Figure 24-1.

FIGURE 24-1

By default, the Record
Macro dialog box
suggests the name
Macro1 for your first
macro.

You can start recording a macro either by choosing Tools Macro
and then Record or by double-clicking on REC in the status bar at
the bottom of the Word window. If you prefer, you can add a button
to any of your toolbars that will let you choose the Tools Macro
Record command with a single mouse click; alternatively, you can
define a keyboard shortcut that will let you choose the command
by pressing a shortcut key. For details on customizing toolbars, see
"Customizing Toolbars" on page 288. For details on defining a keyboard shortcut, see "Keyboard Customization" on page 917.

After bringing up the Record Macro dialog box, you can type a name for
the macro, such as *EraseWord*, in the Record Macro Name text box. Alternatively, you can accept Word's default macro name for now—Macro1, in this
case. (The next time you record a macro, Word will suggest the name Macro2,
and so forth.)

If you use the default name (or any other name, for that matter),
you can rename the macro at any time by choosing Tools Macro and
then choosing Organizer to open the Organizer dialog box. You
would then highlight the macro name you want to change and
choose Rename. We'll cover this in a bit more detail in "How to rename a macro" on page 818.

To jump ahead of our example a bit, once you give the macro a name, you
can choose OK and perform the task you want to record—in this case typing
⌘-Shift-Right arrow and then ⌘-X or F2. To stop recording, you can, among
other choices, double-click on REC in the status bar, or choose Tools Macro

and then Stop Recording. Once the macro is recorded, you'll be able to delete a word, or part of one, and put it on the Clipboard simply by moving the cursor to the appropriate word and running the macro. But before you actually record the macro, there are some issues you will want to consider.

## Rules for macro names

Word has a few simple rules for naming macros. The name must start with a letter of the alphabet, and it can contain only letters and numbers. If you type an invalid character, such as a space, in the Record Macro Name text box, Word will dim the OK button in the dialog box; you will not be able to close the dialog box to record the macro until you type an acceptable macro name.

## Macro descriptions, template assignments, and shortcuts

In addition to typing a name, you can optionally add a description for the macro before you record it, using the Description text box at the bottom of the Record Macro dialog box. You can also assign the macro to a template and specify a shortcut key, menu item, or toolbar button for running the macro.

As with the macro name, you can change descriptions, template assignments, shortcut keys, menu assignments, and toolbar button assignments at any time. We'll show you how to change a description in "How to change a macro's description" on page 818. We'll show you how to change a menu assignment or shortcut key in Chapter 28, "Customizing Menus, Keys, & Templates," starting on page 896, and how to change a template assignment in Chapter 27, "Templates," starting on page 883. Changing toolbar buttons works the same way for macros as for Word's built-in commands and is covered in "Customizing Toolbars" on page 288.

You can define all three kinds of shortcuts—keystroke, menu assignment, and toolbar button—for any macro. But once you start defining them, you won't have the option of coming back to the Record Macro dialog box to change the macro name, description, or template assignment. So be sure you're satisfied with these before you complete the procedure of specifying a shortcut.

### How to enter a macro description

As you can see in Figure 24-2, the Record Macro dialog box includes a Description text box where you can enter a description for the macro.

**FIGURE 24-2**

The Record Macro dialog box lets you give your macro a description as well as a name.

You don't have to give your macro a description. If you do, however, and you attach the macro to a menu, Word will display the description in the status bar when you highlight the menu choice. Similarly, if you attach the macro to a toolbar button, Word will display the description in the status bar when you move your mouse pointer over the toolbar button.

You can write a macro description of up to 255 characters—substantially longer than will fit in the Description text box without scrolling. However, you should try to limit the description so it will fit. As you'll see when you run the macro, keeping the description short enough to see all of it at once will make it easier to find the right macro when you can't remember its name. And if you attach the macro to a menu, keeping the description short will ensure that you can see the entire description on the status line. For our example, we'll use the description *Delete a Word to the Clipboard*, as also shown in Figure 24-2. Note in passing that as you type a description in the text box, you can start a new line by pressing Return.

## How to set a macro's template assignment

Immediately above the description box in Figure 24-2 is a text box labeled *Make Macro Available To*. The choices you'll see in the pull-down list depend on which templates you're using with the current document.

If you're even slightly familiar with the concept of templates—which we discussed briefly in Chapter 2 and also in Chapter 9—you probably already know that you can store macros in the Normal template to make them available to all of your documents. Alternatively, you can store them in the current supplementary template so they will be available to only the documents that are based on that particular template. The Make Macro Available To box is where you specify which template to store the macro in. For a detailed discussion of templates, see Chapter 27, "Templates," starting on page 883.

Word will also let you load a template as a global template. When you create a macro, however, Word does not give you the option of storing the macro in any global templates that happen to be loaded. If you want to move the macro to one of your global templates, you have to use the Organizer, which we'll describe in Chapter 27.

If your current document is based on the Normal template, the only choice in the list for the Make Macro Available To box will be All Documents (Normal), as in Figure 24-2. If you are using a supplementary template, however, you'll also see a choice for documents based on that supplementary template. If the template is Letters, for example, you'll see the choice Documents Based On Letters. If you have more than one choice available, simply select the template you want to store the macro in.

If you choose to assign a keystroke, menu, or toolbar shortcut to a macro, as we'll describe in the next three sections, you'll find that you can also store these shortcuts in either the Normal template or the current supplementary template. For example, the Keyboard card in the Customize dialog box, shown in Figure 24-3, provides an option for selecting the template: the Save Changes In box in the lower right corner.

Be aware that if you change the setting for storing the shortcuts, the change does not affect where Word stores the macros. You can, for example, assign a shortcut key to the Normal template that runs a macro stored in some other template—call it Letters. If you then attach the Letters template to a document, the shortcut key will work. If you don't attach the Letters template, nothing will happen when you use the shortcut key.

There are some situations in which this can come in handy. Suppose you have two templates, Letters and Memos. You might want macros in both that serve the same function but behave differently; for example, you might want to start the letter off with a letter format and the memo with a memo format. You can create two macros with the same name and store each in the appropriate template. You can then assign a shortcut key to the macro name in Normal. That shortcut key will run the memo version of the macro when you attach the Memo template and the letter version when you attach the Letter template. This feature should be used with care because it can easily become confusing. For the rest of this discussion, we'll ignore the Save Changes In list box.

There are any number of reasons why you might want template-specific macros. For example, if you create a separate template for each of several users, you can write a different set of macros to match each individual's working habits and store each set in its own template. Until you're completely comfortable with templates, however, and unless you have a good reason for doing otherwise, we strongly recommend that you store your macros in the Normal template. For most of this discussion, we'll assume you are using only the Normal template so that choosing where to store the macro is not an issue.

## How to assign a macro to a shortcut key

As you can see in Figure 24-2, the Record Macro dialog box includes three items in the Assign Macro To box: Toolbars, Menus, and Keyboard. You can choose any of these to open the Customize dialog box (shown in Figure 24-3). Once you've opened the dialog box you can move freely between the Keyboard, Menus, and Toolbars option cards. However, the item you choose in the Record Macro dialog box determines which card you'll see when you first open the Customize dialog box. For purposes of this example, we'll start with the Keyboard card. If you choose it, Word will respond with the Customize dialog box, as shown in Figure 24-3.

**FIGURE 24-3**

To assign a shortcut key to a macro you are about to record, open the Customize dialog box by choosing Keyboard in the Record Macro dialog box.

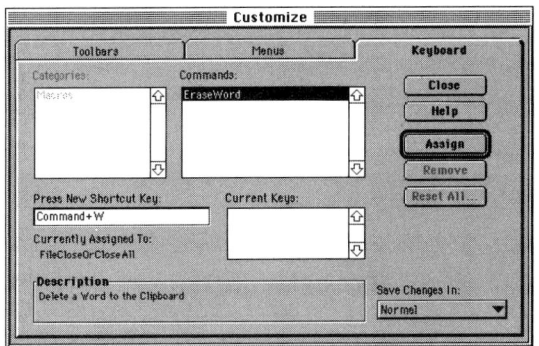

When you open the Customize dialog box from the Record Macro dialog box, the only item Word will let you customize is the macro you're about to record. That's why the only category in the Categories list box in Figure 24-3 is Macros, and the only command in the Commands list box is EraseWord, the name of the macro as we've typed it.

To assign a shortcut key, simply make sure the cursor is in the Press New Shortcut Key box and press the appropriate keys. If you choose a shortcut key that's already assigned, Word will let you know. In Figure 24-3, for example, we've used ⌘-W as the shortcut key. Note that Word has responded below the text box with the message that the shortcut key is already assigned to FileCloseOrCloseAll. If you use a shortcut key that isn't already assigned, the message will read *Currently Assigned To: [unassigned]*.

If the shortcut key you used is already assigned and you don't want to change the assignment to the new macro, simply press the Delete key and enter a different keystroke. For this example, we'll stay with ⌘-W. When you're satisfied with the entry, choose Assign, and Word will list the key in the Current Keys list box. If you change your mind, you can then highlight the key in the list box and choose Remove to tell Word to remove the key from the list. When you close the Customize dialog box, Word will take you directly to the editing screen to record the macro, whether you've assigned a shortcut key or not. (If you want to specify a menu or toolbar assignment for this macro, choose the tab for that card in the Customize dialog box before you close it.)

You can assign as many shortcut keys as you like to the macro you're about to record. Word will display each one separately in the Current Keys list box. If you close the dialog box before choosing the Assign button, however, Word will not assign the shortcut key to the macro—even if a shortcut key name is showing in the Press New Shortcut Key text box.

You can define shortcut keys by using Control, ⌘, Control-Shift, or ⌘-Control in combination with any alphabetic character; any number; the unshifted characters on any of the punctuation keys (period and comma, for example); any function key; or the Del, Delete, Home, End, Page Up, Page Down, or the arrow keys. You can also use ⌘-Shift in combination with any of these but the number keys. Even better, Word 6.0 will let you define two-keystroke assignments—for example, Control-P followed by P, which we will indicate as Control-P,P (with Control-P counted as one keystroke). For the second keystroke, you can use a key by itself or in combination with Shift.

## How to assign a macro to a menu

To assign the macro to a menu, you can choose Menus, rather than Keyboard, from the Record Macro dialog box shown in Figure 24-2. Alternatively, if you've just finished assigning a keystroke but haven't closed the dialog box yet, you can choose the Menus tab to move to the Menus card. Either way, you'll see the Customize dialog box with the Menus card, as shown in Figure 24-4.

Because you opened the Customize dialog box from the Record Macro dialog box, Word will limit your choices on the Menus card primarily to customizing the macro you're about to record. (We say "primarily" because you can choose the Menu Bar button to customize the menu bar itself.) That's why the only category in the Categories list box in Figure 24-4 is Macros, and the only macro available to work with is EraseWord, the macro we're about to record. For purposes of this discussion, we will ignore the Menu Bar button. But you can find details on customizing the menu bar in "Renaming, Adding, and Deleting Menus" on page 914.

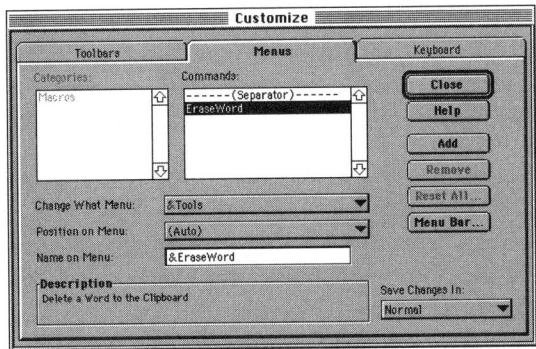

**FIGURE 24-4**

To assign a macro you are about to record to a menu, choose Menus from the Assign Macro To box in the Record Macro dialog box, or choose the Menus tab from within the Customize dialog box.

The three items you need to be concerned with on the Menus card are the boxes labeled *Change What Menu, Position On Menu,* and *Name On Menu.*

As you can see from the partial list showing in Figure 24-5, you can use the Change What Menu list box to pick from a large number of menus. In addition to the menus on the menu bar, the list includes the File and Help menus, which show when no document is open, and a lengthy list of shortcut menus—the context-sensitive menus Word displays in response to holding down the Control key while clicking the mouse button. The first step in assigning a macro to the menu is to choose the menu to use.

**FIGURE 24-5**

The Change What Menu list box lists all the menus on the menu bar plus all of Word's context-sensitive shortcut menus.

The list available in the Position On Menu box changes to match whatever menu you've chosen in the Change What Menu box. The choices in this list give you complete control over where to put the new menu item in the menu; for the moment, we'll accept the default choice of (Auto). For a detailed discussion of how to control the position of a menu item, see "Customizing the Menus" on page 904.

As a default, Word enters the macro name in the Name On Menu text box. You can accept this or change it. If you want the ability to choose the item from a drop-down menu with a keystroke (which you activate by pressing F10 or ⌘-Tab), be sure to type an ampersand (&) immediately before the character you want to use.

If two or more menu items on any given menu have the same trigger character—meaning the character that tells Word to choose that menu command—pressing the character will not tell Word to run the command. Instead, repeatedly typing the character will cycle through all of the menu commands that use the same character. And to run the command from the keyboard, you'll have to highlight the command in the menu and then press Return. If you want to designate the command and choose it in a single keystroke, you'll have to make sure that you choose a trigger character that isn't assigned to anything else on the same menu. A reasonable choice for the EraseWord macro, for example, would be to put the macro on the Edit menu, name it Delete Word, and put the ampersand in front of the W so that it reads *Delete &Word.*

After you've designated which menu to change, what position to put the menu item in, and what name to use, choose the Add button to assign the item to the menu. If you like, you can then repeat the process, adding the item to other menus; you can even use a different name on each menu.

## How to assign a macro to a toolbar

Assigning a macro to a toolbar is even easier than assigning it to a shortcut key or menu. If the Record Macro dialog box is still open (as shown in Figure 24-2), you can start by choosing Toolbars. Alternatively, if you've already opened the Customize dialog box, you can simply choose the Toolbars tab. In either case, you'll see the Customize dialog box with the Toolbars card, as shown in Figure 24-6.

**FIGURE 24-6**

To assign a macro you are about to record to a toolbar, choose Toolbars from the Assign Macro To box in the Record Macro dialog box, or choose the Toolbars card in the Customize dialog box.

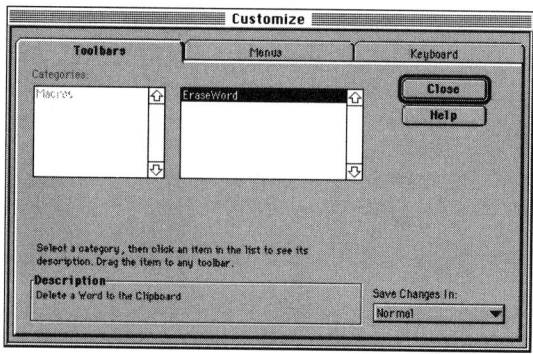

When you open the Customize box this way, Word will limit you to customizing the macro you're about to record. As you can see in Figure 24-6, the only category available in the Categories list is Macros, and the only macro available is EraseWord, the one we're working with. Note too that you're limited to putting the macro button either on a toolbar that's currently displayed or on a new toolbar. To add one of Word's built-in toolbars to the screen while the Customize dialog box is open, hold down the Control key and click on any part of any visible toolbar except on a button. Word will open a pull-down menu with a list of built-in toolbars. Simply highlight the toolbar you want to open, and release the mouse button. As you might expect, you can also move the toolbar button later.

To create a button for the macro and place it on a toolbar, simply click on the macro name and hold down the mouse button. Word will respond by showing the outline of a button at the mouse pointer. You can then drag the button to an appropriate position on any visible toolbar. If you want to place the button between two existing buttons, for example, point to the space or border between the two toolbar buttons and release the mouse button. Word will rearrange the existing buttons to insert the new one. To create a new toolbar, drag the button to any spot outside the dialog box where there isn't already a toolbar.

After you define the position for the new button, Word will open the Custom Button dialog box, shown in Figure 24-7. Choose a button icon from the dialog box by clicking on the icon you prefer, and then choose Assign to assign the icon to the newly created button. Note, in passing, that you can also choose Edit from the Custom Button dialog box if you want to change the way a button looks. For details on the button editor, see "How to add a button" on page 290.

**FIGURE 24-7**

After you indicate where you want a new toolbar button, Word will open this dialog box, and you can pick an icon for the button.

## How to create the macro

After you choose OK in the Record Macro dialog box or finish specifying options in the Customize dialog box, Word will return you to the editing screen.

Notice that the REC indicator in the status bar (as shown in Figure 24-8) is black, rather than grayed, indicating that you are recording a macro.

**FIGURE 24-8**

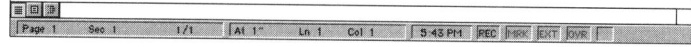

When you are recording a macro, Word changes the indicator REC in the status bar to black lettering.

The next step is to manually choose the commands that you want Word to record. In the example of our EraseWord macro, you would simply press ⌘-Shift-Right arrow and then either ⌘-X or F2. Note, however, that you can perform just about any task while recording a macro that you can normally perform in Word, using either the keyboard or the mouse. The only exceptions are that you can't use the mouse to move the cursor or to select text. Word indicates this by showing the mouse pointer as a transparent left-pointing arrow, rather than the usual I-beam shape, while in the text of your document.

## How to correct mistakes

If you make a mistake while recording a macro, you can easily make a correction. If you type the wrong text character, for example, you can press the Delete key to back up, and you can then type the correct text. Instead of recording both the mistake and the correction (at least in this particular case), Word will record only the result—the final group of characters you type before choosing a command or moving the cursor. (We'll discuss what Word actually records in more detail in Chapter 25.)

If you accidentally change your document by choosing the wrong command—from a menu, the ruler, or a toolbar—you have two choices: You can stop the recording and start all over again, or you can correct the mistake with another command. For example, if you use the Formatting toolbar to change some 12-point text to 18-point and then realize you wanted to change it to 14-point instead, you can use the toolbar again to change the text to 14-point. Word will record the correction as well as the original mistake. You can then edit the macro at any later time to eliminate the mistake. We'll show you how in the final section of this chapter.

## How to end the recording of a macro

After you finish performing the task you want to turn into a macro, you need to stop recording. Word offers three choices for stopping. We mentioned two of these earlier in this chapter: choosing Tools Macro and then the Stop Recording button, and double-clicking on REC in the status bar. The third choice is to click on the Stop button on the Macro Record toolbar. As you may have noticed, when you start recording, Word adds a two-button toolbar to the screen, as shown in Figure 24-9. The left button in this pair is the Stop button. Click on it once to stop recording.

**FIGURE 24-9**

When you start recording a macro, Word displays the Macro Record toolbar.

The right-hand button on the Macro Record toolbar is the Pause button. If you click on this while recording a macro, Word will suspend recording so you can give commands or take other actions without recording them as part of the macro. This can be handy. For example, you may realize after starting the macro that the cursor is in a different position from where it should be. You can click on the Pause button and then move the cursor to the correct position. To resume recording, click on the Pause button again.

As shipped, Word offers only one way to give the Pause Recorder command—the Pause button on the Macro Record toolbar. If you would like to have the command available from the keyboard, you can open the Customize dialog box and assign a different shortcut key to the command. Choose Tools Customize, and then the Keyboard card. In the Categories list box, highlight All Commands, and then in the Commands list box, highlight PauseRecorder. Next position the cursor in the Press New Shortcut Key text box, and press the shortcut keys you want to use—just as you would assign a shortcut key for a macro. To finish, choose Assign. For more details on using the Keyboard card for assigning keys to commands, see "Keyboard Customization" on page 917.

## Running a Macro

After you've created a macro, you can run it in one of four ways: with the Tools Macro command or—if you've assigned one—by using a shortcut key, a menu command, or a toolbar button. We'll look at each of these in a moment, but before we do, a little background might be helpful.

## What happens when Word runs a recorded macro

When Word runs a recorded macro, it repeats the actions you performed while recording that macro. If you chose menu commands or made dialog box entries while recording the macro, you won't see Word open the menu or the dialog box when you run the macro, but you will see the effects of those actions. For example, if the macro opens several files with the File Open command, you will not see the File Open dialog box at any time. The macro will simply open the files for you.

## Running macros with macros

It's worth noting also that a macro can run another macro. If a given macro tells Word to run a second macro, Word will run the second macro and then return to the first. As you might expect, Word will resume the main macro from the point where it left, rather than going back to the beginning.

## A word of caution

Be aware that a macro that doesn't do what you intended can have disastrous effects. For example, it can erase a portion of a document you didn't want to erase. When you're creating macros that have the potential to do harm, save your active document and test the macro before going on. And with that warning, let's look at how to run a macro.

## How to run a macro with the Tools Macro command

To run a macro with the Tools Macro command, first position your cursor where you want it to be when you run the macro. With the EraseWord macro, for example, you'll want to put the cursor at the appropriate position to delete everything from that position to the end of the word.

Now choose Tools Macro to open the Macro dialog box, shown in Figure 24-10. Make sure that the Macros Available In option is set correctly. If the option is set to Word Commands, for example, the Macro Name list box will show Word's built-in commands rather than macro names.

When you want to run a macro, you'll find at least three choices for the Macros Available In box: Word Commands, as just described; Normal (Global Template); and All Active Templates. If the Normal template is the only one attached to your document, the second and third choices yield identical results. With either one, the Macro Names list box will show the macros in the Normal template. If you have a supplementary template attached to the current document, you'll also find a choice for that template, which will show the current supplementary template's name as part of the option name. Choose this one, and the Macro Name list box will show only those macros in the supplementary template. If you have a supplementary template attached and you set the option to All Active Templates, you'll see a list of all macros currently available in all current templates.

**FIGURE 24-10**

You can use the Macro dialog box to run a macro or a built-in command.

Unless there are so many macros that you want to limit the number you have to deal with at once, you'll most often want the Macros Available In option set to All Active Templates.

With the Macros Available In option set appropriately, type the name of the macro you want to run, or choose it from the list box. If you entered a description for your macro when you recorded it, Word will display the description in the Description box at the bottom of the dialog box, as shown in Figure 24-11 on the next page.

If you can't remember the name of the macro you want, you can browse through the descriptions by highlighting macros in the list box. Note also that if the descriptions are short enough to fit within the Description box, you can easily see the entire description for each macro as you browse through the list.

After you enter the appropriate macro in the Macro Name box, choose Run to run it. If you've chosen the EraseWord macro, Word will delete all text from the cursor to the end of the word the cursor is in and place the text on the Clipboard.

**FIGURE 24-11**

If you enter descriptions for your macros, Word will display them when you select the macro name in the Macro Name list.

# How to run a macro with a shortcut key, a menu item, or a toolbar button

Running our sample macro with the Tools Macro command isn't worth the effort, since it takes more work than giving the commands manually. If you've assigned a shortcut key, however, you can get exactly the same effect by positioning the cursor and typing the shortcut key—⌘-W if you followed our example. Clearly, running the macro with a single key combination is an immediate improvement over Word's built-in commands on a simple macro like this, where you are substituting one keystroke for two. For touch typists, the gain is even greater because the one keystroke doesn't force you to take your hands from the home keys—as you must if you use the built-in commands. With more complex macros, even the Tools Macro command can save time, and the advantages of a shortcut key are multiplied further.

If you've assigned the macro to a menu item or a toolbar button, you can run it the same way you would run a built-in Word command: Simply choose the macro from the menu, or click on the button. As with the Tools Macro command, this saves little or no work in our sample macro, compared with choosing the commands manually. With more complex macros, however, the advantages are obvious, particularly for those who prefer the mouse to the keyboard. Even for those who prefer the keyboard, however, using the menu or toolbar button may be the better choice for a macro you don't use often enough to remember the shortcut key. Ultimately, the best way to run a macro is a matter of individual taste.

# Saving a Macro

Word does not save your macros to disk when you record them or change them. Unless you instruct Word otherwise, it holds the macros in memory while you continue working. It will eventually save the macros to disk in one of three ways, depending on which template you've assigned the macro to and on whether you've set Word to prompt before saving the Normal template. (To see or change the current setting for prompting, choose Tools Options and then Save. If the Prompt To Save Normal check box is checked, Word will prompt you before saving the template.)

If you created or changed a macro assigned to the Normal template, Word won't save the macro to disk until you choose File Quit or File Save All. At that point, if Word is set to save the Normal template without prompting, it will simply save the template, macros and all.

If Word is set to prompt when saving the Normal template, however, it will respond with a message box asking whether to save the changes to the template Normal.

If you've assigned the new or changed macros to a supplemental template, Word will ask whether you want to save them when you close the document attached to that template or when you choose File Save All. In this case, Word will always show you a message box asking whether you want to save the changed template. You can then choose Yes, No, or Cancel, as appropriate.

## How to save a macro with the File Save All command

The problem with holding all macros in memory is that you can lose them if you have a system crash. As we just suggested, however, you can force Word to save all your current files on command—including any new or changed macros. Simply choose File Save All. As described above, for each file and template currently open that has any change since the last time you saved, Word will display a message box asking if you want to save the changes. You can choose Yes or No for each, or you can return to your document without saving by choosing Cancel in any of the message boxes.

# Modifying a Macro's Properties

After you create a macro, you can modify the macro's properties, including its name and description. You can also modify the macro itself by editing it. And you can delete a macro.

## How to rename a macro

To rename a macro, first choose the Tools Macro command to open the Macro dialog box. Then choose the Organizer button to open the Organizer dialog box, shown in Figure 24-12, with the Macros card showing.

You can use the Macros card in the Organizer dialog box to rename macros, among other options.

Next highlight a macro name in the list of macros on either the left or the right side of the Organizer dialog box, as appropriate. Choose the Rename button, and Word will display the Rename dialog box, shown in Figure 24-13. You can then type the new name and choose OK. Word will replace the old name with the new one in the list of macros. Close the Organizer dialog box to return to the editing screen.

The Rename dialog box lets you change a macro's name.

## How to change a macro's description

To change a macro's description, choose Tools Macro to open the Macro dialog box, and enter the name of the macro in the Macro Name box. You can then move to the description text box and simply type the new description.

If you press the Esc key or click on the Cancel (or Close) button before you leave the Description text box, Word will ignore any changes in the description that you've typed. However, if you move out of the text box first—by pressing Tab or by clicking with the mouse—or if you choose any button (except Cancel or Delete), Word will accept the changed description.

## How to delete a macro

To delete a macro from the Macro dialog box, enter the name in the Macro Name box, and choose the Delete button. Word will ask you for confirmation. Choose Yes, and Word will delete the macro. Once deleted, the macro is gone—at least in the sense that you cannot use the Edit Undo command to recover an accidental deletion.

## How to recover a deleted macro

If you delete the wrong macro, you may still be able to recover it. Keep in mind that if the macro was ever saved to disk, it's still there, in the appropriate template file. That means there's a simple way to get it back. But use it only if you are absolutely sure that you haven't made any other changes to your macros or AutoText entries since you last saved the template to disk.

If the macro was stored in a supplemental template, close all files that are using that template, and choose No when Word asks if you want to save the changes to the template. If the macro was stored in the Normal template, choose Tools Options and then Save, and make sure the Prompt To Save Normal check box is checked. Then exit Word, and choose No when Word asks whether to save the changes that affect the Normal template. The next time you use the template, the macro will still be there.

This route to recovering accidentally erased macros offers a good argument for saving macros to disk with the File Save All command each time you create or change a macro. This may be a tedious chore if you have a slow computer, but it's a good habit to get into if your system is fast enough to save the changes in a reasonable length of time.

# Editing a Macro

We've mentioned several times that you can edit macros as well as record them. This editing feature is essential for writing macros from scratch—a topic we'll cover in the next chapter. But the ability to edit macros can be helpful even if you're interested only in recording them. In particular, you can edit recorded macros to eliminate mistakes.

In truth, you don't have to fix mistakes. As long as the macro accomplishes the task, you can use it as is. Consider the example of accidentally changing some text to an 18-point font while recording a macro and then correcting it to 14-point. If you create such a macro, complete with the mistake and the correction, you will find that it works just fine for changing highlighted text to 14-point. However, the macro will change the text to 18-point first, just as you did when you recorded it. And the macro will run somewhat faster if you delete the extra step.

To practice fixing a macro, start by creating one that includes a mistake. Select some text, choose Tools Macro, and then choose the Record button. Give the macro an appropriate name, such as FourteenPt; type a description if you like, and assign the macro to a shortcut key, menu, or toolbar button. Then choose OK or close the Customize dialog box to start recording. Format the text with the Format toolbar, first as 18-point, and then reformat it as 14-point. (If you format it a different way, your screen won't match our sample in Figure 24-14.) Finally, stop recording—by choosing Tools Macro and then the Stop Recording button, or by double-clicking on REC in the status bar, or by clicking on the Stop button on the Macro Record toolbar.

To edit the macro, choose Tools Macro to open the Macro dialog box, enter the macro name in the Macro Name text box, and choose Edit. Word will open a macro editing window similar to the one shown in Figure 24-14.

Word records your actions as a series of WordBasic instructions. The first line of the macro is Sub MAIN, and the last line is End Sub. These two lines mark the beginning and end of the macro and must be included as part of every macro. Between the beginning and ending lines are the macro instructions. In this case, the two instructions between Sub MAIN and End Sub are simply the two font commands. The first sets the font to 18 points; the second sets it to 14 points.

As you can see in Figure 24-14, the macro editing window is similar to a document window. The window name is Global: FourteenPt because the macro we're looking at is named FourteenPt and is stored in the Normal template. Notice that the Macro toolbar has changed in appearance from the one that was on the document screen during macro recording; it now contains 12 buttons and a pull-down list, and it appears below the Standard and Formatting toolbars (or below the menu bar if you've set Word not to display any toolbars). We'll discuss these buttons in the next chapter.

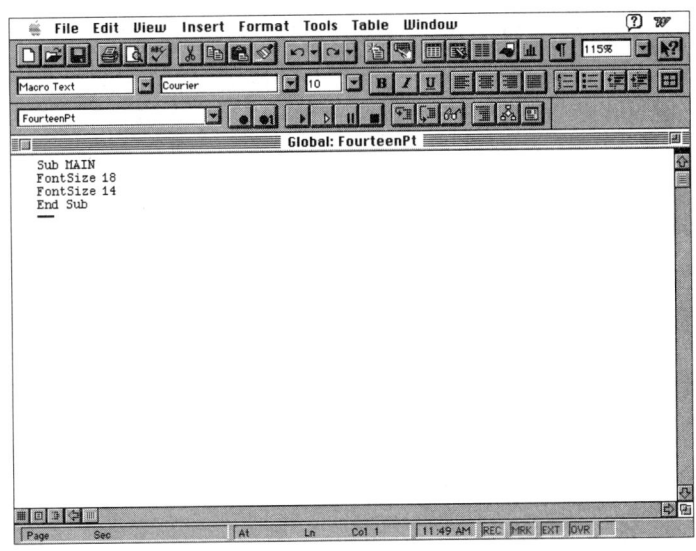

**FIGURE 24-14**

Word's macro editing window lets you review and edit your macros.

Word will dim most of the commands on the menus while you're in a macro editing window. For example, all commands on the Insert and Table menus will be grayed. However, you'll find that all of the commands you need for editing are still available.

The mechanics of editing a macro are the same as for editing a document. For example, you can use the Edit Cut, Edit Copy, and Edit Paste commands to move and copy text within a macro, between two macros, or between a macro and a document window. In fact, the macro editing window works much like a standard document window in most respects, including such details as letting you activate another window with the Window menu. Similarly, you can close a macro editing window by choosing File Close.

Far more difficult than the mechanics of editing a macro is knowing what changes to make. For complex macros, this means learning WordBasic and some elements of programming. For fixing mistakes in a simple macro such as FourteenPt, however, it's often easy enough to spot the offending command and delete it. In this case, you want to delete the command FontSize 18 and leave the command FontSize 14 unchanged.

To fix the FourteenPt macro, delete the command that sets the font to 18-point so that the screen looks like Figure 24-15 on the next page. Then choose File Close. When Word asks whether you want to keep the changes to Global: FourteenPt, choose Yes. (But remember that this doesn't save the changes to disk; it saves them only in memory.)

**FIGURE 24-15**

The corrected version
of FourteenPt still starts
with Sub MAIN and
ends with End Sub.
These starting and
ending markers must
be in every macro.

After you correct a macro, you should test it to verify that it still works. In
this case, if you select some text and run the macro, it should go directly to
14-point size, without stepping through the 18-point size first.

This introduction to the mechanics of editing macros barely opens the door
on the subject. Unfortunately, issues of programming are beyond the scope of this
book. In the next two chapters, however, we'll open the door a bit wider and give
you a look at some of the possibilities available with macros.

# TOPIC FINDER

# 25

# An Introduction to Writing Macros

f you've worked through the introduction to macros in Chapter 24, you should know enough about macros by now to be able to record and use your own. But as useful as you will find recorded macros to be, you will be limited in what you can do with them. To get beyond those limits, you'll need programmed macros.

A programmed macro may simply use features that Word's Record Macro feature has no way to record, as we'll show shortly. But the essence of a programmed macro is that it includes programming logic. Before choosing the File Open command, for example, a programmed macro might stop to ask whether to list all files or just Word documents. Depending on your answer, it would then list the appropriate files. The commands that let the macro ask questions and respond to the answers provide the programming logic.

All of Word's macros—whether recorded or written from scratch—are stored as WordBasic commands. WordBasic is a programming language that's drawn from Microsoft Basic but that also includes commands specifically designed for word processing—for example, setting font size.

Programming, of course, is a subject that's easily worth a book (or several books) of its own. We won't presume to try to teach even the fundamentals of programming in just one or two chapters. However, in this chapter, we will cover the mechanics of using Word's built-in tools for creating, testing, and fixing macros. In the process, we'll cover some aspects of programming, and we'll show you some simple but useful macros along the way.

Even if you're already familiar with programming concepts, you'll still need to learn the proper syntax for WordBasic's various instructions. Word's online Help contains a complete reference to WordBasic syntax. To use this reference, open the Help menu, choose Microsoft Word Help, and then choose the topic Programming With Microsoft Word. If you'd like detailed instructions on WordBasic programming, you might want to order the *Microsoft Word Developer's Kit, second edition.* The first part of the *Microsoft Word Developer's Kit* includes an instruction manual for programming in WordBasic that starts at the beginner's level. You can purchase a copy of the kit wherever computer books are sold, or refer to the supplemental offer card that came in your Microsoft Word package. For those who want to roll up their sleeves and delve into macros further, we'll recommend some additional books at the end of our introduction to macros, in the last part of Chapter 26.

In this chapter, we'll look primarily at the mechanics of writing, editing, and testing macros. We'll start with an example that the Record Macro feature simply can't create.

# Limitations of the Record Macro Feature

If you've been working with Word for any length of time, you've probably developed some techniques that take advantage of Word's built-in features, but go a little further. For example, suppose you make extensive use of the Edit Find command to move around in long documents, searching up or down as appropriate to find the part of the document you want to get to.

In that case, it would be handy to have a pair of macros that open the Find dialog box. One would automatically set the Search direction to Up, the other to Down. Both would wait for you to enter the text to search for. Both seem like simple macros that you should be able to create by recording. Unfortunately, you can't.

To keep this discussion simple, we'll focus on just the macro for setting the search direction to Down. If you try recording the macro with the Tools Macro Record command, your first inclination will probably be to choose Edit

Find, choose Down from the Search pull-down list, and then either click on the Stop button or choose Tools Macro and the Stop Recording button. However, Word will not let you stop recording from within the Find dialog box. If you move to the document by clicking on it with the mouse, Word will let you use either of these commands to stop recording, but it won't record anything. You might next try closing the Find dialog box before you stop recording, either by choosing Cancel immediately, or by searching for some text first, and then choosing Cancel. If you make either choice and then stop recording, you'll find you don't have the macro you want.

To see what these macros look like, choose Tools Macro to open the Macro dialog box; highlight the macro name, and choose Edit. If you chose Cancel in the Find dialog box before you stopped recording, or you moved to the document to stop recording, you'll see the macro shown in Figure 25-1. If you searched for some text first (such as Test Text in our example), you'll see a macro similar to the one shown in Figure 25-2 on the next page.

**FIGURE 25-1**

If you choose Cancel in a dialog box while recording a macro, the macro won't refer to the dialog box.

## What Record Macro records

What both of these macros have in common is that they show the final result of what you did. In the first case, you chose Cancel in the dialog box. Because you didn't complete the command, Word didn't record one. The only statements in the macro are Sub MAIN and End Sub. As we discussed briefly in

FIGURE 25-2

If you record a macro that gives a command through a dialog box, the macro will record only the result.

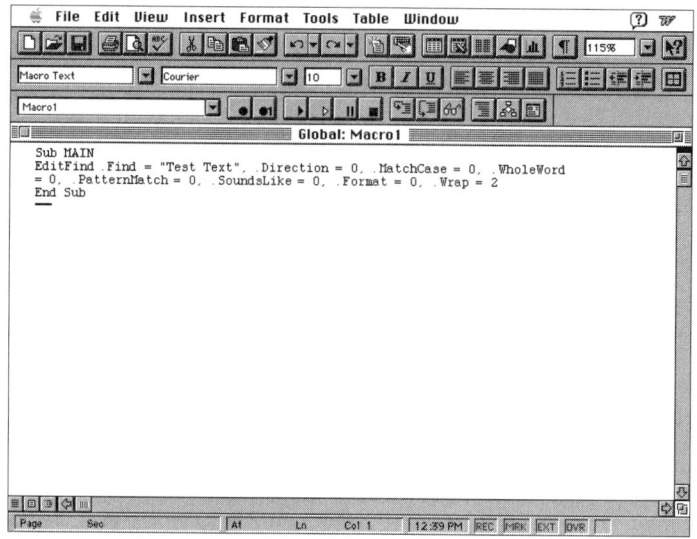

Chapter 24, these are beginning and end markers, and you must include them in all macros, so Word supplies them automatically.

In the second case, you actually searched for some text, so Word recorded the command to open that specific file. Roughly translated, the EditFind command in Figure 25-2 tells Word to search for the words *Test Text* between the current cursor position and the end of the file, without paying any attention to case, whole words, pattern matching, Word's sounds-like search feature, or format. The command also tells Word that if the search started anywhere but at the very beginning of the document, Word should ask whether to search from the beginning when it reaches the end.

In this second example, you will get exactly the same result whether you entered the text to search for or it was already there, whether you had to change the search direction or it was already set the way you wanted it, and whether you had to remove checks from the check boxes or they were already empty. The point is, Word records only the results of your commands, not how you got there.

Neither of these macros does what you set out to do, which is to open the Find dialog box, set the search direction, and wait for you to enter the text to search for. For that, you need to write a macro on your own.

# Writing a Macro from Scratch

To write a macro from scratch, you first need to open a macro editing window. Start by choosing the Tools Macro command, and then type the name for the new macro in the Macro Name text box. (You can also add a Description if you like.) Next choose Create; Word will open a macro editing window that looks much like Figure 25-3.

Except for the macro name and the blank line between the Sub MAIN and End Sub statements, Figure 25-3 is essentially identical to Figure 25-1. The window is initially empty except for these beginning and end markers, which Word automatically provides for you. You write the macro by inserting WordBasic instructions between the markers.

**FIGURE 25-3**

When you open the macro editing window to write a new macro, Word provides the Sub MAIN and End Sub statements.

Note also that when you create a macro from scratch, Word does not give you the chance to assign a keyboard shortcut to it—which Word does allow when you record a macro. We'll explain how to assign a keyboard shortcut to the macro in Chapter 28, "Customizing Menus, Keys, & Templates," starting on page 903. If you follow us through this discussion and create these macros as you go, you still can run the macros from the Tools Macro dialog box.

## Macros that use Word's dialog boxes

Now that you know how to write the macro, the only issue is deciding what to write. What you need, in this case, is a way to tell Word to open a dialog box and then stop and wait for you to enter some text. Learning how to work with dialog boxes is an important technique in WordBasic because dialog boxes are central to Word.

 You should be aware that, as of the time we wrote this book, the FindText.Direction statement as used below was not working. However, it's supposed to work, and we assume that Microsoft will, in fact, get it working at some time.

Start with the screen shown in Figure 25-3. Next, type the following statements between the Sub MAIN and End Sub markers:

```
Dim FindText As EditFind
FindText.Direction = 0
Dialog FindText
EditFind FindText
```

The first line in this macro uses the WordBasic Dim statement to create and open a dialog record named FindText. (You can use the Dim statement for other purposes too, but we'll look only at its usefulness for creating a dialog record.) In effect, it creates FindText as a carbon copy of Word's built-in Edit Find dialog box, complete with a set of empty fields that match the fields in the Find dialog box. Of particular interest for our purposes is the Direction field, which we want to set to 0, the setting for *Down*.

The second line sets the Direction field of the FindText dialog record to 0, after which the Dialog statement in the third line opens the dialog box, using the current values for FindText. At this point in running the macro, you would enter the text you want to search for in the Find What text box, and then choose Find Next. The last line, finally, runs Word's built-in EditFind command, using whatever choice you've entered in the dialog box.

## Handling errors

The sample macro is not quite complete. If you run the macro as it stands, and then choose Cancel to close the dialog box without searching for any text, Word will respond with an error message. You can get around the problem, literally, by adding a command to skip over the command instead of displaying the error message.

WordBasic provides an On Error control structure. On Error takes one of three forms:

```
On Error Resume Next
On Error Goto LABEL
On Error Goto 0
```

The first two choices turn off Word's error messages for the rest of the macro or until WordBasic sees the On Error Goto 0 statement—whichever comes first. The On Error Goto 0 statement sets Word back to its default state—showing error messages in response to errors. Use it in a macro only when you've used one of the other two formats earlier and you need to turn error messages back on.

The first of the three forms, On Error Resume Next, tells Word to ignore any errors and simply continue the macro. The second format lets you control program flow. Think of it as a trip wire. When you set it up, it tells Word to jump to a different part of the macro altogether if it trips over an error.

In this macro, you want Word to skip to the end of the macro if it encounters an error. Enter the line

```
On Error Goto ForgetIt
```

In this example, you can enter the On Error statement anywhere before the Dialog FindText statement. However, it's good practice to place the command just before you want it to come into play (just before the line *Dialog FindText,* in this case) so you don't inadvertently trigger the jump in response to some other error.

## Remarks

Until you've tested a macro and made sure it works, it's not a good idea to turn off the error messages.

In this particular case, you'll want to enter *On Error Goto ForgetIt* but also mark the line so Word will ignore the statement for now. You can do that by adding a single quotation mark (an apostrophe) or the REM statement at the beginning of the line with the On Error statement.

> REM is short for Remark, and it is a valuable tool. It lets you add notes to a macro that can remind you of the purpose of each section should you need to revise the macro at some later date. Put the *REM* or apostrophe anywhere in a line, and Word will ignore everything that follows it on that line.

When you use REM or an apostrophe, as in this example, to tell Word to temporarily ignore a line, the technique is usually called "REMming out the line" because you are telling Word to treat the line as a remark rather than a statement. Once you know the macro works correctly, you can delete the REM or apostrophe and "turn on" the On Error statement. Be aware, however, that in some circumstances, Word will add a paragraph return and an apostrophe later in the same line that you've REMmed out. So when you delete the REM or apostrophe from a line, you may need to clean up the other items Word has added to the line.

## Labels

In addition to using the On Error statement, you'll need to add the label ForgetIt so that Word knows where to jump. In this case, you want it to jump to the end of the macro, so you need to enter the label immediately before the End Sub statement. (There's no need to REM out the label because it simply marks the location.) When you finish writing the macro, it should look like the one in Figure 25-4.

FIGURE 25-4

**FIGURE 25-4**

The FindForward macro includes commands for handling dialog boxes.

WordBasic will recognize a label only if it's followed by a colon. Note also that WordBasic will recognize labels only if they start in the first position of the line. If you're writing a complicated macro, with some lines indented for readability, be sure not to indent the lines with labels.

As we've already suggested, once you've created or modified a macro, you'll want to test it to make sure it works. In this case, you should still have the macro editing window open, and you can simply choose the Start button—the one with the small filled-in triangle pointing to the right—from the Macro toolbar. (Word will show the Macro toolbar when you open the macro editing window. The toolbar will stay visible unless you turn it off by choosing View Toolbars and removing the check mark from the Macro check box.) If you've typed everything correctly, you'll be rewarded with the Find dialog box, as shown in Figure 25-5.

FIGURE 25-5

When you run the
FindForward macro, it
should take you to the
Find dialog box and set
the search direction to
Down.

Word will not check a macro for syntax errors (errors caused by
mistakes in the statements you've written) until you run the macro,
at which point you'll get an error message if you've made a mistake. If there is a syntax error, Word will highlight the line in the
macro where it found the mistake.

When you're satisfied that the macro works, you can edit out the REM or
apostrophe at the beginning of the On Error statement, and then close the
macro editing window. Word will ask whether you want to keep the changes.
Choose Yes, but remember that choosing Yes does not save the changes to
disk. If you want to save the macro immediately so it's safe for future use,
choose File Save All. And note, finally, that the other macro in this pair—for
searching backwards through your text—would be almost identical. Simply
substitute *.Direction = 1* for *.Direction = 0.*

# Some General Considerations for Macros

The FindForward macro is a bare-bones introduction to writing a macro.
We'll go a little further into programming issues in the next chapter. First,
however, we'll look at some general considerations you ought to be aware of.

## Choices for running a macro

As we've already mentioned in this chapter—and as we covered in some
depth in Chapter 24—there are several ways to run a macro. In addition to the
Start button on the Macro toolbar—which is only available when you have a
macro open for editing—choices include the Tools Macro Run command, and
assigning a macro to a shortcut key, a menu, or a toolbar button.

You'll find each of these possibilities discussed in Chapter 24, "Recording
Macros," starting on page 801; and you'll find the menu and shortcut key
choices covered again, from a slightly different approach, in Chapter 28,
"Customizing Menus, Keys, & Templates," starting on page 903.

Still another option is to create a MACROBUTTON field as part of a document and then run the macro by choosing the button. We covered the MACROBUTTON field in Chapter 20, "Fields," starting on page 639.

## Auto macros

Even these four choices for running macros don't exhaust all the possibilities. In fact, there are five other ways to run a macro, using Word's Auto macros.

> Word recognizes five special names for macros—AutoNew, AutoOpen, AutoClose, AutoExec, and AutoExit. Use any of these names, and the macro will run automatically in response to a specific event. The AutoNew, AutoOpen, and AutoClose macros can go in any template, including Normal, and they apply to documents that use the particular template. The AutoExec and AutoExit macros go only in Normal, and they apply to all documents.

### AutoNew

The AutoNew name tells Word to run the macro each time you create a new document. For example, suppose you have a memo template that uses FILLIN fields to prompt for the recipient and subject of a memo. (See Chapter 20, "Fields," starting on page 639, for a discussion of the FILLIN field.)

You'll want Word to request the information to update these fields as soon as you open a new document based on that template. To handle this automatically, create a macro named AutoNew, with the two statements

```
EditSelectAll
UpdateFields
```

between the Sub MAIN and End Sub statements. As their names imply, EditSelectAll tells Word to select the entire document, and the UpdateFields statement tells Word to update all fields in the selection. Save this AutoNew macro in the appropriate template, and Word will automatically prompt you for the memo's recipient and subject every time you start a new memo based on that template.

### AutoOpen

An AutoOpen macro will run every time you open an already existing document. For example, suppose you share a computer with someone who prefers different view options for the screen than those you prefer. You might like the ruler displayed, for example, while he or she likes it hidden. Each of you can create your own personalized templates with AutoOpen macros that set the screen the way you like it. Your AutoOpen macro would display the ruler every time you opened one of your documents; the other person's AutoOpen macro would hide the ruler. (We'll explain how to create separate templates in Chapter 27, "Templates," starting on page 883.)

## AutoClose

As you might expect from the name, an AutoClose macro runs every time you close a document. You can use an AutoClose macro in combination with AutoOpen. For example, suppose you want your view options set a particular way for one kind of document only. You could use the AutoOpen macro to set the options appropriately each time you open a document based on a particular template and then use the AutoClose macro to reset the options the way you normally prefer them.

## AutoExec

AutoExec is similar in concept to the AutoOpen macro, except that it can go only in Normal, and it runs every time you start Word. You can, for example, use AutoExec to set Word to customized settings each time you start the program. Other possibilities include automatically opening the last file you loaded (with the instruction *File1*), automatically loading a set of files that you are working with for a large project (use the macro recording feature to record which files to load), or automatically running the File Open command, with the macro

```
Dim FileNow As FileOpen
On Error Goto ForgetIt
Dialog FileNow
FileOpen FileNow
ForgetIt:
```

## AutoExit

AutoExit is similar to AutoExec in that it goes only in Normal, but it is exactly opposite in that it runs whenever you quit Word rather than when you start it. If you create an AutoExit macro, running the macro becomes the last thing Word does when you close the program. You can use the AutoExit macro to automate any task that you want to perform every time you leave Word.

# Testing, Modifying, and Debugging Macros

If you write or edit many macros, you'll find that they often don't perform the way you expect them to. This is such a truism that a programmer friend of ours insists that the first pass in writing a program should really be called *bugging*. The process of fixing the bugs, of course, is called *debugging*. Word provides several debugging tools for its macros.

## The Macro toolbar

As already mentioned, the Macro toolbar shows up automatically whenever you open the macro editing window. Assuming Word's default settings—with the Standard toolbar just below the menu bar, and the Formatting toolbar just below that—the Macro toolbar shows up just below the Formatting toolbar.

As you can see in Figure 25-6, the default version of the Macro toolbar includes 12 buttons and one pull-down list.

**FIGURE 25-6**

Whenever a macro editing window is open, Word adds the Macro toolbar to the top of the window—even when the macro editing window is not active, as shown in the second figure.

Taken together, the Macro toolbar buttons provide a complete tool kit for creating, modifying, and debugging macros. We'll look at each button shortly, but it will help to know a little about the Macro toolbar itself first.

As shown in Figure 25-6, Word displays the Macro toolbar whenever the macro editing window is open—whether it is the currently active window or not. This holds true even when the macro editing window isn't showing.

The ability to use the debugging tools regardless of which window is active, and regardless of the window arrangement, is a valuable feature. The FindForward macro that we discussed earlier will work equally well from any window and with any arrangement. However, if a macro includes an Edit Go To command, for example, you cannot test it in the macro window itself. Word will not make the Go To command available to a macro within a macro editing window.

For reasons that will become clear when we look at the buttons on the Macro toolbar, the preferred window arrangement for testing a macro is usually to adjust both the macro editing window and the document window so you can see both at once, as in Figure 25-6. If you have only those two documents open, you can get this window arrangement simply by choosing Window Arrange All.

There is one more issue to be aware of when you debug a macro. Make sure that the name of the macro you're debugging appears in the text box on the left side of the Macro toolbar. If you've opened only one macro editing window, that won't be a problem because only one macro will be active. If you've opened more than one, however, Word will show the name of the currently active macro in the text box. To activate a different macro, simply activate that macro's window, then return to the document editing window. Alternatively, you can open the pull-down list and choose the macro you want to activate.

Finally, before running the macro, go back to the document you want to test the macro in and, if the starting position is important to the macro's function, be sure to move the cursor to an appropriate position. Then you can run the macro, using the appropriate debugging tool.

## Word's macro editor tools

As already mentioned, Word's Macro toolbar offers a complete tool kit for creating, modifying, and debugging macros. First on the toolbar is a pull-down list, followed by four groups of buttons. Unfortunately, the meanings of the icons on the buttons are less than immediately obvious. But as with all toolbars, if you have the ToolTips feature turned on, you can point to each button with the mouse and see the name for the button you're pointing to. (You can turn the ToolTips feature on and off by choosing View Toolbars and then adding or removing the check mark from the Show ToolTips check box.) Figure 25-7 shows the Macro toolbar and its button names; we'll use those names throughout this discussion to identify each button.

FIGURE 25-7

The Macro toolbar.

As we explained in the section before this, the text box, called the Active Macro text box, shows the name of the active macro, meaning the macro that will be affected by most of the toolbar commands. Click on the Macro toolbar Start button, for example, and it's the active macro that will start running.

Going from left to right along the toolbar, the first group of two buttons are Record and Record Next Command; you can use these to create a macro, or part of one, by recording. The next two groups—of four and three buttons—consist of debugging tools: Start, Trace, Continue, and Stop in the first group, and Step, Step Subs, and Show Variables in the second. The last group consists of a miscellaneous assortment of tools: Add/Remove REM, Macro, and Dialog Editor. Here's a detailed look at each of these 12 buttons.

## The Record button

The Record button is exactly equivalent to choosing Tools Macro and then Record; in either case, you'll open the Record Macro dialog box. You can then enter a macro name; add a definition if you like; optionally assign a shortcut key, menu item, or toolbar button; and then record the macro. While you're editing a macro, you can use this feature to record a set of instructions that you'd like to incorporate into the macro you're editing.

When you're finished recording, you can open the new macro and copy the commands you've recorded into the macro you've been working with, using Word's standard Cut, Copy, and Paste commands. And you can then delete the macro you've recorded. Alternatively, when you finish recording the macro, you can store the newly recorded macro if you want to keep it as a separate macro, and add a command to the macro you're working with to run the newly recorded macro. The command to run the macro takes the form

```
ToolsMacro .Name = "Macroname", .Run
```

where *Macroname* is the name of the macro.

### The Record Next Command button

As the name suggests, the Record Next Command button will record the next command you give, and only that command. Unlike the Record button, the Record Next Command button will insert the single command into the active macro editing screen at the current cursor location. Be sure your cursor is located at the beginning of a line—and the correct line at that—when you give the command. Otherwise, you'll have to move the new command after you record it. In general, you'll want to place the cursor in the correct position in the macro editing window, switch to a document window to start recording, and then give the command. That way, the command will affect only the document in the document window, rather than the macro itself. Use the Record Next Command button when you're writing or editing a macro and you want to add a command without having to write the whole command yourself.

### The Start button

The Start button tells Word to run the currently active macro. Choosing Start is equivalent to highlighting the macro name in the Tools Macro dialog box and then choosing Run. Use this for testing when you have a short macro, or you think there are no bugs left and expect the macro to run problem-free.

### The Trace button

The Trace button is similar to the Start button in that it tells Word to run the entire macro in a single step. However, when you use Trace, Word highlights each instruction in the macro before executing it. The best way to take advantage of the Trace button is with macros that stop every so often to ask a question. The stopping points will help bracket the source of the problem. Note that if you're having trouble isolating a problem, you might even want to add a few stopping points in the macro strictly to help debug it. You can add these with the Input statement or with dialog boxes, both of which we'll discuss in Chapter 26, "Dialog Boxes & Other Macro Magic," starting on page 853.

### The Continue button

The Continue button works along with the two Step buttons—Step and Step Subs. Both Step buttons tell Word to run just the next step in the macro. (We'll discuss the differences between the two Step buttons in a moment.) Choose the Continue button when you've stepped through part of the macro and want Word to execute the rest of the macro without pausing.

## The Stop button

Like the Continue button, the Stop button works along with the two Step buttons—Step and Step Subs. As just pointed out, both Step buttons tell Word to run just the next step in the macro. Choose the Stop button when you've stepped through part of the macro and want Word to stop executing the macro. If you click on Stop and then click on one of the Step buttons, Word will start at the beginning of the macro again.

## The Step button

The Step button tells Word to execute a single instruction and then pause. If you're running the macro from the macro editing window, or if you've set up your screen to display both the macro window and a document window, then Word's first step for running the macro will be to highlight, but not execute, the first instruction following the Sub MAIN statement. Choose Step again, and Word will execute the first instruction and highlight the second. You can then step through the macro one instruction at a time and see the effect in the document window of each highlighted step in the macro editing window. The Step feature is useful in finding out where a problem is.

Note that if you've set up your screen to show the document only, the Step command will still step you through the macro one instruction at a time, but you won't see the instruction highlighted at each step. This can still be useful. If you spot the point where the macro goes awry, simply switch to the macro editing window. The culprit will (in most cases) be the instruction just before the currently highlighted instruction. (However, be aware that the instruction "just before" the current one may not be on the line just before it, since some macro commands tell Word to jump to different parts of the macro.)

## The Step Subs button

The Step Subs button is similar to the Step button in that it tells Word to execute the macro one step at a time. You'll see the difference between the two only in macros that include subroutines.

Briefly, a subroutine is a section of a macro that performs a particular task and is separated out from the main body of the macro. In long macros, you'll often need to repeat a given set of instructions in several different places. A subroutine lets you enter those instructions once and then call on them as needed from different points in the macro.

The Sub MAIN and End Sub markers define the MAIN subroutine that Word requires in every macro. Additional subroutines take the same form. A subroutine called TRYTHIS, for example, would have the beginning marker

```
Sub TRYTHIS
```

and the end marker

```
End Sub
```

In general, a macro with multiple subroutines takes the form

```
Sub MAIN
    instruction 1
    instruction 2
    TRYTHIS
    instruction 3
    TRYTHIS
    instruction 4
End Sub

Sub TRYTHIS
    instruction a
    instruction b
End Sub
```

When you run this macro, Word starts with the first instruction in the MAIN subroutine. When it reaches the instruction TRYTHIS, it jumps to the TRYTHIS subroutine, runs the instructions in that subroutine, and then goes back to MAIN, picking up at instruction 3. When it reaches the second TRYTHIS instruction, it runs the subroutine again and then, once again, goes back to MAIN, this time picking up at instruction 4.

## Step vs. Step Subs

The difference between the Step and Step Subs commands is in how they deal with subroutines. If you use the Step button, Word will branch to the subroutine and run through its instructions one at a time. It will then return to MAIN and continue where it left off. If you use the Step Subs button, Word will run the entire subroutine in a single step and then return to MAIN, to continue one step at a time. Use the Step Subs command when you already know that the subroutine is fully debugged and is clearly not the source of the problem.

Because you can run a macro from a macro, you can also treat the second macro as a subroutine when designing your macros. Unless the macro you call on is also open in its own macro editing window, however, Word assumes the macro is already debugged, and it will run the macro in a single step whether you are using Step or Step Subs.

## The Show Variables button

The Show Variables button matters only when you're running macros that contain variables. (A *variable*, in case you're new to the term, is any piece of information that varies. For example, any answer you give to a macro that asks a question is a variable.) If a given macro uses variables, the Show Variables button will let you see the current value for the variables at any point while you're stepping through the macro, as shown in Figure 25-8. You can also set a new value for the variables so that you can, for example, test unusual situations easily.

Use the Show Variables button to open the Macro Variables dialog box, to see or set the current values of any variables in the macro.

Choose the Show Variables button while stepping through a macro that includes variables, and Word will open the Macro Variables dialog box.

## The Add/Remove REM button

The Add/Remove REM button will add or remove a REM, or remark, statement, at the beginning of all currently selected lines. More precisely, it will add a REM statement to the beginning of a line if one isn't already there, and it will remove a REM statement from the beginning of a line if it finds one there.

As we discussed earlier in this chapter, REM is short for "remark." If you add a REM statement anywhere in a macro, Word will ignore everything that follows on that line.

You can use the REM statement to write comments in the middle of a macro that will help document what you're doing so that you can make sense of it later. You can also use it to temporarily turn off the effects of a line, which can be useful when you're trying to track down a problem. Such lines are generally referred to as being "REMmed out."

Note that although you can type a REM statement into a line at any point, the Add/Remove REM button will only add or remove a REM at the beginning of a line. To use the button, extend the selection to all lines that you want to add a REM statement to or remove a REM statement from. You don't have to select an entire line—the command will work as long as the selection extends into that line. Then click on the Add/Remove REM button to add or remove the REM statement.

 Note that the Add/Remove REM button does not recognize apostrophes, even though Word otherwise treats an apostrophe as exactly equivalent to the REM statement. If you add an apostrophe to the beginning of a line and then move the cursor or selection to the line and click on the Add/Remove REM button, Word will add a REM statement to the beginning of the line. If you click on the button again, Word will remove the REM statement and leave the apostrophe, so the line will still be REMmed out.

### The Macro button

Clicking on the Macro button is exactly equivalent to choosing Tools Macro: Word will open the Macro dialog box, and you can use any of the features available through the dialog box. We covered many of these features in Chapter 24, "Recording Macros," starting on page 801.

### The Dialog Editor button

The Dialog Editor button is exactly equivalent to opening the Word Dialog Editor from the Finder. Click on this button, and Word will open the Dialog Editor program, a tool for helping you create dialog boxes. We'll cover the Dialog Editor in Chapter 26, "Dialog Boxes & Other Macro Magic," starting on page 853.

## How to change the Macro toolbar buttons

One problem with the Word 6.0 Macro toolbar—especially if you don't use it too often—is that the meaning for the icons is less than obvious. Turning on the ToolTips feature helps identify the icons, but you might also want to consider changing one or more of them to text buttons, as shown in Figure 25-9.

**FIGURE 25-9**

If you like, you can change the Macro toolbar buttons to text so you can easily see what each one is meant for.

First make sure the Macro toolbar is showing by opening any macro to edit. (Choose Tools Macro, highlight a macro name, and choose Edit.) Then open the Customize dialog box by choosing View Toolbars and then the Customize button; or by pointing in the toolbar area of the screen, holding the Control key down, clicking the mouse button, and choosing Customize. Next, to bring up the context-sensitive menu shown in Figure 25-10, point to the Macro toolbar button that you want to change, and hold the Control key down while clicking on the button. Pick Choose Button Image to open the Custom Button dialog box.

**FIGURE 25-10**

To see this context-sensitive menu, open the Customize dialog box, choose the Toolbars card, and hold down the Control key while clicking on any toolbar button.

In the Custom Button dialog box, shown in Figure 25-11, type the appropriate text in the Text Button Name text box, and choose Assign to change the button to text. Repeat these steps for each button.

**FIGURE 25-11**

Use the Custom Button dialog box to define a text button.

Depending on the screen size that you have, you may then have to adjust button size to make all of the buttons fit on the screen easily. To change button size, click on a button (with the Customize dialog box still open), and then point with the mouse to the edge of the button. When the pointer changes to the Vertical Split pointer, you can click and hold down the mouse button to adjust the size of the toolbar button.

When you're done, close the Customize dialog box, and choose File Save All to save the changes to the toolbar. For more details on using the Customize dialog box to modify a toolbar, see "Customizing Toolbars" on page 288.

Changing to text buttons helps identify each button, but given that writing a macro mostly involves typing at the keyboard, you might like the convenience of giving commands from the keyboard as well. If you like, you can assign a shortcut key to each command by choosing Tools Customize, and then the Keyboard card, from any editing window. The commands you need to match are shown in Figure 25-12. For details on assigning keystrokes, see "How to assign a macro to a shortcut key" on page 807 and "Keyboard Customization" on page 917.

> **T**
> **I**  To make the keystrokes easy to remember, you can show each one
> **P**  as a capital letter when you define the text buttons.

| Word Command | Macro Toolbar Button Name |
| --- | --- |
| ToolsRecordMacroStart | Record |
| RecordNextCommand | Record Next Command |
| StartMacro | Start |
| TraceMacro | Trace |
| ContinueMacro | Continue |
| StopMacro | Stop |
| StepIn | Step |
| StepOver | Step Subs |
| ShowVars | Show Variables |
| MacroREM | Add/Remove REM |
| ToolsMacro | Macro |
| DialogEditor | Dialog Editor |

**FIGURE 25-12**

Use this list of commands as a reference to help you assign shortcut keys
to the buttons on the Macro toolbar.

## How to print a macro

One last important debugging tool Word offers is the ability to print a macro. This can be particularly helpful for macros that are too long to fit on the screen at once. To print the instructions in a macro, first use the Tools Macro Edit command to load the appropriate macro in a macro editing window. Then choose File Print to print the macro the same way you would print any Word document.

# A Dozen Quick 'n' Dirty (but Useful) Macros

Ultimately, when it comes to working with macros, there is no substitute for jumping in and trying the real thing. Here are 12 macros that we find useful in our own day-to-day word processing. All of these were chosen so you can create them either with the Record Macro feature (if you recognize the keystrokes that go with the commands) or by typing them in a macro editing window. Consider this a starter set for your own macro collection.

## Some navigation macros

With all the choices Word gives you for navigating through a document, it still misses one feature that can be important for touch typists—the ability to move the cursor without taking your hands off the typing keys. Macros provide an easy way to add this missing feature.

The solution comes in two parts. First, you need macros that duplicate the navigation commands you need most often. At a minimum that includes up, down, left, left one word, right, and right one word. Second, you need some way to run the macros.

The first part is easy. The instructions for the six macros are in Figure 25-13. We've omitted the Sub MAIN and End Sub statements from each macro. However, note that, as with all macros, each of the six in the table must begin with a Sub MAIN and end with an End Sub statement; all you have to do is type the text listed in the Instruction column on a line between those two statements.

| Macro Name | Purpose | Instruction |
|---|---|---|
| CursorDown | Move down one line | LineDown 1 |
| CursorLeft | Move left one character | CharLeft 1 |
| CursorRight | Move right one character | CharRight 1 |
| CursorUp | Move up one line | LineUp 1 |
| CursorWordLeft | Move left one word | WordLeft 1 |
| CursorWordRight | Move right one word | WordRight 1 |

**FIGURE 25-13**

Six macros for moving the cursor.

To keep all similar macros together in the Macro Name list box as shown in Figure 25-14, we suggest giving them names that start similarly as in the Macro Name column of Figure 25-13: CursorDown, CursorLeft, CursorRight, CursorUp, CursorWordLeft, and CursorWordRight.

FIGURE 25-14

Because Word lists
macro names in
alphabetic order, we
suggest giving similar
macros similar names,
as shown with the
navigation macros,
all of which start
with Cursor.

The more interesting problem is how to run these macros. One of the simplest ways is to assign the macros to Control- or ⌘-key combinations, in a kind of geographic mnemonic. For example, if you look at the E, X, S, and D keys, you'll see that they sit at four points of the compass, as shown in Figure 25-15.

You can easily remember the keys if you assign CursorUp to E, CursorDown to X, CursorLeft to S, and CursorRight to D. Carrying the logic one step further, you can assign CursorWordRight to F and CursorWordLeft to A.

**FIGURE 25-15**

You can assign the
navigation macros in a
geographic mnemonic
layout.

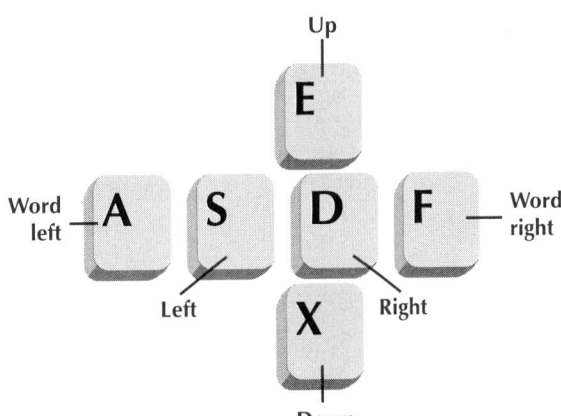

You may recognize this as the famous (or infamous, depending on your point of view) WordStar diamond. You should also note that in Word as shipped, none of these keys are already assigned to other purposes in combination with Control, but all are assigned in combination with ⌘. (⌘-S is assigned to FileSave, ⌘-D is FormatFont, ⌘-E is CenterPara, ⌘-X is EditCut, ⌘-A is EditSelectAll, and ⌘-F is EditFind.) For most users, that makes the Control-key combinations a far better choice for assigning to macros.

In any case, if you choose to record these macros, you can assign them to keys while recording them, as we've discussed in "Recording a Macro" on page 802. If you choose to write the macros in a macro editing window, you can assign them to keys with the techniques we'll discuss in "Keyboard Customization" on page 917.

## How to cut a word, line, sentence, or paragraph

Whether you're typing or editing text, it's often useful to cut a word, line, sentence, or paragraph—often with the intention of moving it elsewhere. Word has tools for most of these tasks, but here again, there's no easy way to use them without taking your hands from the typing keys. What's more, you generally need at least two steps—one for selecting the text and one for cutting it. And in some cases, as with DeleteWord, the built-in command throws the text away rather than storing it on the Clipboard.

Figure 25-16 shows the macro instructions that will let you select and cut text in a single step. As before, we've given the macros similar names, all starting with *Cut*. This makes the names easier to remember and ensures that Word will group them together in the Macro Name list box so they'll be easier to find. As before, the table does not show the Sub MAIN and End Sub markers that each macro must include.

| Macro Name | Purpose | Instructions |
|---|---|---|
| CutWord | Cut text from the current cursor position to the end of the current word and store the text on the Clipboard | WordRight 1,1<br>EditCut |
| CutLine | Cut the entire line the cursor is currently in and store the text on the Clipboard | StartOfLine<br>EndOfLine 1<br>EditCut |
| CutSentence | Cut the entire sentence the cursor is currently in and store the text on the Clipboard | ExtendSelection<br>ExtendSelection<br>ExtendSelection<br>EditCut |
| CutParagraph | Cut the entire paragraph the cursor is currently in and store the text on the Clipboard | ExtendSelection<br>ExtendSelection<br>ExtendSelection<br>ExtendSelection<br>EditCut |

**FIGURE 25-16**

Four macros for cutting to the Clipboard.

As with the navigation macros, you'll want to assign these macros to keys that make sense to you so you can easily remember them. We suggest trying to link macros in groups. For example, you might want to assign the Cut macros to Control-C combinations, using Control-C,P for CutParagraph, Control-C,S for CutSentence, and so on.

Notice in passing that all of these macros end with the EditCut command, which puts the deleted text on the Clipboard. If you'd rather throw the text away, you could end the macros with EditClear—although this might be dangerous for anything longer than a line of text.

A more interesting variation would be to define the selected text as an AutoText entry called *Temp* and never use *Temp* for anything else. That way, you can cut text without disturbing whatever is currently on the Clipboard. You can record the procedure as part of creating the macro, or you can replace the EditCut statements with

```
EditAutoText .Name = "temp", .Add
EditClear
```

This will define the AutoText entry Temp as the currently selected text and then delete the text from your document. If you take this route, you can paste the text elsewhere by choosing Edit Autotext, entering Temp in the Name text box, and choosing Insert.

## How to transpose a letter or a word

Finally, Figure 25-17 on the next page shows two macros for transposing text. The first will transpose two letters—when you've typed *intreesting*, for example, rather than *interesting*. The second will transpose two words—a useful feature if you want to unsplit an infinitive or move a misplaced modifier. Once again, the table does not show the Sub MAIN and End Sub statements; you should make sure they are in the actual macros.

To use the first macro, position the cursor between the two letters you want to transpose. To use the second, position the cursor anywhere in the second word. When you run the TransposeChar macro, it will select the character to the right of the original position and then use the MoveText command to move the character to its proper location. The TransposeWord macro does essentially the same thing with an entire word. Note, however, that as written, the TransposeWord macro assumes that it will select and move a space after the word as well. That means it will not work properly if the second word is followed immediately by a period, comma, or other punctuation mark.

| Macro Name | Purpose | Instruction |
|------------|---------|-------------|
| TransposeChar | Transpose two characters | CharRight 1, 1<br>MoveText<br>CharLeft 2<br>OK<br>CharRight 1 |
| TransposeWord | Transpose two words | ExtendSelection<br>ExtendSelection<br>MoveText<br>WordLeft 2<br>OK<br>WordRight 1 |

**FIGURE 25-17**

Two macros for transposing text.

To fix that shortcoming, you need more sophisticated macro commands than we have yet discussed. In particular, you need to know how to test the character after the word to see whether it is a space, and then tell the macro to do one thing or another depending on what it finds. You may recognize this as a description of an If...Then...End If statement. And that's part of what we'll look at in the next chapter.

# TOPIC FINDER

# 26

---

# Dialog Boxes &
# Other Macro Magic

---

n Chapter 25, we looked at the mechanics of recording, writing, and debugging macros, but we made only passing mention of programming logic and WordBasic commands. In this chapter, we'll look at how to use the WordBasic programming language to build macros that you can interact with. We'll also discuss how to make the best use of dialog boxes, through both WordBasic programming and the Dialog Editor, which comes with Word.

## Interacting with Macros

In Chapter 25, we showed how to write a pair of simple macros for opening the Find dialog box and automatically setting Word to search either forward or backward through your text. It's worth taking this example one step further to see how a macro can ask questions, get answers, and then respond to the answers by following one set of commands or another.

Suppose, for example, that instead of creating one macro to search forward and one to search backward though your text, you'd rather create one macro for both purposes. In that case, you'll probably want the macro, which we'll call Search, to stop and ask which way to search before it opens the Find dialog box. More precisely, you'll need a macro that will ask which direction to search in, store the answer, and then set the search direction to match your answer. As with most possibilities in programming, there is more than one way to get the same effect. We'll start with the simplest approach, and then move on to discuss some more elegant alternatives.

## The Input command

One way to get the macro to ask a question is with the Input command. The command takes the form

```
Input "Any question you want to ask", VariableName$
```

where *VariableName$* is any name you want to use for this particular variable. A variable, as the name implies—and as we mentioned in the last chapter—is any piece of information that varies. In this case, it's your answer, since the variable's contents will depend on your response to the question. The $ at the end of the variable name indicates that this particular variable will consist of text rather than a numeric value. Such text variables are usually called *string variables.*

If you create a macro with this one line (between the Sub MAIN and End Sub statements, of course) and then run the macro, the question inside the quotation marks will show up at the bottom of the Word window, complete with a question mark, as shown in Figure 26-1.

**FIGURE 26-1**

When a macro reaches an Input command, it reads the text included in quotation marks in the Input command and shows that text at the bottom of the Word window.

Note that the question will appear on the bottom line of the screen, where the status bar is displayed, even if you've set Word to hide the status bar. If the horizontal scroll bar is showing, the question will take its place. If neither the status bar nor the horizontal scroll bar is showing, the question will show up in its own bar at the bottom of the Word window.

Suppose that with the Search macro, you'll usually want to search forward, and only occasionally need to search backward. In that case, you'll want the macro to interpret a blank entry to mean that you want to search forward. You'll also want the macro to accept a text entry that specifies a search back through your text. The question should reflect that. And the command as you add the entry to the Search macro might be

```
Input "Search in which direction: F(orward) or B(ack) (Blank entry
searches forward)", Direction$
```

 You can create a reasonably long question. However, be sure that it will fit on one line across the bottom of the screen. Note, too, that you will generally want to keep the command itself on one line in the macro editing screen. We've broken it into two lines here only because it won't fit on one line in this book.

When you run the macro and it reaches the Input command, it will show the question and pause until you answer. At that point, you'll type either an *f* for Forward or a *b* for Back and press Return or simply press Return to indicate that you want to search forward.

## If...End If

Of course, asking a question—and even answering it—doesn't do much good unless the macro knows how to interpret the answer. And that brings us to the If...End If construction.

The If...End If statement offers one way to tell a macro to branch to different commands, depending on a current condition. In its simplest version, the statement takes the form

```
If Condition Then Statement End If
```

This roughly translates to "If some particular condition holds true, then do some particular task; otherwise, ignore that task and move on."

If...End If constructions can also include ElseIf and Else clauses. These take the form

```
If condition1 Then
    Statement1
ElseIf condition2 Then
    Statement2
Else
    Statement3
End If
```

This version roughly translates to "If some particular condition (Condition1) holds true, then do whatever is in Statement1 and pick up the macro after the End If. If Condition1 does not hold true, check to see whether Condition2 holds true. If so, do whatever is in Statement2, and then continue the macro after the End If. If neither Condition1 nor Condition2 holds true, then do whatever is in Statement3, and continue the macro after the End If."

As you can see, you can build a wide variety of actions into the If...End If statement. There is no limit to the number of ElseIf conditions that you can include in a single statement.

## Conditions

The conditions in the If...End If statement are built from a comparison of some sort—typically, a comparison of a variable to some fixed value. For example, the macro may test to see whether the variable *Direction$* is blank. One appropriate comparison would be

```
If Direction$ = "" Then Statement1...
```

which would tell Word to continue with Statement1 if the variable is blank. Another appropriate comparison would be

```
If Direction$ <> "" Then Statement1...
```

which would tell Word to continue with Statement1 if the variable is not blank.

You can also define compound conditions with the logical operators And, Or, and Not. These operators mean the same here as they do in standard English. The compound Condition1 And Condition2 holds true if both Condition1 and Condition2 are true. ("If it's sunny and if I get an hour off from work, then I'll meet you on Friday.") Similarly, the compound Condition1 Or Condition2 holds true if either condition is true. ("I'll meet you on Friday come rain or shine.") The compound Condition1 Not Condition2 is true if Condition1 holds true but Condition2 doesn't. ("I'll meet you on Friday if it's sunny but not if it's the thirteenth.")

Figure 26-2 shows the available comparisons for conditional commands. (These are usually called *relational operators*, but are given in the Word Help system as *comparison operators*.)

| Symbol | Meaning |
|--------|---------|
| = | Equal to |
| <> | Not equal to |
| > | Greater than |
| < | Less than |
| >= | Greater than or equal to |
| <= | Less than or equal to |

**FIGURE 26-2**

Relational operators for conditional commands.

## Putting the Search macro together

We've now covered all the pieces we need for the macro we want to build. Choose Tools Macro, enter a new macro name, such as Search, in the Macro Name text box, and choose Create. Now start with the commands for defining, but not opening, the Search dialog box, as in the macro we built in Chapter 25.

Be aware that as of the time we wrote this book, the FindText.Direction statement as used below was not working. However, it's supposed to work, and we assume that Microsoft will, in fact, get it working at some time.

The first three lines will be the same as in the original macro we wrote in Chapter 25.

```
Dim FindText as EditFind
FindText.Direction = 0
On Error Goto ForgetIt
```

As we discussed in Chapter 25, the first two lines create a dialog record called FindText that matches EditFind but sets the Direction field to 0. The last line ensures that you won't see an error message if you cancel the macro. Instead, you'll jump to the label ForgetIt (which comes later in the macro). As we also discussed, it's not a good idea to turn off the error messages until you're sure the macro works, so you'll want to REM out the line until you've tested the macro. Simply add an apostrophe at the beginning of the On Error line, and Word will ignore it. (Alternatively, you can add the remark command, REM, at the beginning of the line, either by typing *REM* or by placing the cursor or selection in the line and clicking on the Add/Remove REM button—the third from the right on the default version of the Macro toolbar.) For a more detailed look at each of these three lines, take a look at the section

"Macros that use Word's dialog boxes" on page 830. For more information about remarks and about REMming out lines, see "Remarks" on page 831.

Next you need to add the Input command so the macro will stop and ask which direction to search in:

```
Input "Search in which direction: F(orward) or B(ack)  (Blank entry
searches forward)", Direction$
```

After the Input command, use the If...End If statement to tell the macro to test the value of *Direction$* and decide what to do next:

```
If Direction$ ="b" Then
    FindText.Direction = 1
End If
```

The first line of the If statement tests the value of *Direction$*. If it is *b*, the macro goes to the next line and sets the Direction field to *1*, or *Up*. If *Direction$* is anything else at all—presumably meaning you pressed *f* or pressed Return by itself—the macro will jump to the End If statement (leaving FindText Direction set to 0) and continue with the next line. (Notice that we checked for a lowercase *b*. Be aware that Word makes a distinction between uppercase and lowercase letters.)

The rest of the macro includes the remaining three lines from the FindForward macro in Chapter 25:

```
Dialog FindText
EditFind FindText
ForgetIt:
```

As we discussed in Chapter 25, the first and second lines here open the dialog box and search for the text, using the information you designated in the dialog box. The third is the label you told the macro to jump to with the On Error command.

After you type all of these commands between the Sub MAIN and End Sub statements, the macro should look much like the one shown in Figure 26-3. Notice how indenting some lines makes the macro easier to read. In particular, notice that the line within the If...End If structure is indented, to indicate that the If...End If statement controls whether Word runs that command. You do not need to indent lines this way, but if you do, your macros will be easier to read and edit.

Keep in mind that you should not indent lines in a macro that contains labels. If you do, Word will not recognize the labels. So make certain that lines with labels are not indented.

**FIGURE 26-3**

The Input and If...End If statements in the Search macro tell the macro to ask you a question and act on your answer.

# Error Trapping

Note that if you accidentally press some key other than the *f* or *b*, and then press Return, the macro will continue just as if you had pressed *f* or pressed Return by itself. If you like, however, you can have the macro look for your typing mistakes and refuse to accept them—a technique known as error trapping. In this case, you'll want the macro to refuse to accept any input other than an *f*, *b*, or Return by itself.

To add error trapping to this macro, simply add the label

```
DoItAgain:
```

before the Input command, and change the If...EndIf statement to

```
If Direction$ <> "f" and Direction$ <> "b" and Direction$ <> "" Then
    Goto DoItAgain
ElseIf Direction$ = "b" Then
    FindText.Direction = 1
End If
```

With these changes, if you accidentally press anything other than the *f*, *b*, or the Return key by itself, the macro will cycle back to the Input command and ask you to re-enter the information.

## How to run the macro

You can test the Search macro by choosing the Start button on the Macro toolbar. (The Start button is the one with a right-pointing, filled-in triangle, the first button in the second group from the left.)

If you typed everything correctly, Word will ask you the question from the Input command by way of a prompt at the bottom of the screen. Press Return, or press *f* and then Return, and Word will respond with the Find dialog box, with the search direction set to down. Press *b* and then Return instead, and the dialog box will show up with the search direction set to up.

If you made any errors in entering the macro, Word will show you an error message, and you'll get the chance to practice with Word's debugging features that we covered in the last chapter, in the section "Testing, Modifying, and Debugging Macros" on page 835.

When you're sure the macro works, you can delete the apostrophe or *REM* from the beginning of the On Error command to turn off error messages.

## Some variations: The InputBox$() function

Macros are nothing if not flexible. While you still have the Search macro fresh in your mind, you should consider some variations that might better match the way you work. In particular, you may want to change the macro so it asks its question within a dialog box. Word offers a simple way to create the dialog box with the InputBox$() function. To use a dialog box, modify the original Input line to read

```
Direction$ = InputBox$("Search in which direction: F(oward) or B(ack)?
(Blank entry searches forward.)", "Search Direction")
```

If you replace the Input command with this InputBox$() function and then run the macro, you'll see an input box similar to the one in Figure 26-4.

**FIGURE 26-4**

The InputBox$() command offers much the same function as the Input command, but by way of a dialog box.

> In the InputBox$() command in the macro itself, there are two sets of quotation marks within the parentheses. As you can see in Figure 26-4, Word uses the text in the first set for the question it asks and the text in the second set as the title for the box. You can optionally add a comma and then a third text item within another set of quotation marks. Word will use the third item as the default entry for the InputBox$() text box.

## Message boxes

There are two commands in WordBasic that don't have direct relevance to the Search macro but are similar enough to the Input and InputBox$() commands to be worth mentioning here: MsgBox and MsgBox().

Briefly, the MsgBox command takes the form

```
MsgBox "Any Message", "Any Title", Type
```

where *Type* is a number that represents button and icon choices, as we'll explain shortly. The MsgBox() command takes the form

```
SomeVariable = MsgBox("Any Message", "Any Title", Type)
```

As you can see, the structure of the two commands is similar. In fact, if you enter the same message, the same title, and the same type, they will produce identical dialog boxes. Figure 26-5 shows the dialog box you'll get with either command, with the message Any Message, the title Any Title, and Type set to 0.

**FIGURE 26-5**

MsgBox and MsgBox() both show message boxes like this one.

The difference between the two is that the MsgBox() version returns a number as a variable that you can then test and use to control the macro behavior—in an If...End If statement, for example. We'll come back to that variable in a moment. To understand it, you first have to understand Type.

MsgBox and MsgBox() share a set of predefined features that you can designate by number. These include six sets of button types and four choices of icons (plus no icon as an additional choice). If you've chosen a set with more than one button, you can also designate which button is the default.

Figure 26-6 on the next page lists these predefined buttons and icons for MsgBox and MsgBox(). To designate your choices, pick from the list and total their values. For example, if you want the OK button (0) and no icon (0), Type is 0, the default value. If you want Yes and No buttons (4), an information icon (32), and the second button as the default (256), Type is 4 + 32 + 256, or 292.

| To Designate... | Add This to the Type Value... |
| --- | --- |
| **Buttons** | |
| OK button | 0 |
| OK and Cancel buttons | 1 |
| Abort, Retry, and Ignore buttons | 2 |
| Yes, No, and Cancel buttons | 3 |
| Yes and No buttons | 4 |
| Retry and Cancel buttons | 5 |
| **Icons** | |
| No icon | 0 |
| Stop icon | 16 |
| Attention icon | 32 |
| Attention icon | 48 |
| Information icon | 64 |
| **Default button** | |
| First (rightmost) button | 0 |
| Second button | 256 |
| Third button | 512 |

**FIGURE 26-6**

Predefined buttons, icons, and default buttons for the MsgBox and MsgBox() commands.

## MsgBox results

There is little point in defining a MsgBox to contain more than one button. The command does not return a number, and therefore gives you no way to tell the macro to test or act on the result. However, MsgBox() will return −1 for the rightmost button, 0 for the next button, and +1 for the next button. You can then use conditional comparisons to find out which button was pressed and a control statement such as If...End If to have the macro proceed accordingly.

For example, suppose you create a message box with the command

```
PressedWhat = MsgBox("Continue?", "Paused", 4)
```

This will create a message box with the title Paused, the question Continue? and Type 4, with buttons for Yes on the right and No on the left. Choosing Yes, the rightmost button, will set PressedWhat to a value of −1. Choosing

No, the next button to the left, will set PressedWhat to 0. Since there are only two buttons, these are the only two choices for PressedWhat.

After using the MsgBox() command, you can use an If...End If statement to test which button was pressed. The statement would take the form

```
If PressedWhat = -1 Then
    DoTheseInstructions
ElseIf PressedWhat = 0 Then
    DoTheseInstructionsInstead
End If
```

and the macro would then follow one set of instructions or the other, depending on which button was chosen.

## The GetCurValues command and branching execution

One other technique worth passing mention is using the current values in a dialog box to control what your macro does. If you've been working through this entire discussion on macros, you've already seen how to use the Dim...As statement to create a dialog record. For example,

```
Dim FmtFont As FormatFont
```

creates a dialog record named FmtFont, with a set of empty fields to match the fields in the FormatFont dialog box. The GetCurValues statement will let you set the values in the dialog record to match the current settings in the dialog box. The two lines

```
Dim FmtPara As FormatParagraph
GetCurValues FmtPara
```

create the record FmtPara, get the current values for the FormatParagraph dialog box, and store those values in the appropriate FmtPara fields. You can then use an If...End If statement to test the value of the FmtPara fields and control what the macro does.

Suppose, for example, that you want to put a border around paragraphs that you have previously indented $1/2$ inch from the left. You could create a macro that moves forward one paragraph, gets the current values for that paragraph, and tests the values with a command similar to this:

```
If FmtPara.LeftIndent = .5 Then...
```

(Actually, this If statement won't work as shown. We'll explain why in a moment.) If the paragraph is indeed indented $1/2$ inch, the macro can branch to commands that add a border. If it isn't indented, the macro can branch to commands that don't add a border.

# How to use the quotation mark as part of a text string

As we just pointed out, the If statement we breezed past at the end of the previous section will not work as shown. In fact, Word treats LeftIndent—and other paragraph indention settings—not as numeric values, but as text. That means you not only have to enclose the value in quotes to indicate that it's text, you have to give the entire value of the text string. Note too that for any given setting for a left indent, the actual text will vary, depending on how you've set the Measurement Units on the Tools Options General card: for inches, centimeters, picas, or points. A ½-inch indent, for example, can show as *3 pi* for picas, *1.27 cm* for centimeters, or *36 pt* for points. Using inches creates an additional complication, since Word uses the quotation mark as the symbol for inches. If you simply type *"0.5""*, Word will report a syntax error. Instead, you have to represent the 0.5" as

```
"0.5" + Chr$(34)
```

This translates to "0.5" followed by the ASCII character 34, which is the quotation mark. The line would read as follows:

```
If FmtPara.LeftIndent = "0.5" + Chr$(34) Then...
```

# Loops: The While...Wend statement

The example of moving ahead one paragraph at a time and testing the current format for each paragraph assumes that the macro can loop back to the beginning of its own commands, move ahead to the next paragraph, test the new paragraph's format, and so on. One of the more common kinds of loops uses the While...Wend statement, which takes the form

```
While Condition
    Statements
Wend
```

This roughly translates to "While the specified condition holds true, keep repeating all the instructions between the While and the Wend. When the condition no longer holds true, pick up the macro after the Wend."

In this particular case, the most reasonable condition for repeating the loop would be that you haven't yet reached the end of the document. Word provides a simple way to specify this condition by way of two special bookmarks and the ability to compare bookmarks with the CmpBookmark(s) command.

# How to test for the end of the document

The two bookmarks are \Sel, which is the current selection, and \EndOfDoc, which is the end of the document. The CmpBookmarks() command can compare the two and determine whether they match. The appropriate command is

```
CmpBookmarks ("\Sel", "\EndOfDoc")
```

More precisely, the CmpBookmarks() command compares the two bookmarks and returns a number. That number will be 0 if the two bookmarks are exactly equivalent, or some other number if they are not. (For example, 1 means the first bookmark is entirely below the second, and 2 means the first is entirely above the second.) The other numbers that CmpBookmarks() returns are of no importance for our purposes. What does matter is that Word uses the number to determine whether the condition is true or false. In particular, you can make the CmpBookmarks() command the condition in a While construction, in the form

```
While CmpBookmarks ("\Sel", "\EndOfDoc")
    Statements
Wend
```

In this example, until CmpBookmarks() returns the number 0, Word will consider the condition to be true and will keep repeating the loop. When the macro reaches the end of the file, CmpBookmarks() will return 0 and the macro will move past the While...Wend statement.

## Putting the FormatBorder macro together

Finally, taking all this into account, we wind up with the macro shown in Figure 26-7 for putting borders around already indented paragraphs. As written, the macro assumes you're using inches as your measurement units.

**FIGURE 26-7**

This macro demonstrates how a While-...Wend statement can keep repeating a set of commands until a given condition is no longer true.

Note that most of the macro's action takes place within the While...Wend statement. First the macro creates a dialog record called FmtPara; then, on each pass through the loop, it gets the current values for that record and tests the record to see whether the left indent matches the criterion for adding a border. If so, it adds the border. If not, it skips to the End If statement, goes to the next paragraph, and starts again. When you reach the end of the document and the macro leaves the While...Wend loop, the MsgBox command notifies you that you're at the end of the document. And that brings us back to the subject of dialog boxes.

# Designing Custom Dialog Boxes with the Dialog Editor

Up to now in this chapter, we've been looking at message boxes and dialog boxes that are built in, in one way or another. But even though you can accomplish much with Word's standard dialog boxes and predefined message boxes, you can accomplish even more by designing your own dialog boxes from scratch.

For example, suppose that rather than use Word's annotation feature, you'd prefer to enter notes directly in your document, and you want to use colors to indicate the purpose of each note—dark green, say, to indicate a note to a co-author, blue to indicate the source for information you've already confirmed, and red to indicate notes to yourself for information you have to confirm.

If you add many notes, changing color through the Format Font dialog box, you'll find that the multiple steps you need to run through each time quickly become tiresome. A better alternative is to build your own dialog box that offers a more straightforward approach to changing text color. The finished dialog box might look like the example in Figure 26-8.

WordBasic offers commands that will let you design a dialog box any way you like, with option buttons, check boxes, push buttons, text boxes, and so on. You can then use the If...End If statement (or a similar WordBasic construction) to test the entries in the dialog box and act on them. As you might

**FIGURE 26-8**

This dialog box is designed to make it easy to mark text in your choice of colors.

expect, creating a dialog box by typing the appropriate commands in a macro editing window can be a chore. Word provides an easier alternative with the Dialog Editor. In the next few pages, we'll show you how to build a dialog box, using the Mark Text dialog box as an example.

## How to run the Dialog Editor

The Dialog Editor is a separate program from Word. If you specified the Custom/Complete installation when you installed Word, the Setup program automatically installed the Dialog Editor as well, in the Macros Folder located in the same folder as Word. Unless you've deleted the program file since installation, you can run the Dialog Editor from the Finder by double-clicking on the icon (or name if you've set the Finder to view names rather than icons). If you specified the Typical installation, you will need to run Setup again to add the Dialog Editor to your system. The Dialog Editor is included under the Tools option.

You can also run the Dialog Editor from within Word by clicking on the Dialog Editor button, which you'll find on the Macro toolbar. Remember that to see the Macro toolbar, you need to have a macro editing window open. You can edit an existing macro by choosing Tools Macro, entering the macro name in the Macro Name box, and choosing Edit. To edit a new macro, choose Tools Macro, type a name in the Macro Name text box, and choose Create. In either case, Word will add the Macro toolbar to the top of your screen when it opens the macro editing window. The Dialog Editor button is the rightmost button. When you click on it, Word will start the Dialog Editor, if it's not already running, and will then take you to the Dialog Editor window.

## How to use the Dialog Editor

When you start the Dialog Editor, the screen will look much like the one in Figure 26-9 on the next page, with File, Edit, and Item menus and a blank dialog box in the center of the screen. (Note that to keep the screen as uncluttered as possible, we've set the Macintosh to hide other applications, by choosing Hide Others from the Application menu.)

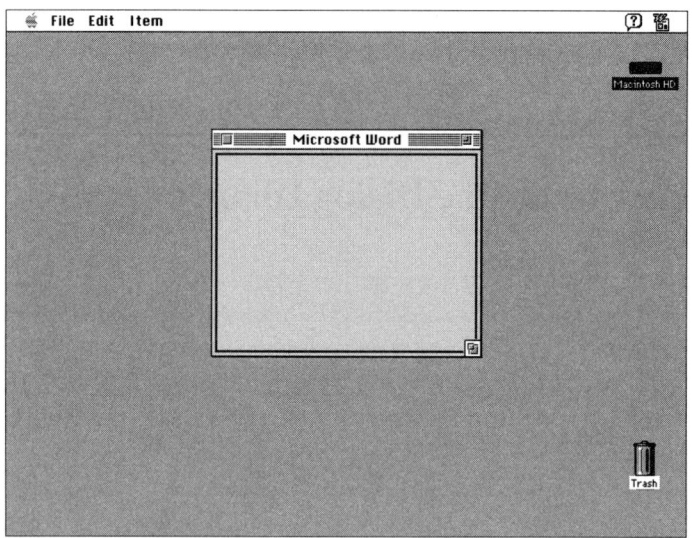

**FIGURE 26-9**

The Dialog Editor starts
with a blank dialog
box in the center of the
screen.

You can think of the Dialog Editor almost as a drafting program. Its various options provide images of option buttons, OK buttons, Cancel buttons, push buttons, check boxes, and other dialog box components. You can define a label for each item, resize the items, and move them around until the dialog box looks the way you want it to. When you're finished, simply copy the dialog box to the Clipboard (it copies as a set of text macro instructions) and then paste it into your macro editing window in Word.

There are essentially five steps in using the Dialog Editor: creating each item, positioning and resizing each, editing the text for each, copying the definition to the Clipboard, and pasting the definition into your macro. When you're actually creating a dialog box, these five steps won't separate out so neatly. You can easily move back and forth among the first three steps while in the Dialog Editor. Less obvious is that you can further modify the definition after it's in your macro. You can even move it back to the Dialog Editor by way of the Clipboard and change it there. For purposes of this discussion, however, we'll assume you're doing everything from beginning to end in a straightforward, step-by-step manner.

## How to create items

Whenever you start creating a new dialog box, either by starting the Dialog Editor or by choosing File New while in the Dialog Editor, the Dialog Editor starts you off with a blank dialog box in the center of the screen. You can then add items with the Item menu. As shown in Figure 26-10, the choices on the Item menu include Text, Text Box, and Group Box, each of which inserts the appropriate item in a single step. In addition, you can choose Item Button to open a dialog box that will let you add any of several types of buttons; Item List Box to open a dialog box for adding various kinds of lists; or Item Picture to open a dialog box that will let you add a picture to the dialog box you're building.

**FIGURE 26-10**

The Dialog Editor's Item menu includes commands for adding text, a text box, or a group box to your dialog box, as well as commands that will open dialog boxes for adding buttons, lists, and pictures.

As you can see in Figure 26-10, the dialog box for adding buttons will let you add an OK button, a Cancel button, a push button, an option button, or a check box to the dialog box you're building. The dialog box for adding lists will let you add a standard (scrollable) list box, a combination text box with attached list box (Combo Box), or a drop-down list box.

The New Picture dialog box, also shown in Figure 26-10, offers five different picture types to choose from: File, AutoText Entry, Bookmark, Clipboard, and Resource. As the names imply, these five choices let you insert pictures into your dialog boxes from any of five sources, using a picture that's stored in a file on disk, in an AutoText entry, in a document that's marked with a bookmark, on the Clipboard, or as a resource. (The Clipboard option assumes that the macro has copied a picture to the Clipboard earlier in the macro.) If you create a dialog box with each of these picture items, you'll find that all five of them use variations on the WordBasic Picture command.

All of these items will work the same way in your dialog boxes as they do in the built-in dialog boxes in Word. To add any of them, simply choose the appropriate item. The Dialog Editor will insert the item in the dialog box that you're building. You can proceed, item by item, until you've added all the items you need.

For our example dialog box, we'll need four option buttons—one for each color we plan to mark text with, plus one to return to the default setting of Auto for color. We'll also need a group box to group the buttons together, an OK button to tell Word when the option button is set properly, a Cancel button to give us a way to cancel the dialog box without changing text color, and, finally, a picture item which we'll use to add a picture of crayons. After you add these items, the Dialog Editor window will look much like the one in Figure 26-11.

**FIGURE 26-11**

This is how the Dialog Editor window will look after you have added four option buttons, a group box, an OK button, a Cancel button, and a Picture item.

When you're grouping option buttons (or any other items, for that matter) in a group box, it helps to add the group box in the Dialog Editor first and then add the option buttons. If you add the option buttons first, you'll find that if you try moving the buttons inside the group box, the box will overlay the buttons on screen and hide them, rather than function as a box that sets off the group of buttons. If you accidentally create the items in the wrong order, however, it's easy enough to fix the problem.

First select the option button (or other item) you want to move to the group box, and cut it using either of the standard Macintosh cut commands: Edit Cut or ⌘-X. Then select the group box you want the item in, and paste the item back into the dialog box with either of the standard paste commands: Edit Paste or ⌘-V. The Dialog Editor will paste the item back in the same position you deleted it from, but if you now move the item into the group box, it will appear inside the box rather than be hidden by it.

## Shortcuts for adding new items

Although choosing items from a menu is a lot faster than typing each WordBasic command into a macro editing window as text, going through three levels of menus can also be a chore. The Dialog Editor provides shortcuts that make creating a dialog box easier.

In general, whenever you add an item to a dialog box, the Dialog Editor leaves that item selected. You can also select any item at any time by pointing to it and clicking with the mouse or by using the Tab key to cycle through all the items, including the dialog box. The Dialog Editor makes an educated guess about what you might want to add next, basing its guess on the item currently selected. You can then add new items simply by pressing Return.

In most cases, pressing Return when you have an item selected in the Dialog Editor yields another of whatever item is selected. For example, if you have an option button selected when you press Return, you'll get an additional option button. There are some exceptions, however. Knowing them will speed dialog box creation considerably. Figure 26-12 lists the exceptions.

Note also that, in some circumstances, the Dialog Editor will place a newly created item at the same position as an item that already exists. You'll then have to move the item to see the one that's hidden beneath it.

| If This Item Is Selected... | Pressing Return Will Add... |
| --- | --- |
| OK button | Cancel if none exists or a push button |
| Cancel button | OK if none exists or a push button |
| Push button | OK if none exists, then Cancel if none exists, and then a push button if both an OK and a Cancel button exist |
| Group box | Option button |

**FIGURE 26-12**

Pressing Return in the Dialog Editor will not create a duplicate of the selected item in these cases.

As you can see from Figure 26-12, you can create the items in the sample dialog box by starting with a group box and then pressing Return four times to create four option buttons; then add either an OK button or a Cancel button, and press Return one more time to create the other button. Finish up by adding the Picture item, choosing File in the Take Picture From box.

## How to delete items

As you're creating items for the dialog box, you may accidentally create more items than you want, or you may simply decide you want to get rid of one or more items. To delete an item, select it with the mouse or Tab key and then press Del or choose Edit Clear. In fact, all of the standard Macintosh editing keys for cutting and pasting that you're used to in Word will work in the Dialog Editor as well. You can also use commands from the Edit menu by selecting an item and then choosing Edit Cut, Edit Copy, Edit Paste, Edit Clear, or Edit Duplicate. Edit Duplicate is the equivalent of choosing Edit Copy followed by Edit Paste.

## How to position and resize items

After you've added all the items that you want in the dialog box, the next step is to position and size each item. A good way to start is by changing the size of the dialog box itself, shrinking or enlarging it so you can arrange the items inside the box in a visually attractive layout. In the case of our sample dialog box, you might want to make the group box a bit smaller so it surrounds only the option buttons, and you'll want to move the OK and Cancel buttons away from the group box. When you're done, the window should look much like the one shown in Figure 26-13.

**FIGURE 26-13**

You can also use the Dialog Editor to move items around and create a visually attractive dialog box.

### How to adjust size with the mouse

Since adjusting position and size is basically a graphical task, you'll almost certainly find that the mouse is the most natural way to approach it—although you may want to use the keyboard commands for fine-tuning. In most ways, adjusting size with the mouse is similar to adjusting a window size. Simply move the mouse pointer to the edge or the corner of the dialog box or item. When the pointer changes to a double-headed arrow, drag the edge or the corner to change the item's size. When the object is the size you want, release the mouse button.

With OK, Cancel, a push button, or a text box, you can adjust only width—not height—unless you change the Auto default. Similarly, you cannot change the height or width of option buttons, check boxes, or text unless you change the Auto default. We'll cover the Auto default in "The Auto size selection and adjusting height and width" on page 876.

## How to adjust position with the mouse

As you move the mouse pointer over items in the dialog box, you'll notice that it takes the shape of the four-headed arrow pointer, as shown in Figure 26-14. Whenever you see the four-headed arrow pointer, you can hold down the mouse button and drag the item the pointer is on. Simply drag the item to the new position and release the mouse button.

**FIGURE 26-14**

The four-headed arrow pointer indicates that you can hold down the mouse button and drag to move an object.

## How to adjust size with the keyboard

If you prefer using the keyboard to adjust size, or if you want the finer control available keystroke by keystroke, press the Tab key until you've selected the item that you want to adjust. Then hold down the Shift key and press one of the arrow keys (Up, Down, Left, or Right) to adjust the size. To move in larger increments, you can hold down the Option key along with the Shift key while pressing the arrow key.

As with the mouse, you'll find that with some items—OK, Cancel, and push buttons—you can adjust only the width; with other items—option buttons, check boxes, and text—you cannot adjust either width or height.

## How to adjust position with the keyboard

To move an item using the keyboard, once again select the item with the Tab key. Then use the arrow keys to adjust position. Note that you can move in larger increments by holding down the Option key as you use the arrow keys.

# A special note about the dialog box

Be aware that whenever you start a new dialog box definition, the Dialog Editor assumes you will want the dialog box horizontally and vertically centered on the screen. And it anchors the box there unless you tell it otherwise. In general, there is no reason to move the dialog box. If you want to move it, however, either double-click on the box or select it and choose Edit Info. The Dialog Editor will show you the Dialog Information dialog box, as in Figure 26-15 on the next page. If you clear the Auto check boxes under Position, you'll then be able to move the dialog box, much as you would any other item. In this case, however, you would use the standard Macintosh conventions for moving a document window—clicking on the title bar and dragging the window to the new position.

The Dialog Information dialog box holds all of the information about the dialog box item.

Note that as long as the dialog box is anchored at the center of the window, any time you change the size by dragging the size box, the Dialog Editor will reposition the window so it will still be centered, as shown in Figure 26-16. After you clear the checks from the Auto check boxes, however, the window will stay where the dotted outlines indicate when you adjust the size.

By default, the dialog box is anchored at the center of the window. When you change the size by dragging the size box, as shown in this figure, the Dialog Editor will reposition the window to re-center it, as shown in the figure on the facing page.

*(continued)*

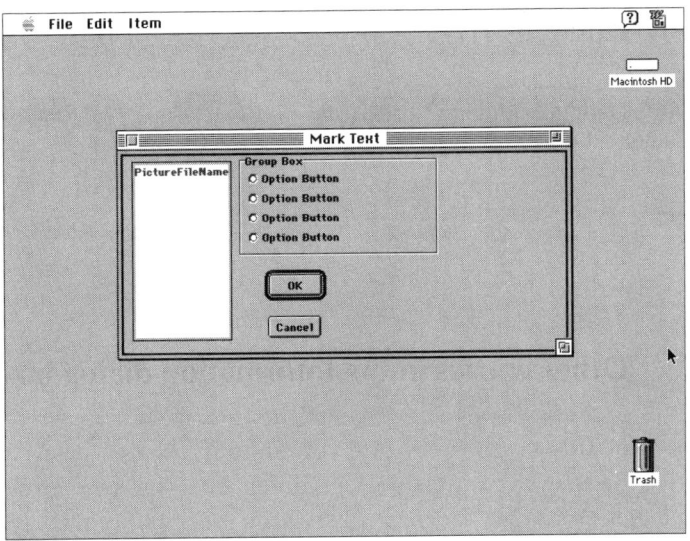

**FIGURE 26-16** *continued*

## How to edit the text for each item

At this point, if you've been working along with our example, you have all the items you want arranged the way you want them. But they still have generic labels, such as Option Button. To edit the text for an item, either double-click on the item or select it and then choose Edit Info. The Dialog Editor will show you a dialog box much like the one in Figure 26-15, though the dialog box will vary slightly depending on the item. For example, an OK button must have *OK* and a Cancel button must have *Cancel* for the text, so you won't be able to change the text choice for either of these buttons. Similarly, the name of the dialog box will change, depending on the type of item you're editing information for. The name of the dialog box for an option button, for example, is Option Button Information.

The entries for each kind of item also have slightly different purposes, even though the Information dialog boxes are similar. For example, for the Dialog Information dialog box shown in Figure 26-15, anything you type in the Text$ text box will become the title for the dialog box. For a group box, the text becomes the label for the box. For an option button, the text becomes the label for the button. And for a picture, the text identifies the source of the picture. In this example, we've entered *Mark Text* as the text for the dialog box; *Color to Mark Text* as the text for the group box; *Dk Green (Note to Co-Author), Blue (Source of Info), Red (Things to Check),* and *None (Return to Default)* for the four option buttons; and the filename for the graphic as the text for the picture. Figure 26-17 on the next page shows the result.

FIGURE 26-17

The finished dialog
box as it appears in the
Dialog Editor.

## Other entries in the Information dialog box

Most of the other entries in the Information dialog box are beyond the scope
of this discussion, but you should be aware of what they are in general.
Briefly, each Information dialog box shows information about the selected
item that will become part of the macro statement for that item. For example,
the X and Y text boxes under Position define the position of the upper left corner of the item. Similarly, Width and Height define the size of the item.

As with any macro command, the statement for each dialog box item must
follow a precise syntax. Because command syntax is beyond the scope of this
book, there is no point in explaining each item in the dialog box. However, it's
worth noting that the Dialog Editor itself supplies most of the syntax for you.

When you adjust the position and size of each item, the Dialog Editor
automatically supplies the correct syntax for defining that position
and size. You'll note that if you've followed our example, the Dialog
Editor entered *OptionGroup1* in the OptGroup text box for all four option buttons. This identifies the option buttons as being part of the
same group, ensuring that you cannot select more than one at a time.

Be aware, however, that the Dialog Editor is only an aid to creating dialog boxes, not the final arbiter. You'll find that after you've
created dialog boxes with the Dialog Editor, you'll occasionally
have to clean up a few stray errors manually. And that means that if
you want to make best use of the Dialog Editor, you'll have to learn
macro syntax—an issue we'll touch on in the section "Where to Go
from Here" on page 880.

## The Auto size selection and adjusting height and width

Earlier in this chapter, we pointed out that you can't change the height of OK
buttons, Cancel buttons, push buttons, and text boxes unless you change the
Auto default. More specifically, if you look at the Information dialog box for

any of these items, you'll see that the Auto option button next to the Height text box is checked. If you want to adjust the size of any of these items, simply clear the Height check box. Similarly, if you look at the Information dialog box for option buttons, check boxes, and text, you'll find the Auto check boxes for both Width and Height are checked. Here again, if you want to adjust the size for these items, simply clear the appropriate check box.

## How to copy the definition to the Clipboard

After you've created the dialog box with the Dialog Editor, you have to move it to the Clipboard. The procedure is similar to moving text or objects to the Clipboard while you're working in Word. Assuming you want to move the entire dialog box, simply choose File Quit. Word will prompt you to save changes to the Clipboard. Choose Save.

> If you have already defined a dialog box in your macro editing window, you can copy just a part of the dialog box from the Dialog Editor by selecting only the portion you need to add to the macro. Most often, however, you'll want to move the entire dialog box. Also note that you can't save a dialog box as a separate Dialog Editor file.

## How to paste the definition into your macro

When you copy the dialog box definition to the Clipboard, it's copied as text. In fact, if you look at the Clipboard at this point, it should look much like the one in Figure 26-18.

**FIGURE 26-18**

When you copy a dialog box definition from the Dialog Editor to the Clipboard, it shows up in the Clipboard as text.

```
                                    Clipboard
BeginDialog UserDialog 392, 181, "Mark Text"¶
        GroupBox 143, 0, 246, 93, "Color to Mark Text"¶
        OptionGroup .OptionGroup1¶
                OptionButton 149, 13, 233, 18, "Dk Green (Note to Co-Author)", .OptionButton1 ¶
                OptionButton 149, 31, 178, 18, "Blue (Source of Info)", .OptionButton2 ¶
                OptionButton 149, 48, 183, 18, "Red (Things to Check)", .OptionButton3 ¶
                OptionButton 149, 67, 203, 18, "None (Return to Default)", .OptionButton4 ¶
        OKButton 180, 110, 65, 20 ¶
        CancelButton 179, 148, 65, 20 ¶
        Picture 12, 6, 122, 164, "Macintosh HD:Microsoft Word 6.0:Clip Art:Crayons.pict", 0, .Picture1 ¶
EndDialog ¶
```

To paste the dialog box definition into a macro, you only have to go to your macro editing window, place the cursor where you want to insert the definition, and give the Edit Paste command. At this point, you'll have a dialog box definition that starts with a Begin Dialog UserDialog statement and ends with an End Dialog statement. To actually use the dialog box as part of a macro, you'll have to add more commands. In particular, you need to add the following two lines after the End Dialog statement just to get the dialog box to appear on the screen:

```
Dim MarkText As UserDialog
Dialog MarkText
```

The first line creates a dialog record called MarkText to match the defined dialog box. The second puts the dialog box on the screen.

As we've already mentioned, you may still have to debug the definition itself. For example, the Dialog Editor will let you create a definition that consists of nothing but option buttons. However, if you try to use that definition, Word will respond with the WordBasic error message "Dialog needs End Dialog or a push button," which means that WordBasic couldn't find at least one of these items (in this case a push button, since the Dialog Editor automatically adds the End Dialog statement). The reason for the error message is that if you use only option buttons with no OK button, Cancel button, or other push button, there is no way to leave the dialog box once you open it.

## What to do with a dialog box once you have one

Throughout this discussion of the Dialog Editor, we've concentrated on the mechanics of the process. But even though this is not a book about macros, it would be pointless to go through all of these steps without giving at least some idea of how to take advantage of a dialog box.

Figure 26-19 shows the full macro we've been discussing in our example, after we've modified the lines created by the Dialog Editor and added other commands. If you look through it, you may find that you can apply many of these techniques to your own macros.

**FIGURE 26-19**

This macro for marking text will ask you to choose a color for the currently highlighted and following text, and will set Word accordingly.

Note first that the macro consists of two main sections: the dialog box and the If...End If statement that tests which option button you've specified in the dialog box and then sets the font color accordingly.

The dialog box section was produced primarily by the Dialog Editor and then modified slightly. Note the syntax for each item in the dialog box. For example, the line

```
OKButton 180, 110, 65, 20
```

completely defines the OK button. The first two numbers (180 and 110) specify the upper left corner of the OK button, as measured from the upper left corner of the dialog box. The second two numbers (65 and 20) specify its size. More generally, the OKButton command takes the following form:

```
OKButton DistanceFromLeft, DistanceFromTop, Width, Height
```

You can also add an optional identifier at the end of the command, but we'll ignore that in this discussion.

The statement that produces the Cancel button is identical in form to the OKButton statement, differing only in that it starts with *CancelButton* rather than *OKButton*. And the other commands for dialog box items are similar. The OptionButton command takes the form

```
OptionButton DistanceFromLeft, DistanceFromTop, Width, Height, "Label"
```

and the group box statement takes the form

```
GroupBox DistanceFromLeft, DistanceFromTop, Width, Height, "Label"
```

The Picture statement has just a bit more information in it, taking the form

```
Picture DistanceFromLeft, DistanceFromTop, Width, Height, "PictureName",
Type, .Identifier
```

*Type* here indicates whether this picture is stored as an AutoText entry (Type 1), identified by a bookmark in the current document (Type 2), taken from the Clipboard (Type 3), stored as a resource (Type 4), or, as shown in Figure 26-19, stored in a separate file (Type 0). PictureName is the name of the file, AutoText entry, bookmark, or resource, depending on the picture type. If you were using Type 3, taking the picture from the Clipboard (as you might in a macro that had already copied a picture to the Clipboard), the PictureName would be given as a null value, with two double quotes and nothing inside them. The identifier gives you a way to refer to the picture in other commands.

 The OptionButton and the GroupBox statement both allow an optional identifier at the end of the command, as does the OKButton. (But here again, we'll ignore the identifier in this discussion.)

The option buttons are all defined as being within OptionGroup1 simply because they immediately follow the line

```
OptionGroup .OptionGroup1
```

You could create a second group of mutually exclusive option buttons by adding the line

```
OptionGroup .OptionGroup2
```

before a second group of buttons. Also part of the dialog box section are the two lines

```
Dim MarkText As UserDialog
Dialog MarkText
```

As we discussed earlier in this chapter, these lines create a dialog record called *MarkText* and put the dialog box on the screen. In addition, you'll note that we've added the line

```
On Error Goto SkipIt
```

before calling up the dialog box. As we've also discussed earlier, if you choose the Cancel option in the dialog box, this On Error statement tells the macro to jump to the label SkipIt rather than show you an error message.

The If...End If statement tests to see which button you chose. Note that by default, Word assigns the first button to 0, the second to 1, and so forth. Depending on which one you chose, the macro uses the appropriate FormatFont command to set the color of any selected text, or any text you type at the cursor position. After setting the color for the text, the macro continues after the End If statement and ends.

# Where to Go from Here

At this point, you should have a pretty good idea of how to build some useful macros. However, even these three chapters on macros provide only an introduction to the subject. To learn more, you need a reference to all of the macro commands in Word and the syntax for each command.

## Help for macros

You can find much of the information you need in the Word Help file. If you choose Microsoft Word Help from the Help menu, choose Programming with Microsoft Word, then Contents, and then the Statements And Functions Index, you'll find an alphabetic list of WordBasic commands that you can then choose from to see the proper syntax and examples for each. Alternatively, rather than choosing the index, you can choose the Statements And Functions By Category option. Then you can choose the category of command you are looking for (such as Branching And Control) and browse through the choices to find the right command when you're not sure which one to use.

You may find that having the commands in the Help file is not as convenient as having them in a reference book. If you want a reference book, the *Microsoft Word Developer's Kit, second edition*, is a good one to start with. This book includes both a complete reference to macro commands and a detailed set of instructions for macro programming. You'll find more information on the book, and how to get it, in the Word Help system. Here again, choose the topic Programming With Microsoft Word from the main contents of the Help system. Then choose The Microsoft Word Developer's Kit option for the information.

If you decide to roll up your sleeves and get serious about learning WordBasic, there's one other book you should be aware of: *Hacker's Guide to Word for Windows,* by Woody Leonhard and Vincent Chen, published by Addison-Wesley. Although this book was written for Word for Windows, the macro languages in the Windows and Macintosh versions of Word are nearly identical, so you can learn a great deal from the book. The *Hacker's Guide* is filled with useful nuggets of information that you won't find elsewhere, documenting bugs and peculiarities in the way Word and WordBasic work. Even better, the book is fun to read, which is quite an accomplishment for a book on programming. The *Hacker's Guide* also includes a complete reference to WordBasic commands. Also worth reading is *Take Word for Windows to the Edge,* by Guy Gallo, published by Ziff-Davis Press. *Take Word for Windows to the Edge* takes a more straightforward approach to the subject, but it, too, is filled with useful information. Somewhat surprisingly, although the two books necessarily deal with overlapping subject matter, they are different enough to make both worth having.

We've essentially completed our introduction to macros, but we're not quite finished with the topic of macros in general. In the last chapter of this book, we'll show you how to make macros even more useful by assigning them to key combinations and menus. (We'll also explain how to rearrange Word's default key assignments and menus.) Before we discuss these finishing touches about macros, however, we'll take a slight detour in the next chapter, to look more closely at Word's templates. Read on.

# TOPIC FINDER

# 27

# Templates

e've already worked with templates in Chapter 2 and Chapter 9. We've discussed how to create a new document based on any given template and how to attach a different template to any document, and how templates differ from Apple Stationery Pads. Templates are central to Word, and you need to know at least a little about them for everything from creating a new document to customizing Word's menus.

In this chapter, we'll discuss templates in more detail. We'll show you how to create and edit your own templates, and we'll discuss some of the possibilities for using templates.

## Creating a New Document Template: The Mechanics

Word offers several choices for creating a new template. You can create one from scratch, you can base it on an existing document or an existing template, or you can use a wizard to generate a template.

The point of using templates is to let you create what amounts to different default settings for different kinds of documents. For example, you may want a default of single spacing for letters but double spacing for reports. If you don't have preprinted letterhead, you may want to create a heading in a letter template so that Word will automatically add it to the first page of each new letter. Word's templates are also capable of far more sophisticated automation.

## NEW! How to change the User Templates folder

With Word 6.0, you can define the folder you want to use for your templates. To see the current setting for the User Templates folder, choose Tools Options, and then the File Locations card, shown in Figure 27-1. To change the setting, choose User Templates in the File Types list box, and choose Modify to open the dialog box shown in Figure 27-2. You can then use the pull-down list at the top left of the dialog box, combined with the scrollable list just beneath it to specify a different folder on your system. (Note that you can choose the Desktop button to go back to Desktop level.) When you're done, choose Use Selected Folder to accept the new setting and return to the File Locations card, or choose Cancel to return to the File Locations card and keep the original setting.

**FIGURE 27-1**

The File Locations card in the Options dialog box shows a list of Word's current settings for file locations.

**FIGURE 27-2**

Choose Modify on the File Locations card to open this dialog box and change the locations where Word searches for particular kinds of files.

While working in the dialog box for modifying file locations, you can also create a new folder for your templates if you like by choosing the New button. Word will open the dialog box shown in Figure 27-3. Type the new name in the Name Of New Folder text box, and choose Create to create the folder and return to the dialog box for modifying locations. Alternatively, choose Cancel to close the dialog box without creating a folder first.

**FIGURE 27-3**

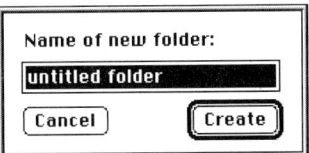

To create a folder while in the dialog box for modifying file locations, choose New to open this dialog box.

## How to create a new template from scratch

To create a new template from scratch, choose File New, choose the Template option in the New box, and choose OK. Word will open a new document window with the title Template1. If you open additional new templates during the same session, Word will number them sequentially—Template2, Template3, and so on.

With the template showing on screen, you can modify it as you would any other document. You can add, edit, and format text; define styles, AutoText entries, and macros; change format settings; change the View menu options; and more. In Chapter 28, "Customizing Menus, Keys, & Templates," starting on page 903, we'll show you how to redefine the menu and shortcut key assignments as well.

Note that any formatting you add to text that's part of the template carries over to documents based on the template. The same is true of any formatting you define with the Document Layout or Columns dialog box. To set template-specific defaults for font, paragraph, tabs, borders and shading, and language, you can redefine the Normal style and other styles. For any given document based on the template, you can override any of these formatting instructions by redefining the format while working in that document.

### How to save a template file

You save a template by choosing File Save or File Save As, just as you would save any standard document; Word will display the usual dialog box for saving. When saving templates, Word automatically sets the folder to whatever you've defined as the User Templates folder.

If you like, you can use the dialog box to specify a different folder. If you change the folder, however, Word will not be able to find the file automatically for you later. As a general rule, unless you have a good reason for doing otherwise, you should accept the default folder and simply type in a filename.

After you type a name for the template, choose Save to save it. If Word is set to prompt you for summary information, it will then open the Summary Info dialog box. (To use this feature, choose Tools Options, go to the Save card, and check the Prompt For Summary Info check box.) You can then type the summary information and choose OK to finish saving. Word will return you to the editing screen, where you can make further changes if you like. After you finish with the template, choose File Close to exit from the template file and save your changes.

If you try to save a template under the same name as an existing template, Word will ask whether you want to replace the existing template. Choose Replace or Cancel, as appropriate.

After you save the template in the folder specified for User Templates on the File Locations card, Word will add it to the Template list box whenever you give the File New command to start a new document. Similarly, Word will add the template name to the list of filenames when you choose the File Templates command and then choose Attach to open the dialog box for attaching templates, shown in Figure 27-4.

**FIGURE 27-4**

The dialog box for attaching templates is similar to the dialog box for opening files and will help you find a template to attach to the file you're currently working on.

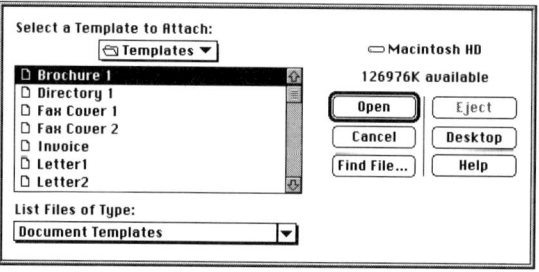

## Template security and passwords

As already mentioned, you can bypass Word's default setting for template location. This can serve as a mild security measure if you want to hide the template from other users. If you put the template in some other folder, Word will not add it to any list of template files; you won't be able to choose it from the list of templates when you're creating a new document, and it won't appear in the list of files in the dialog box shown in Figure 27-4.

If you know the filename, however, you will still be able to designate the template. After creating a file, choose File Templates Attach, then use the dialog box to move to the proper folder, and choose the template from that folder. The dialog box looks and works the same way as the dialog box for opening files.

Note that you don't have to hide a template to keep others from using it, however. Word's file-level password security, which we discussed in Chapter 2, applies to templates as well, and it offers stronger security than simply changing the template's location. You can add a password to a template at any time. With the template open, simply choose File Save As and then Options, and type a password in the Protection Password text box. Word will show your keystrokes as bullets, and ask you to type the password a second time to confirm it. You can remove the password by opening the file and choosing File Save As; then choose Options, delete the bullets in the Password Protection text box and choose OK.

**NEW!**

If you add a *protection* password, you'll have to enter the password whenever you open the template to edit it, whenever you try to attach the template to a document file, and whenever you open a document file that has the template already attached. Note that a template password is case sensitive when you open a template; Word will not accept Hello, for example, as a match for HELLO. However, it is not case sensitive when you open a document the template is based on.

You can also create a *write reservation* password for template files—either instead of or in addition to a protection password. Write reservation passwords work much the same way with templates as with documents; users who don't know the password can open the file, but they can't modify it. With templates, though, using only a write reservation password will also let you attach the template to a file, so you can use the template even though you can't modify it.

A write reservation password can be useful for templates that you create for others, particularly templates that are meant to establish a companywide or groupwide standard—for AutoText entries or style formats, for example. You may want to let users take advantage of a particular set of macros, AutoText entries, and so on, without letting them modify any of the template's customizations. You can add a write reservation password much as you add a protection password: With the template open, choose File Save As and then Options. Then type a password in the Write Reservation Password text box. For more information on both kinds of passwords, see "File Save As options" on page 42.

## How to create a new template from an existing document

At times you'll want to create a template from an existing document. For example, you may create a memo, a letter, or a fax cover sheet for one-time use and then decide later that you want to reuse the format. To convert a document to a template, start by opening the document and choosing File Save As. Next choose Document Template in the Save File As Type list box, and specify the folder for the template, using the pull-down list and scrollable list above the Save Current Document As text box. To finish, choose Save.

## How to base a new template on an existing template

As you develop a collection of templates, there will be times when you will want to base a new template on one that already exists. For example, after you develop a letter template, you may want a memo template that shares many of the same features but uses a different format for date and address. Rather than create an entirely new template, you can start with the first template and change just those items that you need to change.

One way to create the new template is to start by choosing File New and choosing Template in the New box; then, in the Template list box, highlight the template you want to start with. Choose OK, and Word will create a new template that includes all the customizations of the template you're basing it on. Make any changes you want, and choose File Save As, giving the template an appropriate name.

Alternatively, you can choose File Open to open the existing template and then use the Save As command to save it under a new name. If you choose this route, we recommend that you save the template under the new name immediately, before making any changes. This will ensure that you don't inadvertently save the changed file under its original name.

## How to create a template by copying a document or template file

You can also create a new template by copying an existing template or document to a new filename using the Finder's File Duplicate command. Be sure to store the new file in the User Templates folder unless you have a specific reason not to. After you copy the file, you can open it in Word and edit it, as we'll discuss later in this chapter.

## How to create a template using a wizard

Finally you can create a template by using one of the wizards that come with Word. In Chapter 9, we described how to use wizards to create individual documents as you need them. If you use the same format repeatedly, however, working through the wizard's questions each time can become tiresome. Instead, you can create a given format once and then save it as a template by choosing File Save, typing an appropriate name, and specifying Document Template in the Save File As Type box.

Once you've created a template, you can use the format whenever you like without having to answer all the wizard questions again. Simply open a new file and specify the appropriate template.

 One advantage to creating templates from wizards, rather than using the wizard each time, is that you can customize the template file further if you like; for example, you can format some part of a letter differently than the wizard formats it—and you need to make the changes only once. If you use the wizard to produce a new document each time, you have to add the same customizations repeatedly.

# Editing a Document Template

After you create a template, you can open it and modify it just as you would any standard Word document, using either the File Open or the File Find File command. Be sure Word is set to look in the User Templates folder (as we discussed earlier in this chapter) and that it is set to list all files, readable files, or document templates in the List Files Of Type box. If you use the File Open command, for example, set Word to look in the proper folder, and set the List Files Of Type box to Document Templates. Word will show you a list of template files, as in Figure 27-5. Highlight the template file you want, choose OK, and Word will open the file. You can then make whatever changes you'd like, saving the file as you go.

**FIGURE 27-5**

Changing the entry in the List Files Of Type box to Document Templates tells Word to show you a list of all document template files in the current folder.

Select a Document:

Templates ▼

- Brochure 1
- Directory 1
- Fax Cover 1
- Fax Cover 2
- Invoice
- Letter1
- Letter2

List Files of Type:
Document Templates

⬠ Macintosh HD
126976K available

Open   Eject
Cancel   Desktop
Find File...   Help

☐ Read Only
☐ Confirm Conversions

## The effects of an edited template on an already existing document

After you modify a template, any new documents based on that template will include all the modifications you've made—whether to text, format settings, styles, AutoText entries, macros, toolbars, menu assignments, or key assignments. When you open an already existing document that was based on the original template, however, that document will not include all changes.

This makes sense because there are some features—notably, boilerplate text and format settings—that you'll usually want to have frozen after they're in a document. And indeed, Word will not apply the changes you make to a template's text, format, or style definitions to already existing documents. However, any changes you make to the template's AutoText entries, macros, toolbars, menus, or key assignments will show up in any file that uses the template, whether the document was created before or after those changes were made.

If you've changed or added style definitions in a template, and you want to include those changes and additions in already existing documents, you can, using the Organizer feature. We'll cover the Organizer feature on page 896.

## How to deˊ     template

As we've mentioned, Word defaults to storing document templates in the folder defined for User Templates in Tools Options on the File Locations card. To delete a template, simply delete the appropriate file from the folder by opening that folder from the Finder and dragging the file to the trash.

Because Word lists the available templates based on the files it finds in the User Templates folder, deleting the template file will eliminate the template name from all list boxes that offer a choice of templates.

## Normal, Supplementary, and Global Templates

As you may have noticed, we haven't yet drawn any distinctions in this discussion between the Normal template, supplementary templates, and global templates. Briefly, as we've discussed elsewhere, Word attaches the Normal template to all documents, and you can use the Normal template to store any customizations that you want available to all documents. Any template other than Normal can function as either a supplementary template or a global template.

Unfortunately, the way Word 6.0 uses the term *global* can be confusing. In **NEW!** some earlier versions of Word (but not in earlier versions of Word for the Macintosh), *global* was essentially synonymous with the Normal template. And even Word 6.0 refers to Normal as a global template in some lists and message boxes. However, the only global behavior that the Normal template shares with templates you designate as global is that its customizations are available to all files. Among the differences:

- When you designate a template as global, you can load or unload the template at any time. The Normal template is always loaded.

- When you designate a template as global, you cannot add or modify any customizations unless you edit the template file directly, attach it as the supplementary template, or use Word's Organizer. The Normal template lets you add or modify customizations while working on any document.

- When you designate a template as global, Word adds it to a list of check box items in the Templates And Add-Ins dialog box, as we'll discuss shortly. And if you try adding it to the list a second time, Word will merely ensure that the check box is checked. The Normal template is not on that list. And if you try adding it you'll see a message stating that Normal is already open as an add-in program.

Given all these differences between Normal on the one hand and templates that you designate as global on the other, it's important to be clear on the distinction between them.

You may choose to think of Normal as a special kind of global template with its own set of features. But given that the two kinds of templates are so different, we think it's less confusing to put them in separate categories, with Normal the only representative of its category. For purposes of this discussion, we'll use global template to mean those templates that you designate as global. When we want to talk about the Normal template, we'll call it the Normal template, or simply Normal.

The difference between a supplementary template and a global template lies not in the template file itself but in how you make it available to your document.

Figure 27-6 on the next page shows the Templates And Add-Ins dialog box, which you can open with the File Templates command. In the figure, we've designated Letter1 as a supplementary template by entering the name in the Document Template text box. (You can either type the filename in the text box or choose Attach to open a dialog box to find and designate the file to use.) In Word's terminology, this is called attaching the template, a term that can apply either to Normal or to any supplementary template.

**FIGURE 27-6**

The Templates And Add-Ins dialog box lets you change the currently attached template and designate which global templates to load.

Notice that Letter2 is also a choice in the Global Templates And Add-Ins box, with a check box next to its name. If you attach some other template to the file, using the Document Template text box, you can still make some of the customizations in Letter2 available in the current editing session by checking the check box—which tells Word to load Letter2 as a global template. We'll discuss the differences between using the template as a supplementary template and using it as a global template in a moment.

> Also notice the Add and Remove buttons. You can use these to add or remove filenames from the list of global templates. To add a file to the list, choose the Add button; Word will open a dialog box that you can use to designate a file. To remove a name from the list, simply highlight the name and choose Remove. (You can also add a name to the list automatically by storing a template in Word's Startup folder, as we'll discuss in a moment.)

## Normal and supplementary templates vs. global templates

For any given file, you can designate either the Normal template or any supplementary template as the attached template, although Word will attach the Normal template in any case, even when you attach a supplementary template. The key point, for the moment, is that when you *attach* a template, you attach it on a file-by-file basis. And the attached template is always loaded when you open the file it's attached to.

Global templates are not linked in any way to individual files. They are, rather, available or not available to all files you have open during the current editing session. For example, suppose you've created a template file called Names, with names and addresses included as AutoText entries. If you add the file to the list of global templates in the Templates And Add-Ins dialog box, as we described in the previous section, and check the template's check box, you'll find that the AutoText entries are available to any file you have open at the moment. Clear the check box, and the AutoText entries will disappear, no matter what file you move to or load. If you save a file when you have the check box checked, Word will not save the information about which global templates you had loaded. When you open the file again later, you'll find that the template is available only after you add a check to the template's check box in the Templates And Add-Ins dialog box.

## How to load global templates automatically

As we've already mentioned, you can have Word load a template as a global template whenever you start the program. Simply place the template file in the Word Startup Folder (6) folder—by default, the Startup folder is located in the Preferences folder within the System folder. When you start Word, the program will add the template name to the list of global templates in the Templates And Add-Ins dialog box, and it will automatically load the file as a global template.

You can find out which folder is currently the Startup folder and you can change it if you like, using the same techniques as for the User Templates folder. For details, see "How to change the User Templates folder" on page 884.

## How to customize the three kinds of templates

One of the most important differences between the Normal and supplementary templates on the one hand, and global templates on the other, shows up when you create customizations—such as an AutoText entry or a macro. When you customize any element of a document you're working on, you have the choice of saving the customization in the Normal template or in the document's supplementary template if there is one. You don't have the option of saving the customizations to a global template.

Most relevant dialog boxes, such as AutoText and Record Macro, include a pull-down list box to let you designate where to store each item as you create it. The box is labeled with some variation of Make This Available In, and the list of choices includes some variation on All Documents (Normal). If you choose this option, Word will store the customization in the Normal template and make it available to all documents. (Note, however, that you can override the Normal template's customizations with supplementary template customizations, as we'll explain shortly.) Any supplementary template attached to the currently active file will also be on the list as a choice for storing each customization. If one or more global templates are loaded, however, you won't find them on the list.

Your choice of where to store customizations determines when you can use them. For example, if you want a given macro available whenever you're using Word, store it in the Normal template. If you want it available only when working with letters, say, and out of the way otherwise, put it in a supplementary template for letters, along with other related customizations.

If you're not sure where to store a given customization, it's generally best to store it in the Normal template. If you decide you want it elsewhere, you can always move it by using the Organizer feature that we'll describe later in this chapter. And in the meantime, it will always be available.

Sometimes you may want to store a customization in a global template. Don't be stopped by the mere fact that Word doesn't offer global templates as an option. You can store the customization in the Normal template and then use the Organizer feature to move it to the template you really want it in.

## Priorities among templates

The interaction of Normal, supplementary, and global templates can become complicated—particularly if you have conflicting customizations, such as a macro in a supplementary template with the same name as one in the Normal template. If there are any differences among templates, the supplementary template takes precedence over the global templates, and, in general, the global templates take precedence over the Normal template. (Note that this general rule isn't strictly true in all circumstances, but it's a useful rule of thumb in any case.)

## Special considerations for the Normal template

Creating or modifying the Normal template is just like creating or modifying a supplementary template—with one important difference. Even if you have no

Normal file in your Word program, Word still attaches the Normal template to every file. In essence, a predefined Normal template is built into Word. And if Word doesn't find a Normal template file on disk, it provides the built-in Normal template automatically, then saves it to disk when you exit Word.

You can load the Normal template and modify it just like any other template. You can also take any template you've created and save it as Normal in the template folder. Word will recognize the name and use the file as its Normal template. In short, there is a real, but exceedingly subtle, difference between working with Normal and working with a supplementary template. But the mechanics of modifying the Normal template differ hardly at all from the mechanics of modifying other templates.

# Why Use Supplementary and Global Templates?    NEW!

We've already suggested some reasons for using supplementary and global templates—creating one template for letters and one for memos, for example. Remember also that you can customize more than just text and default formats; you can create customized menus, special-purpose macros, specialized AutoText entries, and even field-based forms for each template.

Consider, for example, some menu commands you might add to a letter template: a Signature Block choice on the Insert menu and choices on the Format menu for block format, double-spaced format, and one-and-one-half-spaced format paragraphs. These formatting choices might use macros to set margins, paragraph spacing, and first-line indents with a single menu command. The possibilities are limited only by your imagination.

Global templates, in contrast, let you create a set of customizations that you can use along with the Normal template and any number of supplementary templates. For example, you could create a template with a set of names and addresses stored as AutoText and designate it as a global template. That would make the names and addresses available to you when you're writing memos or letters, but let you avoid loading the names and addresses—and cluttering up the AutoText choices—when you're working on a report.

If more than one person uses your copy of Word, you may each prefer different customizations. Each of you can store your own set of customizations in a personal template and load those customizations as global templates. That way, each of you can have your customizations available for the files you work on, and still use other templates as supplemental templates for particular kinds of files.

Word's flexibility is one of the program's great strengths, but when it comes to templates the flexibility can also be confusing. Here are some simple rules of thumb for using the three kinds of templates. We recommend that you follow them until you understand templates well enough to devise your own approach:

■ Use the Normal template to store customizations (macros, styles, AutoText entries, and so on) that you want available to all documents.

■ Use supplementary templates to store customizations that you need only for specific kinds of documents—for example, one supplementary template for letters and another for memos.

■ Use global templates for customizations that you want available to a wider range of documents than you would use a supplementary template for but that you don't want to store in the Normal template.

## NEW! Organizer: Moving Styles, AutoText, Toolbars, and Macros Among Templates

As you take more and more advantage of multiple templates, you'll occasionally find that you've stored a style, macro, AutoText entry, or toolbar in the wrong template and that you need to move it. The Organizer dialog box, shown in Figure 27-7, makes it easy to move and manage any of these customizations.

**FIGURE 27-7**

The Organizer dialog box will help you manage your styles, AutoText entries, toolbars, and macros.

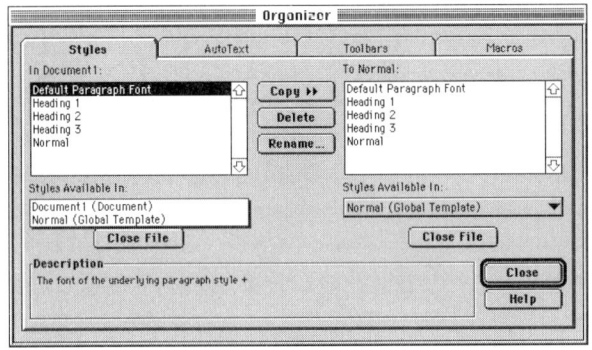

# The Organizer dialog box

Word offers several routes for reaching the Organizer dialog box. You can choose File Templates, or Format Style, or Tools Macros, and then, in each case, choose the Organizer button. Whatever route you take, you can choose any of the four cards—for Styles, AutoText, Toolbars, or Macros. We'll start with the Styles card.

## How to manage styles with the Organizer dialog box

The Styles card, shown in Figure 27-7, consists of four areas. The left side includes a list box containing the names of all styles in a particular file—in this case, Document1 (the file that was active when we opened the dialog box).

Just below the list box is a pull-down list box labeled Styles Available In. The list always includes the active document, the Normal template, and the supplementary template (if any) attached to the active document. If you change the entry in the Styles Available In box, the label on the list box above it changes to match the newly chosen filename, and the list of styles changes to show the styles stored in that file.

Just below the Styles Available In box is the Close File button. If you choose this button, Word will remove all the choices for the Styles Available In box, so the box and the list above it will be blank; the Close File button will change to read Open File, as in Figure 27-8. If you choose the Open File button, Word will respond with the dialog box for opening files, and you can choose another file.

**FIGURE 27-8**

If you choose the Close File button in the Organizer dialog box, Word will clear the Styles Available In box and the list above it. The button will change to an Open File button, which you can use to choose another file.

 If you open a document file with the Organizer, Word will always list that file, as well as any attached templates, in the Styles Available In box. If you open a template file, Word will list the template file itself, as well as Normal.

The second area on the Styles card is on the right side, and is essentially identical to the first, even down to the labels on the Styles Available In box and the Close File button. Here again, the list box shows a list of the styles stored in the file whose name is showing in the Styles Available In box. Below that is the Close File button. The list, text box, and buttons all work exactly the same way as the equivalent elements on the left side.

The third area on the Styles card consists of the three buttons between the first two areas: Copy, Delete, and Rename. These buttons perform the functions you would expect from their names; we'll discuss them in a moment.

The fourth area, at the bottom of the card, consists of a box labeled Description, a Close button (to close the dialog box), and a Help button. As long as only one style is highlighted on either the left or the right side, this box will give a description of the highlighted style. This can be helpful as a reminder of what each style does, particularly if you have two styles with the same name in two different files; by selecting each in turn, you can see the differences between them.

**How to delete a style.**   To delete one or more styles from a template or a document, first load the file you want to delete the style from. You can load the file on either the left or the right side of the Organizer dialog box. Then highlight the style or styles you want to delete, and choose the Delete button. Word will respond with a dialog box asking whether you want to delete the style. Answer Yes, No, Cancel, or Yes To All, as appropriate. (The Yes To All choice applies only if you have selected multiple styles. If you choose it, Word will delete all selected styles at once. Choose Yes, and Word will delete only the specific style named in the dialog box question, and it will then ask the same question again for the next highlighted style.)

**How to rename a style.**   To rename a style in a template or a document, start once again by loading the appropriate file on either the left or the right side of the Organizer dialog box. Then highlight the style you want to rename, and choose the Rename button. Word will respond with a Rename dialog box. You can then type the new name and choose OK, or you can choose Cancel to return to the Organizer dialog box without changing the name.

**How to copy a style.**   To copy a style from one template or document to another, first load both the source file (containing the style to be copied) and the destination file, using the left and right sides of the Organizer dialog box. Then highlight the style or styles you want to copy, and choose the Copy button. Unless there is a style in the destination file with the same name as a style you've told Word to copy, Word will simply copy the styles, adding them to the style list in the destination file. If there is a duplicate name, however, Word will respond with a dialog box asking whether you want to overwrite the existing style. Answer Yes, No, Cancel, or Yes To All, as appropriate. (As when deleting styles, the Yes To All choice applies only if you have selected multiple styles. Choose it, and Word will copy all styles with duplicate names at once. Choose Yes, and Word will copy only the specific style mentioned in the dialog box question and then ask the same question again for the next selected style with a duplicate name.)

**How to move a style.**   To move a style, first copy the style, and then delete it in the source file list, using the steps already described for copying and deleting.

Notice that the Copy button in Figure 27-7 includes two arrowheads that point to the right. Their direction indicates the direction the styles will be copied in. You can use the arrows to help avoid confusion. If you select style names on the left side of the dialog box, the arrows will point to the right. If you select names on the right, the arrows will point to the left.

## How to manage AutoText, toolbars, and macros with the Organizer dialog box

As we've already mentioned, the Organizer dialog box works essentially the same way with all four cards. In fact, as you can see by comparing Figure 27-7 to Figures 27-9, 27-10, and 27-11, the only differences among the cards are a few minor changes in labels; the Styles Available In label, for example, becomes AutoText Available In, Toolbars Available In, or Macros Available In, as appropriate. Deleting, renaming, copying, and moving AutoText, toolbars, and macros follow exactly the same procedures we've described for managing styles.

**FIGURE 27-9**

The AutoText card is almost identical to the Styles card shown in Figure 27-7, as are the Toolbars and Macros cards shown in Figures 27-10 and 27-11 on the next page.

**FIGURE 27-10**

The Toolbars card is the third card in the Organizer dialog box.

**FIGURE 27-11**

The Macros card is the fourth card in the Organizer dialog box.

We've now covered all the highlights of templates in this whirlwind tour. But before you spend too much time working with multiple templates on your own, take a look at the next chapter, where we'll show you how to redefine menus and shortcut-key assignments, two important capabilities for customizing Word and designing your own templates.

# TOPIC FINDER

# 28

# Customizing Menus, Keys, & Templates

 o matter how comfortable you may be with the logic of Word's menu structure and with the default keyboard assignments, you may wish some features were arranged differently. For example, Word puts the Page Numbers command on the Insert menu and the Header And Footer command on the View menu. You might prefer to have both on the same menu, since page numbers are a type of header or footer.

Similarly, you might prefer to assign shortcut keys differently from their defaults. Perhaps you'd prefer to assign all your formatting keys to Control combinations so that you could use J for justified paragraphs, L for flush left, R for flush right, and C for centered, rather than the default ⌘ plus J, L, R, and E (⌘ plus C is assigned to EditCopy).

With Word, you can rearrange the menus and key assignments at will.  You can also add your own macros to the Word menus and assign macros to your choice of shortcut keys. Better still, Word offers a feature that will let you assign easily remembered two-key mnemonics to your macros and the built-in commands. If you want both mnemonics and reminders, there is even a way to create two-key or three-key mnemonics that prompt you if you forget the keystrokes. We'll cover all of this, and more, in this chapter.

# Customizing the Menus

You may find that Word's default menu structure seems intuitive and well organized—or you may feel that some menu items should be on different menus. Even if you like every default menu choice, you may want to add some of Word's built-in commands or your own macros as additional choices. You can make any of these changes with the Menus card, which you can reach by choosing Tools Customize and then choosing the Menus card.

## NEW! How to create a practice template

Before you change any menus, we recommend that you create a special template to practice with. If you make accidental changes to Normal or another template, you may have trouble getting back to the original menus without losing AutoText entries or macros that you've created.

As we discussed in Chapter 27, if you used the Custom/Complete Installation option when you installed Word, the program automatically created several template files and put them in the default User Template folder. Unless you've moved them or erased them, they should still be there.

As we also discussed in Chapter 27, you can create a practice template easily by using the File Duplicate command in the Finder to copy the Normal template, and then giving it another name, such as *Practice* or *Custom.* You can also create the new template file from within Word. Simply use the File Open command to open Normal, then choose File Save As and save it under the new name. For the rest of this discussion, we'll assume that you're using the name Practice for your practice template.

After you create the Practice template, open a new document by choosing File New and entering *Practice* in the Template box, as shown in Figure 28-1.

**FIGURE 28-1**

You can attach the Practice template to a new file by entering *Practice* in the Template list box when you create the file.

Alternatively, if you already have a new file open, you can attach the Practice template to it by choosing File Template to open the Templates And Add-Ins dialog box, shown in Figure 28-2.

**FIGURE 28-2**

Use the Templates And Add-Ins dialog box to designate a template to attach to your document.

You can type a template name in the Document Template text box directly, or you can choose the Attach button to open a dialog box which will let you find and specify the template. The dialog box for attaching templates works just like the dialog box for opening files. When you designate a file in the Attach Template dialog box and then choose Open, Word will attach the template.

Note that if you designate Normal as the template to attach, Word will detach any currently attached supplementary template.

## The Customize dialog box

Starting with a new, blank document with the practice template attached, choose Tools Customize, and then choose the Menus card. Word will open a dialog box similar to the one shown in Figure 28-3. Starting from the Menus card, you can add, delete, or rename menus and menu items; move menu items to different menus; and assign built-in commands, macros, AutoText entries, and styles to menus. You can, in fact, completely redesign Word's menus and menu structure.

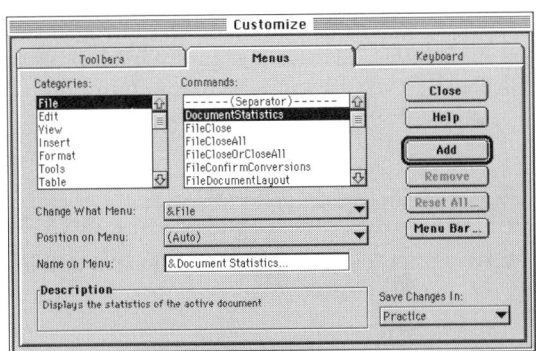

**FIGURE 28-3**

The Menus card in the Customize dialog box will let you redesign Word's menus.

## How to tell Word where to store your menu customizations

Notice first the Save Changes In pull-down list in the lower right corner of the Menus card. The possible settings for this choice are Normal and the document's supplementary template if one is attached—in this case, Practice. The setting for this option determines not only where Word will store any changes you make, but also what you'll see in the list boxes.

 If you've added a menu or menu item to Practice, and you set the Save Changes In box to Practice, Word will show you the added entries in the appropriate list box. If you then change the setting to Normal, Word will no longer show the entries. Choose Normal here both to store your changes in the Normal template and to have lists for Change What Menu, Position On Menu, and Name On Menu show the current settings for the Normal template. Choose the supplementary template name to store your changes in the supplementary template and to have the lists display the current settings for the supplementary template.

If you created the Practice template by copying Normal, as we suggested, you won't see any difference between the lists when you move between the two settings. But that's only because the two templates are still identical. Make sure that the Save Changes In choice is set to Practice, since that's where you'll want all your changes to go for now. Throughout the rest of this chapter, we will refer to Practice, the practice template, and the supplementary template interchangeably.

## How to assign an item to a menu

The Menus card in Figure 28-3 includes two list boxes, labeled Categories and Commands. It also includes two pull-down lists, labeled Change What Menu and Position On Menu, plus a text box labeled Name On Menu.

In Chapter 24, we explained how to assign a macro to a menu when you record the macro. The techniques are exactly the same when you want to assign an existing macro, a command, or any other item to a menu. Briefly, you use the Change What Menu pull-down list to specify the menu to assign an item to, the Position On Menu list to assign a position for the menu item, and the Name On Menu text box to specify the name of the menu item. For an introduction to using these three items, see "How to assign a macro to a menu" on page 808.

The two elements we didn't deal with in Chapter 24 are the Categories list box and the second list box, labeled Commands in Figure 28-3. As the name suggests, the Categories list box lets you specify the category of the item you will be assigning to a menu. Categories include all the standard menus—File, Edit, View, and so on—plus Drawing, Borders, Mail Merge, All Commands, Macros, Fonts, AutoText, and Styles.

As you might expect, the category you choose in the Categories list box determines the options available in the second list box. If you choose Macros in the Categories box, for example, Word changes the label for the second list box to Macros and will list all the macros in the current template (meaning the template specified in the Save Changes In box). If you choose Styles, Word will change the label for the second box to Styles and will list all the styles in the current template.

After you choose a category, you can scroll through the second list box, looking for a particular command, macro, style, AutoText entry, or font. If you don't know what a given command or other item does, you can view a description in the Description box at the bottom of the dialog box, as shown in Figure 28-4.

**FIGURE 28-4**

If you choose a category in the Categories list, and then choose an item from the second list box, Word will display an explanation for that item in the Description box at the bottom of the dialog box.

Items listed as commands are also part of the WordBasic macro language. Note also that if you are looking for a specific command but you aren't sure which category to look under, you can see a list of all commands by choosing All Commands in the Categories box.

Once you've chosen a category and chosen an item from that category in the second list box, assigning the item to a menu is essentially identical to assigning a macro to a menu when you record a macro. Simply choose the menu you want to add the item to from the Change What Menu list, choose a position for the menu item from the Position On Menu list, and enter a name for the item in the Name On Menu text box. Then choose the Add button to add the item to the menu.

## How to assign a position to a menu item

It's worth noting that the Position On Menu pull-down list provides complete control over the placement of each item. The first three choices on the list, shown in Figure 28-5, are Auto, At Top, and At Bottom. At Top and At Bottom are self-explanatory; the Auto choice is less so.

The Position On Menu pull-down list provides complete control over the placement of each menu item.

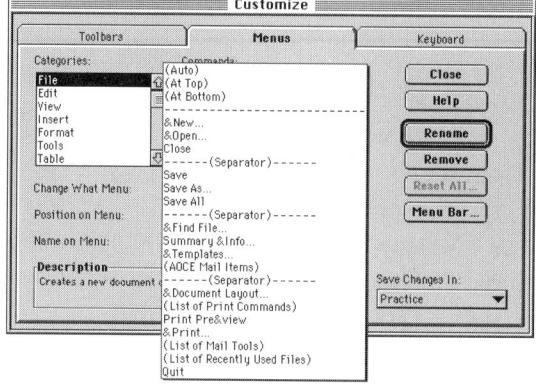

Word has its own idea about where each menu item should go. For example, if you add the Document Statistics choice to the File menu, Word will, by default, add it just below the Templates choice. You can then remove the Document Statistics choice from the menu if you like and add it back at, say, the bottom of the menu. But if you choose Auto for the position when you add it back, Word will put it just below the Templates choice again.

In general, the Auto choice maintains the logical categories of the menus as originally designed. If your menu customizations are minor, you're generally best off using the Auto choice for position. If you've made extensive changes in your menu structure, however, you probably won't want to use Auto.

In addition to letting you specify a menu position At Top, At Bottom, and Auto, Word will also let you designate any specific menu position you like. If you move through the Position On Menu list below these first three choices, you'll find that it's simply a list of all current menu items in the order they appear on the menu. If you choose an item from this part of the list, the Add button will change to Add Below. And if you want to add a new menu item to a specific position, you can simply designate the item that you want just above the new item, and choose the Add Below button.

## How to assign a name to a menu item

As soon as you designate an item to add to a menu, Word will enter a default name for you in the Name On Menu text box. You can accept the default name or not. And keep in mind that if you want to be able to choose an item from a drop-down menu with a keystroke (after pressing F10, then opening the menu), you have to enter an ampersand just before the character you want to use. Keep in mind also that if you've defined the same trigger character for two or more items on a menu, typing the character repeatedly will move the highlight from choice to choice rather than giving the command.

## How to delete a menu item

There may be times when you'll want to delete a menu item that you never use or that just doesn't make sense to you. Suppose, for example, that you've added some macros to your Tools menu, and you want to cut down the size of the menu by deleting the Language choice because you never use it.

To delete the Language choice, first give the Tools Customize command and then choose the Menus card. Next, choose &Tools in the Change What Menu list so the items on the Tools menu will show in the Position On Menu list. Next open the Position On Menu list and choose &Language, the item you want to delete, as shown in Figure 28-6. And finally, choose the Remove button. Figure 28-7 shows the Tools menu before and after this change.

**FIGURE 28-6**

If you specify a menu in the Change What Menu box, and an item in the Position On Menu box, and then choose Remove, Word will delete the item from the Position On Menu list and from the menu as well.

**FIGURE 28-7**

The before and after versions of the Tools menu. The default menu is on the left. The changed menu, with the Language menu item removed, is on the right.

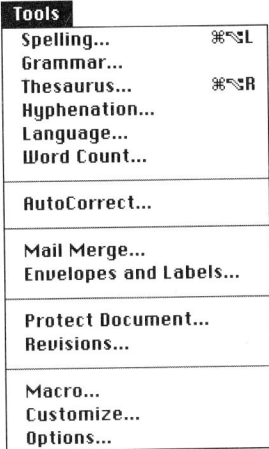

When you choose the Remove button, Word will delete the highlighted command from the menu without asking for confirmation. If you accidentally delete the wrong item, you can restore it easily enough. Use the Categories and Commands list boxes to specify the item, and make sure the correct menu name is showing in the Change What Menu box. Then specify a position in the Position On Menu box (choose Auto to restore a standard command to its default position), and choose Add.

Word offers a shortcut that you need to know about for removing menu items—if only to avoid it. If you press ⌘-Option-hyphen (using the hyphen on the typing keys rather than the minus on the numeric keypad), the mouse pointer will change to a thick horizontal bar—a minus sign. If you then open a pull-down or a context-sensitive menu, you can remove almost any item from that menu by clicking on it with the mouse button. You can also remove a menu item by opening a drop-down menu with F10 and then a keystroke, and then either typing the menu item's trigger key or highlighting the item and pressing Return.

We find this shortcut to be more dangerous than helpful. If you generally give menu commands from the keyboard, you'll find it far too easy to accidentally press the shortcut key combination and end up removing a menu item the next time you try to give a command. And even if you don't consider this a problem, the shortcut is clumsy to use for extensive menu redesign. As soon as you remove a menu item, Word will return to its usual behavior. So if you need to remove several menu items, you have to retype the shortcut key for each item you remove.

We firmly recommend that you delete this shortcut key assignment with the technique we'll discuss in "How to delete shortcut keys" on page 921. The key is attached to a command called ToolsCustomizeRemoveMenuShortcut in the All Commands category. Note too that there is a companion shortcut for adding menu commands. This second shortcut, ⌘-Option-equal sign, isn't as dangerous, but it's also clumsy to use. Type the key combination, and the mouse pointer will change to a plus sign. You may want to remove the shortcut key from this command as well. The relevant command is ToolsCustomizeAddMenuShortcut.

## How to rename a menu item and change the trigger key

There may also be times when you simply want to rename a menu item or change the trigger key for selecting an item. For example, Word's Format menu as shipped uses C for Columns and E for Change Case. If you give the menu commands by keyboard, you might prefer to rename Change Case to Upper/Lower Case and assign U as the trigger key. Alternatively, if you rarely use columns but often need to change case, you might like to keep the names and change the trigger keys, assigning C for Change Case and perhaps L for columns.

To change the name of an item, the trigger key, or both, first use the Categories and Commands list boxes to find and highlight the command you want to change. Word will automatically fill in the appropriate entries in the Change What Menu, Position On Menu, and Name On Menu boxes. To change the name or the trigger key, type the new or changed name in the Name On Menu box. For example, if you want to change the Change Case command to Upper/Lower Case and use U as the trigger, highlight the FormatChangeCase command, and then change the Name On Menu text to &Upper/Lower Case, as shown in Figure 28-8. Word will replace the Add button with a Rename button, which you can choose to complete the change. Figure 28-9 on the next page shows the Format menu before and after the change. To change only the trigger key (to C, for example), you would change the text from its original Change Cas&e to &Change Case.

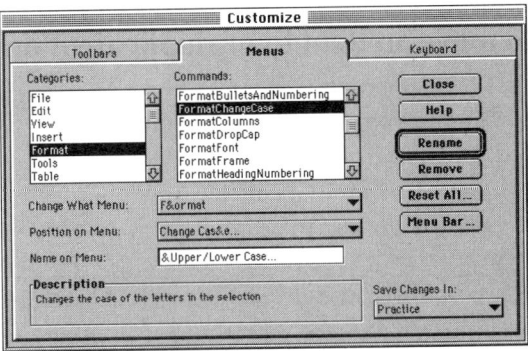

**FIGURE 28-8**

To change the menu name for a command, find and highlight the command, type the new name in the Name On Menu text box, and choose Rename.

The before and after versions of the Format menu. The default menu is on the left. The changed menu, with Change Case renamed as Upper/ Lower Case, is on the right.

When you're looking for commands that are on the default menus, the command names will usually be a combination of the menu name and the menu-item name. The command for Change Case, for example, is FormatChangeCase; the command for Columns is FormatColumns. You can find these commands in the Commands list box by highlighting the menu name in the Categories list box and then looking through the alphabetic list in the Commands list box.

## How to move an item to or duplicate it on another menu

There are times when you may want to move a menu item. For example, you might want to move the Page Numbers command from the Insert menu to the View menu, where its close relative, Header And Footer, is located. Alternatively, you might prefer to create a duplicate command on the View menu and leave the original on the Insert menu so that you can give the command from either menu. This sort of multiple route to a given dialog box is already built into Word in many cases (with some of the Options cards, for example), and it helps minimize the number of times you'll search for a command because it's not where you expect it to be.

To duplicate a command, simply add it to another menu, using the standard procedure for adding menu items. You can add the same command to as many menus as you like, using the same name and trigger key or different names and trigger keys, as you prefer. To move a command, simply delete the item from one menu and add it to another.

## How to change the position of a menu item

Although Word does not provide a specific command for changing the position of an item on a menu, you can still move any item however you like. Here again, you only need to delete the menu item and then add it back—in this case, to the same menu but in a different position.

## Macros, fonts, AutoText, and styles on menus

 **NEW!**

As we've already mentioned, the Categories list also includes choices for macros, fonts, AutoText, and styles. As you might expect, you can add, delete, rename, or otherwise modify items in any of these categories, by following the same procedure as when working with Word's built-in commands.

## How to use separators

If you create new menus or heavily modify Word's existing menus, you'll want to pay attention to separators—the horizontal lines that separate different sections of each menu and group related commands together. The default version of the File menu, for example, starts with all of the commands for opening and closing a file directly—New, Open, and Close—followed by a separator, followed by the commands for saving a file directly—Save, Save As, and Save All—followed by another separator.

You can add and delete separators in much the same way that you add and delete menu items. To add a separator, choose the (Separator) line in the Commands list box, as shown in Figure 28-10. Then use the Position On Menu box to specify the command that you want the separator to go below, and choose Add Below. To delete a separator, use the Position On Menu box to specify the separator you want to delete, and choose Remove.

**FIGURE 28-10**

To add a separator, highlight the (Separator) line in the Commands list box, specify the position for the separator, and choose Add Below.

 Whatever choice you make in the Categories box, the (Separator) item will be the first choice in the second list box.

### The Reset All button: Handle with care

The button second from bottom on the Customize Menus card is the Reset All button. You'll want to use this with care, if at all. As its name implies, this button resets every menu change you've made. If you choose it, Word will ask for confirmation before actually resetting the menus, but once you answer yes, you have no option for undoing the change.

Note that the Reset All button does not reset menus back to where you started in the current session. It resets everything back to Word's defaults. In short, if you've customized your menus, choosing this button throws all of your customizations away. Note, however, that the reset applies only to changes stored in the template currently specified in the Save Changes In box.

### How to recover from an accidental Reset All

As with macros and AutoText entries, Word doesn't try to save menu changes to disk until you choose the File Save All command, close the document that uses the supplementary template (if one is attached), or exit from Word and close the Normal template. To recover a supplementary template as it was last saved on disk, simply close all files that use that template, answer No when Word asks whether to save the changes, and reload the file or files you're working with. To recover the Normal template, first choose Tools Options, then choose the Save card, and make sure there's a check mark in the Prompt To Save Normal check box. Then exit from Word and answer No when Word asks whether to save changes to Normal. The next time you start Word, it will reload the Normal template in its previous form.

As we pointed out in Chapter 24, this approach to recovering a template also loses any other changes you've made since the last time you saved the template to disk. And it provides a good argument for using the File Save All command whenever you've made changes you're satisfied with. Note also that it's a good idea to keep a backup of your template files, just as you should keep backups of your data files—whether on floppies, tape, removable cartridges, or another hard disk.

# Renaming, Adding, and Deleting Menus

One of Word's most intriguing customization capabilities is that it will let you redefine even the menu names on the menu bar. In fact, you can add up to 42 additional menus to the menu bar, for a total of 50 menus. (Be aware, however, that you can only see as many menus as will fit across the screen at once on one line.) You can also delete and rename menus.

This feature is particularly useful if you're familiar with some other word processor and its menu logic, since you can recreate the menus you're used to. And if you've always thought you could do better than anything you've seen elsewhere, this feature, combined with the menu customization we've already discussed, will let you design your own menus from scratch.

## How to rename a menu or change the trigger key

Renaming a menu or changing the trigger key is much like renaming a menu item or changing its trigger key; the difference is that you make the changes in a menu through the Menu Bar dialog box, shown in Figure 28-11. To open the Menu Bar dialog box, first choose Tools Customize, and go to the Menus card. Then choose the Menu Bar button.

**FIGURE 28-11**

The Menu Bar dialog box will let you add to or rename the menus on the menu bar.

To change a menu name or the trigger key, first highlight the menu name in the Position On Menu Bar list box. Then type the new name for the item in the Name On Menu Bar text box, with an ampersand just before the letter you want to use as the trigger character. If you want to change the Format menu so that you can open it by typing F when the menu bar is active, for example, select F&ormat in the Position On Menu Bar box, and type &Format in the Name On Menu Bar box. Finish by choosing the Rename button. You can then make another change, or choose Close to close the Menu Bar dialog box, and Close again to close the Customize dialog box.

As with menu items, if you have more than one menu with the same trigger character, pressing that key will highlight one of the menus but not open it; pressing the key repeatedly will cycle through the choices. To open a menu, you have to press Return when the menu name is highlighted.

## How to add a menu

Just as renaming a menu is similar to renaming a menu item, so too is adding a menu similar to adding a menu item. With the Menu Bar dialog box open, use the Position On Menu Bar button to define the position where you want the new menu. Choose First to put it in the leftmost position on the menu (just to the right of the Apple menu) or Last to put it at the rightmost position before the Balloon Help. If you want to place the new menu between two existing menus, highlight the menu name that you want to have immediately before the menu you're adding.

After choosing the position, type the name for the menu in the Name On Menu Bar text box, along with an optional ampersand to indicate the trigger key. Finally, choose the Add button (which will change to Add After if you've highlighted one of the menu names in the Position On Menu Bar box). You can then close the Menu Bar dialog box to return to the Menus card and use the techniques we've already described to add menu items to the menu.

## How to delete a menu

Deleting a menu with the Menu Bar dialog box is straightforward. Simply highlight the menu in the Position On Menu Bar list box, and choose Remove. Word will respond with a message box asking for confirmation. Answer Yes to confirm the deletion or No to return to the Menu Bar dialog box without deleting the menu. Note that removing the menu also removes all menu items assigned to it.

## How to move a menu

Because deleting a menu removes all the menu items assigned to that menu, you can't easily move a menu by deleting it in one place and adding it in another. However, deleting and re-creating a menu is easier than you might expect. After deleting the menu and adding a replacement in another position, close the Menu Bar dialog box to return to the Menus card in the Customize dialog box. Then choose the appropriate category in the Categories list box, and work your way through the commands in the Commands list box, being careful to choose only those commands that you want on the menu.

If you are moving a standard Word menu, the names of most of the commands you want will closely match the combination of the original menu and menu item names. For example, ViewNormal is the command for the Normal choice on the View menu, and ViewOutline is the command for the Outline choice. There are some variations, however; the command for the Page Layout choice, for example, is ViewPage.

## Strategies for renaming menus

Although Word gives you the ability to completely redesign the menu system, it's important to exercise some restraint. In particular, you should approach any changes with an overall design in mind. For example, you might want to keep the menus pretty much as they are, but with menu names that let you press F10 and then the first letter of each menu name to open the menu. For example, you may find it cumbersome to press O for the Format menu and A for the Table menu.

One possibility is to keep the default names but move the ampersand to the beginning of each word. If you take this approach, you'll have two menus that use F—File and Format—and two that use T—Tools and Table. As we pointed out earlier, if you then press F10 and then either of these letters, Word will highlight the first menu name with that letter. To get to the second menu, you'll have to press the letter again. And to open either menu from the keyboard, you'll have to highlight it first and then press Return.

Although there is nothing wrong with this approach, you might prefer to rename the menus altogether to avoid the conflict in trigger keys. For example, you could rename the File menu to &Document, the Table menu to &Table, and the Tools menu to &Utilities so that each menu starts with its own unique trigger key.

As should be clear, there is no reason why you have to maintain Word's original menu logic. In fact, you can name the menus in any way that makes sense to you. If you decide to redesign the menus from scratch, we recommend that you invest some time in designing a menu structure first. But don't be afraid to experiment—it's easy enough to go back to the default menus.

If you create a completely new set of menus for the menu bar, be careful not to close the Customize dialog box until you've added the ToolsCustomize command to one of your new menus or assigned it to a shortcut key. Otherwise, you won't be able to reopen the Customize dialog box to add commands to the menus.

# Keyboard Customization

If you're like most people, you'll use the mouse a lot while you're learning Word because it's easier to point and click with the mouse than to remember arbitrary key combinations such as ⌘-F2 for File Print Preview or ⌘-K for Format AutoFormat. If you're a touch typist, however, using the keyboard to give a command is far faster than taking your hands from the home keys, reaching for the mouse, giving a command, and then finding the home keys again.

Word comes with a large number of shortcut keys defined. However, you can change any of them. Choose Tools Customize and then the Keyboard card to assign (or reassign) keys to built-in commands, macros, fonts, AutoText, and styles.

In addition, you can assign shortcut keys to a class of items that Word lists as Common Symbols. These include foreign-language characters such as ç and é, typographical aids such as single and double curly quotes for better-looking output (' ' and " " instead of ' and "), and such common symbols as ™ for trademark and © for copyright. In all cases, you can assign the shortcut keys both to items that come with shortcut keys defined and those that don't.

## The Options Keyboard dialog box

The Keyboard card in the Customize dialog box is similar to the Menus card that we discussed earlier in this chapter.

As we suggested in the beginning of the section on customizing menus, if you want to work through our examples as you read this discussion, or otherwise experiment with key assignments, we recommend that you start with a new, blank document with the Practice template attached. Then choose Tools Customize and choose the Keyboard card to open the dialog box shown in Figure 28-12.

**FIGURE 28-12**

You can use the Keyboard card in the Customize dialog box to assign shortcut keys.

### How to tell Word where to store your keyboard customizations

The Save Changes In box in the lower right corner of the dialog box works the same way for key assignments as the equivalent box in the Menus card works for Menu assignments. Your choice of either Normal or the supplementary template determines both what you see in the Current Keys list box and where Word stores any changes you make. If you choose Normal, the Current Keys list box will show the current settings in the Normal template, and Word will store your changes there; if you choose the supplementary template, the list will show the current settings in the current supplementary template, and Word will store your changes there instead.

Here again, if you created the Practice template by copying Normal to the new filename, you'll start out with identical key assignments in the Normal and Practice templates. If you switch back and forth between the two, you won't see any difference in the Current Keys list box. After you make changes, however, you will see differences.

## The Categories, Commands, and Current Keys list boxes

The Categories box and the second list box, which is labeled Commands in Figure 28-13, are essentially identical to their counterparts on the Menus card. And as with the Menus card, the title on the second list box changes to match the category you've selected: Macros, Fonts, AutoText, Styles, or Common Symbols. We described these list boxes in detail in "How to assign an item to a menu" on page 906.

The one difference between these two boxes and the two on the Menus card is the additional category Common Symbols, which we've already discussed—at the very beginning of the keyboard customization section.

We've also covered most of what you need to know about the Press New Shortcut Key and Current Keys boxes in Chapter 24. Briefly, the Current Keys list box will show the shortcut keys currently assigned to whatever item you've highlighted in the list box just above it. To assign a shortcut key, move to the Press New Shortcut Key box and press the keys you want to use. Word will show the key names in the Press New Shortcut Key box and add a message just below the box either showing the command the key is currently assigned to, as in Figure 28-13, or stating that the key is currently unassigned, as in Figure 28-14 on the next page. You can then either assign the keystrokes to the new command by choosing the Assign button or press Delete to remove the entry and then press different keys instead. For a more detailed look at this part of the Keyboard card, see "How to assign a macro to a shortcut key" on page 807.

**FIGURE 28-13**

If the keystrokes you enter in the Press New Shortcut Key box are already assigned to a command, Word will tell you which one.

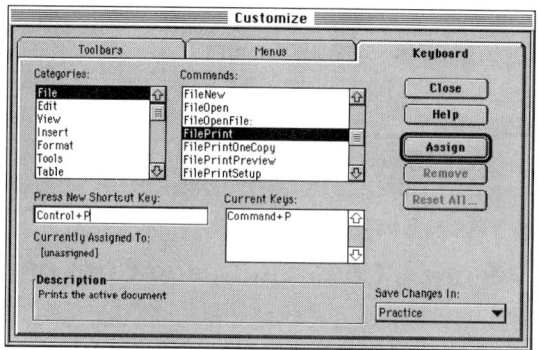

**FIGURE 28-14**

If the keystrokes you enter in the Press New Shortcut Key box are not already assigned to a command, Word will tell you so.

The Currently Assigned To line in the Keyboard card is all the warning you get when reassigning a key. Be sure to look at this line before choosing Assign to ensure that you're not reassigning a shortcut key that you may need later. In general, it's best not to reassign keys unless you're sure you'll never need the original assignments. In particular, we recommend leaving the default keys alone until you're ready to design your own fully customized interface.

As we discussed in Chapter 24, you can define shortcut keys using Control, ⌘, Control-Shift, ⌘-Control, or ⌘-Control-Shift in combination with most other keys, including any alphabetic character, any number, the function keys F1 through F15, and most other keys on the keyboard (including Del, Delete, Home, End, Page Up, Page Down, or the arrow keys). In addition, you can use ⌘-Shift in combination with any of these but the number keys. Finally, you can include the Option key for even more choices.

You can also define two-keystroke assignments, such as Control-P followed by P, which we'll indicate as Control-P,P. For the second keystroke, you're limited to using a key by itself—as in Control-P,P—or in combination with the Shift key, which we'll show as Control-P,Shift-P. (Note that if you define a shortcut as Control-P,P, you must type the P without the Shift key—even if you haven't defined a Control-P,Shift-P shortcut. However, you can type the shortcut even if Caps Lock is on. Similarly, if you define a shortcut as Control-P,Shift-P, you must press the Shift key even if Caps Lock is on.)

You can also create multiple shortcut keys for any command. This capability may seem superfluous, but it can come in handy. For example, suppose a colleague sometimes uses your computer. One of you likes using function keys and has all of Word's default shortcut keys memorized, including such arcane choices as ⌘-F2 for Print Preview. The other prefers mnemonic shortcuts and wants to use, say, ⌘-P,P for Print Preview. The ability to define multiple shortcut keys for each command lets each of you use the shortcut keys you prefer. Note, however, that if two users have completely different ideas about how to customize Word, it would make more sense to create two separate templates—one for each user.

The ability to assign two-keystroke shortcut keys to a macro does more than simply increase the number of key combinations available. It also makes it easier to make mnemonic key assignments. With one-key shortcut keys, you will quickly run out of mnemonics and be forced into arbitrary choices that are hard to remember. With two-keystroke shortcut keys, you can use extensive mnemonics that make it much easier to remember your shortcut keys.

For example, you could create a number of printing macros and have them all start with ⌘-P: ⌘-P,S to print the current selection, ⌘-P,P for the current page, and so on.

The trick is to use the first keystroke to group macros into conceptual categories that are easy to remember—in this case, all printing macros. But, just as important, be sure to reserve the first keystroke for only those macros. Once you establish ⌘-P for printing macros, don't use it for macros meant for other purposes.

## How to delete shortcut keys

Deleting, or removing, key assignments is even easier than adding them. Suppose you decide, after you've added ⌘-P,P as a shortcut key for FilePrintPreview, that you don't want to use it after all, since it means you can no longer use the default ⌘-P for printing the active document. Simply highlight FilePrintPreview in the Commands list box, highlight the shortcut key you want to remove in the Current Keys list box, and choose Remove. Figure 28-15, for example, shows ⌘-P,P highlighted prior to deletion. Note that you cannot select multiple shortcut keys to delete more than one at a time.

**FIGURE 28-15**

To delete a shortcut key, highlight it in the Current Keys list box, and then choose the Remove button.

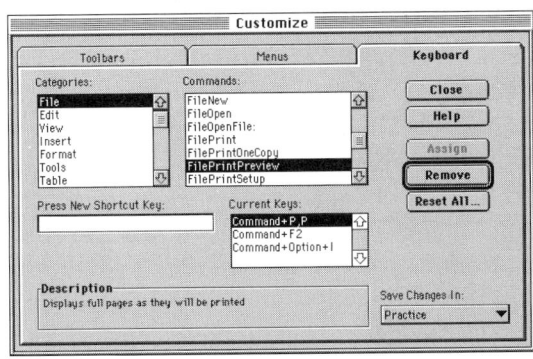

## How to assign shortcut keys to macros, fonts, AutoText, styles, and common symbols

When you highlight any of the items in the Categories list, Word will change the label on the second list box as appropriate for the category, and will show a list of all the specified items. You can then assign shortcut keys to, or remove them from, any of these items.

For macros, AutoText entries, and styles if you choose Normal in the Save Changes In box, Word will display all of the specified items stored in the Normal template. If you choose the supplementary template, Word will display all of the specified items stored in both templates. This makes sense because if you have a macro, say, stored in the Normal template, you can assign a shortcut key to it in the supplementary template, and you can assign different keystrokes in different templates. That lets different users each use their own preferred shortcut keys for any item stored in the Normal template.

### The Reset All button: Handle with care

The Reset All button on the Keyboard card works just like its counterpart on the Menus card. Here again, you'll want to use this button with care because it resets every key assignment you've made in the currently selected template. And here again, the reset goes back to Word's defaults, not to the settings you had when you started the current session.

As with the Reset All button for menu assignments, the Reset All button on the Keyboard card applies only to changes stored in the template currently specified in the Save Changes In box.

> Most important, as with the menu assignments, if you accidentally choose the Reset All button, you can go back to the last settings you saved on disk. The technique is identical to the one we described in the section "How to recover from an accidental Reset All" on page 914.

# How to save menu and key assignments

The reason you can recover from accidentally choosing the Reset All button is that Word doesn't save your menu or key assignments to disk when you make those assignments. Rather, Word follows exactly the same strategy that it does with AutoText entries and macros.

Word holds the changes in memory; unless told otherwise, it will eventually save the changes to disk in one of two ways. If you made the changes in the Normal template, Word will wait until you exit from the program with the File Quit command. It will then simply save the Normal template or, if you've set the program to prompt before saving Normal, it will announce that you've made changes in Normal and ask whether you want to save the changes. (To set Word to prompt before saving changes, choose Tools Options, choose the Save card, and add a check to the Prompt To Save Normal check box.) If the changes are in a supplementary template, Word will ask whether to save them when you close the document attached to that template or when you exit Word, whichever comes first. In either case—for the Normal or supplementary template—you can choose Yes or No, as appropriate, to tell Word to save or not.

It's generally much safer to save your changes as soon as you can. You can force Word to save all current files—including any changes to menu and key assignments—by choosing File Save All. For each currently open template that you've changed since the last save, Word will show you a message box asking whether to save the changes. You can choose Yes or No for each one individually, or you can bypass all remaining message boxes and return to your document without saving by choosing Cancel.

### How to print key assignments

After you define some custom key assignments, you may want to have a reference sheet handy with a list of all the assignments. To print a list of your current key assignments, choose File Print and open the Print pull-down list. Choose Key Assignments, and then choose Print. Word will print a list of customized key assignments for the Normal template and for any currently attached supplementary template.

# Another Kind of Two-Key Shortcut

As we've already discussed, Word's ability to define shortcut keys with two keystrokes rather than one opens the door to much more useful shortcut keys. However, even with Word's two-keystroke shortcuts, you can't type the mnemonic shortcuts if you forget the mnemonics.

This can be a problem with macros that you use in bursts—using them frequently when you use them, but only using them for occasional projects. Odds are that when you use macros that fall in this category, you'll want shortcut keys for their speed. But if you haven't used them in a while and have forgotten the shortcuts, you would probably find it easier to read the commands off a menu. Fortunately, Word can solve even this problem, letting you have your shortcut keys and read them too.

Figure 28-16 on the next page shows the macro we developed in Chapter 26 when discussing custom dialog boxes. If you find it difficult to understand how this macro works, you might want to look back at "Designing Custom Dialog Boxes with the Dialog Editor" on page 866 before you read the rest of this section.

FIGURE 28-16

When you run this macro, it displays a dialog box with option buttons that let you choose a text color.

```
Sub MAIN¶
Begin Dialog UserDialog 392, 181, "Mark Text"¶
    GroupBox 143, 0, 246, 93, "Color to Mark Text"¶
    OptionGroup  .OptionGroup1¶
        OptionButton 149, 13, 233, 18, "Dk Green (Note to Co-Author)".
.OptionButton1¶
        OptionButton 149, 31, 178, 18, "Blue (Source of Info)",
.OptionButton2¶
        OptionButton 149, 48, 183, 18, "Red (Things to Check)",
.OptionButton3¶
        OptionButton 149, 67, 203, 18, "None (Return to Default)",
.OptionButton4¶
    OKButton 180, 110, 65, 20¶
    CancelButton 179, 148, 65, 20¶
    Picture 12, 6, 122, 164, "Macintosh HD:Microsoft Word 6.0:Clip
Art:Crayons.pict", 0, .Picture1¶
End Dialog¶
Dim MarkText As UserDialog¶
On Error Goto SkipIt¶
Dialog MarkText¶
If MarkText.OptionGroup1 = 0 Then¶
    FormatFont .Color = 11¶
ElseIf MarkText.OptionGroup1 = 1 Then¶
    FormatFont .Color = 2¶
ElseIf MarkText.OptionGroup1 = 2 Then¶
    FormatFont .Color = 6¶
ElseIf MarkText.OptionGroup1 = 3 Then¶
    FormatFont .Color = 0¶
EndIf¶
SkipIt:¶
End Sub¶
```

Briefly, this macro lets you set text color for currently selected text, or text you're about to type, by specifying the color with an option button. When you run the macro, it opens a dialog box like the one shown in Figure 28-17. The dialog box has four option buttons, one for each of the three colors you can use for marking the text, and one to return the color to the default setting of Auto. When you choose one of the buttons, and then choose OK, the macro sets Word for the appropriate text color.

FIGURE 28-17

The macro in Figure 28-16 displays this Mark Text dialog box.

## Push buttons

The part of this macro we're primarily concerned with here is the dialog box. We are going to replace the option buttons with push buttons, and then we'll change a few other items that relate to this primary change. The result will be fully equivalent to assigning two-key macros. In fact, it will have some advantages that two-key macros don't have.

A push button is similar in many ways to an OK button or a Cancel button in a dialog box: Choosing it closes the dialog box and initiates a specific action. You can build push buttons into dialog boxes by applying the same techniques we discussed in Chapter 26 for custom dialog boxes. In this case, we'll simply replace the option buttons that are already there with push buttons of the same name.

The syntax for push buttons is nearly identical to the syntax for option buttons, so we'll start by replacing the word *OptionButton* with the word *PushButton* in the four places where it occurs in the macro.

We'll also delete the lines for OptionGroup and GroupBox, since push buttons aren't grouped together the way option buttons are. And we'll add an ampersand in front of the first character in each button name. The ampersands in button names work just like the ampersands in menu names. When Word puts the dialog box on the screen, it will underline the character just after the ampersand in the macro. The user can then choose the button from the keyboard by pressing the key for the underlined character.

You also need to change the part of the macro that determines which button you choose. The original macro tests to see which option button you chose. As you would expect, the push buttons need a different command.

First you have to change the Dialog statement from

Dialog MarkText

to

Button = Dialog(MarkText)

Next you have to change the If...ElseIf...End If statement to

```
If Button = 1 Then
        FormatFont .Color = 11
ElseIf Button = 2 Then
        FormatFont .Color = 2
ElseIf Button = 3 Then
        FormatFont .Color = 6
ElseIf Button = 4 Then
        FormatFont .Color = 0
Else
        Goto SkipIt
EndIf
```

Notice the addition of an Else statement at the end. This is needed with the PushButton commands to tell Word to skip over the color-changing step if you choose the Cancel button instead of either push button. (Notice also that push buttons, unlike option buttons, start numbering from 1, not 0.)

You should also delete the OK button in this example; it no longer serves any purpose because the macro will react immediately to any of the push buttons. Finally, you should delete the On Error statement, which also no longer serves any purpose. You should leave the Cancel button, however, so that you can close the dialog box without changing text color if you open it by accident. After you finish, the macro should look like the one shown in Figure 28-18. (We've also adjusted the size of the first button to make it a bit easier to read.) The dialog box you see when you run the macro should look like the one in Figure 28-19.

**FIGURE 28-18**

This macro will create a dialog box that includes only push buttons and a Cancel button.

**FIGURE 28-19**

Using this dialog box, with push buttons only, is the equivalent of assigning a second key to a macro.

## The final flourish

All that remains now, to get the magic of two-keystroke macros combined with on-screen menus, is to assign a shortcut key to the macro that opens the dialog box, using the techniques we described earlier in this chapter. Because this macro is meant for marking text, you might use Control-M. And that's it. You can now press Control-M,R to call up the dialog box and change text color to red, or you can press Control-M,B to call up the dialog box and change the color to blue, and so on.

Nor is this all. Early on in discussing push buttons, we mentioned that building the equivalent of multiple-keystroke shortcut keys with push buttons had advantages over being able to assign two keys directly. In fact, there are two advantages.

First, there is no need to limit yourself to two-key mnemonics. You can build a macro that opens more than one dialog box so that you could, for example, press Control-M,T,R to mark text as red, and Control-M,T,B to mark text as blue.

More interesting is that the dialog box provides what amounts to a Help screen for your shortcut keys. If you remember the full mnemonic and if you can type the keystrokes quickly enough, the dialog box will flash only briefly on your screen. But if you hesitate after Control-M, Word will show you the dialog box complete with the push buttons for all macros and commands that are available through that dialog box. If you organize your macros with dialog boxes and group your shortcut keys in ways that make sense to you, you don't have to remember each key sequence. You need remember only the first key; you can pick the rest from the dialog box.

You can combine both advantages of push button–based mnemonic shortcuts to create what amounts to a master dialog box that will function as a Help system for all of your shortcut keys. Simply define a dialog box that includes push buttons for all other shortcut-key dialog boxes and that will call them up for you. Then assign any shortcut key you can easily remember to this master dialog box.

If you remember the shortcut key for any other dialog box, you can go to that box directly. If you forget the key, you can open the master dialog box, pick the dialog box to go to, and then pick the shortcut key in that box. This is particularly useful for shortcut keys that you don't use regularly but that you need to use repeatedly when you're using them at all—such as shortcut keys for building an index.

If you've followed the discussion through Part Five, by now you know enough to build what amounts to your own user interface for Word. Odds are you'll never need to customize the program so completely, but you'll be able to customize it as much as you need to. And as you'll discover, that's one of the real advantages of Word.

# Index

## Special Characters

& (ampersand), 575, 576
* (asterisk)
    in format switch (\*), 654–56, 790
    as multiplication operator, 763
    as wildcard character, 100, 575, 576
@ (at sign)
    in Date-Time Picture switch (\@), 659
    in pattern matching, 101
\ (backslash), 575, 576, 641, 740
^ (caret)
    as exponent operator, 763
    in pattern matching, 101
: (colon), 740, 743
, (comma)
    as field delimiter, 691, 758–59
    as logical OR, 576
© (copyright symbol). *See* special
    characters
{ } (curly brackets), 101, 641
/ (division operator), 763
… (ellipsis), 151
= (equal-to operator), 764, 857
= (Formula) field, 642, 762–63, 764, 765,
    770–72
>= (greater-than-or-equal-to operator),
    764, 857
> (greater-than symbol)
    as operator, 764, 857
    in pattern matching, 101
<= (less-than-or-equal-to operator), 764,
    857
< (less-than symbol)
    as operator, 764, 857
    in pattern matching, 101
\! (lock result switch), 652
– (minus sign), 762, 763
<> (not-equal-to operator), 764, 857
\# (numeric picture switch), 657–59
( ) (parentheses), 101, 764
% (percent sign), 763

+ (plus sign), 762, 763
? (question mark) as wildcard character,
    100, 575, 576
" " (quotation marks)
    in file searches, 575–76
    in text strings, 691, 864
® (registered trademark symbol). *See*
    special characters
; (semicolon), 743
[ ] (square brackets), 100–101, 306
~ (tilde), 576
™ (trademark symbol). *See* special
    characters

## A

About Balloon Help command, 23
About Microsoft Word command, 10
ABS function, 765
accelerator keys. *See* trigger keys
action fields, 640, 671–76
addition operator (+), 762, 763
addresses. *See* envelopes; labels
Advanced Search dialog box
    Location card, 573–74
    Summary card, 574–79
    Timestamp card, 578–79
ADVANCE field, 565
aliases, 414, 570–71
alias icons, 5
Align Drawing button, 525, 529
aligning frames, 494–96
aligning table rows, 369–70
aligning tables, 368–69
aligning text
    centered, 206, 210, 214
    flush left, 206, 210, 214
    flush right, 206, 210, 214
    with Formatting toolbar, 206
    horizontally, 206, 210, 214

indexes, *continued*
    formatting page numbers in, 742
    inserting entries for, 739–40
    in long documents, 747
    marking all occurrences of a term, 742
    for master documents, 564, 747
    multilevel, 741
    for multiple-file documents, 747
    overview, 737
    page ranges in, 739–40
    partial, 744
    splitting large, 744
    styles for, 743
    term vs. topic entries, 740
    updating, 744–45
INDEX field, 744
indicators, 18–19
INFO field, 666, 670
initials, author, 306, 308–9, 670–71
InputBox$() function, 860–61
Input command, 854–55
Insert Annotation command, 306
Insert Break command, 456, 477, 478
Insert Caption command, 735, 785
Insert Cells dialog box, 358–59, 364
Insert Chart button, 15, 542
Insert Columns button, 362, 364
Insert Cross-Reference command, 791, 794
Insert Database command, 593–94, 605
Insert Data dialog box, 598
Insert Field command, 643–46
Insert File command, 604–5
Insert Footnote command, 312
Insert Form Field command, 715
Insert Frame button, 525
Insert Frame command, 484, 486, 515, 539
Insert Index And Tables command, 726, 729, 744
insertion point, defined, 7. *See also* cursor
Insert menu, 9, 10
Insert menu (Microsoft Graph), 543, 545
Insert Merge Field dialog box, 692–93, 701
Insert Microsoft Excel Worksheet button, 14
Insert mode, 79

Insert Object command, 531, 534, 542, 607–8
Insert Page Numbers command, 154
Insert Picture command, 509, 605
Insert Picture dialog box, 509–11
Insert Rows button, 357
Insert Symbol command, 144–45
Insert Table button, 14
Insert Table dialog box, 332–33
INT function, 768
italic text, 224, 226

## J

joining paragraphs, 80, 81
jumping to. *See* Go To dialog box
jump terms, 25
justifying text, 206, 210, 214

## K

Keep Lines Together option, 215, 477
Keep With Next option, 216, 477
kerning, 230
keyboard. *See also* shortcut keys
    aligning text with, 210
    assigning keys to macros, 807–8
    changing fonts with, 228
    changing indention with, 209, 210
    changing line spacing with, 210–11
    changing margins with, 200, 201
    choosing menu options with, 11–12
    copying text with, 88, 91
    cutting and pasting with, 88, 91
    deleting key assignments, 921
    formatting characters with, 226–28
    formatting paragraphs with, 209–12
    getting context-sensitive Help with, 26
    making key assignments, 919–21, 923–27
    moving cursor with, 66–70
    moving text boxes with, 499
    moving text with, 91
    navigating tables with, 344–45
    printing key assignments, 245, 429, 923

**M. David Stone** has been working with and writing about personal computers since 1981. He was Computers Editor at *Science Digest* and is currently a contributing editor at *Windows Sources* and at *PC Magazine*, where he writes the word processing section of the Solutions column. His work has also appeared in *Computer Shopper*, *PC Sources*, and *InfoWorld*, among other publications. His other computer-related books include *Getting the Most from WordStar and MailMerge*, *Microsoft Word Power Pack*, and *Getting Online*, which was a primary selection of the Small Computer Book Club.

**Alfred Poor** writes in his "electronic cottage" in Bucks County, Pennsylvania. As a contributing editor with *PC Magazine* and *Computer Shopper*, he has reviewed hundreds of products, including dozens of word processing programs. His articles have also appeared in *PC Week* and *PC Sources*. He is the author of three other books: *New Life for Old PCs*, *The Data Exchange*, and *The Hewlett-Packard LaserJet Printer Handbook*.

he manuscript for this book was prepared and submitted to Microsoft Press in electronic form. Text files were prepared using Microsoft Word 2.0 for Windows. Pages were composed by Microsoft Press using Aldus PageMaker 5.0 for Windows, with text in Palatino and display type in Optima Bold. Composed pages were delivered to the printer as electronic prepress files.

*Cover Graphic Designer*
**Rebecca Geisler**

*Cover Illustrator*
**David Lemley**

*Interior Graphic Designer*
**Kim Eggleston**

*Interior Graphic Artists*
**Sandi Lage, Lisa Sandburg, Penelope West**

*Principal Compositor*
**John Sugg**

*Principal Typographers*
**James Kramer, Anne Taussig**

*Indexer*
**Julie Kawabata**

# Create a Book

Create dozens of great-looking documents quickly. See "Wizards: Automated Documents," *page 294.*

Create a decorative first letter. See "How to create a dropped capital letter," *page 539.*

Place text in a shaded box for emphasis. See "How to adjust frame settings," *page 489.*

Wrap text around a picture or other object. See "How to adjust frame settings," *page 489.*

Create margins that allow for binding. See "Document Formatting," *page 193.*

Create a bulleted or numbered list. See "Numbering Paragraphs and Creating Lists," *page 445.*

Create fancy type effects. See "Creating Font Effects with Microsoft WordArt," *page 533.*